Hanuman

"Vanamali Devi has done a beautiful and inspiring job of making Hanuman a palpable life, worthy of love, devotion, and respect."

NAYASWAMI KRIYANANDA, AUTHOR AND SWAMI
OF THE GIRI (MOUNTAIN) BRANCH OF
THE ANCIENT SWAMI ORDER

"Vanamali's work is Universal and helpful for people in all walks of life."

SHIVARUDRA BALAYOGI MAHARAJ

Aum Sri Ganeshaya Namaha!

Salutations to
Lord Ganesha!
May He remove all obstacles on the path of this scribe
and enable her to write this book on
the *lilas* of
Sri Hanuman.

HANUMAN

The Devotion and Power
of the Monkey God

VANAMALI

Inner Traditions
Rochester, Vermont • Toronto, Canada

Inner Traditions
One Park Street
Rochester, Vermont 05767
www.InnerTraditions.com

Originally published in India in 2010 by Aryan Books International under the title *Sri Hanuman Lila*

Library of Congress Cataloging-in-Publication Data
Vanamali, 1935–
 [Sri Hanuman lila]
 Hanuman : the devotion and power of the monkey god / Vanamali.
    p. cm.
 Includes passages in Sanskrit (romanized).
 Originally published in India in 2010 by Aryan Books International under the title Sri Hanuman lila.
 Includes bibliographical references and index.
 ISBN 978-1-59477-337-2 (pbk.)
 1. Hanuman (Hindu deity)—Legends. I. Title.
 BL1225.H3V36 2010
 294.5'113—dc22

                                                         2009053206

Printed and bound in the United States by Versa Press, Inc.

10 9 8 7 6 5 4 3 2

Text design and layout by Priscilla Baker
This book was typeset in Garamond Premier Pro with Kingsbury used as a display typeface

To send correspondence to the author of this book, mail a first-class letter to the author c/o Inner Traditions • Bear & Company, One Park Street, Rochester, VT 05767, and we will forward the communication or contact the author at **www.vanamaliashram.org**

Aum Anjaneyaaya Vidmahe.

Vayu putraaya deemahi,
Tanno Hanumath prachodayaath.

I contemplate on Anjaneya,
I meditate on the son of Vayu,
May He give me enlightenment.

◆

Dedicated to my dearest friend, Nilli,
one of the greatest bhaktas *of Sri Hanuman.*

Benediction given by Sri Neeb Karoli Baba
as conveyed by his chief disciple Sri Siddhi Ma.

Hanuman sama nahi bad bhagi
Nahi kou Ram charana anuraagi,
Pavana tanaya bala pavana samana
Buddhi viveka vijnana nidhana
Kavana so kaaj katthin jaga maahi
Jo nahi chod tatha thum pahi.

There is no one as fortunate as Hanuman,
No one who has as much love for the feet of Rama,
Son of the wind god, who equals him (the wind) in strength,
Repository of intelligence, discrimination, and understanding.
O Dear One! If you shower your grace
No task is difficult in this world.

HANUMAN CHALISA BY TULSIDAS

Contents

Aum Sri Ramaaya Namaha!

Foreword

Sri Vanamali is a rare being. She is a Devotee of the Lord in all his forms who has been blessed with the compassionate desire to communicate his *lilas* (divine acts of play) to the English-speaking world.

In the West, there are many new devotees who desperately need access to the revered ancient Scriptures of India. Sri Vanamali comes as the cool breeze of grace, filling the hearts and minds of the thirsty devotees with the stories of the Lord's joyous play. In this book on Sri Hanumanji, as in all her other books, she gives us access to the inner worlds of our Beloved's *lilas*.

Sri Hanuman is the greatest of all devotees of the Lord. He is a *jnani* (one in complete knowledge) in the fullest sense of the word. He has merged with his Lord, Sri Rama, in his own being, and he sees his Lord in everything and everyone. His realization of the truth does not end there.

As Sri Krishna says,

> *And when he sees me in all and sees all in me,*
> *Then I never leave him and he never leaves me.*
> *And he, who in this oneness of love*
> *Loves me in whatever he sees,*
> *Wherever this man may live,*
> *In truth, he lives in me . . .*
>
> BHAGAVAD GITA, CHAPTER 6

This is the key to understanding Sri Hanuman. He serves Sri Rama in all beings by removing the obstacles to those beings realizing the truth in themselves. He sees that, in fact, there ARE no "other" beings, only Rama. Motivated by love born of Truth that manifests as compassion for beings who believe themselves to be separate, he works tirelessly to remove their suffering.

Another mystery of Sri Hanuman was revealed by Sri Neem Karoli Baba to one of his great old devotees, Dada Mukerjee. A small party of devotees had, along with Maharaji, climbed to the top of Hanuman Dhara in Chitrakut. They rested by the spring that comes out from the rock at the top of the hill.

Maharaji said to Dada, "This is where Hanumanji came to calm himself and to cool himself off after burning Lanka."

Then after a few seconds he said very softly, as if to himself, "Of course, Hanumanji was always at peace."

No matter what he was doing—burning Lanka, destroying the demons, singing Ram Naam, or serving the devotees—Hanuman was never outside of Sri Rama's being.

May the Lord be gracious to all.

SRI KRISHNA DAS

Sri Krishna Das is well known to all lovers of music, especially in the West, for his numerous recordings of heartrending devotional lyrics. Even though he is known as Krishna Das, he could just as easily be called Ram Das or Hanuman Das, since he is a devotee of both.

Aum Sri Hanumathe Namaha!

Introduction

Yatra Yatra Raghunatha Kirtanam
Tatra Tatra Krita Mastaka anjalim
Bashpavari pari purna lochanam
Marutim nammascha raakshasantakam.

I bow to Maruti, the destroyer of demons,
Who stands with folded palms,
In all the places where the glories of Sri Rama are sung,
Shedding tears of devotion and joy.

RAMACHARITAMANAS BY TULSIDAS

Modern science may claim to have traced the mechanical laws of evolution, but the ancient *rishis* (sages) of India discovered the spiritual law of eternal values called the Sanatana Dharma (eternal law), the divine thrust inherent in the human psyche that enables it to attain greater heights of evolution. This is the great contribution that India has made to the world, one that inspires in human beings a strong desire to shake off their humanity and bring to light the inherent divinity within. This is what is known as enlightenment. Age after age, India has produced enlightened souls who have continuously renewed and refreshed this great *dharma*—the Sanatana Dharma—and made it available to the whole of the human race. The sages wanted our country to progress not just materially but through a constant inner renewal of the cosmic law of righteousness that is guided by the wisdom embedded in our heritage.

The great verse epics of our country called the Mahabharata and Ramayana, and the massive assemblage of narratives known as the Puranas, are thus storehouses of wisdom, and by reading them, our spiritual evolution will be hastened. Truth is a matter of direct realization by our own individual efforts, but the sages gave us many different methods to attain it. These saints were great souls who were far above the vulgar herd who merely want to see their names emblazoned in anything they write. Thus, their names remain a mystery. We can show our gratitude to them only by trying out the many paths they gave us.

We find a great urge on their part to share their vital experiences with all those who have the hearts to understand. This experience is the highest available to the human psyche and is known as *brahmajnana* (knowledge of Supreme Spirit or Brahman). The knowledge by itself is not the aim of life. It has to become a living understanding in which we actually experience the unity of life underlying all living beings— in fact, the entire cosmos. From this is born an overwhelming love for the whole of creation and a burning desire to see human beings free themselves from the strangling limitations and illusions of this waking world of our common experience. This type of love is totally unselfish, characterized by a deep desire to share one's most cherished possession with the whole of humanity. Thus, we see that the *rishis* tried every means in their power to enable our tragic and ignorant human race to acquire that which was the sumum bonum of human life. Every human being is nothing but a reflection of the divine. Involvement in the illusions of this world alone stops us from realizing our divinity.

The Upanishads give us the path of *jnana,* or spiritual wisdom, which is difficult for many to follow. They appeal only to those who are already endowed with great spiritual leanings. However, it is said that the Absolute, Timeless, and Formless Presence descends to this mortal plane in the form of the gods for certain mysterious purposes of Its own. This is known as the *lila,* or the play of god. The sages who came after the age of the Upanishads were determined to cater to the majority of human beings who might not have had any spiritual leanings at all. They resorted to bringing the truths of the Upanishads forcibly to the minds of the average human being in the form of stories. The sage Vyasa, author of the Mahabharata, was the greatest of these storytellers. He said that if we listen carefully to a story, we will never be the same again. The story, especially if it has some spiritual basis, will worm its way into our heart and break down our self-constructed barriers to the divine. Even if we start off by reading these stories as entertainment, one or two of them will eventually slip through our defenses and explode the hard shell of our humanity to disclose our divinity. These stories have an inexhaustible vitality in them so that people are never tired of hearing them. They can be listened to or read and pondered over, and thus are capable of promoting in the listener a deep understanding of life, death, and destiny. Every story had implicit in it a moral value that is likened to the fragrance of a beautiful flower. The *rishis* taught us that all forms are the letters of a form-word-power alphabet of a language that can help us to realize our spiritual reality, unconditioned by any form yet the supreme source of all forms.

The path of *bhakti,* or devotion to a personal God, is forcibly brought out in the epics and Puranas, which tell stories of the great incarnations and of the numerous gods of the Hindu pantheon who are completely in tune with the truth of life. The culture of the Indian subcontinent was developed in the climate of these great epics. Every child was taught to emulate the classic examples given therein and thus bring his or her own life to perfection. The Hindu mind had no difficulty in picturing the Supreme in the form of either animal or human. Thus we find Ganesha, depicted as a human being with the head of an elephant, and Hanuman, who was a monkey.

Hanuman is one of the most beloved figures in the Hindu pantheon of gods called Kimpurushas, mystic beings that are half-human and half-animal. He is the symbol of utter and selfless devotion to his supreme deity, Sri Rama, the seventh incarnation of Lord Vishnu, scion of the solar race, the pinnacle of human perfection. Hanuman's entire strength came through the repetition of the name of Rama, the greatest *mantra* for this age of Kali, which if chanted with devotion, is said to give liberation from the coils of mortal life. Every temple of Rama has a figure of Hanuman seated at his feet and bowing to him. Wherever the Ramayana is read or recited, a seat is left vacant for Hanuman, since it is believed that he is always present at the reading of the story of his beloved master.

Perhaps the Western reader can best be introduced to the Ramayana by recalling Homer's *Odyssey,* another well-known ancient epic, in which the Greek hero Odysseus goes through many trials and adventures before reuniting with his faithful wife Penelope. But Rama, as an incarnation of the god Vishnu, second of the Vedic triune gods, is on a divine quest. He subdues the demon king Ravana and restores the balance of good and evil on Earth. The lecherous and prideful Ravana represents the monster we can become when we give our baser instincts full reign. By contrast, Rama is seen as the supreme glory of mankind and teaches us how to behave with valor, dignity, compassion, and chilvalry. He is the epitome of a great ruler and husband. His wife Sita is the embodiment of earthly grace, beauty, and virtue. Rama has been described as the sun, or divine consciousness, and Sita as the light of its warming rays on Earth. As Sita says in Valmiki's Ramayana, 5.21.15, "I am as inseparable from Rama as radiance is from the sun." Together, they make up the ideal couple and the verses describing their love are some of the most beautiful ever written. Hanuman, son of the wind god, is the breath that unites them. As a lowly simian, he would not be expected to embody total self-control and discipline, and yet by concentration of mind, he accomplishes just that, ever steadfast in helping his lord Rama to defeat the demon king and rescue Sita. He shows the reader that if he too concentrates his mind on the divine and never wavers, he can control his baser instincts and merge with supreme consciousness. Hanuman is sometimes described as the world's first Superman and, as such, his stories can be appreciated even by young children. He accomplishes feats of amazing strength, but it is his personal commitment to principles of valor and justice, along with his humble demeanor, that help make him such an admired figure. In India today, there exist popular cartoons depicting the many breathtaking feats of Hanuman. However, as stated, the figures of Rama, his wife Sita, the monkey god Hanuman, the demon god Ravana, and others who figure prominently in the Ramayana are all part of a most profound philosophical and religious allegory that can be appreciated on a variety of levels, and this is why these exciting stories have endured through many millennia.

The Sanskrit word *sadhana* refers to any method by which the aspirant, or *sadhaka,* can establish contact with the inner realms of being. One of the easiest methods of *sadhana* is known as *japa,* or the repetition of the name of God in whatever form we picture him. Hanuman gives us the image of an animal that attained perfection solely by chanting the name of Rama, his personal deity, and of the utter and complete self-abnegation of his interests to that of his Lord and god Rama. Humility and selflessness are measures of our knowledge. The more we know, the more we realize how little we know and how little we can do by ourselves.

As stated, according to legend, Hanuman is the son of the wind god. Air sustains all living beings. One can exist without food, spend days without water, but it is impossible to exist even for a short time without air. Air is life. Therefore, Hanuman is also called Pranadeva, or the God of Breath or Life.

Vaishnavites, or followers of Vishnu, believe that the wind god Vayu underwent three incarnations to help Lord Vishnu. As Hanuman, he helped Rama, as Bhima, he assisted Krishna, and as Madhvacharya (1238–1317), he founded the Vaishnava sect known as Dvaita.

In Hindu symbolism, a monkey signifies the human mind, which is ever restless and never still. This monkey mind happens to be the only thing over which man can have absolute control. We cannot control the world around us, but we can control and tame our mind by ardent discipline. We cannot choose our life, but we can choose the way we respond to it. Truly, Hanuman is symbolic of the perfect mind and embodies the highest potential it can achieve. He is the true picture of the *sthitha prajna* (man of steady intellect) of the Bhagavad Gita (literally, Song of God) and had perfect control over his mind. The name Hanuman gives a clue to his character. It is a combination of two Sanskrit words, *hanan* (annihilation) and *man* (mind), thus indicating one who has conquered his ego. According to *yoga* (a physical or mental technique practiced to facilitate union with the Divine), the body is only an extension of the mind. Hence Hanuman, with perfect mastery over his mind, had the most developed body. He is sometimes called Bajarangabali (one whose body is like a thunderbolt and whose movements are like lightning). He is so strong that he can lift mountains, so agile that he can leap across the sea.

His strength is proverbial, and thus he is the patron of physical culture. His image is enshrined in gymnasiums all over India and wrestlers worship him before commencing their practice. The *yogasana* (yogic position) known as *surya namaskara,* or salutation to the sun god, is a mixture of all the main *yogic* postures combined with devotion, and it was composed by Hanuman in honor of his celestial *guru,* Surya. Vayu, his celestial father, taught him *pranayama,* or the science of breath control, which he in turn taught to human beings.

The scriptures refer to several events where Hanuman exhibited his power over the celestial bodies, including the sun and Saturn. Hence he gained power over the *navagrahas,* or nine planets of Hindu cosmology. These planets are Ravi, the sun; Soma, the moon; Mangal, Mars; Buddha, Mercury; Brihaspati, Jupiter; Shukra, Venus; Shani, Saturn; the bodiless, Rahu (the north node of the moon) and the headless, Ketu (the south node of the moon). Their alignment in the astrological chart is supposed to decide a person's destiny. In many of his images, Hanuman is shown trampling a woman and holding her by her braid. This woman embodies Panavati, or baneful astrological influences.

Sorcerers manipulate cosmic powers to invoke malevolent spirits. People normally call upon Hanuman to protect them from such people. When Ravana invoked two such sorcerers, Ahiravana and Mahiravana, Hanuman turned the tables on them and invoked the power of Kaali to subdue them. Many practitioners of Tantra worship him because he has many *siddhis,* or supernatural powers, such as the ability to change his size and the ability to fly, which he gained through his strict *brahmacharya* (celibacy) and *tapasya* (austerity). Thus he displays the dual characteristics of *bhakti* (devotion) and *shakti* (divine energy). Either one or the other is given prominence in his shrines.

He is also the patron of Ayurvedic healers, since he played a vital role in saving Lakshmana's life by bringing him the magic herb from the Himalayas. He later saved Shatrughna's life with the same herb. Lakshmana and Shatrughna were twins who were also Rama's younger brothers.

As a warrior, Hanuman has no parallel. He uses both strength and guile to overpower the enemy. This was exhibited many times during the war with the king of the demons, Ravana. He used both brawn and brain to achieve victory over his enemies.

Hanuman was also a master diplomat. He knew how to speak sweetly and make others see his side of the matter without the use of force. Hence, he was the spokesman for Sugriva, the monkey king, when he approached Rama to find out his intentions. Again Sugriva sent him to try and subdue Lakshmana's anger at his own lapse. Rama sent him as his envoy to Sita twice—once to the island fortress of Lanka carrying his signet ring, and again to fetch her after the war. He also sent him to his brother Bharata to find out his intentions before setting foot in Ayodhya. All those who came into contact with him were most impressed by his diplomatic method of talking and by his beguiling ways.

Hanuman impressed both Rama and his antagonist Ravana by his mastery over language: his impeccable grammar, his choice of the right word at the right moment and in the right context, and his perfect diction.

Strangely enough, he was also a great musician. He had been blessed by the goddess Saraswati and was thus able to play on the lute and sing lyrics in praise of Rama. He was the first to sing *bhajans* (songs of adoration) and *kirtans* (songs of praise). His music was an outpouring of his great love for his beloved master and hence even had the power to melt rocks.

Hanuman is the perfect example of a student. He was totally focused, hardworking, humble, determined, and brilliant. He flew to the solar orb in his determination to obtain the sun god, Surya, as his *guru*. However, he never flaunted his brilliance and scholarship but always sat at the feet of Rama—ever the humble servant.

Hanuman had no desire for name or fame. He preferred to live in mountains and caves. As mentioned, he practiced total celibacy, which was very strange in a simian. Even when he lived in the palace, he behaved like a hermit, never indulging his senses. This was what gave him so much spiritual power.

He was also a *hatha yogi* since he practiced *yogasanas* (yogic postures) and *pranayama* (control of the breath). He was a *laya yogi* (one who practices the yoga of immolation, dissolving into the Supreme), since he knew how to control his mind with *mantras* (sacred sounds) and *yantras* (sacred symbols). Thus, as mentioned, he acquired many *siddhis*, or supernatural powers.

If *yoga* is the ability to control one's mind, then Hanuman was the perfect *yogi*, having perfect mastery over his senses, achieved through a disciplined lifestyle and as discussed, by a strict adherence to celibacy and selfless devotion. He controlled his mind through absolute faith in the divine. Every event in his life was a gift from his master to be accepted without question. His life is a classic example to be followed by all devotees of God in any form. He shows us how a devotee should spend his or her life so as to reach the Supreme. He symbolizes the pinnacle of *bhakti*, and Hindus consider him to be the eleventh *avatara*, or incarnation, of Rudra or Lord Shiva. Once it is said that Narada asked Brahma whom he considered to be the greatest devotee of Vishnu. No doubt the sage was hoping that his name would be suggested. However, Brahma directed him to Prahlada, the king of *asuras* (demons) for whose sake Vishnu had taken a special *avatara* as Narasimha (the man-lion). Prahlada, who was himself a great devotee of Vishnu, with characteristic humility told him to go to Hanuman, whom he thought to be the greatest devotee of Vishnu since he chanted the name of Rama constantly.

Hanuman was a perfect *karma yogi* (one who practices the *yoga* of action), since he performed his actions with detachment, dedicating everything to Rama, his God. He was totally free from any desire for personal aggrandizement. In the whole of the Ramayana, there is no incident in which he did anything for himself. All his feats were for the sake of others. When he described the war to his mother, she chided him for not killing Ravana and rescuing Sita by himself, for that would have made him more famous than Rama. Hanuman replied that his life was not given to him to gain fame for himself but for serving Rama. His utter selflessness comes into great prominence when he saw how dejected the writer Valmiki was by his work. Without hesitation, he threw his own immortal classic into the sea.

Hanuman spent his entire life in the service of others. First he served Sugriva, then Rama. He personifies *bhakti* through *dasa bhava*, or the attitude of the servant. This type of devotion is the perfect instrument to destroy the ego. He performed his duties humbly, modestly, and with great devotion. He chose not to marry and have a family of his own so that he could devote himself entirely to the service of others. He never exceeded his orders even when he was capable of doing so. For instance, he could easily have killed the demon Ravana and conquered the island of Lanka on his own, as his mother said, but he refrained from doing so since he wanted to be a true servant and obey his master's orders.

He is one of the seven *chiranjeevis* (those who live until the end of this cycle of creation). He is noted for his mighty intellect and is thought to be the only scholar who knows all the nine *vyakaranas* (explanations of the Vedas). He is thought to have learned the Vedas from the sun god himself. He is the wisest of the wise, strongest of the strong, and bravest of the brave. He had the power to assume any form he liked, to swell his body to the size of a mountain or reduce it to a thumbnail. One who meditates on him will attain power, strength, glory, prosperity, and success in life.

Hanuman is the epitome of wisdom, self-control, devotion, valor, righteousness, and strength. His indispensable role in reuniting Rama with Sita is likened by some to that of a teacher helping an individual soul realize the divine.

Rama himself describes Hanuman thus: "Heroism, cleverness, strength, firmness, sagacity, prudence, prowess, and power have taken up their abode in Hanuman."

Sage Agastya endorses this view and said to Rama, "What you say regarding Hanuman is true, O Raghava! None else is equal to him in might, speed, or intelligence."

He is easily reachable just by chanting the *mantra* "Rama." Conversely, it is also held that the easiest way to attain Lord Rama is to worship Hanuman.

He is worshipped on Saturdays and Tuesdays, which are associated with Shani and Mangal, or Saturn and Mars. Both these planets are associated with death and war and known to disrupt human life by their malefic influence. His offerings are simple—*sindoor* (red lead), *til* oil (sesame), husked black gram and garlands of a certain tree (*Calotropis gigantica*) in the north, and garlands of betel leaves in the south. Also in the south, his idols are often pasted with butter that, strangely enough, never melts, even during the hottest summer. He is also adorned with garlands of rice and savory lentil doughnuts (*vadas*).

The reason for the vermillion paste will be given in the chapters below. But esoterically speaking, red is the color of strength and virility. *Til* oil is used by wrestlers and gymnasts to massage their body. Butter and dal are sources of protein and generate energy, stamina, and muscle.

The two scriptures that are read by all Hanuman devotees are the Sundara Kanda of the Ramayana, where he discovered Sita in Lanka, and the forty verses of the Hanuman Chalisa by Tulsidas, the great sixteenth-century poet. And as mentioned earlier, wherever the Ramayana is read, a special seat is always reserved for Hanuman since the belief is that he will always be present at such a reading.

What are his physical characteristics? Is he the black-faced *langur* or the red-faced *bandar*? Sometimes he is described as a golden monkey with a red face. His face is supposed to have turned black when he wiped his face with his tail after destroying Lanka.

His tail is arched upward and is the symbol of strength, agility, and virility. He wears earrings made of five metals: gold, silver, copper, iron, and tin. He came to the world already adorned with these. Normally, he wears only a loincloth in the manner of wrestlers and bodybuilders. His images usually show him saluting Rama or standing guard and displaying his strength as he holds the mountain in one hand and his mace in the other.

The Hanuman Chalisa declares categorically that there is no blessing that he cannot bestow. Sita granted him the power to bestow the eight *siddhis* and nine types of wealth on others. However, the greatest boon one can ask of Hanuman is the uplifting of the spiritual qualities that he himself is known for.

> *Having polished with the dust of my master's feet the*
> *   mirror of my heart,*
> *I narrate the pure fame of Raghupati (Rama), who*
> *   bestows life's four desires.*
> *Considering myself to be devoid of intellectual merits,*
> *I invoke Sri Hanuman, the son of the wind god.*
> *Bestow on me strength, intelligence, and knowledge.*
> *Remove my bodily ailments and vicious qualities.*
> *(And allow me to write this book.)*
>
> HANUMAN CHALISA BY TULSIDAS

Aum Sri Hanumathe Namaha!

1

Mahavira

The Historic Hanuman

More man prabhu biswasa,
Ram the adhik Ram kar dasa.

My heart, Lord, holds this conviction,
Greater than Rama is Rama's servant.

Ramacharitamanas by Tulsidas

Our first meeting with Hanuman, the monkey god, is in the great epic of Valmiki, The Ramayana. It occupies a unique place in Hindu culture because of the representation of Rama as the ideal man and Sita as the ideal woman. Of all the great religious texts, it is one that has gripped the imagination of not only the Indian continent but of many other countries of the Far East, where it has had far-reaching effects on various cultures. In fact, out of all the numerous works of Hindu literature, the Ramayana is perhaps the only one that is known to every Hindu. There are many saints in India who have attained self-realization simply by chanting the name of Rama. Hanuman is the classic example of this intense devotion. He was the chosen messenger, warrior, and servant of Rama. He lived only to serve Rama. In fact, he is such an integral part of the epic that the saying, "Where Rama's story is, there is Hanuman," is commonly repeated.

However, it is a matter of conjecture as to how this remarkable "being" suddenly appeared in Valmiki's epic without previous precedent either in the Vedas or Puranas. These extraordinary beings, which came to help Rama in the Ramayana, made their first appearance in the book of Kishkinda, a part of the Ramayana, and they were called *vanaras,* or monkeys. But most obviously, these creatures were not ordinary monkeys. They had immense strength, and some had supernatural powers and the ability to change forms at will. Though Valmiki's *rakshasas* (malevolent, cannibalistic spirits) have precursors in Vedic literature, his *vanaras* do not. Ravana had asked for the boon that he should not be killed by the gods or any other superhuman beings, but he did not mention humans and monkeys in this list since he thought they were far below his consideration. So it appears that the *vanaras* were created to fulfill this particular necessity. Many of their leaders were begotten through *vanara* women by the gods in order to assist Rama.

Thus Hanuman was a *vanara,* or monkey. He represents a stage of evolution lower than the *chandala,* or outcaste. He rose to the stature of a god through sheer strength of character and one-pointed devotion.

In the story, we see that Hanuman combines simian agility and energy with human sagacity, eloquence, and devotion, and he eventually emerges as one of the epic's most complex and fascinating characters. Was he a creation of Valmiki's genius, or is there mention of him in the Puranas or in the ancient Vedas, held to be the storehouse of all lore concerning the gods?

Some people might say that he owed his greatness to the fact that he was the son of the wind god. If this is true, then in the Mahabharata, all the Pandavas who were sons of the gods should have been deified, but none rose to Hanuman's heights. We consider the Pandavas to be mortals, but no one thinks of Hanuman as a monkey or even a human. He is a god! Actually, Valmiki does not give us a portrait of his early life, a depiction of which might have led to an understanding of his deification. We are left to conjecture this from his perfected portrait. Hanuman himself explains the secret of attaining spiritual perfection:

> *Na mantradikritastata,*
> *Na cha naisarngiko mama,*
> *Prabhava esha samanyo,*
> *Yasya yasyachutho hridi.*

> Neither by the repetition of mantras
> Nor by inherited tendencies,
> Did I gain perfection,
> But only through unwavering concentration
>   of the mind on god.

Hanuman states very clearly that his greatness was due to his constant effort and not due to his inborn character, that of an ordinary monkey. *Brahmajnana* is possible for all. *Moksha,* "liberation," is everybody's birthright. In his case, Hanuman declares that his entire spiritual development was attained by single-pointed devotion to god. He who constantly thinks of the Supreme becomes Supreme. Absolute surrender to god is the secret of spiritual perfection. Spiritual transformation cannot be brought about by the mere chanting of *mantras* or offerings in temples and other superficial rituals. It is also not something that can be inherited. An infant, whether begotten by god or man, is still an animal. Evolution only aids its physical growth. Spiritual growth is impossible without effort. Learning and discipline must be present if one is to reach this higher form of evolution. An imperfect body is made perfect when it is made into an instrument of god. Then even our shortcomings will turn into advantages. When the entire personality is molded into the Supreme, even shortcomings become helpful. So we find that it was his monkey nature that helped him to cross the ocean, reach Lanka, discover Sita, and bring the message back to Rama. He had no private enjoyments. The good results of his actions always went to other people. Thus, Valmiki portrayed a remarkable character in Hanuman, a model for all those who aspire toward liberation.

In his technique of creating real, down-to-earth beings who are nonetheless capable of deification, Valmiki exceeds Vyasa, the author of the Mahabharata. The characters of the Ramayana are a happy combination of historic realism and religious symbolism, appealing both to the religious-minded and secular person. With the sole exception of Krishna, none of the other characters in the Mahabharata lend themselves to deification. In order to prove his divinity, Vyasa allows Krishna to perform miracles and exhibit his cosmic form many times. However, Valmiki's portrait of Rama is in black and white with no embellishments. He never allowed his poetry to become the handmaid of mysticism. Rama is the Maryada Purusha, or the perfect human being, who by his exemplary adherence to the cosmic *dharma* became a god, and Hanuman is an ordinary simian who, by dint of his unflinching devotion to Rama and extraordinary attention to his duty, also became a god.

According to the Hindu point of view, there is no objective world out there. The whole manifested world is a subjective phenomenon created by our own selves. As humans, we have the unique ability to condition our minds. In other words, we have the power to change the way we perceive life. And by changing our perception of life, we have the power to change our world. When Hanuman entered Rama's life, he changed Rama's world. He transformed a crisis (the loss of Sita) into an opportunity to rid the world of Ravana. He transformed a victim into a hero.

Even though Hanuman does not appear in the earlier Shruti Vedas, the two gods from whom he claims paternity are both from these Vedas—Vayu, the god of wind and Rudra, the god of destruction. Rudra is both one and many and is the prototype of the later Puranic Shiva. Hanuman's association with Vayu is shown in his swiftness. In Ayurveda, or the Vedic science of healing, illness is declared to be the imbalance between the three humors of the body: *vata* (wind), *pitta* (sun), and *kapha* (moon). Of the three, *vata* plays a crucial role in the upkeep of the body. Many diseases, including rheumatism, gout, epilepsy, and paralysis, are attributed to an excess of the wind factor. Hanuman is closely linked with this essential humor as depicted in the delineation of his characteristics later on. Some of his important names are Vayuputra, the son of Vayu, the wind god, and Vatamaja, born of Vayu. All bodily functions are controlled by the five winds, or *vayus*. These are *prana, apana, vyana, samana,* and *udana.* They take care of the different autonomic functions of the body such as breathing, digestion, excretion, and so on. There is one figure of Hanuman with five heads that correspond to these five winds. Thus it is said that he is in charge of our involuntary functions and so devotion to him will give us health.

Of course, apart from this, the present-day picture of Hanuman came only after the advent of the Valmiki Ramayana, so his debut in the Hindu pantheon of gods is very recent. He belongs to the category of the "second generation" deities. However, as his devotees point out, in most regions of India there are far more shrines to Hanuman than to his exalted master. Actually, out of the trinity of Brahma, Vishnu, and Shiva, it is only Shiva whose offspring seem to have sprung into prominence and in some cases even usurped their parents' high status. The three well-known sons of Shiva are Ganesha, Kartikeya, and Dharma Shasta or Ayyappa. Hanuman also claims to be the son of Shiva. In fact, he is said to be the eleventh Rudra, as was mentioned before. Ravana was a great devotee of Shiva, and thus it appears strange that his son could have become his enemy. The story that circumvents this particular dilemma has it that Ravana had once sacrificed his ten heads to Shiva but had not appeased the eleventh Rudra, no doubt because he didn't have another head!

All the sons of Shiva seem to have exerted a great fascination on the Indian mind. Ganesha is universally acclaimed and worshipped by all sects of Hindus. He has even gone across the seas, and you see many devotees of Ganesha even in the west. Kartikeya used to be very popular in the north at one time, but now his temples are almost exclusively found in the south and in Sri Lanka. He is known as Skanda, Murugan, and Swaminathan in the south. Ayyappa is a fairly modern advent. His main temple used to be in Kerala alone, in the place known as the

Shabari Hills. He is the god for this age of Kali since he is supposed to have been born from both Shiva and Vishnu and has both their powers. His popularity is increasing in many other states in the south and now you find temples even in Delhi. Hanuman, on the other hand, used to be more popular in the north since he is almost the hero of Tulsidas' Ramacharitamanas (Hindi Ramayan), the sixteenth-century Awadhi version of the Ramayana, perused daily by most Hindi-speaking people. But now we find that his worship is becoming more and more popular in the south. At one time there were no separate temples to him, but now some of his biggest temples are found in the south, like the ones at Namakkal and Suchindram. He displays a versatility that is greater than that of the other second-generation deities. Ganesha has certain specialities, but he is not an embodiment of boundless mercy, self-sacrifice, or ascetic rigor like Hanuman.

Hanuman has legs in both camps—Shiva and Vishnu. His father is Shiva and he is the greatest devotee of Vishnu in his *avatara* as Rama. Therefore he became very popular with both Shaivites (those who follow Shiva) and Vaishnavites (those who follow Vishnu). Like the other sons of Shiva, he has a plethora of birth stories. Ganesha, as has been mentioned, is universally adored in both northern and southern India and is perhaps the most popular. However, Hanuman seems to be a close competitor in the popularity polls, though possibly Ganesha has a slight advantage over him since it has been declared in the Puranas that he has to be worshipped first before starting any venture. Of course, Hanuman is a specialist to whom people turn for the specific services in which he excels. He is capable of warding off all evil portents and planetary disturbances, so he is slowly creeping into prominence. In fact, in Maharashtra, which is predominantly a state devoted to Ganesha worship, we find that Ganesha's shrines are outnumbered almost four-to-one by those to Maruti, as Hanuman is sometimes known, since he is the son of the wind god, and the name Maruti is a form of the Sanskrit word for wind. Many scholars are of the opinion that Hanuman worship is an outgrowth of *yaksha* worship. The *yakshas* (nature spirits) are the guardians of the wealth of the earth and are known for their great strength and swiftness. Their figures were often carved outside temples and villages, as *dwarapalas,* or guardians of the gate, and also as *kshetrapalas,* or guardians of the temples and villages. Now we find that Hanuman's figure has replaced the early figures of *yakshas* and is always found outside temples and villages. Kubera, the king of the *yakshas,* is always depicted with a mace (*gada*) in his hands, and of course, this is the only weapon that Hanuman carries. After Rama left the earth, Hanuman retired to the Himalayas, to a place close to a lake owned by the *yakshas,* thus showing his affinity to them. This is where he met his half-brother Bhima.

A number of monkey idols have been unearthed in the excavations of the Indus civilization, which might suggest the worship of such a monkey god from those times, but the clues are very slight. The Rig Veda is purported to contain numerous allusions to Hanuman in the Samhitas as well as in the Satapatha Brahmanas. Some of the hymns are thought to contain allusions to the events of the Ramayana. There is one specific Rigvedic passage in which some mention is made of a tawny yellow bull-monkey called Vrishakapi. Indra's wife complains that this monkey has usurped her husband's portion of the Vedic offerings. The name Vrishakapi occurs in the Purana known as Harivamsa, in which he is identified with the eleventh form of Rudra. This name is also found in the Mahabharata in the Vishnu Sahasranama (thousand names of Vishnu), as one of the names of Vishnu. Documentation on Hanuman worship dates back only to about a thousand years, and thus he is considered to be only an infant as far as Indologists are concerned. In fact, some of his most significant manifestations have appeared only in the last few centuries.

The largest amount of material on Hanuman is, however, found in the Puranas. Mention of him is made in the Agni, Vishnu, Kurma, Garuda, Brahmavaivarta, Narasimha, Kalki, and Bhagavata Puranas. The Agni Purana gives instructions for constructing an image of Hanuman with two feet pressing down an *asura* and with two hands, one of which holds a *vajra,* or thunderbolt. The elaborate story of Ahiravana, which is not found in Valmiki's epic, is found in the Shiva Purana. This Purana also includes another variant of his birth in which his mother is impregnated with Shiva's seed, thus making him an *amsa,* or portion of Shiva himself. In another passage, he is called an *avatara* of Rudra. This link with Shiva is mentioned in the Skanda, Padma, and Naradiya Puranas. The last Purana also offers a *mantra* for Hanuman's worship and describes the *yantra* to be used in lieu of an icon. It also says that water made potent with the use of this *mantra* will have the power to drive away ghosts and cure maladies like fever and epilepsy. The text also identifies Hanuman as the founder of classical music, and musicians are advised to pray to him in order to attain perfection. The Purana also describes Hanuman as the embodiment of the combined power of Shiva and Vishnu. However, it is a fact that the majority of the earlier Puranas do not mention Hanuman, and even if they do, it is only in the context of retelling the Ramayana.

Mention of him is made more in the group of Puranic texts known as the Shiva Puranas. From early times, his worship has been upheld by the Shaivite ascetics. Like Shiva, he displays ascetic tendencies and does not care for fame or fortune. Shaivites believe that both Shiva and Vishnu descended on earth as Hanuman and Rama to destroy the unrighteous Ravana, who had misused the power that Shiva had bestowed on him. Without Hanuman, Rama would have been helpless. It was Maruti (Hanuman) who found Sita, built the bridge to Lanka, and helped Rama to fight and kill Ravana. However, he never claimed any honor for himself and always remained in Rama's shadow. His attributes are most appealing to *yogis*. He is physically immortal and linked with many herbs, and he has many *siddhis* sought after by *yogis*. As we know, he was also held to be a strict celibate, and due to his supernormal powers of strength and fleetness, he is worshipped by wrestlers and athletes.

Vaishnavites naturally worship Hanuman as the embodiment of *bhakti* to Rama, the sixth incarnation of Vishnu.

Shaktas, or worshippers of Shakti, the Divine Mother, worship him since the Devi (goddess) is thought to have been very pleased with him when he helped unite Sita with Rama. Kaali was very pleased with him when he killed the sorcerer Mahiravana and offered his blood to her. He is thought to be the guardian of a woman's chastity since he never looked on any woman with lecherous eyes.

In Tantric tradition, Hanuman is seen as the perfect Tantric who has acquired all the eight *siddhis*. After he rescued Rama from the great sorcerer Mahiravana, he was also considered to be a master of sorcery and also one who can protect people from black magic.

As we will discuss later when touching upon the Adhyatma Ramayana, Vedanta views Hanuman as the personification of *bhakti,* which is instrumental in uniting Sita (here representing the *jivatma,* or individual spirit) with Rama (here representing the *Paramatma,* or Supreme Soul*)* after destroying Ravana (here representing *ahamkara,* or ego).

Tales of Hanuman reached Southeast Asia through the merchant ships sailing from the east coast of India. Hanuman and Rama are very popular characters in the art of ancient Cambodia, Vietnam, Thailand, Burma, Bali, and Malaysia.

Buddhist monks took the story of the monkey-hero to China where he became extremely popular as the Golden Monkey. However, his character in these countries is totally different from the Indian Maruti. There he lived a hedonistic life and terrorized everyone, including the gods, and was eventually tamed by the Buddha himself.

Hanuman is thought to be the original narrator of the story of Rama. Not only was he was an eyewitness to the events he describes, but his motive in telling the tale was purely to extol his Lord Rama. However, tradition has it that this tale survives only in fragments, filtered through the lenses of human storytellers such as Valmiki, Kampan, Tulsidas, and so on.

Victory to thee, O Hanuman,
Ocean of wisdom and virtue,
Hail to thee, O Lord of monkeys,
Illuminator of the three worlds.

HANUMAN CHALISA BY TULSIDAS

Aum Sri Hanumathe Namaha!

ॐ

Aum Anjaneyaaya Namaha!

2

Anjaneya
Son of Anjana

Hanuman Anjana sunu,
Vayuputro mahabala,
Rameshta Phalguna sakha,
Pingaksha amitavikrama,
Utathikarmanaschaiva,
Sita—shoka vinashaka,
Lakshmana prana datha cha,
Dasagreevashcha darpaha,
Evam dwadasa naamani,
Kapindrascha mahatmana,
Swapakale pateth nityam,
Yatrakale visheshata,
Tasya mrityu bhayam nasti,
Saravatra vijayi bhavet.

Hanuman, the son of Anjana,
The powerful son of Vayu,
Friend of Rama and Arjuna,

The red-eyed doer of impossible deeds,
The dispeller of Sita's sorrow,
Giver of Lakshmana's life,
Foe of the ten-headed one,
One who meditates on this noble monkey with
    twelve names,
In the morning,
And at the time of travel,
Will never be frightened of death,
And will ever be victorious.

HANUMATH DHYANAM

The ancient *rishis* placed great importance on the choice of names. There is a mysterious connection between a word and its meaning, and this is the foundation of the *yoga* known as *japa,* or continuous repetition of the names of any deity. Hanuman, is supposed to have gained all his powers from the continuous *japa* of the *mantra* "Rama." The name that he is most commonly known by is Hanuman, and this has two meanings. One meaning is that he has (*man*), a prominent or disfigured jaw (*hanu*). This came about as a result of his jumping for the sun as a child. Another meaning is one whose ego or mind (*man*) has been destroyed (*han*). His second most common name is Anjaneya, or the son of Anjana, as well as Ajaniputra. He has many names derived from his father Vayu. He is known as Vayuputra, Pavanaputra, and Pavakatmaja as well as Maruti, all of which denote him as the son of Vayu, the Vedic wind god. He is also known as Kesarisutha, the son of Kesari and Kesarinandana, Kesari's darling, in which he is linked with his simian father, Kesari. Strangely enough, he has no names that link him with Rudra. When he is called on for protection, he is known as Bajarangabali, which is actually a corruption of the Sanskrit word *vajra* (thunderbolt) along with *anga* (limb), denoting one whose limbs are as hard as the thunderbolt. Another popular name is Sankata Mochana, or the one who releases us from sorrows and dangers. He is also known as Veera and Mahavira, both denoting his great powers. Sometimes he is referred to as Panchavaktra, or the five-faced one, and Kapiswara, or lord of monkeys.

There are many stories connected with the birth of Hanuman. He claims paternity to two gods and a simian father also, but there has never been any argument about his mother. Many of his epithets, as we have seen, identify him as the "son" of someone, but he has only one name that connects him with his mother. She has always been accepted as Anjana.

Even though he is normally considered as the son of the wind god Vayu, one story goes that he was actually the son of Shiva and Parvati and was born from Shiva's seed.

Shiva was not present when Vishnu took on the form of Mohini in order to outwit the demons. When he heard of Mohini's exquisite beauty, he was eager to see her. He went to Vaikunta, the abode of Vishnu, and asked him to reveal her form to him. When he saw Mohini's world-enchanting form, it is said that even Shiva, the supreme ascetic, fell in love with her. He chased her and embraced her. At that time, his seed, formed out of his great *tapasya,* slipped out. His semen, which was gleaming on a leaf, was caught by the seven sages, or *sapta rishis.* When the propitious time came, they gave the seed to Vayu, who took it to the forest where Anjana was doing *tapas.* She was seated on a hill worshipping Shiva and asking him to bless her with a son. The wind god approached her as a gentle breeze and slipped the celestial seed through her ear into her womb. In due course, the baby monkey who was called Hanumat (in Sanskrit) was born out of Shiva's seed.

In the Ananda Ramayana, Hanuman is said to be Rama's brother, born of the same sacred potion that made Dasaratha's wives pregnant. Anjana had been worshipping Shiva for many years in order to get an exemplary son. Shiva told her that he was pleased with her *tapasya* and would be born to her as the eleventh Rudra. He told her to raise her cupped palms to heaven and wait patiently. Meanwhile, Dasaratha, the king of Ayodhya, was performing the *putrakamesti yaga* in order to have children. As a result, he received a celestial pudding to be distributed among his three wives. Having partaken of the sweet, they gave birth to Rama, Lakshmana, Bharata, and Shatrugna. By divine ordinance, Vayu, in the form of a hawk, is said to have swooped and pecked a bit of the pudding from the hands of the youngest wife, Sumitra. He dropped it into Anjana's outstretched palms while flying over the hill where she was engaged in worship. She consumed the sweet morsel and Hanuman was born to her as a result. This actually made him Rama's half-brother.

Another story goes that Anjana was the daughter of sage Gautama and his wife Ahalya. The latter was seduced by Indra, the king of gods, who approached her in the form of her husband. When Gautama returned, he cursed both of them. Ahalya believed that her daughter had told on her to Gautama and cursed her to become a monkey. Anjana decided to perform austerities in order to overcome the effects of the curse. She was so absorbed in her *tapas* that an anthill started to grow over her. The wind god Vayu took pity on her and fed her regularly through a hole in the anthill. Meanwhile, Shiva and Parvati used to sport in the forest, taking on the form of various animals. Once when they were in monkey form, Shiva's seed was ejaculated and Parvati could not bear the intensity of his seed. So Vayu picked it up and carried it to Anjana. Three months later, Hanuman emerged from her mouth in the form of a baby monkey. (This story will be elaborated upon in another chapter.)

The Valmiki Ramayana gives a different version of the birth of Hanuman. The celestial maid Punchikasthala was cursed by a sage and had to be born on earth as a monkey, but she had the power to assume human form at will. Once, when she was wandering along the mountainside in her beautiful human form, her garments were lifted up by the wind. Vayu was enamoured by her lovely limbs and ruffled her clothes and entered into her. Anjana sensed this violation and was about to curse her unseen paramour when the god appeared before her and promised her that not only would there be no loss to her chastity but she would also get a powerful son equal in strength to himself.

The story as given in the Shiva Purana is a little different. Once

Parvati heard her husband repeating the *mantra* "Rama" and asked him the reason. Shiva replied that the *mantra* was very potent, since it designated the ultimate reality that had taken the form of an earthly prince and was an *avatara* of Vishnu.

"Parvati! Rama is very dear to me and I am going to incarnate myself on earth in order to serve him." Parvati protested at this but Shiva said that he would send only an *amsa* (part) of himself. Shiva decided to take on the form of a monkey since it is humble, with simple needs and a simple lifestyle, and needed no observance of the rules of caste and stages of life. This would give him maximum scope for service. Initially, Parvati was shocked at this, but Shiva convinced her that the monkey form was the ideal one for avoiding the lure of *maya*. Parvati asked to accompany him and volunteered to become his tail, for the wife is an ornament of her husband as the tail is of a monkey. Shiva agreed to this and that is why Hanuman's tail is so beautiful and imbued with *shakti,* the power of the goddess.

Another story goes that Ravana and Kumbhakarna were incarnations of two of Shiva's attendants; hence, he was obliged to protect them. However, they became arrogant due to the boons they had received from Brahma and started to harass the gods who appealed to Shiva to protect them. Shiva's anger was fully roused when Ravana imprisoned Mahakala, the lord of death, and Shani, the planet Saturn. This is another reason why he decided to incarnate as Hanuman.

In the time of the Manu Swayambhu, a sage called Shilada did penance to please Shiva and requested that he would like to have a son like him. Shiva agreed to this, and his eleventh manifestation was born as his son Nandi. The son performed penance and obtained the boon that he would be born as Shiva's devotee in the form of a bull. While Ravana was rampaging across the earth, he had the temerity to go to Kailasa. Nandi stopped him from entering, and Ravana ridiculed and taunted him, telling him that his face resembled that of a monkey! Nandi cursed him that he would meet his end through a monkey's intervention. Later he requested Shiva to be allowed to be born on Earth as Hanuman, "the bull" among monkeys.

One more story in the Shiva Purana says that the wind god Vayu assisted Shiva in slaying the demon called Jalandhara. Shiva offered him a boon. Vayu requested that Shiva be born on Earth as his own son, and Shiva agreed.

Vishnu wanted Shiva's help in order to slay Ravana, so he prayed to Shiva and performed a *puja* (ritual) to him by offering red lotuses, each having a thousand petals. Shiva appeared and informed him that he had already given the boon to Anjana that he would be born as her son and would certainly help him in his *avatara* as Rama.

Since he has been credited with a great number of birth stories, naturally many texts also set different dates on which he is said to have been born. Actually, eight different dates have been given, and these are enumerated below. All birth dates are gauged according to the Hindu lunar calendar.

1. Chitra Purnima, or the full moon of the month of Chaitra (March/April).
2. Chitra shukla ekadasi, or the eleventh day of the bright fortnight of Chaitra.
3. Kartika Purnima, or the full moon of the month of Kartika (October/November).
4. Kartika Amavasya, or the new moon of the month of Kartika.
5. Shravana shukla ekadasi, or the eleventh day of the bright fortnight of the month of Shravana (July/August).
6. Shravan Purnima, or the full moon of the month of Shravana.
7. Margashirsha shukla trayodasi, or the thirteenth day of the bright fortnight of the month of Margashirsha (November/December).
8. Ashvin amavasya, or the new moon of the month of Ashvin (September/October).

Out of these, two have come to enjoy wide prominence. The most popular is the full moon in the month of Chitra, which heralds spring. This sets Hanuman's birthday five days after that of Rama, who was born on Chitra *navami,* or the ninth day of the bright fortnight of Chitra. This also places his birthday in *uttarayanam,* or the waxing sun, when it is moving northward toward the Himalayas and the world of the gods.

However, in Ayodhya, the birthplace of Rama, his birthday is celebrated six months later, on the new moon of the autumn month of Kartika. This is also known as *yaksha amavasya,* which again points to his connection with the *yakshas,* as has been pointed out before. This date comes in *dakshinayana,* or the night of the gods, when the sun heads south toward the realm of the dead and hence is considered to be waning. These two birthdates give Hanuman a foothold in both halves of the ritual year, one which is associated with the bright forces, or *devas,* and the other with the world of the dead and elemental forces.

It is claimed that he was born either on a Tuesday or a Saturday and thus these two days are kept aside for his worship. As mentioned, according to Indian astrology, these two days are most inauspicious since they are governed by the malignant planets, Mangala, or Mars, which presides over Tuesday, and Shani, or Saturn, which presides over Saturday. Worshippers of Hanuman are automatically protected from the evil effects of these planets.

> *You are the incomparable emissary of Rama and the*
>   *abode of might,*
> *You are also known as Anjaniputra [Anjana's son] and*
>   *Pavanaputra [son of the wind].*

HANUMAN CHALISA BY TULSIDAS

Aum Sri Hanumathe Namaha!

3

Kesari Putra

Son of Kesari

Sarvarishtanivaarakam, Shubhakaram,
Pingakshamakshapaham,
Sitanweshana tat param, kapivaram,
Kodindusurya prabham.

Greatest among monkeys,
With the effulgence of a hundred thousand suns,
Capable of removing all troubles,
With red-tinged eyes,
Who is renowned for having discovered Sita.

HANUMAN STOTRA

The Puranas give graphic pictures of the many *lokas,* or astral realms, where dwell different types of beings. The *apsaras* were celestial dancers and normally lived in Indra's court. Punchikasthala was one such *apsara.* As a child she was adopted by Brihaspati, the *guru* of the gods, who took her to his own *ashrama* and brought her up as his daughter. She had a highly spiritual nature and was sweet and kind to all. Even as a child, she busied herself collecting flowers for his *puja* and making herself generally useful to all. Thus she grew up in this background of spirituality where she hardly ever saw any young men and certainly none who were not spiritually inclined. She was as sweet and untouched as one of the flowers that blossomed in the *ashrama* gardens. She never wandered beyond the precincts of the *ashrama,* so she had no idea of the normal behavior of young people. Thus she grew up totally untouched and unaware of human nature. At the age of seventeen, she was a raving beauty but had no idea of her own charms. One day, as chance would have it, she wandered beyond the boundaries of the *ashrama* into the forest in order to pick better flowers and thus please her father. Just then, her gaze was transfixed by the sight of some *gandharvas* (celestial singers) who were sporting in the lake and jousting with each other. Never had she seen such handsome bare bodies. Her whole body flamed with desire when she beheld these beings. Her upbringing was totally forgotten. The flowers she had collected fell unheeded from her hands and she sat spellbound, watching the play of these celestial beings. She yearned with all her heart to get such a being as her husband.

In the evening, Brihaspati noticed her absence and went in search of her. He was shocked to see her standing mesmerized by the erotic scenes that were being enacted in front of her eyes. So absorbed was she that she was totally unaware of his arrival.

"Punchikasthala!" he thundered. "What are you staring at? Have you forgotten that you are an *ashramite?* These types of scenes should not be viewed by you. Come back, my child, and promise never to come to this place again or else I may have to ask you to leave this *ashrama.*"

For the first time, she did not meekly agree with her father. In fact, she was even bold enough to retort.

"What have I done that you should scold me so harshly? All I did was to gaze at these beings. They are so glorious to behold. I have never seen anyone like them!"

Brihaspati understood her feelings and gazed sadly at her.

"My child!" he said. "We are *ashram* dwellers. Our only aim in life is to attain self-realization. The life of the normal ego-centered individual is shunned by us. But I realize your weakness. You are young and perhaps unable to overcome your feelings for a family life. Let it be. I will send you to the mortal world where you will be born as a monkey. In the short span of the life of a monkey, you will be able to assuage your desire for sex. After that, you will be able to renew your original form and return to this world."

Punchikasthala fell at his feet and begged him to retract his curse. Brihaspati looked fondly at her and said, "The curse of a saint is always a blessing. It is always meant to fulfil a deep divine purpose, and my curse is no exception to this rule. You will be the mother of a male monkey who will be glorified in the whole world as the greatest of *bhaktas* (devotees). He will be renowned for his valor, intelligence, and adherence to *dharma*. He will be the supreme devotee of Lord Vishnu in his *avatara* as Rama, king of Ayodhya. The moment he is born, you will regain your former body and be able to return to these heavenly regions."

Seeing her pleading look, he continued, "It is better for you to get rid of these lower desires now in the form of a monkey where they will be totally exhausted in the shortest possible time and then return to this *ashrama* where you can continue your former practices and gain liberation. You will be known as Anjana and will be able to assuage your thirst for sex with a handsome monkey of your choice. At the appointed time when you are united with your husband, the wind god Vayu will deposit the seed of Lord Shiva in your womb, and thus you will have a baby with all the qualities of Lord Shiva and the speed and strength of the wind god."

Everything happened as the sage had predicted. Punchikasthala was born in a tribe of monkeys as the daughter of the chief called Kunjara. She was named Anjana. However, she remembered her past life perfectly and was not happy at leading the life of a normal monkey. As soon as she was able to, she left the tribe and penetrated deep into the forest. She wandered hungry and thirsty without finding anything to eat. At last, she came upon a huge tree filled with luscious fruit. She jumped up the tree, but just a she stretched her hand to pluck the fruit, she heard an ethereal voice.

"Anjana! You should not eat anything until you have bathed and said your prayers. You have come to this forest with a purpose. In order to fulfill this, you should live the life of an anchorite. Do *tapasya* to Lord Shiva and Parvati to give you a wondrous son and deliver you from your curse."

Anjana was glad to follow this advice from a divine source. From that day onward, she strictly adhered to the life of an anchorite. She would get up early in the morning, take her bath, and sit meditating on the divine couple Shiva and Parvati. It was only after doing this that she would pluck the fruits and leaves of trees to assuage her hunger.

One day she was rudely awakened from her austerities by a hideous noise. The whole forest seemed to be in a state of unrest. Birds were screaming and flying around in fear, and even the animals in the forest seemed to be running for their lives. Suddenly she saw the enormous figure of a *rakshasa* (giant cannibal) standing in front of her. Trembling with fear, she started to get up and run. But the creature accosted her.

"O beautiful one!" he roared. "Why are you running away from me? I will not harm you. My name is Shambasaadan and I'm the king of this forest. However, I am prepared to marry you and give you everything you desire. Come close to me and let us make love. Life is too short to waste time doing useless austerities!"

With this profound pronouncement, he made a lunge at her. Anjana escaped his clutches and ran for her life. Since she was a monkey, she could swing from branch to branch, but her sinister suitor was not to be put off so easily. He was so huge that he trampled over trees and bushes in hot pursuit. Half-crazed with fear, Anjana cried out to her guardian deities to save her from this new calamity. To her amazement, just as he made a lunge to catch her, he was felled to the spot. She was astonished at this miraculous reprieve and went to investigate if he were really dead. She saw a huge cobra slithering off.

Just then a voice warned her that Shambasaadan was only unconscious and might recover soon. She bent over, peered at his face, and saw signs of life. Not waiting to investigate further, she ran deeper into the forest. At last, tired and desperate, she came upon an *ashrama*. She threw herself at the mercy of the anchorites there and begged them to save her from this predicament.

Seeing her distress, they gave her water to drink and told her to take refuge there. When she mentioned the name Shambasaadan, they quivered with fear and told her that he was a cruel *rakshasa* who terrorized the whole forest. They could not practice their fire rituals without fear of his coming and despoiling everything.

"The only one who is capable of vanquishing him is a heroic monkey called Kesari." Hearing this, Anjana prayed to her favorite deities to send Kesari and enable him to kill the *rakshasa* who was harassing all the *ashramites* and holding the forest in thrall. She spent the night in prayer.

It is said that Kesari had once killed a mighty elephant that was troubling the sages and hermits. That is how he got the name Kesari, which means "lion." He was also called Kunjara Südana (the elephant killer).

The next morning, the whole *ashrama* came to life and all of them felt some new hope in their breasts. They started to prepare their morning rituals—their *yajnas* and *yagas*. These were Vedic rites in which offerings were made into the blazing fire accompanied by *mantras* and secret incantations for the well-being of the world and for their own spiritual progress. They were a bit worried about starting it since Shambasaadan came very often to put an end to their rites. They were waiting anxiously, not knowing whether to start or not, when a mighty monkey came into their midst. He was tall and handsome and looked as if he were capable of routing anyone. He told them not to fear but to start their rituals and he would guard them as he had done of yore. He looked enquiringly at the newcomer in their midst and the *rishis* introduced Anjana to him. This was the hero Kesari about whom they had told her. She took an instant liking to him and felt that he was truly capable of saving all of them from the scourge of the *rakshasa*. Without further ado, he jumped onto one of the trees and stayed hidden behind the leaves.

Just then, there was a tremendous uproar and the whole forest became petrified. The birds squawked and flew hither and thither; the deer ran off in different directions, not knowing where to flee. Suddenly, the hideous form of the *rakshasa* appeared. Immediately, he spied Anjana shaking with fear and trying to hide in a corner of the compound.

Putting out a huge, hairy hand, he caught her and pulled her toward him. He was reeking of stale blood and sweat, and she shivered with disgust as he drew her closer. In a disgustingly intimate voice, as if to seduce her, he said beguilingly, "Ah! My little dove! Why do you try to flee from me? Don't you know that I'm crazy about you? You can never escape me. I'll follow you to the end of the world if necessary. Come! Let us go away, and we will live in luxury and happiness. These cowards don't have the power to save you, but I'll protect and guard you always."

The terrified Anjana shrieked and cried out, "Save me! Save me! Is there no one who can save me from this beast?"

"God himself is helpless before me! So who can save you now?"

Just at that moment, the mighty Kesari jumped out of the tree with a loud roar and landed right in front of the *rakshasa*.

"O Shambasaadana!" he roared. "If you value your life, let go of the girl!"

Hearing this, Shambasaadana put Anjana to the ground and said, "O! Are you the one who has come as her protector? I'll make mincemeat of you first and deal with her later."

Taking this opportunity, Anjana ran into the hermitage and closed the door.

The *rakshasa* laughed long and loud as he saw Kesari standing before him with an arrow fixed to his bow ready to let fly at him.

"O, you stupid monkey!" he said. "Are you so presumptuous to suppose that you can save this girl and the *ashramites*? I'll make short work of you and the ashrama and then make off with the girl."

So saying, the *rakshasa* plucked a huge tree from the forest and threw it at Kesari. The latter immediately split the tree in mid-air with his arrow and felled it to the ground before it could cause any damage.

This infuriated the *rakshasa,* who uprooted a small mound nearby and hurled it at Kesari. Once again, Kesari shattered the mound with his arrow. The *rakshasa* couldn't believe his eyes. He flew at the monkey as if he would throttle him with his bare arms. Kesari rained a whole host of arrows at him.

The latter knew that he had met his match, so he resorted to his magic tricks and took on the form of a maddened elephant. He caught the fleeing *rishis* and threw them around, destroyed their ashrama, and defiled their *yajna kund (container for sacred fire)*. Anjana saved herself by hiding in the hollow of a huge tree.

All that time, Kesari had been raining arrows at the mad elephant, but they merely grazed the skin of the animal and fell to the ground. The enraged pachyderm now turned his full fury on him. He plucked the bow from him and stamped on it. Kesari immediately took the form of a little monkey and flew into the air. He landed with great force on the forehead of the elephant. This is supposed to be an elephant's weakest point. He then proceeded to pound this tender spot with adamantine fists. Try as he might, the elephant could not shake off the little monkey who was hammering on his weak point with such force. So he immediately changed his form back to that of a *rakshasa*, plucked off the monkey, and dashed him to the ground.

Kesari regained his normal stature and started pelting the demon with his arrows. Even though blood was oozing from the wounds, he seemed to be completely unaffected and laughed in scorn. Anjana felt desperate and mentally begged Lord Shiva to save Kesari. Immediately, she felt a response.

Shiva told her that the *rakshasa* could not be killed with anything but his own blood. She asked how this could be managed. The reply was that she should think of a ruse herself.

She cogitated deeply on the matter. Suddenly, she spied an arrow that had fallen a little distance from the place where the two heroes were engaged in a desperate battle, which they both knew would be a fight to the finish. She could see that Kesari's strength was flagging. Spurred by this, she crept forward, rescued the arrow, and smeared it with the blood that had fallen from the *rakshasa*. Now she was on the lookout for an opportune moment to pass this to Kesari.

The demon now assumed the form of a gigantic buffalo and came with lowered horns to gore Kesari. The latter immediately fixed two arrows on his bow and aimed them at the buffalo's eyes. It was a real bull's-eye, and the buffalo reeled and bellowed in pain.

Anjana took this opportunity to rush to Kesari's side. She whispered Shambasaadana's secret to him, gave him the blood-smeared arrow, and told him to shoot the arrow at the earliest opportunity. By this time, the demon had realized that his best bet would be to discard the buffalo form and with it the fatal injury to its eyes. Anjana hardly had time to run off when Shambasaadana rushed at Kesari, shouting imprecations all the while.

He raised his huge iron mace above his head and flourished it.

"This will make an end of you once and for all, you puny little monkey!" he shouted.

Before he could hurl the fatal weapon, Kesari prayed to Lord Shiva and let fly the arrow that Anjana had given him. The arrow poisoned with Shambasaadana's own blood flew unerringly toward its mark and buried itself in the demon's heart. Shambasaadana gave a mighty roar and started reeling with pain. At last, he fell with a tremendous thud that made the whole earth shudder.

The relieved *rishis* now rushed out with shouts of joy and praised Kesari, thanking him for having rescued them from this constant pestilence. Once more they could conduct their rituals without fear of being molested by the demon. Kesari told them to thank Anjana, for she was the one who had disclosed the secret of the demon's weak point, and had he not been told of it, he would never have managed to kill him. The *rishis* now turned to Anjana and thanked her also.

"How can we show our gratitude to you both?" the *rishis* asked. They discussed the matter among themselves and then came and spoke to Anjana.

"My child! Will you be prepared to do our bidding? It is something for your own good."

Anjana promised to obey the *rishis,* no matter what they said.

The *rishis* then smilingly asked her, "Will you consent to marry Kesari?"

Anjana bent her head shyly. They took this as a sign of consent. Kesari also professed his willingness to this happy alliance, and the wedding was conducted on a modest scale by the joyful *ashramites.*

> *O valorous one! With body like a thunderbolt,*
> *Exterminator of evil thoughts and companion to the*
> *good.*

HANUMAN CHALISA BY TULSIDAS

Aum Sri Hanumathe Namaha!

4

Vayu Putra

Son of Vayu

Lankadwipa bhayankaram, sakaladam,
Sugrivasammanitam,
Devendradi samastha devavinutam,
Kakasthadutam bhaje.

I worship the emissary of Rama,
Who is worshipped by all the gods starting with Indra,
Who subdued the terrible island of Lanka to Sugriva's
    great delight.

HANUMAN STOTRA

Some years passed before their passion for each other was fully abated. Swinging from tree to tree, Kesari would pluck the sweetest and most luscious fruits for his beloved, and thus they spent many happy years. However, their love did not produce any fruit. This again was her *guru's* blessing, for he had told her that the moment she held her first-born in her arms, she would be free from the curse and be able to return to her heavenly abode. He wanted to give her a chance to exhaust all her desires for physical pleasures before granting her a child. A time came when Anjana started to feel unhappy at the thought that, though she had spent so many years as a wife, she still had not become a mother. Kesari knew the cause of her unhappiness, and he told her that it was best that they should undergo some penance in order to be blessed with a son. Anjana told him that the only way was to do *tapas* to Shiva and Parvati and they would surely grant their wish for a noble son. Thus the couple prayed intensely to the divine couple to grant their desire. They had only one meal during the day. They no longer slept with each other. The whole day was passed in deep prayer and *puja* to the divine couple. Summer came, and then the rainy season, followed by autumn and finally winter. But the couple continued their *tapasya* unabated.

At last the divine pair decided to bless this couple who were so engrossed in their worship. They took on the form of monkeys and came and ate up all the fruits and food that had been spread out for the morning ritual. Kesari was annoyed when he saw the mischievous antics of the two monkeys and was all set to drive them off when Anjana stopped him. "My Lord!" she said. "I don't think these are ordinary monkeys. I believe they are Shiva and Parvati who have come to bless us. So let us start worshipping them." Kesari agreed with her, and they started to worship the monkeys as Shiva and Parvati.

They were seated deep in meditation when they heard a voice saying, "O Anjana! O Kesari! We are pleased with your prayers and austerities and will certainly grant your desire. Deep in the forest, there is a huge mango tree. Go there daily and circumambulate this tree and pray to Shiva to grant your desire. Within a week, you will find a wondrous mango on the tree. Let Anjana eat this fruit, and she will be blessed with a baby boy who will be equal in strength to the wind god Vayu."

The couple was delighted to hear this and prostrating themselves, thanked Shiva and Parvati for their blessing. Immediately they started to search the forest for this wondrous tree and very soon found it in the middle of a grove. The next morning they did their ablutions and proceeded to worship the tree, circumambulating it three times and doing *puja* as prescribed by the divine pair. This went on for seven days. On the eighth morning when they reached the tree, they were told by a divine voice to prepare themselves for the emergence of the celestial fruit. At that moment, the whole tree was lit up by a heavenly radiance that slowly started to descend. The radiance proved to be a majestic celestial being that was holding the fruit in his hands. He came to a halt in front of the couple. They stood wonderstruck by the vision before them.

The Being now spoke. "O Kesari! Have no fear! Accept the fruit that I have brought you and give it to your wife Anjana. Let her eat it, and she will surely conceive a child."

In a tremulous voice Kesari asked, "We are indeed most grateful to you. Pray deign to tell us your identity."

The Being replied, "I'm Vayu. I have come here at the behest of Lord Shiva. This mango contains his seed as well as my powers. Have no fear. Accept this fruit in your hands and invest it with your own prowess and give it to Anjana to eat. You will get a son who will be renowned in all the three worlds as the strongest, the bravest, and the foremost in devotion." Thus Hanuman was endowed with the best of both divine and simian qualities.

Kesari accepted the fruit and held it to his heart and prayed that all his strength would go into the fruit. He than handed it over to his wife, who accepted it with great devotion. She took the mango in her hands and prayed to Lord Shiva and to Vayu. Then she fell at her husband's feet and asked for his blessings also. Only then did she eat the divine fruit. Immediately, she was impregnated. The fetus soon started to grow within her womb. It was filled with all three qualities: divine, mortal, and animal. Kesari looked after her with great love and care. As the fetus within her started to grow, Anjana was filled with a heavenly radiance. At last she knew her time had come. It was Tuesday, the full moon day of the month of Chaitra. She bathed in the stream and prayed to her favorite deities, then lay down on a bed of freshly plucked leaves and flowers that Kesari had lovingly arranged for her inside a bower. Very soon, she gave birth to a beautiful baby monkey. As soon as he was born, he let out a loud roar. Kesari was anxiously waiting outside and as soon as he heard the roar, he came inside to take in the beautiful scene of his son being fed by his wife.

Many exceptional traits marked his birth. He did not come into the world as a naked little monkey. His golden-colored furry body was adorned with supernatural ornaments. He had a tight red loincloth, a sacred thread of twisted *munja* grass, and a pair of heavy, elaborately carved earrings. The normal sacred thread worn by humans is made of cotton thread, but the one worn by Anjana's son was made of a wild, coarse grass, or *munja,* which resembled a rope made of hemp. This was a kind of omen of his future life as a celibate and an ascetic. It was also suggestive of his animal origin as well as his humility.

His earrings were said to be invisible to the eyes of most mortals. His mother told him that only the one who would be his Master would be able to perceive the earrings. Rama, of course, was the only one who did see them. These earrings have an interesting legend connected with them.

At the time of Hanuman's birth, the undisputed leader of the monkey world was Vaali, a strong and powerful ape. When Vaali came to know that Anjana was pregnant with a child who was bound to develop into a dominant rival, he decided to put an end to all competition while the child was still in its mother's womb. He created a dart using five metals: gold, silver, copper, iron, and tin. When the unsuspecting mother was asleep, he sent the missile into her womb. A normal child may have succumbed to this dastardly attack, but not one born of Shiva's fiery seed. As soon as it touched the baby's body, the dart melted and transformed itself into a pair of beautiful earrings. Thus wearing the trophies of his first battle, fought while still in his mother's womb, Hanuman entered this world.

At that moment, Shiva and Parvati took the form of monkeys and arrived to bless Anjana's son. Vayu also arrived to gaze at his son. All those who had contrived to produce the child arrived to bless him. Vayu told the parents to call him Maruti.

How Shiva's seed came into the mango is another story. Shiva was the eternal ascetic who had conquered lust. He had reduced Kama, the God of love, to ashes. However in order to please his wife Parvati and fulfill her desire for sexual pleasures, Shiva took on the form of a male monkey and Parvati of a female monkey, and thus they sported in the woods, hanging from the branches, swinging about, and making love in a wild and abandoned manner, as monkeys are wont to do. At that time, Parvati discovered to her dismay that she was expecting a child. Her first-born had an elephant's head, so she was not at all anxious to have another in the form of a monkey. She confided her fears to her Lord. Shiva teased her about this and told her that all creatures were one with him and a child born of his seed would indeed be perfect in every way, whatever his form. She was not convinced and begged him to remove the seed from her womb and transfer it to a more fitting receptacle. Shiva called Vayu to come to his aid and told him to take the seed and place it in a suitable womb. Vayu took the seed and impregnated the mango and further endowed it with his own powers and bestowed it to the pious couple who were praying for a son.

> *Golden-hued and splendidly adorned,*
> *With heavy earrings and curly locks.*

HANUMAN CHALISA BY TULSIDAS

Aum Sri Hanumathe Namaha!

5

Maruti

Flight to the Sun

Kyatha Sri Rama dhuta, pavanatanubhava,
Pingalakshashikhavan,
Sitashokapahari Dashamukha vijayi,
Lakshmana pranadhata.

You are known as the son of the wind and messenger of
    Rama,
With red eyes,
Dispeller of the sorrows of Sita and vanquisher of the ten-
    headed one,
And the giver of life to Lakshmana.

HANUMAN STOTRA

Indeed, having both Shiva and Vayu as his illustrious fathers, Maruti was no ordinary child. He was restless, spirited, energetic, and inquisitive. He was obviously endowed with awesome strength, and the scriptures abound in tales expounding his remarkable feats. One of his most remarkable feats, recounted in all his tales, has to do with his jump to the sun. In fact, this amazing achievement is the one that gave him his most popular name—Hanuman.

The baby was a voracious eater. His appetite could never be totally appeased. The poor parents did their best to satisfy him, but he was never completely satisfied and was always demanding more food. By the time he was a year old, he started climbing and eating all the fruit in the surrounding area. One day, Anjana took him with her to the river and allowed him to do whatever mischief he wanted on the banks while she had her bath. After having eaten as many fruits and shoots from the trees as he could get, he was still hungry. Suddenly, he spied the huge orange orb of the sun rising in the sky and thought to himself that this must be an exceptionally big type of fruit. He called out to his mother to come and have a look at this new fruit. She thought that it must be some fruit on a tree and told him to go for it. Undaunted, the child gave a magnificent leap and soared up to the sky toward the orb of the sun. When Anjana came out of the river after her bath, she couldn't see her son and looked anxiously for him. At last, she spied him flying toward the sun. She shouted to Kesari to come and see what their son was up to. He jumped toward the little fellow to try and catch him but was unable to do so and fell back, dejected. The parents didn't know what they should do now.

The celestials watched his progress with wonder. "Neither the wind god nor Garuda or even the mind can move as swiftly as this son of Vayu. If this is his speed as a mere babe, what will be his speed when he becomes a youth?"

The wind god was also closely following him to protect him from the danger of getting scorched. The sun god realized that he was an innocent child. He also knew of the great purpose that Lord Vishnu in his form as Rama would accomplish through him and thus he did not harm him.

Unfortunately, that day happened to coincide with the day of the solar eclipse when Rahu (the north node of the moon, associated with malefic forces) was supposed to swallow the sun. Suddenly, Maruti saw Rahu shaped like a serpent making his way toward the sun in order to devour him. Mistaking him for a huge worm, the inquisitive monkey dashed toward him and attempted to catch hold of his tail. Rahu fled for his life and sought shelter at the feet of Indra, the lord of the gods. He spoke angrily to Indra, "You have allotted the sun and the moon to me for appeasing my hunger on certain days, and now I find that my share has been given over to some other creature. Today is the night of the new moon, and this is the day on which I have been told to devour the sun. Now look what's happened! Here comes another creature to thwart me."

Indra picked up his deadly thunderbolt, mounted his white elephant named Airavata, and went toward the impudent monkey. The clouds rumbled and lightning thundered across the vast skies in an expression of Indra's wrath. But neither this scary scenario nor the mighty-armed Indra on his high mount was sufficient to induce even a trace of fear in the heart of the little monkey. On the contrary, the spectacle only added fuel to his excitement. He decided that an elephant was just what he needed as a vehicle and tried to grab it. He caught hold of its trunk and leaped on its back. Taken aback by the sudden appearance of a baby monkey behind him, Indra was all set to strike him with his thunderbolt. Vayu arrived on the scene at this opportune moment and tried to stop him, but Indra was not to be deterred.

"He is only a child! What sort of a god are you that you are prepared to wage war against a small child?"

Indra retorted, "He may be a child, but he tried to swallow Surya and catch hold of Rahu, and I merely came to their aid."

Vayu did his best to dissuade him, but Indra hit Maruti on the chin with his bolt and left a mark on it forever. Hence, Anjana's child got the name Hanuman. *Hanu* means "chin" in Sanskrit. But even Indra's thunderbolt was unable to kill him, although the impact threw him off the back of the elephant. As he hurtled through the air, unconscious, his father Vayu sprang to his rescue and caught him in mid-air.

The sight of his beloved son lying helpless in his arms infuriated the wind god. He drew in a mighty breath and sucked away all the air from the cosmos. "Let all those who have harmed Anjana's son choke to death," he thought out aloud. Vayu went into seclusion, taking the atmosphere with him. All living beings began to get asphyxiated. There was panic in the cosmos. Without air, life on every level was threatened. Nothing stirred in the universe. The recitation of the Vedas by the Brahmins ceased and the stomachs of the gods began to shrink.

Anjana and Kesari waited in vain for their child to return to them from the sky. When there was no sign of him, they started to weep and beat their breasts in sorrow.

"Ha Shiva! Ha Parvati! We had to go through so much of trouble to get a son, and now he has been cruelly parted from us. What have we done to deserve this?"

Seeing their sorrow, Vayu appeared before them and comforted them.

"Your son is safe with me. I'm keeping him with me for some time in order to teach Indra and the other gods a lesson. Don't worry. I'll bring him back to you safely."

Hearing this assurance, the parents were pacified.

However, since Vayu the wind god refused to blow anymore, the whole earth started to suffer. Unable to breathe, creatures started to suffocate and die. Very soon it looked as if the whole world would perish. Indra felt very sorry for his impetuous deed. He knew that he alone was responsible for the whole thing. He should have desisted from using his thunderbolt even though he had been egged on by Rahu. All the gods now ran around desperately trying to find out the whereabouts of Vayu. He could be found nowhere. They ran to Shiva and Vishnu and begged for their help. They were aware of everything and knew exactly where Vayu was hiding the child. They went to the netherworld along with Brahma. Vayu was very happy to see them and prostrated himself. He told them the whole story of how his son had been ill-treated by Indra and Surya.

Brahma, Shiva, and Vishnu pacified him and all the gods gave him many blessings. As soon as Brahma touched him, Maruti revived. Now all the gods vied with each other to give him boons.

Indra took off his garland of lotus flowers and placed it around the baby's neck and said, "Since this infant's chin has been broken by my thunderbolt, he shall in the future be known as Hanuman [one who has a disfigured chin]. He will also be invulnerable to my thunderbolt."

The sun god now said, "I bestow on him a hundredth part of my brilliance. Moreover, when the time comes for him to study, I myself shall impart the knowledge of all the Vedas and *shastras* (scriptures) to him. There will be none superior to him in the knowledge of the *shastras*."

Varuna, the god of waters, gave him the boon that he would never need to have any fear from water.

Agni, the god of fire, promised never to harm him.

Yama, the god of death, now said that he would be immune to all diseases and would never come under his sway, and that he would have the ability to choose the time of his death.

Kubera, the king of the *yakshas,* said that his mace would never be able to kill him in war and that he would always remain unwearied during battle.

Shiva gave him the supreme boon that he would be a *chiranjeevi* and would never be able to be killed by any of his weapons.

Viswakarma, the divine architect, now pronounced that he would be impervious to any weapon made by him.

Brahma gave him another boon, that he could never be killed by the *brahmastra,* the weapon that bore his name, and also gave him physical immortality for the duration of a cosmic eon. Turning to the wind god, he said, "Your son will be invincible. He will be the terror of his foes, and give freedom from fear to his friends. He will be able to change his form at will and go wherever he pleases with the speed of his choice. Whatever he does will turn out to be glorious."

Vishnu now turned to the wind god and said, "This son of yours will become a great Vishnu *bhakta.* No one will be able to vanquish him. He will be like a brother to my *avatara* as Rama and his wife Sita, who is Lakshmi incarnate."

All the gods now said that there would be no one on Earth or in Heaven that could equal Maruti in strength and speed.

Brahma concluded the session by bestowing on Hanuman a strength greater than even Vayu and Garuda and endowed him with a speed faster than even the mightiest wind.

After receiving blessings from all the gods, Vayu returned in triumph to the earthly regions whence all creatures revived and started to breathe normally once again. Vayu took Hanuman to his earthly parents and related the whole story to them. They were delighted to hear of the wondrous boons their dear son had acquired. They were also happy to hear his new name, though not so happy to see the mark on his chin. However, they decided that it suited him.

Another version of the same story as given in the Valmiki Ramayana describes how Vayu saw Anjana on the hill in Kishkinda and fell in love with her. He gently stole away her clothes and embraced her. Naturally, she objected violently to the loss of her chastity, so he assured her that there would be no loss to her chastity and blessed her with a wonderful son who would be endowed with his own strength and vigor. She felt the babe within her move, so she went to a cave and gave birth to a lovely baby monkey. He had white fur, a red face, and brownish-yellow eyes. Reluctantly, she left him in the cave and returned to her husband.

The baby was hungry. Dawn was approaching and still no one came to feed him. The sky grew lighter and lighter, and at last he saw the glorious sun rise into the air like a big ripe mango fruit. Instinctively, he knew that monkeys were frugarians and that this was food for him. He crawled out of the cave and crouched down and leaped toward the sun. Vayu came from the north and blew cool fresh air over him so that he would not be scorched by the heat of the sun. This was the day of the solar eclipse, and as the baby monkey approached the sun, the disembodied head of the *asura* Rahu advanced to swallow the sun. Closer and closer he came with wide open mouth and was astounded to see this strange creature approaching the sun. Hanuman decided that Rahu was another fruit and lunged toward him. Rahu ran to Indra for protection and both of them returned, mounted on the Airavata, Indra's elephant. Hanuman was delighted to see them and wondered at the amount of strange creatures in the sky! He dashed toward the elephant, despite Indra's shouts to keep off. Indra was furious at the audacity of the creature and struck him with the flat side of his thunderbolt. He fell unconscious to the earth. The rest of the story is similar to the one recounted above.

After this incident Hanuman was overflowing with vigor due to all the boons he had received from the gods, and he was up to all types of mischief. Sometimes he teased the meditating sages in the forests by snatching their personal belongings and disturbing their well-arranged articles of worship. He broke their sacrificial ladles and vessels and interrupted their oblations and tore up their bark cloths. He stole their water pots and sandals and pulled their beards when they were meditating and tossed their sacred stones into the ponds. Since no one dared to stop him, he became bolder, smashing their vessels, tearing up their scriptures, and dropping huge boulders on the hermitages. Time and time again, both Kesari and Anjana forbade him from doing such mischief, but knowing himself to be invulnerable from the curses of Brahmins, Hanuman continued his pranks. The sages knew of the boons that had been given to him, and they put up with his behavior as long as they could. At last, finding his antics unbearable, they placed a curse on him. They declared that Hanuman would forget his own prowess and would be able to recollect it only when others reminded him of it. Immediately, Hanuman forgot his divine powers and began to behave like an ordinary monkey.

At one time, it is said that he even harassed the children of the gods. When they appealed to Indra, he advised them to seek instruction from Hanuman himself about the art of wrestling so that they would be able to fight with him when necessary. So, in this story he became the *guru,* and they learned from him the esoteric secret of wrestling of which he was a master.

In the Sundara Kanda, Jambavan, the big bear, had to remind Hanuman of his abilities and encourage him to go and find Sita. It was only then that Hanuman remembered his unusual talents and accomplished the impossible, making the amazing leap to Lanka. During the course of the war, he demonstrated some of his phenomenal abilities, but each time it was Jambavan who reminded him and prompted him. This story also goes to show that Hanuman is a deity whose dormant *shakti* can be activated through hymns. The motif of forgetting and remembering is suggestive of the journey of the *jivatma* back to self-knowledge.

The sun is two thousand leagues away,
Yet you swallowed him, taking him to be a
    sweet fruit.

HANUMAN CHALISA BY TULSIDAS

Aum Sri Hanumathe Namaha!

6

Kesari Nandana

Hanuman's Education

Anetho bheshajatre,
Lavanajalanidhe,
Laghane deekshito ya,
Veera Sreeman Hanuman,
Mama manasi vasath,
Karyasiddhim tanotu.

O powerful Hanuman!
Who crossed the ocean so easily,
Do thou remain in my mind,
And allow me to accomplish everything.

HANUMAN STOTRA

When Hanuman was five years old, Kesari decided that it was high time his son got a formal education. The sage Agastya told them to send him to the sun god Surya.

"The sun is the source of all light and knowledge and has already blessed Hanuman. He will surely accept him as a pupil."

Anjana was not too happy at sending her son so far off. However, Kesari urged her that this was the best thing for their child, and thus Hanuman was sent to the sun god for instruction on the Vedas and all allied subjects. Kesari chose Surya as his son's teacher because the sun is the sole *karma sakshi,* or the eternal witness of all the deeds of human beings.

Hanuman did not remember his great powers and innocently asked his mother how he would reach the solar orb. She reminded him that he was the son of the wind god and immediately, he soared into the sky.

Hanuman respectfully approached the chariot of the solar deity. Aruna was the name of his charioteer and he allowed Hanuman to approach his master and prostrate himself to him.

"You see everything there is to see in the universe and therefore, you know everything there is to know. Please accept me as your pupil."

Surya hesitated, for he remembered only too well what had happened the last time Hanuman came near him, and he felt quite nervous about accepting him.

"I don't have the time," he said. "You see, I move across the sky in this chariot night and day, always facing forward and never slackening my pace. How can I possibly give you instruction?"

Hanuman cheerfully replied that he did not see any problem in this. "You can teach me as you ride across the sky. I will face you and move backward, matching my pace with yours so that I can get instruction straight from your lips."

The sun god agreed reluctantly, for he was well aware of Hanuman's divine nature and exceptional abilities. He also knew that he was born knowing everything and all he needed to do was stimulate his memory.

Happy at being accepted, Hanuman placed his body into orbit around the sun. He enlarged his body, placed one leg on the eastern ranges and the other on the western ranges, and turned his face toward the sun. Pleased with his persistence, Surya started to teach him. Hanuman kept moving backward in order to remain facing Surya continuously. As he taught, Surya was impressed by the zeal and determination of his student. Hanuman rotated like a planet before the chariot of the sun god, withstanding the awesome glare, until he became well versed in the 4 books of knowledge (the Vedas), the 6 systems of philosophies (*darshanas*), the 64 arts, or *kalas,* and the 108 occult mysteries of the *tantras.* He flawlessly memorized each *mantra* and verse in the shortest possible time. It is said that Hanuman rivals the sage Brihaspati, the *guru* of the gods, in all the branches of learning as well as in the practice of austerities.

Having become a master of all that he had set out to learn, it was now time for him to pay for his education and give the fee known as *guru-dakshina.* Surya demurred and said that having such a devoted pupil was payment enough for him, but when Hanuman insisted on giving something to express his gratitude, the sun god asked him to look after the welfare of his son Sugriva, who was the stepbrother of Vaali, the king of monkeys. Thus Surya gave a most precious gift to his son Sugriva, for without Hanuman, Sugriva would not have been able to accomplish anything.

There is another version of the same story. When Hanuman reached the sun god's chariot, he found that he already had a great number of other pupils. These were the tiny sages known as the Valakhilyas, who were a thousand in number. When Hanuman humbly asked the sun to accept him also as one of his pupils, these hot-tempered sages informed their *guru* that they would not study the Vedas in the company of a monkey! Surya did not know what to do, for he feared the curse of these irascible sages. This was when Hanuman devised the ruse of running backward in front of the sun so that he could learn everything without being compelled to join the company of the narrow-minded sages! As a result of facing the solar orb for so long, his face became black.

Another version relates how Hanuman was so intelligent that he was able to learn the whole wisdom of the Vedas in a mere fortnight. The sun god, however, was loath to part with his exceptional pupil, who was a part of Shiva himself. So he repeatedly caused Hanuman to forget what he had learned so that the lessons were dragged on for many months. However, Hanuman pleased him so much by his docility and devotion that he released him and gave him the boon that henceforth those who invoked Hanuman's name would never forget their lessons!

Another story goes that when he was asked by his parents to seek the sun as his *guru,* he merely seated himself in meditation and continuously repeated the *gayatri mantra,* the great *mantra* that invokes the supreme intelligence as reflected in the sun. He sat in meditation the whole day, following the course of the sun across the sky until it set in the west. At the end of the day he was perfectly blessed with all knowledge. Actually, the ancient *rishis* had the ability to absorb whatever information they wanted from the ether. Knowledge of Veda exists in space in the form of sonic vibrations. The *rishis* had inner antennas that were capable of picking up these vibrations. These vibrations are very subtle and always exist in space. They can be compared to the television and radio signals with which we are familiar. The *rishis* did not need any external aids like the ones we use to pick up signals. Hanuman practiced the same technique.

The parents were still eager to find an earthly *guru* for him and did not know whom to approach. One day, when Hanuman was playing in the forest, he saw a ferocious tiger approaching him. The tiger pounced on him with a menacing growl, but Hanuman was undeterred. He jumped ten feet into the air and landed on the tiger's back, catching him in a merciless hold. He opened the gaping jaws and tore them apart. The tiger was exhausted by then and Hanuman rode on his back effortlessly. However, before he could go far, the tiger collapsed.

Just then there appeared before Hanuman a hunter wearing a tiger skin and adorned with a necklace of tiger claws. A bow and quiver were slung across his broad shoulders. Seeing his form, Hanuman felt a great love well up in his heart. He fixed his admiring gaze on him without blinking.

The hunter laughed and asked, "Aren't you frightened of me? I might be a monkey hunter. I might catch you and take you back with me!"

Hanuman gazed fearlessly at him and replied, "I have no fear of anyone, but I would like to know who you are. I haven't seen anyone like you around here."

The hunter replied, "I'm a hunter and I live far away in the Snow Mountains. If you are not frightened of me, I am willing to teach you many interesting things."

"My parents are on the lookout for a tutor for me," said Hanuman. "Come with me, and I'll take you to them."

Anjana and Kesari were shocked to see their darling son coming hand-in-hand with such a rough-looking fellow. They were even more shocked when Hanuman told them that he wanted to go with his new-found friend to learn the arts.

"Are you out of your mind? Just looking at him, one can see that he is an uncultured and uneducated boor. How can such a fellow teach you anything?" asked Kesari.

"Father, how can you make such statements about someone you don't know? I want him as my *guru*."

"Doesn't the pupil have any say in the choice of a *guru*?" asked the hunter.

"Maybe he has," Kesari replied, "but he's only a child, and I'm not interested in keeping you as his *guru*!"

"Shouldn't you test my prowess before branding me as an uncultured brute?" persisted the hunter.

Anjana and Kesari were amazed at these words of the hunter. They looked at each other and Kesari said, "I don't think this is an ordinary hunter. I think we should give him a chance to prove his mettle."

So saying, he challenged the hunter to a duel with his weapons. The hunter was undeterred but said that they would need an umpire to decide the winner. Kesari suggested Anjana. The hunter laughed and said that she was hardly a good choice, since obviously, a wife would always choose her husband as the winner even if he were defeated. Kesari admitted the truth of this and mentally called upon Vayu to help him. Immediately, Vayu appeared in a gust of wind and agreed to do the umpiring.

Now Kesari girded up his loins and charged at the hunter with upraised fists, pounding his chest. He threw him a few lengths away. Anjana was delighted to see her husband's feat and applauded him. However, her happiness was short-lived. The hunter coolly rose up and came up to the huge figure of Kesari. He caught hold of him and threw him easily into the air. Kesari landed with a thud that knocked him out. Anjana ran to his aid and massaged his body until he slowly regained consciousness. He managed to rise up painfully and was all set for another bout, but Anjana begged him not to have another encounter with the hunter. Kesari could not bear to admit defeat and shot a glance at the hunter, who seemed to be having a quiet laugh at his expense.

"Let us try our prowess with weapons now," Kesari said.

The hunter immediately stood ready with his bow and arrow. Kesari also took up his bow and shot arrow after arrow at the hunter, who parried them all with ease until he eventually shot down Kesari's bow so that he stood defenseless.

Anjana realized that this was no ordinary hunter. She closed her eyes and brought her favorite deity to mind. When she opened them, she saw that the hunter was none other than Shiva himself. Hastily she plucked some flowers and ran forward, placing them at the hunter's feet. Hanuman also brought some flowers and placed them at his chosen *guru*'s feet. The hunter placed his palms on the boy's head and blessed him. Turning to Kesari, he asked with a laugh, "Now do you have any more objections to my becoming your son's tutor?"

Kesari fell at his feet and begged him to pardon him. "It is our great good fortune that you have come here in person and agreed to become our son's *guru*. Because of this we have had the good fortune to see you with our own eyes. Pray forgive my transgressions and take our son as your pupil."

Shiva agreed and touched the boy's tongue with his ring. Lo and behold, the child started to sing a paean of praise to the Lord. He then whispered the sacred syllable (*pranava mantra*) in the child's right ear by which Hanuman became a fully enlightened being. Next, he told

Hanuman that Saraswati, the goddess of the arts, would grant him proficiency in music when the time came and when he so desired it.

The parents were delighted to hear all this and prostrated themselves again and again to the Lord.

Thus Lord Shiva taught Maruti all the esoteric knowledge of *mantras* and *yantras* and various other spiritual secrets. It is said that Vishnu taught him *bhakti yoga* (the yoga of devotion), *samkhya yoga* (the yoga of wisdom), and *hatha yoga* (the yoga of physical purification). Parasurama, the sixth incarnation of Vishnu, is supposed to have taught him the secrets of wrestling.

Now his father Vayu took over his teaching. First of all, he taught him the esoteric secrets of *pranayama,* or the science of breath control. He then taught him to fly like a bird and jump vast distances. One day he presented him with a beautiful lute and told him to sing and praise the Lord with this accompaniment. Hanuman was delighted and spent the evening hours known as *sandhya* (twilight devotions) singing to God. Once, while he was bathing in a forest pool he heard the dulcet sounds of a nightingale and thought to himself that he would really love to sing like that. Just then he remembered the words of Shiva who had encouraged him to pray to the goddess Saraswati if he wanted to be a master of the fine arts. As soon as this idea came to his mind, he jumped into the pool and stood waist-deep in water. He prayed to the goddess to grant him a boon.

Hearing his fervent plea, the goddess appeared and shook him slightly so that he opened his eyes. She then told him to ask for any boon.

He bowed low before her and asked her to grant him knowledge of all the fine arts as well as the ability to sing. Smilingly, she agreed to his request and told him to take up the lute and start singing. Having prostrated himself before her, he took the lute, sat under a tree, and started to sing. Hearing his melodious voice accompanied by the lucid notes of the lute, even the wild animals came near to listen. Celestial beings passing in the sky also stopped to enjoy the music.

Just at that time Narada, the divine sage, who was a famous singer and a great devotee of Lord Vishnu, happened to pass by and was struck by this sight. He thought he was the only one who played on the lute and sang for the Lord, and he was not too pleased at this intruder into his particular field. He came down hurriedly to the ground to find out what was so special about Hanuman's voice that made the whole forest go into a state of ecstasy. He approached the young devotee and tapped him on his shoulder. Hanuman opened his eyes and saw the sage standing with his lute in front of him. Narada told him who he was and Hanuman bowed with all humility before him. Narada then asked him to sing another song for him. Hanuman agreed and began to sing. When he heard his dulcet notes, Narada was totally immersed in the music, and when he stopped, he felt truly humbled and said, "O Hanuman! I came to test your ability and now I'm convinced that you are a great master of music. I see that the goddess Saraswati has indeed blessed you with all her gifts. Let me add my blessings to hers. You are certainly superior to me."

Hearing this, Hanuman fell at the feet of the divine sage and said, "O noble one! Surely none can compare with you in devotional singing. Your fame has spread over all the three worlds. I'm nothing compared to you."

Narada was pleased both by Hanuman's humility as well as by his divine voice. Having blessed him, he rose up to go but was dismayed to find that the lute he had placed on a rock had become stuck to the boulder that had melted at the sound of Hanuman's music!

Turning to Hanuman, he begged him to sing once again so that the rock would melt once more and free his lute. Hanuman did so, and the celestial sage was able to retrieve his lute. In the age of Dwapara, all solid things like rocks were purported to have melted when they heard the ravishing notes of the flute that Lord Krishna played in the forest of Vrindavana. The same was the case here. Having realized Hanuman's greatness, Narada blessed him once again and went on his way.

Some years passed in this delightful fashion. However, the time was fast approaching when this idyllic time would come to an end. One day when Anjana was immersed in meditation, she heard a voice from within her calling, "Punchikasthala! Punchikasthala! Your time for reprieve has come. You may now return to your celestial abode!"

When she heard this, a flood of memories arose in her and her past life became vivid in her mind. "I'm not a monkey called Anjana. I'm the celestial maiden known as Punchikasthala. I am the adopted daughter of Brihaspati, the *guru* of the gods. I am now freed from my curse and can return to my father's *ashrama.*"

But somehow this thought did not bring her any joy. Her eyes filled with tears.

Her husband Kesari came near her and asked her the reason for her tears. Baby Hanuman came close and hugged her and promised never to get into any mischief. At this Anjana burst into tears and hugged him close.

"My darling son! It's time for me to return to my abode and leave you. But I cannot bear the thought of leaving you and going back."

Neither her son nor her husband could figure out her meaning.

"What are you saying? I don't understand. Where do you have to go? This is your home."

"My Lord!" She said, "In reality, I'm not Anjana but an *apsara* called Punchikasthala. I belong to the *ashrama* of Brihaspati. I took the form of a monkey due to a curse. Now I have been reprieved from it and given permission to return home. But the thought of parting from you and my beloved son is tearing me apart."

"O Anjana! I cannot live without you. I will definitely not allow you to go anywhere," cried Kesari.

"My beloved husband! None can change the course of destiny. You will not be able to stop me. So please give me leave to go."

Her son now spoke true words of wisdom. "O Mother!" he said, "Go in peace. You are absolutely right in saying that none can stop the wheel of destiny."

The wind god Vayu now appeared, comforted her, and said, "Don't grieve about your son. We are all here to see to his welfare. If you have to go, go in peace."

The heroic Kesari could not bear this parting. "I cannot live without you, beloved! Wherever you go, I will follow."

Hearing her husband's oath, Anjana closed her eyes for a few minutes and meditated on her *guru*. Mentally, she begged him to allow her to go to the mountain of Kanchana in the Himalayas, along with her husband, in order to practice *tapasya*. She clasped Hanuman in her arms, kissed his forehead, and gave him to Vayu. Then turning to Kesari, she said, "My Lord! I feel the same way as you. If you want to accompany me, clasp me in your arms."

He did as bidden and to the amazement of her son, they both rose up into the sky and then turned into two balls of light. He watched in wonder as they slowly disappeared toward the north. Brihaspati granted her wish, and they both went and stayed at the mountain known as Kanchana.

> *Thou art the son of Shiva and Kesari's joy,*
> *Your glory is sung throughout the word.*
>
> HANUMAN CHALISA BY TULSIDAS

Aum Sri Hanumathe Namaha!

Aum Manojavaaya Namaha!

7

Jitendriya

Conqueror of the Senses

Manojavam Marutathulyavegam
Jitendriyam buddhimatam varishtam,
Vathatmajam vaanarayudhamukhyam,
Sri Rama dhutam shirasa namami!

I bow to the messenger of Rama,
Who was the son of Vayu and the best among monkeys,
Who had his senses under perfect control and was highly
   intelligent,
Who was as fast as the mind and as swift as the wind!

HANUMAN STOTRA

After his parents left, Hanuman was left solely in the care of his foster
father Vayu. After some years in the forest, Hanuman thought to himself that there must be more to life than just eating and playing in the
forest. He mentally asked his father Vayu to come to his aid and told
him that he was anxious to see the world and meet great saints. Vayu

agreed to his request and said, "Indeed, it is time for you to go from here. However, I'd like you to get married first before going anywhere. Then you can go to the kingdom of the monkeys known as Kishkinda. The king of that state is a great and powerful monkey known as Vaali. He has a brother called Sugriva. Befriend him and you will certainly gain fame and fortune."

Hanuman bowed low before his parent and said firmly, "My Lord, I am not in the least interested in a family life. I have taken on a vow of chastity, and I hope I will never have to break it. However, I'm pleased by your other advice. I will certainly set out for the kingdom of Vaali without further ado."

He bade a fond farewell to his playmates in the forest and started out toward Kishkinda. He traveled through the trees as monkeys do. After some time, he was very thirsty and hungry. He spied a stream below him and came down to drink the water. Hardly had he scooped some water in his palms than he heard a horrendous voice saying, "No one is allowed to drink this water without my permission!" Hearing this, Hanuman let the water fall from his hands and looked around for the person who had spoken. Seeing no one, he said, "Who are you? Why are you hiding in the foliage like a coward? Why don't you reveal yourself?"

At these words the whole forest was shaken by the sound of a roar and the horrible figure of a *rakshasa* appeared before Hanuman. He was not to be deterred by this figure and asked him who he was.

The *rakshasa* replied, "Why should I introduce myself to you? You have trespassed on my land and now I will certainly make my midday meal out of you!" So saying, he opened his cavernous mouth and prepared to swallow Hanuman whole. His mouth emitted the stench of blood. Before he could catch him, Hanuman made use of the powers given to him by his father, Vayu, and enlarged himself so that he stood face-to-face with the *rakshasa*. The demon was a bit astonished to see this feat by the little monkey, but he knew a few tricks himself, so he also became larger and larger and made a lunge at Hanuman with these words: "Now let me have my lunch!"

Immediately, Hanuman magnified his body to double the size of the *rakshasa* and gave him one kick, which felled him to the ground. But the demon rose up with redoubled vigor and the two of them fought for a long time without either being vanquished. Hanuman now realized that this was not an ordinary *rakshasa* and begged Lord Shiva to come to his aid. He picked up a piece of *dhruva* grass and breathed the *mantra* of the great weapon of Shiva known as *paasupatha*. This he threw with all his might at the demon who was hurled a few yards away. His body fell on a rock and was smashed to smithereens. Out of the pieces there rose a divine form, which came toward Hanuman and bowed low before him.

"My Lord!" he said, "I was a *gandharva* in my previous life and became a *rakshasa* due to a curse. Thanks to you, I have been redeemed from this!"

Hanuman wanted to know how he was cursed. The *gandharva* replied, "Once I tried to kidnap the daughter of a *rishi* and he cursed me that I would become a *rakshasa*. When I begged him to release me from this curse, he told me that I would meet my end at the hands of one who was born from Shiva's seed. At that time, I would be released from my curse. So now I see that you are the one who was foretold by the *rishi*."

The *gandharva* now blessed Hanuman and proceeded on his way. Hanuman also was able to quench his thirst in the clear waters of the stream and take his fill of the fruits before progressing on his journey.

Maruti now continued his journey through the subcontinent of Bharatavarsha. He met many great sages on the way and got their blessings. He also encountered fierce beasts and strange birds and saw many lovely trees and flowers. At last he reached a huge forest known as Vidarshana that was so dark and menacing none dared to go through it, even during the day. It was thought to be the haunt of *rakshasas* and other night wanderers and was also inhabited by many wild beasts.

Hanuman contemplated on Lord Shiva and fearlessly entered the forest. As he walked on, he was beset by stinging mosquitoes and other poisonous insects. Vines and tendrils wound round his feet and tried to stop him from proceeding. As evening approached, he could hear the menacing growls of wild beasts all around him. He decided to spend the night in a tree, but all through the night he could hear the heartrending roars of an elephant in pain. With the break of dawn, he hurried to the site of the cries and discovered a magnificent elephant half in and half out of the river. His rear legs were firmly planted in the water and try as he might, he seemed unable to get out of the water and drag himself to the bank. Hanuman felt very sorry for the royal beast and went close, peering into the water to find out what was preventing the elephant from getting out of the water. He was shocked to see that one of the creature's legs was cruelly gripped in the strong jaws of a crocodile. The huge crocodile was slowly but surely dragging the elephant down into the water. Blood was oozing from the elephant's feet and flowed like a red stream in the river. The elephant lifted up its trunk and cried piteously. Feeling sorry for the noble animal, the fearless son of the wind god leaped into the water.

He grasped the tail of the reptile and pulled it. However, the crocodile refused to let go and dragged him along with the elephant further into the water. Hanuman immediately realized that this was the wrong thing to do. He let go of the tail, jumped nimbly on its back, and grasped its jaws, which were locked on the elephant's legs. Using his enormous strength, he tore open the jaws and thus freed the elephant from its agony. The crocodile was incensed with the pain and the thought of its lost prey. It thrashed its tail violently in the water and turned with gaping, bloody jaws at its new enemy. Anjaneya immediately swam to its rear, grasped its tail, and dragged it to the banks. Before the creature could gather its wits, he once again grasped the tail, swung it above his head, whirled it round, and hurled it a hundred yards away. It crashed to the ground and died immediately.

Suddenly to his amazement a beautiful maiden rose out of the crocodile body, came near him, and bowed low.

"Who are you, and how did you come to take on a crocodile's form?" he asked.

"O Anjaneya!" she said, "I am an *apsara* called Ambalika. I belong to the court of Indra, the king of gods. Once, as I was bathing with a group of my friends in the pellucid waters of a Himalayan lake, we happened to see a group of young ascetics meditating on the banks. We were smitten by their looks and approached them, trying to entice them with our songs and dances. At last they opened their eyes. They cast their compassionate glance on us and advised us strongly to leave them alone if we did not want to be cursed. My friends hurriedly left the place, but I lingered on, smitten by the beauty of one of the ascetics. Again and again, he warned me not to try him further, but I refused. At last he cursed me that I would become a cruel crocodile and live in a mud pool in the forest of Vidarshana. I begged him for reprieve, and he relented and told me that I would be saved by the son of the wind god, born of the seed of Shiva! I see now that you are the one predicted by the ascetic. I would like to give you a boon for having saved me. You will never have to fear from drowning. Water will not be able to harm you. Now please give me leave to go!"

Hanuman was amazed to hear her story and told her to go on her way.

After this episode he continued on his journey. After passing through many forests and crossing many mountains and rivers, he arrived in a forest at the outskirts of the kingdom of Kishkinda. From afar he could hear the roars of wild beasts and the trumpets of elephants. He jumped onto a tree in order to have a look at what was happening and found that a noble-looking monkey was surrounded by wild elephants and other beasts and was slowly losing ground. Undaunted, Hanuman jumped into the fray and routed the elephants.

The monkey asked him, "Who are you that appeared at the right moment to save me?"

"I am Anjaneya, the son of Anjana, but people also call me Hanuman. But tell me who you are. You seem to be pretty exhausted. How did you get into this predicament?"

"My name is Sugriva, and I am the younger brother of Vaali, the king of this land. This forest is the hideout of a fierce *rakshasa* called Mayavi. My brother and I had decided to get rid of him once and for all. My brother told me and my friends to come by this trail while he went by another. Though we managed to locate Mayavi, we were unable to kill him. After a fierce fight, he killed all my friends. Turning to me, he said, "I will let you off since I have no quarrel with you. It's your brother Vaali whom I'm after!" However, as soon as I escaped from him, I was attacked by beasts, as you saw. I was too tired by then to defend myself and had you not come, I would have been in a bad state!"

Hanuman smiled and said, "O Sugriva! You and I are meant to be friends. We have a long history before us!"

"I don't understand what you mean," said Sugriva.

"Time will reveal my meaning to you. I have given a promise to your father, Surya, to be your friend. However, tell me about Mayavi. Who is he? Is he such a terrible creature?"

"What a question!" said Sugriva. "He's indeed a mighty warrior. Only my brother will be able to vanquish him."

Hanuman smiled when he heard this and said, "There is nothing and no one that one cannot conquer in this world if one controls the mind. However, we will talk of all this later. We were fated to meet and our friendship is only starting. You need some rest and after that we will continue on our way."

Sugriva embraced him and begged him to be his friend forever. He invited him to his kingdom of Kishkinda.

Seeing him to be in no fit state for travel, Hanuman carried him with ease on his back until they came to a river where they bathed and refreshed themselves. Then Hanuman brought some fruits from the forest and after partaking of that meal, they rested for the night in the trees.

During the night they talked of many things. Hanuman asked Sugriva to tell him the story of his birth and that of his brother Vaali.

Once there was a very chaste woman called Shilavati. Her husband Ugratapas caught leprosy, but she continued to look after him very lovingly. Once he told her that he wanted to have intercourse with a courtesan. Undaunted, Shilavati decided that it was a wife's duty to fulfill her husband's desires, however unreasonable. Since he was in a pitiful state and unable to walk, she proceeded to carry him in a basket on her head to the courtesan's house. On the way she passed the field where a great sage called Mandavya had been impaled on a stake by the king's orders through false charges. The sage could not bear to see how this noble woman was being exploited by her vile husband. He cursed him that he would die before the break of dawn! Shilavati immediately countered the curse by praying that the sun would not appear the next morning. Such was the power of her chastity that it happened as she wished.

Next morning the sun did not appear at his normal time. His charioteer called Aruna came to collect him and found him to be immobile. He decided to visit the world of Indra until the sun god was ready to start on his daily round. When he reached Indra's heaven, he found the gate barred to all men. Indra was holding court with his *apsaras* (heavenly dancers), and they were enacting a drama for him. He gave orders that only women were to enter. Aruna came just at this time and was disappointed to hear this edict. He was determined to see the celestial show and thought of a ruse to get in. He changed himself into a woman and slipped in unnoticed, mingling with the flock of dancers. But Indra, who was noted for his eye for beauty, immediately spied the glamorous new maiden in their midst. He dismissed the other dancers and stopped Aruna at the door when he tried to slip out with the rest of the dancers.

Indra was used to getting any woman he wanted and he tried to beguile poor Aruna, who didn't know what to do. Finally, she had to disclose her secret. Indra was mad when he heard this and said that she would have to pay the price for having deceived the whole court like this. Aruna was forced to agree, and Indra forcibly took her. A lovely baby boy was born out of this union. Since Aruna couldn't possible take the child with her, Indra gave her to Ahalya, the wife of the sage Gautama, to bring up.

In the meantime, due to Shilavati's great austerity, the sun could not rise. The whole world was in darkness. At last, the gods found out the reason for this strange state of affairs. They approached the sage,

Atri, the father of Ugratapas, and urged his wife Anasuya to go and beg Shilavati to withdraw her wish. The latter stopped her prayers and allowed the sun to come out.

When the sun looked about for his charioteer, he was nowhere to be found. He was quite cross with him for being so late. Aruna tried to slip in unnoticed but Surya accosted him and asked him the reason for his tardiness. Aruna was forced to tell him the whole story. Surya pardoned him but was struck with a desire to see the form that had enchanted Indra. Aruna tried his best to dissuade him, but Surya insisted, and at last he had to give in to his wishes. The inevitable happened, and Surya fell for her charms and made love to her. Another beautiful baby boy was born of the union, and this child was also given to Ahalya to look after. One day, when Ahalya was playing with the children, both of them insisted that they should be carried on either hip. She became quite cross and called, "You little monkeys! How can you torment me like this?"

Her husband came in just in time to hear her say this. He became quite angry at her behavior and said, "If that is your wish, let both of them turn into monkeys!"

A sage's word must always come true, and so the two boys turned into monkeys. Ahalya was very unhappy at the fate of her two lovely boys. However, a sage's anger is always short-lived, and her husband prophesied that the two would become mighty beings.

Indra heard about the fate of the two boys, had them brought to his court, and gave them shelter. The child born to him was named Vaali because he had a very long and powerful tail, and the son of Surya was named Sugriva since he had a beautiful neck.

There is another story connected with the birth of the two brothers Vaali and Sugriva. Once upon a time, the creator Brahma came down to the earth and rested on the mountain called Meru, which is the axis on which the earth revolves. At that time a tear fell from his eye, and when it touched the ground, the very first monkey (*vanara*) was born. Brahma named him Riksha and stayed with him for a while. The little monkey played on the hill and ate all the fruit he wanted.

Every evening he returned to Brahma and laid some flowers at his feet. One day Riksha saw his reflection when he bent to drink from a lake. He thought it was the face of an enemy trying to grab him and pull him into the water. He jumped into the lake to attack the adversary. He didn't know that it was a magic lake, and when he came out of the water, he found that he had been changed into a female. He was a most entrancing female monkey and as she stood on the hillside of Meru, both Indra and Surya fell in love with her. That same morning, first Indra and then Surya came down and made love to her.

Children of the gods are born very quickly. The monkey girl had two golden babies. That afternoon, as she washed them in the lake, they splashed water all over her, and by the time they were clean, she found that she had changed sex once again and become Riksha.

He took his sons to Brahma. They named Indra's son Vaali and Surya's son Sugriva.

Brahma gave the kingdom of Kishkinda to Riksha. Kishkinda was a dense forest rich in fruit trees and inhabited by various wild animals. Brahma created many other *vanaras* with the power of flight and speech and asked them to make friends with the bears. The two brothers were inseparable and as they grew older, the father taught them all the arts at his command. When Riksha died, many other contenders to the throne arrived, but Vaali killed or maimed every other challenger and became the undisputed ruler of the monkey world. He declared himself to be the sole Lord of all the trees and the female monkeys of Kishkinda. His authority was unquestioned, and as one who had successfully earned his dominant place among the apes, Vaali was not obliged to share the spoils of power with anyone. However, being of a magnanimous nature, he shared everything with his younger brother Sugriva, who was his second-in-command and who in turn served his elder brother faithfully. Indra gave his son a victory garland of little golden lotus flowers that would make him invincible.

Once Vaali heard of the churning of the milky ocean by the gods and the demons (one of the most celebrated tales of Hindu mythology, full of rich allegory) and decided to go and see this event for himself.

All of them reached the banks of the ocean of milk. When he saw that his father Indra and the other gods were flagging, it is said that Vaali took over the churning himself. Such was his strength that he could single-handedly accomplish what the two protagonists were unable to do. Indra was mighty pleased with his son's prowess. For having helped them, the gods blessed him with immeasurable strength. Another boon they gave him was that anyone who approached him for a fight would lose half their strength, which would come to him.

Many precious things appeared out of the ocean. Two beautiful damsels also appeared. They were known as Tara and Rumi. Vaali accepted Tara as his chief wife, and Sugriva chose Rumi. The brothers returned joyfully to their kingdom and reigned in peace for a long while. In time, Vaali had a son called Angada.

Vaali was a great devotee of Shiva, and every day he went to all eight directions, bathed in the oceans, and worshipped Shiva in all his aspects. At one stride, he could cross the seven seas and reach the mountain known as Charuvala, which lay beyond the seas. When he moved, it was with the force of a typhoon. No lance could pierce his chest. When he strode across the earth, the mountains shook and the storm clouds scattered in all directions, afraid to precipitate rain. All nature feared him and even Yama, the god of Death, was afraid to approach him. Thunder softened its voice and even lions refrained from roaring in his presence. Once it is said that he picked up the ten-headed Ravana and tucked him inside his tail!

Supremely wise, virtuous, and clever,
You are always eager to fulfil any mission of
Rama's.

Hanuman Chalisa by Tulsidas

Aum Sri Hanumathe Namaha!

Aum Brahmachaarine Namaha!

8

Sugriva Mitram

Friend of Sugriva

Buddhirbalam Yasho dhayryam,
Nirbhayatwam arogata,
Ajadyam vaak padutwam cha,
Hanumatha smaranaath bhaveth.

One who meditates on Hanuman will become famous
    and obtain
Great intelligence, strength, courage,
Freedom from fear and disease,
As well as expertise in talking.

Hanuman Stotram

Hanuman now accompanied Sugriva to Kishkinda and was introduced to Vaali. Sugriva described how Hanuman was solely responsible for having saved him from the wild beasts. He also told him about his greatness. Vaali was at first rather suspicious of Hanuman, whom he had tried to kill as a baby since he feared that he might possibly be a usurper to his throne, but when he heard that Hanuman was a good singer he insisted on hearing him sing. Hanuman took up the lute and started strumming it. When he began to sing, the whole court went into a state of ecstasy. As the music wafted out, all the monkeys left their respective work and crept in, mesmerized by his voice. Vaali was charmed and told him that he could remain in his land forever.

Sugriva took Hanuman on a tour of their land. When they reached the mountain called Rishyamukha, Hanuman was struck by the serenity of the place and told Sugriva that this mount was indeed very holy. Sugriva agreed but sadly said that it was out of bounds for his brother Vaali. Hanuman enquired about the reason for this, so Sugriva told him the whole story.

Once there was a demon called Dundubhi who managed to get many boons from the creator Brahma. One of these boons was that he could never be killed by any weapon. Having got these boons, he proceeded to vanquish the gods and disturb the sages and kings of the land. His hands were always itching for a fight, and he could never find a worthy opponent. Unable to bear his urgent desire to try out his strength, he rose from the netherworld, thrashed through the ocean, and swam ashore. He thrust his horns into the sand and bellowed to the waves, "Fight me!" But the waves just kept coming on and on. They didn't care whether he was there or not.

The long, watery arms of the sea hissed and swelled round Dundubhi's feet. They appeared to be warning him to go back or else drown. A huge wave now rose up foaming and frothing, steadily coming closer and closer. Dundubhi thought it better to retreat.

Then he went to the snowy Himalayas, white as Shiva. He rushed up the snow-clad slopes and battered the sides with his horns. The mountain King Himavan turned his rocky face and looked glassy-eyed at the irate buffalo. He was clothed in a white robe of snow and falling water with a belt of ice. In a booming voice he said, "Don't bring war to this untouched country. Why harm my men of peace? The strong will never get angry because we know that our serenity is our armor. Now go and leave me in peace."

Hardly had he said this than a huge cloud of mist and snow covered him and he disappeared from view. The mountain seemed to disappear along with Himavan. The ice and sleet cut into Dundubhi, biting and crushing him so that he ran screaming and never stopped until he reached the cave fortress of Kishkinda.

He desecrated all the fruit trees in the forest surrounding the fortress. He then stuck his enormous head into the cave city and roared. Vaali came out on his balcony and told him to go while he still had life to do so. Dundubhi challenged him to fight. Vaali put on his golden garland and came charging out of the gates, and both of them had a duel in which neither was able to vanquish the other. At last, Vaali used his superhuman strength and caught hold of the buffalo's horns as he came charging at him with lowered horns. He whirled him above his head and flung him as far as he could. Dundubhi could hardly stand up, but Vaali followed him. He kept picking him up and whirling him round and round. At last, he dashed him on the ground. The demon started vomiting blood and finally died in agony. Vaali's rage was still unabated. He lifted up the carcass and threw it many leagues away, where it fell with a tremendous thud on the mount on which stood the *ashrama* of the sage Matanga. As the carcass passed over the head of the sage, it splattered blood all over him. Rudely disturbed in his meditation, the irate sage rushed out and was met by the gory sight of the huge carcass of the buffalo demon.

He made a dire pronouncement. "If the one who has done this despicable deed ever comes within four miles of this hallowed place, his head will burst into a thousand pieces! Let all the monkeys who are camping in this place who belong to his tribe also depart instantly or they will all be turned into rocks!"

"That is why my brother never dares to come to this beautiful place," said Sugriva. Hanuman thought a while and told Sugriva that one day this very mount would be a sanctuary for him. Beyond that, he refused to reveal anything, even though Sugriva pressed him.

Dundubhi had a friend called Mayavi, who was the son of the architect of the demons called Mayan. He was furious at the fate of his friend and swore to avenge his death. He had come to Kishkinda and challenged Vaali for a fight. At that time Vaali had chased him off. Sugriva had also accompanied him but Vaali had told him to go off, and that is how Sugriva came to meet Hanuman. Vaali was sure that he had gotten rid of the nuisance once and for all, but the demon was not to be deterred so easily. Once again he came to the gates of the cave fortress of Kishkinda and woke everyone with his bloodcurdling roars at midnight. The monkeys tried to drive him off, but he shooed them off like flies. At last, they appealed to their king. Vaali took up his arms and went out of the gates, but the demon was nowhere to be seen. Well versed in the magic arts of his father, he had simply disappeared from the scene. Vaali shouted to him to reveal himself. "Coward that you are, why don't you come and fight with me like a hero? What is the use of hiding yourself?"

Hearing this, Mayavi came out of his hiding place. He saw that Vaali was flanked by Sugriva and Hanuman and laughed in scorn. "Are you such a hero that you can't fight by yourself and have to ask for help from two others?"

Turning to his brother and Hanuman, Vaali asked them to return to the palace, since this duel was to be between him and Mayavi alone. Hanuman complied but Sugriva refused to leave.

Turning to Mayavi, Vaali said, "This will be a fight to the finish between us. I will not let you return alive from this place."

Mayavi laughed in derision when he heard this and said scornfully, "I will finish you off first, and then kill your brother and son and become the king of Kishkinda!"

Without wasting time in useless verbal combat, Vaali lunged at Mayavi with his bare fists. Then ensued a mighty battle between the two. At last Mayavi realized that once again he had misjudged the powers of his opponent. He ran off into the forest with Vaali in hot pursuit. Sugriva also followed, since he feared for his brother. Vaali caught up with Mayavi, and they had another fierce battle in the middle of the forest. To Sugriva's amazement, the two heroes fought on without showing any signs of fatigue for one whole day and night. As dawn appeared, Vaali saw that Mayavi showed signs of fatigue, so he pressed on, determined to kill him at all costs. The demon knew he was beaten and fled beyond the edge of the world into a subterranean passage. Vaali followed, but before entering he turned to Sugriva and said, "Please wait for me here. I will surely kill him and return. But if for some reason he kills me, then don't wait. Seal the mouth of the cave with a stone and return to the kingdom, or else he will come out and kill you. Remember if he is killed, milk will flow out of the cave and if I am killed, it will be blood, so if you see blood, close the cave with a stone and save yourself. You are certainly no match for him!"

Sugriva stayed at the mouth of the cave, waiting anxiously for his brother for one whole year. At last, one day he heard a thunderous sound coming from the cave, and soon after that a stream of blood started to flow. Sugriva was sure that the sound was his brother's death-cry and that the demon had killed him. The stream of blood confirmed his suspicions. Crying bitterly for the fate of his brother, he sealed the mouth of the cave with a huge boulder and made his way to the kingdom where everyone was awaiting their victorious return. The monkeys wept when they heard the whole story. Sugriva was sunk in gloom and the *vanaras* feared that the kingdom was going to ruin. The ministers urged him to take over the kingdom and at last he was forced to agree.

However, the truth of the matter was that Vaali had actually killed Mayavi but a traitor to the last, the demon had wrought his magic and changed the milk that was oozing from him into blood so that he could create dissension between the brothers. When Vaali came to the mouth of the cave, he found to his consternation that it had been firmly sealed. He couldn't believe that his brother had betrayed him in this cruel fashion. He concluded that his greed for the throne must have prompted him to act in this pitiless manner. Using his mighty strength, he kicked the boulder aside and came out like a tornado. He was filled with an uncontrollable rage against his brother. He went outside the gate and roared with anger. The citizens shuddered when they heard this roar. They ran to Sugriva and informed him that Vaali had arrived at the gate! Sugriva couldn't believe his ears. Surely he had seen blood flowing out of the cave! Could this have been a trick of the malicious demon? Before he could go to the gate, Vaali rushed into the court, foaming at the mouth. Without much ado, he picked up Sugriva like a bit of straw from the throne on which he was sitting and threw him a hundred yards away.

"Ungrateful wretch!" he shouted. "You thought you could kill me and steal the throne for yourself. You are a hundred times worse than Mayavi. If you fear for your life, then make yourself scarce. If I ever find you hanging around here again, that will be the end of you!"

So saying, he ran after Sugriva and before he could raise himself up, he pounced on him. He boxed and pounded him in the presence of all the courtiers and officials. Sugriva tried to explain that he was innocent, but Vaali gave him no chance to say anything. No one dared to stop Vaali in his terrible rage. He seized Sugriva by the scruff of his neck and tried to smash his head against a rock. Sugriva managed to slip out of his hands and flee but was hotly pursued by his brother. At last he was inspired to go to the mountain of Rishyamukha, which he had shown to Hanuman long ago. Vaali was filled with rage at the fact that he couldn't follow him. He pulled out a few trees in his fury and threw them at his brother. Sugriva was prostrate with grief and anger and hid inside a cave to lick his wounds and try to figure out what he should do next.

Vaali returned to Kishkinda and took up the reins of the kingdom once again. Frustrated in his attempts to punish Sugriva, he killed his brother's children and forcibly acquired Sugriva's wife Rumi. So Sugriva lost both his kingdom and his wife!

When Sugriva followed his brother to the cave, Hanuman decided to leave Kishkinda and went to the forest to meditate. Very soon he found that his mind was peaceful and under control. He started to look like a veritable sage.

This was the time when Vaali was chasing Sugriva who ran and took shelter in Rishyamukha, which was forbidden territory for his brother. One of these trees that Vaali uprooted and hurled at Sugriva fell in front of Hanuman when he was meditating and made him open his eyes. He thought for a while and realized that everything had come to pass as he had foreseen. His friend had been thrown out of Kishkinda and had taken refuge in Rishyamukha. Without wasting another moment he went and met Sugriva and comforted him.

"Don't worry, Sugriva! Truth shall prevail. Even though you are down now, good times are ahead of you. Meditate on god and don't harbor ill-will toward your brother, and all will go well."

Sugriva followed his advice, and the two of them spent their time on the mountain. Soon, some of his other friends joined them.

However, Vaali could never forgive his brother, and every day he would climb the hill opposite Rishyamukha and terrorize his brother with abuses, threats, and displays of strength. He would scream and shout, beat his chest, gnash his teeth, and hurl abuses at his brother. As mentioned before, Vaali had the habit of bathing in all the oceans of the world. Effortlessly he would jump from ocean to ocean and take his bath every morning. Every time he flew over Rishyamukha, he would give a mighty kick on the head of the hapless Sugriva if he happened to be standing below him. One day Hanuman decided to stop this vile practice once and for all. As Vaali passed overhead, he jumped and caught hold of his long tail and tried to drag him down. His idea was to make him fall on the mountain and thus destroy himself as per the curse of the sage. However, Vaali was noted for his amazing strength and was a good match for Hanuman, who had infinite powers but had to be prompted by someone before he could use them fully. Vaali realized that the person who had caught him must be Hanuman since Sugriva would not dare to do this, so he thought that the best thing would be to carry Hanuman back to Kishkinda and kill him there. However, they were equally matched, and neither could make their plot work. At last they decided to make a pact with each other. Hanuman told Vaali that he would release him if he promised not to keep harassing Sugriva. Vaali agreed, provided Sugriva would promise to never return to Kishkinda or make claims on the throne. It was only then that Hanuman let him go. Vaali was pleased with this pledge since he had feared that Hanuman would be another contender to his throne.

In Valmiki's Ramayana, Hanuman makes his debut in the Kishkinda Kanda. He played a very subdued role in the beginning of the *kanda* (portion of a book) in which his momentous meeting with Rama took place. Sugriva never knew that Hanuman's strength was superior to his brother's. Had he known of it, he would have asked Hanuman to fight with Vaali instead of approaching Rama. But both of them were ignorant of Hanuman's exceptional powers and thus Sugriva appealed to Rama. In fact, without the curse of the *rishis,* the entire course of the Ramayana war might have been different, for Maruti could have fought the war single-handed.

> *Rama, Lakshmana, and Sita eternally abide in*
> *your heart,*
> *Nothing delights you so much as to listen to the*
> *Lord's stories.*

Hanuman Chalisa by Tulsidas

Aum Sri Hanumathe Namaha!

Aum Ramabhaktaaya Namaha!

9

Ramadasa

The Famous Encounter

Aum Namo Hanumathe,
Rudravataaraaya,
Vishwarupaaya,
Amitha-vikramaaya,
Prakataparaakramaaya,
Mahaabalaaya,
Suryakoti samaprabhaaya,
Ramaduthaaya namo Namaha!

Prostrations to Hanuman, the messenger of Rama,
The avatara of Rudra,
Who could take on the form of the whole universe,
Who had amazing powers,
Who performed incredible feats,
Whose strength was unbelievable,
And who was as brilliant as a thousand suns!

HYMN TO HANUMAN

Months passed in this way. Sugriva was always bewailing his loss, but Hanuman always gave him good counsel. In the meantime, destiny was already weaving her inextricable strands, and the time was slowly but surely approaching when Sugriva's fortunes were going to turn for the good. Once when Sugriva and Hanuman and some of the other monkeys were sitting on a rock, they saw a chariot flying over the mountain toward the south. A beautiful woman and an enormous man were in the chariot. The woman was crying piteously, and as soon as she saw them, she tore off a piece of her upper garment, tied her ornaments in a bundle, and threw it down. The monkeys picked up the little bundle that she had thrown and kept it safely in their cave.

Far away in Ayodhya, which was the capital of their land, many strange things had happened. The king of the land was Dasaratha, and he had four sons called Rama, Lakshmana, Bharata, and Shatrugna. Rama was the incarnation of Vishnu and was an exemplary person. He had married Sita, the daughter of King Janaka, king of Videha, who was noted both for her beauty and her conduct. It so happened that Dasaratha decided to crown Rama as king since he was getting old. However, before the event took place, due to a series of strange misunderstandings, the king was forced to give in to his favorite queen Kaikeyi's pleas to send Rama to exile in the forest for fourteen years and install her own son Bharata in his stead. The poor king had given her two boons long ago, and the queen took this opportune moment to ask him to fulfill his promises. The king was most reluctant to give in to her demands, but she threatened to kill herself if he refused. When Rama heard of this, he decided to carry out his father's promise even if it meant giving up his kingdom. His wife Sita and his brother Lakshmana insisted on accompanying him to the forest, and the three of them set out without further ado. The king could not bear this parting and died soon after.

Kaikeyi's son Bharata was away when all this happened. When he returned, he was furious with his mother and refused to accept the throne. He went after his brother, whom he loved dearly, and begged him to return. However, Rama refused to comply with his wishes and told him it was his duty to go and do as his father had wished. Bharata reluctantly returned but refused to sit on the throne meant for his brother. He kept Rama's sandals on the throne and lived the life of a sage outside the city, in a hut like his brother.

In the meantime, Rama, Lakshmana, and Sita spent an idyllic time in the forest roaming around and meeting many sages. Unfortunately, in the last year of their exile, Ravana, whom as we know was the wicked *rakshasa* king of the island of Lanka, saw Sita. He fell in love with her, abducted her, and took her off to his island retreat. Sita had thrown her bundle of jewels when they passed over the hill of Rishyamukha where Sugriva and Hanuman were sitting.

Rama was desperate and did not know how to get her back. Lakshmana tried to comfort him, and they went from place to place trying to locate her whereabouts. They met an old woman saint called Shabari, who advised him to go and meet a monkey called Sugriva who would help him. With this in view, the brothers went on their way to the hill of Rishyamukha.

Before proceeding to the famous encounter between Rama and Hanuman as given in the Valmiki Ramayana, we will share another very sweet story in which it is said that Rama met Hanuman when they were both very young children.

Knowing that Vishnu had taken an incarnation as Rama, Shiva longed to have a glimpse of him and watch his childhood pranks. He took on various disguises in order to gain entrance to the palace. He pretended to be an astrologer, a mendicant, and a bard in order to have a look at the child, but he was unsuccessful in all his attempts. A last he decided to take on the guise of a monkey trainer and go with a monkey. So he went to Anjana's cave and asked her to send her son with him. Anjana recognized him as her favorite god. She bowed low to him and brought Hanuman before him. Maruti also thought that he looked very familiar. In fact, the thought flashed across his mind, "He and I are one!"

Shiva put a leash round the baby monkey's neck and apologized to him for the discomfort. They went to Ayodhya and drew crowds wherever they went. Maruti held everyone spellbound with his clever tricks. They reached the palace gates where the gatekeeper scornfully told them to clear off. Shiva, in his guise as a *madari* (monkey trainer), just stood there playing on his drum. Inside the palace, Rama, who was just four years old, heard the sound of the drum and started to throw a tantrum, and Dasaratha commanded that the *madari* be admitted. In the palace courtyard, the two of them performed for the royal princes. This was no ordinary show, for the drummer was Nataraja, Lord of dancers, now dancing in the form of an ordinary monkey trainer. Vishnu, who makes the entire universe dance to his tune, clapped his hands in delight, oblivious to all but the monkey's antics. He gazed wide-eyed at the drummer and the dancing monkey. No one in the court except the royal *guru* Vasishta guessed the secret, and he bowed his head in reverence to Shiva.

When the dance was over, the entertainers were given rich gifts, but when they prepared to leave, Rama began to cry and insisted that the monkey be left behind. The mother felt embarrassed to ask the *madari* to give up his source of livelihood. All at once the drummer vanished and the monkey jumped into Rama's arms. After that, Hanuman became Rama's constant companion. During the day he served the princes and joined in all their games. He would fetch balls for them, disentangle kite strings, and fan them while they played board games. He would row for them when they went on the river and guard them when they went swimming in the Sarayu River. He would retrieve arrows when they practiced archery and climb trees to pluck fruits for them. As a reward for all this, he was allowed to sleep in Rama's bed and eat the leftovers on his plate. He was even allowed to ride on his shoulder. He remained with him as the royal pet until the time when Vishwamitra came to take Rama to save his *yaga*, or fire sacrifice. At that time, Rama secretly instructed Hanuman to go to Kishkinda, enter Sugriva's service, and await his coming.

The story as given by Valmiki follows the course of Rama's and Lakshmana's journey through the subcontinent and their meeting with the tribal woman Shabari, who instructed Rama to approach Sugriva.

Sugriva was sitting with Hanuman and his other ministers under a tree when they spied Rama and Lakshmana coming up the hill. Sugriva, as usual, was filled with misgivings and feared that Vaali had sent them to kill him. Hanuman climbed on top of a peak and observed the two who were approaching. At the very first sight of Rama, he was filled with an ecstasy, the reason for which he was unable to say. He felt as if he were seeing god. He cupped his palms together above his head and bowed to him. Turning to Sugriva, he told him that he was sure that these people had not been sent by Vaali and that they were not coming with bad intentions. However, Sugriva was not convinced of this and told Hanuman to go down in disguise and find out their intentions. Hanuman took on the form of a young Brahmin and went down to the brothers. This was indeed an encounter that was to have far-reaching consequences, not just for Hanuman but for the whole world of devotees for all time to come.

As he approached them, an unaccountable feeling of joy overcame him. His mind was clear and pure and none of the suspicions of his chief darkened his thoughts. The birds seemed to be chirping more musically than usual. The soft and gentle breeze from the south wafted a divine fragrance toward his nostrils, which he thought was a benediction from his father. The creepers that were entwining the trees seemed to shed their flowers in his path. Never for a moment did he realize that this was to be the turning point of his life and that he was about to meet his master whom he would serve faithfully for the rest of his life!

With one jump Hanuman came close to where the two were coming and changing his identity, he went near and bowed to them.

Of the many facets of Hanuman's personality, the outstanding quality that attracted and endeared him to his master Rama was his power of eloquence. As he approached the brothers for the first time, Hanuman felt a thrill of joy, and all his faculties of intelligence, discretion, observation, and power of speech surfaced. Paying homage to both the brothers, he addressed them in a soft and pleasing manner. Valmiki has given a beautiful description of this in his Ramayana:

"How have you two ascetics of remarkable vigor, unfailing prowess, most austere vows, and excellent appearance come to this region? Your looks are that of some royal sages or of gods. You seem to be searching for something. Your presence adds charm to this lake of sparkling waters. Having eyes resembling the petals of a lotus and wearing a rounded mass of matted hair, you two gallant men resemble each other! You seem to be heroes come down to this Earth from Heaven!"

Seeing that the brothers still remained silent, Hanuman decided to disclose his identity. "I am a monkey named Hanuman and have been sent by the virtuous king of monkeys called Sugriva. He seeks your friendship and has asked me to negotiate for him." Actually, the astute Hanuman added that last bit himself for he realized that these people were capable of helping Sugriva.

Valmiki portrays Hanuman as a model speaker who, by the magic of his words and their skilful presentation, was able to win the heart of Rama, a stranger.

Rama was struck by the Brahmin's demeanor and totally captivated by his sweet speech. He told Lakshmana that no one could speak in this way unless he had mastered the Vedas. He noted that there was no defect in his countenance, eyes, forehead, brows, or limbs.

"O Lakshmana! He has delivered a wholesome, distinct, and remarkable speech, grammatically correct, fluent, and delightful to hear. Even the mind of an enemy with uplifted sword will be moved by his speech."

This first impression that both had about each other developed into a mutual attraction, binding them together for life in a saga of selfless service, sacrifice, and devotion. All the subsequent events in the epic only served to bring them closer, deepening their love, admiration, and understanding of each other.

From this moment onward, Hanuman enshrined Rama as the Lord of his heart. He accepted him alone as the supreme Lord. His mind and intellect were totally surrendered to him.

This life of selfless service and single-pointed devotion to his Master hastened his spiritual unfoldment. In the devotional literature of the world, Hanuman's *bhakti* to Rama has no parallel. He will ever remain the purest and most exalted *bhakta* the world has ever known. Valmiki says that even a very casual mention of the name of Rama was enough for his eyes to well up with tears of profound joy and for his palms to fold before him.

Lakshmana now said to Hanuman, "Know us to be the sons of the great king Dasaratha of the land of Kosala. This, my brother, is his eldest son Rama, and I'm his brother Lakshmana. Just at the time when he was going to be anointed king of the land, he was disinherited of his sovereignty by some unpardonable trick of destiny and came to live in the forest with me and his consort Sita. She is a veritable Lakshmi and deserves to live in a palace adorned with all jewels and comforts. However, she chose to follow him to the forest. Unfortunately, a *rakshasa* whose name is not known has abducted her and taken her to his stronghold. We have come here in search of her. We were told by the great sage Shabari that we should enlist the support of a monkey chief called Sugriva who would be able to help us in our search."

He added that Sugriva's name had also been told to them by a giant called Kabandha whom they had released from a curse.

"We are indeed happy to hear that you are Sugriva's minister. By the pleading of such an envoy, all the objects of the sovereign in whose service he happens to be employed will be accomplished. My noble brother is the ruler of this land but by a cruel fate he has been forced to take on the life of a mendicant, and we will be happy to accept help from your master Sugriva in order to find his consort."

Hanuman said, "The noble Sugriva is in the same predicament as your brother. He has been deprived of both his throne and his spouse by his brother, exiled by him, and forced to take refuge on this hill. He will certainly help you to find Sita."

Lakshmana now turned to his brother and said, "Brother, it looks like we have arrived here at the right time and the right place to meet the right person. Let us go with him and meet Sugriva."

Hearing the story of Rama's selfless renunciation of the throne, Hanuman's initial admiration turned into great respect and love. He realized that Rama was no ordinary person but a great being, worthy of veneration.

Rama willingly agreed to meet Sugriva, but Hanuman knew that the brothers would be unable to scale the impossible slopes of Rishyamukha, so he resumed his monkey form and bowed before the two brothers.

As soon as Hanuman assumed his simian form, Rama noticed the glittering earrings and remarked on them to Lakshmana, who was quite puzzled because he could not see them. However, Hanuman heard him and remembered his mother's words that only the one who would be his master would be able to see the earrings. He was thrilled and knew that the instinctive feelings that had welled up in him at the sight of Rama had been right.

His heart overflowed with joy. He took the two brothers on either shoulder and jumped with them up the hill to the peak where Sugriva was sitting with his other ministers.

Placing Rama and Lakshmana down before Sugriva, he said, "I would like to present to you Rama, the scion of the race of Ikshvaku, and his brother Lakshmana, who are both sons of the emperor Dasaratha. In order to keep his word to his wife, Kaikeyi, the king was forced to banish Rama to this forest. He came accompanied by his brother and his wife. Unfortunately, his wife was stolen by some *rakshasa,* and he has come here seeking your aid in finding her."

Sugriva, who had been suspiciously watching their approach, now came forward with outstretched arms and clasped Rama's hands in his own, saying sweetly, "I'm indeed honored that you have come to me to seek my aid. Let us clasp our hands in friendship and take an oath to help each other. If you promise to help me kill my brother Vaali and restore my wife and throne, I shall surely swear to help you to find your wife!"

After hearing Sugriva's story, which resembled his, Rama said, "*Dharma* is the law of civilization, based on duty, not desire, which ensures social stability. He who upholds *dharma* is an *arya,* or noble, and he who does not is a *rakshasa.* Vaali is an animal, a barbarian who is no different from Ravana. Both believe that might is right. Both have become kings by force, and they do not respect the sanctity of marriage. If civilization is to be established, people like Vaali and Ravana need to be destroyed."

Hanuman immediately lit a fire. He had Rama and Sugriva stand on either side and forge a pact of friendship with the blazing fire as witness. They worshipped the fire with flowers and went round it three times, swearing to help each other. After this, they clasped each other in their arms and swore eternal friendship.

Sugriva broke off a flower-laden bough and placed it on the ground as a seat for Rama, and Hanuman did the same for Lakshmana.

Now that they were comfortably seated, Sugriva narrated his pitiful tale to Rama and begged him to kill Vaali who had insulted him and treated him so unfairly.

Rama smiled and said, "My arrows, sharp like the fangs of a serpent, will descend on your brother and finish him off in no time. So have no fear."

Sugriva now told Rama, "I have heard from Hanuman how the *rakshasa* has stolen your beloved spouse. Rest assured that wherever he might have hidden her, in the bowels of the earth or the vaults of heaven, I shall deliver her to you. Therefore, cast away your grief, for you shall surely get your beloved back! I think she must have been abducted by Ravana. In fact, I feel that it was she who was being dragged away in his aerial vehicle."

Rama was amazed to hear this and eagerly asked him to narrate the tale.

Sugriva said, "While Hanuman and I were sitting on this mountain with four others, we saw an aerial vehicle passing overhead. I think it was Ravana who was inside. He was carrying a most beautiful woman in his arms. She was wriggling and crying out loudly, 'Rama! Lakshmana! Save me! Save me!' Seeing us standing below, she tore off a piece of her upper garment, tied her jewels in it, and dropped it down without Ravana noticing. We have kept it safely, and I will show them to you, and you will be able to know if they belong to your wife."

Rama was greatly excited when he heard this and asked Sugriva to show it to him immediately. Sugriva went into the cave where they lived and brought out the bit of cloth and gave it to Rama. Rama opened the scarf and saw his beloved wife's jewels inside. He pressed them to his bosom. Tears started to flow from his eyes, and he could no longer speak. At last, he controlled himself and turning to Lakshmana, he showed the jewels to him and said, "Lakshmana, don't you recognize these jewels as belonging to the princess of Videha?"

Lakshmana replied, "I do recognize her anklets, which I used to see every time I bowed at her feet, but my eyes never went beyond that to her neck."

"O Sugriva!" said Rama. "Do you know where that wretch has carried away my queen? His end is approaching fast, for I shall surely follow him and kill him."

Sugriva said, "I'm not sure where his abode is situated, even though I know that he is the mighty king of Lanka, but I swear to you that my monkeys will discover his whereabouts and recover Sita. It ill-befits a noble soul like you to give way to your grief like this."

At that moment far away in Lanka, Sita felt her left eye tremble by itself and the same thing happened to Vaali in Kishkinda, and Ravana's ten left eyes also trembled. This is considered to be a good sign for females and a bad omen for males.

Hearing this, Rama checked his grief and listened to the sad tale told by Sugriva about the injustice that had been done to him by his brother. He assured him that he would kill Vaali. However, Sugriva was not quite convinced, for he knew his brother's amazing powers and feared that the slender Rama would not be a match for him.

Falteringly, he spoke. "I realize that you have great strength, but constant harassment has made me timorous. I'm not sure if you can beat the mighty Vaali in combat. Actually, he is so powerful that once he even subdued the mighty Ravana." He went on to tell Rama about this feat.

Once the mighty night wanderer, Ravana desired to conquer the heavens and bring Indra, the king of the gods, to heel. He called his eldest son Meghanatha and told him his wish.

Meghanatha said, "O Father! Why do you hesitate to ask me such a thing? You have only to say one word and you know that I shall obey you. Come, let us go to Indra's heaven and capture him."

Thus the two of them went to Indra and challenged him to a fight. Indra was a bit reluctant since he was not sure of the outcome; however, since he could not refuse, he agreed. Very soon it became apparent that Ravana was going to be defeated. His son Meghanatha immediately stepped into the fray and effortlessly subdued Indra. He tied him and threw him before his exultant father. It was after this feat that Meghanatha got the new name of Indrajit (conqueror of Indra). Ravana took Indra back to his stronghold and tied him to a pole in the middle of the courtyard for all to see. He then looted the heavens and reveled in his greatness.

Indra's pitiable state was reported to Brahma by the sage Narada. It was Brahma who had given many boons to Ravana and made him invincible, so he felt a bit guilty. He went to Lanka and made Ravana release Indra. The latter was most ashamed of the whole affair and crept back to heaven hoping that the other gods had not heard of this shameful episode.

However, Narada came there soon afterward and told him of a way by which he could get even with Ravana. "Your son Vaali is the one person who can humble Ravana's pride," he said. "Leave it all to me. I'll see that justice is done!" So saying, Narada departed to Lanka, where he was welcomed by Ravana. There he fanned the flames of Ravana's pride by telling that there was a monkey called Vaali, who was Indra's son, who went about telling everyone that he would get even with the person who had humiliated his father! Ravana was indignant at this and swore to kill this impertinent monkey. He was all set to go to Vaali armed with all his weapons and accompanied by an army. Narada laughed to see these preparations and said, "He is only a monkey. You don't need all these weapons and army to subdue him. All you need is a rope. You can creep up behind him and tie him up before he knows what's happening!"

So Ravana desisted from taking his army and weapons and went in search of Vaali. Narada, who didn't want to miss the fun, offered to accompany him. They crossed the southern sea and found Vaali deep in meditation on the shore, since, as we know, he was in the habit of jumping from sea to sea every morning to do his morning ablutions and prayers.

Seeing his enormous frame, Ravana was a bit daunted, but Narada egged him on and told him to creep up behind, catch his tail, and then bind him without difficulty. Now, a monkey's tail is his greatest strength, and Vaali's tail was very special. In fact, he had been named Vaali because of the extraordinary length and strength of his tail. *Vaal* is the Sanskrit word for tail.

Ravana crept up from behind and caught his tail. Vaali did not stir from his prayers but simply caught hold of Ravana's hand in his tail. Then Ravana put out his other hand and that also met with the same fate. Very soon, Vaali had bound Ravana's whole body in his tail, and he continued uninterruptedly with his prayers! Narada thought it expedient to leave the place as fast as he could.

Vaali's tail had wound tightly round Ravana's whole body, holding him in a fierce grip so that only his face was to be seen. Keeping Ravana thus bound in his tail, Vaali went from ocean to ocean, and each time he had a dip, Ravana was submerged again and again in the salty water! This went on for many months. At last his son Indrajit became anxious about his father's whereabouts and was all set to go and fight with Vaali. Again, Narada arrived on the scene and told him not to confront Vaali since the latter had really no enmity with Ravana but was waiting for Indrajit to present himself, as he was the one who had bound his father. Narada told Indrajit that Vaali would definitely kill him if he went. He advised him to wait patiently until Vaali released Ravana of his own accord.

As foretold, Vaali grew tired of having Ravana hanging on his tail and released him. Ravana was completely subdued and begged his pardon. Vaali agreed on condition that he and his son would not go and make a nuisance of themselves to his father Indra in heaven. In return, Vaali promised that he would never make war against Ravana nor side with those who wanted to conquer him.

This was the story told to Rama by Sugriva, since he wanted to make Rama understand Vaali's great strength. He also added that Vaali had a boon that he would automatically get half the strength of anyone who confronted him. This is one of the reasons that Rama chose to kill him from behind a tree.

Every arduous task in the world,
Becomes easy thanks to your grace.

HANUMAN CHALISA BY TULSIDAS

Aum Sri Hanumathe Namaha!

10

Pranadeva
The Killing of Vaali

Aum Hanumathe Rudravataraaya,
Ramasevakaaya,
Ramabhakti tatparaaya,
Ramahridyaaya,
Lakshmana shakti nivaranaaya,
Lakshmanarakshakaaya,
Dushta nigrahanaaya,
Ramadhutaaya, namo Namah!

I bow to Hanuman, the messenger of Rama,
The avatara of Rudra, in the service of Rama,
Totally engrossed in devotion to Rama,
Ever keeping Rama in his heart,
Who saved Lakshmana and gave him back his powers,
And who is the destroyer of the wicked!

HYMN TO HANUMAN

Hanuman whispered to Lakshmana that Sugriva had told them this story only because he doubted Rama's ability to kill him. He did not dare to ask him for a show of strength, but he would be happy if Rama showed some of his prowess. Lakshmana told Rama of Sugriva's fears. Rama laughingly went up to the enormous skeleton of the demon Dundubhi, lifted it up with his toe, and flung it to a distance of about eighty miles! Sugriva was a little appeased by this feat, but he still spoke doubtfully.

"This carcass was filled with blood and flesh and ten times as heavy as it is now when Vaali lifted it and flung it here. Now it's only a bare skeleton. I wonder if I could ask you to perform one more feat and thus assure me of your might. Vaali's arrow could pierce a *sal* (ironwood) tree, which has a huge circumference, without any difficulty. Here are seven *sal* trees growing in a row. If you can pierce one of them and split it into two, my fears will be laid to rest once and for all."

Rama smiled, and without a word he fitted his arrow to his mighty bow, known as the Kodanda. The arrow was gold-plated, thicker than a finger, half as long as a staff, marked with his name, decorated with the feathers of the fastest birds, and tipped with iron. The *sal* trees were as thick as turrets. The arrow flew from the bow and split not one tree but all seven trees, and then pierced the earth. It is said to have gone to the subterranean world and then returned to its own quiver!!

Sugriva couldn't believe his eyes. He felt most ashamed at having tested Rama's powers like this. He prostrated himself at his feet and begged his pardon for having doubted him.

Standing with folded palms before Rama, Sugriva said, "I am now fully convinced that you can kill even Indra, the king of the gods, if you so choose, so why not his son Vaali? Let us proceed straight away to Kishkinda and you can meet him face to face."

They went through forests and mountains fragrant with sandal-wood and came to a grove of most beautiful trees from which arose a fragrance of oblations being offered into the fire. Rama asked Sugriva what that grove was and to whom it belonged.

Sugriva said, "This hermitage belonged to seven sages known as Saptajanas. They used to practice severe penance here for many years.

They slept on water and subsisted on air alone. They never stepped out beyond this grove. When the time came for them to depart from this world, they were given bodily liberation. However, this grove is still sacrosanct. None dare enter it. One can hear music and ethereal voices singing from within. The perfume rising from sacred wood fires lighted during *yajnas* permeates the air, as you can see. Let us all bow from here to those glorious sages and obtain their blessings before proceeding."

All of them bowed low in front of the holy place and then walked on. When they reached the outskirts of Kishkinda, Rama and the others concealed themselves behind the trees of the thick forest that surrounded Kishkinda.

Rama now told Sugriva to go forward alone and challenge Vaali for a duel. "I will stand aside unseen and shoot my arrow into him at the right moment."

In light of the fact that Sugriva had told him about Vaali being able to take over half the strength of his opponent, Rama decided to shoot him from behind a tree. Another reason given for this strange act was that Rama feared if he confronted Vaali, he might refuse to fight with him, since he had no quarrel with Rama, and then he would not be able to keep his pledge to his friend Sugriva. So Rama told Sugriva to go and challenge his brother and he and Lakshmana would follow close behind him. Sugriva mentally prepared himself and boldly went to the gates of Kishkinda, bellowed loudly, and challenged his brother to a duel. Enraged at hearing his brother's roars, Vaali got up with such force that the base of the cave sank and his eyes spat fire. Grinding his teeth in anger, he slapped his thigh and clapped his hands so that the sound echoed through the valleys. He charged out with such speed that the ornaments round his neck snapped and scattered their gems all around. Vaali came out of the cave looking like the morning sun rising over the horizon. He grabbed Sugriva, who was certainly no match for him, and bashed him to a pulp. With great difficulty Sugriva managed to extricate himself from Vaali's iron grip and take to his heels. He ran all the way back to Rishyamukha before Vaali could finish him off.

In the meantime, Rama had been keenly watching the fight and found to his dismay that he couldn't distinguish between the two brothers, who looked like two peas in a pod. Fearing to discharge his arrow in case he killed Sugriva instead of Vaali, he desisted. He followed Sugriva, who was in a very poor state.

Sugriva could hardly speak, yet he whispered, "If you didn't want to kill my brother, why did you not refuse at the very outset instead of letting me get battered like this? Fully believing your word, I challenged him and see what has happened!"

Rama tried to pacify him. "My dear friend," he said, "how can you think that I have betrayed you? Your brother and you resemble each other in stature, costume, and embellishments. Even your roars sound similar. Both of you were clasped in each others arms trying to strangle each other. How could I shoot my deadly arrow when I knew that I might kill you instead of him? Please do return to Kishkinda and challenge him once again, but this time you must wear a garland by which I will be able to distinguish you."

He told Lakshmana to take a liana from the mountainside, which was covered with flowers and looked like a beautiful garland, and put it round Sugriva's neck. Battered and bleeding though he was, Sugriva licked his wounds and proceeded toward Kishkinda, followed by Rama, Lakshmana, Hanuman, and a few of his other friends.

Rama urged Sugriva to go and challenge Vaali fearlessly once again, as now he was sure that his arrow would find its mark.

Sugriva went and roared outside the gates. Vaali was in his seraglio lolling about with his wives when he heard the roar. He couldn't believe his ears. His amorous mood gave way to one of violent loathing. How could Sugriva, whom he had just reduced to pulp a few hours ago, dare to come and challenge him again? He was filled with a blind rage. He was determined to finish off his brother once and for all. He had been a real thorn in his side for a long time and once he was dead, he could enjoy the company of his wife Rumi without feeling any guilt. He was well aware of his crime in consorting with his younger brother's wife while her husband was still alive. He had somehow stifled his conscience, for he was infatuated with Rumi even though his own wife

Tara was very beautiful and wise. With Sugriva out of the way, he could have Rumi without any pangs of shame, for the law allowed a man to marry a deceased brother's wife in order to protect her! Thinking thus, Vaali gave a big bellow of disgust and rage and rushed out.

The intelligent Tara stopped him as he was going and gave him some sage counsel.

"My Lord!" she said. "This brother of yours was beaten by you and ran off with his life just a short while ago. How is he emboldened to return and roar like this without the assurance of help by some powerful ally? The crown prince Angada, your son, gave me the following report. He said that two young and expert warriors, known as Rama and Lakshmana, the sons of the emperor Dasaratha, have entered this forest and formed an alliance with Sugriva. I'm sure Sugriva has been emboldened by their protection or else he would never have dared to accost you like this. Please don't go now. Tell him to return tomorrow morning, and then you can fight with him if it pleases you. Better still, you can make friends with him and allow him to return to the court. Be kind to him. Return his wife to him. She is very unhappy here. Somehow my heart sinks within me and I see only bad omens. I beg of you not to go now."

Vaali's time had come and he just would not listen to reason. Moreover, he was anxious to appropriate Rumi all for himself. Brushing off Tara's detaining hand, he ordered her to return to the other women. She placed Indra's golden garland round his neck and embraced him sadly, for she had a premonition that she would never see him alive again.

Vaali brushed her aside and rushed out. He glared angrily at Sugriva and charged at him like an infuriated bull. They started to grapple in deadly earnest. Sugriva's strength was flagging, and he looked around desperately for Rama, wondering why he was not coming to his aid. Vaali lifted him above his head in order to dash him on a rock and thus end his career! The golden necklace was shining round Vaali's neck. Rama had no trouble in recognizing him. He saw Sugriva's agonized look. He stretched his powerful arrow on his bow and let it fly with a tremendous twang. It found its mark on Vaali's breast and felled him as easily as it had felled the *sal* trees. The full moon shone with all its splendor and lighted up the huge fallen body of Vaali, which was now bleeding and weak. Vaali had never thought even for a moment that there was any weapon or power on heaven or earth that could conquer him in a fight. He was invulnerable, according to the promise of the gods, yet here he was, laid low on the bare ground of his own kingdom with just one arrow. He was really anxious to know who this exceptional warrior was who was able to kill him with one arrow. His name must be on the arrow. With his last remaining strength, he pulled the arrow out of his chest. Blood gushed out of his heart like a spring that had been dammed for a long time. Everything was blurring before his dying eyes and he had to hold the arrow close to his eyes before he could spell the name "Rama" on it. For a moment, gratitude filled his heart. All creatures had to die at one time or other and far better for him to die at the hands of Rama, who was thought to be an *avatara* of Vishnu, than by the weapon of a *rakshasa, asura,* or wild animal. This feeling was swiftly replaced by anger at the way he had been killed. He looked up feebly as Rama and Lakshmana approached him. Summoning his waning strength, he upbraided Rama for his act.

"You are supposed to be the scion of the line of Ikshavku and noted for your adherence to *dharma*. How could you have killed me from behind a tree when I was fighting with my brother? When Sugriva challenged me for the second time, my wife Tara warned me not to go, for she feared that he was being helped by you, but I told her that I had no fear of you since I knew you would not stoop to any type of unrighteous act. What have I done that you should have killed me from behind? I hear you are looking for your wife. I could have killed that wretch Ravana and brought her back to you singlehanded. I have already defeated him once and spared his life, but this time I would not have done so. Why did you have to ally yourself with this worthless Sugriva?"

Vaali had exhausted himself by this speech, and he fell back gasping for breath. Rama waited patiently for Vaali to have his say for he knew that on the face of it, he had every right to berate him. At last when Vaali had stopped, he spoke to him with compassion in his eyes.

"O Vaali! How dare you speak to me about *dharma* and *adharma* (unrighteousness) when you are living a life steeped in sin? Your younger brother, who is full of good qualities and loves you very much, should have been treated by you as a son. Without giving him a chance to clear his name, you beat him up and banished him to Rishyamukha in order to keep his wife. According to the law of this land, anyone who is guilty of sleeping with his brother's wife when he is still alive is punishable by death! You have continued your enmity with your brother only to fan your own lust. Sugriva is as dear to me as my brother Lakshmana. I have sworn friendship with him and publicly made a pact to kill you and restore his kingdom and his wife. What sort of a friend would I be if I did not keep my promise?"

Vaali considered Rama's words and realized that he spoke the truth. He bitterly regretted his cruelty to his younger brother, whom he should have treated as a son. He also knew that his action in having stolen his wife was despicable.

"O Rama!" he said. "You have spoken rightly. I'm not worried about myself. Death is inevitable for all, but I'm worried about my son Angada. Please consider him as your own son and see that he is looked after properly. Please don't let my beloved wife Tara be insulted by Sugriva. She is wise and good. I realize that I'm fated to meet death at your hands and that is why I refused to listen to her when she urged me to desist from fighting."

With his last breath Vaali took off his gold chain, which had miraculous powers, and put it over Sugriva's neck. He begged him to forgive him for all he had done to him and told him to look after Angada as his own son as well as his beloved wife Tara. Sugriva felt such remorse for his act that he couldn't say a word.

Rama promised to see that Sugriva gave the best treatment to Angada and Tara. Hearing of the tragic end of her husband, Tara now ran to his side along with her son Angada. Casting herself over his body, she bewailed his fate. Rama urged her to get up and see to the obsequies, but she refused to budge from the place. Taking up the fatal arrow that had killed her husband, she threatened to plunge it into her own heart and had to be forcibly stopped by her attendants.

Hearing her cries and his brother's kind words, Sugriva lost whatever courage he had. He told Rama that he would also immolate himself on his brother's pyre and that Angada could help find Sita. Neither Rama nor anyone else could console him.

At last Hanuman approached Tara and told her in gentle tones, "An embodied soul always reaps the good and evil fruit of his actions done in the past. The body is like a bubble on the water. It might burst at any time and is not worth grieving for. Your duty now is to look after your son Angada who is solely dependent on you. It is your responsibility to see that the last rites are done for your husband in the proper way. That's the only thing you can now do for him."

Rama spoke sternly to Sugriva and told him that he had done this only at his request, and for him to wash his hands of the whole matter was not a manly thing to do. It was his duty to see to the obsequies of his dear brother rather than opt to perish in the flames. He commanded Sugriva to bring a palanquin and take his brother's body to the riverside. At last Sugriva did as he was bidden. The monkeys brought out the royal hearse, which was like a chariot without wheels. They dressed their dead king in jeweled clothes, placed his body on a bier covered with flowers, and placed it on the pyre that had been prepared for him. Angada set fire to it and all of them offered water and did all the usual rites that had to be done for a departed soul.

By the law of the jungle, after Vaali's death his killer would automatically become king with the right to kill Vaali's children and to claim his wives. However, Rama wanted to make the *vanaras* leave their old laws and adopt the law of *dharma*. So he told Sugriva to ask the monkeys whether they were agreeable to have him as king. When they agreed, Sugriva asked Tara if she was willing to be his queen. When she agreed, he adopted Vaali's son Angada and made him the heir to the throne. Thus did Rama make the monkeys change their ways and follow the rule of righteousness.

It was at this time that Hanuman, determined to conquer his animal instincts, took a vow of celibacy and service. By the vow of celibacy, he crushed the desire for sensual pleasures and by that of service, he trampled the tendency to inflate his ego.

After this, Hanuman approached Rama, stood with folded palms, and spoke these words to him: "O Lord, by thy grace, this kingdom has now been acquired by Sugriva. Pray enter the palace and crown him king."

Rama refused to enter the city, since he said that he had given his word to his father not to enter any city for the duration of fourteen years. However, he gave all instructions as to how Sugriva should be anointed king and how Angada should be crowned as the prince regent. He advised Sugriva on the duties of a good king. "Whatever you do, let it be based on the sanctioned codes of good conduct. Never hurt anyone with your words, even if it be an enemy."

Sugriva said, "I want to serve you. Please command me." Rama said, "The rainy season is coming. At the end of it, bring your army and come help me find Sita."

Hanuman begged to be allowed to accompany Rama and serve him during the four months of the rainy season. Again, Rama had to decline his offer.

"Your presence is absolutely necessary for Sugriva. He will need your support and judgment. Come to me after four months, and I'll tell you what you can do for me." He and Lakshmana decided to spend the approaching four months of the monsoons in a cave nearby. At the end of the four months, Sugriva promised to gather all the monkeys and start on the great quest to find Sita.

Sugriva duly entered the city in state and was crowned as king with Angada as the crown prince. Tara also drew what comfort she could from the fact that at least her son's well-being was being looked after.

> *You rendered great service to Sugriva,*
> *Arranged his meeting with Rama and gave him kingship.*

HANUMAN CHALISA BY TULSIDAS

Aum Sri Hanumathe Namaha!

Aum Ramadhutaaya Namaha!

11

Ramadhuta

Messenger of Rama

Anjana garbha sambhuta,
Kapindra sachivottama,
Rama priya namastubhyam
Hanuman raksha sarvada

I bow to the beloved of Rama,
Born from Anjana's womb,
Greatest of simians,
Hanuman! May thou look after everyone's welfare.

HYMN TO HANUMAN

Rama and Lakshmana now spent the four months of the monsoon season, from July to October, in a cave on the mountain called Prasravana. The sun now started to move south. Dark clouds heavily laden with water covered the skies so that the sun was not to be seen at all. The heavens burst and gushed down the mountainside and deluged the fields. The birds were silent. No animal stirred outside while the waters poured and roared. Wild vegetation covered the landscape with monstrous creepers and vines. The sky was perpetually overcast. The persistent gloom and dampness were reflected in Rama's heart.

"The skies are weeping at the fate of my beloved, as indeed I am, too," thought Rama. For four months, the brothers were confined to the small cave with nothing to do but watch the continuous downpour going on outside. Those four months were months of torment for Rama, since he was always imagining his beloved Sita's state and how anxious she must be about his whereabouts and whether he would come to rescue her. But there was nothing he could do about it since the monsoon season was not suitable for any sort of travel.

The rains ended at last and the sky began to clear. Rama was waiting anxiously for Sugriva's arrival, but almost a month passed and still there was no sign of him. Seeing his unhappiness, Lakshmana said, "Brother, I think that the ungrateful monkey has totally forgotten the promise he made to you. I will go and remind him forcibly of his duties!"

Lakshmana was not a calm person by nature and the four months of confinement inside the cave had not improved his temper in any way. And now the sight of his brother's agitation made his blood boil. He strapped the quiver to his shoulder, took up his bow, and strode toward Kishkinda, looking like a thundercloud. Rama cautioned him not to get angry and to try conciliatory methods with Sugriva.

In the meantime, Hanuman was always conscious of his duty and couldn't bear this delay any longer. Sugriva was always closeted in the harem with his wives, drinking and cavorting and making merry. He had totally forgotten the passage of time. His bedroom was so gorgeous and comfortable that he had hardly left it for the past four months. He wasn't even aware of the storms raging outside. He was surrounded by his beautiful wives with long tresses and heavy breasts who provided him with all comforts and sang and danced for him. Having been denied all the pleasures of the senses for such a long time, Sugriva found it impossible to control his appetite for food and sex. He was lying in a euphoric daze when Hanuman entered the harem where he had never gone before.

"O Sugriva!" he said. "It ill befits you to forget the promise made by you to Rama. Because of him, you are now enjoying all these luxuries. The rainy season has long passed, and you have not redeemed your promise. Therefore, issue orders immediately to the monkeys that they should assemble for the great endeavor of finding Sita."

Hearing these words of his able minister, Sugriva aroused himself a little and told Hanuman to send word to all the monkeys and bears in all the lands under his sway to come and assemble at Kishkinda in a week's time.

"Let my entire army be assembled under their generals without delay so that Rama may not think that I have been lagging in my duties." Having made this effort, Sugriva sank back into the arms of his wife.

Lakshmana walked with purposeful strides to Kishkinda. The earth shook with the force of his angry steps. The entrance to the city was through a cave that was guarded by monkeys so that no one could enter without permission. Seeing Lakshmana, they took up trees in order to stop him from entering. When he saw this, he became doubly incensed. Seeing his fury, they fled in all directions. They ran to Sugriva and told him of Lakshmana's violent mood. The king was totally inebriated and lost to the world in the arms of his brother's wife. He hardly knew what they were saying. The monkeys now ran to Angada, who hurriedly came out of the gate to meet Lakshmana in order to try to pacify him. Lakshmana ordered him to call his uncle immediately. He could hear the sweet strains of music and signs of revelry floating in the air, and when he thought of the agony that his brother had endured these past four months, his blood boiled. Angada was scared out of his wits and ran to inform his uncle and mother of the situation.

Hanuman also went to him and apprised him of the gravity of the situation.

"Rama is a wonderful friend, but he will be like a malefic comet if aroused to wrath. It is your tardiness that has made Lakshmana come here in search of you. You have to go and pacify him." But Sugriva was totally intoxicated and in no condition to meet Lakshmana. "What crime have I committed? Why should he be angry with me?" whined the tipsy monarch.

"You must admit that you have allowed time to elapse. You have lost track of the seasons in your ardor. Rama has been counting the days to go in search of his wife. Pained in heart and mind, he has sent Lakshmana to remind you of your promise. Please go and talk sweetly to him."

Sugriva did not dare to go and face him, so he begged Tara to go and pacify him since he knew that Lakshmana would not display his anger before a woman. Tara was also in a state of inebriation. Her gait was unsteady and her hair and clothes disheveled.

In the meantime, Lakshmana had forced an entrance into the palace and noted the abundance of wealth and luxury. His heart burned with rage when he thought of his dear brother's plight and how this ungrateful monkey was enjoying himself, oblivious to the woes of his master. He was loathe to force an entrance into the inner apartments.

Tara met him just outside the harem and pacified him with her sweet words.

"Why, O Prince, are you so angry? Who has been foolish enough to kindle your wrath?"

Lakshmana replied, "Your husband seems to have forgotten all the rules of *dharma*. Lapped in lust, he has forgotten the promises he made to my brother. If you wish to do him some good, go and tell him to rouse himself from this orgy of lust and help Rama. Ingratitude leads to the destruction of the best of men. We have been betrayed by one whom we considered a friend!"

Tara replied in a sweet and gentle tone. "O Prince! Please don't be angry with Sugriva. You know that *kama* (lust) is a powerful emotion. Even *rishis* have fallen beneath its spell. What need be said about a mere monkey, who is fickle by nature and who has been denied these pleasures for many years? Please pardon him for his apparent indifference, which has been caused by weakness. Actually, he has already ordered the army to be mobilized, and soon thousands of monkeys from all over the country will assemble here to start out on their quest to discover Sita. Please return to your dear Lord and apprise him of the situation."

Lakshmana was slightly appeased by these words and turning to Hanuman, he asked him if it were true that the monkey hordes had been commanded to come. Hanuman assured him that he himself had despatched messengers to all the great monkey strongholds in the subcontinent and very soon all of them would come.

By this time Sugriva had got himself under some sort of control. He accompanied Lakshmana, went to Rama, prostrated himself at his feet, and begged his pardon for his seeming tardiness. Rama was always the soul of compassion, and he immediately forgave Sugriva and embraced him. Just then Jambavan, the king of bears, arrived. He was an old dark bear with a crown and earrings of gold, with smoky gray eyes, huge paws, and long arms, and he stood on two feet. He pointed out to Rama the monkey troops that had started to arrive from all over the world. The whole hillside was covered with tree folk. They came in millions, lion-tailed, dark-faced, red-bottomed, white-furred, and golden-haired, ranging from all parts of the country from the Himalayas to the tip of the southern sea. The entire world's tree folk answered Sugriva's call and crowded round their king to await his commands.

Sugriva was delighted and pointed out the different types to Rama.

"Look over there at the white tree-dwelling monkeys who can change their forms at will. Note the tall blue coconut monkeys who are as strong as elephants, the yellow honey-wine monkeys with sharp teeth, the charcoal monkeys born to the daughters of the *gandharvas,* who worship the sun, the gray apes from the woods skirting the edge of the world who are handsome from eating only berries, the black ones with snaky tails from the caves on the banks of the Ganga, the red ones with lion manes and all the great bears of the earth, dark as gloom, brown, black, and terrible in combat. They have all answered my call and are ready to do your slightest bidding."

Rama was very pleased to see them. Since Sugriva did not know the exact whereabouts of Lanka, Rama asked him to choose four leaders who could take their troops to the four quarters and begin the search for Sita without further ado. The general called Vinata was sent to scour the eastern regions.

"Dawn first appears bright with brilliant glory in the east and people living there also become golden-colored. Search everywhere, but stay away no longer than one month from today." One-quarter of the monkeys followed him. The ground trembled as they left.

Another batch led by Sushena, his father-in-law, was sent to the west.

"Explore the west for Sita. That is where the sun's light ends and the lady of the night has her home. Follow the cool forest streams that flow from the high cold lakes, search the kingdoms and empires, the plateaus and wastelands. There live the *gandharvas*. But don't let any creature see you. Do not go farther than where the sun goes. Return here within a month."

Satabali, the white furred bear, was told to proceed north.

"Go to the enchanted lands of the Himalayas where the mountain of Kailasa rises pale and silver as the moon and go to the palace of Kubera, the Lord of wealth. Examine the icy slopes of the Himalayas and listen to the music of the Apsaras and the Nagas who live beneath the ground. Turn back from the dark and fearful northern border of the country and let not more than a full month pass before you return." With him went the third quarter of the monkey warriors.

At last he called Hanuman and Angada and told them to proceed to the south. Jambavan also lumbered in after them and all sat on rugs before Sugriva.

Sugriva said, "We saw Ravana fly south with the princess. I make Prince Angada the leader of the batch. Pavana Putra, the son of the wind, will surely find her." He then took out a scroll, gave it to Hanuman, and said, "Memorize this and give this message to the demon king when you meet him."

Hanuman turned to Rama, who was sitting beside Sugriva, prostrated himself at his feet, and begged him to bless him. Rama placed his lotus palms on Hanuman's head and blessed him. He then took him aside and gave him a perfect description of Sita so that he would know her when he saw her.

"O Hanuman," he said. "I feel sure that you will be the one to find Sita. Look at her feet, and you will find that her toenails glow like rubies. Her heels have been compared to a quiver. As for her waist, it is delicate and unseen. However, it is enough for you to observe her feet. They are incomparable. When you see her, give this ring to her so that she will know that you are not a spy but have come as my messenger. It is the signet ring of the Ikshvakus, and she will surely recognize it." Rama then gave a description of how she spoke, how she walked, and how her voice would sound. He also narrated some anecdotes to him that only he and she knew so that she would have no doubt that Maruti was indeed her husband's messenger.

Hanuman respectfully listened to every word that Rama spoke. He had a very good portrait of Sita in his mind now and he felt that when he saw her, she would look familiar to him. He took the ring, reverently placed it on his head, bowed low to Rama, and departed to the south, followed by a host of monkeys led by Angada and Nila.

Even before a month had passed, the generals who had been sent to the east, west, and north returned despondently and declared their inability to find out anything concerning Sita. All of them felt sure that Hanuman alone would accomplish the impossible.

Hanuman proceeded to the south with his party and passed many forests and rivers. The stipulated time of one month was coming to a close, and the monkeys were exhausted and hungry since they had just passed a forest that was totally denuded of fruits and roots due to the curse of a sage. They had crossed chasms and ravines and forests and thickets. They couldn't find even a drop of water to drink. Exhausted and dispirited, they collapsed on the hillside. Just then, Hanuman noticed two birds with water dripping from their wings coming out of a cave. He told the monkeys that there must be water and fruits inside and decided to follow the birds. It was pitch dark in the tunnel, so they walked single file, one catching the tail of the other, until they suddenly came to a wonderful grove with trees of gold under one of which was sitting a woman ascetic. At first they thought that this must be Sita, but Hanuman observed her carefully and could not detect any of the signs given by Rama. He approached her in all humility and begged her to tell him the story of the cave and this wondrous place.

She told them that her name was Swayamprabha and that she was the guardian of this cave, which belonged to her friend Hema, the *apsara*. The demon king Ravana had married Mandodari, Hema's daughter. Swayamprabha now plied them with fruits and nuts to eat and delicious honey drinks until they were satiated. She was very lonely and did everything to charm the monkeys and make them stay on. Even Jambavan, the wise old bear, succumbed to her allure and forgot about their mission. Only Hanuman remembered and told her the whole story of their search, and courteously asked her whether he could do anything for her in return for her hospitality. She begged him to marry her and stay on in the cave and she would give him anything he wished for. He sternly refused her offer and insisted that he would have to leave with or without his companions. Seeing his determination, she promised to help them. She told him that this was a magic cave and no one who entered it ever got out alive. However, she took pity on them and told them to close their eyes and she would transport them out of the cave. When they opened their eyes, they found that they were standing on the shore of the southern sea. The perfume of sandalwood from the Malaya Hills swept over them. Around them stretched the lifeless sands without a single fruit tree and before them the emerald green ocean, stretching to the horizon. The island of Lanka was nowhere to be seen.

Angada looked at the sun and realized that much more than a month had passed since they had entered the cave. He was utterly dejected. None of them knew what they should do now. Hungry and helpless, the monkeys groaned in despair. Angada looked at the dejected monkeys and said, "I'd rather starve myself to death than return and face Sugriva's wrath!"

The rest of the monkeys and bears swung their arms up and down and cried, "We will die with you!"

Hanuman told Angada not to be a coward and that it was better to return and face Sugriva, who was sure to be kind to them. Angada had painted a lurid picture of Sugriva to all the other monkeys, and all of them agreed that it would be better to fast to death. Nothing Hanuman said could persuade them to change their minds.

They lay on the seashore with their heads facing south.

In the meantime, a huge vulture by the name of Sampati heard their talk and came out of the cave where he was living. Seeing the monkeys lying in rows on the beach, he congratulated himself on finding that his food had been supplied to him by the kind gods.

"Today fortune has indeed favored me. I have not eaten for days, and here are some delicious monkeys, all laid out in neat rows, waiting for me to go and gobble them up!" With these words, the bird started to hop toward them, since he didn't have any wings.

When they saw this enormous bird hopping toward them with the sole purpose of devouring them, the monkeys started lamenting their fate. They who had decided to starve to death now appeared to be frightened of being eaten alive!

Angada started wailing, "Just look at our fate. This bird looks like Yama, the god of death himself, coming to make an end of us. It is said that all birds and animals love Rama. Even the old vulture Jatayu was prepared to give up his life for Rama's sake! Then why should this bird try to kill us and stop us from helping Rama?"

Actually, Sampati was the brother of Jatayu, who had helped Rama during his exile and who had been killed by Ravana while trying to stop him from abducting Sita. As soon as Sampati heard the word "Jatayu," he stopped in his tracks and enquired from Angada as to what he knew of Jatayu, who was his younger brother. He asked him to help him down from the rock since his wings had been burned. Angada now became a bit bolder and helped the old vulture to climb down the rock, and then he narrated the whole story of Rama and of their own search for Sita.

Sampati's eyes filled with tears when he heard of his brother's fate, and he wept bitterly. Angada asked him how he knew Jatayu, and Sampati recounted his own story to them.

"Jatayu was my younger brother. When we were young, we had a competition to see who could fly higher, and we flew straight at the sun. When I saw that Jatayu was getting burned due to the scorching heat, I flew over him and protected him so that he escaped, but I fell to the ground with my wings totally burned. I have not been able to fly ever afterwards and I have never met my dear brother since. My life has been one long suffering since then, and I have kept myself alive because I have been told that my redemption would come when I heard the story of Rama."

As soon as he heard Angada's tale of Rama, the old vulture sprouted wings and soared into the sky like a young bird, much to the surprise of all the monkeys. They were astonished at the miraculous power of the story of Rama. Sampati swooped down once again and told them that he had seen Sita being abducted by Ravana. Angada begged him to tell them all he knew.

Sampati said, "One day while I was sitting on this rock, I saw a beauteous young lady being carried away by force by one of the night wanderers who was undoubtedly their king—Ravana. She was trying her best to wriggle out of his grasp, but he held her in a fierce grip. She was crying out piteously for Rama and Lakshmana."

Hearing this, a flash of hope dawned in the hearts of the monkeys and they crowded round the old vulture and begged him to tell them all he knew.

He continued, "Ravana is the son of Vishravas, who was the son of Pulastya, one of the seven sages. He had two wives. One was a *yakshi* who gave birth to Kubera, and the other was a *rakshasi* who gave birth to Ravana. This city of Lanka, which I can see with my keen vulture's vision, was built by Kubera. Ravana was jealous of his brother. He did austerities to Shiva and was given a sword with which he defeated and drove out his brother and appropriated the island for himself. He also grabbed Kubera's aerial car, the Pushpaka. Riding on this flying chariot and wielding his divine sword, Ravana indulged in an orgy of rape and plunder. Once he had kicked a hermit and called him a monkey. The enraged hermit cursed Ravana that monkeys would indeed be the cause of his death."

Peering to the south, Sampati assured the monkeys that with his keen vulture's vision, he could see Sita sitting in a grove surrounded by *rakshasis*. Sampati blessed the monkeys and told them that they would surely be successful in their search. He advised them to select one out of their clan who would be able to leap to Lanka and give them news of Sita.

Angada and the other monkeys now became hopeful once again that their mission would be successful and started making plans as to who could jump farther and who would be able to go to Lanka and get news of Sita.

Angada now asked each of the monkeys how far he was capable of jumping. One said he could jump ten miles, another twenty, and another thirty, and so on. But they all proclaimed their incapacity to jump a hundred *yojanas,* or eight hundred miles! Angada himself said that he felt sure he could jump all the way to Lanka but feared that he would not be able to make it back.

Jambavan, the great old bear, was noted for his sagacity and strength. The incarnation of Rama was taken to annihilate Ravana and before he took birth as Rama, Vishnu asked the creator Brahma to create a number of monkeys who would be able to help him in his mission. The story goes that Brahma cogitated over this for a while and then he felt sleepy and yawned. Out of his mouth jumped a small creature that later became the wise old bear, Jambavan.

Another story about his birth goes as follows. Once when Brahma was reclining on his lotus seat, there suddenly appeared two huge demons before him called Madhu and Kaitabha. Seeing them, Brahma was frightened out of his wits and started to perspire. Jambavan is said to have been born out of those divine drops of perspiration. He was a great devotee of Vishnu and is purported to have taken birth along with Vishnu in each of his incarnations. In this manifestation, he had taken on the form of a bear in order to help Rama. Though he had possessed mighty powers before, he was old and weak now and confessed his inability to do this amazing deed.

All the while Hanuman was sitting apart, gazing at the sea and

chanting the name of Rama. While all the other monkeys were brag-
ging about their prowess, Hanuman alone sat silent, deep in some reverie of his own.

Jambavan now went to him and said, "O jewel among monkeys!
Why are you remaining silent? Don't you know that you are the son of
the wind god? You have the ability to jump as far as you wish. In fact,
even as an infant you jumped over twenty thousand miles in order to
catch the sun! You alone among us have the power to accomplish this
impossible task. Rise up and soar into the air and leap over the vast sea,
for you can easily do this."

As we know, Hanuman had been cursed by the *rishis* that he
would never remember his extraordinary powers and would have to
be reminded of his strength by someone before he could put it to use.
Hanuman listened intently as Jambavan spoke. "Only in you are found
strength, good sense, and valor. In you alone does one find perfect
adaptability to the exigencies of place and time. Scholar in ethics, in
you alone is there perfect morality." These are the words that Valmiki
makes Jambavan say while he exhorted Maruti to undertake the impossible task of crossing the mighty ocean. Hanuman rose up and with his
usual modesty, he bowed to the aged bear and told him that he was
prepared to do as commanded.

"Your words give me so much courage that I feel that I can vanquish the entire race of *rakshasas* single-handed if they will not hand
over Rama's immaculate wife. The span of this ocean seems quite
insignificant to me. The grace you have conferred on me and my Lord's
command are like two wings that will carry me across this vast expanse
of water with the greatest of ease. I will fly to Lanka as swiftly as the
powerful arrow released by Raghava. If I fail to locate Sita in Lanka,
with the same speed will I fly to the abode of the *devas*. If I fail again,
I will bind and bring Ravana and hand him over to my Lord." His
supreme confidence in his ability to achieve what he had been told to
do came from his total dedication to his Master.

Hearing his vow, the gods extolled him thus, "One in whom
undaunted courage, foresight, balance of mind, and skill are found, as in

you, will never feel any tediousness in any work that he undertakes."

Our mind needs to be constantly reminded of its divine potential and of the fact that it can achieve phenomenal heights provided it realizes its divine destiny. It needs to be reminded that nothing can be performed by itself and that everything is done by the divine power operating within us. Thus, Hanuman is symbolic of the perfect mind and embodies the highest potential it can achieve.

> *Hanuman releases all afflictions of those*
> *Who concentrate on him in thought, word, and*
> *deed.*

HANUMAN CHALISA BY TULSIDAS

Aum Sri Hanumathe Namaha!

Aum Mahakayaaya Namaha!

12

Sundara
The Book of Beauty

Atulita baladhamam,
Hemashylabha deham,
Bhanujavana Krishanyam,
Jnaninaamagraganyam,
Sakalaguna nidhanam,
Vanaraanaam adhishtam,
Raghupathi priyabhaktam,
Vatajaatam namaami.

I bow to the son of the Wind,
Whose strength is incomparable,
Whose body has a golden sheen,
Like the color of the sun,
Foremost of the wise,
Filled with all noble qualities,
Greatest among simians,
The beloved devotee of Rama.

SRI HANUMATH STOTRAM

113

Reminded of his powers, Hanuman was suddenly filled with his own strength and expanded himself until his head almost reached the heavens. His face glowed like the rising sun, energy throbbed through his powerful limbs, and his eyes blazed like planets. His breath rumbled like a volcano that was about to erupt. His tail was held above him like the banner of the war god Kartikeya. All those who saw him trembled in fear. Birds squawked and scattered in all directions, wild animals hid in their caves, and even the fish darted to the bottom of the ocean. The monkeys alone were unafraid and watched, spellbound by this feat. They cheered wildly and jumped up and down with joy.

From his gigantic height he spoke to them, "Fear not, O Monkeys! I come from the loins of the wind god who is mighty beyond measure. I can circumambulate the mountain Meru and can overtake the blazing sun. My form as I leap across will resemble that of Lord Vishnu in his incarnation as Trivikrama (the one who measured all the three worlds in three steps). I shall cross the sea in a matter of moments and see Rama's queen and bring her back if possible. I shall now go to the top of this mountain, which alone will be able to sustain my weight as I jump."

In his exuberance, he jumped from peak to peak and crushed their tops as easily as breaking off the stem of a flower! The other monkeys watched open-mouthed at this display of power. He then jumped to the top of Mount Mahendra, which was the highest spot on the beach, and prepared to make the leap across the sea. Under the force of his weight, the mountain shuddered and released its waters; animals ran around crying in terror. Hanuman composed himself and fixed his mind on Rama and repeated the magic *mantra,* "Rama, Rama." He then folded his palms, looked to the east, and received the blessings of his father the wind god. He flexed his muscles and slapped them in the way of wrestlers. He then squatted on the ground with hands on the ground and one foot stretched behind like a racer and gave a mighty roar as he leaped into the sky. Trees and bushes were uprooted by the force of his jump and scattered their flowers on him as if in benediction. His tail, which was curled above him, looked like a banner as he coursed through the sky. Clouds parted to make way for the amazing son of the wind god. Sea creatures rose to the surface to watch in wonder at this astonishing feat. He could touch the sky above and see the glimmering sea below.

Midway between Jambudwipa (India) and Lanka lies the mountain known as Mainaka. Varuna the Lord of the sea saw him passing and thought to himself that he should do something to help the messenger of Rama. So he told the mountain, which was submerged in the ocean, to rise up and offer some rest to Anjaneya. Mainaka did as commanded, and suddenly Hanuman saw the golden peaks of the mountain rising up from the ocean, blocking his passage. The mountain took a human form and begged him to accept his hospitality and that of the king of the ocean and rest awhile before proceeding on his journey.

With his single-pointed devotion to duty, Hanuman refused to accept the mountain's appeal and told him firmly that the time allotted to him was very short and he was bound to accomplish his purpose and return as fast as possible, so he simply touched the mountain with his hand in acceptance of the welcome offered to him and sped on his way, anxious to reach Lanka before the sun touched the western horizon. The mountain now sank back and renewed its former position in the ocean.

The gods then decided to test Hanuman and told Surasa, the mother of the serpents, to intercept him so that they could ascertain his strength. She promptly took on a huge and hideous form and stood arms akimbo in front of Hanuman as he was skimming across the sea.

"The gods have ordained that no creature can cross the southern sea without entering into my mouth. Today they have given you to me as my food, so I shall eat you up." This was one of the reasons that no creature ever made its way to Ravana's stronghold.

So saying, she opened her cavernous mouth and prepared to swallow him. Hanuman spoke sweetly to her and begged her to allow him to pass since he was the messenger of Rama and had urgent business on hand. He promised to return to her after accomplishing his purpose. She was adamant and said that he would have to pass through her

mouth before proceeding. Hanuman was angry at her lack of understanding and doubled his size. Surasa promptly opened her mouth even
wider and Hanuman again doubled his size, but Surasa kept opening
her mouth even wider. The intelligent Hanuman then reduced his size
to that of a thumb, entered her mouth, and came out again through
her nostrils!

"Now that I have fulfilled your vow that none can pass without
entering your mouth, please allow me to pass," he said.

The gods were happy to see Hanuman's quick wit and intelligence,
and they told Surasa to give him passage. She said, "Move forward, O
high-souled Hanuman, foremost of monkeys. Proceed on your way and
enable Rama to reunite with Sita!"

Hanuman bowed and coursed along the sky with the speed of
wind, trailing clouds of glory behind him.

At this time, another demoness known as Simhika, who lived in
the sea and was able to catch her prey by catching their shadow on
the water, saw Hanuman flying and thought to herself that the gods
had blessed her with a good dinner that day. She seized his shadow,
and Hanuman felt himself being dragged down. He was wondering
what had happened to him when the creature rose up from the water
and prepared to devour him. Hanuman instantly grew to enormous
proportions, but the creature also widened her mouth and flew at
him. He immediately reduced his size, fell into her mouth, and tore
out her vital parts with his sharp nails. He then expanded himself
and split her apart so that she fell dead in the ocean. The fish rushed
up to eat her carcass.

As Hanuman soared into the sky once again, all the gods and divine
beings extolled him. "You have indeed performed a most meritorious
deed in having killed this terrible creature. He in whom firmness, true
vision, understanding, and skill exist, can never fail in any undertaking.
May you accomplish your purpose and return soon, O Son of Vayu!"

Very soon after that Hanuman spied the island of Lanka, looking
like a jewel set in the heart of the ocean. He observed the forests, rivers, cascades, and flower gardens with which it was surrounded. The

city was built on a level place just below the highest summit of the three-peaked hill known as Trikuta and looked as if it rested on clouds. Actually, this peak was a piece of the fabled Mount Meru. Once upon a time, it is said that Vaasuki, the holy serpent on which Vishnu reclined, had a contest with Vayu, the god of wind. In order to prove his prowess, the snake curled himself round Mount Meru and refused to budge. Vayu was furious and blew with all his might, with the result that the whole world was thrown into chaos. The gods ran to Vishnu and begged him to intercede. Vishnu ordered Vaasuki to release his hold on the Mount. The snake uncoiled one of its twists and immediately Vayu tore off a piece of the Mount that was exposed and blew it far off into the ocean. He dropped it in the southern sea and in course of time, it came to be called Trikuta. Soon after this incident Kubera, the son of the sage Vishravas, wanted to build himself a city. His father told Vishvakarma, the architect of the gods, to build him a city on top of the peak of Trikuta. It was a beautiful city and was called Lanka. Ravana was another son of Vishravas. He gained many boons from Brahma and became puffed up with pride. Just as Sampati had said, he waged war against his brother Kubera, drove him out of the island, and grabbed it for his own.

Hanuman descended on the summit of a hill and beheld the stunning city of Lanka with its rooftops gilded with gold by the setting sun. The splendor of Ravana's city left him breathless. If it was so beautiful from the outside, how splendid would it be from inside, he wondered. He noticed that the city was fully protected by the sea, which girt it on all sides. It had four gates facing the four directions, and the walls surrounding it were made of gold. Lanka was strongly fortified and surrounded by moats and trenches crawling with poisonous serpents. The hillside was covered with trees and flowering bushes and the mansions were glittering in the evening light. He could also see the clean, white roads bordered by green, luscious-looking grass. Situated as it was on top of the hill, Lanka looked as if it was floating on air, as there were so many clouds surrounding it. The warm wind playing over his face smelled of pepper, cloves, and fragrant spices.

Maruti nimbly jumped from rock to rock as he made his way toward the northern gate. The moat that ran round the walls was filled with man-eating fish.

Elephants stood under the stone gate arch and fierce-looking *rakshasa* bowmen looked out from the roofs and turrets. Hanuman wondered if it would be possible for Rama to breach the ramparts of this city, even if he managed to cross the sea with his army of monkeys. "Even my father, the god of wind, would find it difficult to enter this city undetected," he thought to himself. However, he decided that his immediate job was only to find out the whereabouts of Sita and give a full report to his master. He realized that he could never enter Lanka in his present form, guarded as it was by fierce *rakshasas*. He pondered awhile as to how he was to accomplish his purpose of finding the princess of Videha, Sita. He waited for darkness, which fell like a mantle over the city. A pale moon floated across the sky accompanied by her attendant stars, and Lanka loomed above him like a dream. He reduced his form so that he became as small as a cat and tried to creep through the northern gate. "A cat can go anywhere it wants to in the night," he thought to himself.

Lankini was a warrior maiden who had once guarded the abode of Brahma. He had cursed her for her arrogance and told her that she would have to leave his celestial realm and guard the city of the demons until a monkey defeated her and released her from his curse. She kept a vigilant watch outside the gates of Lanka while all others slept soundly inside. She stood with arms akimbo before Maruti and obstructed his passage.

"Who are you, O denizen of the forest?" she asked. "These portals are protected by the forces of Ravana and guarded on all sides, and none may enter them without my permission."

Hanuman countered with another question. "Who are you, O gentle goddess? Why are you so anxious to stop me?"

She was not pacified by his humble demeanor or his disguise and retorted, "I am the personification of the city of Lanka, O monkey, and it is my duty to guard it from all intrusion. Prepare to die, for I will kill you now."

Unruffled by this declaration, Hanuman said meekly, "I have merely come to view this city of which I have heard many splendid accounts."

Lankini had blazing eyes and mighty arms bearing every type of weapon. She was not impressed by his sweet words and laughed in derision. "Without overcoming me, you will not accomplish your purpose, O monkey!" With these words she boxed him on his cheeks.

Hanuman was incensed by this and without saying a word he closed his left fist and gave her a glancing blow that felled her to the ground.

Stunned by the blow as much as by the loss of her dignity, Lankini spoke.

"Spare me, O jewel among monkeys! I shall leave this place and allow you to enter. The creator Brahma spoke the following words to me when he kept me here: 'One day you will be felled by a blow of a mere monkey. When that time comes, know that the fate of the city is doomed as well as that of Ravana's!' I see now that the time foretold by Brahma has come. You may enter the city and go about your business. You will surely find the virtuous daughter of King Janaka." Saying this, Lankini left Lanka for good.

There is another story about the guardians of Lanka. Ravana was such a great devotee of Shiva that both he and Parvati had come to live in Lanka, thus making the island invulnerable. When the gods, headed by Indra, complained to Brahma about Ravana's tyranny, he went to Lanka and begged the divine pair to withdraw their protection. Shiva agreed to take birth as a monkey who would be instrumental in bringing about Ravana's destruction, and Parvati took the form of Kaali and was installed in a temple at the gate. When Hanuman entered Lanka, he saw the temple of the three-eyed goddess holding divine weapons and flanked by eight *yoginis*. She challenged him and revealed herself as the cosmic mother in all her terrible manifestations. Hanuman responded by manifesting his own cosmic form, which contained the energies of all the gods. She recognized him as the son of her own Lord Shiva and bowed to him. Maruti begged her to leave the island, for no one would be able to conquer it as long as she protected it. The goddess agreed to leave and asked him to see to it that the nine nights of her worship (*Navaratri*), which usually occurred in autumn, would also be performed in spring. Hanuman agreed to do this, and she left the island for good.

> *What a wonder that you kept the signet ring of the*
> *Lord in your mouth,*
> *And leaped across the sea.*

HANUMAN CHALISA BY TULSIDAS

Aum Sri Hanumathe Namaha!

13

Pavana Putra

Search for Sita

Ullankhya sindho, salilam, salilam,
Ya shokavahnim janakatmajaaya,
Adaaya tenaiva dadaha Lankaam,
Namaami tam pranjalir-anjaneyam.

I bow to Anjaneya,
Who leaped over the waters of the sea,
And removed the sorrow of Janaka's daughter [Sita],
And burned the city of Lanka.

Sri Hanumath Stotram

Having got rid of the guardian of the city, Hanuman leaped easily to the top of the ramparts and surveyed the sleeping city spread like a carpet beneath him. The town was planned with meticulous care and neatly laid out streets, flanked by superb mansions from which floated peals of laughter and sounds of various musical instruments. The latticed windows were studded with diamonds and shone in the moonlight. Palaces gleamed in the silvery sheen of the moon. Hanuman glided unnoticed along the well-swept roads scattered with rose petals and sprinkled with sandalwood oil and flanked on either side with magnificent buildings of various shapes and sizes. It was the last full moon of autumn and the moon rose in all its glory. Midnight is the time when the night wanderers go out to eat the flesh and drink the blood of their victims. In Lanka, it was the time of enjoyment and revelry, the time to drink and make love and be merry. Hanuman heard the sounds of every type of indulgence, the music of lutes and horns and the low beat of drums, with chattering voices and ogres clapping time. Along with this were the deep melodic chants from the Vedas by the Brahmins who were kept especially for this purpose. On the streets carrying lighted torches, he saw the night patrols of *rakshasa* warriors. Some were clad in rich and regal heraldry, some in feathers and quills, and some were rotting, with raw skins, while others walked naked with shaven heads. They were armed with studded bludgeons and knives and spears and javelins. These were the warriors who had conquered the heavens and the netherworlds along with Ravana's son Indrajit.

In the course of his cosmic conquests, Ravana had subdued many of the Vedic gods and made them work as his servants. However, he had dealt really harshly with two of the most dangerous of these deities and imprisoned them at the southern edge of Lanka. The south is thought to be the most inauspicious cardinal direction. In his inspection of the city, Hanuman came to the southern tip and found a grotesque black figure chained to a rock. Hanuman approached him and asked him who he was and why he had been chained.

"I am Kaala, Lord of Death. Ravana has chained me here with a belt that has been secured by Rudra's *mantra*."

Hanuman, who was Rudra's son, went close and touched the belt, which instantly came apart and released Kaala, who was so grateful that he gave him the boon that anyone who remembered Hanuman would have no fear of death.

Just then, Hanuman heard a pathetic cry for help. He followed the sound and found Shani, the malefic planet Saturn, who had also been imprisoned by Ravana. The deity had been chained by his feet to the ceiling of the cave and was hanging like a bat with his face to the wall so that his evil gaze could not fall on anyone. Maruti broke the chain and freed him.

The grateful Shani told him that even though the blue sapphire is believed to give protection against his evil influence, the blue-colored Lord Vishnu is the sapphire of sapphires, and all Vishnu's devotees would be automatically protected. He then gave the boon to Hanuman that all those who worshipped him would not be troubled by Shani and gave him the title Sankata Mochana, which as mentioned earlier means "the one who delivers from sorrow." However, later stories show the spiteful Shani attacking his benefactor who was forced to deal with him more firmly.

As he reached the center of the city he saw a smaller wall, which ran in a great circle and was made of sixteen colors of rose gold. This wall enclosed the palaces and gardens of the Demon King. Hanuman jumped over the wall and landed in a garden. Bright lamps burned on golden posts and the gravel on the paths was made of jewel dust. There were small temples everywhere from which the perfume of incense flowed. The temples were surrounded by arbors and pavilions. In the center of the park was the spired palace with golden domes and walls studded with gems and scattered with diamonds. Hanuman slipped past hooded watchmen and fierce night birds that were trained to scream if they were disturbed. He went round the palace and there, in a huge courtyard, he saw the fabled aerial chariot known as the Pushpaka that Ravana had stolen from his brother Kubera. It was breathtakingly beautiful, made entirely of flowers—the chariot of spring, driven by the mind and resting on air, two fingers above the ground. He got into it and gazed spellbound at the interior. It would take a whole month to explore it. There were hills and lawns and flowers and golden benches and everything that you could fancy. There was even a swimming pool with a splashing fountain!

At last Hanuman decided to get down and explore the palace grounds further, since it was obvious that Sita was not in the chariot.

He saw another huge courtyard where Ravana's garrison was housed. He peeped into all the palaces of Ravana's great generals. He noted the huge numbers of horses and elephants.

Then he decided to follow his nose, since the smell of wonderful types of food and wine assailed his nostrils. Boldly he entered the hall from where the delicious aroma was flowing and noticed the golden walls studded with precious jewels. The palace thronged with ravishing princesses whom Ravana had abducted. The whole place was lighted up as if it were day, by lights burning inside golden lamps. The scene was one of total revelry and debauchery. Hundreds of voluptuous-looking females sprawled about in various states of dishevelment. Some lay on the carpets with flowing hair and scattered jewels, some were dancing, and some drinking. The red dots on their foreheads were often smeared by their lovers' hands, their girdles loosened, clothes crushed, and garlands trampled. Pearls gleamed in the lamplight between their heavy breasts and heavy gold earrings hung from their ears. Some women were applying *sandal* (sandalwood tree) paste on their bodies as well as those of their lovers. Others remained with their arms entwined round their beloved's necks. They were all in a half-intoxicated state and their breath smelled of liquor made from cloves. They were all enchanting to look at, elegantly clad, fragrant with perfumes, with curved eyes, long lashes, and sidelong glances guaranteed to entice men. All the most beautiful women from various parts of the world had been captured and brought to Lanka by Ravana. It appeared as if his main job had been to course through the length and breadth of the worlds in his aerial vehicle, grabbing the virgin daughters of the *nagas, gandharvas, daityas,* and *rishis.* All of them had cried and struggled when they were captured and had sworn to kill themselves, but in the end they had succumbed to his fatal charms, for his expertise in the art of lovemaking was proverbial. He had been cursed by their parents over and over again as well by the women whom he had brought forcibly to the palace. Hanuman looked at all of them and knew instinctively that none of these could be Sita. He imagined her to be pale and emaciated, pining for her husband, looking like the full moon seen through a cloud.

He stepped over alabaster floors and sprang up a stairway of lapis and burnished gold until he reached the end of a hall paved with silver that ended in a jade door with cut amethyst handles. This was the entrance to Ravana's bedroom. Softly he turned the handle and entered. The room was lit with flaming lamps of gold and covered with sleeping women. Each woman was lovelier than the next. They were sleeping deeply after an evening of drinking, dancing, and music. Their fragrant hair was loose and their jewels scattered. Their girdles had come loose and their silken robes fell unheeded to either side. The city of Lanka, the palace, and Ravana's female consorts, all described as extremely enticing, are meant to remind us of the disabling power of unchecked desire, a desire that is to destroy Ravana.

Suddenly he spied Ravana, chief of the night wanderers, reclining on a cot made of crystal, ivory, sandalwood, and gold. The cot was unbelievably beautiful, and he stood for a while admiring it. The white umbrella of royalty was above it. The demon king lay fast asleep on the bed. He was a magnificent figure of a man with huge, powerful arms and a broad chest covered with white silk. He had ten devilishly handsome heads adorned with long, heavy gold earrings. He was clad in the purest of white garments and was sound asleep. On one side was a table with the leftovers of a magnificent repast of exotic foods. Hanuman went closer and helped himself to some delicious fruits. Being a monkey, he did not care for cooked foods. After his tasty repast, he surveyed the rest of the room.

Four lovely women stood at the four corners of Ravana's bed and fanned him gently. Many charming women were sleeping in abandoned positions all round him. Some of them were clutching musical instruments, which they must have been playing for Ravana. Suddenly Hanuman spied a most attractive woman sleeping on a couch set apart. She was so beautiful that for a moment he thought she must be Sita, but he soon realized that Rama's wife would never adorn herself like this nor would she be able to sleep so deeply. He realized that the woman must be Mandodari, Queen of Lanka. She was Ravana's chief wife and renowned for her beauty and chastity.

Long ago Ravana had heard that Shiva's wife Parvati was the most beautiful woman in the world. Wanting to possess her, he performed many austerities to please him. Shiva was pleased and granted him a boon. Ravana immediately asked for Parvati! Shiva was forced to allow him to take her to Lanka. When she saw him coming to get her, Parvati decided to teach him a lesson. She caught a *manduka* (female frog), transformed it into a beautiful female, and called her Mandodari. Ravana saw her and, thinking it was Parvati, took her off to Lanka and made her his chief queen. Like all female frogs, Mandodari came to consort with Ravana only at the start of the rainy season, but she was a most faithful wife and always gave him unconditional support.

But generally, she is known as the daughter of the great King of Danavas, known variously as Maya, Mayan, or Mayasura. He was the chief architect of the creatures of the netherworld. And her mother was the beautiful celestial dancer, Apsara Hema. Mandodari is widely respected for her kind and pious nature, and always thought to be the better half of Ravana.

A lesser-known story concerning Mandodari makes her out to be Sita's mother. Once Ravana performed a grand *yaga*, using the blood of sages as a sacrificial offering. Thousands of sages were beheaded and their blood collected in a jar that Ravana gave Mandodari for safe-keeping. During the night, Mandodari got up with a raging thirst and accidentally drank up the contents of the jar. The blood of the sages entered her body and made her pregnant. In due course, she gave birth to a daughter. Oracles prophesied that the baby would be the cause of Ravana's destruction. Due to her love for her husband, Mandodari threw the baby into the ocean. The sea god Varuna saved the baby and placed it into the arms of the earth goddess. The baby lay in a field, inside a golden pitcher, until Janaka, king of Videha, found her while plowing the field at the commencement of a sacrifice. He named the child Sita, since she was found in a *sita*, or furrow. And so fittingly, Sita is of the earth as Rama is of the heavens, and their union joins the individual to the infinite.

It should be noted that in this instance as elsewhere, there exist several versions of some events from the Ramayana, as Valmiki's epic was clarified or embellished upon by various minds throughout the ages according to the social, philosophical, religious, political, artistic, and regional concerns of the day.

When he first came into the hall, Hanuman had felt slightly embarrassed at the thought of being forced to look at all these voluptuous females in seductive poses, but then he realized that though he was moving among such extraordinary beauties, his mind was totally unaffected and untouched by any of them. The *vanaras* as a race were not noted for their continence! But unlike other monkeys, Hanuman was a *brahmachari* (celibate) and had never thought of consorting with any woman.

Not wanting to waste time, he pressed on through the portrait gallery and many other places but was unable to find Sita. He became totally despondent and did not know where to look for her. He started to suspect that Ravana might have killed her. He thought he had completely exhausted all the places where he could possibly find her. It would be better to die rather than return to Rama with this tragic news. Tears rolled down his eyes at the thought. At last, just at that moment when he decided that he would have to return with his mission unaccomplished, he saw a grove that he had not seen before. It was filled with many types of trees; prominent among them was the *ashoka*. He leaped onto the wall that enclosed the grove and surveyed the garden, which was filled with all types of trees laden with fragrant blossoms. Many flower-laden creepers embraced the trees, and everywhere there was a fresh and wonderful fragrance, most unlike the artificial perfumes found inside the palace. There was a charming pond that had steps inlaid with gems and covered with lotuses. It was obviously a favorite haunt of the demon king, since it was so well tended. Hanuman jumped onto an *ashoka* tree, concealed himself among the thick foliage, and surveyed the garden. The night was passing and he still had not discovered Sita. The birds were beginning to wake up and they flew up into the clouds, chirping angrily at being disturbed by Hanuman's frolics. The sun glided down the Trikuta peak and slipped into Lanka, setting the golden walls afire. The temple bells started to ring, and inside Ravana's bedroom, the bards sang songs of praise to waken the Lord of Lanka.

Rama had told Hanuman that Sita was extremely fond of flowers, and he hoped that she might come to that enchanting grove for a walk. The garden, with its flowering shrubs and waterfalls and ponds, seemed to be made for her. Looking around in the light of the setting moon, he saw a small temple with white pillars. The steps were of coral and the surface covered with gold. It gleamed in the moonlight. As he peered closer, he suddenly spied a woman and knew unmistakably this was Sita—the beloved of Rama. She looked like the crescent moon, pale and wan. She was emaciated through fasting and was clad in a soiled yellow garment and devoid of all ornaments. Her lovely eyes were filled with tears that dropped unceasingly to the ground. Sorrow seemed to be her constant companion. Her long black hair was tied in a simple braid that fell to her thighs. She, who had been a stranger to sorrow, now knew only grief. Unwashed and unkempt as she was, she resembled a flame covered with smoke, and Hanuman knew instantly that this was indeed Sita, the darling of Rama, the princess of Videha. She was surrounded by *rakshasis* (female demons). Hanuman was filled with sorrow to see the beautiful queen of Ayodhya in such a sad plight. She who had been protected by the lotus-eyed Rama was now being protected by *rakshasis* with crooked eyes and deformed bodies! She was surrounded by these horrendous monsters, some with one eye or one ear, some without ears, some with noses on their foreheads, some hairy, some bald, some hunchbacked, and some with faces resembling goats, foxes, camels, and horses. Some had huge ears covering their bodies and some three eyes. Some had hanging bellies and flapping lips and voices like rasps. Some were leering, others grim. All of them without exception were misshapen and frightening to behold. Ravana had especially chosen them to frighten Sita into submission to his will. Surrounded by these hideous creatures, Sita was seated at the foot of one of the trees, the picture of despair with her head in her hands.

It is thought that symbolically, the misshapen ogresses may represent the base desires that surround our pure soul and keep us enslaved, until, with the help of wisdom and devotion, we escape. Hanuman is the embodiment of wisdom and devotion. The monsters are depicted as being so very repulsive in order to highlight desire's terrible hold. One of the meanings of the word *sita* is "whiteness," or purity, from the Sanskrit root *sit*. And it is the release of the pure soul from the world of monstrous desire that is one of the central dramas of the Ramayana. Sita, whose loveliness is internal as well as external, is Beauty itself made manifest on Earth, (she is the daughter of the Earth). This much-beloved section describing Sita in the garden is called The Book of Beauty (Sundara Kanda).

Hanuman thought to himself, "This is indeed Sita. Neither the lack of ornaments nor the fact that she is clothed in rags and is frail and emaciated can hide the fact that she is a raving beauty. She is as beautiful as Rama described her—exquisite eyebrows, graceful, rounded breasts, lips as red as a berry, peacock blue throat, slender waist, lotus petal eyes—all these are visible through her screen of sorrow."

She sat on the bare ground like a female ascetic, bound in a net of grief, the picture of shattered hope. Though parted cruelly from her husband, her mind was full of him alone. Her lips were constantly murmuring the *mantra,* "Rama, Rama." This was indeed the woman for whom Rama was pining. Hanuman could see that she belonged only to Rama, body, mind, and soul.

"She is meant only for Rama and he for her. Their love for each other is so great that it is only because of it that they have managed to remain alive. All Heaven's stars may fall, and Earth may break apart. Fire may burn cold, and waters run uphill, but Sita will never turn from Rama!" Hanuman prostrated mentally to Rama and whispered, "Lord, I have found her!"

He was overcome with sorrow at the sight of the princess of Videha who had been parted so cruelly from her husband. "Fate is indeed all powerful," he thought to himself, "or else why should this innocent lady have to suffer like this? She was protected by no less a personage than her illustrious husband, along with Lakshmana. Her husband killed thousands of *rakshasas* at Janasthana for her sake because Ravana's sister was threatening her, and now she is held captive by that very Ravana, surrounded by these hideous women, with no privacy even to weep. She has no eyes for this beautiful garden. Her eyes are in her heart and her heart is with Rama."

Hanuman was just wondering how he could present himself to Sita when he heard the sound of music coming from the palace. It was the time known as Brahma Muhurtam. With the break of day, the bards began to chant the Vedas to wake up the demon king of Lanka. Drums started booming and lutes began playing to welcome the dawn. The perfume of incense spread over the city from the fire sacrifices that were being performed everywhere. Ravana was greeted with many women fanning *chouries* (yak tail fans) and ghee lamps. As soon as he woke up, his first thought was of Sita. Day and night he could think of nothing but Sita. Even though he had so many beauties from all the three worlds in his harem who were willing to give in to his passion, his mind was always fixed on her who refused even to look at him and treated him with utter scorn. He had never met with such resistance from any woman in all his life, and he certainly had a lot of experience with females of every type. Her resistance only served to whet his appetite. It was a challenge to him, and he was determined to make the citadel fall at all costs. He was sure that no woman could resist him for long and that it could only be a matter of time before she succumbed like all the others. He would happily have forced her to comply with his desire, but he had been cursed that if he took a woman without her consent, his head would burst, so he had to desist. Every morning as soon as he woke up, he was irresistibly drawn toward the grove and hurried there before he attended to any of his state matters.

Anjaneya looked up as the noise of bugles and cymbals came closer, and then he saw Ravana approaching with a bevy of belles. Most of them looked sleepy due to the intoxication of the night, but they hurried after their Lord, carrying *chourie* fans, golden lamps, cushions, and pitchers of wine. When he came close to the tree on which Sita was leaning, he commanded the *rakshasis* surrounding her to push off and also told his entourage to stand apart so that they would not be a witness to his ardent wooing! Hanuman came down the tree a little in order to have a closer look at the King of Lanka. He concealed himself behind the leaves and peered through the gaps. He had only seen him when he was asleep. Now he looked even more magnificent. He was clad in the finest of white garments, which billowed like a cloud behind him, and he was adorned with many fantastic ornaments, all meant to charm the heart of any female.

Hearing the tread of his feet as he approached, Sita quivered with fright and loathing. Despite her pitiable condition, her beauty shone like the full moon seen through a cloud. One single braid fell over her left shoulder as she tried to cover herself with the pitiful remnants of her clothes, and she crossed her arms in front of her in a desperate attempt to cover her breasts from Ravana's piercing, lustful gaze.

Looking at her pitiable efforts to cover herself, Ravana said, "O Princess of Mithila! Why do you try to hide your beauty from my eyes? I am sure there is no one in all the worlds here as exquisite as you. Why do you shun my gaze and turn away from me? You should be clad in the finest of silks and adorned with costly jewels, yet you sit on the ground, wearing only a soiled rag, eating nothing and trying to hide your beauty from me by crossing your arms. Even thus, you put all the other ladies of my harem to shame. I would exchange all of them for one smile from you! I abducted you only because I fell prey to your unbelievable beauty. Pray listen to my appeal. Your husband is a coward; otherwise, he would have come to rescue you long before this. Don't waste your youth and beauty in pining for him. Accept me, and I will make you my foremost queen and give you the whole world if you so desire it! Your lovely hair is matted, your silk garment is soiled and torn, and you are half-starved and emaciated, yet you continue to fascinate me. Night and day I am haunted by your face. Can't you see that I am crazy with love for you? After having met you, I cannot bear to look at my other wives. Youth and beauty are short-lived. Do not waste both in unnecessary sorrow. Come, shake off your grief and accept my love. Rise up, dress yourself in lovely silks and satins. Wear jewels and perfumes. This bare ground is not a fitting couch for your flaming beauty. You have seen me and my glory. What has Rama got to compare with this? He is only a mendicant, clad in bark, with not even a kingdom to call his own. Take it from me that you will never see him again. You probably consider my action to be unrighteous. But in the code of the *rakshasas,* it is quite acceptable to take another man's wife for his own. Why are you torturing yourself like this? I can easily force you to comply with my will, but I have been patient because I want you to come to me of your own accord. I want your love and not just your body. I have never said this to any other woman. But your time and my patience are running short. I gave you one year in which to make up your mind and the time is almost up!"

Not once did Sita look at Ravana during this impassioned speech. Though she was terrified of Ravana and sickened by his sensual talk, she clutched at the remnants of her tattered pride along with her tattered clothes. Without raising her eyes, she picked up a straw from the ground, placed it before her and spoke to it as if addressing the king of Lanka! It was a graphic reminder to him of her attitude—that she cared two straws for him!

With utter scorn, she said, "O you of poor intellect! Know me to be the beloved of Rama, scion of the race of Raghu. Do not keep your mind on me. Fix it on your own consorts. Having one of impure heart as its ruler, the city of Lanka as well as the whole *rakshasa* clan will perish in the flames of my husband's wrath. He is the repository of all virtues. How can I who am his wife bear to even look at another man? If you want to save yourself and your clan, try to propitiate him. He is kind and compassionate to those that surrender. But he is as severe as he is compassionate, and if you don't surrender to him, his arrows will descend like serpents on you and destroy you completely! Remember how he destroyed your whole garrison in Janasthana single-handedly. Why are you bent on destroying your race? An entire kingdom can perish if its ruler becomes the slave of his passions. Lanka is doomed. What a fool you are to think that you can tempt me with gold and riches. Rama is to me what sunlight is to the sun. Restore me to him and thus earn my gratitude, if you will, but never hope to earn my love, for that is irrevocably given to Rama! How will he not destroy you, who have dared to abduct his beloved wife? You boast of your courage, yet you crept into the hermitage in disguise and stole me away when my husband was not there! Was this the action of a brave man? Soon shall my Lord come and rescue me and shoot deadly arrows at you, which will suck your life's blood. So beware! You and your clan will be totally wiped out!"

Ravana was furious at her words and retorted angrily, "The kinder I am to you, the more intolerable you become. It's only my love for you and the fact that you are a woman that makes me refrain from killing you straightaway. I have given you twelve months to make up your mind. Out of that only two months remain. After that, you either share my bed or become my breakfast. If you still refuse, death shall be your lot! My cooks will make mincemeat of you for my breakfast!"

Despite the fact that she was quaking inside, Sita retorted angrily, "O vile wretch! Your days are indeed numbered. Is there no good man here to advise you? I wonder why your tawny eyes do not drop off when you gaze at me lustfully. Why does your tongue not drop off when you speak such words?"

Ravana looked at her with his amber eyes smouldering with anger. "O woman, you are devoted to a man who is beset with ill luck and devoid of resources. I shall get rid of you today itself. You do not deserve any compassion!"

Then turning to the *rakshasis* who were stationed there to guard Sita, he spoke harshly. "It's your duty to see that this woman submits to my will before the day is over. Threaten her, cajole her, and if all fails, use force or whatever you think is necessary, but see to it that she submits to my will!" With these words, Ravana angrily strode off to his own palace to be fawned over and waited upon by his numerous wives, all of whom were distasteful to him now.

A few of the women who had followed Ravana felt sorry for Sita but none dared say anything. Some took the opportunity to ingratiate themselves in his favor. They entwined their soft arms round his neck and offered themselves in lieu of Sita, but he shook them off angrily and strode off, making the ground tremble with the force of his strides.

You possess the elixir of Rama bhakti,
And remain eternally his true servant.

Sri Hanuman Chalisa by Tulsidas

Aum Sri Hanumathe Namaha!

Aum Sita Shokavinaashakaaya Namaha!

14

Sankata Mochana

Dispeller of Sorrow

Markadeya mahotsaha,
Sarvashoka vinashaka,
Shatrun samhaara mam raksha,
Shriyam dapaya-me prabho.

O Lord! Pray give me all auspiciousness.
Thou art the greatest among simians,
One who can take away all sorrow,
Save me from being troubled by enemies.

HANUMATH STHUTI

The *rakshasis* who had been asleep when Ravana came were now wide awake and eager to do as he told them. All this time they had desisted from doing any harm to Sita since that had been his bidding, but now that they had got orders from him to act as they wished, they rushed to her. All of them were deformed and ugly, and they pounced on Sita gleefully and started to torment her with their sharp tongues.

"What a stupid woman you are that you will not listen to a great soul like Ravana. He is prepared to put aside his own wife, Mandodari, and make you his favorite consort. Yet, stupid fool that you are, you refuse his kind offer. At his command, the trees scatter flowers and the clouds release rain. The sun and the moon would stop shining if he did not wish it. You are a brainless idiot not to agree to his wishes!"

Sita replied angrily, "You are giving me cheap and sinful advice. Destitute and deprived of his kingdom though he is, I will ever remain faithful to my husband. You may kill me and eat me if you will, but I will not budge from my resolve!"

Another declared loudly, "Ever since I saw her, I have had an irresistible desire to feast on her luscious breasts and berrylike lips, and her delicious liver and spleen. Come, let us have an orgy. Bring out the wine, and we will chop her into little bits and feast on her!" So saying, she licked her chops and drooled from her thick black lips. Sita shrunk back in fear and disgust and started to weep uncontrollably.

Hanuman, who was hiding in the foliage, could not contain his anger and sorrow to hear the *rakshasis* upbraiding and torturing Sita like this. But he knew that this was not the right time to reveal himself.

Sita was now crying like a stricken deer. All the pent up feelings that she had repressed before Ravana now broke loose and she burst into heartrending sobs. "O Rama! O Lakshmana! Where are you? When will you come for me? This heart of mine must surely be made of iron that it doesn't break even though I'm in agony. What a vile wretch I am to keep on living even though separated from my beloved and leading such a miserable existence. I realize now that death will not approach a person until the appointed time has come or else how can I continue to live in the midst of these cruel creatures, in the palace of this lecherous man, parted from my beloved Rama?" So saying, she sank to the ground and burst into uncontrollable sobs.

Again she raised herself, for she was filled with doubts. "How will my Lord know that I am here, and how will he cross the ocean and come here? My death grows near. But I'm not afraid. Far better for me to die than fall to the lures of this wicked Ravana! It looks as if I will see Yama before I see the lotus-eyed Rama!"

Hearing her laments and the cruel words of the *rakshasis*, an old ogress called Trijata now approached Sita. She kept the others at bay and told all of them of the dream she had.

"Listen, O *rakshasis*! I just had a dream in which I saw Rama coming in a golden palanquin, clad in white raiment and wearing celestial garlands. Sita was then reunited with her beloved husband. I saw Ravana with shaven head, falling from his aerial car. He was dripping with oil, attired in black, and had a red garland round his neck. Again I saw him being pulled by a woman on a chariot drawn by asses. He was totally intoxicated and out of his wits. The woman in black was drawing him in a southerly direction. His son Indrajit and brother Kumbhakarna were also following him. Only his youngest brother Vibhishana was left here. I saw Lanka being burned up by an agile monkey who was Rama's envoy."

"Therefore, I adjure you to take care of Sita. See that no harm befalls her or else you will also suffer the same fate as Ravana and his clan!"

Hearing this, the *rakshasis* disbanded and returned to their posts, and Sita sat alone under the tree. She had reached the end of her tether. She felt she just could not go on anymore. Physically and mentally, she was at her lowest ebb and decided to make an end of her life before Ravana came again. Taking out the cloth that was wound round her waist, she decided to hang herself with it before Ravana could torture her to death. However, just at that very moment, she felt some auspicious omens on her body. Her left eye, arm, and thigh started to throb. These are considered to be extremely favorable omens for a woman, so Sita's heart took courage and she desisted from her desperate attempt.

Hanuman had been watching everything from his vantage point and decided that the time had come for him to reveal himself and try to comfort Rama's wife.

He thought to himself, "I have been told to find out her whereabouts and also ascertain the strength of the enemy, but I would be failing in my duty if I did not give her some comfort before leaving or else the daughter of Janaka may well give up her life before Rama comes. I might frighten her if I jump down in my monkey form for she is already terrorized by these misshapen *rakshasis*."

Hanuman thought deeply over the matter and then decided on a plan to allay Sita's fears. In a very sweet voice he started singing the whole story of Rama's life, ending with his being sent as an envoy. Sita was thrilled to hear his tale and looked around anxiously to see where the voice came from. Brushing her disheveled hair aside, she looked up at the tree and tried to find the person who was responsible for bringing this ray of hope into her stricken heart. The thick foliage hid him from her sight. Her eyes roved in all directions, but she couldn't find him. Meanwhile, the *rakshasis* had given up their efforts to persuade her. Some had gone to tell Ravana and the rest were snoring under the trees in ungraceful postures.

Hanuman took this as an opportune moment and jumped lightly down to a branch where he could be seen. At last her anxious eyes spied him—the messenger of Rama, harbinger of hope and happiness. She beheld a small, cute monkey with white fur and red face closely watching her from among the leaves. His eyes were like liquid gold and he was smiling at her. He looked harmless, but she still had her doubts. She had been cheated and tormented so many times in the past few months that she was always suspicious of everything and everyone. Sita was sure that she was dreaming and cried out to Rama to save her.

"What can be the cause of this apparition? Surely it must be another trick of the wicked Ravana."

Hanuman guessed what was going on in her mind and decided that it was high time for him to appear before her. He nimbly leaped down and stood with folded palms before her. He then raised his palms above his head and extolled her.

"Who are you, O fair lady of exquisite limbs? Are you a goddess or a celestial being?

Tell me, for whom are you grieving? If you are indeed Sita, the wife of Rama who was stolen by Ravana, please tell me."

Sita was elated when she heard these words and cried out, "Yes, indeed, I am the daughter-in-law of the great Dasaratha and the wife of the noble Rama. My father is the king of Videha, and I am called Sita. I accompanied my husband to the forest and was kidnapped by Ravana and brought here. He has given me two more months to succumb to his passion. If Rama does not come before that, I will end my life. But tell me who you are, who has brought me the nectar of Rama's name that has put new life into me?"

Hanuman tilted his head, listened attentively to these words, and then spoke humbly to her. "My lady!" he said. "I have come as an envoy of your husband. He is alive and well and is waiting for me to tell him of your whereabouts. He grieves for you night and day and has sent me, as his messenger, to tell you that he will come for you very soon and kill Ravana and rescue you."

A thrill of pure joy shot threw Sita when she heard these comforting words of Anjaneya. She had been living in the darkness of despair for so many months that she had almost given up all hope of rescue. However, when he tried to get closer to her, she who had been cheated so many times by Ravana began to suspect that he was Ravana again, coming in another form to seduce her. Her mouth went dry, her limbs grew weak, and she sank to the ground, unable to cling to the branch she was holding.

"O Ranger of the Night! I know you are capable of assuming many forms. Yet I feel that you are not he. Somehow I can't explain it, but for once delight has sprung in my heart, which makes me believe that you are actually what you claim to be, in which case may good befall you. Speak to me once again of Rama. Let me hear it even though it might be a dream. The very thought of Rama brings delight to the universe, so what does it not do to me?"

In order to put her mind at rest, Hanuman prostrated himself full length before her and refused to look up.

"My sweet lady! Have no fear. I have been sent by your noble husband to comfort you. He will come shortly, accompanied by the heroic Lakshmana. They are always thinking of you and talking about you.

They have made a pact with Sugriva, the king of monkeys, and I am his minister Hanuman."

At last she was convinced that he was indeed a messenger from Rama. Sita then asked him to describe the features of Rama and Lakshmana. When Hanuman gave these details, she was highly gratified.

"Rama has broad shoulders, mighty arms, a charming countenance, and lotus-petal eyes. He has a voice deep as thunder and a dark blue complexion. He is full of splendor, is greatly adored by all who meet him, and is steadfast in his vow of chastity. He is devoted to truth and righteousness. His brother Lakshmana is equal to Rama in strength and charm and has a golden color. They had been ranging the earth searching for you before they came to the mount of Rishyamukha and met Sugriva. When Rama saw the jewels that had been dropped by you, he nearly swooned with joy. He had to be revived by me. My Lady! That scion of the race of Raghu burns for you as much as you burn for him. Have no fear, for that tiger among men will surely come and rescue you. Now tell me, what may I do for you before I return?"

Sita was delighted to learn of her husband's grief at her loss, even though she was upset that he had to pass through such tortures of the mind. She was thirsty for news of her husband and asked Hanuman to tell her everything that had happened to him after she was abducted—what did he do and where did he go and how long would it be before he reached Lanka, and so on. Eagerly she lapped up every scrap of news that Hanuman gave her. He was only too happy to speak of Rama his god. He told her of how the monkeys had seen her being carried off by Ravana and had picked up her jewels, which she had thrown to them, and all the other incidents ending with his finding her. At the end of the recital, he stood respectfully with folded palms before her. Sita's joy knew no bounds. She was now convinced that he had indeed come from her beloved. Tears of happiness replaced the tears of sorrow that had been flowing in torrents down her cheeks. Hanuman now handed over to her the precious signet ring that Rama had given him to inspire confidence in her. She took the ring that had adorned her husband's finger and pressed it to her bosom. She was speechless with delight. Her whole demeanor now blossomed like a plant that had been watered after long months of no rain. With eyes filled with gratitude, she looked at this adorable little monkey who had brought new hope to her barren heart.

"You are indeed a jewel among monkeys. How did you cross this enormous sea and go round the city of Lanka without being discovered? You are no ordinary monkey. May you be blessed. Now tell me more about my Lord." Hanuman now told her the two stories only she and Rama knew and that Rama had told him in secret so that she would know that he had been sent by her husband.

After their wedding, when they were returning in the chariot, Rama had gently rubbed his feet over hers. To his horror, he found that her lotuslike feet were so sensitive that even this gentle pressure made them red. Later on when they were in the forest, he said to her, "O my gentle princess! Remember the time when I stroked your feet with mine on our way back from our wedding and your feet became swollen and red? How is it that you have no problem now placing those delicate feet on these hard stones and thorns?"

He also mentioned another incident that happened soon after their marriage. Rama had asked her to massage his feet. Before doing so, she had removed her jewel-studded bangles. He had then questioned her as to why she did this and she had replied, "My Lord! I have heard it said that when Visvamitra took you to the hermitage of the sage Gautama, he asked you to place your foot on a stone that turned into a woman called Ahalya who had been cursed that she would remain a stone until you placed your divine feet on her. Think of the fate of my poor jewel-studded bangles if you place your feet on them."

Sita was overcome with emotion when she heard these stories known only to her and Rama and she was convinced that Maruti (Hanuman) was indeed the messenger of Rama.

Hanuman felt himself to be deeply privileged to hear such intimate stories from both parties. Once again he comforted her. "The only reason your Lord has not come is because he did not know where you were. His mind is ever fixed on you, so have no fears on that score. He lives in a cave and hardly eats or sleeps. He does not care for anything anymore and is always lost in thought. Even when he falls into a fitful sleep due to exhaustion, he wakes up crying, 'Sita! Sita!' Whenever he sees something that is pleasing to you, he sighs and is inconsolable. As soon as I return he will come with a huge army of monkeys and bears. Have no fear. Live in hope, my Lady, your deliverance is nigh!"

Sita was thrilled to hear that Rama's desire for her was as great as hers for him. "Dear monkey! Your words bring both happiness and unhappiness to me. When I think of his unhappiness, I become sorrowful too. Both happiness and sorrow are the outcome of one's actions in a past life. Please tell my Lord that my time is fast running out. I have only two more months to live. After that, I will become the repast of that night wanderer. His brother Vibhishana and another *rakshasa* called Avindhya warned Ravana of the dire consequences of his action in having abducted me and told him to return me to my Lord, but Ravana's time is drawing to a close and hence he cannot listen to reason. Please tell my Lord to come soon, for life is unbearable without him."

Hearing this pitiful plea, Hanuman's heart melted with sorrow and he told her, "O noble lady! Please don't give way to further grief. Climb on my back, and I will transport you this minute back to Rama. Have no fear."

Sita was both touched and amused at hearing this offer of the little monkey. Thinking of him as only a baby monkey, she was quite unaware of his prowess.

"Dear little monkey," she said, "your good nature has made you suggest the impossible. How can a tiny creature like you carry me across the sea?" Hanuman now decided to inspire confidence in her and started growing to an enormous size right in front of her eyes.

"I have the capacity to carry the entire city of Lanka over the sea if I want to, so have no fear, for I will surely transport you without any difficulty!"

Sita was astonished to see his size and said, "Indeed, I realize that you are no mean monkey but the true son of the wind god. However, I don't think it's proper on my part to go with you. When they see me being borne away by you, these evil *rakshasas* may pursue you and cause you to drop me into the raging sea. Moreover, I was abducted by the cruel Ravana and kept here in his domain for so many months. It is only right and proper that my husband should come and rescue me after killing him, or else Rama's fame may suffer. Besides, I keep my Lord enshrined in my heart always and don't wish to touch any other man on my own accord. I was forced into contact with Ravana when I was helpless. Therefore, O gallant monkey! Bring him here with all speed, for I don't think I should go with you."

Hanuman agreed with her and said that it was only his eagerness to see her reunited with her husband that had made him make such an improper suggestion. He could well understand her delicacy in touching another male. So he begged her to give him some token by which he could convince Rama that he had indeed seen her.

As proof of the fact that he had met her, Sita handed over to Hanuman her hair ornament, the *chudamani*. "Seeing this jewel, my Lord will be reminded of the three most important people in his life: my father, his father, and myself. This was given to me as part of my dowry by my father in his father's presence." With these words she handed over to him the precious ornament that she had carefully kept hidden in her clothes.

Then she recounted two incidents in their lives in the forest known only to her and Rama.

With sobs choking her throat, she said, "Remind him of the time when we had bathed in the river near the mountain of Chitrakuta and he rested with his head on my lap. He went to sleep and a crow came and pecked my breast. I threw a clod of mud at him and shooed him off, but he would not leave me alone and came and pecked me again and again. I started to cry and Rama woke up and teased me about my fears and comforted me, and then we lay down in each other's arms and fell asleep. But that vile crow was biding his time and swooped down and clawed my breasts. The hot drops of blood fell on my Lord's face and woke him up. He was furious and looked around for the culprit who had dared to do this to me, and he saw the crow sitting on a branch. He recognized the crow to be Jayanta, the son of Indra. Rama immediately took up a blade of *kusa* grass, invoked it with the power of Brahma, and threw it at the crow. It flew off in fright, but the *astra* (weapon) followed him wherever he went. He found no asylum anywhere, and at last returned to Rama and begged him to withdraw the missile. Rama said that the *brahmastra,* once invoked, had to do some damage, and so he took away the crow's right eye and spared his life. How is it, O Hanuman, that he who invoked the might of the *brahmastra* against a crow who harmed me now remains silent when this demon has dared to abduct me?"

And then she said, "Remind him of the time when he smeared the red dot on my forehead and powdered a red stone and put a red dot on my cheek as a joke!"

Sita's eyes filled with tears when she recounted these two stories, which were known only to her and Rama. With tears choking her voice she told Hanuman, "How can I reward you, who have given me back my life? I was ready to end my wretched life when you came and instilled confidence and hope in me. You are indeed a son to me. Tell my Lord, O noble monkey, that I will not live another month more. If he does not come by the end of the month, I shall take my life before that ogre can touch me."

Hearing this impassioned appeal, Hanuman assured her that Rama's only thought was of her alone. "Fear not, O gentle Lady! Rama and his brother will soon come and kill the *rakshasas* and rescue you. I have seen with my own eyes how desolate Rama is without you, so have no fear on that score. Before you know it, he will be here with the monkey army and totally exterminate these terrible night wanderers!"

He took the jewel that she handed over to him and pressed it to his heart. He then went round her thrice, bowed low to her, and asked her permission to leave.

"Keep good cheer, O gentle princess! I will soon return with Rama and the monkey hoards that will kill the *rakshasas* and rescue you. Do not give in to grief but remain full of hope, for there is no one in the whole world whom Rama cannot overcome!" So saying, Hanuman bowed to Sita once again and took his leave.

As he fell at her feet, Sita blessed him with all her heart. "O Anjaneya! Your name and fame will be remembered in the world as long as the names of Rama and Sita remain. We will never accept any worship in which your name is not included." She placed her palms over his head in blessing and gave him leave to depart.

The goal of all mystical yearning is the union of the individual soul with the universal soul. In the Adhyatma Ramayana, an ancient Sanskrit philosophical poem that is embedded in the Brahmanda Purana and thought to have been written by Vyasa, the author of the Mahabharata, Sita is said to represent the individual soul (*jivatma*) that has been separated from the universal soul (*Paramatma*) symbolized by Rama. In this beautiful interpretation, the character of Hanuman shows the ability of *bhakti* to annihilate the *ahamkara*, or ego (Ravana), and reunite the two.

Sheltered by you one gains all delight,
Protected by you, one fears no one.

SRI HANUMAN CHALISA BY TULSIDAS

Aum Sri Hanumathe Namaha!

Aum Vajrakayaaya Namaha!

15

Bajarangabali

The Burning of Lanka

Sri Rama bhaktakula moulim-achintya-veeryam,
Sri Rama sevaka janavana lola chittam
Sri Rama nama japalina hridam kumaram,
Vande Prabhanjana sutham Raghurama dasam.

Hail to thee, O son of Anjana! Servant of Rama,
Greatest of all Rama *bhaktas,* possessed of unbelievable
　　powers,
Whose mind ever delights in doing service to Rama,
And chanting the names of Rama.

HANUMATH STHUTI

Hanuman was loathe to leave Sita, and she on her part felt desolate at parting from him who had given her hope and a reason to live after all these bitter months of anguish. He decided that though he had achieved his main purpose, which was to find Sita, he would have to prove his worth to her so as to bolster up her courage. He was so angry with Ravana that he decided to ravage his favorite garden before he left. He set about this destruction in a most methodical manner.

Like a raging tempest, he uprooted every tree and trampled it with his enormous feet. He muddied the ponds, crushed the rocks, and laid waste the entire garden that was so pleasing to Ravana. The creepers were torn from the trees, the temple smashed, the pools splattered with the copper-colored buds of the *ashoka* trees, and the lakes churned and made muddy. The little hillocks were ground to powder, and the beloved garden of Ravana was made into a desolate waste. Having desecrated the garden, he climbed to the top of the archway to the garden and waited expectantly for things to happen. He did not have long to wait. There was a great commotion in the garden itself. The birds were screeching in terror and the deer and peacocks were running around crying and bleating piteously. The *rakshasis* were woken up from their sleep by a noise resembling a hurricane, created by Hanuman. They rushed to Sita and asked her who this gigantic monkey was who was bent on destroying the garden. She pleaded ignorance of the whole matter. The women ran to Ravana and reported what had taken place. They said that they suspected that Sita knew who he was but refused to divulge his identity. He had destroyed every part of the garden except the grove in which she sat.

Ravana was furious when he heard of the destruction of his pleasure gardens and ordered the palace bodyguards to go and subdue the creature. The army approached Hanuman, who had stationed himself on top of the archway to the garden. He was really pleased to see the approaching troops. He lashed his tail on the ground and filled the whole of Lanka with the horrendous sound. The troops rushed at him from all sides and attacked him with numerous weapons. He grew in size, clapped his hands on his shoulders in the manner of wrestlers, and spoke in a thunderous voice, "I'm Hanuman, the servant of Lord Rama. Not a thousand Ravanas are capable of withstanding my powers. I will return only after devastating Lanka." He then proceeded to break off a bar that was protruding from the arch and thrashed the demons that had come to catch him and made them run for their lives.

Ravana couldn't believe that his troops had been defeated by a mere monkey. He ordered Jambumali, the son of his chief general, to go and flog the monkey. Jambumali got into his two-wheeled chariot drawn by three white, mountain ponies. He held a red bow decorated with solid gold flowers. Hanuman made short work of his troops and then jumped nimbly onto the spire of the temple and started to destroy it. The guards tried to drive him off but Hanuman uplifted a pillar and thrashed them soundly. The he shouted loudly, "Hail to Rama! Hail to Rama!" in a resounding voice.

At this point Jambumali assaulted Hanuman with thousands of arrows, some of which were aimed at his mouth. Hanuman uprooted a tree and hurled it, but it was cut to pieces by the demon's arrows. In great rage, Hanuman took the iron bar that he had used previously and hurled it at his enemy's chest. It pierced him and he fell down dead.

The news made Ravana mad with rage and he commanded the seven sons of his chief minister to go and kill the monkey. Hanuman jumped into the air, avoided the arrows of the seven, rained rocks on their heads, and killed them all. He then despatched another five generals who had been sent by Ravana. Streams of blood began to flow down the main highway of Lanka leading to the palace, carrying the mangled bodies, legs, and arms of the slain. Ravana was quite bewildered by this unexpected turn of events, and despite the remonstrations of his wife Mandodari, he sent his youngest son Aksha Kumara to subdue the monkey. Mounted on a beautiful chariot drawn by eight horses, the young prince set off from the palace, eager to prove his prowess. He wore golden armor and looked like the rising sun. He let fly many arrows at Hanuman, who resembled a blazing fire and was covered with blood. Hanuman couldn't help but admire the young man who seemed to be a replica of Ravana. But he had no recourse but to fight with him even though he was loathe to do so. He decided to frighten him off the field by destroying his chariot. He jumped into the air and pounced down on the horses and felled them with his fists and broke his chariot. The valiant prince now rose into the air and started discharging arrows at Hanuman. The latter was full of admiration for the boy but decided that he could not afford to show any leniency. He caught hold of his legs, swung him round many times, and hurled him far off in the hope that he might survive and run away. However, the prince never rose up. Hanuman then jumped back to his stronghold on top of the arch to await the next person who would be sent by Ravana.

Ravana couldn't believe that his dear son had been killed by this dreadful monster. He was filled with remorse at having sent him to his death. He decided to summon his eldest son, the valiant Indrajit, to go and capture the monkey alive since he wanted to find out who he was and why he was causing such destruction. He feared that there was something unusual about this monkey and that was the reason why his army could not handle the situation. He walked through a tunnel under the city wall, which ended in a secret door that led to a hidden grove in the woods. There under a banyan tree sat his son, Indrajit, immersed in his esoteric practices. Ravana stood for a while in silence until Indrajit got up and saluted him. Ravana said, "My son! You are the pride and hope of our race, invincible in battle. You are not only proficient in weapons but also have command of all types of magic powers. A gigantic monkey is on the rampage and has killed many of our best warriors. I don't think it is an ordinary monkey, and it appears that it cannot be subdued with weapons, so you must use your other tricks and capture him alive."

"Rest assured, father! I shall capture him for you."

So saying Indrajit, the son of Mandodari, got into his celestial chariot and sallied forth with no fear in his heart. He was raven-haired, dressed in blue and yellow silk, his skin dark red, and he had a yellow flower in his hair. His eyes were dark green with cat's pupils, and a golden chain was wound nine times round his waist. He held a round, blue, steel shield in one hand and a bow backed with gold serpents in the other, and a sword in a silver sheath on his belt. He who had subdued Indra felt pretty sure he could capture a monkey without much effort. However, he realized that this was no ordinary monkey and could not be killed with ordinary weapons. He climbed to another tower as tall as the one on which Hanuman had perched himself and sent an arrow with the *mantra* invoking the mystic noose known as *naga pasha*. These were actually ropes made of snakes. Hanuman fell to the ground, tied invisibly hand and foot and unable to move.

Anjaneya realized the magic potency of the noose that was binding him and decided to remain silent. The stupid forces of Indrajit could not see the subtle ropes that were binding him and brought their own ropes and chains and bound him up. The moment the gross ropes touched his body, the subtle effects of the *mantra* were nullified. Indrajit was angry to see the folly that had been committed by his men but wondered why Hanuman made no effort to set himself free. He decided to wash his hands of the affair and returned to his lair in the forest to continue with his interrupted rituals. Hanuman wanted to be taken before Ravana, so he allowed Ravana's henchmen to parade him along the streets of Lanka. Some people abused him and some threw stones at him while others jeered and made jokes. Hanuman took it all without turning a hair. They dragged him and teased him and tortured him, but he put up with all these insults.

At last he was dragged before the ten-headed Ravana, who looked dazzling in all his finery. He was clad in the softest of white silks, which looked like billows of surf on the seashore. He sat on a throne covered with doeskin, set in the center of a long indoor altar, made of a golden frame filled with earth. He wore ten crowns of flaming red flowers and gleaming gold. A gold chain hung from his neck forged of flat, heavy links from which were hanging golden devil faces with diamond eyes, open ruby lips, and long, shiny, ivory teeth. His green eyes were gleaming with strange lights and looked piercingly at Hanuman. For a few minutes Maruti was dazzled by his charisma and could not help feeling that had he not been so cruel, Ravana might well be competent to become the ruler of all the three worlds.

Ravana looked deep into the tawny eyes of the monkey and some unknown fear gripped his heart. He remembered the incident long ago when he had tried to approach Shiva, his favorite deity. At that time, Shiva's bull vehicle had stopped him. This had infuriated him so much that he had shouted at Nandi, "O you monkey! How dare you try to stop me from entering?"

Nandi had cursed him in return. "Beware, O Ravana! You have called me a monkey, and one day a monkey will be the cause of your downfall!"

This had infuriated Ravana even further and in his arrogance, he had put one finger under the mountain of Kailasa, the abode of Shiva, and tilted it perilously. Parvati had been frightened. In order to comfort her and to quell Ravana's pride, Shiva had simply pressed the mountain down with his big toe and crushed Ravana's finger! Ravana is supposed to have placated Shiva by composing the extraordinary hymn known as the Shiva Thandava Stotra.

Tulsidas describes Hanuman's entry into Ravana's court thus:

"The monkey observed the glory of Ravana's court. Even the gods and the regents of the quarters stood meekly with folded palms, anxiously watching his changing expressions. Hanuman, however, stood like a colossus and was totally unperturbed by the sight of the powerful demon king! He was no more disturbed by the sight of his power than Garuda by the sight of snakes!"

Ravana wanted to insult him and did not even offer him a seat that was due to him as a messenger. All the others were given seats. Hanuman decided that the insult was to his master and not to him. He thought of Garuda, the eagle vehicle of Vishnu who was the enemy of snakes, and chanted his *mantra*. Immediately the snakes released him from their noose. Hanuman shook himself, lengthened his own tail, and coiled it into a seat that was much higher than Ravana's throne. He seated himself with dignity on this self-made seat and looked down on Ravana from this high position!

For a moment, as he looked into the amber eyes of the monkey, Ravana thought that this was the time foretold by Nandi so long ago, but he shrugged off the incident as being of no consequence and asked his minister to question the *vanara* about his reason for coming to Lanka. The minister asked, "You have nothing to fear, O monkey, if you tell the truth. Have you been sent by Indra, king of the gods? What is your motive in penetrating this impenetrable fortress and destroying the garden? If you speak the truth, you will be let free."

Hanuman replied firmly and boldly to Ravana's questions. His only motivation was to change Ravana's heart so that he would release Sita and avoid war.

Maruti looked intently at Ravana and said, "I am the servant of Lord Rama, prince of Ayodhya and prince among men. I have come here to speak with you. You have abducted his beloved wife, and he has asked me to ascertain her whereabouts. I devastated your garden only so that I would be brought face to face with you. I am incapable of being bound by nooses or killed by missiles. I allowed myself to be bound only to see you. You are well acquainted with the laws of *dharma* and know how injurious it is to steal another person's property. By your great austerities you have won many boons, including the one that neither gods nor demons nor yakshas or any other celestial beings can kill you, but you did not add human beings in your list since you thought no human being could kill you. But remember, Rama is a human being and he is being helped by monkeys, who again were not in your list! Therefore I ask you to listen to reason and return Sita to her husband or else you, as well as your whole clan, will be mercilessly slaughtered by my Master! He is the equal of Vishnu in prowess and since you have wronged him so woefully, he will not spare you. Listen to me and let Sita go, and save yourself and your country! Sita spells death for you and your clan. Let her go and save yourself when you can!"

In all his answers, Hanuman wanted to stress the fact that by himself he was incapable of performing any of the acts attributed to him. His strength and inspiration were due to Rama and Rama alone!

Ravana's bloodshot eyes rolled with rage and shot flames of red and gold. He ordered the monkey to be executed forthwith. However, his younger brother Vibhishana intervened and said, "Brother, you know the dictates of *dharma,* and you know that it is most improper to kill an envoy. You will surely lose your fame and your store of merit if you commit this heinous act."

Ravana was even angrier at hearing this and insisted that this monkey who had done so much harm to his city and killed his son deserved to be put to death. Vibhishana begged him to reconsider his decision and said that the only way he could lay hands on the two princes and lure them to Lanka would be to let the monkey go.

Ravana thought about this and agreed that this was a point to be considered, but he insisted that the monkey should be mutilated. "A monkey's tail is his prize possession, so let his tail be set on fire at once and let him return with a burned tail to be the butt and scorn of his friends and relations!"

Ravana issued a command that the monkey's tail should be lighted and that he be paraded round the entire city so as to provide some fun for the populace, who loved the sight of anyone being tortured.

The demons were delighted at this order, which was entirely to their liking. All the time when he had been dragged to the court, they had been shouting fiendishly, "Kill him! Roast him! Eat him!" and so on. Now they fell on his tail with glee and started to wrap it in oil-soaked rags before setting it on fire. While his tail was being swathed, Hanuman made it grow out of all proportion. It became longer and longer until it circled the entire city of Lanka ten times. The confused demons ran around in circles trying to wrap the tail in cloth and found that even though they collected all the scraps and bales of material in the whole of Lanka, they could not cover this colossal tail that simply grew and grew! The citizens were forced to surrender their clothes and the women their *saris*. When they had exhausted the entire amount of cloth in Lanka, they were at a loss to know what to do. Hanuman laughed to himself and at last allowed his tail to be covered. Then they brought huge cauldrons of oil and soaked his tail in oil before setting it on fire. Hanuman was delighted and immediately lashed his blazing tail, killing all those surrounding him! Then he controlled himself and allowed them to bind him and sling him on a pole and take him round the city. He did this so that he could make a mental map of the entire city and take in those things that had not been obvious to him in the darkness of the night when he had wandered through the streets.

All the *rakshasas* lined the streets of Lanka with their womenfolk, everyone anxious to see this spectacle. Some of the *rakshasis* ran gleefully back to Sita and reported the whole matter to her. Sita was filled with sorrow when she heard this. She closed her eyes and prayed to the god of fire to reduce the heat on Hanuman's tail. Thereupon, to Hanuman's surprise, he found that the fire on his tail had no power to burn him!

After having made a mental map of the city, Hanuman flexed his muscles and easily broke the bonds that had been tied round him. He jumped onto the city ramparts with his flaming tail and decided that it would be good to destroy Lanka and thus reduce Ravana's pride. "This fire that has been used to punish me has been denied its food, so I will give it some sustenance."

In one of his most Rudra-like acts of destruction, he began to jump over the tops of the buildings like a flaming meteor. Bounding from house to house, he set fire to each of them in a methodical manner until at last the whole of Lanka was a flaming conflagration. The only places he avoided were the mansion of Vibhishana and the *ashoka* grove in which Sita sat. Very soon the flames changed the beautiful city of Lanka into a cremation ground. There was pandemonium everywhere. People were screaming and running around, women and children were wailing, horses and elephants were stampeding. The wind began to spread the blazing fire through the length and breadth of Lanka. The flames shot up to the skies and appeared like the fire of universal destruction. The mansions made of pearls and gems with lattices of gold cracked with loud reports and toppled to the ground like card houses. The gold plating on the buildings melted and streams of molten gold trickled toward the sea. Houses along the streets collapsed, and gates and grills snapped and smoked. Screams and shouts rent the air as the terrified citizens ran hither and thither in their effort to escape from the conflagration. The whole of Lanka was like a flaming torch. It was an awesome spectacle.

"Surely this is not a mere monkey but Rudra in disguise in his form as Mahakala, or the Great Time spirit of destruction!" cried the *rakshasas*. Hanuman sat on top of the ramparts and surveyed his work with glee. At last he was satisfied that he had completely destroyed Lanka, so he jumped into the sea to cool himself off and put out the fire on his tail.

This is the only time that we find Hanuman resorting to his monkey nature and engaging in an act of wanton destruction. When his temper had cooled a little he was filled with remorse for what he had done.

"What have I done?" he thought to himself. "An angry man is capable of committing any crime. He alone can be called a sage who controls the anger in his mind and does not retaliate even when provoked. I am truly a sinner. If Sita has been destroyed along with this fire, then I have killed my Lord also, for he will not live a moment without her. My journey would have been in vain. The whole of Lanka has been reduced to ashes. Is it possible that Sita is still alive? By virtue of her asceticism and her exclusive devotion to her husband, it is possible that fire itself cannot touch her."

As he was thinking this in deep remorse, he saw some astral beings winging their way over him and talking among themselves. "Strange indeed that the whole of Lanka is in flames and the only place left unscathed is the grove where Sita is sitting!" He was overjoyed to hear this and jumped to the grove in order to find out if this were indeed true. He found her still sitting under the tree, exactly as he had left her. Both of them were delighted to see each other and Sita begged him to stay another day with her.

"Your very sight, O dear monkey, brings consolation to my heart. If you go, I'm tormented with doubt as to when you will return. Are the other monkeys capable of leaping across the sea as you have done? How will my Lord accomplish this feat?"

Again Hanuman comforted her and assured her that Sugriva was no mean monkey but was able to accomplish wonders, and very soon she would see the monkey hordes cross the ocean and Rama coming to rescue her. Sita was full of hope when she heard this and reluctantly agreed to his departure.

> *You showed your small, slight form to Sita,*
> *Then assuming a terrible form you burned the city of*
> *Lanka.*

SRI HANUMAN CHALISA BY TULSIDAS

Aum Sri Hanumathe Namaha!

16

Shoora

The Faithful Servant

Yasyasthi Ramakarunamrita vaibhavena,
Lokaavasaana Samayavati dheergham-ayur,
Tam veera purusha kalagranimajaneyam,
Vande prabhanjanaasutham Raghurama daasam.

Hail to thee o son of the wind! Servant of Rama,
O Anjaneya! Thou art indeed a powerful person,
Who by the grace and blessings of Lord Rama,
Will continue to live until the end of the world.

Raghuramadasashtakam

The gods were delighted at Hanuman's mighty deeds and the grand-sire, Brahma himself, gave him a letter to give Rama, which contained a detailed account of his exploits in Lanka. In this account of his adventures it is said that Sita returned Rama's ring to him together with her hair ornament. So Maruti had three precious articles with him to give to Rama. After all the adulation he received from the gods and from Sita, it is only natural that Hanuman felt a twinge of pride at his accomplishments.

He was eager to get back to Rama. He turned round to have a last look at the city. The fabulous city of Lanka, which had appeared like a gleaming pearl pendant set in the heart of the sky, now lay in shambles at his feet. He felt a pang of compunction but decided that Ravana deserved it. He now sprang to the highest peak in Lanka and grew in size. He fixed his mind on Rama, whom he was longing to see, repeated the powerful *mantra* of Rama, and took a flying leap from the peak toward the northern shore of the sea. Hanuman looked like a mountain with wings as he sailed across the sky. He saw the sea surging beneath him as he turned his face north and sped on his way. He passed with ease through the crimson-tinted clouds and coursed through the sky like an arrow. By the time he reached the mainland he was feeling very thirsty. He looked down and saw an *ashrama* with a lake beside it. He went down and found a sage seated in meditation. Hanuman humbly approached the sage and requested to be allowed to drink from the lake. The *yogi* nodded his head. Hanuman placed his three treasures next to the sage and went to the lake to drink. While he was at the lake, an ordinary *vanara* bounded out of the bushes, picked up Rama's ring and dropped it into the sage's water pot. When Maruti returned, he found that the ring was missing and questioned the sage as to what had happened. The *yogi* said not a word but pointed to his water pot. When Hanuman put his hand into the pot he was stunned to find that it was filled with rings that were exact replicas of the one that Rama had given him. Hanuman asked the sage to kindly tell him which was the one he had brought. At last the sage broke his silence and said that all of them belonged to Rama. When Hanuman looked bewildered, he went on to say that in each of the eons known as Treta, Hanuman would come and drink water from his lake and a monkey would come and pick up the ring and drop it in his water pot. Hanuman was naturally stunned and asked in a meek voice, "How many rings are there in the pot?"

The sage smiled and said, "Why don't you count?"

Hanuman began to count and soon found that it was countless! It was then that he realized that he was not unique. In the Lord's creation, one age follows another. Many others had come before him and many others would follow. This was enough to obliterate whatever pride he had felt in his achievements. Later on when he met Rama, he found that the ring was already on his finger. Rama smilingly admitted to Hanuman that he himself had taken on the form of the sage in order to take away even the smallest trace of pride in his devotee. Hanuman fell at his feet and begged him never to let him fall prey to pride again. Rama granted him this boon. Thus, in this evocative scene of the rings in the water pot, one finds a good example of strong images used to powerfully convey an abstract lesson.

Hanuman now rose up into the air and continued with his interrupted journey. When he neared the spot where he had left his friends, he gave a massive roar to announce his approach.

"Ah! Hanuman has been successful in his mission, as is obvious from his roar," said the other monkeys. Feeling overjoyed, they sprang from treetop to treetop and peak to peak in the usual way of monkeys, eager to be the first to welcome the returning hero. Hanuman landed on the mount of Mahendra from which he had jumped. The other monkeys joyfully gathered round and placed their little gifts of roots and fruits in front of him as a token of their appreciation. They made him sit and encircled him and pelted him with questions. Hanuman bowed to Jambavan and Prince Angada and narrated his tale. The excited monkeys embraced him and sprang from rock to rock with upraised tails.

Angada praised him and said, "There is no one equal to you, O Hanuman! You have given us back our lives and only because of you Rama will be united with Sita."

Again and again he had to repeat his story to the excited monkeys, who were all gathered round him and chattering with joy. Every detail was heard with great delight by the monkeys. The crown prince Angada now said that it would be best if they all went to Lanka and rescued the princess of Videha and took her back to her Lord. Jambavan put him off this impetuous scheme by saying that it was Rama's duty to rescue her and they had only been told to find her. The faster they returned and gave the message, the better it would be for Rama.

They decided that Jambavan was right, and the whole troop started on their return journey. Their enthusiasm lent wings to their feet, and the monkeys made the return back to Kishkinda in half the time. They were all anxious to get there soon and be the first to break the pleasant tidings to Rama. At the entrance of the town there was an orchard called Madhuvana that was filled with fruit trees and flowers laden with nectar. It was a haven for bees who buzzed around collecting nectar and making hives. The garden belonged to Sugriva and was guarded by his uncle. The monkeys begged the prince to allow them to taste the fruits and honey and were given permission by him. That was all they needed. They devastated the orchard and got pleasantly drunk on the honey, much to the disgust of the caretaker. Monkeys are normally difficult to control and these monkeys, who were the color of the honey that they had imbibed in vast quantities, played havoc in the garden, pelting each other with the combs, squashing the fruits, and rioting wildly. Here, as in other instances in the Ramayana, the antics of the simian army serve as a kind of comic foil when contrasted with the self-composure of Hanuman, highlighting his excellent qualities all the more and throwing into light our foolishness whenever, much like the monkey army, we give in to our own impulsive natures.

Sugriva's uncle was the guardian of the grove, and he tried his best to stop them, but they paid no heed to him. The whole garden was filled with intoxicated monkeys reeling about in different states of inebriation. At last he threatened that he would go and report the matter to Sugriva. Sugriva was seated with Rama and Lakshmana, and the guard narrated the whole story, insisting that the monkeys be severely punished, but contrary to his expectations, Sugriva told him not to worry about them. In fact, he seemed rather pleased.

Turning to Rama, he said, "My Lord, I feel sure that these monkeys have accomplished your purpose and that is why they are so bold as to desecrate the king's orchard. There is no doubt that Hanuman has discovered Sita!"

Rama and Lakshmana were filled with delight to hear this. Sugriva told his uncle to return to Madhuvana and send Hanuman and the other monkeys to him without delay.

He went immediately to Madhuvana and bowed humbly to Angada.

"You are the crown prince, and I was told by Sugriva that you could have your fill of honey. Pray forgive me and the guards for having tried to stop you. You have been asked to return to Kishkinda straightaway."

Like stones shot from a catapult, Angada immediately leaped into the air, followed by Hanuman and the others. Seeing them coming, Sugriva told Rama, "I feel sure that Sita has been traced by Hanuman. None but he is capable of accomplishing this task. He is endowed with intelligence, valor, and capability. Moreover, Angada would not have dared to ransack the honey grove that was bequeathed to me by my grandfather had he not accomplished their purpose."

Even before he reached Rama, Hanuman shouted, "Seen have I Sita!" He phrased his sentence in this way because he knew that Rama's heart was filled with expectation and until he heard the word "seen" he would be in agony. Hanuman wanted to spare him even this one moment of pain if he could and thus he cried out, "Seen have I Sita!"

Hanuman now landed close to where Sugriva and Rama were sitting and bent low over his feet. He reported that Sita had been found and was in sound health and filled with devotion to her husband. By this time Angada and the other monkeys were also longing to have their say and jostled each other in their anxiety to tell the tale that they had heard secondhand from Hanuman. Rama looked lovingly at them and said, "I'm sure you have all done very well, but now I would like to know more about Sita. What did she say? Did she send any message or token for me?"

Hearing this, the monkeys turned sheepishly to Hanuman and begged him to continue with the story.

Hanuman bowed low before Rama and told him the whole story of his conquest of Lanka and his meeting with the lovely, lonely princess of Videha who was eating her heart out for her beloved husband.

"O Valiant Prince! Your consort has been detained in a grove by that night wanderer, Ravana. She is forlorn and remains absorbed in you alone. She sleeps on the bare ground and is pale and wan like a lotus flower at the approach of winter. She told me two incidents that are known only to you." He went close to Rama and whispered in his ear, "One is about the crow Jayanta, who pecked her breasts, and the other is about the red dot you playfully placed on her cheek. She also asked me to give you this jewel that she used to wear in her hair and that she had preserved carefully without it being noticed by the *rakshasis*. I offered to bring her to you on my back, but she refused to leave in such a secretive manner. She said that she would wait until her husband came and rescued her after killing the one who had treated her so abominably. At the end she told me to tell you this, "O Son of Dasaratha! Fallen as I am into the clutches of this ogre, I will not survive beyond a month!"

All the while when Hanuman was speaking, Rama's eyes were overflowing with tears. He clutched her jewel to his breast. A flood of memories swept over him and he said, "My heart melts at the sight of this jewel, which was presented to her by my father-in-law, King Janaka, at the time of our marriage and was fastened on her head by her mother. It is a precious jewel that was given to him by Indra, king of the gods. I remember clearly how charming she looked with her hair adorned with this jewel. Repeat to me once again, O Hanuman, every incident of your meeting with her. I can't hear enough about her. She says she can't survive another month without me, but I won't be able to survive even for a moment without my dark-eyed darling!

"Who else but the son of the wind god could have achieved such a stupendous task? Not only did you fly over the ocean and give solace to Sita, but you also laid waste the whole of the city of Lanka! The best type of servitor is the one who not only accomplishes everything his master told him to do but uses his intelligence and does even more."

As Valmiki tells it, Rama said, "No one endowed with a body, whether a god, a human being, or a sage, has put me under such obligation as you have done, O Hanuman! My mind shrinks from facing you, for at the moment I have nothing to repay you."

He continued, "Listen to me, my son! I have thought over the matter and I have concluded that the debt I owe you can never be repaid! At present I have nothing to reward you except this embrace." So saying, Rama clasped Hanuman to his chest and hugged him.

Hanuman's eyes filled with tears at this mark of love from his master. He fell at his feet and said, "O Lord! You have given me the supreme gift. What else do I need?"

Turning to Lakshmana, Rama said, "Let us not waste even a moment, now that we know where she is."

He then looked at Sugriva and asked him if he had any ideas on how to cross the ocean. Sugriva told him not to give way to despair and that his monkeys would easily construct a bridge across the sea by which all of them could cross without any difficulty. Rama now urged him to order the army to start on their march to Lanka, since they had only one month!

Before starting their journey to the south, Rama questioned Hanuman once again about the fortifications of Lanka, the number of entrances, and the type of missiles they possessed.

Hanuman answered, "My Lord! First of all, Lanka is surrounded by the sea, which itself is a natural fortification. Then, it is built on a hill encircled by a thick forest and a river. It also has artificial fortifications of moats and walls. A high protective wall of gold, inlaid with jewels, surrounds the city. These walls are again encircled by fathomless moats infested with poisonous serpents and alligators. Each gateway has a drawbridge by which the moats can be crossed. The central drawbridge at the northern gate is strongly garrisoned and extremely strong. The city has four main gates with strong doors closed with massive bars. At the entrance to the gates are stationed enormous catapults, capable of discharging darts and huge boulders. Hundreds of huge sharp-edged steel clubs bristling with iron spikes are kept ready at every gate. Ravana himself reviews his forces now and again. Lanka is thus extremely difficult to get into."

"Inside, the city is packed with horses and elephants in ruts. Thousands of *rakshasas* carrying poisoned darts and swords are stationed at the eastern gate. An army of foot soldiers along with horses, elephants, and chariots are garrisoned at the southern gate. A million *rakshasas* carrying swords and shields are stationed at the western gate. A hundred million of Ravana's crack regiment coming from noble houses are at the northern gate. Finally, hundreds and thousands of men are stationed in the central military barracks. These drawbridges, gates, and walls were smashed and burned by me as well as many of the stately mansions of the nobility. Actually, there is no need to try and take the whole of the monkey army across to Lanka. Just a few of us can easily go and get Sita for you since most of the fortifications have already been broken by me. However, it is possible that they have all been repaired. If it's your wish that all the monkeys should be transported, then that also can be done. We await your command!"

Rama immediately ordered Sugriva to start their march at the propitious time when the sun was at its zenith. This is an auspicious hour known as *abhijit* and spells victory for anything that is commenced at that time.

"Today is a very propitious day and now is the hour to start, so let us not delay any further. The lid of my upper right eye is twitching, and for a man this is a most favorable omen. Let the monkey known as Nila accompanied by a *lakh* (hundred thousand) of agile monkeys march at the head of the army and choose the best route. Let him lead the army through a route full of fruits and roots and honey and fresh water. Be vigilant since the enemy might try to poison our water sources. If there are any weak limbs in the army let them remain at Kishkinda, for we have a formidable task ahead of us. Let some of the best generals guard the left and right flanks of the army. The mighty Jambavan and a few of the others shall guard the rear. I myself shall ride on Hanuman's back and Lakshmana on Angada's, and we will remain in the center so that we will be able to move faster."

Sugriva immediately gave orders according to Rama's instructions, and the mighty contingent of assorted monkeys started to move forward with great enthusiasm. They set out in a southerly direction. Some were leaping in all directions in order to guard the army from all sides;

others were breaking branches and clearing a passage. All of them were shouting and screaming in excitement and feasting on fruits and fragrant honey. Nila was the commander-in-chief of the army and held the monkeys in check lest they should do any mischief while they passed villages en route as they pressed forward like the tide of the sea. The monkeys had to cross mountains, rivers, and deserts as they advanced toward the southern sea.

There was great excitement amidst the *vanara* hoards that leaped from tree to tree, shouting and waving their tails in glee. They bounded and hopped and swung from branch to branch, plucking trees and waving banners of flowering creepers, sparring and playing pranks on each other and feasting on fruits and honey. They were all in high spirits. Mile after mile they covered effortlessly, camping beside lakes and traversing hills and forests, until they reached the southern sea.

All the while Lakshmana pointed out to Rama many good and auspicious signs and thus kept up his brother's spirits. At last they reached Mahendra Mountain. Rama and Lakshmana climbed the mountain and beheld the turbulent sea stretching before them as far as the eye could see.

Rama gave orders that the monkeys should camp on the beach while they made plans about the method of crossing the sea. The noise made by the monkeys drowned the roar of the sea! Thousands and thousands of monkeys arrived and camped on the shore. In fact, they appeared like another ocean. They stared fascinated at the storm-lashed waves and wondered how they would cross it!

Looking at this formidable array of water, Rama said to his brother. "O Lakshmana! They say that grief decreases with the passage of time, but in my case it seems to be just the opposite. Every moment away from my beloved increases my agony. The time stipulated by her is passing away. Every moment is precious, and I have no idea how to transport this army across the ocean. I only survive because I know that she is still alive." Lakshmana comforted him as best as he could, and they spent the night on the beach.

Feeling the wind on his face, Rama said, "O gentle breeze, please blow over my beloved's face and then return and caress me while her touch is still warm upon you. She must have called for me time and time again as she was being carried away over the sea. I am tormented at the thought of her helplessness. Now that I know where she is, I am on fire to see her. I long for her smile, her gentle glances, and her caressing voice. She was always slim, and now with this continuous fasting, she must be weak and emaciated. I am aching for the day when I can kill that fiend and clasp her to my bosom!"

Sri Rama praised you highly and said,
"You are as dear to me as my brother Bharat."

Sri Hanuman Chalisa by Tulsidas

Aum Sri Hanumathe Namaha!

Aum Mahatmane Namah!

17

Mahatman

Ravana's Council of War

Shatruchedaika mantram
Sakalamupanishadvaakya sampujya mantram
Samsarothara mantram
Samuchita samaye
Sanganiryana mantram.

The only mantra for vanquishing foes,
The mantra that contains all the truths of the Upanishads,
The sole mantra by which we can cross the ocean of
    existence,
The mantra that will save us at the time of death.

Sri Hanumath Stotram

Looking at the dreadful destruction done to his city by Hanuman, Ravana was stricken with sorrow. He called his councillors together and asked them for a plan of action. His spies had informed him of the approach of the monkey contingent. He felt sure that Rama would succeed in crossing the sea. Ravana called a council of war and said, "Our impregnable and glorious citadel has been laid waste by a mere monkey and some of our best men have been killed. How are we to proceed? We have to come to some fast decision before the enemy reaches the farther shore as they are sure to do."

Unfortunately, he did not realize that he was surrounded by sycophants and toadies. All they knew was to bolster up his already bloated ego. One of Ravana's generals now spoke confidently. "O mighty ruler! You have conquered everything from the heavens to the nether regions. There is no one in all the three worlds who doesn't tremble at the very mention of your name. Why should you fear Rama? His army is only composed of monkeys and bears. How can it be compared with yours? Your son Indrajit is also said to be unconquerable. You don't have to stir from this stronghold. He will annihilate the enemy hordes single-handed even before they cross the ocean. That would be the best thing to do."

Now Prahasta, the commander-in-chief of his army, spoke. "You have only to command me, Sire, and I shall personally cross the ocean and destroy the army of monkeys."

"This assault of our city by a mere monkey is not to be tolerated," declared another *rakshasa*. "I shall dispose of Rama and his army in a trice and will return before night sets. You have only to give the command!"

Many of the valiant heroes of Ravana's army now made the same claim and insisted that they would go single-handed and destroy Rama's army. These words of comfort by his ablest men made Ravana feel very confident. He cast his glance on all of them in approbation.

After listening to all their boasts, Vibhishana, Ravana's youngest brother, now spoke. "Dear Brother! We should not be led away by vain boasts. It is not good to underestimate the power of the army. Ever since Sita arrived here, evil portents have been seen. You have many sycophants, O King, who are ready to please you with evil advice. Send back Sita and save yourself and your people. We would all like to live in peace and harmony. Rama is no mean enemy, as you might think! He is a dangerous opponent."

Ravana dismissed Vibhishana's advice scornfully. "I see no cause for fear from a mere mortal like Rama, supported by a motley crew of untrained monkeys. They will be helpless against our well-trained and powerful army." With these words he insultingly dismissed his younger brother.

All of them now thought of a plan that would make Rama turn back. Ravana ordered the sorceress Benjkaya to take on Sita's form and pretend to be dead. The corpse was cast adrift on the sea and washed ashore close to Rama's camp. When it was brought before Rama, he turned pale, for he recognized the necklace as belonging to Sita.

"Ravana must have killed her and cast her body on the sea," he cried and fell to the ground in agony.

Hanuman, however, sensed that something was wrong. He ordered the monkeys to make a pyre and place the corpse on top and light it. As soon as the flames began to lick the body, it jumped up and ran toward the sea! Hanuman caught her and forced her to reveal the whole foul plot to Rama.

After having told Rama the whole story, she fell at Hanuman's feet and begged him to marry her, for she could no longer return to Lanka. Hanuman declined the offer but promised to give her shelter in Kishkinda. Thus she spent the rest of her life in Kishkinda singing the praises of her savior!

When he realized that his trick had been seen through, Ravana dismissed the council for the day. When he returned to his own palace, he brooded over his younger brother's words, but due to his infatuation for Sita he could not accept it. In fact, day and night he could think of nothing but Sita. The more he thought her, the more determined he became to keep her with him at any cost.

He knew that war was imminent, so he decided on another council of war. The ten-headed king of the *rakshasas* got into his golden chariot and drove to the assembly hall in state where he was met with a blare of trumpets. All his best troops lined the roads to the hall to honor their king. He ordered the foremost of his generals, including his younger brother Kumbhakarna, who normally slept for ten months of the year, to be woken up and brought to the hall forthwith. They came one by one and bowed at his feet.

Ravana ordered Prahasta, his commander-in-chief, to see to it that all four parts of the army—cavalry, elephant brigade, chariots, and infantry—were stationed at all the four gates in readiness for any attack. He then spoke to that assembly of *rakshasas* who were eager to please him in whatever way they could.

"All of you must know that I have abducted Sita, the consort of Rama. It appears as if she is some enchanted being conjured by the demon Mayan who is full of magic tricks. Looking at her fair and lovely countenance, I have become a slave of passion and am no longer my own master. Having been told of our stronghold by the monkey Hanuman, it appears that Rama and Lakshmana are already encamped on the other shore with their army of monkeys. I know that we have nothing to fear from these mere mortals leading a host of irresponsible monkeys. However, it is best to be prepared for whatever may come and thus we must immediately devise a plan to kill those two wretched brothers."

His brother Kumbhakarna was already annoyed at being woken up from his beautiful slumber and when he heard this declaration of passion by Ravana, he flew into a mighty rage and said in a thunderous voice, "You did not choose to consult any of us before you abducted another man's wife! That was the time when you should have asked our opinion. Actions that are undertaken by a monarch that run counter to the principles of *dharma* (righteousness) are sure to produce only misfortune! However, since I am your brother, I shall endeavor to set right what you have wrongly performed! Let them come and I'll make short work of them! After having killed Rama and Lakshmana, I shall devour his monkey hordes! With Rama out of the way, I'm sure Sita will succumb to your will! But remember that I do not approve of all this!"

Ravana was silent even though he did not care for the frank manner in which his brother spoke. However, he knew that he was indispensable to their army and so kept his peace. Then spoke another mighty general called Mahaparshwa.

"Who is it that can dare lord it over you, O thou mighty sovereign of all the three worlds? Who is it that will not drink a pot of honey after having procured it? Make Sita submit to your will even if you have to use force to do so. In the meantime, all of us shall reduce your enemies to smithereens!"

Ravana now divulged his dire secret to them. "In days of yore, I ravished a celestial nymph called Punchikasthala. She ran to the creator Brahma like a stricken deer. He knew what had happened and cursed me thus, 'If you dare to violate any other woman without her consent, your head will be split into a hundred pieces.' This is why I have not so far forced the charming princess of Videha to my bed. However, there is no doubt that Rama does not know my prowess and that is why he is marching into a death trap. I am not capable of being defeated, even by the gods. What then to speak of a mere mortal helped by a pack of apes and monkeys!" With these words he roared uproariously with mirth. The rest of the court except for his two brothers joined him, and the whole court dissolved into laughter at this ridiculous picture of the great Ravana being defeated by a pack of monkeys and bears! But Ravana had forgotten the boon he had received from Brahma. As we know, he had asked for immunity from death from all types of heavenly and demonic beings. In his arrogance he had refused to consider human beings and monkeys as worthy of being possible opponents and now they were the very ones who were advancing purposefully toward him.

It is said that Punchikasthala swore to take revenge on Ravana and that is why her son Hanuman destroyed his precious city and was instrumental in the destruction of not only Ravana but of his whole hierarchy.

Hearing the boastful words of Ravana and the others, Vibhishana made a last bid to save him from his doom. "I beg of you, O brother, to listen to me and give Sita back to Rama before the monkeys invade this island. You know what one monkey was able to do to your wonderful city. Think of our fate when thousands of them start pouring in. Sita is a deadly serpent that has wound itself round your heart. She will be the cause of your death! Give her back before you and your people are destroyed totally!"

Turning to the other ministers, he said, "It is the duty of a minister to advise a king wisely and save him from the consequences of his own folly, if possible. Why are all of you determined to bring about his downfall and the destruction of your race?"

Ravana's eldest son Indrajit now spoke hotly. "This younger uncle of mine seems to be the only one in the race of *rakshasas* who is not endowed with courage, virility, prowess, and fortitude. His nature is quite different from ours. He is a coward and your name will be in the dust if you listen to him. Why should he try to frighten us? Even Indra, the wielder of the thunderbolt, was cast by me to the ground! I even dashed his elephant to the earth and set all the celestial hosts into panic! Do you think I am incapable of subduing two insignificant mortals?"

Vibhishana listened to his nephew's talk without rancor. "My dear boy, I am afraid you are not able to distinguish between right and wrong. You are a mere boy and your intelligence is not steady. Though you profess to love your father, you are actually doing great harm to him by encouraging him in his folly!"

Ravana was furious when he heard his brother's well-intentioned words.

"It is better to live with an avowed enemy than with a relation who is jealous and secretly works to bring about your ruin. Fire and weapons I do not fear, the dangerous ones are the near and dear. Bees fly away after sucking the last drop of honey from a flower, so the unworthy give up a relationship that has ceased to be profitable. You alone, my brother, do not like to see the whole world honoring me! Had you not been my brother, you would not be alive now. A curse upon you! You are a disgrace to our race!"

Vibhishana did not like to stay to get any more curses and said, "You are my elder brother and thus command respect. Whatever I said was meant only for your good. It is always easy to find people who will try to please you with honeyed words, but there are very few who will dare to tell a king the unalloyed truth to his face. I'm afraid I cannot tolerate your inequities any more. You are surrounded by sycophants and fools. A man in the noose of death can never listen to the salutary advice given by well-wishers. However, I wish you well. May prosperity attend you. For my part I cannot stay any longer with one who is steeped in *adharma*!" So saying, he rose up into the air along with his four ministers and went to the other shore, where he hovered over Rama's camp.

It is said that the three brothers Ravana, Kumbhakarna, and Vibhishana typify the three types of *gunas,* or modes of nature—*sattva, rajas,* and *tamas.* Vibhishana was the example of *sattva,* or the quality of harmony and goodness, Ravana of *rajas,* or passion, and Kumbhakarna of *tamas,* or inertia, sloth, and stupor. As an important character in the story, Vibhishana shows us that even a demon can turn against evil and toward good if he aligns himself with supreme consciousness, and through his brave act of defying Ravana, it is he who will inherit the city of Lanka.

> *Vibhishana heeded your council and became King*
>   *of Lanka,*
> *As the whole world knows.*

SRI HANUMAN CHALISA BY TULSIDAS

Aum Sri Hanumathe Namaha!

Aum Bhaktavatsalaaya Namaha!

18

Bhaktavatsala

Rama Gives Sanctuary

Anjananadanam veeram,
Janaki shokanashanam,
Kapishamaksha hantaram,
Vande, Lanka bhayankaram.

Salutations to the courageous darling of Anjana,
Who removed Sita's sorrows,
King of monkeys whose very look could kill hundreds,
And conquer the terrible city of Lanka.

HYMN TO HANUMAN

Sugriva was filled with suspicion when he saw the five *rakshasas* looking like miniature mountains hovering in the sky. He suspected that they had been sent by their ten-headed king to kill them.

Vibhishana spoke from the air. "I'm Vibhishana, younger brother of Ravana. I advised him again and again to return Sita to Rama, but he refused to see reason and thus I have sought refuge in Rama!"

Hearing this appeal, Sugriva ran to Rama with this news and warned him not to take him at face value since he was a *rakshasa*.

"It is wise never to trust these night wanderers. He is also Ravana's brother. He may be a spy sent by Ravana to find out our strong and weak points or he may even strike us himself in the middle of the night since he has four stalwarts at his command. Like an owl that waits for the opportune moment and then destroys the whole clan of crows, he will join us and wait for the right time and annihilate us. I think it best that he and his friends should be killed before they do harm to us."

All the other monkey heroes like Angada, Nila, and others tended to view Vibhishana with suspicion and advised that he should be watched carefully and his movements noted and anything of a suspicious nature immediately reported to Rama.

Rama looked enquiringly at Hanuman, who as usual had remained silent. When thus requested by Rama, Anjaneya said, "Vibhishana does not have the looks of a deceitful person to me. His mien and voice are open and pleasing. I think he has decided that it would be going against the law of righteousness to stay with one as debased as his brother. Moreover he must have heard of your glory and your adherence to *dharma*. Hence he has defected. One who comes as a spy would not announce himself as he has done. He was the only one who pleaded my case with Ravana and begged him not to kill me when I devastated the garden. This is my humble opinion and now, my Lord, you can take whatever decision you like to take."

Rama was delighted to hear Hanuman reflect his own views on the subject and said, "I fully endorse what the noble Hanuman has said about Vibhishana, even though I know that the rest of you are fully devoted to me and that's why you have given me this advice. However, on my part I have taken a vow that I will never turn away a person who has surrendered to me or taken refuge in me. Whatever his intentions may be, if he appears to have come in a friendly spirit it is my duty to accept him."

Sugriva, the prudent, spoke once again and warned Rama of the dangers of accepting the brother of the ten-headed Ravana who was sure to prove perfidious and untrustworthy and deserved instant death.

With a slight smile Rama said, "A righteous man may be born even in a clan of *rakshasas*. The scriptures enjoin us to welcome even an enemy who comes to one's door asking for protection. Such a person should be protected even at the cost of one's own life. I would be guilty of a great crime if I did not give him asylum."

After saying this Rama made his oft-quoted vow, "I promise to give security to all living beings that come to me even once and seek my protection. I will do this even if Ravana himself comes! O Sugriva! Let Vibhishana be brought before me at once and let him be treated on equal terms with me."

Sugriva spoke, "My Lord! You are too noble. I am sure he is a spy. It would be safer to kill him."

Rama replied with a smile, "I know that you speak out of your love, but the code of *dharma* says that one who has taken refuge should never be abandoned. My principle is to give succour to anyone who comes and declares that he wants to join me. His character is immaterial. Go and bring him here."

Sugriva bowed to Rama and went and gave an assurance of safety to Vibhishana, who immediately descended on the beach and fell at Rama's feet.

"I am Vibhishana, Ravana's youngest brother, and have sought refuge at your feet for you are capable of giving shelter to all created beings. I have come to you after having abandoned my city, friends, and relatives. Now you are my all. My life and welfare are in your hands. I have surrendered my joys and sorrows and my very life at your blessed feet. Please accept me as your devoted slave."

Rama was touched by his devotion. He smiled tenderly at him, bade him welcome, and gave him permission to stay. Afterward, he asked him about Ravana's strengths and weaknesses.

Vibhishana was only too happy to oblige. "I am capable of giving you many hints about Ravana and his generals. My eldest brother has a boon that he cannot be killed by the gods or demons or celestial beings or serpents or birds. My powerful second brother, Kumbhakarna, is an exceptional warrior. The commander of the forces, Prahasta, is an indomitable soldier. Ravana's eldest son, Indrajit, has invincible armor and is clothed in iguana skin, which cannot be pierced by arrows. Having propitiated the god of fire, Indrajit has the ability to remain invisible when fighting. The army consists of tens of thousands of ogres able to change their form at will, living on flesh and blood. As for Ravana, he has defeated even the gods in battle."

Rama listened carefully to this account and then said with a smile, "Indeed, I am well aware of Ravana's exploits, which have been recounted to me by various persons. However, I give you my word that I shall not return to Ayodhya without killing this monster who has abducted my wife. I will then crown you as king of Lanka! Though he may run and try to hide in all the worlds, Ravana will not be able to escape the fury of my arrows. Until I achieve this, I will not enter Ayodhya. I swear this in the name of my three brothers."

Vibhishana fell at his feet and assured him that he would give him all assistance in this noble endeavor. "I swear in the name of *dharma* that I will assist you in all ways to the best of my ability, but the one thing that I will not do is to kill my own people!"

Rama embraced Vibhishana and asked Lakshmana to bring water from the sea to anoint him as king of the *rakshasas*. Water was forthwith brought and poured over Vibhishana's head by Lakshmana, in the formal ritual known as *abhishkekam,* in the presence of all the monkeys, in order to proclaim him as king of the night rangers!

In the meantime, Ravana sent a spy to try and make friends with Sugriva and encourage him to return to Kishkinda and thus desert Rama. The spy took the form of a monkey and tried to ingratiate himself with Sugriva. When he felt that he had his confidence, he took him aside and told him that his master was Ravana, who was really very anxious to make friends with him since he had been a friend of his brother Vaali. He told him to take his army and return to Kishkinda and win Ravana's favor for all time. Sugriva was so angry to hear this that he jumped on him and nearly choked him to death. The other monkeys came running to find out what the commotion was about, and when they heard of the spy in their midst, they would have torn him to pieces, but he shouted to Rama to save him since he was only an envoy. Rama immediately ordered the monkeys to release him, and he flew away squawking in fear and reported the matter to Ravana.

Rama now asked Vibhishana for a stratagem to cross the ocean. Vibhishana told him that for this he would have to ask Sagara, the Lord of the ocean, to help him to make a bridge that would carry his army across.

"This ocean owes its very existence to the Sagara brothers who belong to the Ikshvaku clan and are your ancestors. Therefore, he is bound to help you."

When Rama heard this salutary advice, he lay on the beach, facing the east with his arm as a pillow, on a mat of *kusa* grass, and started meditating on the Lord of the ocean. When Sagara did not appear after three days and nights of meditation, Rama lost his temper and told Lakshmana, "Do you see, O Lakshmana, how this haughty ocean refuses to show himself even though solicited so politely by me? Forbearance and politeness are misconstrued for weakness in this world. But mark my word, today I shall dry up this ocean with all its wealth. My arrows shall suck up the waters so that it will remain dry so my army can cross it without difficulty!"

So saying, Rama let fly his potent arrow deep into the sea, causing consternation among the aquatic creatures. The waves were as tall as mountains. The earth trembled and quivered in agony. The sky became pitch black and meteors flashed across the firmament even as lightning flashed. The ocean throbbed and moaned in pain. Lakshmana caught Rama's arm before he could release his second arrow. However, since it had already been mounted, it had to be discharged.

"Shoot it in the opposite direction," said Hanuman. Rama shot it to the North, and the place where it fell came to be known as the Thar Desert!

Seeing the confusion caused in his waters, the sea god Sagara rose out of the water clad in red robes and wearing a garland of pearls and red flowers. The darkness caused by Rama's anger lifted due to the radiance of the jewels round Sagara's neck. His hair was covered with seaweed and water kept pouring down his long gray hair and beard. He rose up to the surface of the ocean on the crest of a wave. Slowly he came to the shore and approached Rama and stood humbly in front of him with folded palms kept above his head. He was decked with many jewels and ushered to the shore by waves. Coming near Rama, Sagara spoke.

"My Lord, you are known to be the abode of kindness and mercy. I did not appear before you earlier because I cannot go against my nature. As you know, earth, fire, air, and water have their own specific qualities. I cannot go against these. I am fathomless and incapable of being swum across. However, I will allow your monkeys to make a bridge and keep the stones afloat and thus give them a safe passage so that they may not be harmed by crocodiles and other reptiles. Let the two brothers known as Nala and Nila be allowed to make a bridge across the sea. They have been given a boon that any stone they place on the water will be able to float." With these words, the sea god melted back into the ocean.

Nila and Nala now came forward and told Rama to order the monkeys to collect material for the construction of the causeway.

The monkeys were delighted to get orders from Rama and immediately ransacked the forest for trees and boulders, which they dragged to the shore and threw into the sea. The two brothers, Nala and Nila, were remarkable engineers and saw to it that the rocks and trees brought by the monkeys were kept in the right places. The enthusiastic monkeys uprooted trees and brought huge boulders. Rocks as large as hills were carried on their willing shoulders and thrown into the sea. However, they were dismayed to find that the rocks, though floating, quickly dispersed on the choppy waters. Hanuman quickly thought of the brilliant idea of writing the Sanskrit words *ra* and *ma* on alternate stones and allowing the crack between them to stand for the long vowel *aa*, which in Sanskrit is written like the cardinal number "1."

Maruti said, "The Lord's name is the greatest of all *mantras* and the bridge will be made in an unbroken line of Rama *mantras*!"

Work was progressing very satisfactorily, with Hanuman supervising everything and working harder than any of the others. However, their enthusiasm dampened when they found that once again the stones refused to stay together and drifted away in all directions! Hanuman decided to investigate the reason for this. He dived into the ocean and found that the fish were responsible for dismantling the bridge. He shook his tail vigorously and thrashed the waters, thus paralyzing the fish.

He then confronted Swarna-matsya, the golden mermaid, queen of fishes, and demanded an explanation.

"I was ordered by Ravana to disperse the stones," she said. Then looking closely at Hanuman, she said enticingly, "Who are you? You seem to be strong and handsome and intelligent. What have you got to do with this war between Rama and Ravana? Marry me and enjoy life as it is meant to be enjoyed. Together we will rule the sea, unconcerned with the worries of the world above!"

Hanuman replied, "Of what use is my strength, beauty, and wisdom if they are of no use to others? He who uses his abilities only for his own aggrandisement is a fool. As for me, I live for my master Rama. I have no life apart from him." So saying, Hanuman declined her offer and rose to the surface. The queen was impressed by Hanuman's selflessness and ordered all her creatures to help him in building the bridge. The fish, serpents, seals, and sea monsters held the stones together and the bridge to Lanka started to take shape.

Hanuman continued to work twice as hard as any of the others, constantly repeating the magic *mantra* of Rama as every stone was placed and the work went on with great speed. The bridge was a hundred leagues long and ten leagues wide. On the very first day one-fifth was completed. In this way, the monkeys, guided by Nala and Nila, managed to span the ocean and complete the bridge in five days! Even now, parts of this amazing bridge can be seen in the ocean off the coast of Dhanushkodi, which is the modern town closest to Sri Lanka.

Rama was amazed to see the miracle of the floating stones and asked the monkeys how it was done. They replied that it was only due to the power of his own name, which Hanuman was engraving on every stone. Rama was intrigued and thought to himself that if his name could produce such miracles, then surely he himself should be able to do the same. So he quietly moved to another part of the beach and started to throw some stones in the water. Much to his disappointment, none of them floated. When he turned round, he found that Hanuman had been standing at a safe distance and watching the entire proceedings. Rama was a bit abashed and asked Hanuman the reason why he did not have as much power as his name.

Hanuman's interpretation was in accordance with his devotion.

"My Lord!" he said, "anything that you choose to hold in your hands will be saved and anything that you let go will naturally fall. The stone that slips from your grasp will obviously have to sink!"

Rama now joined Lakshmana near the bridge and watched the work. It is said that a small squirrel that was anxious to help Rama used to jump into the water and roll on the sand and then go and shake off the dust on the bridge, since that was the only effort it was capable of making. Hanuman picked up the little fellow and asked him what he was doing. The little one reared itself up beside the mighty monkey and said, "The causeway is made with a lot of ragged rocks. My Lord's tender feet will get torn when he walks on it, so I thought I would make a nice soft sandy surface for him to walk on!" Hanuman was amazed at the little creature's devotion, which seemed to exceed his own. He took it to Rama, who kept it on his lap so that it could nestle close to him. Rama comforted the little one by passing his three fingers over its back. The Indian squirrel (chipmunk) bears the mark of Rama's fingers on its back to this day. It has three lines on its back. Rama calmed its fears and told it that its tiny efforts were as valuable to him as the gigantic achievements of the monkeys. The sand he had brought was as precious to him as the rocks of the *vanaras*. Thus the little squirrel also found a place in Rama's heart.

Another interesting legend connects Hanuman with the baleful planet Saturn (Shani). It is believed that Saturn visits each individual at least once in his lifetime for a period of seven and a half years. Just as the bridge was being built, it was time for Saturn to come into Hanuman's horoscope. He requested Shani to postpone his visit until he had successfully assisted Rama in regaining Sita. But despite the fact that Hanuman had freed him from Ravana's dungeon, Saturn, true to his nature, was adamant and Hanuman had to comply with the law of nature. He allowed Saturn to sit on his head as his hands were busy carrying stones and uprooting trees and his legs were too humble to seat such an exalted personage.

For a few minutes Saturn happily settled on Hanuman's head and watched the proceedings with glee. The mighty monkey continued with his work, piling heavy boulders and stones on his head in an apparently casual manner and carrying them to the construction site. After a while Saturn found it impossible to bear the load of the heaped boulders on top of him and wanted to climb down. Hanuman insisted that he complete his mandatory seven and a half years. Saturn pleaded for release, saying that the seven and a half minutes that he had spent on Hanuman's head felt like seven and a half years. Hanuman smiled and allowed him to go. Since then it is believed by all worshippers of the monkey god that those who are suffering from the ill effects of the seven and a half year stay of the malefic planet will definitely get a remand from their sentence if they worship Hanuman.

By the fourth day of construction, the monkeys had uprooted all the mountains and stones in South India and started to fly north to uproot the peaks there. Hanuman also flew to the Himalayas, where he was struck by the sight of a lofty mountain called Dronachala. However, he found it impossible to uproot and realized that it was made of a black stone called *saligrama,* which is used in the worship of Vishnu. Hanuman told the mountain that he wanted to use it to help the *avatara* of Vishnu called Rama and he would be touched by Rama's feet. At this, the mountain allowed itself to be uprooted but en route Maruti was met by Nala and Nila, who told him that the causeway was complete and that Rama had ordered all monkeys to drop the mountains they were carrying and return immediately to camp. Many monkeys were on their way at that time, carrying mountain peaks. On hearing Rama's order, they dropped the peaks over the whole of South India and thus created the present day topography of the land. Hanuman, however, was still far to the north and when he heard Rama's order, he set the mountain down in the forest of Vrindavana near the Yamuna River. The mountain was crestfallen at being denied the chance to worship Rama and reminded Hanuman of his promise to take him to Rama.

Maruti was in a dilemma. Was he to break his promise to the mountain or disobey Rama's orders? He flew back to Rama and told him the whole story. Rama comforted him by saying, "Return to the mountain and tell him that the time for us to meet has not yet come. I will return to the earth in the next age of Dwapara as Krishna and will play with my friends on top of this mountain. I will even lift it up with my little finger and hold it aloft. It will be known as Govardhana and will be worshipped as an embodiment of myself."

Hanuman delivered this message and the mountain was satisfied and waited for the advent of the Lord as Krishna in the *yuga* (epoch) known as Dwapara.

Rama was anxious to install a *lingam* (stone symbol of Shiva) and pray to him for success in his endeavor before crossing the bridge. In one day, the two brothers Nala and Nila made the small dais on which the *lingam* was to be installed. Rama entrusted Hanuman with the work of bringing a really auspicious *lingam*. Hanuman immediately set off for Kailasa from where he hoped to get a *lingam* from Shiva himself. However, he was unable to return at the appointed time. The priests warned Rama that the auspicious time was about to pass. So Rama himself made a beautiful *lingam* of Lord Shiva with sand, and it was installed at the correct time. All the monkeys were thrilled to see this. Anjaneya arrived soon after with a beautiful stone *lingam* given by Shiva and was most disappointed to see that the function had taken place without him. Seeing his despondent look, Rama comforted him and told him to remove the *lingam* that he had kept and to install his own instead. Anjaneya did his best to remove the *lingam* but was unable to do so. He even tried to wrap his tail around it and pull it up but his tail broke instead. Rama lovingly moved his hand over his tail and restored it to its original beauty and size.

He told him, "O son of Vayu! Do not be distressed. Our endeavor would have been unsuccessful had I not worshipped the *lingam* at the appointed time. Hence I was unable to wait for you. A *lingam* once installed by me cannot be moved; however, I give you permission to install this *lingam* that you have brought to the east of this dais. The main entrance will be kept there so that anyone who comes to worship at this place will have to offer worship at your *lingam* first. Hanuman was very happy to hear this. This place where Rama installed the *lingam* is known as Rameswaram (Rama's Lord Shiva) and is a famous place of pilgrimage to this very day.

There is another strange story about the installation of the *lingam*, which shows the Indian ability to give credit even to an enemy if it's called for. It is said that at the time when Rama wanted to install a *lingam*, there was no priest to officiate. He asked Hanuman to fly to Lanka and request Ravana, who was a great devotee of Shiva, to come with a Brahmin and do this service. Ravana agreed but said that Sita would also have to be present since the sponsor of the ritual should have his wife beside him. So Sita was fetched from the garden and Hanuman, accompanied by Ravana and Sita, went in the Pushpaka Vimana, Ravana's flying chariot, to the mainland. Rama asked Ravana to suggest a source for the *lingam* and Ravana suggested Kailasa. Hanuman was sent to procure the required *lingam* but was unable to return in time. Ravana insisted that the ceremony had to be conducted at the auspicious hour and Sita moulded a *lingam* out of the sand. Ravana observed all the rites punctiliously and even intoned Rama's *sankalpa,* or intention for which the ceremony was being conducted—the slaying of Ravana and the rescue of Sita!! The rest of the story is the same as above.

The causeway was complete and the installation over. Even the gods came to survey it, and from above it looked like the central parting of the hair of a woman, so elegant and beautiful was it! Now it was time to cross. Rama and Lakshmana blew their conches and saluted Durga, the goddess of war. Hanuman let out a war cry, filling the hearts of the monkeys with confidence. Sugriva now invited Rama to climb on Hanuman's back and cross the bridge while Lakshmana rode on Angada's back. They led the way followed by rest of the *vanara* hordes who followed, dancing and bounding with joy. They leaped into the air and jumped into the sea and swam for a while. They made such a clamor that the noise of the sea was successfully shut out. It was if the sea held its breath while the army crossed.

As they approached their destination, Ravana hurled two missiles and destroyed the two ends of the bridge. Rama and his troops were stranded in the middle, unable to cross to Lanka or return to Jambudwipa. Hanuman immediately came up with a brilliant solution. He increased his size and stretched himself over the gap, placing his hands on the shore of Lanka and his feet on the edge of the bridge. The monkeys scrambled over his back and jumped onto Ravana's stronghold. As Rama walked over Maruti's back he said, "I'm indeed blessed today for my Lord's feet have stepped on my back."

At last they set foot on enemy territory. Rama was touched by the enthusiasm and devotion of the monkeys and their innocent love. Sugriva was all set to put up camp on the other side in a place that abounded with fruits and roots and clear water. However, Rama saw many evil portents bidding dire consequences for the whole earth and told Sugriva that they should immediately march toward Lanka instead of dallying there at that pleasant spot. Thus the monkey hordes continued to advance until they came in sight of the ramparts of Lanka. They drew up in military formation even though it was night. The full moon slowly rose up to display the huge army of monkeys who were camped on the mountainside.

Rama looked up at the city of Ravana with its turrets of gold and silver and thought of his beloved Janaki (Sita) who was a prisoner of love in that city of hate. He was lost in thought for a long time. At last he roused himself and talked to Sugriva and the commanders about their plan of action for the next day.

> *You are the ever vigilant guard at the door of*
> *Sri Rama.*
> *No one can enter without your consent.*

Sri Hanuman Chalisa by Tulsidas

Aum Sri Hanumathe Namaha!

19

Mahatejasvin

The Siege of Lanka

Dehadrishtya tu daasoham,
Jeevadrishtya twadamshakam.

When I identify myself with my body, I am your servant,
When I identify myself with my ego, I am a part of you.

VALMIKI RAMYANA

In the meantime, the spies sent by Ravana had returned and told him all the details about the enemies and how Hanuman had made it possible for them to pass over the bridge that had been broken by his missiles. He felt a bit dejected and decided to survey the enemy camp for himself, so he climbed up the turret of his palace, which was as tall as ten coconut trees kept one on top of the other. He leaned over the wall and saw to his amazement that the whole land beyond his citadel was filled with monkeys of all shapes and sizes. He brought the spies with him and asked them to point out the leaders of the army.

Pointing at one of the monkeys, they said, "That huge monkey with the thick neck and golden hair, who is boisterous and facing us, is Sugriva, son of Surya. The yellow-haired one, who is roaring like a lion and lashing his tail again and again, is the crown prince Angada. The one who stands surrounded by a valiant army is Nila, the one who built the bridge. The white monkey in the forefront is Hanuman, son of Kesari, who is also known as the son of the wind god Vayu. As you know, he is the one who crossed the sea and set fire to Lanka. This prince among monkeys is able to change his form at will and is richly endowed with might and physical charm, and he cannot be swayed from his course even as the powerful wind cannot be forced to change its route. As a baby he saw the rising sun and, thinking it to be a fruit, he jumped three thousand leagues toward it. He is totally devoted to Rama and is the scourge of his enemies, as you well know."

One of the spies then went on to point out the various other commanders of the *vanara* army so that Ravana could have an idea of whom they were.

"Now, O King! Observe those black, ferocious bears that live on mountains. Their leader is that old, shaggy bear, Jambavan, who once helped Indra in his war with the demons. His troops are extremely ferocious, can scale huge mountains, and are totally unafraid. All of them are valiant, powerful, and daring and all are ready to lay down their lives for Rama!"

"Observe this valiant prince, O King, with matted hair and dark blue in color, with lotuslike eyes, the scion of the race of Ikshvaku, foremost among those who know the Veda, expert in the use of the mystic missile of Brahma (*brahmastra*), whose wrath is like the wrath of Death and whose consort Sita, was abducted by you from Janasthana. His arrows can slice the earth and pierce the sky. Observe him closely, for he is Rama, your archenemy, who is advancing toward you, determined to kill you at all costs!"

"The one who stands on his right, fair in color, with broad chest, coppery eyes, and dark curly locks is Lakshmana, Rama's younger brother, who is totally devoted to him. He is foremost in the wielder of weapons and unforgiving toward the enemies of Rama. He is ever prepared to lay down his life for his brother's sake. Observe closely, O King, your brother Vibhishana, who stands on Rama's right side and who has already been installed as King of Lanka by Rama! He is furious with you and is longing to come to grips with your army."

Ravana was furious with his servitors who spoke so highly of the enemy army.

"How dare you speak to me like this? You are my dependents, and I can kill you for singing the praises of my enemies like this. Leave my presence immediately and never let me see you again!" So saying, Ravana dismissed them and sent some other spies to find out Rama's plans for the day. However, they were also spotted by Vibhishana and would have been tortured by the monkeys had not Rama intervened and allowed them to go free. They returned singing Rama's praises.

Ravana decided to try a final trick to make Sita succumb to his charms! He called the court magician and asked him to make a replica of Rama's head as well as a replica of Rama's famous bow, the Kodanda. The magician carried these two objects and accompanied the king to the *ashoka* grove where Sita was sitting, the very picture of dejection.

Brandishing Rama's head before her, he said, "That good-for-nothing husband of yours was killed by my general while he was camping outside the gates of Lanka. Evidently your stock of spiritual merits was not enough to save him. Lakshmana as well as the foremost of the generals of their army have all been killed."

He shot a piercing look at her through his crystal green eyes and continued, "I see that you don't believe me. I anticipated this and have brought your husband's head to convince you!"

He ordered the magician to come forward. He arrived promptly with Rama's head stuck on a pole. This gruesome article was placed before Sita. Ravana took the bow and threw it in front of her and said, "Here is the famous bow of Rama. Surely you recognize it." Then, leaning forward, he whispered words meant for her ears alone: "Now will you agree to be mine?"

Sita gave one look at the head and shrieked, "O my beloved Lord! Have you deserted me? The astrologers had predicted a very long life for you. How did you meet this untimely death when you were well versed in the science of warfare? Why don't you look at me, O prince? Why don't you answer me?"

Turning to Ravana, she said, "Kill me with the same weapon with which my husband was killed and lay my body over his on the battlefield. I shall follow him wherever he may be." So saying, the poor lady fell to weeping and lamenting.

Just then, one of Ravana's generals came and demanded his immediate presence at the council hall, for a matter of great importance had to be discussed. As soon as Ravana left, both the magic head and the bow vanished, much to Sita's astonishment.

Just then Vibhishana's wife came and told Sita not to worry since it was a trick of Ravana's and her husband was alive and preparing to attack Lanka. She revived Sita and told her to listen to the sounds made by the approaching army. Sita was most grateful to her and asked her to go and find out what plans Ravana was making and whether he would release her now that he realized that her husband was already camped outside the city. Vibhishana's wife returned soon after and appraised Sita of the situation.

"O Princess of Mithila! Ravana is not prepared to let you go until he dies. He will certainly not release you through fear, so deep-rooted is his infatuation for you. However, fear not, your husband will come soon enough and kill the ten-headed monster and rescue you!"

In the meantime Rama, accompanied by Lakshmana and the other chieftains, decided to climb to the top of Suvela Mountain in order to have a closer view of the city of Lanka, which had been built on top of Trikuta Mountain. Suddenly he saw Ravana standing on the ramparts clad in all his finery, adorned in scarlet robes, and fanned on both sides by beautiful females, surveying the camp of the *vanaras*.

Seeing this, Sugriva could not control himself and suddenly sprang from one peak to the other, landing next to the astonished Ravana.

"I am Sugriva, the friend and servant of Rama. You shall not be spared by me this day!" With these words, he leaped on him, snatched his crown, and threw it on the ground.

Ravana was taken by surprise and said, "I will deprive you of your beautiful neck in a moment." So saying, he caught hold of him and threw him on the ground. Sugriva bounced up like a ball and there was a small skirmish. However, Sugriva realized his mistake and hurriedly jumped back to the Suvela peak. The monkeys cheered their leader, but Rama chided him gently for his brash act and told him never to repeat such a thing again. Had he been killed or caught the results would have been disastrous for them.

He then told him to send Angada as a messenger of goodwill in order to give Ravana a last chance to save his people. Such an act was in accordance with the laws of a righteous combat. Hanuman said that in his opinion nothing on earth would make Ravana change his mind. However, Rama insisted that on his part there should be no deviation from the path of *dharma* and he should by all means give the demon a chance to change his mind even at this last minute, if he so wished.

Angada was longing to have a close look at Ravana and hardly had he got his orders than he leaped to the assembly hall where Ravana was meeting with his ministers.

In the sunlight he looked like a fiery golden ball when he landed lightly in front of the Demon King.

"Who are you?" he asked.

"I am Angada, the son of Vaali and the messenger of Rama, Prince of Ayodhya." As soon as he heard these words, Ravana rose up and welcomed Angada warmly.

"My dear child! You are the son of my good friend. You are like a son to me. But I don't understand why you should be befriending a person who killed your father in an unfair manner. Stay with me and I'll treat you like my son, Indrajit, and give you all comforts. You are the son of a noble father and should not consort with such riffraff!"

"O King of *rakshasas*! Who are you to give advice to me when you yourself are steeped in sin! I have merely come to give you Rama's message. He has given you an ultimatum. Either you should return the princess of Videha to him and beg his pardon or else go out of the palace gates and confront him in a battle to the finish. The choice is yours—to live honorably or die dishonorably!"

Ravana was furious at this message and ordered the messenger, to whom he had proclaimed eternal love a few minutes ago, to be caught and put to death immediately!

"I will not blow out like a light with these windy words!" he said. He bent down and thrust his snarling face close to Angada. His eyes were aflame and his brows knit into a huge frown. He reached out for Angada, who was quivering with fear, but at the last moment, he merely brushed him with his hands and ordered his guards to catch him.

Angada caught hold of the four guards who rushed forward to seize him, leaped with them onto the wall of the palace, and threw them down on the ground. He then took a flying leap onto the turret of the palace and broke it in two. He stood there and roared like an infuriated bull and then nimbly landed back in front of Rama and the other monkeys who were highly delighted at his antics. He then gave an account of all that had happened in the court.

"So Hanuman was right," thought Rama. "Ravana will neither relinquish Sita nor will he come for an honorable combat until he is forced to do so."

Hanuman ordered the monkeys and bears to howl and growl menacingly and challenge the *rakshasas* to a fight. The thunderous noise made by them filled the air and frightened the residents of Lanka who were used to a life of voluptuous debauchery and were not happy at having been asked to fight. They started raising their voices asking Ravana to give up Sita and allow them to live in peace.

"Our civilization is doomed," they said, "unless the king complies with our wishes."

Ravana was livid when he heard this. "They are only a pack of monkeys and bears," he shouted. We will hang their heads as trophies on our walls. Their skins will provide clothing for your wives and their flesh will provide food for your children. Mount your chariots, let loose our dogs, and let us drive off Rama's rabble!"

Rama asked Sugriva to choose the generals who were to attack from various gates.

Very soon the entire space between the walls and the moat was filled with monkeys. In fact they seemed to have formed a solid wall round Lanka. This news was forthwith taken to Ravana who immediately told his forces to stop them from entering the gates. He himself climbed up on the ramparts and was astonished to find the whole grounds outside the gates swarming with monkeys, all eager to fight. The green fields had changed to brown. He suddenly spied Rama seated on Hanuman's back urging the monkeys to destroy the barricades and invade the town. He had never expected that a puny human being helped by a pack of simians would ever be able to come close to his precious city, and now it looked as if they would soon get inside the gates. At that instant Lakshmana pointed his bow at Lanka, Ravana raised his mace above his head, and the commander of his armies waved his sword. He ordered the gates to be opened and let loose hundreds of wild hunting dogs followed by fierce *rakshasas* mounted on war chariots. He was sure that his well-trained army would easily rout a pack of unruly monkeys. The big north gate of Lanka opened, and the youngest third of the *rakshasa* army rushed out.

The monkeys fell back in fear, but Hanuman led the attack and threw a huge stone at the *rakshasa* who was in the forefront, knocking him down senseless. Thus emboldened, the monkeys rushed forward, armed with sticks and stones, determined to overcome the army of the night wanderers. The bears frightened away the dogs and startled the horses. The monkeys leaped into the chariots, kicking, punching, and biting the *rakshasas* who were ill prepared for this type of warfare.

The monkeys now started filling up the moat with stones and branches so that their troops could cross easily. Then they started scaling the walls in various places. They grabbed trees and logs and stones for weapons and jumped onto the streets of Lanka shouting, "Victory to Rama! Death to the demons!" and so on. Very soon the whole place was alive with a mass of leaping, screaming *vanaras* bent on destruction.

The army of the night rangers now tried to stop the monkeys

from advancing. All of them were decked in golden armor and carried swords and bows and arrows. They rushed forward with bloodcurdling roars and swooped on the *vanaras*. They attacked them with flaming brands, javelins, pikes, and axes while the monkeys retaliated with trees and rocks, as well as their nails and teeth!

The young generals of Ravana's army now sallied forth, mounted on huge horses, elephants, and chariots. All the horses and elephants had golden trappings, and the heroes were dazzling in gold and silver coats of mail, while the monkeys had nothing but their fur to protect them!

Since they did not have chariots, Rama rode into battle on Hanuman's shoulders and Lakshmana on Angada's. Soon the battle-field was covered with dust. Blood of the *vanaras,* bears, and *rakshasas* flowed in streams on the ground. The air was filled with the din of drums, bugles, and war cries. Banners were torn, chariots were smashed, and weapons cast here and there. Bones were broken, flesh was torn and eyes gouged out as the monkeys clawed and scratched and jumped on the backs of *rakshasas*.

Ravana stood on the highest tower in Lanka and surveyed the devastating scene. His troops were being driven back into the citadel and he feared that the ancient prophecy made by Nandi would come true and he would have to face defeat at the hands of the monkeys. Hanuman saw Ravana, took a flying leap, and landed on his head. He then danced on all his heads and kicked his ten crowns to the ground. The monkeys roared their approval while the *rakshasas* hung their heads in shame. Before Ravana could catch him, he had leaped back into the fray.

The first day's battle went on into the night, which was the time when the night rangers were most powerful. The darkness was lit up by the brilliance of the gold-tipped arrows that were shooting across the sky. The night prowlers were jubilant at the advent of night.

Ravana said, "Let the young warriors take rest. Arm the veterans."

Demon soldiers knelt before fires praying for victory. They strung their bows, donned their armor, and put garlands over them blessed by the priests with mantras for safety. Ravana gave his general Prahasta a few drops of *soma* juice and blessed him. Little flames started to come out of Prahasta's eyes. He bowed before Ravana and said, "I'll drive away the monkeys and isolate Rama and feast on his flesh."

He bowed to Ravana and got his blessings and mounted his chariot, which had wheels of gold that shone like twin suns. Sixty-four horned serpents drew the chariot, which bristled with swords and harpoons. His flag had a snake of emeralds and a lion of topaz sewn onto blood red silk. Prahasta flexed his muscles and rolled his bloodshot eyes. The north gate opened, and he led out the veterans, the grand army of the *rakshasas*. The soldiers followed with bells tied on their arms and legs. They charged at the animals that fled in terror. Nala alone faced Prahasta's chariot. He dodged thousands of arrows that were flung at him and threw a boulder that overturned the chariot. The demon broke free from his chariot and lunged at Nala with his mace. He dodged the blow and pulled out one of the wheels of the chariot, striking Prahasta on the heart. The mace fell from his hand and Prahasta fell down dead. The time was midnight. The *rakshasas* tore their hair in shame and returned leaderless to Lanka.

The monkeys and bears carried their dead and laid them in the forest. Many of the demons had died, but since Ravana did not want anyone to know how many had fallen, he ordered that their bodies should be thrown into the sea.

Ravana immediately ordered his son, Indrajit, as well as his foremost generals to go out and tackle the simian army. They challenged Lakshmana and the others to duels. Indrajit fought with Angada, Lakshmana with Virupaksha, and Hanuman with Jambumali. They were two of the most trusted generals of Ravana's army.

Angada was determined to come to grips with Indrajit, the son of Ravana. He was a master magician and prince of illusions. He was Ravana's golden boy who could take on any form at will. It was said that only Mandodari, his mother, knew his actual form. Angada wounded Indrajit and killed his charioteer and horses. Rama and the others applauded Angada for his feat, for they all knew the might of Indrajit.

In the meantime, the wily son of Ravana leaped into the air and disappeared into the clouds. From this vantage point he sent the deadly *naga pasha,* or noose of the serpents, by which he bound the two brothers. The serpent ropes coiled round the necks of the brothers, choking them until they became unconscious. Enmeshed by these magic cords, lacerated all over their bodies with Indrajit's deadly arrows, Rama and Lakshmana lay on the ground drenched in blood, with hardly a sign of life except for an occasional feeble twitch. There was panic in the *vanara* army. They fell into a mood of dreadful despondency when they saw their heroes in this pitiable state. They jumped to the sky searching in vain for a glimpse of Indrajit, but he remained invisible. All they could hear was his mocking laughter. Only Vibhishana could see him, and he was also helpless against the snake arrows. Indrajit was jubilant, for he was sure he had killed the brothers. Having created havoc in the rest of the army, he returned to his father and gave him the happy news of the death of the Kosala brothers.

The monkeys crowded round the fallen princes and gave vent to their grief. They felt that the fact that the very first day of war went so badly was a bad sign for them. However, Vibhishana approached them and told them not to grieve, for he did not think that they were dead. He told them to protect the princes for he was sure they were only unconscious. Jambavan told them that Rama was Vishnu incarnate and could certainly never be killed by anyone.

> *You took a colossal form and killed the demons.*
> *Thus you fulfilled the mission of Sri Rama.*

SRI HANUMAN CHALISA BY TULSIDAS

Aum Sri Hanumathe Namaha!

ॐ

Aum Ravana-maradanaaya Namaha!

20

Vatamaja

The War Continues

Na mukhe netrayovapi
Lalade cha bruvosthata,
Anyeshwapi cha gaatreshu,
Dosha samvitita kwachit.

I can see no fault of expression anywhere on his face or even
his eyes,
Forehead, eyebrows, or in any one of his limbs.

VALMIKI RAMAYANA

Ravana was elated at the thought of the death of Rama and immediately ordered that Sita be taken in an aerial car and shown this scene so
that she would believe. "Tell Sita to forget her husband and come to me
since she has no other recourse open to her but to accept my love and
become my wife!"

Sita could not believe what the *rakshasis* told her, so they forced her
to enter the aerial car and took her to the battlefield. She wept at seeing

the devastation on the battlefield and the scores of monkeys who lay dead. In the midst of this sea of corpses of the dead and dying monkeys she saw her beloved husband and his brother lying on a bed of arrows, their bodies bleeding and inert. She could no longer see clearly due to the tears that were flowing in torrents from her eyes.

She started to moan and curse her fate. "How is it that my Rama, who killed all the *rakshasas* at Janasthana single-handed, was unable to counteract the deadly arrows of the evil-minded son of Ravana? Our *guru* Vasishta prophesized that Rama would perform many *ashwamedha yagas* (horse sacrifices) and win great fame as a king. He also said that I would never be a widow and would be the mother of heroic sons. How is it that all these sayings have proved false? Of what use are the lotus marks on my feet, which proclaim that I will be a queen. I have all the twelve auspicious signs of a noble woman on me. My body is symmetrical, my teeth even, my navel set deep in my stomach. My breasts are full and skin and hair soft. My complexion is pearly and soles touch the ground when I walk yet this calamity has overtaken me!"

One of the *rakshasis* who was kinder than the rest and had befriended her before now comforted her with these words, "My lady, please do not weep. Your Lord is certainly not dead. In fact, neither of them is dead. See how the *vanaras* are guarding their bodies. They appear to be waiting for them to recover. There is a glow about their faces that would not have been there if they were dead. Take this opportunity to have a good look at the face of your beloved from whom you have been parted for such a long time. Forget your sorrow and take heart!"

Sita was thrilled to hear this. She observed the two of them carefully and confirmed what the kindly *rakshasi* had said. She raised her palms and saluted Rama and then returned.

"Only the divine eagle, Garuda, can break these ropes and release the brothers," said Jambavan.

Hanuman had been standing quietly all the while, for he was convinced that Rama and Lakshmana were not dead. He sat down facing the east and started chanting the Garuda *mantra*. Garuda was Lord

Vishnu's eagle vehicle and the avowed enemy of snakes. Hardly had he finished chanting when a tempestuous wind arose in the sky and whipped the waves and made them rise to the sky. Trees were snapped like sticks and flung far off to the sea and animals ran hither and thither. Suddenly they saw Garuda, the king of birds, who resembled a blazing fire, cleaving his way through the storm-tossed sky. The storm had been caused by his enormous wings. Seeing him, all the snakes that had bound Rama and Lakshmana released their deadly hold on them and slithered off in terror. Both of them now stirred and sat up as if from a deep sleep. Garuda came close to them and stroked their faces lovingly with his wings and instantly their wounds vanished and luster returned to their faces. Their splendor and majesty were redoubled. Garuda embraced them warmly and Rama said, "When you touched me with your wings I felt as if my father was caressing me. Because of you we have been saved from this deadly snake noose. Pray tell me who you are."

The eagle said, "I am Garuda, the son of Vinata, and I am the vehicle of Lord Vishnu. I am your constant companion and will always be hovering about you even though you are not aware of it. These snakes were converted into arrows by the magic mantras of Indrajit. I am the only one who could have saved you from this noose of snakes. I am their ancient enemy and that is why they vanished as soon as they saw me. Fear not, O Rama! You and your brother are destined to destroy your enemies and have a glorious future. Your strength lies in your adherence to *dharma,* and you will be victorious even though your enemies are treacherous. Now please give me leave to go. Whenever you need me, just think of me and I'll be there."

The monkeys chattered and shouted with delight when they saw this miraculous recovery. They thrashed their tails and thumped their kettledrums, beat their clay tom-toms and whooped with joy. Ravana heard these sounds and was quite puzzled. "How can they be so joyous when Rama lies dead?" he thought. He ordered his spies to go and find out the truth and was amazed when they returned with the news of the miraculous escape of the two brothers.

Ravana now ordered one of his best generals called Dhumraksha, the fiery-eyed one, to take a huge contingent and destroy the opposing army. He had the voice of a braying donkey and was mounted on a wonderful chariot driven by donkeys with harnesses of gold and heads resembling those of a wolf and a lion. He sallied forth through the western gate, which was being guarded by Hanuman, accompanied by a host of *rakshasas* armed to the teeth and all wearing coats of mail. The monkeys were itching for a good fight and charged at the army as soon as it appeared through the gate. Dhumraksha, who was in the forefront, dispersed the monkeys in all directions with a shower of arrows. Infuriated at this, Hanuman took up a huge rock and flung it at Dhumraksha's chariot. He leaped out of the chariot in the nick of time and the chariot and the donkeys were smashed by the rock. Hanuman now started hurling trees and rocks at the *rakshasas* and then charged at their leader. Dhumraksha took up his huge mace studded with sharp spikes and hit Hanuman on the head with it. Hanuman brushed off the blow and retaliated by hurling a huge broken pillar at his opponent. This was the end of the *rakshasa*. He fell senseless to the ground and the others ran back to report the matter to Ravana.

Ravana now sent his next champion, Vajradanta, or the one with teeth like diamonds. His diamondlike fangs were long and sharp and hung over his lower lips. He was accompanied by a number of soldiers on elephants, horses, donkeys, and camels. He was decked in lovely armlets and a diadem and had a coat of mail. His forces now came out of the southern gate, which was being guarded by Prince Angada, who immediately came forward to battle with the demon. There followed a terrific fight between the monkeys and Vajradanta's army. He sent a thousand arrows at the prince who retaliated by hurling a tree at his opponent. He then charged forward and shattered Vajradanta's chariot and forced him to jump out and face him on an equal footing. The demon held a huge shield and sword, while Angada had only a tree. They wheeled round each other, waiting for an opportunity to close in. When the ogre collapsed, Angada jumped and grabbed his fallen sword and lopped off his huge head. The panic-stricken army now ran back to their fortress and reported the whole matter to Ravana.

The next general to be sent by Ravana was Akampana. Mounting his huge golden chariot decked with jewels, he sallied forth accompanied by a huge army of soldiers. He caused great carnage to the monkey host until at last all the great leaders ran off in terror. Seeing this, Hanuman entered the fray. The monkeys were gladdened when they saw his mighty form and untroubled demeanor, and all of them rallied back around him. Akampana greeted him with a volley of arrows. Unperturbed by this, Hanuman tore up a huge crag and hurled it at the *rakshasa* who split it into smithereens with his arrows. This enraged Hanuman, who tore up a huge tree and rushed at Akampana, who kept raining arrows at him. Undeterred by this, Hanuman brought the tree down with all force on Akampana's head and killed him instantly. The rest of the *rakshasa* army were in total disarray. With loosened hair and shrieking with fear at seeing the gigantic figure of Hanuman, they took to their heels in panic while the gleeful monkeys chased them with sticks and stones.

Ravana was slowly beginning to realize that he was not facing an ordinary foe. One by one all his great generals seemed to be dying. Now he called his commander-in-chief, who had advised him to wage war against Rama, and told him that he was depending on him to defeat the foes. He set out, with a thunderous roll of kettledrums and a blast from scores of trumpets, in his enormous chariot decked with jewels and accompanied by thousands of soldiers all armed to the teeth. They rushed at the monkeys and fought with swords, javelins, double-edged swords, pikes, arrows, mallets, maces, iron bars, spears, axes, and bows and arrows while the poor monkeys defended themselves with only trees and rocks.

They were met by Nila, the commander-in-chief of Sugriva's army. The two commanders met in a grim combat. Nila met the volley of arrows with closed eyes. He then grabbed a huge tree and shattered the demon's bow and chariot with it. The demon jumped down with his mallet and rushed at Nila and gave him a mighty blow on his head. Even though he was bleeding badly, Nila took a huge rock and hurled it at his head, which broke into pieces. The army was sadly demoralized at the death of their commander-in-chief and fled to Lanka.

Ravana decided that he would have to enter the battlefield himself. His wife Mandodari approached him and begged him to reconsider his decision and to make peace with Rama. Ravana was outraged at this suggestion.

"Ravana has never bowed his head before anyone and will not do so now. But have no fear, O Mandodari! By this evening I will have killed the Kosala brothers and avenged the death of my commanders."

Ravana sallied forth accompanied by a huge army of invincible warriors, all of whom looked like huge mountains. Seeing the approach of this army, Rama asked Vibhishana to point out the leaders to him. Vibhishana pointed out the various commanders to him and said, "There comes Ravana, king of the night rangers in the chariot with the white umbrella! He is accompanied by ghosts and ghouls with hideous forms, having rolling eyes and heads of tigers, camels, elephants, and horses. He is decked with a diadem and his ears have huge swinging earrings. He is the one who humbled the pride of Indra himself."

Rama gazed at him for a long moment and said, "Indeed he is a glorious figure. Such radiance! Like the sun at noon! He seems to be endowed with all the qualities of a great hero. Yet I cannot help but pity him, for he is coming closer to his death!"

Ravana was discharging his deadly arrows at the monkeys who charged at him.

Seeing this, Sugriva could not help himself. He tore a rock and sent it hurtling at Ravana who saw it coming and splintered it with his arrows. He then hurled his javelin at Sugriva, who fell to the ground. Seeing this, the monkeys fled toward Rama, who picked up his bow and decided to face Ravana himself. Lakshmana stopped him and begged him to allow him to go. Rama agreed, for he felt the time had not yet come for him to come into close combat with Ravana.

In the meantime, Hanuman rushed at Ravana's chariot and said, "You have been granted many boons but none that will protect you from monkeys. Now allow my right hand to teach you a well-deserved lesson."

Ravana replied, "Strike once and earn everlasting fame for having hit the great Ravana and after that, I will destroy you."

Hanuman raised his fist and smote him on the chest. Ravana reeled under the blow and retaliated with a similar punch on Hanuman's chest.

Ravana said, "Well done, O monkey! You are an adversary worthy of my praise."

Hanuman retorted, "Woe to my valor, since you are still alive. Why don't you strike again? And then I will send you to the abode of Yama!"

His eyes inflamed with anger, Ravana brought his right fist down with all his might on Hanuman's chest. Seeing Hanuman reeling under the blow, the *rakshasa* king did not wait to see more and drove his horses forward to confront Nila, the commander in chief of Rama's army. He discharged scores of arrows at him. Nila was the son of Agni, the god of fire. With great agility he reduced his size and leaped to the top of Ravana's chariot and then to the top of his crown, and then kept hopping from place to place so that Ravana's arrows could never pierce him. Rama and Lakshmana were astonished to see the antics of this monkey. At last Ravana invoked the fire missile and flung it at Nila, who fell to the ground. But since he was the son of the fire god, the missile could not kill him. Ravana thought him to be dead and turned toward Lakshmana. There ensued a formidable battle between the two. At last Ravana hurled a javelin at him, strengthened with a powerful *mantra*. It pierced Lakshmana's chest and made him swoon.

Filled with rage, Hanuman darted at Ravana and gave him a mighty blow on his chest with his fist, which made him fall to the floor of his chariot and lose consciousness. Hanuman immediately lifted up Lakshmana and brought him to Rama. Very soon, both Lakshmana and Ravana recovered from their swoon. Rama decided to face Ravana himself, and Hanuman begged him to sit on his shoulders like Vishnu sitting on Garuda.

Thus seated on the huge monkey, Rama charged at Ravana and said, "You shall not escape me wherever you may go and hide."

Ravana retaliated with a shower of gold-tipped arrows that covered Hanuman as well as Rama. The latter was furious at seeing Hanuman in this state and let fly a most potent arrow at Ravana's chest that made him reel so that his bow fell from his nerveless grasp. With another arrow, Rama tore off Ravana's crown and made him fall from his chariot. Seeing him dazed and without any weapons, Rama took pity on him and told him to go back to Lanka and return in another chariot when he was a bit refreshed.

Ravana returned to Lanka with his pride crushed, his bow broken in two, his horses and charioteer killed, his crown shattered, and his body pierced all over with Rama's deadly arrows.

> *You alone can contain your glory,*
> *The three worlds tremble at your roar.*
>
> Sri Hanuman Chalisa by Tulsidas

Aum Sri Hanumathe Namaha!

21

Daityakulantaka

The Fall of Kumbhakarna

Shirasi praharad virasthada, vayusutho bali,
Nadenakampalyachaiva rakshasaan sa mahakapi.

The valiant and mighty son of the wind god then dealt a
  blow on his [the asura's] head,
And made the ogres tremble with his roar.

Valmiki Ramayana,
Yuddha Kanda (Book of Battle)

Ravana was completely demoralized by the scene he had just gone through. Far from appreciating Rama's generosity in letting him go, he was filled with humiliation and thoughts of revenge. He sat and brooded on his golden throne and recalled all those painful incidents in his life when he had insulted so many people and had been cursed by them. He remembered Brahma's warning to beware of humans for he had not asked for immunity from them! He also remembered the curse of Punchikasthala and Nandi, the vehicle of Shiva, and many others. His ministers crowded around him to find out his commands. At last he roused himself from these mournful thoughts and told them that the only way open to them was to rouse his brother Kumbhakarna from his sleep. He had been summoned to the council nine days ago and had gone back to sleep.

The *rakshasas* were terrified of calling Kumbhakarna before the stipulated time. However, the king's orders had to be obeyed. As they neared Kumbhakarna's subterranean abode they were blown back by the breath coming out of his nostrils! His mouth was like a yawning cave and his snores shook the rafters and made them rattle. His breath reeked of alcohol and blood for he had drunk and eaten his fill nine days ago before falling into a deep stupor. The *rakshasas* who went to wake him carried wagonloads of buffalo and boar meat and buckets of blood and marrow and barrels of strong wine. They plastered his uncouth body with *sandal* paste and perfume and garlands. They made thunderous noises calculated to waken the dead, while others blew loudly on conches, bugles and trumpets. Some used sticks and rods to prod him awake but he slept on, blissfully unaware of the tortures being done to his body! Then they fell to biting his ears and tearing his hair and jumping up and down on his stomach. At last the monster showed some signs of animation and gave a great yawn. Those who had been pulling his beard fell into his cavernous mouth and had to be fished out before he closed it. Furious at having been interrupted in his slumber of only nine days, he gave a mighty shout that made all of them flee in terror before he caught and started eating them. However, when he saw the mountains of food heaped before him, he was a bit appeased and started greedily chomping his way through it. The *rakshasas* slowly crept back and informed him that his brother wanted him urgently. Having licked the pots and eaten the buffaloes that drew the carts containing the food, Kumbhakarna proceeded to dress himself with great care before going to the council hall to meet the king. The earth shuddered with every step he took. His gargantuan body occupied the whole width of the street.

Ravana was delighted to see him and informed him of the critical events that had taken place in Lanka while he was in the throes of blissful slumber. Kumbhakarna laughed heartily at Ravana's description of the *vanara* army and said, "My dear brother, I warned you of the consequences of your infatuation for that woman just ten days ago in the council hall, but you would not listen to me. The king who follows the rules of *dharma* and listens to the words of the wise will reap the rewards of his good deeds, but the one who discards these words and acts according to his own perverted understanding will have to bear the consequences of his actions. Both Vibhishana and I advised you once, but you would not listen. It is still not too late. Try to avert this crazy war and make friends with Rama. I hear that you have already lost your best generals and have been publicly humiliated. Will you not stop until your head is cut off from its shoulders?"

Ravana's lips quivered with rage and his eyes became like hot coals shooting sparks of fire. He shouted at Kumbhakarna, "An elder brother should be honored like a father. How dare you try to advise me? What has happened has happened. I am not prepared to go back on anything I have done. If you have ever held me in esteem or love, then tell me what to do now. Try to correct the results of my past indiscretions instead of harping on them!"

Kumbhakarna realized that his words were like a red rag to a bull, so he pacified him with sweet words.

"Don't worry, brother. I will pulverize the whole lot of them just by walking in their midst. I will make mincemeat of those puny princes. Just let me get my hands on them. I will tear them apart with my bare hands. I need no weapons. Cast off your worries and go into your harem and make merry with your wives. Once Rama is dead, Sita will be yours."

Ravana was delighted to hear this and placed many precious necklaces round his monstrous neck and sent him off with his blessings.

That night Rama could see the shadow of Kumbhakarna, dark and menacing, striding behind the walls like walking death. Kumbhakarna's eyes were like cartwheels and his teeth like elephant tusks. He donned his bronze armor and golden helmet. His belt was as large as the chain on the drawbridge. He came to battle after having quaffed two thousand barrels of wine and a few thousand barrels of hot buffalo blood to give him strength. He entered the battlefield with great enthusiasm, flourishing his iron spear, which was spitting flames from its tip. In front of him walked the person carrying his black banner with the wheel of death on it. He was followed by a mob of excited, shouting *rakshasas,* brandishing tridents, javelins, and clubs. He looked like a colossal black thundercloud as he stepped over the walls instead of coming through the gate, and the monkeys fled in terror.

Seeing him coming, Rama questioned Vibhishana, "Who is this colossus who is now approaching us?"

Vibhishana replied, "He is the son of sage Vishravas and the younger brother of Ravana. His appetite is so enormous that even while he was still an infant, he was in the habit of devouring thousands of creatures of all types for his breakfast and an equal amount for lunch and dinner with a few snacks thrown in at odd times. At last, all the creatures of the world appealed to Brahma. The grandsire [Brahma] cursed him that he would sleep for the rest of his life. Ravana intervened for the sake of his brother, and Brahma modified his curse and said that he would sleep for six months at a time and then wake up for a day, so that his insatiable appetite could be appeased, and then go back to sleep for another six months! Had he not been cursed in this fashion he would have eaten up all the life on this earth a long time ago. He can easily make one mouthful of our entire army!"

Brahma had promised that on the day when he woke up after six months of sleep even the gods would not be able to defeat him in battle. However, if he was aroused from sleep on any other day, he would surely be killed. In his eagerness to have his brother fight for him, Ravana forgot the warning and ordered his brother to be called.

Kumbhakarna stepped over the wall and advanced like a mountain on the move, his eyeballs rolling like chariot wheels. When he saw Vibhishana fighting in Rama's army, he was furious and shouted at him.

"Whatever Ravana's faults may be, he is still our brother. By fighting for his enemies you have turned against your family. Your treachery disgusts me!"

So saying he rushed at Vibhishana, who immediately took refuge behind Rama. The monkeys fled in terror on seeing his advancing form, which resembled a thundercloud.

Angada tried to rally the fleeing monkeys by telling them that he was only a war machine that had been trained to fight and that they could easily conquer him. They started to rain rocks and boulders and trees on him, but they glanced off him like feathers from a rock. The monkeys tried to jump on him and bite him, but he brushed them off like flies. In fact, he hardly noticed them and walked on, crushing those who happened to get under his enormous feet. Angada rallied all those who were turning tail and encouraged them to return and face the monster, but they were so terrified that they did not stop in their tracks. From the air Hanuman rained mountain peaks, rocks, and trees of every kind on Kumbhakarna's head, but he intercepted them easily with his pike. Hanuman now came to the ground and struck him hard on the chest. This made the giant reel a bit, and he retaliated by striking Hanuman on the breast with his pike. Such was the force of this blow that Hanuman burst into a loud cry of anguish, much to the delight of the *rakshasas* and the dismay of the monkeys.

However, he quickly rallied himself, gave a mighty leap, jumped onto his shoulder, and bit off his ear, which made Kumbhakarna howl in pain.

All the other *vanara* leaders now surrounded Kumbhakarna and battered him, but the colossus hit them viciously right and left and all of them fell to the ground. The other monkeys were now filled with rage and jumped on him from all sides and started to bite him and tear him with their nails. They scrambled up his trunklike legs like locusts, scratching and biting. He simply lifted them from the ground and stuffed them into his mouth. Some of them escaped through his nostrils and some through his ears. Now Angada accosted him, but the monster gave him one blow with the back of his hand, which made him fall down senseless.

Then Sugriva came forward and challenged him. Kumbhakarna

was enraged and hurled his pike at him. Had it hit him, he would surely have died, but Hanuman bounded forward, caught it in midair, and broke it in two, even though it weighed as much as a mountain. The monkeys rejoiced to see this sight and rushed forward. However, Kumbhakarna picked off the top of a rock and flung it at Sugriva, who became senseless. He caught hold of him in his arms, kept him under his armpit, and walked on. Hanuman wondered if he should grow to his enormous size and rescue him but thought it better to wait until Sugriva came to his senses and rescued himself or else he would feel very despondent at having been defeated by the ogre. Very soon Sugriva came out of his swoon, clawed viciously at the ogre's massive ears, bit off his nose, and ripped his thighs with his nails. Kumbhakarna swore and dashed him on the ground. Sugriva got up painfully and loped off to Rama before the monster could catch him again. Kumbhakarna was by now famished and started to devour monkeys, *rakshasas*, fiends, and bears alike. Seizing huge handfuls of monkeys, bears, and ogres, he simply stuffed them all into his cavernous mouth.

Seeing the panic in the *vanara* army, Lakshmana came forward to try and stop this terrible destruction, but his arrows could not penetrate the stiff, curly hair that covered the mammoth's body wherever his armor did not. Kumbhakarna brushed him aside, saying, "I will deal with you after having finished off your brother," and strode on. Lakshmana refused to let him pass and rained arrows at him until his mace fell from his hands, but he continued to move forward like a huge road roller, crushing everything in his path. Though he was without any weapon, he played havoc among the monkeys with his fists and hands. At last he came face to face with Rama and gave a bloodcurdling roar that made all the monkeys fall down senseless.

Rama shot an arrow with bent knots, which struck Kumbhakarna on the chest and penetrated through his armor so that blood started to pour out of the wound. He was so furious that flames shot out of his mouth. Even though the wound was fatal, his hatred for Rama kept him alive, and he advanced toward Rama, bellowing with pain and rage. Lakshmana now spoke to Rama.

"This fellow is totally out of his senses now and doesn't know if he's killing his own people or ours. It is best if our monkeys climb on him and pester him so that he doesn't annihilate those on the earth."

The monkeys were delighted to get this order and jumped on him from all sides, driving him thoroughly crazy with their antics. In the meantime, Vibhishana, carrying his mace, darted in front of his elder brother. When Kumbhakarna saw him, he said, "Get out of my way before I kill you. I am so confused with lack of sleep and food as well as thousands of wounds that I no longer know who is friend and who is foe. But you, I know, are my younger brother. You are the only fortunate one among us who had the temerity to stand up to Ravana in order to vindicate your desire for truth and righteousness. You alone will be responsible for perpetuating our race. By the grace of Rama you will become sovereign over our people and uphold our traditions."

Hearing this, Vibhishana retired to a corner of the battlefield, his eyes bathed in tears. Kumbhakarna turned round to see Rama standing in front of him and took a huge boulder and hurled it at him. Rama splintered it with five arrows and said, "Brave *rakshasa*! I am Rama, son of Dasaratha. Take a good look at me, for soon your eyes will not be able to see!"

Kumbhakarna laughed and said, "I'm not one of your puny *rakshasas* who can be killed by you. I am Kumbhakarna, destroyer of the gods." So saying, he wielded his mace and killed thousands of monkeys. Rama invoked the wind god and sent an arrow with a broad razor head that severed the arm carrying the mace and made it fall along with the mace with a monstrous sound, crushing many monkeys in the process. Undeterred by this, the monster tore up a tree with his other arm and lunged at Rama, who cut off that arm also with another well-aimed arrow. It fell to the ground, carrying with it many trees and crushing both monkeys and *rakshasas*. But still the colossus kept advancing and shouting, "No one can slay me. No one can stop me!" He kicked and stamped and killed hundreds of monkeys with his enormous feet.

Rama now cut off both his feet with two crescent-shaped arrows. He was not put off even by this and stomped forward on the stumps of his legs with enlarged mouth belching fire. Rama now filled his mouth with gold encrusted arrows so that he could not speak or close it. Finally he sawed off his gigantic head with an arrow, shaped like a razor. His diademed head, brilliant with lovely earrings, fell to the ground with a horrendous noise, bringing down with it some of the buildings on the causeway and even parts of the defensive wall.

Far off in Lanka, Ravana heard this horrifying sound and a shaft of pure terror shot through him. He could not imagine that his monstrous brother could have been killed. The mountainous head rolled down the hillside and dropped into the ocean in a whirlpool of blood, making the waves rise up in huge gory billows and killing the whales. It was nearing dawn and Rama stood silhouetted against the eastern sky. Kumbhakarna, the terror of the world, the sole hope of Ravana, lay dead in a lake of blood and fat on the gory battlefield strewn with heads and arms and dead monkeys and *rakshasas*.

> *You are the protector of sages and saints*
> *The destroyer of demons and the darling of Rama.*

Sri Hanuman Chalisa by Tulsidas

Aum Sri Hanumathe Namaha!

22

Lakshmana Pranadhata

Savior of Lakshmana

Tejo, dhriti, yasho, dakshyam,samarthyam,vinayo naya,
Pourusham vikramo buddhir yasminethani nityada,
Hanumansthena harena, shushubhe, vanararshabha,
Chandrashuchayagourena shwetamrena yatachala.

The dark-eyed lady [Sita] forthwith conferred that necklace
   on the son of the wind god.
In whom energy, firmness, renown, dexterity, competence,
   modesty,
Prudence, virility; prowess, and intelligence are to be found.

VALMIKI RAMAYANA, YUDDHA KANDA

The *rakshasas* ran back and reported the news to Ravana.

"O king!" they said. "Your brother, who vied with Yama, the god of death, in destroying people is now reduced to a headless and limbless mass with his trunk half-submerged in the ocean and the rest of the body blocking the main gate of Lanka!"

Ravana fainted when he heard about his beloved brother's death. When he recovered he ran to the wall and saw his brother's body and limbs blocking the gate. He sat with his head in his hands and bemoaned his loss. He couldn't believe that a mere mortal could have killed his gargantuan brother.

"This is entirely my fault. I banished Vibhishana, who was like my conscience, and now my other brother who loved me so much lies dead."

Ravana hung his head and wept. Hearing him wail like this, three of his younger sons came forward and cheered him up.

"O father! Why should you be overpowered by grief like this? The creator Brahma himself has bestowed on you an invincible coat of mail, an arrow and bow, and a chariot drawn by a thousand donkey-faced fiends. What need is there for you to fear? We will go to the battlefield today and slay your enemy for you."

All his four sons were capable of flying through the air and adept in conjuring tricks. They entered the arena, vying with each other to exhibit their prowess.

Flaunting their flaming lances they dashed into the midst of the monkeys, creating havoc. Though the princes were all valiant, one by one they were crushed to death by Angada and Hanuman. Angada killed Narantaka, Hanuman smashed Devantaka, and Trisira and Lakshmana had a gruelling battle with Atikaya and eventually killed him.

The heroes who had set out so enthusiastically in the morning now lay like felled trees on the battlefield. Ravana could not bear it. He started to wonder if there was any truth in what he had heard about Rama—that he was Narayana (Vishnu) incarnate who had taken on a human birth in order to kill him. He began to feel anxious about the safety of the city and gave orders that all precautions should be taken to avoid any infiltration by the simians.

As he sat sunk in gloom with his head in his hands, his golden boy, Indrajit, son of his favorite wife, Mandodari, now came to him and tried to cheer him up. Ravana looked into Indrajit's quiet eyes and felt a great relief.

"My beloved father!" he said, "Why should you worry when I am here to help you? Today the sun and the moon and all the gods shall witness my immeasurable powers. I will go this very minute and punish your opponents. Before the end of this day, victory will be yours!"

Ravana cheered up considerably on hearing this. He looked with loving eyes at his golden boy. His skin and hair were the color of gold and there were golden flecks in his eyes. His armor and helmet were of gold as well as his shoes and belt. He was as beautiful as his mother and Ravana was delighted to hear his promise.

"There is no one on earth who can defeat you, my son. My blessings are upon you."

Indrajit bowed low before his father and went to his enchanted garden, where he kindled a fire, poured oblations into it, and worshipped Agni, his favorite deity. Soon enough, there rose out of the fire a golden chariot drawn by four tigers. The fiery chariot was decorated with the golden faces of demons and deer. His flag was that of a lion with sapphire eyes. Indrajit wrapped himself in his invisible coat of mail, got into his chariot of illusions, and set out immediately, followed by a mighty army riding on elephants, horses, and donkeys, bristling with weapons of every type.

Vibhishana shaded his eyes and looked at the blue sky, but even he could not see Indrajit. Through the clouds, Rama and the monkeys could hear the creaking of chariot wheels and the flash of gold weapons. They could hear flag bells ringing and tigers growling, but of the warrior there was no sign.

Indrajit began raining arrows over the *vanara* host who began to fall in thousands. The whole field was strewn with dead and dying monkeys. Though all the monkey leaders did their best, they were hampered by the fact that they could not see him, since he was an expert in the art of illusory warfare. How could they fight against an invisible enemy? Through the dark clouds of illusion, they could hear the sound of his chariot and the twang of his bow. Sometimes they could see the flash of his golden armor and the streak of his golden spear, but of him they could see nothing. One by one all the great *vanara* heroes—except for Hanuman and Jambavan— fell to Indrajit's deadly arrows. A flaming ax flew through the sky and killed Sugriva. Thirty-three crescent-shaped arrows killed Angada and an iron hook crushed Nala's chest. Ten diamond-shaped arrows pierced the king of bears and a barbed spear tore Vibhishana's shoulder. Hanuman flew into the clouds. He couldn't see his opponent, but he saw a flaming sword flying toward him like lightning. He grabbed the sword, but it changed into a young woman who cried for mercy so he let it go and it changed back into a sword and cut him down to the ground. The whole field was covered with the dead and dying.

Rama stood among his dead friends and tried to aim his arrows at his unseen enemy, but it was to no avail. At last only Rama and Lakshmana were left standing. Indrajit's arrows continued to rain down on them so that no space was left on their bodies that was not covered with wounds.

Rama turned to Lakshmana and told him to be careful. Hardly had he said this than Indrajit shot a poisoned-tipped arrow at Lakshmana that pierced his shoulder. Instantly his skin turned blue and he fell down senseless. Another arrow made Rama also fall unconscious. Exulting in his day's work, Indrajit withdrew all at once to his city and filled his father's heart with delight by his report of the day's work. He then went to his grove of trees outside Lanka and got out of his chariot. It disappeared along with the tigers in a ball of flame. Indrajit remained under the banyan tree, closed his eyes, and went into *samadhi* (a super-conscious state).

With the advent of night, Vibhishana stirred. He grasped the spear in both hands and pulled it out. He was trembling with effort and pain. Slowly he drew himself up and surveyed the ground, strewn with dead monkeys. He knew that Hanuman could never be killed and scrutinized the field for him. At last he saw a blur of white. He went toward it and found Hanuman sitting up covered with sword cuts. Together they searched the field and found Jambavan, who appeared to be close to death but was still breathing. Vibhishana knelt down and gave him some water and asked him, "O King of Bears! Are you still alive?"

"I'm alive, but I can't see. Tell me, is Hanuman alive?"

Vibhishana growled in anger and retorted, "You show no regard for Rama, only for that white monkey!"

Jambavan said, "If Hanuman lives, the army lives. If he is dead, we are all dead."

The three of them now painfully walked through the field and came upon the inert forms of Rama and Lakshmana. All of them were totally bereft at this sight. After some time Rama slowly came to consciousness. However, Lakshmana still appeared inert and lifeless. Seeing this, Rama was filled with sorrow.

"If Lakshmana dies, I have no desire to live. It is possible that I might find another wife like Sita, but I will never find another brother like Lakshmana. I cannot return to Ayodhya without him. What will I tell his mother Sumitra? I too shall follow him to the abode of death. Life has no meaning for me without my beloved brother."

Vibhishana told him not to despair and said that Ravana's court physician should be brought immediately, for he had many mystic herbs and *mantras* at his command. Night had already fallen and without a word, Hanuman flew into Lanka and woke up the physician, who was fast asleep in his house. Vibhishana had already told him that even though he was a *rakshasa,* he was first and foremost a physician who was true to his vocation and would do his best to revive whoever went to him, whether friend or foe. Hanuman explained the matter to him.

Without giving him time to think over the matter, he carried him in his arms and deposited him in front of Vibhishana, who asked him to revive Lakshmana. He looked at him carefully and said, "The only thing that can help him is the miracle herb known as *mritasanjivani*. This is capable of awakening the dead. However, poison has already pervaded his entire body and unless he gets the proper treatment before sunrise, he will surely die."

Rama and the others were delighted to hear that he knew of a remedy and asked him to apply it immediately.

He said, "I'm afraid I don't have it. It can only be found on the peak called Dronagiri, which lies between Kailasa and Manasarovar, high in the Himalayas. This peak is covered with medicinal herbs and casts a matchless splendor on all sides. Right on top of that peak there are four flaming herbs illuminating all directions. *Mritasanjivani* is capable of restoring the dead to life, *vishalyakarani* is capable of healing all wounds inflicted by weapons, *suvarnakarani* restores the body to its original complexion, and the great herb called *sandhani* is capable of joining severed limbs and healing fractured bones. If someone among you can get these four, I can revive all those who have fallen here, but it has to be brought immediately, before the setting of the moon and the rising of the sun. Only then will I be able to revive them. Every minute is precious. If anyone is capable of getting it, then the prince and the others can be saved."

Hearing this, everyone looked expectantly at Hanuman, and Jambavan prompted him and said, "O son of Anjana! You are the only one who can save Lakshmana's life as well as the lives of your countless friends who have fallen today. Go immediately to that golden peak filled with medicinal herbs and bring back the four mystic herbs."

Jambavan had the great quality of reminding people of their true worth. His words led them to realize that they were capable of anything. Very few people have this ability. In fact, many try to criticize and ridicule another person's capacity and thus make him out to be less than he is! The character of the sagacious and trustworthy Jambavan is thus prized as one who can remind us of our connection with our divine selves, as opposed to one who elicits our base instincts. He reminds us that it is best to surround ourselves with those who can recall us to our highest natures.

Without losing a moment, Hanuman grew in size until they could no longer see his head. Chanting the name of Rama, he sprang to the Trikuta peak and then kicked off and went like a huge cloud toward the Himalayas. As he was traveling with the speed of lightning, he crossed the sea and traveled over Kishkinda, Dandaka, and the Vindhya Mountains to enter Aryavarta. As he flew over Kosala, the residents of Ayodhya mistook him for a flying monster. They begged Bharata to save them. He shot an arrow and forced Hanuman to descend to the ground.

"Who are you?" asked Bharata sternly. When Maruti identified himself and spoke of his mission, Bharata's eyes filled with tears. He embraced him and said, "I'm Bharata, Rama's unfortunate brother. I'm happy to get some news of him but filled with sorrow at Lakshmana's plight. I wish I could help you in some way, but I'm afraid I can't leave Ayodhya."

"If you can help me to reach Dronagiri very fast and make up for my lost time, that would be more than enough," said Hanuman.

Bharata meditated on Rama and mounted an arrow on his bow. He asked Maruti to sit on the arrowhead. Chanting a *mantra,* he shot the arrow with such speed that it ripped through the clouds and reached the foot of the mountain known as Dronagiri.

The news of Hanuman's rescue operation was brought to Ravana by his spies. He immediately called his great friend Kalanemi, who was an expert conjurer, and told him to go to the mount called Dronagiri and stop Hanuman by fair means or foul from getting the required herbs.

Kalanemi reached the mount before Hanuman. He created a hermitage and changed himself into an old ascetic and pretended to be meditating. Hanuman felt very thirsty and when he looked down, he saw the hermitage next to a lake and decided to go down and drink some water. He was surprised to see a *yogi* there and asked him politely if he could give him some water. The ascetic welcomed him and predicted that he would be successful in his attempt. He offered him water from his own water pot in which he had mixed poison. Hanuman refused the offer and asked permission to drink from the lake where he could also take a bath. The sage agreed and said he would give him a *mantra* that would enable him to recognize the herbs. Hanuman was surprised at the ascetic's knowledge of his mission and went to the lake as he was bidden. As he entered the water in pitch darkness, he found that his foot had been caught by a crocodile, which was slowly dragging him down. He realized that the creature was really big and strong. Time was running short, so he exerted all his strength and shook his leg free. He then caught the crocodile's mouth and pried it open and split it in two and threw it far off. Immediately a beautiful damsel appeared out of its body and said, "Salutations to you, O son of wind! I am actually an *apsara* from the celestial regions who had been cursed by a sage to take on the form of a crocodile. He told me that I would be released from my curse when the son of the wind god came and killed me. I am deeply grateful to you for rescuing me, but I have to warn you that you are in grave danger. That man who is posing as an ascetic is actually the great conjurer called Kalanemi who has been sent by Ravana to thwart you in your attempt to get the herbs, so please be on your guard and never accept water from his water pot." With these words the damsel disappeared.

Hanuman returned to the hut of the ascetic and bowed before him. He took the lighted lamp that was in front of him and suddenly hurled it at the man's head and dashed it to the ground and killed him. Immediately the hut and all the other things that had been an illusion created by the demon vanished, and Hanuman was left alone in the pitch darkness of the night on the mountaintop.

In the meantime, Ravana feared that Hanuman would return in time and ordered the sun to rise and the moon to set before their appointed time. Maruti was horrified to see the moon slipping rapidly toward the horizon and the first light of dawn appearing beyond the hills. He realized that this was just another plot by Ravana. He rushed to the horizon, caught the moon between his jaws and trapped the sun in his armpit!

Time was running short and without wasting another moment, Hanuman jumped to the peak called Dronagiri. As he was flying over he saw the whole peak aglow with a divine radiance. He realized that this was the place where the herbs grew, but as he came down the radiance disappeared and he couldn't find what he was looking for since the only clue he had been given by the physician was that these herbs would glow in the dark. But it seemed as if the herbs did not want to be picked and had hidden themselves. Hanuman was angry at their behavior and decided to break off the whole peak since dawn was fast approaching and his beloved Lakshmana's life was ebbing fast. There was no time to speculate. Without a moment's hesitation he grew in size until his head brushed against the sky. He then plucked the entire peak as easily as breaking off a flower from its stem and flew with it to Lanka where everyone was expectantly awaiting his arrival. All the gods, birds, beasts, reptiles, and fish that saw Hanuman flying across Jambudwipa and crossing the sea to Lanka with the hill in his hand were wonderstruck by this spectacular sight.

He circled the battlefield like a huge eagle and slowly started to come down. Such was the potency of the herbs that when the heady perfume of the *mritasanjivani* penetrated Lakshmana's nostrils, he stirred and turned round as if from sleep. All the other monkeys also recovered. Hanuman was still circling round the field, not knowing where to land and place his precious burden. The royal physician Sushena told him where to keep it. He scoured the slopes of the hill and found the life-giving herbs.

"Now all I need is the divine pestle and mortar that Ravana keeps in his inner chambers," he said.

Hanuman immediately made his way into Ravana's apartments. However Ravana had foreseen Sushena's need for a pestle and had hidden it next to his bedside table, determined not to let it out of his sight. Maruti noticed that Mandodari was sleeping soundly next to the king and thought of a plan to distract Ravana. He slipped under his bed and tied Ravana's hair to the bedpost. He then grabbed the pestle and mortar and ran toward the door. Ravana woke up in an instant and tried to run after Hanuman but was yanked back to his bed by his hair. He tried to untie the knot but failed because Hanuman had cast a spell. The knot would not be undone until Mandodari had kicked Ravana on the head with her foot!

Hanuman chuckled as he watched the mighty king of the *rakshasas* shaking his wife awake. He bowed his crowned head before her and begged her to kick him. Hanuman had a hearty laugh and then sped back to Sushena and gave him the pestle and mortar.

Sushena immediately made a paste of the magic herbs and smeared it all over Lakshmana's body. The juice seeped through his skin and entered his bloodstream and counteracted Indrajit's poison. He woke up as if from a long sleep and jumped to his feet, looking more radiant than ever.

Suddenly Rama noticed that neither the sun nor the moon could be seen in the sky.

"What happened to these celestial orbs?" he questioned.

Hanuman looked a bit sheepish and opened his mouth to let out the moon and released the sun from his armpit. As the sun and moon returned to their celestial orbits, Rama and Lakshmana embraced Hanuman. They were totally bereft of words and did not know how to express their gratitude.

Jambavan then told Maruti to take the mountain back to its original position since, if it was kept on the battlefield, the *rakshasas* would also make use of it. So Hanuman once again returned to the Himalayas. He put the mountain back in its place and came back before dawn broke over the ocean. Actually, this whole episode was known only to Rama, Vibhishana, Jambavan, Hanuman, and the physician who was taken back to his home in Lanka.

Rama was so happy that he hugged Hanuman close. He blessed him and said, "Without you there will be neither Rama, nor Sita, nor the Ramayana. May you be blessed and live forever!"

One might wonder how it was that none of the fallen *rakshasas* revived. This was because Ravana had commanded that all the dead in the demon army should be thrown into the sea so that no one could count their number and thus taint his reputation.

The monkeys were jubilant at their recovery. That whole day none of the *rakshasas* appeared for a fight since Ravana was sure that their leaders were lying dead. By nightfall the monkeys were determined to stake their claim as victors. Urged by Sugriva, the whole hoard pushed their way into the fortress, carrying flaming brands and torches, and started on their journey of destruction. Once again Lanka went up in flames as the excited monkeys jumped from house to house and palace to palace, setting fire to everything. Ravana was woken up by the wailing of the citizens and the acrid smell of smoke. He could not believe that the monkeys were carrying on the war without Rama. Surely his cousin Kalanemi must have stopped Hanuman from bringing the famous herb, so what made the monkeys rejoice and how could they dare to come within the walls of Lanka without their master? His ministers came and gave him the happy news that Rama and Lakshmana were very much alive and all of them were ready to fight. When he heard this, he immediately summoned Kumbhakarna's sons, Kumbha and Nikumbha, and asked them to go and avenge the death of their father.

The night stalkers issued forth once again, determined to slay their father's killer. They were both powerful warriors, and the *vanara* host started falling like autumn leaves. Three of their leaders, including Angada, had fallen in a faint. Hearing this, Sugriva went to the front and accosted Kumbha. "I am full of admiration for the way in which you handle your weapons. I see in you a combination of your father and uncle—the solidity of one with the dexterity of the other. I don't feel like killing you since you are surely a jewel among your race, but I have no option, since we are on opposite sides, so let us fight to the finish."

Though Kumbha was pleased by Sugriva's praise, he didn't like the insinuation that he was superior to himself. He rushed at him with a bellow and the two of them started wrestling with each other until the earth shook and the leaves fell off the trees. At last with a powerful blow, Sugriva felled him to the ground and killed him.

Seeing the death of his valiant brother, Nikumbha rushed at the monkeys and slew them by the hundreds. Seeing their plight, Hanuman came to their rescue and punched him forcibly on his chest. Nikumbha flung a huge iron pestle at Hanuman. Everyone expected him to fall, but to their astonishment the pestle shattered into a million fragments on his adamantine chest. Hanuman now rushed at Nikumbha and after grappling with him for a while, he threw him on the ground and sat on his chest until he suffocated to death. The *vanaras* set up a roar of jubilation.

When he heard the news, Ravana was at a loss to know what he should do. He couldn't believe that the enormous strength and modern weapons of his army counted for nothing in the face of these long-tailed tree folk, armed with only sticks and stones. Not one of them was capable of wielding a sword or using a bow and yet they seemed to be gaining the upper hand.

At last he went to his beloved son Meghanatha and exhorted him once again to go and try his hand at killing the two brothers.

Indrajit said, "O Father! For your sake I killed him once, but it appears as if the whole of Nature is supporting him or else how could he be still alive? Remember, father, that in your youth, you ruled the world supported by *dharma*, but now you rule through *adharma* alone. The very gods tremble at the mention of your name and the curses of the saints whom you have killed have taken on the form of this battle that will be the end of you. You have made the whole of creation suffer through your inequities. It is the collection of your wrongs that is devouring us. The fear and anger of the helpless has taken on the form of this army of animals. The day you abducted Sita, you took death on your lap. *Dharma* is on the side of Rama. *Dharma* alone rules this world. Those who go against it will have to perish at some time or other. However, I am your son and will do your bidding. I shall kill the Kosala brothers as I promised to do."

Ravana said, "You are my beloved son who once conquered the gods. Now fight for me on Earth as you fought in Heaven."

> *You brought the nectarine herb and revived the life*
> *of Lakshmana.*
> *Rama embraced you with deep joy.*
>
> SRI HANUMAN CHALISA BY TULSIDAS

Aum Sri Hanumathe Namaha!

Aum Raudraaya Namaha!

23

Kapindra

The End of Indrajit

Lakshmana samare veera sasajendrajitam prati,
Aindrastrena smayuchya Lakshmana paraviraha.

Drawing up to his ear that arrow charged with the mantra
   of Indra,
The heroic and glorious Lakahmana let it fly at Indrajit.

VALMIKI RAMAYANA, YUDDHA KANDA

Indrajit now thought of an ingenious plan to dupe Rama. Using his magical powers, he made an identical living image of Sita and placed it in his chariot and drove to the battlefield surrounded by his army. The monkeys rallied around and forged forward to meet him. They were led by Hanuman, who was carrying a huge boulder. Suddenly he stopped short, for he recognized the pitiable and miserable figure of the princess of Videha. She was wearing the same soiled yellow garment that she had on when he saw her last, but it could not dim the radiance of her ethereal beauty. She was sitting forlorn and unhappy as if she did not care what was happening to her. Hanuman could not tear his gaze away from her grief-stricken face. He had no idea why Indrajit had brought her in his chariot to the battlefield. He did not dare to attack Indrajit in case he did some harm to her. Seeing him, Indrajit grabbed hold of Sita's long braid and started to berate her with his sword. She called out loudly, "Rama, Rama," and burst into heartrending sobs.

Tears of blood dropped from Hanuman's eyes to see the princess of Videha being treated so cruelly. "O ruthless one! What has the princess of Mithila done to you that you should treat her so cruelly? Such an act is not worthy of even a barbarian and you claim to be the grandson of the sage Vishravas!"

Indrajit laughed scornfully when he heard this tirade and drove toward Rama. He shouted to him to watch carefully while he made an end of the woman who was the prime cause of the destruction of the *rakshasas* and who was the cause of his father's infatuation. Taking hold of her hair, he lifted her up and decapitated her. He gave a gruesome laugh and said, "Behold, O Rama! Your darling wife has been killed by me. Vain is your exertion now to get her back. The war is over. Go back to your country!" Seeing this gruesome scene Rama totally lost all will to live. He collapsed on the ground and bewailed the loss of his beloved wife.

Hanuman could not bear to see this. Taking up an enormous boulder, he rushed at Indrajit, followed by all the monkeys. There followed a sharp and furious encounter in which Indrajit disappeared from the field. Hanuman immediately realized that this whole thing was a trick of Indrajit's to subdue Rama. He immediately took the form of a bee and went to the *ashoka* grove, where Sita was sitting with her head in her hands, and convinced himself that she was indeed alive. He instantly returned to Rama and gave him the happy news.

As he was saying this, Vibhishana came forward and wanted to know what the commotion was about and why Rama looked so sad. When he heard the story, he laughed and said, "How can you possibly believe such a thing? Don't you know the extent of Ravana's infatuation for Sita? He is prepared to sacrifice his country, his sons, and his people for her sake. How can you believe even for a moment that his son would dare to kill a woman who is so dear to his father? This whole thing was planned by Indrajit, the master magician. He enacted this drama so that he could go and complete his *yaga,* which will make him invincible. If he is allowed to finish this ritual, there will be no holding him back. No one will be able to kill him. There is not a moment to be lost. Let Lakshmana come with me, and I'll take him to the spot where that misguided son of my brother is conducting his *yaga.* Brahma has told him that by performing this sacrifice he will become invisible and invulnerable. That is why he thought of this master plan to delude you into believing that Sita was dead!"

Rama immediately told Lakshmana to go with Vibhishana and intercept the *yaga.* He armed himself and took Rama's blessings before leaving. He was accompanied by Vibhishana, Hanuman, and a host of other monkeys.

Vibhishana told Lakshmana that he would repeat some *mantras* by which the invisible grove would become visible. Suddenly the whole mountainside became dark as if it were shielded by some huge black umbrella. In and through this gloom, Lakshmana saw a grove of ancient, gnarled trees, plunged in darkness and shadow. Vibhishana proceeded toward this sacred grove where Indrajit was conducting his black magic rituals in order to invoke the great cosmic powers. His army was stationed between his hideout and the approaching army of monkeys. Hanuman immediately sprang to the forefront, confronted the enemy host, and engaged them in a fierce combat while Vibhishana took Lakshmana to the secret grove that none but the *rakshasas* could see. "The god of fire will give him a magic chariot yoked to tigers, which will make him invulnerable. Hurry! We have to disrupt this ritual."

Vibhishana touched Lakshmana, who was then able to see Indrajit kneeling before an altar in the grove, invoking the aid of his favorite god. He was pouring ghee into the fire with a double ladle of black iron and muttering incantations. His back was turned to them. The black sacrificial goat was tied to a stake and was bleating piteously. Wearing a crimson robe with his hair all disheveled, Indrajit beat the earth with his javelin, and out came thousands of serpents that coiled themselves round his arrows, which were piled near the altar. His ax fell with deadly accuracy on the neck of the goat and severed it neatly so that it fell in a pool of blood. He held the ladle filled with goat's blood above his head, ready for the final invocation. As the flames leaped higher and higher, the tawny figures of the tigers could be seen snarling and growling, waiting for their cue to leap out of the flames, drawing the invincible chariot. Vibhishana nudged Lakshmana, who sent an arrow straight at the upraised ladle and split it in two just as it was descending for the final offering.

His arrow screamed like an eagle, which was the deadly enemy of snakes, and the Nagas hissed and slithered back to the netherworld from which they had come. Agni the Lord of Fire rose from the sacred *kund* (pool) and seven tongues of flame shot out of his mouth. His eyes roved round the scene and he gave a secret smile. His form faded from the altar and the fire sank back into the hearth. There were no signs of either tigers or chariot.

Indrajit swirled round with a terrible imprecation and snarled at Vibhishana. "You traitor! You have betrayed me. You call yourself my uncle yet you have disclosed all my secrets to the enemy. Without you, he would never have found out this place. You have eaten the salt of my father's table and yet you have defected to the enemy's side! You are a disgrace to our race! It's better to be a slave in one's own country than a Lord in the enemy's side by licking his boots. One who abandons his own people and adopts the ways of his enemy is a traitor, and I should kill you first before killing Lakshmana! May your new friends forsake you when your old ones have died!"

Vibhishana retorted, "You are the wicked son of my wicked brother, and I will have nothing to do with either of you. All these years my brother has reveled in sinful acts. His anger and arrogance are proverbial. All these years I have borne up with it because I was helpless. Though I was born in the clan of the *rakshasas,* my instincts were always those of a human being. If I have abandoned you all now, it is because I am fed up of living a life of unrighteousness and wish to take up a noble path. You are a foolish, impulsive boy, bursting with pride, but beware! Both you and your father are doomed and so is this fabulous city of Lanka!"

By now Jambavan and his army of bears had joined Hanuman, and they began to harass Indrajit's army. The commotion was so great that he was forced to put an end to his verbal combat with his uncle and come out through the secret tunnel into the open forest. The demon prince was furious at having to end his ritual. He came out looking like the god of death. He was wearing silver armor and carried a silver sword. Light glinted from his sliver helmet and silver bow. A quiver of silver arrows and a silver dagger hung at his side. He climbed on his huge chariot, which was most artistically decorated and drawn by silver white horses. His hair was flowing behind him and his huge bow was kept taut and ready. He saw Lakshmana, who was seated on Hanuman's shoulder facing him with his own bow drawn and ready. Indrajit hurled insults at him and swore to make an end of him before the day was over.

Lakshmana replied scornfully, "O son of Ravana! Make good your boast in a noble fashion. So far you have fought a secret battle, remaining invisible all the time. This is the way adopted by thieves and cowards and not heroes! Make good your boasts now in the open when I'm facing you, and let us see who is stronger."

Indrajit said, "Today you shall see my power. All I ask is for a single combat!"

"So be it," said Lakshmana.

Indrajit immediately let fly his arrows at Lakshmana. The deadly arrows went and buried themselves on Lakshmana's body, making him bleed profusely.

"O son of Sumitra! Today jackals and vultures will have a grand feast. So prepare for the end."

"Give up your empty words and enforce it with action, O devourer of human flesh!"

With these words both of them started shooting long, painful arrows tipped with golden feathers at each other, each more deadly than the other. Indrajit jumped out of his chariot and shot one thousand arrows at Lakshmana, who cut them down as they flew at him. He then shot seven arrows and slit Indrajit's silver armor so that his coat of mail fell down like a cluster of stars. Both warriors were well matched and so swift were their hands that none could see them take an arrow or draw their bows. Arrows flew so rapidly that the sky became dark. Indrajit seized a poisoned javelin and hurled it at Lakshmana, who cut it down before it reached him. The silver boy now raised his bow again. Swift as a thought, Lakshmana cut it down before the arrow was shot. Ravana's son then threw a demon dart that separated into splinters and pierced Lakshmana all over his body. However, Indrajit was not capable of an open combat like this. He had always fought invisibly and soon he showed signs of flagging under Lakshmana's determined onslaught. Vibhishana advised Lakshmana to press forward since the mighty warrior appeared to be losing ground.

Lakshmana charged forward, but Indrajit rallied himself and taunted him.

"Have you forgotten our last encounter when I made you and your brother lie flat on the ground? This time I will not let you go as easily but will despatch you fast to Yama's city!"

With these words he discharged seven shafts at Lakshmana and ten at Hanuman. Then he turned toward his uncle and let fly a hundred arrows at him. Thus they started another formidable battle that went on for hours, with others looking on in amazement. Vibhishana now incited the other monkey chiefs not to lose time watching but to try and drive off Indrajit's army.

The two protagonists were set for a fight to the finish. Their brilliant arrows, charged with incantations, flew across the sky like meteors and collided in mid-air with earth-shattering explosions, each negating the other. Beasts and birds flew hither and thither and the very air seemed to hold its breath in fear. Lakshmana sent four silver-tipped arrows that instantly felled the four beautiful caparisoned white horses. As the chariot started to swerve violently, another crescent-shaped arrow neatly severed the charioteer's head from his shoulders. For a second Indrajit faltered but undaunted, he took up his bow again and shot thousands of arrows at Lakshmana's forces. The monkeys quickly took shelter behind Lakshmana. Under cover of the darkness, Indrajit went back to the city and returned with another chariot. Lakshmana was wonderstruck at the swiftness with which he returned. Within minutes Lakshmana smashed this chariot also. Lifting his javelin high above his head, the night stalker whirled it round and round so that the blade seemed to become a blazing wheel. Lakshmana did not wait for him to release it but shattered it with a hundred arrows. Night was falling fast and Vibhishana advised Lakshmana to put an end to Indrajit since he would grow stronger with the advent of darkness.

At last Lakshmana took out the arrow given to him by the sage Agastya, which was charged with the power of Indra, and prayed to the weapon. "If it be true that Rama, the son of Dasaratha, has never swerved from the path of *dharma,* if it is true that he has ever been truthful, has ever been loyal, and is absolutely unrivalled, then let this arrow kill Indrajit, the son of Ravana!"

So saying, he let fly the *mantra*-charged arrow at Indrajit. It flew like a streak of lightning straight to its target and before he could counter it with one of his own, it neatly severed his handsome head so that it fell on the ground, looking like a silver lotus. Like the bright sun setting behind the hills lay the head of Mandodari's glorious son. The vanquisher of Indra was killed with the missile of Indra himself. For a moment his body seemed to stand against the light. Then it fell with a thud. In death his corpse reverted to its original *rakshasic* form. There was nothing beautiful about it. His face was set in a snarl with long protruding fangs. The gods rejoiced at his death, for he had been a terrible scourge to them. The *vanara* army set up a roar of victory that could be heard by both Rama and Ravana. The *rakshasa* army fled in dismay, leaving their weapons behind.

Monkeys and bears hugged each other. Vibhishana, Hanuman, and Jambavan returned to Rama and gave him the news of the glorious combat that had ended in the death of the famous son of Ravana. Rama hugged his brother and praised him for his amazing feat. He immediately ordered the physician to come and administer to his numerous wounds.

Indrajit's body was covered and carried to the king's palace, but no one dared to tell Ravana. At last his minister Suka went to him and said, "Your son has been killed by Lakshmana."

Ravana sank to the floor in a swoon. Then he roused himself and weeping, said, "My son! My beloved son! There was no one like you in the whole world. You could defeat every enemy you encountered, yet you have been killed by that puny human being. How is it possible? Without you, this entire earth seems to be an empty place. Life has lost its charm for me. Where have you gone, leaving me and your mother and your beloved wife?"

Indrajit's wife was called Sulochana. She was the daughter of the celestial snake known as Ananta, on whom Vishnu reclines. As we know, Rama was the *avatara* of Vishnu and Lakshmana of Ananta. So when she came to know that her beloved husband had been killed by the *avatara* of her father, Sulochana was grief-stricken. She rushed to Ravana's assembly hall and accused him of having caused the death of her husband. Ravana was still in a state of shock. He refused to believe that his invincible son had died and continued to talk to the corpse as if it were alive. Indrajit, who had once captured Indra and brought him in chains to his father, now lay dead, killed by an arrow that had been charged with the might of Indra himself.

Indrajit's mother, Mandodari, and his wife, Sulochana, threw themselves over the body and started weeping. When the time came to cremate his body, Sulochana threw herself on the blazing pyre like a chaste wife and immolated herself.

As an aside, it should be noted that the practice of self-immolation is an ancient one. Followed by various cultures on several continents, it was not universal throughout India's history. Lauded in symbolic terms only, the practice has long been banned in India.

Ravana, in the meantime, started ranting and raving. He forgot that he was the sole cause for the destruction of all his sons. His sorrow turned to anger, as it normally did with him, and he decided to kill Sita in truth and not as a trick, for she was the cause of it all. He forgot that he had no one to blame but himself. It was his cruel and unjust act that had brought calamity on his whole race as prophesized by Vibhishana. Tears like liquid fire rolled down his cheeks. Picking up his sword, he rushed out of the *ashoka* grove determined to kill Sita, who was still devoted to Rama. His ministers and wives rushed after him. They had seen him angry before but that was nothing compared to what they saw now. Like a malefic comet approaching Venus, he flew at Sita with upraised sword. She saw him coming and realized that this time he was not approaching with words of love but with the sword of hate, and that he meant to kill her as easily as he had professed to love her. How easily swayed are the minds of the wicked! One day, they profess to love and the next day they begin to hate. Sita was ready to die since she was convinced that Rama had died. Luckily for her, one of Ravana's ministers, who was saner than the rest, approached him and said, "My Lord! How can you contemplate such a sinful deed!? It was bad enough that you abducted her. How can you think of killing her now when she is helpless and at your mercy? Leave this poor, defenseless woman alone and turn your fury against the one who killed your son. Today is the fourteenth day of the dark lunar fortnight. Tomorrow is the night of the new moon, the most auspicious night for night rangers like us. That is the time for you to march against Rama, and after having killed both of them, you can return victoriously and claim Sita as your own!"

Luckily for Sita, Ravana seemed to find this advice palatable. He checked his stride and stood for a moment lost in thought. Then without another word to anyone, he turned round and marched back to his assembly hall.

> *May Sheshnag, the thousand-headed divine*
> *serpent, sing your praises.*
> *Saying thus, the Lord of Lakshmi embraced you!*

SRI HANUMAN CHALISA BY TULSIDAS

Aum Sri Hanumathe Namaha!

24

Mahabala

Journey to Patala

Think of Vaidehi as your mother and Rama as your father,
Where Rama dwells there is Ayodhya,
As wherever there is the light of the sun, there is day.

SUMITRA TO LAKSHMANA IN THE
RAMACHARITAMANAS OF TULSIDAS

Ravana was totally demoralized by his favorite son's death. He was at a loss to know what to do. Then he suddenly remembered his other sons, Mahiravana and Ahiravana, who were ruling in Patala, the lowest of all the seven worlds. They were born to Mandodari but their serpentine appearance was so terrible that it frightened even Ravana, so he cast them into the ocean. There they were adopted by the snake demoness Simhika and taken to the serpent world. They performed intense *tapas* to Mahakaali and acquired supernatural powers. She also gave them the boon that one day their father Ravana, who had insulted and abandoned them, would call on them for help. They had married the daughters of the king of Patala and become kings in turn. Ravana suddenly thought of them. He went to Patala, the netherworld, and asked them to help him. They both said, "Don't underestimate your enemy. He is Vishnu incarnate. It would be better for you to make truce with him."

The brothers were great devotees of the goddess Kaali, and Ravana slyly told them that they were missing a golden opportunity to please the goddess by offering the heads of the two handsome and virile princes!

"Think of the powers she will grant you if you make this sacrifice," he said.

Hearing this, they decided to help their father.

In the meantime, the ever-watchful Vibhishana heard of Ravana's visit to Patala. He called Hanuman and told him to be on his guard, for these two night wanderers were great practitioners of black magic and sorcery and were capable of taking on many forms in order to fool people. Hanuman told him to have no fears and he would see to it that no danger came to Rama and Lakshmana. Hanuman lengthened his tail to enormous proportions and wound it round and round the camp so that the site became a fortress, and he sat in front so that no one could enter without his permission. The sorcerers came there and didn't know how to get in and kidnap the brothers. They cast a spell by which all the monkeys who were guarding the fortress went to sleep.

However, Hanuman remained awake, and they still did not know how to get in as he remained guarding the entrance. Then they thought of a brilliant idea. Mahiravana disguised himself as Vibhishana. He went to Hanuman and told him to lift his tail a little and let him in. Naturally, Hanuman wanted to know where Vibhishana had gone at that time of night. He was under the impression that he was inside. The false Vibhishana said that he had gone to the seashore for his ablutions. Hanuman thought it a bit strange that Vibhishana wanted to take a bath at that time of night; however, he allowed him to go in. Mahiravana went to the place where Rama and Lakshmana were sleeping and threw a spell over the whole camp so that everyone fell unconscious. His brother had slipped in invisibly when Hanuman lifted his tail. So the two of them easily lifted the brothers on their shoulders. They made a tunnel to the netherworld and transported them to Patala.

When the monkeys roused themselves from the spell, they discovered that Rama and Lakshmana were missing. There was uproar in the camp, and they ran to give this news to Hanuman.

"Did any stranger enter the fortress made by your tail in the night?" asked Sugriva.

"Only Vibhishana came at night," said Hanuman.

Hearing this, Vibhishana came forward and exclaimed, "I certainly did not go out of the fortress at night. I was inside the camp all the time. It must have been the Ahi-Mahiravanas about whom I warned you. They must have taken the princes to Patala. You are the only one who can get them back, O Hanuman! Don't delay. Go immediately."

"Fear not. Wherever he might have hidden them, I will discover their whereabouts and bring them back," said Hanuman.

Just then they saw the tunnel that the Ahi-Mahiravanas had made. Hanuman jumped into it without a second thought. The tunnel ended in a forest. There he heard a conversation between two birds. The female bird was sulking and the male was trying to cajole her with these words: "My Dearest! Please don't be angry with me. Tomorrow night Ahiravana and Mahiravana will be making a human sacrifice of two brothers in their Kaali temple in Patala. After it is over, I promise to bring some tasty morsels of human flesh for you."

Hearing this, Hanuman immediately concluded that the two brothers were incarcerated in Ahi-Mahiravanas' dungeon. With the proverbial speed of wind, he reached the netherworld known as Patala, which was the residence of the *asuras*. There he saw a huge fortress. He was wondering how to enter. He decided to make himself tiny so that he could squeeze in through some small door. Just then some ladies came outside and he heard them talk about the two handsome humans who had been brought there to be given as a sacrifice to Kaali. Hanuman was determined to find out where his Lord had been incarcerated.

As he went around the fortress, he suddenly found a door guarded by a handsome young monkey. He went to him and asked him to allow him to enter.

"Who are you, and why have you come here?" asked the young monkey.

"I have come to rescue my master Lord Rama and his brother, who have been stolen by your masters, the Ahi-Mahiravanas."

"You'll have to fight with me before you can enter. But beware, I am Makaradwaja, son of Hanuman, and you won't find it easy to beat me!"

Hanuman burst out laughing when he heard this. "What a stupid monkey you are to tell such stories. I am Hanuman, and I am an eternal celibate. I have neither wife nor child."

When he heard this, the young monkey threw himself at Hanuman's feet and asked him to bless him. "Blessed is my life, now that I have seen you," he said.

Hanuman shook him off and said, "You must be a *rakshasa* kept by Ahiravana in order to hinder me. Now stand up and tell me where they have been hidden. If not, I'll kill you."

Makaradwaja begged him to listen to the story of his birth, which had been told to him by the sage Narada.

"At that time when you were returning through the air after having found Sita, a drop of your perspiration fell into the sea and was swallowed by a crocodile that became pregnant with your seed. The crocodile was caught in a fish net and brought to the court of my masters. They cut open its stomach and I came out of it. They decided to adopt me and made me the guardian of their gate. That is why my name is Makaradwaja [part crocodile, part monkey]."

"This is certainly a wondrous tale," Hanuman said. "I suppose if this was told to you by the celestial sage Narada, it must be true. I am indeed very happy to meet you, but I have no time to lose, so tell me where your master has kept the two princes. Did you know that he has captured Rama and Lakshmana and brought them here?"

"I didn't know who they were, but I know that he brought two hermits who were unconscious and has kept them under custody to be taken to the temple. They will be offered as sacrifices to Kaali tomorrow morning."

"I must rescue them immediately," said Hanuman.

"Father, forgive me, but if you want to enter the fortress, you will have to fight me and tie me up so that my master will not suspect me of having betrayed him. I am as loyal to my master as you are to yours," said the monkey fearlessly.

Then followed a fight between father and son in which Hanuman defeated Makaradwaja and tied him up before proceeding to the temple where Rama and Lakshmana were to be sacrificed. The boy told him that before he could kill his masters, he would have to put out five lamps that were placed in five different directions in the temple. Apparently their life force was kept in these lamps, and they could never be killed just by cutting off their heads.

Hanuman thanked him and took the form of a bee, getting into the fortress through the keyhole. He then went to the Kaali temple and hid himself in a small monkey form that was inside the idol of Kaali.

The temple was slowly starting to fill with people coming with different types of offerings to the goddess. The brothers now came with the two unconscious princes and threw them at Kaali's feet. They were slowly starting to recover from their swoon. The demons beseeched the goddess to accept this final offering of two humans so that she would be pleased to grant all their wishes. Hanuman was furious when he saw this and started eating all the things that were kept in front of the idol, much to the astonishment of all those present.

"She must like us very much," they thought. "We've never seen her eat all these sweets before." They ordered more sweets to be brought, all of which were consumed by Hanuman as fast as they were brought.

The two demons then said in pious tones, "Now we will offer you the blood of these two humans." So saying, one demon grabbed Rama by his topknot and the other grabbed Lakshmana. They prepared to chop off their heads. At that moment Hanuman, pretending to be the goddess, spoke from inside the idol.

"Leave everything here and go out. Let the temple be cleared of all people. I will eat these humans by myself."

The brothers were amazed at Kaali's words. But they immediately cleared the temple and went out, closing the door.

Hanuman directly came out of the idol and bowed to Rama and Lakshmana, who had almost recovered from their swoon. Very soon they became fully conscious. They were astonished to see where they were. Hanuman bowed low to Rama and told him the whole story briefly, since time was passing and the monkeys would be awaiting his return anxiously.

As he came out of the door of the temple, the brothers who were waiting saw him and realized that they had been neatly tricked. They pounced on him. Hanuman kept the two princes down and started to fight with the demon brothers. But however much he tried, he could not put them down. Rama and Lakshmana now came forward, for they had fully recovered, and started to help Hanuman. But the brothers seemed invincible. With every blow they appeared to grow stronger. They laughed in scorn to see the bewildered look on Hanuman's face. Then suddenly he remembered his son's words. He told Rama and Lakshmana to keep them at bay and ran back to the temple. He looked around and saw the five lamps as described by Makaradwaja. He immediately assumed his *panchamukha* (five-faced) form and put out all five lamps simultaneously. Of these five faces, there were the three incarnations of Vishnu—Varaha (boar), Narasimha (half-man, half-lion), and Hayagriva (horse-faced). The fourth face was that of Garuda, Vishnu's eagle vehicle, and the fifth was his own face. Having extinguished these five lamps simultaneously, he ran out and killed Ahiravana and his brother easily. He also killed all the other demons who tried to stop him.

Another story about the invulnerability of the brothers is described in a different way. Every time Rama, Lakshmana, and Hanuman killed the brothers, they revived and start fighting again. Hanuman was puzzled and flew to the city, determined to discover the reason for their apparent immortality. He found the Naga princess who was Mahiravana's queen, and she promised to tell him the secret of his invincibility on condition that Rama agree to marry her. Hanuman agreed but placed a counter-condition—that Rama would be relieved of this obligation if the cot on which they sat were to collapse beneath him. The princess then revealed the secret of her husband's immortality. She told him that he owed his existence to seven large bees that were kept in a hive thirty leagues away and that produced nectar that kept the two demons alive. Hanuman flew to the spot and killed six of the bees. He spared the seventh on condition that it go to the princess's room and hollow out the leg of her bedstead. He then returned to help Rama and Lakshmana and killed the demons in no time. Hanuman told Rama the whole secret. Rama went to the princess's room, but just as he sat down on her bed, the frame gave way. He then blessed her to become his wife in another age—the Dwapara Yuga.

Hanuman now took Rama and Lakshmana on his shoulders and started to fly back. When they passed the bound figure of Makaradwaja, Rama asked him who it was. Hanuman said that he was a monkey who professed to be his son. Rama insisted on going down and freeing him. He also anointed him as king of Patala and told him to reign according to the law of righteousness so that the Vedic *dharma* that the demons had destroyed would once again be established.

Makaradwaja fell at Rama's feet and at his father's feet and got their blessings.

Hanuman now returned to Lanka with Rama and Lakshmana and revived the hopes of the monkeys, who had been waiting anxiously for their return.

> *O Hero! Ghosts and demons can never come*
> *near one*
> *Who utters your name!*

SRI HANUMAN CHALISA by TULSIDAS

Aum Sri Hanumathe Namaha!

25

Rudrasya-Soonu

Fight to the Finish

Sa tena shylena brisham raraja shylopamo
gandavahatmajasthu,
Sahasradharena sa pavakena chakrena khe
vishnurivarpitena.

Coursing through the air with the peak,
The son of the wind god, who resembled a mountain,
Looked like Lord Vishnu carrying his flaming discus with a
thousand edges.

VALMIKI RAMAYANA, YUDDHA KANDA

Ravana was rejoicing in the thought that the Kosala brothers must now have been given as a sacrifice to Kaali by his sons when he heard the commotion outside the fortress. He climbed up the battlements to see what was happening and saw Rama and Lakshmana being feted in the midst of the *vanaras*. He just couldn't believe this. One by one, fate was depriving him of all his friends and hopes. But he revived himself and decided to send the last of his generals to the battlefield. The next day he sent his crack regiment of carefully chosen men, famed for their valor, to the battlefield. With them went his remaining commanders—Mahodara, Mahaparswa, and Virupaksha. They were all thought to be invincible warriors.

Armed with all the best weapons of their time, the ill-fated army gathered at the western gate at break of day. Their fires threw off dark smoke. Carrion birds hovered over the sky and jackals barked and howled. Clouds of ash floated over the city of Lanka. Outside the golden walls there was an explosion as Indrajit's enchanted grove went up in flames. The west gate opened, and the drawbridge dropped with a thunderous sound. The sentinels on the walls beheld the bears and apes were watching them, but the *rakshasas* were not afraid and drew out their swords with a grating noise. The two armies met with a terrible clash, and blood flowed like a river. Now Rama told the monkeys to stand aside and tackled them single-handed, as he had fought the army at Janasthana. The army could hardly be seen due to the shower of arrows that engulfed them. Then Rama took up the weapon called the *gandharva* and created a kind of illusion by which many hundreds of Ramas could be seen on all sides. Within an hour he had totally reduced Ravana's crack regiment to nothing.

In the meantime, Ravana's three wonderful commanders were having a hand-to-hand battle with Sugriva and Angada. After some hard fighting, Virupaksha and Mahodara were killed by Sugriva and Mahaparswa was killed by Angada.

There was a loud wail in the whole of Lanka, set up by the wives of the deceased. They blamed Ravana's sister Shurpanekha for being the sole cause of all their troubles, as it was she who had convinced her brother to kidnap Sita. Every house in Lanka was sunk in sorrow. Those houses, from which at one time only the sound of music and revelry were heard, now reverberated with the shuddering sounds of moans and sobs.

Ravana was filled with gloom and foreboding when he heard this news. He consulted the court astrologers who studied his horoscope and decreed that the alignment of celestial bodies was not in his favor. As mentioned, Indian astrology is governed by nine planets known as the *navagrahas*. Ravana thought that by changing the alignment of these heavenly bodies, he would be able to alter his destiny. Mounting his flying chariot, he rose to the skies, captured the nine planets, herded them to his capital, and bound them in chains. He then began a series of rituals that, if successful, would force the planets to realign themselves in his favor.

Vibhishana, who was always alert, saw the fumes rising out of the *yajnashala* (place of sacrifice) where the *yaga* was being conducted and warned Hanuman to try to stop it. He led Hanuman and a band of monkeys through a secret passage to Ravana's sacrificial hall. They found the ten-headed one sitting beside the altar with eyes shut, mouthing *mantras*. The monkeys let out a piercing war cry and rushed into the hall, creating havoc. They stamped out the ceremonial fire, kicked the utensils around, and wiped out the occult diagrams drawn on the ground. Ravana was in deep meditation and remained unperturbed by all this commotion.

"We must stop him at all costs," said Vibhishana, "or else he will succeed in changing the course of his destiny."

Hanuman now came up with a plan. He told the monkeys to go into the inner apartments and frighten Ravana's wives. Undeterred, the monkeys attacked his queens and concubines, pulling their hair, scratching their faces, and tearing their clothes.

They ran to the *yajnashala,* crying to Ravana to help them. Still, Ravana did not open his eyes. The monkeys now gathered around Mandodari. They bared their teeth, beat their chests, and growled menacingly. Hearing her pitiful cries, Ravana opened his eyes and rushed to her defense. With Ravana out of the way, Hanuman ran to the sacrificial hall and liberated the nine planets that had been held captive. For having successfully aborted Ravana's attempts to subvert fate, Hanuman won the eternal gratitude of the planets (*grihas*). Because of this, Hanuman is believed to exercise considerable power over them. He is worshipped by those whose planets are placed in unfavorable positions.

On the eve of his death, the desperate Ravana made one final attempt to gain victory. He went to his *guru* and asked him to prescribe some means by which he would be victorious in the battle that would follow on the night of the new moon. The *guru* advised him to perform another *yaga* to the goddess Kaali, which would make him invincible, but he warned him not to antagonize her for she was capable of saving anyone who prayed to her. He assembled a large number of Brahmins who had been kept as prisoners and who were deeply learned in all forms of *tantric* rituals. He commanded them to invoke the most violent form of the goddess as Kaali. If she were on his side, victory was assured. The Brahmins were to recite a certain hymn to the goddess a thousand times, bracketing each recitation with an appropriate offering in the fire, followed by a request to the goddess expressing Ravana's desire.

Vibhishana learned of this scheme and informed Hanuman, who instantly took the form of a Brahmin and went to help the others who were preparing various things for the ritual. The Brahmins were impressed by him, since they didn't normally get this type of service from the inhabitants of Lanka. In return for his services, they offered him a boon. Hanuman pretended to be dismayed and professed that he wanted nothing except to serve them. But they were insistent that he be given something for his devotion, so he innocently asked them to change one syllable in the final *mantra* they were reciting to procure the favor of the goddess. The Brahmins instantly realized the grave implication of his request, since with the changing of that one syllable, the entire meaning of the *mantra* changed and instead of asking her to help them, they would be asking her to hinder them! They glanced meaningfully at each other, but since they were bound by their oath, they decided to carry on as the little Brahmin wished.

The night-long ritual commenced, but since they were saying the wrong *mantra,* the goddess refused to manifest herself as expected after the recitation of the thousand and first *mantra*. The priests looked around but found that the helpful young Brahmin had disappeared. Ravana lost his temper with them and wanted to know where they had failed. They replied that the goddess was angry with him for all his *adharmic* (unrighteous) acts and had therefore refused to comply with his wishes.

Ravana was furious when he heard this unpalatable truth and rushed at them with sword upraised to kill all of them, but his wife Mandodari caught his hand and stopped him from this heinous crime.

She begged him to make a truce. "What have the Brahmins done? They have only told the truth. All your brothers, our sons, our friends, ministers, and commanders have died. Will you not stop this outrage until the last of your people have died? What have we left to live for? As for myself, I don't want to live after the death of my beloved sons! Will you not listen to reason at least now?"

She begged and pleaded, but Ravana had gone too far to back out now, and he simply waved her off. He thought of another strategy by which he could still vanquish the Kosala brothers. "What Mandodari said is true. All my closest and dearest ones have left me. Tomorrow I will have to face my enemies alone. However, I have never bowed my head before anyone so far and I shall not do so now!"

Mandodari now asked all his wives to undertake a long vow of fasting and complete chastity and keep an all-night vigil so that the goddess would protect their husband. Jambavan heard of this and knew that any vow would come to naught if the women committed adultery even by thought, if not by deed. So he told Hanuman to fly past their palace window in his most handsome form. Ravana's wives noticed him and admired his lithe limbs and graceful movements, and a passing thought came to their minds that they would like to be clasped in his strong arms! This mental infidelity detracted from the power of their vow to protect Ravana, and thus he became vulnerable to Rama's arrows.

After the disruption of his *yaga,* in which he had made a desperate attempt to change the positions of his ill-fated planets, Ravana began to realize the powerful truth that one cannot really change one's destiny. That night as he sadly approached his bedroom, the fascinating Mandodari, daughter of Mayan, the maker of illusions, approached him and softly wound her arms round his neck.

"My Lord!" she said, "Do you have to go to battle tomorrow? Can you not change your mind?"

Gently he pulled her away from him and said, "My faithful one, you know I have to go, but please believe me, I will never let you down."

"You have never let me down, my Lord. From the day you married me, you have given me nothing but delight. How can I forget?"

"You must believe me," said Ravana. "Put your faith and hope in me once more—just once more. I will not let you down."

"You are my beloved husband. I know that you will never let me down."

Ravana held her in his arms once more and said, "Farewell, my love."

She watched him sadly while he climbed up the ramparts of the castle for the last time. He sang the Sama hymns (the second book of the Vedas is the Sama Veda, or Book of Song), in which he was expert. Singing these sacred songs, he had once so pleased Shiva, the Lord of the world, that Shiva had granted him all his desires. And now the whole of nature seemed to be providing an accompaniment for his chants, with the sighing of the wind, the lashing of the waves, and the eerie creaking of the trees as they swayed to and fro, in tune with the rhythm of his chant. He lifted up his foot, brought it down again and again and began to dance. His breath came fast, but he felt calm. He threw back his head, waved his arms, and spun around. The wind was rushing around him, and even the gods came to watch. Blue flames shimmered around his form high above Lanka, and electricity crackled in his long loose hair. Rama and the animals saw him from down below and watched fascinated as Ravana's mighty figure, silhouetted against the sky, swayed and flowed with his own music.

At last, with the approach of midnight, *amavasya,* the night of the new moon, the wind dropped, the waves calmed down, and Ravana came down for his final battle.

The tenderness with which Valmiki describes Ravana's final parting from his wife, and the arresting, dramatic images of his preparation for battle, in which Ravana is treated with a dignity approaching reverence, remind us of his role as fatally flawed tragic hero. Once a great Brahmin and a revered and trusted leader, his wanton pride and excess of appetite had brought him to his doom.

For the first time there was a tinge of fear in Ravana's voice as he ordered the last of his generals to get ready for battle, for he had decided to go himself and avenge the death of all his loved ones. He wore his night armor made of finely woven black steel and donned his dark helmet that hid his face. Over his chariot was raised the battle banner of Lanka, made of golden cloth. Tied loosely on the flagstaff were ten golden arrows, for the ten directions of his empire. The chariot was protected with shields and plates cut from brass. It was equipped with all the latest weaponry and gleaming with jewels. It was loaded with tough, horn-tipped arrows, a long straight sword, and a heavy eight-sided mace. As it was driven to the gate, Ravana leaped into it like a tiger and took the reins himself. He rode out into the streets, and the demon warriors who lined the streets cheered and clapped as he thundered down. He chose to take the fifth gate, the gate of illusion, and rose up like a huge black swan into the midnight sky.

The *vanaras* were watching all four gates, but Ravana, perhaps fittingly, came through the illusory gate in the sky, and he landed in their midst with a thud. As he emerged from the gate, it is said that in the pitch black sky of this dark night of the moon, the wind began to blow, owls started to hoot, and jackals started to howl. Clouds rained drops of blood and horses tripped and fell. Ravana's face lost its customary glow and his voice became hoarse. His left arm and eye started to throb. All these omens were indicative of death.

Paying no heed to any of these omens, he drove at a fast pace through the ranks of the monkeys, accompanied by the remnants of his loyal ministers. In the distance, he could see the golden tips of Rama's bow. He was standing on the ground, totally unafraid. Ravana pushed through the ranks of the monkeys and fought like one possessed. None of the *vanaras* were able to face the onslaught of his fury. Like a lake drying up as summer advances, the simian forces were decreasing as more and more of them fell dead. Ravana hardly glanced at them, for he was bent on reaching Rama. As he saw him approach, Rama asked all the animals to go behind him, for this was the moment he had been waiting for and he preferred to face his enemy alone.

Ravana ordered his charioteer to take him to Rama. He preferred to forget their first encounter, when Rama had treated him so chivalrously. He saw Rama holding his famous bow, the Kodanda, with Lakshmana beside him, and the thought crossed his mind that he looked like Narayana himself with Indra by his side. Since Ravana was seated in his chariot, Hanuman offered to carry Rama, as that would enable him to face him on an equal footing. In the battle that followed, Hanuman skillfully dodged every weapon sent by Ravana so that not even a scratch fell on Rama! Rama managed to shoot an arrow that severed Ravana's head, but to his surprise another head grew back instantly. This happened several times, and Ravana laughed mockingly at the puzzled look on Rama's face. Frustrated, Rama left the field to Lakshmana and sought Vibhishana's advice.

Vibhishana said, "I'm not sure, but it is rumored that there is a pond in Ravana's garden into which a drop of the nectar of immortality fell when Jayanta was carrying it away. The lotuses that grow there are imbued with the power to regenerate the body and heal even the most lethal of wounds. Ravana must be eating these lotuses every time he is injured and thus getting rejuvenated."

Hanuman immediately took the form of a bee and discovered the fabled lotus lake. He swallowed all the lotuses and drained the pool of water, and returned as fast as he had gone.

In the meantime Lakshmana had been longing to come to grips with Ravana and shot a number of shafts at him, resembling tongues of fire. Ravana intercepted them with ease and split them with his own. He then passed over Lakshmana and stood face-to-face with Rama, letting fly a shower of arrows at him. Rama retaliated in kind, and soon the sky was overcast with arrows of various kinds. The shafts were extremely sharp-pointed, adorned with plumes of vultures, and flew with amazing speed. They were well-matched, both equally skilled, and adept in the use of different missiles. Ravana's arrows had the heads of lions, tigers, geese, and vultures as well as jackals and wolves. Rama countered all his arrows with ease, much to the joy of the monkeys.

Again Lakshmana came to the fore and with a single arrow, he felled Ravana's splendid banner, which had been fluttering in the breeze. Lakshmana could still see his sister-in-law's piteous face when she had begged him to go after Rama outside their hut in Panchavati. Keeping this in mind, he severed the head of Ravana's charioteer with a single arrow. Then with five whetted shafts, Lakshmana split asunder Ravana's huge bow, which resembled the trunk of an elephant. Vibhishana now rushed forward and struck his huge horses with his mace and killed them. Ravana was furious and sent his famous Shakti weapon at his brother. Lakshmana intervened and saved him. Ravana decided it was high time he put an end to this impudent brother of Rama's. His green eyes sparkling with copper fire and roaring like a lion, Ravana hurled a javelin made by Mayan, endowed with magic powers. It sizzled through the air, making a horrendous noise. It flew like an awesome meteor at its target. Rama saw it going toward his beloved brother and quickly made a *sankalpa*. "May you prove ineffectual! May your attempt to kill Lakshmana be frustrated." However, though the missile lost its power to kill, it was still potent enough to knock Lakshmana down senseless.

Seeing Lakshmana lying in a pool of blood, Rama was totally unnerved. He ran and took him to his bosom, even though Ravana kept pelting him with his potent arrows. He then shouted to Hanuman and Sugriva to come and take care of Lakshmana since he would not leave until the ten-headed monster was killed. He had many scores to settle with him.

"It is obvious that the world cannot contain the two of us. Either he or I will have to die. You may all take vantage positions on the hill and watch, for this battle will be talked about as long as the world remains, as long as the earth stands above the sea, and as long as living beings inhabit this earth!"

All the pent-up fury he had against Ravana, which he had been bottling up for eleven months, now rose to the surface, and he fought like a mad tusker.

Then followed a tremendous battle between the two. However, the *rakshasas* were night stalkers and with the approach of day, they became weaker, and Ravana perceptibly started to lose his strength. This encounter with Rama was even fiercer than the previous one, and the spectators could only hear the twang of the bowstrings and the clap of their palms as they released the arrows from the bows. At last, stung and pierced by the numerous gold-tipped arrows sent from Rama's flaming bow, Ravana fled from the field. Rama gladly turned his attention to his brother who lay unconscious. He begged Sugriva's court physician to do something to save him. Again he repeated the sentiments he felt at his brother's first calamity.

"If my brother dies, I care not if I win or lose the war. I do not desire the kingdom or even my life. I seem to have lost the desire even to rescue Sita. A wife like her may perhaps be found, but I will never find another like Lakshmana, who was born with me and was like my shadow and who has been my sole support and comfort during these dark days." So saying, Rama sobbed over the body of Lakshmana.

The physician said, "My Lord! Lakshmana's face has not lost its glow, which makes me believe that he is still alive. His skin does not have the darkness that is associated with death. His palms are still pink and soft. Moreover, he has all the auspicious signs of a long-lived man. So please do not grieve."

Turning to Hanuman, he requested him to go once again to the Himalayas and bring back the herbs known as *mritasanjivani* and *vishalyakarani,* which have the property of bringing a person back to consciousness. Before he could complete his sentence, Hanuman had winged his way to the north, but as before, he could not recognize the medicinal herb in question, so once again he lifted the whole peak and carried it back so that the physician could choose what he wanted. When he breathed the healing fragrance of the herb, which the physician crushed and held to his nostrils, Lakshmana woke up as if from sleep with no loss of energy or signs of fatigue. Rama was overjoyed to see him totally recovered. Shedding tears of joy, he clasped him to his bosom and exclaimed, "My dearest brother! My life would have been purposeless without you. Neither Sita nor kingdom would have meant anything."

Lakshmana was embarrassed at this and said, "O Rama, you have taken a vow to kill Ravana today and rescue the gentle princess of Videha. That should be your aim now. Never mind about me. Challenge him to a fight. Before the sun sets, you should kill him."

Then both of them embraced Hanuman and blessed him for having come to their rescue for the second time.

> *Diseases vanish and pain removed,*
> *O Great Hero, when your name is repeated*
> *   constantly.*

HANUMAN CHALISA BY TULSIDAS

Aum Sri Hanumathe Namaha!

26

Virupa
The End of Ravana

All glorious shone forth Raghupati on the field of battle,
In his immeasurable might and manifold beauty,
With the drops of toil on his lotus face,
With his lovely eyes and body specked with blood,
While in both hands he brandished his bow and arrows,
With the bears and monkeys grouped round him.

RAMACHARITAMANAS BY TULSIDAS

Rama knew that his brother spoke the truth, but he went into a reverie and for a moment felt that perhaps he might not be able to defeat Ravana. Seeing him looking utterly exhausted and sitting in deep thought, the sage Agastya came to him and gave him the great hymn known as the Aditya Hridayam. It is a hymn to the sun god, said to have the power to overcome all obstacles.

"O Prince of the solar race—mighty armed Rama!" he said. "Listen to this ancient *mantra,* by which you will be able to vanquish your foe in battle. The presiding deity of this hymn is the sun, and if it is chanted fervently, it will result in the destruction of your enemies and bring you victory and unending bliss. It is guaranteed to destroy all sins and allay all anxiety. Worship the golden-orbed deity of the sun therefore with this hymn, for he represents the totality of all celestial beings."

The all-knowing sage knew that Rama was Narayana incarnate, but he also knew that he was unaware of his divinity, and so he initiated him into the esoteric *mantra* as a *guru* would initiate an ordinary mortal. By the sincere chanting of this holy hymn, not only will material obstacles be removed but also all obstacles on the path of the seeker of eternal truth. He advised Rama to look at the sun and repeat it and he would surely be victorious in battle. Hearing this, Rama was thrilled, and gazing intently at the rising sun, he repeated the hymn with all fervor and sincerity.

"O Lord of Victory! Lord of the East! Lord of the West! O thou immeasurable one! Thou resplendent one! Golden-limbed creator of the universe! Witness of all the actions of all created beings! Again and again I bow to you!"

Rama belonged to the solar race, and as he repeated the hymn three times, the sun burst forth in all his glory, as if he applauded Rama's decision and urged him to hurry up with the deed on hand!

At dawn Ravana also offered prayers to his favorite deity, Shiva, and prepared to ride to the battlefield.

After chanting the Aditya Hridayam, Rama was filled with enthusiasm and challenged Ravana to come out. He was clad in bark with matted hair and walked barefoot.

The demon king watched in scorn as Rama came forward looking like a hermit. Suddenly a star seemed to come down from heaven. As it approached him, Rama saw that it was a brilliant aerial car with weapons that shone like lamps drawn by ten silver gray horses. Its many fan blades were spinning and silver wheels flashing as it landed softly, close to Rama. The charioteer jumped out and bowed to him and said, "I am Matali, Indra's charioteer. These are Indra's rain steeds, the misty runners of the sky. O King of the solar race, Indra as sent me here to take you to victory."

"Welcome to you," said Rama and sprang lightly onto the chariot.

Matali touched the horses and told them to advance. They rushed forward with flashing silver shoes.

Ravana's chariot leaped forward to intercept them. A fierce battle began between the two. The gods assembled in the sky to witness this final scene. The animals and demons took up safe positions to watch this concluding scene.

The charioteers drove their respective chariots in a series of skilful and bewildering maneuvers. Both Rama and Ravana discharged a number of deadly arrows charged with various potent *mantras*. The snake arrows of Ravana, which flew with unerring precision at Rama, spitting poison from their wide open mouths, were foiled by the eagle arrows of Rama. Eagles are the avowed enemies of snakes. The sky became dark with arrows flying in the air, colliding and negating each other with horrendous noises resembling thunderclaps. The world trembled to witness the wrath of Rama. The sun lost its brilliance, and the sea came in huge waves to watch the terrifying spectacle. The terrible frown on Rama's face, which was so seldom seen, made even Ravana tremble in terror. Birds and beasts ran about in panic. Valmiki says that just as the ocean can only be compared with the ocean and the sky with the sky, so the battle between Rama and Ravana can only be compared to the battle between Rama and Ravana!

At last Ravana took hold of a javelin that was covered with spikes and had a sharp point that was sizzling and blazing like a huge fire, as if it were anxious to go and find its rest on Rama's chest, and he sent it flying at Rama.

He roared, "This will make short work of you and your brother, O scion of the race of Raghu!"

Rama immediately countered with a host of arrows, but they were all burned to ashes by the fury of Ravana's javelin. In a trice Rama took up the javelin sent by Indra, which had been kept in the chariot, and hurled it with all force at the oncoming dart of Ravana's. The two weapons collided in mid-air and Ravana's javelin broke into a thousand splinters and fell on the ground, its power totally exhausted. Ravana immediately took another missile and shattered Rama's pennant. Rama turned to Hanuman and said, "O Vayu Putra! Get me another flagstaff immediately and do thou be seated on my flag and terrify the enemy."

Hanuman immediately cut off a branch from a *sal* tree, hoisted it on top of the chariot, and sat on it himself. From this vantage point he cast his eyes on all sides and gave the most ferocious and terrifying roars.

Now Rama spoke to Ravana, "You call yourself a hero after having abducted Sita when she was alone and unattended in the *ashrama*. What chance did she have against brute force? You are nothing but a thief and a molester of women and a coward. But beware! Your head will provide food for hungry vultures and your blood with be lapped by wolves before the day is over!" With these words Rama harassed Ravana with hundreds of arrows.

Ravana was beginning to be unnerved by Rama's unflagging enthusiasm and barrage of arrows and fell into a faint. Seeing the condition of his master, his charioteer skillfully steered the chariot away from Rama. When Ravana came out of his swoon he swore at his charioteer and ordered him to drive fast to the midst of the fray.

"Ravana never turns his back on his enemies," he said. "He does not retreat until he has wiped out his foes!"

"My Lord," said the charioteer, "it is the duty of a charioteer to protect his master. Our horses were tired and you were also fatigued and in a faint. I saw nothing but ill omens and thought it best to bring you away from the situation."

Ravana was pleased with his devotion and presented him with his own bracelet. The charioteer whipped up the horses as commanded by his master and took him in front of Rama once again.

Rama requested Matali to maneuver the chariot to a good position. He raced his horses straight at Ravana's chariot and deflected them to the left just before they collided. As they passed, Rama shot an arrow deep into Ravana's shoulder. The demon king clutched desperately at the flagstaff to stop himself from falling. The chariots turned and faced each other once again. The rest of the army stood like painted figures, spellbound by the awesome scene. Ravana tried to bring down Indra's divine banner and failed, while Rama's arrow found its mark and brought down Ravana's pennon. Ravana was biting his lips and darting sparks from his eyes when he found that none of his arrows were hurting Rama. The latter, on the other hand, had a slight smile on his lips, as his arrows seemed to be finding a sure mark.

There ensued another terrific battle between the two heroes. Matali advised Rama to make an end of the ten-headed demon before the approach of night. Rama then fitted an arrow resembling a venomous snake and sliced off the resplendent head of his opponent adorned with huge earrings. But to his astonishment, in front of his very eyes, there arose another head in the place of the previous one and then another and another as each was cut off.

Ravana's ten heads are meant to convey his enormous ego. With just one head all of us have egos that are impossible to control. Think of the ego of a person with ten heads! When each ego head was chopped off, another reared its haughty hood. It is the same with us. When our ego is put down in one place, we immediately find another place or situation by which we can make ourselves feel important.

Rama was beginning to feel a bit worried, though his face remained calm, and he kept sending a continuous stream of arrows from his bow. Then Vibhishana approached him and whispered to him that Ravana could be slain only with the *brahmastra* that Brahma himself had given him. This was hidden in Mandodari's apartments and without it, the fight could go on forever. Hanuman immediately leaped to Lanka and, taking on the form of an aged Brahmin, he hobbled before Mandodari. She was delighted to see this venerable Brahmin and offered him all hospitality. The Brahmin then warned her that Vibhishana had told Rama of the existence of the only weapon that had the power to kill her husband and that was hidden by her. He advised her to remove it to a new hiding place.

Mandodari became panic-stricken and ran to rescue the arrow from inside the crystal column in which she had carefully hidden it. Hanuman immediately reverted to his own form, grabbed the arrow, and flew back, leaving Mandodari in tears.

Hanuman gave the arrow to Rama and whispered in his ear, "My Lord! Remember who you are. Ravana's moment of death has come. Despatch the *brahmastra* and kill him. Do not aim at his head but at his chest!"

The time destined for Ravana's death had come. But when Rama looked at Ravana's heart, it is said that he saw Sita enshrined within, and inside Sita's heart, he saw himself. He was in a dilemma. What could he do? He waited for that split second when Ravana forgot Sita in his anger against Rama and at that precise moment, he whispered the incantation of Brahma and sent his golden-tipped arrow straight at Ravana's heart. It was the most powerful weapon known to man or god and very few human beings were initiated into its mysteries, for its power for destruction was so great that no one who had not learned to control himself could be trusted with it. Hence in ancient India, scientific knowledge was only given to those who had strong moral and ethical qualities and who could be depended to use it for the good of mankind.

The dart was made of the essences of all the five elements. Flaming like the fire of universal destruction and as fatal as the power of Time, the dart fled from Rama's bow like a streak of lightning and found its mark on Ravana's chest. Piercing his body through and through, it sank into the earth and then swerved and returned to Rama's hand like a meek servant. The invincible bow of the king of demons dropped from his nerveless grasp and his body, full of splendor, fell like a thunderbolt from the chariot. Seeing him fall, the night rangers fled in all directions, shrieking with fear.

The watching gods rained flowers from the sky, and the sun came out from behind the clouds. Ravana's life was fast ebbing away. The mighty king of the *rakshasas,* who had ruled the entire world with the might of his arms alone, now lay dead on the battlefield, a prey to every passing vulture and jackal. He who had no equal in might and valor, he who had terrified the whole world and thus earned the name Ravana (the terrifier), who had pleased Lord Shiva himself by his glorious chanting of the Sama Veda, had been killed by a mere mortal, as had been prophesied. His lust for another man's wife had killed him as well as the curses of all those women whom he had ravished. Even in death, he had not lost his splendor. He looked as dazzling as a fallen sun, glorious even in death.

Lakshmana, Sugriva, and the others crowded round Rama and congratulated him. Vibhishana was suddenly struck with remorse and wept for his proud brother who had come to such an end. Rama comforted him by saying that Ravana had indeed died a hero's death.

"This is the path pursued by the heroes of old," he said. "For a Kshatriya, there is a right way of living and a right way of dying, and he has chosen the right way of dying if not of living—on the battlefield. Vibhishana! All enmity ends with death. Now go and do whatever rites are to be performed for him as per the rules, for there is no one else to do it for him but you."

Mandodari, foremost queen of Ravana, mother of the brave Indrajit, now came running to the battlefield, her hair disheveled, her face streaming with tears, and threw herself over the body of her dying husband.

"How could such a calamity have overtaken you, my noble Lord? How is it possible for a mere mortal to have killed you? This Rama must be divine. The fact that he defeated Khara and Dhushasana single-handed should have convinced you that he was not an ordinary human being. When I heard that he had built a bridge across the sea, I knew that he was not an ordinary mortal. I know now who Rama is. He is the Lord Narayana himself—the Supreme Purusha. He has assumed the garb of an ordinary mortal for the purpose of saving the world, and the gods themselves have assumed the forms of these monkeys. It is Narayana who has killed you, my Lord, not a human being. How can you lie on the bare ground shrouded by dust when you are used to reposing on the softest and most sumptuous of couches? Why do you not speak to me, miserable creature that I am? Once upon a time, you performed many austerities with your senses under perfect control, and now those very senses, like untamed horses, have dragged you to your death. Sita is a noble lady, devoted to her husband. She should have been honored by you, but instead you chose to insult her. Her tears of shame and despair have killed you and not Rama's arrows. What does she have that I lack? In birth, I am her equal, in beauty she is in no way superior, yet blinded by lust, you chose to carve out your dreadful end. You brought death to Lanka the day you brought her here. Now she will be reunited with her Lord and will live happily with him, while I will have to lie on my lonely bed, plunged in sorrow without you. Where has your smile gone, my Lord? Where is the look of love in your eyes when you gazed at me? How proud I was of my good fortune! I was the daughter of the architect of the *asuras,* and my husband, the king of the *rakshasas,* and my son, the most valiant warrior in the whole world. How could I believe that death would rob me of my dearest treasures in one fell stroke?"

So lamenting, Mandodari fainted over the dying body of her husband and the other women had to carry her away. Again and again she ran back to have a last look at her husband's beloved face, which she would never see again. Refusing to go away, she sat on the ground next to him and put his head on her lap, whispering words of comfort to him.

Following close on her heels came the rest of his harem, composed of thousands of ravishing women who had been picked from all over the world, famed for their beauty, whom not even the sun had seen for they had never been allowed to go out in the streets. They ran to the gory battlefield and threw themselves over his blood-stained body and wept piteously.

"Our Lord had been granted immunity from death by Brahma and now he has been killed by a mere mortal. Why did you never listen to us? You abducted Sita despite our advice. She has been the cause of the extermination of the entire race of *rakshasas.* Had she been restored to Rama, all this would never have happened. You spurned the words of Vibhishana. Fate is indeed all powerful. It was ordained that Ravana, the greatest of all monarchs, would be defeated by a mere human being, helped by a pack of bears and monkeys!"

While the rest of the monkeys were celebrating, Hanuman came near Rama and said, "Ravana was a great scholar, even though he was unrighteous. Let us take advantage of his enormous knowledge before he dies." Both Rama and Lakshmana went near Ravana. Lakshmana stood at his head and said, "I have heard that you have a great deal of knowledge. We are the victors, and therefore you should pass it on to us before you die!"

Ravana painfully turned his head away in silence, refusing to answer Lakshmana's request. Now Rama came forward and knelt at the dying king's feet and said softly, "Ravana! I have killed you not out of malice but because it was my duty to save my wife. However, I have great respect for your vast knowledge and would deeply appreciate it if you would share it with me before you die so that it will not be lost to the world!"

Ravana slowly opened his eyes and said, "I accept you as my pupil, O Rama! For you sat at my feet and spoke with all humility as a student should. I'm willing to impart my knowledge to you."

Then to the astonishment of all those who had gathered there, the dying Ravana, with his head on Mandodari's lap, revealed to his enemy Rama the subtleties of philosophy, politics, economics, fine arts, dance, music, drama, and statecraft. Thus the villain became a teacher and the hero a student!

Ravana was fast losing his life breath and could do no more than whisper. At last the mighty hero could no longer speak and his lifeless head was held in a tight grasp by his faithful queen, whose hot tears fell unheeded over his face.

Rama now told Vibhishana to set about the task of cremating Ravana. His body was placed on a pyre made of sandalwood and many other types of fragrant wood and herbs. It was draped with the skins of black antelopes. Curd and ghee were poured on his shoulders and a wooden mortar inserted between his thighs. The corpse was draped with different types of costly silks and garlands. Roasted grain was sprinkled over it. It was then carried in state by everyone and placed on the pyre of sweet-smelling wood. With great reverence, Vibhishana touched the earthly remains of his brother with a flaming torch and set fire to it. He completed all the rites connected with the funeral and gave oblations to the departed soul. Then he went and saluted Rama and told him that everything had been done according to his wishes.

Rama prostrated himself to Indra's chariot and thanked Matali and sent him back. He then asked Lakshmana and Sugriva to take Vibhishana to the city and crown him as king. He did not go himself since his fourteen years of exile were not over. Lakshmana took Vibhishana to the city of Lanka. He placed him on the throne and gave him the ceremonial bath by pouring consecrated water over his head, and thus pronounced him King of Lanka. Only a few citizens were left to cheer the new king. The once populous and prosperous capital of Lanka now looked like a deserted ghost city. Even royal fortune fails at last and turns away from the greatest kingdom.

The great Rama/Ravana war ended on the morning of the fourth day, just past the first night of the new moon, close to the summer solstice when the sun turns in the sky to begin his journey to the north.

> *The ascetic king, Rama, is the ruler of the*
> *universe,*
> *And you are the one who carries out his tasks.*

SRI HANUMAN CHALISA BY TULSIDAS

Aum Sri Hanumathe Namaha!

Aum Uttamaaya Namaha!

27

Uttaman

Trial by Fire

The flame was as cool as sandalwood, as Sita entered it,
Meditating on her Lord.
"Glory to the king of Kosala, for whose feet,
Ever worshipped by Shiva,
I cherish the purest devotion."

RAMACHARITAMANAS BY TULSIDAS

Though the thought of Sita must have been foremost in his mind, Rama sternly subdued it and saw to Ravana's cremation as well as the welfare of the citizens of Lanka by crowning Vibhishana before seeing to the matter that was closest to his heart.

Turning to Hanuman, he told him to go to Sita, give her the happy news, and find out how she was faring. Hanuman was delighted to be given this most pleasant task.

He flew in a flash to the *ashoka* grove, his white fur round his neck ruffled with happiness. He saw Sita surrounded by *rakshasis,* sitting in a forlorn mood, for no one had told her the news so far.

With folded palms, he bowed low to her and gave her the happy news. "Take heart, O divine lady! Rama and Lakshmana are well and happy and have sent me here to give you glad tidings. The ten-headed one has been killed by your husband! Lanka has been placed under the rule of Vibhishana, who will be coming here shortly to pay his respects to you." Sita couldn't say a word, as she was overcome with joy.

At last in a trembling voice, she said, "I really don't know how I am to repay you for the wonderful tidings that you have brought me, my dear monkey! Neither silver, gold, precious stones, nor even the sovereignty of the three worlds can equal in value this message that you have given me."

"This speech of yours, O Mother, so full of love, is the most precious gift I can receive. I have received the blessings of all the gods by these words."

Out of the overflowing gratitude she felt, Sita told Hanuman, "O son of Vayu! You will always be the stronghold of valor, strength, knowledge of scriptures, vigor, prowess, skill in action, forbearance, firmness, stability, and humility. These and many other brilliant qualities will always exist in you!"

Standing meekly in front of Sita, Hanuman said, "My Lady! Believe me, I have spent sleepless nights thinking of your pathetic condition, and now it is my luck that I have been chosen by our Lord to bring you this joyful news. Mother! If you will permit me, I will kill these *rakshasis* who have been torturing you for such a long time."

Sweetly Sita said, "Why should servants be blamed for carrying out the orders of their master? Moreover, it is my fate that has ordained that I should be treated thus. Perhaps I have committed some crime in the past for which I am being punished now. Everyone reaps the fruit of his or her own actions of the past. So spare them, dear monkey. No one is infallible. To err is human. The virtuous do not return evil for evil. It is my duty to condone their conduct, which was forced upon them by a higher authority."

Hanuman bowed to Sita and desisted from killing the *rakshasis*. He then asked her for a message to be given to Rama. Sita told him to tell Rama that she was longing to see him. Hanuman once again bowed and said, "You will undoubtedly see the scion of the race of Raghu very soon."

He leaped into the air and returned to Rama and said, "The princess of Mithila has heard of your victory. At the very mention of your name she became wild with joy and her eyes filled with tears. She is thin and wan with grief and told me to tell you that she is longing to see you, so please go to her."

Rama's eyes filled with tears when he heard this, but he remained sunk in thought for a while. At last he sighed and told Vibhishana to bring Sita to him after she had been given an auspicious bath and clothed in beautiful apparel.

Vibhishana went to the *ashoka* grove and conveyed this message to Sita. She replied, "I want to see my husband now and not waste time in bathing and ornamenting myself."

Vibhishana said that it was his duty to obey Rama's commands implicitly and that he could not take her as she was. Sita contained her impatience to see her Lord and allowed Vibhishana's wife to bathe and anoint her with *sandal* paste and unguents and clothe her in costly apparel. She wore a silk yellow robe and a crown of fresh and fragrant wildflowers. She was even more beautiful than Lakshmi. She then got into the richly decorated palanquin that was kept ready for her and went before Rama. He was still lost in thought and sat with his eyes fixed on the ground.

The *vanaras* and *rakshasas* crowded around the palanquin, eager to have a glimpse of the beauty for whose sake so much trouble had been taken and the whole race of demons annihilated! Vibhishana and the others pushed them back and ordered them to go away, since Rama would want to see his wife alone and in any event, it was not correct for the common populace to view a lady of the royal household.

Rama chided him and said, "A woman's protection should be her purity and chastity and not a wall or a veil. Let them stay where they are and see her if they wish. Let them gaze as much as they want on the beauty of the princess of Videha. Moreover, it is only right that she should be seen by those who fought and died for her sake. Ask her to step out of the palanquin and approach me all alone."

Lakshmana, Hanuman, and Vibhishana were all puzzled by Rama's strange behavior. Vibhishana led Sita, who had covered her face with a veil, to her husband. Like the *chakora* bird drinking in the nectar that drops from the moon, she lifted up her veil and gazed adoringly at his beloved face. It was many months since she had seen his beloved face and as she gazed, she felt her strength returning to her limbs and the glow to her face.

Rama averted his face and spoke in an unusually harsh tone, "I have accomplished what I have set out to do. I have vindicated my honor and kept up the reputation of the fair house of the Ikshvaku clan. I have wiped out the insult that was offered to me and killed the one who abducted you. Hanuman, who leaped across the ocean and destroyed Lanka, has been rewarded. So has Vibhishana who left his brother and took refuge in me. Sugriva and all the other monkey leaders have been applauded for the help they rendered to me."

Sita had been waiting for a year for the moment when her beloved husband would come and rescue her and take her in his arms and comfort her and make her forget the trials that she had gone through. She could not understand why Rama, who had never spoken harshly to her at any time, was now using this tone of voice, and why he was narrating all these incidents and avoiding her eyes. She looked at him with her fawnlike eyes, which were slowly beginning to fill with tears, and Rama's heart was torn with agony and love, but he kept a stern check on his natural emotions and continued to speak harshly.

"Don't think that I have fought this war for your sake. I did it only to save my name and the honor of my race. As you have lived for eleven months in the city of a notorious womanizer like Ravana, do you expect me to believe that he could refrain from ravishing you—you who are so lovely and alluring? That lecherous wretch has feasted his eyes on you and carried you in his arms. Rumors will be rife about you and I cannot take you back. You are now free to go where you wish, O Janaki! I can no longer bear to look at you. Your presence hurts my eyes like blinding sunlight for sore eyes. Now that I have done my duty and rescued you, I owe you nothing more. I belong to a noble house and it does not befit me to take you back. What man born in a noble family would take back a woman who has dwelt in another man's house for eleven months?"

Hearing this cruel speech coming from the mouth of her husband from whom she had heard nothing but words of love, Sita swayed like a creeper that has been torn from its prop. Tears streamed from her eyes, and she looked like a wilting flower. To make matters worse, there was an interested and sympathetic audience to witness this painful scene. She had thought her heart had been broken when she had been abducted by Ravana, but now she realized that it was nothing compared to this frightful ordeal.

At last she said in faltering tones, "Why do you speak such harsh words to me? This is the talk of a common man to a woman of the streets and you are not a common man, neither am I a woman of the streets. If you doubted me, why did you come to search for me and why did you send Hanuman with your ring? Why didn't you tell him that you had no further use for me? Why did you take the trouble of crossing the sea and fighting and killing Ravana? You risked your life and the life of all your friends by coming here. You could have saved yourself a lot of trouble and I could have given up my life then and there, and then I would not have had to hear these cruel words. If I had been touched by that sinner when I was being carried away, it was because I was too weak and helpless to protect myself. How can you blame me for that? Even after living with me for so many years, it looks as if you have never understood me. My thoughts and love have never strayed from you, even for a moment. I might be called Janaki, the daughter of Janaka, but I am really Sita, the daughter of the earth. Did you never consider my exalted birth before passing judgment? Does my love and chastity mean nothing to you? If that was so, why did you come? You have given me leave to go where I want. There is only one place I want to go and that is into the heart of a fire."

Turning to Lakshmana, she said, "Lakshmana, make a pyre for me. It is the only cure for the grief that is burning me more than flames. I have been falsely accused, and I don't want to live anymore. My husband has repudiated me in front of this big crowd of people and asked me to go where I want. There is only one place for me, and that is the world of Yama!" Her voice choked with emotion, and she could no longer speak.

Lakshmana looked angrily at Rama, who stood with his head cast down like a painted statue. No one dared approach him or try to argue with him. Rama made a gesture with his hand and Lakshmana reluctantly went and made a pyre.

Sita circumambulated Rama three times as he stood with a stony face and a dreadful frown on his face, and then she went slowly toward the blazing fire. She stood with folded palms before it and said:

"If it be true that my thoughts have never at any time wavered from my husband, then let this fire, which is the witness of all things, protect me. If I have never been unfaithful in thought, word, or deed to Rama, who is the repository of all virtues, let the god of fire afford protection to me. If the deities of the sun and the moon and my mother the earth, as well as the deities of the four quarters, know me to be of unblemished character, then let the fire god protect me."

So saying, she went three times around the fire and then flung herself into the heart of the conflagration before the horrified eyes of the spectators. All the *vanaras* and the *rakshasas* who had assembled there set up a loud wail of protest. Clad in yellow silk and adorned with gold ornaments, Sita glowed like molten gold in the heart of the fire. Rama turned his face away, for he could not bear to see this pitiable scene. Though his heart was breaking and his eyes were streaming with tears, he did not do anything to save her, she who was dearer to him than his own life.

At that moment there appeared two chariots in the air, and the celestials showered fragrant flower petals from the air. Brahma came down and spoke to Rama. "How can you stand and watch unmoved while Sita immolates herself in the fire? Don't you know that you are Narayana, the primeval being, and Sita is Lakshmi, your eternal consort? You were born to destroy Ravana and establish peace on Earth. Now your task is accomplished and *dharma* has been reestablished."

As soon as Brahma had finished speaking, Agni, the god of fire, stepped forward from the blaze with Sita in his arms. She was dressed in red and looked as lustrous as the morning sun. Even her garland was not singed by the fire. He handed her over to Rama and said, "Here is your wife, the noble princess of Videha, who is totally without blemish. She was never unfaithful in thought, word, or glance. Believe me and accept this jewel among women!"

Hardly had he finished speaking than Indra, king of the gods, appeared next to Sita. He wore a thin cloak of mist trimmed with stars and stood barefoot just a finger's width above the ground. His body cast no shadow and his black eyes never blinked.

He bowed before Rama and said, "O Narayana! Thou art the primeval being. You were born on Earth as Rama in order to save humanity from the inequities of Ravana. Sita is your divine consort Lakshmi. Both of you can never be parted, so take her back, return to your country, and rule in peace." Thus ended Sita's trial by fire.

Indra asked Rama to request a boon, for he had done him a great service by killing Ravana, who had been a thorn in his side for years. Rama immediately asked him to resurrect all those monkeys who had given up their lives to help him.

"May all these long-tailed monkeys and bears recover from their wounds and rise up once again filled with life and enthusiasm. Let fruits and flowers and roots abound wherever these monkeys live."

Indra was only too happy to grant this request, and all the fallen monkeys and bears now rose up as if from sleep.

Tears flowed unchecked down Rama's eyes as he took his beloved wife's hands into his own. "I know that my wife is pure and chaste as unsullied snow. I never doubted her even for a moment, but if she had not undergone this ordeal by fire, people would have spoken ill of her and of me. They would have said that Dasaratha's son, blinded by love for his wife, was willing to take her back even though she had lived so long in the house of another man. I knew full well that Sita was totally protected by her purity. Ravana could never have sullied her. She is to me what splendor is to the sun. As a good man cannot abandon a good name, so also I can never abandon Sita. If I spoke harshly to her and watched unmoved when she entered the fire, it was only to vindicate her name before the eyes of all."

So saying, he lifted up her face to his and looked deep into her lovely eyes as he had been longing to do. When Sita turned her reproachful, tear-filled eyes at him, Rama chided her softly so that none could hear. "O daughter of the earth! My lovely Sita! How could you think even for a moment that I doubted you? Why do you think I trudged through the length and breadth of this country, if not to catch a glimpse of your bewitching face? Why do you think I faced the wrath of the demon king and risked my life, if I did not crave for you? My dearest love, I repudiated you so that none could ever point an accusing finger at my darling."

Hearing this passionate declaration, Sita was slightly pacified and looked up at him with all her love pouring out of her eyes. Thus for a long moment they were lost to the world and gazed long and deep into each other's eyes, much to the joy of all who were assembled there.

Then Lord Shiva came and extolled Rama, telling him that the world owed him a great debt for having exterminated the scourge of Ravana. He blessed him with all success in his life as king of the land of Kosala.

As Sita, Rama, and Lakshmana stood together, they were delighted to see their father, Dasaratha, whom the gods had brought from heaven in an aerial car so that he could see his beloved son once again. The celestials now reminded Rama to return immediately to Ayodhya, for the fourteen years were drawing to a close and Bharata was waiting for his arrival with great anxiety.

In order to end the hostility between the *vanaras* and the *rakshasas,* Hanuman suggested that Sugriva's son should be given in marriage to

Vibhishana's daughter. Everyone approved of the idea and the marriage was conducted in style and blessed by Rama and Sita.

> *You are the dispenser of the eight supernatural*
> *powers*
> *And the nine treasures.*
> *Mother Janaki bestowed this blessing on you!*

Sri Hanuman Chalisa by Tulsidas

Aum Sri Hanumathe Namaha!

28

Sahasravadana

Return to Ayodhya

Tato Ramabhyanujnatam tad vimanamuthamam
Vavande pranato Ramam merusyamiha bhaskaram.

Alighting from their chariots, the citizens stood on the
    ground and looked up
To behold Rama seated in the aerial car like the moon
    in the sky.

VALMIKI RAMAYANAM, YUDDHA KANDA

Vibhishana now approached Rama with folded palms and humbly
asked him to enter the city of Lanka, where everything had been prepared for a royal welcome.

My Lord, I have prepared various types of baths and oils and
unguents for you to refresh yourself. Garments of various kinds and
garlands have all been laid out. Kindly refresh and adorn yourself
before setting out on the return journey."

Rama smiled and said, "You may offer all these precious things to
Sugriva, for my thoughts are all with my dear brother Bharata. The

269

way back to Ayodhya is long and hard and the fourteen years are coming to a close. Bharata has sworn that he will take his life if I do not reach Ayodhya by the end of the stipulated time."

Vibhishana said, "My Lord! I will help you to reach Ayodhya in a single day. My brother Ravana forcibly took the aerial vehicle called Pushpaka from his brother Kubera. It was his prized possession. Please accept my hospitality for a few more days and then you can return to Ayodhya in this vehicle."

Rama was touched by his devotion and said, "Vibhishana, I am well aware of your love for me, but my heart yearns to return to Ayodhya and see my brothers and mothers and the people of Kosala, who must be anxiously awaiting my arrival. However, you may take Hanuman to Ravana's palace and show him the wonders inside while the rest of us take some rest after the battle." So saying, he took Sita's hand in his and went toward the seashore, where they sat close together and she told him of all the sorrows she had gone through.

Hanuman was anxious to know the secrets of the city of Lanka, so Vibhishana led him into Lanka along the empty brick streets to the royal palace. He took him via a secret door to the storeroom. It was locked with ten thousand and one locks, all made with strange, ornate designs. Though the keyholes were of different shapes, Vibhishana opened them all with the same key! The door opened into a huge room that was lit with lamps placed inside glass domes. Hanuman gauged that the room had been dug into the heart of Trikuta Hill. Many shelves lined the wall on which were kept fine linens, patterned silks, and skins of tigers, leopards, lions, and wolves. There were many books made of stone and secret treasure maps. Exquisite vials of perfumes and piles of jewels, gold, and silver filled the shelves.

Vibhishana spoke, "These are the ancient, timeless treasures of our race. In these vaults lie all the lore of old, gathered from the beginning of Time. This room was built by Vishvakarma, the architect of the gods. The *rakshasas* have a great deal of knowledge, which must not be allowed to perish. You are the only outsider who has ever seen or will ever see this room."

Hanuman looked curiously around the room and asked, "Why have you favored me like this?"

"Because you are my first and only friend from another race," said Vibhishana. "Moreover, you are wise and faithful. You put your whole heart into whatever you do and you never seek for any gain. I am really happy to have you as my friend. I know that your heart lies with Rama and you will go with him, but remember that you are always welcome to come here anytime you want."

Hanuman thanked him, and they locked the room and retraced their steps to where Rama, Sita, and Lakshmana were waiting along with the rest of the valiant army of monkeys and bears.

Rama told Vibhishana to fetch the aerial car that would transport them in a day to Ayodhya, as he was keen to see his brothers and mothers as well as the citizens who were waiting so anxiously for him. Vibhishana returned to Lanka and came back with the Pushpaka.

It was a fantastic, flower-bedecked chariot, drawn by white swans. It was like a small city, glittering with gold and silver and adorned with blossoms of every kind and season. Rainbows were made into colored knots over its frame. Inside there were summerhouses and ponds and pools and dining halls. It had benches and beds and a kitchen that supplied every type of food. It was a mind-driven chariot taken forcibly by Ravana from his brother Kubera. It came rolling out on its thousand wheels with all flags flying and wind bells chiming. Vibhishana walked in front of it. He bowed before Rama and requested him to climb into it.

Rama, Lakshmana, and Sita got in without further ado. Even though the Pushpaka was as big as a palace, Rama sat with Sita on his lap, much to her delight. He looked at Hanuman, Vibhishana, Sugriva and all the other *vanaras* and said with tears in his eyes, "I don't know in what way I can repay you all for the love and devotion you have shown to me. Sugriva, please return to Kishkinda with your army. My blessings will always be with you. Angada, my dear child, I can never forget your prowess and as for you, O Hanuman, what can I say? Both of us owe our lives to you. Now please give me leave to return to my own city. I have been in exile for so long that my heart yearns to return."

Sugriva bowed low and said, "Lord, please give us leave to come with you to Ayodhya. We promise not to indulge in any act of destruction, as we monkeys are wont to do. We are most anxious to witness your coronation."

Rama laughed at their eagerness to accompany him and their promise to behave themselves and said, "I am delighted at he thought that I will enter my ancestral city accompanied by those who have helped me most. Sugriva, ask your people to get in."

Vibhishana and the other ogres also expressed the same desire. Rama gladly gave his consent, and the whole party got into the Pushpaka, and still there was enough room in it for another army!

One of the most endearing things about Rama was his great love for all animals of land and air. Monkeys, bears, and birds wander in and out of the pages of the narrative of his life as if it were the most natural thing in the world. His love and regard for his animal friends shows a unique facet of his character.

Rama turned to Hanuman and asked him what reward he wanted for his invaluable services. Hanuman replied, "My Lord! Give me leave to spend the rest of my life in your service!" Rama smilingly agreed.

The divine chariot now rose into the air effortlessly, carried by the four white swans. Celestial flowers rained from the sky as it rose up. The *vanaras* shouted and whooped with joy, peering over the edge at the ground below, which fell with alarming rapidity.

Sita's face glowed with happiness and beauty as Rama pointed out various sites that would interest her, through which they had wandered during their long and painful search. First of all, he showed her the battleground and the spot where Ravana had fallen. And then he pointed out to her the amazing bridge built by Nala, over which they had crossed. He kept reiterating the fact that everything he had done was for her sake alone, as if trying to make up for all the harsh words he had spoken to her previously.

"O Princess of Videha! Observe this roaring, swelling ocean, teeming with all sorts of reptiles and fish that is Varuna's domain. Now we will land on the shore so that you can pray at the temple to Shiva that I had installed."

The plane gently landed on the other side of the bridge so that Rama could worship at the shrine of Shiva that he and Hanuman had consecrated before they set out. At that time he had made a vow to the three-eyed Lord that he would return and pay his homage to him along with his wife Sita.

"Here on this spot, Shiva, the supreme deity, bestowed his grace on me and accepted my worship in the form of Rameshwara (Rama's Lord). This place where the bridge was constructed will be known as Sethubanda and will be adored in all the worlds. This spot will be held as supremely sacred and will be capable of washing away all major sins. This is the place where Vibhishana made his first appearance."

Once again they got into the plane and he pointed out to Sita Sugriva's fortress Kishkinda. Sita immediately asked for the car to be brought down so that they could take Sugriva's wives Tara and Rumi, as well as the wives of the other monkey leaders.

So the chariot landed and the ladies joyfully joined the group. Later Rama pointed out Rishyamukha, where he had met Hanuman for the first time. "There is Lake Pampa, filled with lotuses, where I was reminded of you so painfully and where we met the old lady ascetic Shabari."

"O look, Sita!" he said. "There is our *ashrama* at Panchavati, where you were so cruelly captured. There is the enchanting hut of leaves made for us by Lakshmana close to the holy river Godavari. We abandoned it immediately after you were abducted, for I could not bear to stay there without you." He remained silent for a few minutes reliving the painful scenes of that time and Sita buried her face on his shoulder and wept.

"Here is the delightful forest of Chitrakuta where we spent so many happy days together and where Bharata came to meet us. Now we come to Bharadvaja's *ashrama*, which lies at the most holy confluence of the divine Ganga with Yamuna and Saraswati."

Rama requested the Pushpaka to land. The sage was delighted

to see them, and Rama, who was starved for news of his people, was relieved to hear that all was well in Ayodhya. The sage also went over all the hardships he had undergone, including Sita's capture and his killing of Ravana, for he had known everything by his divine powers. Bharadwaja requested Rama to stay for the day and proceed the next morning, so Rama informed Hanuman.

"I cannot refuse the request of the sage, so please proceed to Nandigrama and give Bharata all the news and that I am coming tomorrow. If his face shows the slightest disappointment at my return and any desire to keep the kingdom, please return and tell me. I will not stand in his way. Even the best of men may be tempted by riches at some time or other."

On his way to Ayodhya, Hanuman stopped at the homestead of Guha, chief of the tribe who had helped Rama to cross the Ganga on his way to the forest, and gave him the happy news. He then flew to Nandigrama and observed Bharata from the air. His hair was bound in matted locks on top of his head and he had a long black beard; he was clad only in bark and the skin of a black antelope and was totally emaciated, for he had been subsisting on fruits and roots alone for fourteen years as his brother must have also done. He had undertaken to guard the kingdom until his brother returned and that he had done to the best of his ability. He ruled the country from the little village of Nandigrama outside Ayodhya. He kept Rama's wooden sandals on the throne and took his orders from them. Bharata considered himself to be merely a regent. He seemed to be keeping alive only for that purpose. In fact, he looked like a *brahmarishi* (sage who has integral knowledge of the Supreme Brahman), sitting with eyes half closed, absorbed in deep meditation. His lips were constantly murmuring "Rama, Rama!" Seeing his condition, Maruti was overjoyed. Assuming the guise of a Brahmin, he approached in all humility, for he realized that he was in the presence of a truly superior human being, the very personification of *dharma,* one who had conquered his senses, one who had no desire for worldly possession and whose only thought was for Rama!

Hanuman repeated the name of Rama loudly in order to catch

Bharata's attention. He immediately opened his eyes and looked at him in surprise.

Hanuman said, "O Prince! I bring you tidings of your brother, Rama, for whose sake you have donned this garb and for whose dear sake you have given up all thoughts of a happy, normal life that you could have well enjoyed. He for whose loss you sorrow night and day, the catalogue of whose virtues you are incessantly reciting, the glory of the line of Raghu, the benefactor of the pious, the deliverer of the saints, has arrived safely. After conquering his foes in battle, with the gods to hymn his praises, the Lord is now on his way with Sita and Lakshmana. He has sent me in advance to tell you that he will be arriving here very soon."

Now, in order to test him, Hanuman said, "However, it is my duty to advise you. Why have you deprived yourself of the kingship that your mother got for you with such difficulty? Why do you feel guilty about accepting the throne? This type of renunciation is only for weaklings!"

Bharata was horrified to hear the Brahmin's advice. "Go away, you wicked Brahmin! Like my brother, I too am an upholder of *dharma*. I would rather die than sacrifice it on the altar of ambition!"

Hanuman was very happy to hear this and revealed his true form to him. He gave him the happy news of Rama's approach.

For fourteen years, Bharata had been waiting for this moment, and now when he heard the news, he swooned with happiness. He recovered himself and embraced Hanuman, saying, "I don't know who you are, but you have brought me the happiest news of my life and thus you are my best friend. Many, many years ago, my beloved brother went away to the forest and all these years I have been waiting only for his return. Tell me how I should reward you."

Hanuman's eyes filled with tears to see such devotion. He had thought that he loved Rama more than anyone else, but now it appeared that there were many who had the same adoration for Rama. "I am the son of the wind god, a monkey, Hanuman by name, a servant of the glorious Raghupati."

On hearing this, Bharata rose up and embraced him. Tears were flowing unchecked down his cheeks, and he could not contain his delight.

"O monkey! Now I remember you are the one who halted here when you were going on your way to get the magic herb to revive Lakshmana. Your very sight has dispelled my sorrows, for today I have embraced a friend of Rama's. Now tell me of my Lord's adventures. Did my brother make mention of this poor servant?"

Hanuman was amazed at Bharata's humility.

"My Lord, you are as dear to Rama as his own life. Believe me, this is the truth!" Hanuman now seated himself beside Bharata on the grass mat and told him all the details of Rama's life after leaving him. At last, he told him that he had reached the *ashrama* of sage Bharadwaja and would be reaching Ayodhya shortly.

Bharata called Shatrugna and all the others, and all of them made haste to prepare the city for Rama's arrival. The city of Ayodhya, which had been like a dead city all these years, suddenly blossomed to life. Once again banners and streamers flew from the battlements of the palace. Musicians restrung their silent *vinas* (stringed instruments akin to lutes). The trees burst into bloom and the streets were sprinkled with rose water and fried rice and decorated with auspicious signs. Once more the fountains started to play and the streams to run and the sound of laughter and rejoicing floated in the air. The citizens donned their best clothes, which had been locked away in their chests for fourteen years, and thronged the streets. The ladies formed a procession, singing and bearing golden salvers laden with curds, *dhruva* grass, turmeric paste, fruits, flowers, springs of the holy *tulsi* plant, and many other auspicious articles. The whole city waited in anticipation for the arrival of her rightful Lord. The king's highway leading from Nandigrama to the city was decorated with auspicious patterns, traced with colored powder, and sprinkled with rose water. Rama's sandals were kept on top of a caparisoned, white elephant, with the white umbrella of sovereignty held above it. Bharata and Shatrugna shaved their beards and cut their hair and dressed themselves in princely attire.

The dowager queens rose up in haste and eagerly questioned Bharata about Rama's welfare. He assured them that he was arriving soon.

Everything was ready and everyone was eagerly waiting when the Pushpaka reached the sacred village of Nandigrama, where the flame of devotion had been kept alight for fourteen years by Bharata. Many of the ladies crowded on the rooftops of houses in order to see the chariot as it descended. The chariot hovered for some time in the air so that Rama could point out the various familiar landmarks to the excited monkeys and *rakshasas*.

"There is Ayodhya, the city of my fathers and the citadel of the kings of the solar dynasty. This city is even more precious to me than Vaikunta, the abode of Vishnu. The dwellers here are indeed very dear to me. There is the Sarayu River, which holds the land of Kosala in its embrace, and there are my dear brothers, Bharata and Shatrugna, saluting me from below. Those are my mothers, Kausalya, Kaikeyi, and Sumitra, who are standing on the palace ramparts."

At the very first sight of the aerial chariot, Hanuman shouted, "Here comes Sri Ramachandra!" The citizens took up the cry, and soon the whole air was reverberating to the shouts of "Jai Sri Rama!"

As soon as the car landed, Rama got out and dropped his bow and arrows and went and fell at the feet of his preceptors, Vasishta and Vamadeva, as well as the other Brahmins.

Bharata now rushed forward and fell full-length at Rama's feet. Bharata could hardly speak when Rama asked about his welfare.

"I was sinking in an ocean of sorrow, but now that I have seen you, all is well with me."

The brothers had a tender reunion that brought tears to the eyes of the watching monkeys. Bharata took the sandals, which were the virtual rulers of the state, and placed them lovingly on his brother's holy feet, saying, "I give you back the kingdom that was given to me to look after. It was a great burden on me, but I have guarded it carefully. Today my mother's name has been cleared, and I have atoned for her sins. Please allow us to conduct the coronation that should have taken place fourteen years ago."

Sugriva and Vibhishana were touched to see this brotherly affection and pained by the thought of their own brothers, Vaali and Ravana, who had treated them so harshly.

Rama agreed to this and then sent the Pushpaka back to Kubera, who was its rightful owner. The flower-bedecked chariot slowly rose up into the air, circled Rama thrice, and then floated away in a northerly direction. Rama turned to the citizens and personally greeted each and every one of them, much to their delight. He then proceeded to the palace where the mothers were eagerly awaiting him. They embraced him in turn with eyes filled with tears of joy.

Urmila was Lakshmana's wife. The goddess of sleep had given her a boon that she would sleep for fourteen years while her husband was away. It is said that during this period Lakshmana did not sleep at all so that he could serve his brother night and day! As soon as Rama and Lakshmana reached the outskirts of Ayodhya, Urmila woke up from her long slumber and bedecked herself in order to meet her husband.

Rama and Lakshmana shaved off their matted locks and discarded their clothes of bark. The three mothers now gave them a ceremonial bath. They washed away every trace of forest life on their bodies and anointed Rama with oil, *sandal,* and turmeric paste. They bathed him in milk, curd, butter, and perfumed water and bedecked him in yellow silk and adorned him with fragrant garlands and gem-studded ornaments of gold. Janaki was also lovingly bathed and dressed by Kausalya, Sumitra, and Kaikeyi. She was clad in heavenly attire and every part of her body was adorned with jewels. Kausalya condescended to dress the hair of the wives of the *vanaras,* much to their delight.

Sumantra, the charioteer, now brought the royal chariot, and Rama and Sita ascended it and were taken in state to the main palace. Bharata asked Sumantra's permission and took over the reins of the chariot. Shatrugna held the white umbrella of royalty over Rama's head while Lakshmana and Vibhishana stood on either side and fanned him with the white-tailed yak fans. Hanuman knelt at his feet. Sugriva came at the back, riding on an elephant. The citizens who were lining the streets went mad with joy and shouted, "Jai (hail) Sri Rama! Jai Sita!

Jai Lakshmana!" Thus they arrived in state at the palace that had been occupied by the kings of the Ikshvaku dynasty for centuries. For the first time in fourteen years Rama entered a city. He had deliberately declined from entering any city all these years. He had not seen either Kishkinda or Lanka from the inside.

Rama then asked Bharata to prepare the best rooms in his own palace for Sugriva and Vibhishana to reside along with their wives. Bharata in turn requested Sugriva to send his people to bring waters from all the holy rivers and oceans of the land for the coronation. Five hundred monkeys sprang to do his bidding and brought water from five hundred different sources! Sage Vasishta was the *guru* of the solar dynasty, and he was the one in charge of the whole function.

He had Rama sit on the jeweled throne of the Ikshvakus with Sita beside him. From golden pitchers, all the great sages poured the consecrated waters, brought from all the sacred rivers and seas of the land, over Rama's head, to the accompaniment of sacred Vedic chants. Shatrugna held the white umbrella of sovereignty over his head. Lakshmana and Bharata stood on both sides, and Sugriva and Vibhishana waved the royal yak tail fans. Hanuman sat at his feet and offered his paws as a footstool. Vasishta now crowned him with a crown studded with precious stones and fashioned by Brahma himself.

The wind god came and presented Rama with a golden garland that was made of one hundred golden lotuses, as well as a beautiful necklace of pearls. The gods and celestials stood in the sky watching the wonderful scene.

Rama now gifted a hundred thousand cows and horses to deserving Brahmins. To Sugriva he presented a golden garland studded with jewels and to Angada, the son of Vaali, a pair of lovely armlets made of diamonds and other precious stones. He then gave Sita the pearl necklace given to him by Varuna, the god of the ocean, which had the luster of moonbeams, as well as many splendid garments and jewels. All the *vanaras* and *rakshasas* were also given many exotic gifts. However, he didn't give anything to Hanuman.

Sita now looked at Hanuman with great love and glanced inquiringly at her husband. Rama knew what was passing through her mind and told her, "O Janaki, you are free to bestow the pearl necklace on the one with whom you are most pleased. Gift it to one who has all the qualities that you think a great hero should have, such as fidelity, truth, skill, courtesy, foresight, prowess, and good intellect."

Sita took out the precious necklace of pearls that Rama had given her and without a moment's hesitation, she put it around the neck of the son of the wind god. Hanuman bowed respectfully and returned to his seat.

He took out the necklace and started to examine it carefully. He smelled it and scratched it and put it to his nose and his ears as if listening to something. He then took each precious bead, cracked it with his teeth, and peered into the shiny fragments before throwing it off as being worthless! Everyone was horrified at this terrible behavior. "What an insult to the queen," said some. "What can you expect from a monkey?" asked another.

Sita couldn't bear to see such monkeylike behavior on the part of one whom she loved so much and who had done so much for her. She asked him to explain himself.

Hanuman looked surprised and replied, "To me, the only thing worthy of respect is the name of Rama. Anything that does not have it is worthless. I examined the beads to see if they had his name written anywhere, then I smelled it to see if his perfume was there, and bit it to see if it contained anything of Rama inside, but there was nothing. This is only an ordinary pearl necklace, and what use is such a thing for a monkey like me? My Lady! I am of course proud that you have chosen me as a fitting recipient for this signal honor, but please forgive me for not wearing it."

The spectators were astonished by this statement and Sita asked him, "O Hanuman! What about your body? Is it not made up of the five elements? What does it have of Rama?"

Hanuman now asked Sugriva to put his ear to his chest, and to Sugriva's amazement, he heard the continuous chanting of "Rama, Rama," coming from Hanuman's heart.

Then, as if to put an end to further dispute, it is said that this great devotee of Rama split his chest open with his nails, and to the astonishment of all, there was Rama enshrined within with Sita beside him! A great gasp of wonder rose up in the assembly and everyone shouted, "Jai Sri Rama! Jai Hanuman!"

Rama came down from his throne, embraced him warmly, and placed his blessed hands on the wound, which healed miraculously at his touch. He then asked him to choose whatever gift he would like.

Hanuman replied, "My Lord! May my supreme affection for you live forever. May my devotion to you be constant. Let my love not be diverted to anything else. May life remain in my body as long as your story remains on the face of the earth. Let me imbibe the nectar of your stories so that I shall be able to ally my longing to see you in front of me. Let me be present whenever and wherever your name is chanted and your songs are sung. This is the only gift that I want." Rama placed his hands on Anjaneya's head and blessed him with all the boons he had requested.

"So shall it be, O Prince of Monkeys! There is no doubt that your fame will endure and life too will continue in your body as long as this story remains current in this world. My stories will abide as long as the world lasts. When I think of all the services you have rendered to me and Sita and Lakshmana, I should be prepared to give up my life for you here and now. But I prefer to remain in your debt forever, O monkey! I pray that I will never get an occasion to repay you for all that you have done, since normally one wants to be repaid only when one is in trouble!"

Rama then hugged Hanuman and blessed him over and over again.

He then presented each and every one with some precious gift. No one was left out, not even the hunchback Mandara, who was the sole cause of his having been banished from Ayodhya, since it was he who had poisoned the mind of Kaikeyi. The whole day long, the citizens and the monkeys ate and drank to their heart's content. That night, for the first time in fourteen years Lakshmana slept in the arms of his wife Urmila.

Rama wanted to confer the title of prince regent on Lakshmana, but he steadfastly refused to play this role and insisted that the post belonged to Bharata alone.

The monkeys were in a state of bliss. They had quite forgotten their forest homes and continued to stay on with the Lord of their hearts. At last Rama called them to him and told them all to return to their homes and take up their allotted duties and maintain their devotion to him. Rama gave a jeweled robe to Sugriva and one to Vibhishana. Sorrowfully, Sugriva and his brood of monkeys returned to Kishkinda and Vibhishana and his people to Lanka. Hanuman, however, opted to stay with Rama, for he could not bear to be parted from him.

Ramarajya, or the rule of Rama, is famed over the whole world up to the present day as being a glorious one. Great spiritual leaders continue to hope that one day, as Mahatma Gandhi once stated, the whole of India will exist in a state of Ramarajya. There was at that time no danger from beasts or snakes or fear of diseases. There were no robbers, for everyone had enough of what was needed. There were no untimely deaths and there were no widows. Every creature was happy and devoted to righteousness. People lived to a ripe old age without suffering from any decrepitude. The rod was never seen except in the hand of a *sannyasin* (one who has renounced the world), the word "beat" had no meaning except to mark the time for a dancer, and the only victory was over one's own self. The land flourished and the people were supremely happy, for they worshipped Rama as god incarnate.

Nature gave lavishly of her bounty. The forests abounded with fruit trees and flowers. The elephant and tiger lived amicably together. Bees laden with honey droned and made pleasant sounds. The Earth was clothed with crops and every river flowed with pellucid water.

All affliction ceases, all pain is erased,
When one recalls the mighty hero, Hanuman.

SRI HANUMAN CHALISA BY TULSIDAS

Aum Sri Hanumathe Namaha!

29

Shubangana

Dharma Triumphs

Sarvam muditamevasid sarvo dharmaparobhavat,
Ramamevanupashyanto Nabhbhyahimsam parasparam.

Everyone was happy and devoted to righteousness,
Looking up to Rama alone, even wild animals did not
 kill one another.

VALMIKI RAMAYANA, YUDDHA KANDA

Soon after their return to Ayodhya, Hanuman asked Rama to accompany him to the Himalayas to meet his mother, who was living an ascetic life absorbed in meditation and prayer. Rama agreed, and they went to Anjana's hermitage. She was delighted to see them and welcomed Rama with all love and seated him on a special mat. Now she asked her son to tell her the whole episode of the war with Ravana and the part he had played in it. Hanuman narrated the whole sequence of events. Strangely enough the story didn't seem to impress her. As he kept describing his own part in it, her brow knitted and her face darkened. At last she gave vent to her feelings and burst out.

"You are not worthy of being my son. You have disgraced your mother's milk. It looks as if my giving birth to you and feeding you with my milk has been of no use. Could you not have prevented the whole war by destroying the city of Lanka and killing Ravana by yourself? You could then have rescued the princess and brought her back to Rama and thus saved him the trouble of going there after undergoing so many hardships! I see that the milk you drank from my breasts has proved unfruitful. I am quite ashamed of you!"

Hanuman was amused by his mother's tirade and told her lovingly that he had only obeyed the orders given to him both by Rama and Sita.

"I would have been overstepping my limits as a servant had I rescued the princess of Videha. She was also of the opinion that her husband should come himself and rescue her after killing the ten-headed monster and thus saving his honor as a king!"

Anjana was a little mollified by this and said, "Ah! Then I'm happy that my milk did not go waste."

All those who were assembled there, especially Lakshmana, was wondering what the potency of her milk was, upon which she kept harping. Understanding his unspoken question, she said, "I will prove to you that my milk is indeed very special." So saying, she squeezed her breast so that a thin stream of milk arched through the air and fell on the summit of the hill opposite. There was a deafening crash as of thunder and to the amazement of the onlookers, the summit split in two!

She laughed and said, "Now do you believe me? Maruti was brought up on this potent milk. Can you doubt his strength?"

The entire entourage returned after having spent some time with Anjana. Many years passed while Rama reigned in Ayodhya with Sita by his side, ably helped by his brothers and ministers and ever served by the faithful Hanuman. There are many stories connected with Maruti during this period that highlight other aspects of his unique personality. He was always seated at the feet of the royal couple, listening intently to every word they spoke. Pleased with his devotion, the divine pair, in this famous passage, revealed to him the secret of their incarnation.

Rama said, "Listen carefully, O monkey, to what I have to tell you, for you have proved yourself to be a fitting recipient to hear this abstruse truth. Know me to be the Supreme Purusha, the eternal, unchanging, infinite spirit. I am that one Supreme Consciousness, totally indivisible. Everything is in fact nothing but that Consciousness."

Sita then continued. "Know me to be Prakriti, cosmic matter, the supreme embodiment of all manifestation. I am the cradle of Time and Space and all things exist in me. Rama is the transcendent Absolute and I am his manifest power. I am that principle that performs all these apparent acts of creation, preservation, and destruction. Actually, all the events that have taken place until now are only the sport (*lila*) of the divine. They should not be confused with Rama's transcendent state, which is changeless, eternal, and imperishable."

Rama continued, "Together we constitute the universe. We validate each other's existence and delight in each other's company. I am the Paramatman, soul of the universe, and Sita is the *jivatman,* the embodied soul. Ravana is the ego that separates these two entities. What unites them is *bhakti,* or devotion. You are the embodiment of *bhakti,* and hence this esoteric secret has been revealed to you."

Hanuman listened intently to this discourse. Next morning when he appeared in court Rama asked him, "Who are you?"

Maruti realized that the question was meant to test him and replied:

"From the point of view of the body I am your servant,

From the point of view of the mind and intellect I am a portion of you, but from the point of view of the *atman* I am yourself!"

Rama and Sita were highly pleased with his beautiful explanation.

Sometimes Bharata and Shatrugna would take Hanuman to their own palaces and make him relate again and again all Rama's wonderful doings, for they were never tired of listening to his amazing tales. But Hanuman would never stay long with anyone else. He would always contrive to return and sit at Rama's feet. He anticipated his every need and would do it before anyone else could.

This behavior of his began to irritate Sita and his brothers, who found that there was nothing left for them to do. At last Rama's brothers went to Sita and complained about the fact that due to Hanuman's amazing attentiveness, there was nothing left for anyone else to do, and they all wanted to serve Rama in some way. Sita had to agree that this was indeed true, so they drew up a daily schedule of all the services to be performed for Rama. Each of them was given some task and nothing was left for Hanuman. This schedule was presented to Rama for his approval and seal. He was a bit suspicious since he noticed that Hanuman's name was not included. However, he didn't say anything. Next day when the court assembled, Hanuman started to press Rama's feet as usual. Immediately Lakshmana pointed out to him that this task had been assigned to someone else. He then flourished the time schedule in front of his face. Hanuman was sadly disappointed to see that his name was nowhere in the picture. Lakshmana cheerfully told him that if any service had been omitted he could do it. Maruti inspected the document carefully and realized that every single thing from the time Rama got up until the time he went to bed had been allotted. At last he thought of a brilliant idea.

"I don't see yawning service," he said.

"What on Earth is yawning service?" asked Lakshmana.

"You know, when anyone yawns, they normally snap their fingers in front of their open mouth in order to ward off evil spirits from entering, so I can take up that service and spare my Lord from the exertion of snapping his fingers!"

"Indeed, why not?" asked Lakshmana.

"Well, then I want it in writing, too, with my Lord's seal on it."

Lakshmana promptly had this done, but little did he realize the consequences of such a demand!

A yawn might come at any moment; therefore Maruti had to be with Rama all the time! He had to sit near him with his eyes fixed on his face so that he would never miss an opportunity to snap his fingers in the advent of a yawn! On that day he even ate with his left hand so as to leave the right free for a yawn! At night he went with Sita and Rama and tried to enter their bedroom, but Sita was firm on this point and told him that he could go and rest. Hanuman was a bit sad since night is the time when most people yawn and he wanted to be sure to fulfill his part of the bargain. But what could he do? He went and sat on the balcony just above their bedroom and closed his eyes and started to repeat Rama's name so that he wouldn't sleep. In the meantime he kept snapping his right hand fingers constantly so as to forestall any yawn that Rama might have. Inside the bedroom Rama found that he was hit by a mighty yawning fit, which didn't seem to stop. Yawn after great yawn split his face into two. Soon he couldn't even close his mouth since the yawns kept coming one after the other. He collapsed on the bed in sheer exhaustion. Sita was terrified and called the physician, ministers, and Vasishta, the royal *guru*. Nobody was able to do anything. Suddenly, Vasishta noticed that one person was missing. He immediately set about searching for Hanuman. He was sure he couldn't be far off, and sure enough, he found him on the balcony intently repeating his *mantra* and snapping his fingers continuously. He shook him awake and brought him to Rama's presence. Maruti was devastated to see the condition of his master and inadvertently stopped snapping his fingers. The effect was immediate. Rama stopped yawning. Now the whole story came out, and Sita and the brothers were most contrite, for they realized that they had done an injustice to this great devotee. All of them fell at Rama's feet and promised that henceforth the zealous monkey would be allowed to perform whatever service he wanted.

Hanuman was as attached to Sita as he was to Rama and would watch all her actions with great attention. Every morning he would observe Sita put a red mark on her forehead and smear the parting of her hair with vermilion powder, enacting a ritual that is the exclusive prerogative of married women in India. He was very curious to know the reason behind this daily ritual.

"I do this for the well-being of my husband, as indeed all married women do," she said with a gentle smile. Hanuman, ever the humble well-wisher of his chosen lord, wondered, "If a virtuous woman like Sita has to apply vermilion in this manner for the good of Lord Rama, I, a mere monkey, need to do more." Thinking thus, he bounded off to the market in haste and bought a big sackful of vermillion powder. He mixed some oil and made a paste out of it and smeared his whole body with it. He entered the court and took his usual place at Rama's feet. Everyone was most amused to see his strange looks. Rama also glanced at him in some amusement and asked him why he had done this. Hanuman looked at him with tears in his eyes and said, "My Lord! May you live for as many years as there are hairs on this servant's body!"

Sita immediately guessed the reason for his strange behavior and whispered in her husband's ear. Needless to say, both Rama and Sita were moved by the purity of his heart. Rama got up from his throne and hugged him and said, "Today is Tuesday, and anyone who offers oil and vermillion to my beloved servant on this day will be blessed by me and have his wishes granted." Since then, idols of Hanuman are colored a rich vermilion red.

As Sita had no children of her own, she used to shower all her maternal affection on Hanuman. Normally, he used to eat only Rama's leftovers. One day she decided to prepare something special for him. She made him sit and started feeding him with all the choice dishes she had prepared with her own hands. Hanuman was ravenous, and the more she fed him the hungrier he became. Sita was a bit dismayed, since all the food she had cooked was gone. It was then that she realized that her "son" was actually the great Lord Maheswara who was capable of consuming the whole creation at the time of cosmic dissolution! She quietly went behind him and wrote the five-syllabled *mantra* of Lord Shiva at the back of his head (Aum Namashivaaya), thus acknowledging his true identity! Immediately Hanuman burped, thus showing he was satiated, and went and rinsed his mouth.

One day Hanuman was strolling through the marketplace when a foolish merchant called out to him. "Hey Maruti! Tell me what Lanka looked like when you burned it."

Hanuman replied that he couldn't describe it but was willing to demonstrate. He asked the merchant to wrap his tail in cloth, dip it in oil, and set fire to it. As soon as he had done this, Hanuman immediately set fire to the merchant's shop, which burned to the ground. He then went to a pool and put out his lighted tail.

The next day the merchant went to court and complained to Rama. "Your monkey destroyed my business!"

Rama asked Hanuman to explain his behavior, and he gave him a true account of the affair. When Rama asked the merchant if this was correct, he admitted it but added, "But I never expected him to burn my shop!"

"O! So you would have been happy to watch another person's shop burn?"

The man hung his head in shame and Rama dismissed the case.

Sometimes Hanuman would take the form of an ordinary monkey and raid the fruit gardens of Ayodhya. No one dared to do anything to him since they never knew if he was an ordinary monkey or Rama's favorite, Hanuman. He used to regularly raid one particular garden with luscious fruits, which some men had been tending carefully so that they could pluck the fruit when it was ripe. They were quite exasperated by the antics of this monkey and decided to catch him and take him to court. If it happened to be Hanuman, they knew that Rama would recompense them and if not, they would be free to berate it as they thought fit. So one day they set a trap and caught him and took him to court. Rama recognized him but pretended not to. He told the boys to take it back and give it whatever punishment they thought fit. Hanuman used his strength and broke out of the trap, but before entering Rama's presence, he caused huge welts to appear all over his body and hobbled into court with a doleful expression. Rama was filled with remorse when he saw him and hugged him. Hanuman then laughed and said, "Well, you played a joke on me by pretending you didn't recognize me, so I also played a trick on you!"

One day in court, Rama decided to tease Hanuman. He wanted to know who his most devoted servant was. Naturally everyone raised their hands but Hanuman raised three by including his upraised tail, which is actually another hand for a monkey. The other couriers were always a bit jealous of Hanuman, so they devised a scheme of bringing up a proposal of marriage for Hanuman, whom they knew to be a lifelong celibate. What started as a joke turned out to be a serious test of obedience.

"O Maruti! Now that the war is over, isn't it time you gave up your celibate life and married and settled down?" Rama asked teasingly.

Hanuman knew that Rama was joking, so he decided to play along with him and said, "My Lord! What good-looking woman would even look at me, much less marry me?"

Rama promptly said, "If I find someone who is ready to marry you, would you agree?"

Hanuman was in a dilemma. He was faced with an ethical crisis— his vow of celibacy against his obedience to his Lord. "If the woman is perfectly agreeable, well, I suppose I will have to agree, since it's your wish."

Someone said, "Since the boy is ill-formed, the girl can be a hunchback and so I propose the hunchback Mandara, queen Kaikeyi's maid, as a fitting bride!"

Hanuman was stunned and said, "My Lord! That woman sent you to the forest for fourteen years! Think of what she might do to me!"

Rama laughed and said, "Don't worry. She's a reformed person now. We will summon her to court tomorrow and see if she agrees!"

Late in the night Hanuman went to Mandara's room and told her of the discussion that had taken place at court that morning. Surprisingly, she seemed rather pleased at the idea and said that she would like to get married. If she couldn't get a man, a monkey was the next best bet. Maruti tried to talk her out of this, but she was adamant. At last, Hanuman lost his temper. He grew to an enormous size and started choking her with his tail to give her a taste of what marriage to him would be like! She was terrified and promised not to agree to the proposal when summoned to court.

The next morning, she appeared before the court, and Rama put the suggestion to her. There was an expectant silence. Hanuman glared at her, and she quickly turned down the offer. Hanuman breathed a sigh of relief and looked at Rama, who was regarding him with a twinkle in his eye, and he realized that the whole thing was a joke on his part.

One day Rama and Sita had an amicable argument as to which of them got greater devotion from Hanuman. They asked him outright, but the wily monkey managed to get out of it by saying that he was devoted to both of them jointly—Sita-Rama. Sita promptly asked him to get her a pitcher of water as she was dying of thirst. Rama immediately countered by feigning a swoon due to the heat and begged Hanuman to fan him. They both waited expectantly to find out which request would be attended to first. The clever monkey expanded both his arms and fetched water with one hand while fanning Rama with the other. This placated both his divine masters.

Once the divine sage Narada, who was noted for his great devotion to Vishnu, visited Ayodhya and asked Hanuman if Rama kept a record of his greatest *bhaktas*. Hanuman wasn't too sure of this, so the sage went and asked Rama himself. The Lord showed him a huge ledger in which Narada's name appeared on the top of the very first page. He was very pleased, but after going through the pages, he was puzzled at not finding Hanuman's name anywhere. He went and reported the matter to Hanuman who said, "Ask him to show you his little diary."

Narada returned and asked the Lord to show him this little book. In this he found that Hanuman was listed first and his own name was not to be found at all. Naturally, he asked Rama about the difference between the two. The Lord replied that the large book was a record of all those worthy souls who remembered him all the time whereas the second book was a record of all those whom *he* remembered all the time! Narada's pride was duly humbled for he had always thought he was the greatest of all devotees.

Narada now enacted another drama to show the glory of the Lord's name. Once the king of Kashi was going to Ayodhya with his full retinue when he was stopped by the sage, who always loved to create some situations for the further play of the Lord. Narada told the king that when he reached the court, he should pay his respects to all the sages except Viswamitra. The king was not at all happy about this but was bound by his promise. Vishwamitra was noted for his volatile temper and furious at the king's behavior, complained to Rama. The Lord took out three arrows from his quiver and vowed to kill the king of Kashi before the end of the day. This news reached the king, who was terrified and ran to Narada, telling him to save him since the whole fault was his. Narada cheerfully replied that he could not hope for a better death than at the hands of Rama. The king was not impressed by this and ran to the river to hide himself from Rama's wrath. Narada followed him and told him not to worry and that he would save him. He told him to sit on his lute and that he would carry him to the Kanchana Mountain.

"Who is there in that mountain that will be able to save me from Rama's wrath?"

"Hanuman's mother, Anjana, is doing *tapas* there. Throw yourself at her feet and beg her to save you. Don't get up until she gives her word."

As instructed, the king threw himself at the feet of Anjana and begged her to save him from imminent death. She promised him asylum and told him that no one could harm him in her presence. Then she asked him to name the person from whom he was running.

At last the king whispered, "Rama is one who has sworn to kill me before the day is over!"

"Rama!" exclaimed Anjana. "He is the soul of compassion! What crime have you committed to make him take such an oath?"

The poor king related the whole incident. Anjana then decided to invoke her son since she had given her word to the king to protect him. Just at this time Hanuman also arrived to meet his mother.

She was very happy to see him. She told him that she was in a great dilemma and begged him to rescue her. Hanuman immediately agreed to take care of whatever the problem might be, but she made him give his word three times before she disclosed the secret. Naturally, Hanuman was astounded to hear the whole story but having promised his mother, he had no other choice but to comply. He immediate transported the King of Kashi to the banks of the Sarayu River, which encircled the city of Ayodhya. He told him to stand waist-deep in the water and continuously chant the name of Rama.

"Remember, you must never get out of the water until I tell you and you must never stop chanting "Rama, Rama.""

The unhappy king had no other recourse but to give his promise. Hanuman now went posthaste to Rama and prostrated himself before him humbly.

Rama looked at him enquiringly and asked, "Is there something you want?"

Hanuman said, "My Lord, please give me your word that I will always be able to protect those who are chanting your name."

"My dearest Maruti! I have already given you this boon. Why are you asking for it again?"

Hanuman insisted that he give his word once again and Rama laughingly obliged. Anjaneya now returned to the river and stood with upraised mace, ready to protect the king of Kashi, who was devotedly chanting Rama's name loudly and clearly. Very soon the news spread that the one whom Rama had sworn to kill before nightfall was being guarded by no less a personage than Hanuman himself!!

Rama soon learned of the whereabouts of the king and went to the river accompanied by the sage Vishwamitra. Hanuman saw him coming and warned the king to keep chanting relentlessly, whatever happened. Rama fixed his arrow on the bow and shot it at the king. The arrow, however, went around the king and returned to his quiver. Rama was astonished to hear a voice from the arrow, "My Lord! I can't kill someone who is chanting your name while Hanuman is around."

Rama refused to listen to this and sent another arrow, which also returned and said, "O King! You have given your word to your devotee that anyone that chants your name will be protected by him. We are only helping you keep to your word."

Vishwamitra was getting angry by this time, so Rama fitted his third arrow to the bow. Hanuman warned the king of Kashi to repeat the sacred *mantra* without even pausing for breath. The king's teeth were chattering with cold, but he repeated the *mantra* continuously.

Just as Rama fitted his third arrow, his family *guru*, Vasishta, arrived on the scene and begged Hanuman to stand aside and allow Rama to redeem his pledge.

"The king will reach Heaven if he dies at the hands of Rama, so don't try to thwart him."

Hanuman said, "But I am indeed redeeming Rama's pledge to me that I can save anyone who chants his name!"

Vasishta was puzzled as to how this dilemma could be solved. He decided that the only one who could do it was Vishwamitra. So he went to him and begged him to forgive the king of Kashi and let Rama off his pledge. Vishwamitra said that he was prepared to do so if the king fell at his feet and promised never to insult anyone in future, especially a sage.

Hanuman told his protégé to get out of the river and throw himself at the sage's feet. The king was shivering so much that he could hardly get out of the river. Still repeating the name of Rama, he went and prostrated himself full-length at the feet of Vishwamitra. He clutched his feet and begged him to forgive him since the whole thing was a drama planned by the sage, Narada, who had a curious sense of humor and who was even now watching the whole scene with great amusement.

Vasishta now told Rama to keep his third arrow back in its quiver. Rama did so just as the sun slipped below the western horizon. Hanuman fell at the feet of his master and begged him to forgive him. All he wanted to do was prove to the world the glory of the Lord's name.

There is another story with the same theme that is well worth mentioning here.

The king of Kashi was called Yayati. He was a great *bhakta* of Rama. Once when he had gone hunting, he met the great sage, Vishwamitra and failed to do reverence to him in the eagerness of the chase. The sage, as is to be expected, cursed him. "I'll see to it that your head falls at my feet!"

Yayati ran after the sage and begged his pardon. He told him that he was quite innocent of the whole affair and that he had been too engrossed in the chase and had not seen him. Vishwamitra was not to be appeased. He went straight to Ayodhya and told Rama, "O Rama! If you are my true disciple, you should see to it that the head of the one who insulted me is brought to my feet!"

"My Lord, who is it that has dared to insult you? Name him and I shall do your bidding immediately."

When Rama heard the name of Yayati, he was shocked, for he knew that he was his true devotee, but after considering the matter carefully, he decided that it was his duty to obey his *guru*'s commands. He sent his minister to Kashi and commanded the king to be ready to have a duel with him. The king did not know what to do, but he decided that it was his duty to obey his Lord, so he started off toward Ayodhya in order to spare Rama the trouble of coming to him. En route he was met by the divine sage, Narada, who was always on the lookout to see more of the Lord's *lilas*. The sage knew that the whole of life was indeed a game of the Supreme and he always did his bit to give interesting twists to the drama of life.

"O King!" he said. "I see that you are proceeding toward Ayodhya in order to spare the Lord the trouble of coming to you. But why do you give in so easily? Don't you want to save your life?"

The poor king nodded his head miserably. He said that he didn't know what he should do in this predicament and was hoping to persuade Rama that he was innocent.

Narada said, "Rama knows that, but he has sworn to do as his *guru* commands, so I advise you strongly not to go to Ayodhya."

"What should I do then?" asked the desperate king.

"You should go to the mountain of Kanchana and take refuge at the feet of Anjana, the mother of Anjaneya. She is the only one who will be able to help you."

"Now we will see some fun," thought Narada as he proceeded toward Anjana's *ashrama*.

Yayati also went as fast as he could to Anjana's *ashrama*. He fell at her feet and begged her to give him sanctuary. She told him not to be frightened and that no one would be able to hurt him in that place. She then thought of her son and asked him to come to her aid.

Hanuman was disturbed by these mental vibrations of his mother and immediately came to her hermitage.

He bowed to her and to the King of Kashi, whom he recognized as a great devotee of Rama, and asked his mother why she had summoned him. She explained the whole matter to him. Hanuman also promised to protect the king. It was only then that they thought of asking him the name of his adversary. When he heard the name of Rama, both Hanuman and Anjana got a shock. They didn't know what to do, but Anjana begged her son to back her word, even if it meant fighting with his beloved Rama. Narada also arrived on the scene, strumming his lute and looking quite delighted.

Both Rama and Vishwamitra arrived shortly after on the scene. Hanuman kept the king behind him and told Rama that his mother had afforded him protection and that he was bound to keep his mother's word.

God and devotee stood looking at each other. At last Rama took up his fire missile and flung it at Hanuman. However, Anjaneya simply absorbed it, as well as all the other missiles that followed. Nothing seemed to affect him. At last Rama took up his famous arrow and said, "I have no recourse but to use this. Prove that you are my devotee and deliver King Yayati, to me for I have to keep my word to my *guru*."

Hanuman replied, "My Lord! I am indeed your true devotee and disciple, so I have to keep my promise to my mother. Here is my breast. Please shoot your arrow at me."

So saying, he bared his breast and stood with closed eyes, repeating the Rama *mantra*.

The arrow flew unerringly, split Maruti's breast, and disappeared into his heart. To everyone's amazement, within his throbbing heart, they saw Rama and Sita enshrined.

Narada now went to the king and told him to run and lay his head at Vishwamitra's feet. This was the right moment to save himself. Even though he was frightened to show himself, the king obeyed the sage and ran and put his head on Vishwamitra's feet and begged him to forgive him for whatever sin he might have unknowingly committed.

Rama turned around, ready to take Yayati's head, but Narada stopped him and said, "My Lord, please desist from killing Yayati. Your *guru*'s curse has been fulfilled. All he told you was to lay the king's head at his feet and this has been done. So you are not guilty of going against your *guru*'s command."

Rama looked enquiringly at Vishwamitra, who was already regretting his hasty action and had forgiven the king long ago. The sage said, "Narada is right, O Rama. The king's head is at my feet, so please consider that you have obeyed my command."

Rama put his arrow back into the quiver and turned to Hanuman, saying, "O Anjaneya! You have conquered me. You are indeed my true devotee. In order to keep your word, you were even prepared to fight with me. In the future, you will be known as Veera Hanuman (Heroic Hanuman).

Hanuman bowed at Rama's feet and said, "It is you who have conquered me, my Lord, from the day you first cast your gracious glance over me. You are ever in my heart and it is you yourself who intercepted the arrow sent by you and saved me. I had nothing to do in this matter."

There is another story about Hanuman that is meant to prove the superiority of the Lord's name.

Once it is said that Rama picked up his bow to kill a person called Kuvachana who had insulted his ancestors. He immediately sought Hanuman's protection. Without going into the nature of his crime, Hanuman promised to defend him at any cost.

When he saw Rama approaching, bow in hand, he realized he had been tricked. Since he had given his word, he placed himself, arms akimbo, between Rama and Kuvachana.

Chanting the name of Rama, Hanuman created an enclosure around Kuvachana with his tail. The enclosure reverberated with the sound of the Rama *mantra*. Try as he might, Rama himself could not breach this fortress.

"More powerful than Rama is the name of Rama," murmured Hanuman.

The gods intervened to end the stalemate. Rama was allowed to kill Kuvachana to avenge the insult to his ancestors. Hanuman was allowed to bring Kuvachana back to life with the power of Rama's name!

> *Whoever brings any yearning to you,*
> *Obtains the fruit of immortal life.*
>
> Sri Hanuman Chalisa by Tulsidas

Aum Sri Hanumathe Namaha!

Aum Samsara-bhayanashakaaya Namaha!

30

Veera

Sita Abandoned

Again and again I beg of thee a boon,
Be gracious and grant it—an unwavering faith in thy
    lotus feet,
And constant communion with the saints.

RAMACHARITAMANAS BY TULSIDAS

It is in the last book known as Uttara Kanda that Valmiki recounts
the previous history of Ravana, the king of the night wanderers. It is
also in this book that the painful episode of Rama's repudiation of Sita
is told. We may well wonder at the intention of the sage in doing this.
Maybe he wanted to compare the polaric differences in the towering
personalities of the two men, both of whom loved Sita so passionately.
One was the lusty, powerful *rakshasa* Ravana, who was prepared to
exterminate his entire race, his brothers, his friends, and even his own
sons in order to quench his infatuation for another man's wife. The
other was the divine personality of Rama, who made the heartrending
decision to subdue his passion for his lawfully wedded wife and place
his duty to his subjects first, who was prepared to sacrifice the one he

loved most on the altar of the cosmic law of *dharma,* which proclaims that a king should put god first, his country next, and his own personal desire last. Ravana perished along with the rest of his tribe while the land of Kosala flourished under the rule of its saintly king!

Sages from all over the land used to come to Ayodhya in order to bless Rama and Sita. He seated them on golden thrones and gave all hospitality to them. Once he questioned them on Ravana's history—how had he become so powerful and what was the story behind his son, Meghanatha, and so on.

Agastya now told the whole story of Ravana. He had been a great devotee of Shiva. He had done great *tapas* to Brahma and had gotten many boons from him. He had asked for invincibility from all types of gods, demons, animals, and celestials, but he had forgotten to add humans and monkeys to his list. Having got all these boons, he became very arrogant and fought with everyone, including the gods. In his pride he even tried to lift up Mount Kailasa, but Shiva pressed the mountain down with his big toe so that Ravana's hand was smashed under it. It was then that he composed the famous hymn to Shiva known as Shiva Thandava Stotra, which pleased Shiva so much that he released his hand and gave him many other boons.

When he was returning, he saw a very beautiful lady anchorite staying in an *ashrama*. She had no ornaments and was clad in bark with matted hair and was doing intense *tapas*. Despite her lack of embellishments she was very beautiful and Ravana was not one who could resist a woman's beauty. He approached her and asked her who she was and why she was doing *tapas*.

She replied, "My name is Vedavati and I am the granddaughter of Brihaspati, the preceptor of the gods. My father refused all other offers of marriage for me and insisted that I should do *tapasya* in order to acquire Vishnu as my husband. My parents were killed by a demon and ever since then, I have been practicing austerities in order to have Vishnu as my husband."

Ravana laughed in scorn and said, "How stupid your father was and how stupid you are to follow his foolish advice and waste your youth. I am as great as or even greater than Vishnu and you would do well to become my wife." So saying, he made a lunge at her. She ran for her life, but he followed her and grabbed her by her hair. She managed to free herself and said, "O you monster! I will give up this body that has been defiled by you. But I will take another body that will eventually bring you to ruin." So saying, she gave up her life in front of his eyes.

The sages told Rama, "That Vedavati was born as Sita and you are the *avatara* of Vishnu."

Agastya then told Rama another story about Ravana concerning the reason he abducted Sita. Ravana had done a number of good things in his life and was a fitting recipient to go to heaven, but due to his atrocities, all the good he had done was negated. Once, during the *yuga* known as Satya, Ravana had asked the great sage, Sanat Kumara, to tell him which of the trinity was capable of giving liberation. The sage told him that Vishnu was certainly the one who could liberate. Anyone who was killed by Vishnu would attain instant emancipation. Ravana's eyes gleamed with interest when he heard this. He asked Sanat Kumara to tell him which was to be the next incarnation of Vishnu so that he could somehow see to it that he was killed by him. The sage told him that in the *yuga* known as Treta, Vishnu would be incarnated at Rama, scion of the race of Ikshvaku, and Lakshmi would take birth as the daughter of the king of Videha and marry him.

Ravana pondered over this matter and decided that the only way he could get liberation through Vishnu in his form as Rama was to make him so angry that he would be forced to kill him. The best way of making him angry was to abduct his wife. Agastya told Rama that this was the secret behind Ravana's abduction of Sita! He also gave him all the other details about the past lives of his son Meghanatha and his wife Mandodari. Thus, all the intricate threads that were woven by destiny to make up the tapestry of their lives were revealed to Rama.

Many years passed while Rama reigned with Sita by his side, helped by his able ministers and beloved brothers. Once when he was sitting with his three brothers and Hanuman, Bharata wanted to put a question to him, but he asked Hanuman to speak for him since he was known to be Rama's favorite.

"My Lord!" said Maruti. "Bharata wants to ask you to speak on the difference in behavior of the noble and the wicked."

Rama replied, "The difference in the conduct of the good and the wicked is like the difference between *sandal* wood and the ax. The fragrant wood imparts its perfume even to the very ax that fells it! For this reason the *sandal* wood is desired by all and has the honor of being put on the head of the gods. The ax on the other hand has its edge heated in the fire and then hammered until it becomes flat!

"O brother! There is no religion like charity and no sin like hatred. There are many types of sinful and noble acts that people might do, but the truly noble look on everything with an equal and loving eye."

His brothers and Hanuman were thrilled to hear his words.

There was an *ashoka* grove next to the palace that was even more beautiful than the one in Lanka. Flowering trees like the *champaka, kadamba, ashoka,* and *sandal* were there as well as fruit trees like mango and pomegranate. After finishing his day's work, Rama would often walk in these fragrant gardens with his adorable queen. One day while they were thus sitting in the grove and talking to each other, Rama noticed that his wife showed all signs of pregnancy. She was wearing a glistening red robe and her skin glowed with an ethereal beauty. Rama was delighted to see this and taking both her hands in his, he led her gently to an arbor in the grove and seated her tenderly on a jeweled seat. He offered her a golden goblet with the nectar of many flowers, untouched by bees. With his own hands he raised the glass to her lips and made her sip the delightful concoction. He embraced his alluring wife with great love and asked her, "My darling one! How radiant you look. I see that you are with child. A son is the only thing that we lack in our lives. I have no doubt that the child will be a wonderful infant. Tell me, my dearest love, how can I make you happier? Is there some wish of yours that is still to be fulfilled? Ask for anything and it shall be yours."

Sita raised her lotus face to his and whispered, "My Lord, I consider myself to be the luckiest woman alive. What further wish can your wife have than to be beside you always?"

But Rama insisted, "My lovely one, I want to make you even happier than you are now, if that were possible. Tell me something I can do for you. I am longing to shower you with everything, for it is said that a pregnant woman should have all her whims humored."

Sita smiled and looked at him with her fawnlike eyes. "Do you remember the forest near Chitrakuta where we used to wander hand in hand? Do you remember the sages and their wives and the peace of their hermitages? I have a great desire to go and visit them once again and eat the wild fruits and roots and drink the pure water of the Ganga and perhaps even stay there for a day or two."

Rama looked adoringly at his beloved wife. There was nothing he could deny her. If anything, his love for her had increased with the passing years. He had never felt the desire to take another consort, as the rest of the kings used to do. In fact the very idea was abhorrent to him. Sita was the most charming woman he had ever known, and he desired none other.

Holding her hands in his, he gazed at her doe-like eyes and said, "O Vaidehi! My beloved wife, you shall certainly go there if that is what you wish. In fact, I will see that you are taken there tomorrow."

Having given his promise to his queen, Rama left her and went to the outer courtyard to talk with his friends, and Sita went to her own apartments, where she was surprised to see her new handmaiden waiting for her. Actually, this woman was none other than Ravana's devious sister, Surpanekha, the cause of all Sita's troubles in the first place, as we know it was Surpanekha who, furious at having been spurned by Rama, had talked her brother Ravana into kidnapping Sita. Now, she had slipped into the palace under the guise of a maid and was plotting to avenge her brother's death. She had endeared herself to Sita and now when she saw her, she playfully asked her to describe what Ravana looked like.

Sita said, "I've no idea what Ravana looked like since I never saw his face. I once saw his shadow as it was cast on the sea on the way to Lanka."

The woman now begged Sita to draw this shadow on the wall and Sita innocently did so. As soon as Sita left the room, Surpanekha completed the drawing and slipped out of the palace. She took good care to spread the news of the painting of Ravana on the wall of Sita's private apartment. Of course, people are ever ready to see evil in their rulers, so the gossipmongers lapped up the tale and embellished it with their own fantastic ideas.

After leaving Sita in the garden, Rama had gone to the outer courtyard to speak to his close friends. In the course of their light banter, he turned to his friend Bhadra and asked, "Tell me, Bhadra, what do the citizens of Ayodhya say about me and Sita and my brothers? Kings are always a subject of criticism for the common folk, and it's always wise to know what they think."

Bhadra folded his palms and said, "Sire, people speak only well about you. Sometimes they discuss the events of the past years, when you achieved the impossible by killing the ten-headed demon and rescuing the princess of Videha. Your exploits are recounted with great enthusiasm by everyone."

"What else do they say, Bhadra? Tell me all. Why do you avert your face? Is there something that you feel should not be reported to me? Have no fear. I want to know the good and the bad. No king can afford to ignore what people say of him, so tell me everything frankly."

In a low, faltering tone, Bhadra said," They also remark that though your action in having killed the *rakshasa* was laudable, your conduct with regard to your wife is shameful. "How could the king have accepted a woman who had been kept on Ravana's lap and who had lived in his palace for so many months? How can the queen forget the indignities she must have suffered? We will have to put up with a similar conduct from our wives. They will be able to go from one man to another as they please and we will be forced to condone them. 'As the king, so the subjects!' This is what the people say in their ignorance."

Rama's whole face changed when he heard this slanderous accusation against him and his immaculate wife. He could not utter a word.

His friends tried to comfort him and said, "Your Majesty! It is the nature of the common people to speak ill of the nobility. A king need not pay heed to such vile accusations."

Rama hardly heard what they were saying. Taking leave of them in his usual courteous manner, he went to the garden and sat immersed in thought. He decided that it was his duty to check on this matter before coming to a decision. That evening, he wore the clothes of an ordinary citizen of Ayodhya and went incognito on a tour of the city. As luck would have it, as he passed the house of a washerman in one of the back streets of the city, he heard the sound of a man's voice raised in anger. He went close to the door and stood outside listening. The husband was berating his wife.

"I have heard reports of your indecent behavior. You have been seen talking to the nobleman who comes for a walk down this street. You may go back to your own home. I will not keep you here any longer. I belong to a respectable family and will not keep a loose woman as my wife. You are free to go where you please."

The poor woman pleaded that she was totally innocent and had only answered some questions the man had put to her. The washerman replied sternly, "Do you think I am Rama to tolerate such behavior? He is the king and can do as he pleases. As for me, I will never keep a wife who has been seen talking with another man."

Rama stood riveted to the spot for a few seconds. He felt like a tree that had been struck by lightning. The tender buds and leaves of hope that had sprouted in his heart after their return from Lanka were scorched and the naked, charred, and blackened branches raised their arms, in mute appeal to the heavens. He felt as if his whole body was on fire. He managed somehow to stagger back to the palace. He went to his private chamber and requested that his brothers come to him at once. They came immediately and were surprised to see his demeanor. He stood with his back to the door, gazing out on a wintry garden. His face was pale and his eyes had a glazed look as he turned around to face his brothers. His hands trembled slightly.

Lakshmana knelt before him and said, "Brother, what is it? Tell me.

Where is the enemy? You know that you have but to command and I shall obey."

Rama spoke in a voice that was drained of all emotion. "Do you know what the citizens are saying about Sita and me?"

All of them hung their heads and Rama continued, "I see that all of you know and have hidden the truth from me all these years, O Lakshmana! You were a witness to the fact that I refused to take her back after the war until her purity was proved by the ordeal in the fire. Yet these people now talk as if I have done a heinous crime. My heart is breaking and I am drowning in sorrow, yet my duty as a king is clear to me. The first duty of a king is to his subjects and not to himself. Sita is dearer to me than life itself, but I have no choice but to abandon her for the sake of my subjects. Lakshmana, take her away in the chariot with Sumantra, and leave her on the other side of the Ganga near the Tamasa River, where we stayed a long time ago. Just yesterday morning she asked me to take her there. Let her have her wish. She will suspect nothing."

Lakshmana jumped to his feet and said, "Rama, you cannot do this to her! She is burnished gold, purified by fire. Please do not ask me to do this. I will do anything else you ask, but not this. Don't you know that she is carrying your child in her womb? How can you bear to do this? Can you not wait at least until the child is born?"

His face carved out of stone, Rama said in a stern voice, "After the child is born you will say, let her stay while she suckles the infant and then you'll say, let her stay until he is five years old, and thus it will go on indefinitely, and eventually Rama would have betrayed his country for the sake of his own felicity."

Bharata and Shatrugna also added their pleas. Rama continued in a hard, loud voice, "I do not want to hear another word from any of you. I want none of your advice. I am your king and I demand implicit obedience."

For a few stunned moments there was absolute silence, except for Rama's heavy breathing, due to his effort to suppress an emotion that threatened to overpower him.

At last, ashen in hue and with a masklike face he said, "Go, Lakshmana! Leave her in a secluded spot on the banks of the Tamasa River near the holy Ganga, close to some hermitage, and return immediately. Don't wait to talk to her. Don't try to explain anything. Let her think the worst of me or else she will die of a broken heart. Don't look at me so accusingly. Anyone who objects to my decision is my enemy. Take her away this very instant, O Lakshmana! If I see her even once, I am doomed. I will be unable to carry out my own command. If I see her fawnlike gaze fixed on me with a beseeching look, I will be lost and not all the slander in the world will enable me to let her go. So go now, before my heart fails me, before emotion weakens my adamantine resolve. Why do you hesitate? It is I, the king of the country, who is commanding you."

His brothers could not speak a word. Lakshmana cursed his luck for having been chosen to carry out this terrible command. His eyes brimming with tears, Rama stumbled out of the room and went to an enclosed spot in the garden where he would not be able to see Sita. He spent the night in the garden, keeping a lonely vigil with the stars. If he went to his room and took his beloved in his arms, he knew that he would never be able to let her go.

Who knew what bitter thoughts passed through his mind? But he was firm in his resolve. *Dharma* was his god and to *dharma* he was prepared to sacrifice his beloved queen and his unborn child. To understand the Ramayana is to understand the meaning of *dharma*.

In India the noble soul is one who is able to minimize his personal interests for the sake of the majority. Liberation from our mortal coils can be obtained only through the unselfish performance of all action. Unfortunately, the modern mind fails to see that a spiritual life demands certain sacrifices of our personal demands. Those who lack this understanding may not be able to understand Rama's behavior. It must be remembered that the Indian mind was always conditioned to place the highest value on the abstract principle of *dharma,* or cosmic law. A king who wants to adhere to this law must, perforce, have to place his country before himself in all situations. This applies to all politicians also. We were happy to applaud the behavior of an English king who was prepared to forsake his country for satisfying his lust for a woman, but in India this would be considered a shameful act. By putting his own petty pleasures before the needs of the country, he would be guilty of having betrayed his country, to which he, as the king, should owe his first allegience.

In India Rama was deified because he put his country before the needs of his own personal interests and was prepared to send away his most beloved wife in order to fulfill his role as the perfect monarch. Valmiki took great care to show the extent of Rama's love for Sita, so as to bring out the enormity of his sacrifice. Moreover, it is also to be noted that Rama refused to take another consort, even though this was customary in those times.

It is because human beings and nations cling to their own selfish interests and shut their eyes to the welfare of other people and other nations that the world has come to such a sorry pass. If all rulers were prepared to follow the way of Rama, every country would be a *ramara-jya,* where even nature bows to the decrees of the monarch and humans and animals are always at peace with one another.

The Ramayana is a book that brings out the true meaning of love in all its aspects. What modern people find hard to accept is that the greater the love, the greater are the sacrifices we are called upon to make. The Ramayana illustrates this very clearly in the lives of all the main characters.

Sita sacrifices her comfortable home and the security of the city to be with the husband she loves, daring to go with him to the dangerous forest where wild animals and demons live.

Rama sacrifices a throne and kingdom, in order to honor the words of his father whom he loves.

Lakshmana sacrifices his own family and household in order to serve the brother whom he loves more than himself. And then later he chooses to sacrifice his own life to avert the curse of Sage Durvasa from his people and his country.

Bharata sacrifices his comforts, which he could easily have enjoyed as regent, and chooses to live the life of an ascetic, refusing to grab the throne for himself. Like Lakshmana, he makes these sacrifices for the love of his brother Rama.

Hanuman sacrifices his own interests again and again for Rama's sake. A classic example of the sacrifice of his ego is the passage in which he chooses to throw his own Ramayana into the ocean to make an old man (Valmiki) happy.

The vulture Jatayu sacrifices his life to save Sita, due to his great love for Rama.

There are many such examples, so it is only to be expected that this story, which is the story of love and sacrifice, should end in the sacrifice of Rama's beloved at the altar of *dharma,* which he places above everything else.

Sita slept alone the night before her trip to the forest. She wondered at her Lord's absence, but then she thought it must have been because he was held up with some official matters. Like a child, she was excited at the thought of the treat in store for her on the morrow. Some of the happiest moments of her life had been spent in the forest with her loving husband, and she was eagerly looking forward to spending at least another night in the hermitage with the loving wives of the sages. She had already tied up a small bundle of gifts for the *ashramites* and their wives, and she was ready to go when Lakshmana arrived and knocked at the door.

Without looking at her, he said in a voice that was totally drained of emotion, "The king, your husband, has commanded me to fulfill your desire to visit the Ganga and the hermitages of the sages. Are you ready to leave?"

Sita was delighted and happily accompanied him to the waiting chariot. It was a grim twosome that set out in the pearly mist of the morn. Neither Sumantra nor Lakshmana could speak a word or even look at her. Sita alone was full of cheer. She turned around for a last look at the sleeping town, not realizing that it was indeed her last look.

Suddenly her heart had misgivings. Everywhere she saw ill omens. Her right side and eye were twitching and she felt weak all at once. In an agitated voice, she asked, "O son of Sumitra! Tell me, is all well with your brother? I have not seen him this morning or in the night. Where was he? I fear something inauspicious has happened."

In a choking voice Lakshmana answered, "The king, your husband, is quite well. He gave orders that you should have an undisturbed night, as you were to undertake a strenuous journey in the morning. He told me to wish you well." More than that he could not say.

By afternoon they reached the banks of the River Gomati and camped at one of the ashrams. Next morning they went forward in the chariot and reached the banks of the holy river. Here Lakshmana could contain himself no longer. He broke down and wept like a child.

"Why are you crying, Lakshmana?" asked Sita. "You are making me nervous. I have been longing to come here and now that you have brought me here, you make me sad by your weeping. Is it because you have been parted from Rama for two days? Then what about me? How much should I cry? I cannot endure life without him. Come, let us hurry and go to the *ashramas* and distribute our gifts, and then we will return. I too am beginning to feel uneasy. I fear something is wrong with my Lord."

Wiping his eyes, Lakshmana brought a boat and escorted Sita to the opposite bank. He then fell at her feet and sobbed his heart out. Sumantra stood on the side, shedding silent tears. Sita was really disturbed at the sight.

"Tell me, Lakshmana, what is the matter? Has something happened to my dear husband? Why didn't he come with us? I was hoping he would also come." Until the end, her one thought was for him, who was her all. She never dreamed that the misfortune the omens foretold was meant for her.

Eyes blinded with tears, Lakshmana looked pleadingly at her. "My noble queen! Forgive me for what I have to do. Rama has entrusted me with the ignoble task of abandoning you here. Better for me to have died rather than carry out this command." So saying, he prostrated himself before her. Sita bent down and gently lifted him up. "What is it, Lakshmana? What are you trying to tell me? What is the reason for my husband's sudden decision?" She could not believe that she was hearing rightly.

"Rumors are afloat everywhere, dear lady, about you and about him. I cannot tell you all. He forbade me to tell you anything. All I can say is that his heart broke when he heard the vile accusations against you. But he is the king. He is *dharma* incarnate. The king's duty is always to safeguard the interests of his subjects. Forgive him and forgive me, also, O gracious Queen of Ayodhya! I can say no more. Night is fast approaching. How can I bear to leave you here all alone with none to protect you? Rama never left you, even for a minute, without asking me to guard you. The only time we both left you was when the wicked king of the *rakshasas* came and abducted you. Now who is there to look after you? May your mother, the earth, give you all protection. May the sky be your canopy. May this holy river look after all your wants. Remember, my Lady, you are carrying the seed of the Ikshvaku line in your womb. It is your duty to safeguard it at all times." Lakshmana feared that in her agony, Sita might put an end to her life.

Listening to Lakshmana's words, Sita looked like a frightened deer and then said in a bewildered tone, "What sin have I committed, that for no reason of mine, my husband should repudiate me twice? Surely I was born for sorrow. Grief alone seems to be my constant companion. Patiently I looked at his forlorn face. Leaving my all, I followed my husband to the forest, inhabited by wild animals and demons. No woman would have done as I did, and now he has abandoned me. Was it my fault that the *rakshasa* abducted me? When the sages ask me what crime I have committed that my husband should abandon me, what should I tell them, O Lakshmana? What wrong have I done? I cannot even take the easy path of ending my life in this holy river, for I will be guilty of breaking the noble line of the Ikshvaku race. Lakshmana, do not grieve. Leave me here and return to the king, my husband, and tell him that his wife wishes him well. A husband is a woman's god and I have always considered him as such. May he find eternal fame by following the *dharma* of a king. More important than my suffering is that his honor should remain intact. Never will Sita be guilty of bringing dishonor to Rama. Farewell, Lakshmana. You have been more than a brother to me. I have deep regard for you. I hold nothing against you. The shades of night are falling fast and you must go, lest my Lord becomes agitated."

Lakshmana fell at her feet once more. He could not speak a word. Slowly he backed his way to the boat and was ferried to the other shore. He turned back to look at her once again and saw her lying on the ground, on the bosom of her mother, weeping as if her heart would break.

Sita looked up and saw the chariot receding into the distance. The plaintive cry of the peacock calling to its mate jarred on her delicate nerves. The Ganga flowed smoothly on, as if to comfort her in her agony. She gazed, mesmerized by the glistening water, and wondered what it would feel like to have it close over her head like a balm, but then she felt the life within her move, and she knew that she could not take the easy way out.

> *Victory, victory, victory to Lord Hanuman,*
> *Be merciful even as is the master.*

SRI HANUMAN CHALISA BY TULSIDAS

Aum Sri Hanumathe Namaha!

31

Ramapriyan

The Ramayana

Tato ardharatra samaye baalaka munidaraka,
Valmike priyamachakyu Sitaaya prasavam shubham.

At midnight the young ascetics gave Valmiki the news of
   Sita's safe delivery,
Hearing which the sage was highly delighted.

Valmiki Ramayana,
Uttara Kanda (The Last Book)

The hermitage of the sage Valmiki was very close to where Sita had
been abandoned. That morning when he had gone to the river for his
morning ablutions, he happened to see two cranes mating. He gazed
with joy at their spontaneous love for each other. Just then a fowler
aimed a fatal arrow at the male bird and shot him, contrary to all the
rules of *dharma*. Pierced by that cruel arrow, in the midst of the act
of love, the bird fell to the ground with a heartrending cry. Wrenched
from her lover, the female bird screamed piteously. Beating her breast

with her wings, she fluttered around, terrified and bewildered. Her piteous cries brought a gush of compassion in the heart of the sage, and he cursed the fowler. As soon as the curse left his lips, he felt great remorse. He was horrified that his compassion for the bird had made him break his vow of nonviolence. The fowler was, after all, only a helpless victim of his own *karma*. He felt very unhappy about the whole episode. Then he realized that that curse had flowed from his lips in a spontaneous verse of four lines with eight syllables. He was struck by the beauty of the verse and told his disciple to memorize it. The sage then continued with his interrupted ablutions and retuned to his *ashrama*. That evening two young brahmacharis ran to him and told him that a beautiful woman had been abandoned near the river and appeared to be contemplating jumping into it and ending her life. Valmiki ran to the river and knew that this was Sita, the wife of Rama, as told by Narada. He escorted her home and told the wives of the sages to look after her, for she was carrying the heir to the throne of the Ikshvakus.

Later, when he sat for meditation, he was still filled with remorse over the episode of the two cranes and his involuntary curse of the hunter. Brahma, the creator, appeared to him and told him not to brood over the strange event because from this incident would arise the inspiration to narrate the story of Rama and Sita.

Brahma spoke, "You will be inspired, O sage, to compose a most memorable poem on the exploits of Rama. His whole life will be revealed to you. Everything that you say in your poem will be based on facts that you have witnessed. You will be able to see each and every one of the glorious episodes in the life of this great *avatara* of Vishnu. You will become famous as the *adi kavi,* the first of all poets. The story of Rama will endure as long as these mountains and rivers stay on the face of this earth. Your fame will resound in the heavens above and the kingdoms below."

Having blessed Valmiki thus, Brahma departed to his own abode. Valmiki then sat down and meditated on the Lord and out of his mouth gushed forth the immortal poem, called the Ramayana—The Way of Rama.

This is how the Ramayana came to be written, from the depths of Valmiki's sorrow at the fate of the two birds who were so much in love with each other and who were parted so cruelly. It does not need much imagination to see the parallel between this story and the fate of the two lovers, Rama and Sita, who were parted time and time again despite their intense love for each other.

The poem took twelve long years to complete, and by then Sita's babies had become twelve years of age. She had been looked after by the women of Valmiki's *ashrama* and had given birth to twins nine months after her arrival. They had been named Lava and Kusha by the sage himself and had grown up as ashramites. They had no idea of their parentage.

Having composed this remarkable poem consisting of twenty-four thousand verses on the life of Rama and Sita, the seer was on the look-out for a person with a prodigious memory who could memorize the entire poem. Just then, Lava and Kusha appeared before him, clad in hermit's garb. Knowing them to be endowed with great intelligence and mastery of music, the sage decided to teach them the entire poem, which they mastered with ease. At an august assembly of sages, the twins sang the whole poem exquisitely, in one voice. The sages were charmed and gave them many boons.

After Sita's banishment, Rama became withdrawn and disconsolate, and when not engaged in official business, he spent most of his time alone. He performed his stately duties by placing a golden idol of Sita on the throne meant for the queen. When his subjects asked him to remarry, he totally refused.

"I have abandoned the woman I love due to your whims, but I will forever remain faithful to her who is my very life."

He denied himself the privileges of a royal life and lived in his palace like a hermit. Though deprived of personal joy, he made sure that there was peace in the country and plenty in the houses of his citizens.

Seeing Rama in this mood, Hanuman decided to go to the Himalayas and reside there, chanting his name. Somehow the life of a hermitage suited his temperament more than the intricacies of a life at court even though it meant that he would have to be parted from his beloved Rama. He imposed this penance on himself for he wanted to experience the anguish that Sita must be going through at this cruel parting from her beloved. Immersed in his *tapas* he did not know what was happening in the world or that Sita had delivered twin boys in Valmiki's *ashrama*.

It was at this time, twelve years after the birth of his sons, that the great sage Agastya visited Ayodhya. Rama asked his advice on how to expiate from the sin of having killed so many people during the war, and especially of killing Ravana, who was a Brahmin. Agastya advised him to perform the *ashwamedha yaga,* or horse sacrifice, which is the biggest of the *yagas* of Vedic civilization. His *guru* Vasishta approved of this idea. He consecrated an auspiciously marked stallion and fastened a golden crown on its brow with the royal proclamation that any ruler who supposed himself to be mightier that the owner of the horse could attempt to halt its progress. But those who were prepared to accept the suzerainty of the king would allow the horse to pass. The royal stallion would be let loose to wander for one year all over the country, followed by the king's army. The question of which of his brothers should follow the horse was solved by Rama. He said Bharata had suffered a lot during his exile and Lakshmana had the unique privilege of accompanying him, so he ordered his youngest brother Shatrugna and his son Pushkala to follow the horse, accompanied by an army of four divisions, including many of the monkey champions who had helped him during the war.

The royal stallion was allowed to wander all over the country. Every piece of land the horse traversed unchallenged came under Rama's sovereignty. Anyone who dared to stop the horse had to stand up to the might of Rama's army. The *yaga* could begin only if the horse returned unmolested and unhampered.

At this time Rama thought to himself that the presence of Anjaneya would no doubt add to the glory of the *yaga*. Since Hanuman was ever immersed in the thought of Rama, he knew immediately that he was wanted. He arrived at the court and asked Rama to command him.

Rama asked him to accompany Shatrugna and see to his welfare. News of the *yaga* spread like wildfire over the whole land. It finally reached the hermitage of Valmiki and was told to Sita as well.

The horse made its way through many lands where it was honored by all the kings. The army followed it and paused at various ashrams, paying obeisance to all the sages. At last it arrived at the *ashrama* of the famous sage Chyavana. Shatrugna begged him to bless them, and the sage started to praise Rama as Vishnu incarnate. He then announced his intention of going to Ayodhya with his family to have Rama's *dar-shan* (an auspicious sight of god or a noble being). Hanuman asked Shatrugna's permission to transport the sage and thus save him from the tedious journey on foot. Shatrugna agreed to this and Hanuman expanded his body and carried the whole party through the air, placing them in Rama's presence in an instant. The sage was delighted and blessed him.

The horse and army now approached the city of Chakranka, ruled by King Subahu, who was a great devotee of Vishnu. His son Damana had gone hunting and when he saw the magnificent horse, he captured it without knowing anything about the matter. The army charged forward and attacked him, but they could not subdue him. He then engaged in a single combat with Shatrugnan's son Pushkala. The prince was a remarkable warrior and soon knocked down Damana. The king heard about this and rode out of the fortress accompanied by his brother and his nephew Chitranga. A fierce battle ensued, with heavy losses on either side. At last Pushkala slew Chitranga. The king started to rain arrows at Hanuman. He responded by binding the king in his tail and throwing him to the ground. Undeterred by this, the king struggled to come to his feet. Immediately Hanuman jumped onto his chest and made him unconscious. In his unconscious state, Subahu saw a wondrous dream in which Rama was seated in his heavenly state surrounded by celestials. When he regained consciousness, he called Hanuman and praised him and called off his forces. He recalled that once he had been cursed by a sage for doubting that Vishnu could take on the *avatara* of a man. The sage predicted that his ignorance would be removed when the Lord's servant struck him with his foot. Subahu invited Shatrugna to his palace and paid him homage. He then paid great reverence to Hanuman for having removed his ignorance and given him *darshan* of the Lord.

The horse then approached the magnificent city of Devapura, whose king Viramani had once propitiated Shiva and received his protection. His son Rukmangada captured the horse and tied him up. Hanuman and Shatrugna ordered the boy to release the horse. When he refused, they were forced to fight with him. His father soon came with a huge army to help the boy. Hanuman now came forward and challenged the king and his brothers. He had a unique method of fighting. He would wrap warriors around his tail, including their chariots and horses, and dash them to the ground. When he saw his army being slaughtered, Veeramani prayed to Shiva, who immediately arrived with his brood of ravenous familiars, to help his devotee. His servant Veerabhadra now seized Pushkala by the feet and hurled him to the ground where he fell dead. Uttering a maniacal laugh he took his trident and decapitated the head of the prince. Anguished by the death of his son, Shatrugna challenged Shiva. Though he fought bravely, he was no match for the divine opponent and fell with an arrow in his heart.

Hanuman was furious and attacked Shiva, abusing him for having killed the brother and son of Vishnu in his *avatara* as Rama. Shiva told him that he had to defend his own votaries and uphold their *bhakti*. Each of them now started to fight with redoubled vigor. Hanuman started to rain mountain peaks and trees on Shiva, who retaliated by hurling fiery darts at his breast. At last Hanuman encircled him in his tail and thrashed him on the ground again and again. Even Nandi, Shiva's bull, was terrified to see this. Shiva released himself and told Hanuman that he was satisfied with his special *puja* and offered him a boon. Hanuman smiled and said that he had received everything he could ever want by Rama's grace, but he begged Shiva to look after Shatrugna and his son while he went to Drona Mountain to get the life-reviving herb that had saved Lakshmana.

He reached the Drona peak on the shore of the milky ocean and was just about to uproot the peak when the *yakshas* appealed to him to stop from uprooting the peak that belonged to them and by the power of which they kept up their immortality. Hanuman graciously agreed and took only a portion of the herbs. He returned to the battlefield and placed the herbs on the breasts of the dead and dying soldiers and reconnected Pushkala's head to his body. He then said, "If my devotion to Rama is unwavering, let the prince revive."

The prince immediately sat up as if from sleep. He then revived Shatrugna also. Father and son now resumed their fight with Shiva and Virabhadra. Seeing them weakening, Hanuman advised Shatrugna to meditate on Rama who alone could save them. Rama instantly appeared on the scene dressed for a sacrifice, holding an antelope's horn in his hand. All of them bowed at his feet and praised him as the Supreme Being. Rama replied that there was no difference between him and Shiva. "He is in my heart and I in his. Only a person of tainted intelligence would see a difference between us." Shiva passed his hand over the dead and wounded and revived them, and all of them joined in praising Rama. King Veeramani returned the sacrificial horse to Shatrugna and the party resumed its journey.

The royal army followed the horse and reached a meadow on Mount Hemakuta or the Golden Peak. The horse suddenly became paralyzed and fell to the ground. Every effort to make it rise up failed. Shatrugna went to a nearby *ashrama* where he met a sage and asked him the reason for this. The sage declared that the horse was possessed by a spirit who was once a Brahmin and had been cursed by some sages. When he begged for reprieve they told him that he would be released from the curse when he heard the story of Rama and that this would take place when he took possession of the sacrificial horse that Rama would let loose. Hanuman sat next to the horse and lovingly recited the whole of the story of Rama in the horse's ear. When he finished, he called on the long-suffering spirit to depart to its proper destination. A divine being now appeared and thanked Hanuman for having released him from the spell. Immediately the horse got up and started grazing contentedly on the meadow.

The next person to attack them and steal the horse was a relative of Ravana known as Vidyunmali. He created a haze through which he spirited away the horse. Then he started attacking Shatrugna and the rest from between the fumes that he had created. Hanuman advised Shatrugna to repeat the *mantra* of Rama and he would undoubtedly be able to overcome the *rakshasa*. Shatrugna now sent the missile known as the *mohastra,* which completely cleared the illusion created by the ogre, after which he was able to kill him easily and retrieve the horse.

The horse next approached the city of Kundalapura ruled by the great king called Suratha, who was a great devotee of Rama. He had received a boon from Yama, the god of death, that he would never die until he had had *darshan* of Rama. When the king learned of the identity of the horse grazing outside his city, he decided to capture it so that he could obtain an audience with Rama. When he heard of this, Shatrugna immediately sent Angada to the king demanding the release of the horse. The king frankly told Angada of his intentions and that he would keep the horse captive until Rama came and gave him *darshan*. Though Angada sympathized with the king, he told him in no uncertain terms that it was his duty to safeguard the horse at all times and if he didn't release it, he would have to face the wrath of Rama's army. Suratha cheerfully told him that in that case he would take all of them as prisoners and never release them until Rama came! Angada returned with this message and preparations for battle began.

The king rode out accompanied by his ten sons and a huge army. Prince Pushkala was captured by Suratha's son Champaka. Hanuman challenged the latter and after a severe fight, he managed to knock him unconscious. He then turned to face Suratha, whom he recognized as a great devotee of Rama. The king vowed to take him prisoner and Hanuman smilingly told him to do so since Rama would definitely come to release him. However, he continued to resist the king, warding off all his supernatural weapons with ease. The king was amazed when Hanuman proved to be impervious even to the *brahmastra*. He then devised a ruse to capture this great devotee. He sent a weapon with the name of Rama written all over it. Hanuman refused to retaliate to this weapon and bowed low before it, allowing himself to be captured.

Once Hanuman was captured, Suratha was able to overcome the rest of the army with ease. All the heroes, including Hanuman, were taken to his throne room as prisoners. The king then asked Hanuman to invoke Rama and request him to come to their aid. Hanuman now composed a long paean of praise to Rama describing his adventures and begging him to come and release them. Rama immediately appeared in Kundalapura, in the king's throne room. Overcome with joy, Suratha fell at his feet and begged him to pardon him for having captured his men. The Lord smiled and displayed his form as Vishnu, clasping the king in his arms. When he glanced at Hanuman and the other fallen heroes, all their bonds fell off. The king, along with his citizens, now worshipped both Rama and Hanuman and thanked the latter for having fulfilled his heart's desire.

The horse then roamed into an *ashrama* on the banks of the Narmada. There in a leaf hut resided the great sage, Aranyaka, who was constant in his worship of Rama. When the members of the royal party paid their respects to him he was overjoyed and delivered a sermon on Rama's glories, including the teachings he had learned from the sage Lomasha.

"There is but one god—Rama; one discipline—his worship; one *mantra*—his name; one scripture—his praise!"

All of them were delighted to hear this, but Hanuman felt a thrill go through him. The sage recognized him as a kindred spirit and embraced him with great joy. Both of them were drowned in bliss.

All of a sudden the horse made straight for Valmiki's *ashrama*. When Lava went to the forest with some of the other children, he saw the horse, and after reading the proclamation, he was determined to show his prowess and tied the horse to a tree. The army followed and ordered him to release it, but Lava refused. The army started to advance, but Lava reached for his bow and cut off their arms. Shatrugna was informed about this and sent his general with another consignment. The general tried to reason with the boy, but Lava said that what intrigued him was the proclamation on the horse's head, which he took as a challenge. A battle ensued in which Lava killed the general and most of his troops. Pushkala and Hanuman arrived on the scene, and Lava felled Pushkala and made him lose consciousness. As soon as he saw the boy, Hanuman thought that this must indeed be his Lord's son, but since his orders were to protect the horse at all costs, he took up a tree and a boulder and hurled them at the boy. But the child shattered them to pieces. Then Hanuman wrapped his tail around him and whipped him into the air, but Lava meditated on his mother and freed himself. He then struck Hanuman so forcefully that he fell to the ground stunned. Shatrugna now came to the front and with great difficulty, managed to wound and bind the boy and put him in his chariot.

The rest of the children who had accompanied Lava were watching all this in great astonishment. When they saw him taken, they ran and told Sita about it. She was quite distraught at the news, but her other son Kusha told her not to worry and he would go and free his brother. By the time he reached the battleground Lava had recovered consciousness. When he saw his brother, he managed to free himself. He jumped out of the chariot, and both of them took up positions and started to ravage the army. When the troops identified themselves as the king's army, the boys merely laughed and very soon they decimated the army. Even Hanuman finally succumbed. However, they desisted from killing him. They tied him with the *naga pasha* and dragged him before their mother to be kept as a pet!

Sita was overjoyed to see her sons return but horrified when she saw their prisoner, whom she recognized at once. She ordered them to release him and tell her the whole story. They gleefully described the whole episode to her of how they had caught and tethered a stallion that belonged to a king called Rama, and how they had killed many people, including some persons called Shatrugna and Pushkala! Hearing this, Sita began to weep and said, "My children! Do you know who they were? They are your uncle and his son, and as for this monkey that you have brought, do you know who he is? He is the great Hanuman, who is the greatest devotee of Rama. He has immense strength."

Lava and Kusha said, "Mother, do you know what message was hung around the horse's neck? 'If anyone with Kshatriya blood dares to capture this horse, he will have to pay the penalty.' O Mother! We know we are Kshatriyas and we thought it our duty to tie the horse and prove our point."

She ordered them to release the horse immediately as it belonged to their father. The boys were surprised to hear this, since they didn't think much of a father who had abandoned their mother. However, they went to do her bidding. In the meantime, Sita conversed with Hanuman, who told her the whole story of why they were there.

"How did two young boys manage to put down a hero like you?" she asked.

Hanuman replied, "O Mother! A son is the very soul of his father. The bright and brilliant faces of these two precious boys are exactly like my beloved Lord's. So when they bound and harassed me, I felt that my Lord was having some fun at my expense. Forgetting everything else, I dissolved myself in that sweet thought and knew nothing else." In this incident Valmiki portrays beautifully the great humility and devotion of this great *bhakta*.

Sita now used the power of her chastity and prayed to god to revive the fallen warriors. All of them rose up and Hanuman and the rest of the army returned to Naimisharanya where the *yaga* was being conducted.

> *Pay no heed to any other deity,*
> *Serving Hanuman, one obtains all delights.*
>
> SRI HANUMAN CHALISA BY TULSIDAS

Aum Sri Hanumathe Namaha!

32

Lokabandu

Ashwamedha Yaga

Tat Sarvamakhilenashu prasthapya bharatagraja,
Hayam lakshanasampannam krishnasaaram
    mumocha ha.

After having sent all the things needed for the sacrifice [to
    the spot where it was being held],
Rama released a black horse possessing all the most auspicious
    characteristics.

Valmiki Ramayana, Uttara Kanda

The *yaga* was conducted on a gigantic scale for one full year after the
return of the victorious stallion that was accompanied by Shatrugna
and Hanuman.

In the meantime, a hundred-headed *rakshasa* called Sahasramukha
Ravana was causing havoc in the country. He was actually a son of
Ravana who had been a baby when his father was killed. When he
came of age he did *tapas* and got a boon from Brahma that only a

woman who was completely chaste in thought, word, and deed would be able to kill him. After having got this boon, he started harassing his uncle Vibhishana in Lanka and Sugriva in Kishkinda. His next target was Ayodhya, and with this in view, he entered Kosala. Rama was forced to send his army to defeat the *rakshasa*. However, the army found itself helpless against this foe. When they heard of his boon, the women of Ayodhya volunteered to enter the battle and stop the demon from advancing. However, there was not even one woman who came up to the high expectations of the boon and thus none of them could stop the progress of the demon. Rama knew that Sita was the only one who could save his city and his people, but he doubted if she would agree to enter the city that had rejected her. So he sent Hanuman and told him to tell her that he was very ill. Naturally, she rushed to Ayodhya where she was stopped by the demon that was standing outside the gates. When he refused to let her enter, she was furious and picked up a blade of grass, charged it with the power of her chastity, and hurled it at the *rakshasa,* who was killed instantly. The citizens now acclaimed her as their savior. She cared not for their acclaim and asked after her husband's health. When she heard that he was hale and hearty, she realized that she had been tricked.

Turning to Hanuman, she said, "Because of you, I have experienced the horror of thinking my husband dead. You will outlive Rama and will also experience the pain of separation." So saying, she returned to the *ashrama.*

Having witnessed the amazing power of her chastity, which none of their own wives seemed to possess, the citizens of Ayodhya were anxious to welcome her back as their queen and requested Rama to bring her back. He was only too willing but did not know how to go about it. In the meantime, the *yaga* was still going on.

Valmiki decided that this was a good opportunity for the boys to meet their father and sent the two boys to the *yaga* to make them sing the whole Ramayana in front of Rama and the others. The children did as they were told and sang twenty cantos in a melodious voice before the noble audience. People were spellbound by the sight of these two hermit boys who sang so sweetly. They also remarked on their uncanny resemblance to Rama, who had looked exactly like them when he went to the forest so many years ago, wearing bark, with his hair in matted locks. Rama was enchanted with the boys and told Lakshmana to give them twenty thousand gold coins and expensive clothes, but the boys refused and said that hermit boys who lived on fruits and roots had no necessity for such things.

Rama was astonished and asked them, "Who composed this poem and how many cantos does it have?"

The boys replied, "The venerable sage Valmiki is the composer of this wonderful poem that recounts the doings of your Majesty. It has twenty-four thousand verses and six kandas. The seventh and last is the Uttara Kanda, which describes events still going on. With your leave, we will recite the whole poem in its entirety to you between the functions of the horse sacrifice."

"So be it," said the king.

For many days, Rama and his brothers, as well as the collection of sages, kings, and monkeys heard the whole splendid story of Rama. All were enthralled by the recital. By the end of it, Rama realized that these boys were indeed his own sons, the children of Sita. All the pent-up emotions that he had bottled up for so many years now surged forward and he was filled with an intense desire to see her once again. He could no longer suppress his feelings. The day that he had banished her, he had enshrined her in his heart and thrown away the key. But these young boys, who looked like him and smiled like her, had broken open the door of his heart and let loose a flood of emotion that threatened to overwhelm him with its intensity. Their smiles brought to his mind only too vividly Sita's charming face. The desire to see her again was too strong to be subdued. Surely the fates would not deny him this final bid for happiness. The citizens had already informed him of their decision to have her back. He sent messengers to the hut of the sage with this request.

"If the Queen of Ayodhya is prepared to take an oath in front of this assembly and thus give proof of her innocence, I am prepared to take her back." Valmiki assented to this.

The next day everybody from all over the realm, as well as the guests who had been invited for the sacrifice, assembled in the *yajnashala* in the forest of Naimisha to watch the final scene in the drama of the lives of their king and queen. Into that motionless crowd of expectant citizens, Valmiki arrived with Sita, the daughter of the earth. Her head was bent to the ground, her palms folded in devotion, her eyes filled with tears and her heart with Rama. At the sight of their queen dressed in bark as befitting an anchorite, yet looking divinely beautiful, the fickle crowd set up a spontaneous cheer of welcome. They who had not made any demur when Rama banished her now appeared eager to take her back.

Valmiki entered the *yajnashala* accompanied by Sita and her two sons, who were the very images of their father, and said, "O Son of Dasaratha! This pious lady was abandoned by you near my hermitage out of fear of the censure of the citizens. For the good of your people, you were prepared to sacrifice your noble wife, whom you loved dearly. However, she is purer than Agni. Fire itself will cool at her approach. If Sita is tainted, then let my austerities be in vain. These twins are indeed your sons as their valor will prove. I assure you that Sita is indeed as pure as gold and totally devoted to you. You may now take her back and no one will say a word against this decision of yours, O noble king!"

Then Rama spoke, "With the gods as witness, the Queen proved her innocence once before in Lanka and I accepted her, but still the people whispered and maligned her, and I was forced to send her away to uphold my *dharma* as king. I hereby acknowledge Lava and Kusha as my own sons and will accept Sita too as my wife, if she proves her innocence once more in front of the people of Ayodhya as she did long ago before the *vanaras* and *rakshasas* at Lanka."

As he said this, Rama allowed himself the luxury of gazing at his beloved wife once more. Bereft of jewels and adornment, dressed in bark, with matted hair tied in a knot on top of her head, stood his queen, the queen of Ayodhya and the queen of his heart. His own heart smote him as he looked at her. Involuntarily he stretched out his hands to her. Without thinking, she put her delicate, pink-tipped palms into his. Despite her lack of adornment, she was still incredibly lovely and he could not tear his gaze away from her. Sita gazed back at him and as their hands and eyes locked in a mutual embrace, they felt as if they were drowning in an ocean of love, mirrored in their eyes. They held infinity in their hands and eternity in their eyes.

A ring of interested spectators had formed a circle around them, but Sita and Rama stood alone within that circle, gazing at each other as if they could not bear to look apart. For twelve long years they had been starved of this pleasure. Time stopped as they beheld Heaven in their eyes. Their whole life passed like a dream in front of their inter-locked gaze and still they could not bear to look away.

At last Sita broke the spell and whispered, "My Lord, do I have your permission to make a public avowal of my purity?"

Rama nodded. Wearing the ochre robes of the ascetics, yet looking as beautiful as a bride, Sita, the daughter of the earth, stepped into the center of the circle and with folded palms she bowed before her mother earth and said, "O Madhavi! Goddess of the earth, beloved mother! If you know that I have never loved any man other than my husband, even for a moment, then please open your arms wide and accept me, your daughter, for I can no longer bear to live in this vale of tears. Grief alone has been my lot in this life and now I long for the comfort of your arms, O mother! Take me to your bosom, as you brought me once out of your womb to the field of my father, Janaka!"

Hardly had she finished speaking when the earth split open with a shudder and out of the chasm there arose a beautiful flower-bedecked throne on which was seated the goddess of the earth in all her bounty, covered with flowers and carrying the nine types of grains in sheaves in her hands.

She opened her arms wide and Sita ran into them and was made to sit beside her on the throne of flowers. In front of the astonished gaze of the spellbound audience, the earth gaped open once more and the throne carrying Sita and her mother slowly descended into the bowels of the earth as the gods rained flowers from above. The earth shuddered and the wind moaned as the gap closed over their heads. The crowd came out of their mesmerized state and a great sigh broke from every mouth.

As she disappeared from sight, Rama woke up from the grip of terror that had paralyzed him. He ran to the spot where she had disappeared and called to her piteously.

Holding a staff picked from the sacrificial ground, he leaned on it as if his body were too weak to stand alone. Bending his head over it, he cried out loud, "O Janaki! O Vaidehi! O Sita! My beloved wife! Why have you deserted me just when I thought I could have you back? Once you were stolen by the wicked Ravana, but I brought you back and then I was forced to send you away again. At that time, I was able to bear the parting only because I knew that you were alive and being looked after somewhere, but now I cannot bear to live when I know that I cannot see you any more. I fear I am being punished for my cruel act in having banished you."

His sorrow turned to anger, and he smote the earth with the staff and said, "O goddess of the earth, return my beloved to me at once. I have suffered enough. I cannot live without her—or open your arms once again and accept me also. I would rather live with her in the bowels of the earth than here as king. Remember I am your son-in-law and have pity on me. You know my valor. If you refuse my reasonable request, I will destroy you, burn your forests, crush your mountains, and reduce everything to liquid!"

All the worlds trembled with fear at the anger and agony in Rama's voice. None dared to approach him.

At last Brahma, the creator, came to him and said, "Rama! Remember who you are. Let me remind you of your divinity. Immaculate Sita will be reunited with you in Heaven for she is none other than your consort, Lakshmi. Do not grieve. Take delight in your children and listen to the rest of the tale of your life, which your sons will recite at dawn tomorrow. It is an exquisitely beautiful poem of a life that was ruled by *dharma* alone. You should be the first to hear it, for it is about you. O Rama! You are not just the foremost of all kings but of all *rishis*." With these words, Brahma vanished.

Rama and his sons spent a night of anguish in the hut of sage Valmiki, grieving for Sita. Valmiki had the unhappy task of comforting all three of them. It is only to be expected that a poem that began with the bereavement of a female bird should end with the bereavement of the human couple. At that time when he had watched the male bird being shot down by the cruel arrow, Valmiki had felt as if he had been pierced by the same fatal arrow. How much more did he feel it now, when he saw the tortured king bemoaning his loss over and over again, throughout the long and lonely hours of an endless night?

The next day, in front of the assembled crowd, Rama asked his children to chant the last portion of the epic. He then distributed wealth to all those assembled there—the Brahmins, the citizens, the tree dwellers, the cave-dwellers, and the night wanderers who had come from Lanka. The *yaga* was over, the people dispersed, and the jungle once more crept over the space that had been cleared for the function.

Rama returned to Ayodhya and spent the rest of his life a lonely ascetic. Without Sita, life had no meaning for him. He never married again but kept the golden effigy of his lovely wife beside him, and he performed ten thousand *ashwamedha yaga*s in order to please his *guru* and the people.

His rule was noted for its exemplary nature. The kingdom prospered and thrived and the citizens rejoiced. Rama and Sita had paid for this glory with their unceasing tears. They suffered so that the rest of the country could rejoice, blossom, and flourish. Never once did the citizens think that the price of their prosperity was the sacrifice of their queen—their land was watered with her tears, their happiness bought with her sorrow. She was the sacrificial offering, tied to the stake of their malice, banished to the forest of their poisonous tongues, and eventually swallowed in the chasm of their doubts! They rejoiced and sported with their wives while their king retired to his lonely chamber every night with only his memories for company. Rama carried on his duties for the rest of his life with his usual charm and adherence to *dharma* and showed a pleasant and happy face to all. Only Lakshmana knew that this was just a facade and inside he was burning with regret at what he had done to his queen and waiting for the day when he could join her in their celestial abode.

After reigning for several years, Rama chose to leave this world. The gods, with Brahma at their head, came to him and said, "O Rama! You have fulfilled your destiny on earth. It is time for you to return to your divine abode."

"So be it," said Rama. He was only too happy to leave this world, which offered no joys to him without Sita.

Brahma continued, "Kaala, the spirit of Time, cannot enter your portals, which are guarded by Hanuman, so send him away."

Rama bowed his head. He then dropped his signet ring in a hole in the ground and requested Hanuman to bring it back. Maruti immediately dived into the hole to search for the ring. The search led him to the land of the serpents (Naga Loka). There he found a huge platter of rings, each exactly like the one worn by Rama. And here we find another version of the lesson learned earlier when the sage had dropped Sita's ring in the water pot.

The Naga King told him, "The wheel of time keeps turning, and each time it comes to the *yuga* known as Treta, Vishnu takes an *avatara* as Rama. Whenever his time on earth comes to an end, his ring falls here and he sends you to retrieve it. This is done to help you to accept the fact that your master's time on earth is coming to an end." Hanuman was filled with sorrow at the thought of his master's approaching end, but he had to bow to the decree of the eternal law.

In the meantime, when Hanuman was away, Kaala, the Time spirit, came to the palace in the guise of an old Brahmin. Rama was waiting for him. He had been waiting for a long, long time. He seated him on a golden seat and politely asked him what he wanted.

"If you want to honor me and the gods, you will have to promise me that our meeting shall be private. Anyone who dares to interrupt us should be put to instant death."

"So be it," said Rama. "Since Hanuman is not here, I'll ask Lakshmana to guard the door so that we can be sure that no one will interrupt us."

He asked Lakshmana to take up the position of the doorkeeper, for anyone who dared to enter would be put to death. Then he returned to the ascetic and asked him to freely say whatever he wished to say without fear of interruption.

"Listen, O king," said the spirit of Time, "I have been sent by Brahma to recall you to your heavenly abode. Your time on earth is over. You have accomplished all that you have set out to do. You are Vishnu! The Eternal, the Immutable, the all-pervading protector of the universe. Your stay among the mortals is over. It is time now for you to return to your heavenly abode."

Rama smiled and said, "I am honored by your visit and happy with your message. I will do as you say."

Just as they were talking, Durvasa the short-tempered sage arrived and demanded an immediate audience. Lakshmana politely barred the way and declared that he had strict orders that no one should be allowed to enter as Rama was giving a private audience to someone. Hearing this, the sage lost his temper and shouted, "Announce my presence immediately or else I shall curse you and your brothers and your whole race, as well as the land of Kosala, so that nothing and no one remains to tell the tale!"

Lakshmana thought for a minute and decided that it was better to sacrifice his own life for the sake of the country, and so he went in and announced the arrival of the sage. Rama was horrified to see him but went out immediately to attend to the needs of the sage.

He asked the sage politely what he wanted and was told that since he had just ended a fast that had lasted for a hundred years, he wanted to be fed sumptuously. Rama saw to it that he was fed lavishly. Durvasa was immensely pleased and showered his blessings on the land, instead of his curses, and returned to his *ashrama*. Now Rama remembered the promise he had made to Kaala and went inside with bowed head, lost in thought. Was this going to be the last sacrifice? Was he being asked to sacrifice his beloved brother, his alter ego, at the altar of *dharma*?

Lakshmana knew what was passing through his mind and said cheerfully, "Brother! Do not hesitate. Kill me this minute. I am prepared for it. I thought it better for me to die rather than that the whole country be cursed by the sage as he threatened to do. If you wish to abide by *dharma,* then kill me, O King! One who does not keep his word will go to hell. In order to keep our father's word, you were prepared to forgo a kingdom. What am I compared to that?"

Rama spoke not a word but summoned his priests and ministers and asked them to advise him, for he had promised the ascetic that anyone who interrupted him would be executed, little realizing that this was going to be his final test.

The priests and ministers were silent since they knew the agony that was passing through the king's mind. At last Vasishta spoke. "If a king does not keep his word, *dharma* will be corrupted and the morals of the country will decline. But banishment can be given in lieu of death, so it is your duty to banish Lakshmana!"

Lakshmana stood with his head thrown back, his eyes gazing fearlessly into Rama's. Rama looked into those adoring eyes that had always regarded him with such love, looked at that beloved form he had known since childhood and that had followed him faithfully like a shadow that can never be parted. He knew that one need not die when parted from a shadow, but what about the shadow? Would it not come to an end when parted from the body? Pain flowed out of his eyes while love flowed from Lakshmana's.

"It does not matter, brother," he whispered. "Command me to leave as sternly as you once ordered me to leave Sita in the forest."

Rama was in anguish. Over and over again he murmured, "Everything passes, everything perishes, nothing will remain. Time is all-powerful. Everything will be swept away in the powerful river of time. I have to abide by my promise; I have to be true to the only thing to which I have clung to all my life—*dharma,* the cosmic law. I have been tested time and time again and I have not failed. Let me not fail now."

He was facing Lakshmana but could not look into his eyes. Instead he fixed his gaze at a spot just above his head and said in an expressionless voice, drained of all emotion, "In honor of truth, in honor of *dharma,* in honor of the law I have always upheld, I banish you, O Lakshmana, forever. You shall never return to this land of Kosala again on pain of death!"

Lakshmana looked lovingly at his brother, whom he had implicitly obeyed all his life and said, "My dearest brother, do not grieve. I have loved you all my life and obeyed you without a murmur. It shall be as you wish. Farewell! And once again fare thee well. We will never meet again in this life. Perhaps we will meet in Heaven."

So saying, he went thrice round Rama and prostrated himself to him; then, he went without a backward glance out of the gates of the palace. He proceeded to the banks of the swiftly flowing Sarayu River, which encircled Ayodhya like a girdle. The thought of a life apart from Rama was unthinkable. Death was preferable to such a life. He did not even consider it. Going to the Sarayu River, he sat in *yogic* contemplation on the banks. He gathered in his vital breaths, withdrew into his *atman,* and merged into the Brahman, the cosmic whole. Thus he sat in deep *samadhi.* Indra, the king of gods, sent his chariot and took Lakshmana, the fourth part of Vishnu, to heaven, where he became one with that essence.

Back in Ayodhya, Rama knew that Lakshmana would never be able to live without him and he himself no longer cared to carry on a life which had ceased to have any meaning for him. He realized that, firm as he had been in his vows of *dharmic* discipline, he had been forced to part, one by one, from all those whom he held most dear. He had always known that life was only a dream, a drama in which he had been called upon to play a part. He had come to the end of his lines. The curtain was going up for the final scene and he had already been given his cue to quit the stage. He called his priests and ministers and announced his decision to them.

"I hereby appoint Bharata as Lord of Ayodhya. The southern portion of this fair land of Kosala will be given to Kusha and the northern to Lava. I myself shall follow Lakshmana."

Both Bharata and Shatrugna refused to live without Rama and decided to follow him. Many of the citizens for whose sake he had sacrificed his all decided that they could not live in a land without their beloved king. Hearing of his decision to leave this world, the monkeys and the bears and Vibhishana from across the sea all arrived and begged to accompany him. Hanuman also arrived from the netherworld, where he had gone to get the ring.

Rama said to Vibhishana, "O Lord of the *rakshasas*! Stay on in Lanka and continue to perform your duty. Rule with *dharma* as your guide. Your kingdom will endure as long as I am remembered on Earth."

Turning to the bear Jambavan, he said, "O wise one! You shall continue to live on this earth until my advent as Krishna, scion of the race of Yadu. Until then, you shall suffer no defeat. When you meet one who is able to defeat you, then you will know that I have returned."

To the others, he said, "All those who wish to follow me may do so. This very day you will enter Heaven along with me."

"What about me?" asked Hanuman, with tears streaming out of his eyes.

"Live long, O Noble Hanuman! Wherever my story is told, wherever the name of Rama is mentioned, you will be there to hear it. This story will be told as long as the sun and the moon shine, as long as people remain on this Earth, and as long as you are there to hear it!"

Most of the people of Ayodhya followed Rama with love and devotion. Even the animals followed him, the cows and goats and elephants, not to mention the monkeys and bears. The very stones on the streets of Ayodhya wept, for they could not follow him, and the trees bent low and brushed his head while he passed. Every creature that could walk or roll or dance or totter followed him. Sumantra was waiting at the banks of the river with the four red horses that he had freed from the chariot. Guha, the hunter king, was also there. The whole procession wound its way to the pellucid waters of the Sarayu River, which circled the land of Kosala like a silver girdle. Rama walked into the icy waters of the river accompanied by all the rest. The waters closed over their heads like a benediction.

Hanuman stood on the banks with closed eyes, from which poured tears in torrents while the heavens opened and the celestials rained flowers.

Brahma spoke, "O gracious Vishnu! Be pleased to return to your celestial abode. Thou art the soul of all—indestructible, immutable and eternal. Be pleased to give up this form of *maya* and resume your *swarupa* [actual form]."

As he finished speaking, out of the waters rose the incredibly beautiful form of Lord Vishnu, holding the discus, conch, mace, and play lotus in his hands. All those who had decided to join him also came out of the waters, endowed with celestial forms, and all rose up to the heavens as the music of the spheres floated down in the velvet twilight.

With the ascension of Rama to his heavenly abode, the twenty-four thousand verses were complete. Back in the deserted city of Ayodhya, Lava and Kusha sang the final verses of the song, to an invisible audienc, the song known as the Ramayana, The Way of Rama, the first poem ever to be composed by the first of all poets—Valmiki.

> *At death one goes to Rama's realm,*
> *Or is born on Earth as his devotee.*

Sri Hanuman Chalisa by Tulsidas

Aum Sri Hanumathe Namaha!

Aum Sathyavachaaya Namaha!

33

Tapaswin

Dwapara Yuga

Sri Raama Raama Raamethi, Reme Raame manorame,
Sahasranama tat tuliam Raama nama varanane.

Repetition of the name of Rama is equivalent to the
chanting of the
Thousand and one names of Lord Vishnu.

As foretold by Sita, Hanuman witnessed the departure of Rama from
this earth and experienced the heartbreak that followed. He returned
to his habitat in the wilds on the Himalayan Mountain. As the years
passed he heard of the deaths of all his friends and loved ones—his
mother, Sugriva, Angada, Vibhishana, Lava, and Kusha. This was the
price he had to pay for being a *chiranjeevi*. All alone on the slopes of
the Himalayas, he meditated in order to experience the ultimate truth.
He remembered the advice given by Sita.

"Rama is the Supreme Purusha, the eternal spirit, Sita is Prakriti, cosmic matter, the embodiment of all manifestation. Together they constitute the entire universe." He witnessed the unending transformations of
matter—birth and death, joy and sorrow, aspiration and frustration, union

and separation. Amidst all this change he remained in the stillness of the *atman,* the serenity of the soul.

It was at this time that he felt the need to record all the glorious deeds of his master to which he had been an eyewitness. The summit of the mountain beneath which he had a cave was composed of sparkling crystalline slabs, and with his diamondlike nails he began to inscribe Rama's story. He recorded his own version of the glorious deeds of his Lord and master, Rama, in the divine language of Sanskrit. He scratched it laboriously with his nails on the rocks. The work continued for a long time and Hanuman, lost in the intricacies of the story, became oblivious to the passage of time.

One day Valmiki came to know that the great Hanuman too had penned the adventures of Rama, engraving the story with his nails on rocks. His curiosity was aroused and he traveled to the Himalayas where Hanuman was residing in order to see this version. The monkey warrior was no doubt an eyewitness to many of the incidents, but was he a poet? He questioned Hanuman about the rumor that he had composed his own Ramayana. Hanuman carried him and placed him on a ledge from which he could read the narration. Valmiki kept reading and reading, scanning the cliffs from top to bottom, climbing and descending now and again in order to see well. Sometimes he laughed loudly and at times his eyes brimmed with tears. Valmiki was overwhelmed by the sheer power and depth of devotion of the amazing narrative. It was truly a lofty work, inspired by great love. After finishing the story Valmiki gazed for a long time into the distance. Joy and sorrow flitted over his face. He was joyous at having had the chance to read such an exquisite work of art and sad because it obviously overshadowed his own work.

Hanuman politely asked him the reason for his sorrow. "O best of sages! Is something wrong? Does the poetry have many faults?"

Valmiki turned to him and said, "It is indeed a marvelous bit of work. Every image, every word is alive and pregnant with devotion. There is not and never can be an equal to it. My version, which I created with such pains over a period of twelve years, is no match for the magnificence of your work and will therefore be despised."

For a moment Hanuman was dumbstruck. Then he said, "Is that all that is bothering you?" He promptly tore the slabs on which he had scribbled the poem on the mountain and piled them on one shoulder. He placed the aged saint on another shoulder and flew to the ocean. When they reached the middle Hanuman called loudly, "May these be an offering to my Lord." With these words, he threw his own version into the sea, where they raised huge waves before disappearing into the depths of the sea. Valmiki watched speechless, overcome with shame and guilt. "It would have been better," he thought, "if he had thrown me into the sea and saved that wonderful story."

But Hanuman seemed unperturbed and cheerful. He returned the sage to his own hermitage in a trice. "Please don't worry about this," he said. "It was just something I did to while away the time!"

The Ramayana is a story of *tyaga,* or renunciation, and this aspect of Hanuman's personality is considered to be far more important than his rhetorical skills. Selfless and compassionate, his loyalty was always to his master and not to any particular telling of the tale, and he willingly drowned his own masterpiece in order to spare a poet's wounded pride. This was the first and greatest Ramayana, called the Hanumad Ramayana, which like the original Veda, was lost and preserved only in fragments.

Hanuman bowed to Valmiki, who blessed him and said prophetically, "O Son of Vayu, in another age I will take birth again and devote myself to your service. I will sing your praises and teach others to do so. I will retell the story you have told, using the language of the common man so that everyone may understand it."

Hanuman smiled and said, "Victory to Lord Rama!"

It is said that Saint Tulsidas, who composed the Ramacharitamanas, was none other than the Maharishi Valmiki, reborn to fulfill his own desire.

Later, one tablet is said to have floated ashore during the time of the great poet Kalidasa, when it was exhibited at a public place. It was in an extinct script, and Kalidasa is said to have deciphered it and recognized that it was from the Hanumad Ramayana as recorded by

Hanuman, and he considered that he was very fortunate to see at least one stanza of this immortal work.

Hanuman's heart was so full of Rama that it was bound to pour out of him in the form of music. He composed verses and set them to music in praise of his Lord. He sang these in his powerful voice and they reverberated across the hills and valleys of the Himalayas. Birds paused in their flight and animals gathered round to listen to Hanuman sing and chant the name of Rama unceasingly, without even pausing for breath.

By this time the *yuga* known as Treta, in which Rama had lived, was long over. It fact, it was almost the end of the next *yuga,* known as Dwapara, in which Vishnu had taken another incarnation on earth as Krishna. Hanuman was the instrument that Krishna chose to curb the pride of many of his attendants. He had many wives but Sathyabhama thought that she was his favorite, little realizing that he was equally affectionate to all. None was specially dear or hateful to him. She considered herself to be very beautiful and had once asked him whether she was not more beautiful than Sita to whom he had been so attached in his previous incarnation. Krishna's vehicle was Garuda and his weapon was the discus called Sudarshana. All of these attendants became very proud of themselves and Krishna decided that it was time to teach them a lesson. Along with them, he also wanted to teach a lesson to the sage Narada and his disciple Tumburu, who thought themselves to be the greatest of all musicians.

Once the two celestial sages came to the court of Krishna and asked him which of them he considered to be the best musician. Krishna smiled and asked them to go to the Himalayas and listen to Hanuman. The two agreed condescendingly and went to the icy slopes where they found Hanuman and asked him to sing. With his usual modesty Maruti said that he was no singer but only wanted to pour out the glories of Rama. But since they insisted, he picked up his lute and started to sing. Narada and Tumburu were enchanted by the music. Such was the power of his voice that the snow began to melt and when he stopped the melted snow became ice. Narada and Tumburu found that they were truly stuck to the ice. They begged Hanuman to release them.

"Why don't you both sing so that the snow melts and then you can free yourselves?" asked Hanuman.

But try as they might, neither of their voices could melt the ice. They realized that their voices were filled with ego while Hanuman sang out of pure devotion. Now they understood why Krishna had sent them to Hanuman.

Another time Narada went to Dwaraka, strumming his lute in order to pay his respects to Krishna. Narada was a great *bhakta*, so Krishna paid him homage. He made him sit and then asked him if there was anything he wanted to tell him.

Narada said, "Well, actually, I came to tell you of how I was insulted by your vehicle Garuda. I had gone to Indra's assembly hall and there everyone paid homage to me except this eagle who said that he saw no reason to respect a person like me who was noted for creating troublesome situations! I didn't curse him since I knew he spoke out of his ignorance, but I thought I might as well mention this to you since I think it is time he was taught a lesson."

Krishna smiled in his usual mysterious fashion, for he knew that his three favorites were filled with pride and he was waiting for an occasion to curb them a little. This was a good opportunity to teach all three of them a lesson. He told Narada to go and call his wife Satyabhama. Narada was bewildered and wondered how Satyabhama, who was herself noted for her arrogance, could help in this matter. However he did as he was bidden and went to Satyabhama's apartment. He asked someone to announce his arrival but was told that she was busy with her toilette and would not be able to see him. Naturally he was quite annoyed at this and he returned and gave the news to Krishna.

"Don't worry, O Narada!" said Krishna with his usual smile. "If she won't come, then you should go to the Himalayas and ask Hanuman to come. As you know, he has been meditating there since Treta Yuga, from the time of my advent as Rama.

Again Narada was puzzled as to why he should be sent off to

Hanuman, whom he had already met once and who had humbled his pride. However, he was always ready to play along with the Lord, so off he went to the icy mountains where Hanuman was meditating. He went close to him and said loudly, "I have been sent by Lord Krishna to call you to come to Dwaraka!"

Hanuman was in deep meditation and did not even open his eyes. Narada repeated the message in a louder voice. At this Maruti opened his eyes and asked, "Who is Krishna? I know no one of that name." He then closed his eyes and lapsed into *samadhi* once again.

Narada was perplexed and thought for a while. Then he realized that Hanuman was Rama's devotee. He probably didn't even know that the present epoch was Dwapara Yuga. He had no contact with the world and probably didn't know about the advent of Krishna. Then he had a brilliant idea. He went close to him and taking out his lute, he started to chant the name of Rama. Even though he was immersed in a super-conscious state, Hanuman started to come closer to Narada without realizing what he was doing. Narada now started to sing of the glories of Rama and began to walk off. Maruti started to follow him with closed eyes. Narada went all the way to Dwaraka and there he stopped his singing. He went to give the news to Krishna. When the singing stopped abruptly, Hanuman opened his eyes and was surprised to find himself in a beautiful garden. He realized that he had been tricked somehow and started destroying the trees in his anger. He mowed down the guards who came to drive him off. The news of a monkey destroying the garden was reported immediately to Krishna. The Lord summoned the eagle Garuda and ordered him to go and chase the monkey from his garden.

Garuda went and saw a monkey sitting with his back to him, munching fruit.

"Vile one!" the eagle screeched. "Who are you and why have you destroyed Lord Krishna's garden?"

Without even turning around, the monkey replied, "As you see, I am a monkey and I'm doing the normal thing that all monkeys do!" Saying this, he resumed his feast of the fruits. Garuda was enraged at this treatment and attacked Hanuman, who quickly wrapped him in his tail and began to choke the life out of him.

With his remaining breath, Garuda gasped, "Lord Krishna has sent me."

"Who is he?" asked Hanuman loosening his grip a little, "I know only Lord Rama."

"They are the same, you fool!" said Garuda in a choking voice.

"Maybe you are right," said Hanuman, "but I only answer Rama's call."

Hanuman had no intention of killing the bird, so he tossed him headfirst into the ocean and bounded off to the southern mountains.

After swallowing a lot of seawater, Garuda revived and made his way back to the court where, with downcast face and dripping plumage, he presented himself before Krishna.

"I see you have been having a dip in the sea!" said Krishna with an innocent look.

Garuda fell at his feet and said, "My Lord! That is not an ordinary monkey. He bound me with his tail and threw me into the ocean."

Krishna comforted him and said, "That monkey is Hanuman, the great *bhakta* of Rama. Go to the Malaya Mountains in the south and call him again, but this time tell him, "Sri Rama is calling you.""

Still proud of his speed, Garuda streaked across the sky to the southern mountains to find Hanuman. He was a bit wary about approaching him and respectfully gave Krishna's message to him. Hanuman, of course, was delighted and told him to go and that he would follow him. Garuda thought to himself, "This monkey may be strong, but he certainly won't be able to match my speed! Wonder when, if ever, he'll reach Dwaraka!" He grinned to himself and took off in a trice and flew at full speed toward Dwaraka.

Krishna decided to welcome Hanuman by taking on the form of Rama.

Turning to his wife Satyabhama he asked her to take on Sita's form and accompany him since that would give greater pleasure to Maruti. She saw to her amazement that Krishna had already taken on the form of Rama, complete with bow and arrows. Then Krishna summoned his discus, Sudarshana, and told him to stand guard outside his door, for he was going to meet an important guest. Bristling with his own importance, Sudarshana stood guard at the door. It took a long time for Satyabhama to finish her toilette and dress like Sita.

After his conversation with Garuda, Hanuman meditated on Rama and reached Dwaraka in a trice. He was just about to enter the throne room when Sudarshana stopped him. Not wanting to waste time in pointless arguments, Maruti simply grabbed the discus and stuffed it into his mouth, entering without any further delay. He couldn't believe his eyes when he saw Rama and Sita awaiting him. When Hanuman saw them, he was totally bewildered. He ran forward and prostrated himself to them.

"My Lord!" he said. "I see now why my meditation was interrupted and why I was brought to this strange place. I have been longing for this blissful vision for a long, long time." Glancing at Satyabhama standing on Krishna's left, he said, "My Lord! Where is my revered mother? Who is this woman standing beside you? She has no resemblance to the princess of Videha."

Satyabhama was truly mortified to hear this. She had always thought herself to be superior to Sita. She hung her head in shame.

Krishna gave a sidelong glance at Satyabhama and, turning to embrace Hanuman, he said, "My dearest devotee! Do you realize that this is already the *yuga* known as Dwapara? Your Rama has incarnated himself in the form of Krishna in this epoch."

With these words, the Lord showed himself to Hanuman as Krishna. Maruti was overjoyed to see this and once again fell at his feet and begged his pardon for having devastated his garden. Narada was, of course, an interested spectator of the whole drama. Just at this moment there was a flurry of wings, and Garuda flew in, huffing and panting. Seeing Hanuman standing before Krishna, he was totally bewildered and hung his head in shame.

Krishna looked askance at him. Then, turning to Hanuman, he asked, "By the way, did someone try to stop you from entering this room?"

Hanuman looked a bit sheepish and said, "Actually, there was some sort of metallic thing that kept buzzing and trying to stop me, but since I was in a hurry to reach you, I didn't wait to exchange blows but simply popped him into my mouth."

With these words, he spat out Sudarshana, who naturally looked very crestfallen. Krishna pointedly looked the other way so as not to give further embarrassment to the three who had set themselves up as his favorites and who were in great need of a set down.

Turning to Hanuman, Krishna said, "O Hanuman, I have incarnated myself in order to establish the rule of *dharma* once again in the world. For this, my chosen instruments are the Pandavas, who belong to the Kuru dynasty. They are five in number and the second brother, Bhima, is your brother since he was born of the wind god, Vayu. They have been banished from the court and will be coming to the Himalayas soon. You will have a chance of meeting both Bhima and Arjuna. You will also be called upon to help them in their war of righteousness. We will meet again on the battlefield of Kurukshetra."

Hanuman took his leave and returned to his solitary mountain fastness.

Krishna now turned to Garuda. He placed his hands over him and made him get up. He gave a quizzical glance at Narada, who was standing close by.

Garuda hung his head in shame and begged Narada's pardon for having slighted him.

"My Lord," he said to Krishna. "I know this is all your game and you wanted to teach me a lesson never to be rude to your devotees. Indeed, now I realize that Narada is one of your greatest devotees."

Sudarshana, in the meantime, had also realized that this was all a game of his Lord to put down his pride and had slunk away in shame. Krishna now glanced at Sathyabhama, who refused to meet his eyes and looked fixedly at her toes. She realized that her beauty of which she was so proud and by which she thought she could enslave Krishna was nothing compared to Sita's. She was slowly beginning to realize the greatness of her Lord who was supreme in himself and a slave to none!

There is another story connected with these three in which Krishna employed Hanuman to destroy their pride. In this story, Sathyabhama, Krishna's proud consort, demanded to have some flowers from Rama's sacred grove in the Himalayas, which was guarded by Hanuman. Krishna sent Garuda to get the flowers, but he was challenged by Hanuman, who stopped him from entering.

"These flowers are meant only for Rama and Sita," he said.

Garuda did not bother to answer him but charged into the grove to pick the flowers. Hanuman simply picked him up and crushed him under his armpit. He flew to Dwaraka so fast that he created quite a tempest, which terrified the citizens. Seeing Hanuman in the sky, they thought he was some demon and ran to Krishna to ask him to protect them. Though he knew who it was, Krishna threw his discus, Sudarshana, to stop him. Hanuman calmly tucked it into his other armpit and landed on the roof of the palace, terrifying the people inside. Krishna explained to them that this was Hanuman, a great devotee of Rama, and if he wasn't pacified he would destroy Dwaraka as he had destroyed Lanka. He told Sathyabhama to dress like Sita, but she took so long that he called Rugmani and asked her to take on Sita's form. She immediately closed her eyes and begged Krishna to allow her to take on the correct form of his beloved in another age, and thus she was a true replica of Sita.

Krishna himself donned Rama's garb and the two of them approached Hanuman, who immediately bowed and placed the flowers at their feet.

Krishna welcomed Maruti and hugged him, and then, with a twinkle in his eye, he asked Hanuman what he was hiding beneath his armpits.

Maruti replied, "A bird came to my Lord's garden and tried to pick flowers, and then when I arrived here some sort of metal wheel tried to stop me, so I took both of them under my armpits."

So saying he produced the bird and the wheel and placed them before Krishna. Both of them looked very crestfallen with their pride duly humbled. Sathyabhama found to her chagrin that Rugmani had already masqueraded as Sita with no difficulty at all. She also realized that the whole drama had been arranged by her Lord to destroy her pride.

> *Whoever recites this a hundred times,*
> *Is released from bondage and gains bliss.*

HANUMAN CHALISA BY TULSIDAS

Aum Sri Hanumathe Namaha!

Aum Veeraaya Namaha!

34

Bhima

The Mahabharata

Tava maya bas firaum bhulaana,
Ta te me nahi prabhu pahichata.

Overpowered by your *maya,*
I as a *jiva* forgot my real nature.
Hence I could not recognize thee, O Lord, appearing in
    human form.

RAMACHARITAMANAS BY TULSIDAS

Since he was a *chiranjeevi,* Hanuman lived through many eons. The
Treta Yuga in which he was born gave place to the Dwapara Yuga, and
Vishnu, who had incarnated himself as Rama in Treta became Krishna
in Dwapara. As predicted by Krishna, Hanuman made many appearances in the *yuga* known as Dwapara and was given a chance to help
the Pandavas.

In the Bhagavad Gita, one of the great philosophical works of
human history, Krishna proclaimed that every time the law of cosmic

righteousness declined in the world, he would incarnate himself to uplift *dharma* and punish those who did not uphold it. In this fight against *adharma,* Krishna's chosen instruments were the Pandavas, who belonged to the Kuru dynasty, which was the ruling dynasty of that time. They were five in number and had extremely noble qualities. The eldest was called Yudhistira, and he was actually the heir to the throne of the Kurus. Bhima was the second and Arjuna the third, while Nakula and Sahadeva were the fourth and fifth. However, their cousins, who numbered one hundred and were the sons of their uncle, Dritarashtra, were bent on destroying them and denying their rightful heritage to the throne. The Mahabharata, written by the sage Vyasa, is mainly the story of the events leading up to the battle between these two sets of cousins known as the Pandavas and the Kauravas. In this battle Krishna sided with the Pandavas and thus they were able to overcome the Kauravas, even though the latter were superior in numbers. Krishna became the charioteer of Arjuna and helped him to win the war. The Bhagavad Gita is the discourse given by Krishna to Arjuna at the beginning of the war and is one of the greatest scriptures in Hinduism.

Each of the five Pandavas is said to have been fathered by a celestial. Bhima, who was the strongest, claimed Vayu as his father. In this way Hanuman was Bhima's brother, since he was also Vayu-putra (son of Vayu).

The five brothers had been cheated at a dice game and banished by the Kauravas to the forest, where they had to spend fourteen years. Arjuna had gone into the deep recesses of the upper Himalayan ranges in order to do *tapas* to Lord Shiva to get the boon of his divine weapons. The other four brothers, accompanied by their wife Draupadi, followed him and came to these remote regions. The sage Lomasha was the one who led them on along this dangerous path where the cruel winds howl and storms constantly ravage the slopes. Draupadi fainted during one of these storms. Yudhistira was anxious to return, but Bhima insisted that they should go forward and summoned his *rakshasa* son, Gatotkacha, who took the exhausted Pandavas through the air to Badarikashrama, the abode of the great sages Nara and Narayana. Here they rested for six days. It was here that Draupadi saw a thousand-petalled lotus that was drifting in the wind. The divine perfume made her reel and she begged Bhima to get more for her.

Bhima was ever ready to do her bidding and departed, roaring and beating a path for himself with his mace through the jungle and destroying much of the flora. He blew his conch loudly and slapped his thighs like a wrestler. Hanuman was living in this forest and heard this commotion. He decided to curb his brother's pride.

After walking a long way, Bhima climbed a high ridge and discovered a beautiful orchard of banana trees that seemed to stretch on forever. He plunged through this like a maddened elephant, shattering and uprooting trees and terrifying the animals and birds. Suddenly in the middle of his path he saw a huge, golden-colored monkey with amber eyes, languidly feeding on the bananas. He heard the commotion made by Bhima's passage and thumped his tail on the ground, producing a sound like thunder. Bhima also heard the sound and considered it a challenge. He charged forward and soon came face-to-face with the monkey, who was lying right across his path.

"His short, thick neck lay on the cross of his arms, his waist over his hips looked slender below his towering shoulder, and he shone as with a flag with his erect, long-haired tail that was slightly bent at the end. His face like the beaming moon showed red lips, a mouth with copper red tongue, pink ears, darting brows and round-tipped protruding tusks. The brilliant white teeth inside his mouth shed luster on it and a massive mane crowned it like a mass of *ashoka* blossoms. Thus he sat, resplendent amidst the golden banana trees, ablaze with his beauty like a blazing fire, staring fearlessly from honey-yellow eyes." This is the description of Hanuman as given by Vyasa in the Mahabharata.

The monkey chided Bhima for his lack of consideration for the creatures of the forest, but the arrogant Bhima merely ordered him to get out of the way or else he would be the next to suffer from the effects of his wrath. The monkey protested weakly that he was too old and tired to move but that he could jump over him if he wished.

Bhima protested, "I believe the divine to be present in all creatures, even an old and prostrate monkey like you, so I will not commit such an act. Otherwise I would have leaped over you as easily as Hanuman once leaped over the sea."

The old monkey's eyes gleamed momentarily and he asked in a weak voice. "Hanuman! Who might that be?"

Bhima replied scornfully, "Everyone knows that Hanuman was the great *bhakta* of Lord Rama and was the son of Vayu, and therefore my own half-brother! As for me, I am Bhima, second of the great Pandavas. Demons tremble at the mention of my name and poets write odes to my strength. Now get up before I kick you aside!"

The monkey seemed unimpressed by all this and languidly continued to peel another banana. He said in a weak voice, "I'm too tired to move, but if you like, you can remove my tail from your path. If you feel you can't do this, then have a banana since it's sure to give you strength!"

Bhima was enraged by this, but he did not like to step over the tail nor did he want to touch it, so he decided to lift it a little with his mace and toss it and the monkey high into the air! When he tried to shove his mace beneath the tail, he found to his surprise that it was hard as iron and when he tried to lift it he nearly fell. He strained until sweat poured down his face and the veins bulged on his forehead. It was only then that he realized that this was no puny monkey as he had thought but some powerful being, much more powerful than him. His pride was duly humbled and he stood before the monkey with folded palms and begged him to reveal his identity.

"Surely you are no ordinary monkey but some god in monkey form. Kindly deign to tell me your name."

Hanuman got up and said, "I am Hanuman, son of Vayu, and you are my brother. I have been lying here waiting for you as I wanted to meet you."

Bhima was overjoyed to hear this, and the two brothers hugged each other with great affection. Bhima told Hanuman that he had been his hero since childhood and that he had always wanted to see him. The brothers embraced each other once again and Hanuman asked Bhima why he was wandering around that lonely forest. Bhima told him that he had come to get the mysterious flower with an intoxicating perfume for his wife Draupadi.

Hanuman said, "The golden lotuses bloom in the lake of Kubera, king of *yakshas*. It is closely guarded by them. You'll have to fight with them if you want to get the flowers."

Bhima replied, "I'm willing to fight anyone to get the flower for Draupadi. With your blessings, I'm sure I'll be successful." Hanuman then blessed him and told him to go to the pond and mention his name to the *yakshas,* and they would gladly give him as many flowers as he wanted.

Bhima now had another request. "I have always pictured you in your youthful form when you crossed the ocean to find Sita. Please bless me with this vision."

Hanuman said, "That form belonged to the age known as Treta. Now it is the Dwapara Yuga. Even though I'm immortal I have to conform to the standards of the current age. Moreover, if I were to assume that form by which I crossed the ocean, you will not be able to endure it."

However, Bhima continued to plead for this vision and finally Hanuman relented. Before he had finished speaking, he changed from an old, gray-bearded monkey to a young and handsome simian. He then started to grow in size before Bhima's astonished gaze until it appeared as if his head would touch the skies. Bhima could hardly see the top of his head, which was as radiant as another sun, so much so that he had to close his eyes as he couldn't bear to gaze at that effulgence. He fell at his feet and begged him to return to his former size. Hanuman resumed his usual form and blessed Bhima, warning him against wanton acts of violence. He told him the secrets of Kubera's lake and offered him a boon. He said that he would destroy the Kauravas and return the kingdom to the brothers if he so wished. Bhima replied that just by meeting him, he was assured of success. Hanuman promised to be present on Arjuna's standard and in Bhima's battle cry. With these words, he disappeared. A wiser and more chastened Bhima found his way to the lake and was able to get the flowers and return to Draupadi without any further mishap.

There is another interesting story of how Hanuman met Arjuna, who was the middle brother among the Pandavas. He was the one to whom Lord Krishna gave the advice of the Bhagavad Gita on the battlefield of Kurukshetra. During the battle Arjuna's pennon had Hanuman sitting on it. There is an interesting story connected with this incident.

During their fourteen years of exile Arjuna went to the Himalayas in order to do *tapas* and propitiate Lord Shiva so that he could get a divine weapon from him, for he knew that a battle between his brothers and his cousins was inevitable. Once while roaming in the forest, he came across a most distinguished-looking monkey meditating under a tree. He was struck by his looks and sat close to him, waiting for him to open his eyes. At last the monkey opened his eyes and Arjuna asked him who he was and why he was meditating here.

The monkey answered, "A monkey's natural habitat is the jungle. I am Hanuman, the servant of Lord Rama. Now would you care to introduce yourself?"

Arjuna went up and touched Hanuman's feet, saying, "I am indeed fortunate to have met you. I'm Arjuna, the middle one [sibling] among the Pandavas. I have come here to meditate and propitiate Lord Shiva and gain some weapons from him. I am glad to have met you, for I have one doubt about Rama. I have heard that he was a great archer and I'm wondering how he could not have constructed a bridge of arrows across the straits instead of having to take the help of monkeys to bring stones and rocks."

Hanuman could hear the arrogance underlying Arjuna's question. It was as if he wanted to prove his superiority as an archer. Hanuman replied, "Making a bridge of arrows would have been a simple task for my Lord, but remember hundreds of gigantic monkeys would have had to cross the bridge, and it's very doubtful whether a bridge of arrows could have supported their weight."

Arjuna replied proudly, "I'm sure I could easily make a bridge that would hold the weight of any number of monkeys."

Hanuman said with a smile, "Here is a pond. Why don't you go ahead and make a bridge of arrows over it? If it can take just my weight, I'll be satisfied and acknowledge your claim. If, however, it doesn't stand my weight, what will you do?"

Arjuna said scornfully, "I'm quite sure the bridge won't break with your weight, but if it does, I promise to immolate myself in the fire. Now tell me what you will do if the bridge holds your weight?"

Hanuman said, "If you prove successful, I promise to sit on your flag in the coming war and lead you to victory."

Without wasting time in more words, Arjuna lifted his legendary bow, the Gandiva, reached into his inexhaustible quiver and started shooting arrows with lightning speed. He linked them and thus created within moments a marvelous span across the lake. Mightily pleased with his feat, he stepped aside and invited Hanuman to walk over it. Hanuman said he would prefer to test the bridge with one foot rather than walk on it and fall into the cold water. Arjuna was furious when he heard this but contained his anger and watched while Hanuman advanced and put one foot gingerly on the bridge. To Arjuna's utter astonishment, the bridge immediately shuddered, cracked and disintegrated and the arrows fell one after the other into the pool! He couldn't believe that just one monkey's foot was enough to make his splendid bridge collapse.

"Now Arjuna," Hanuman asked, "if your bridge can't stand the weight of my one little paw, how do you think it could have withstood the weight of hundreds of monkeys?"

Arjuna was totally demoralized. However, he was determined to keep his word. Silently he collected firewood and made a pyre. Just as he was about to jump in, he was stopped by a *yogi* with matted hair, carrying a staff and water pot.

"You are young and intelligent, as I can see by looking at you. Tell me why you have decided to immolate yourself."

Arjuna told him the whole story and the celibate turned to Hanuman and asked, "Did you have a third person to witness this pledge? In such cases of life and death, it's always normal to have a witness."

Hanuman shook his head and said that in this case there was no need for a witness since he quite believed that Arjuna was an honorable man who would keep his word. The *yogi* insisted that a witness was always necessary in these dire cases and suggested that Arjuna should be allowed to make another bridge and the whole experiment repeated with him as witness. Both of them agreed and once again Arjuna took up his bow, but before starting he made a silent prayer to Krishna to help him. He then made another bridge even stronger than the previous one. Hanuman put his right foot forcibly down on the bridge at one side but found to his astonishment that the bridge hardly quivered. He then started to walk over it with no problem at all. He turned around and came to the middle and jumped up and down on it with all his force, and still the bridge did not stir. He expanded his size and brought his full force down with a crash. The bridge did not stir. He was really puzzled. He thought for a while and knelt down and peered under the bridge and was amazed to find a huge tortoise upholding it. He then turned around to look at the *sannyasin* and saw instead Lord Krishna looking teasingly at him.

Hanuman ran and prostrated himself to him. He realized that his Rama was standing before him in the form of Krishna and that he had taken on his incarnation as the tortoise in order to uphold Arjuna's bridge and stop him from immolating himself. The same love that Rama had for Hanuman, Krishna had for Arjuna.

Seeing the beloved form of his friend before him, Arjuna also came running and hugged him. He realized that once again, Krishna had come to his aid as he had done many times before. Krishna raised him up, looked lovingly at him and said, "Remember Arjuna, that pride should always be curbed. You would have had to pay a heavy price for your arrogance had I not come in time."

Arjuna hung his head in shame and promised to curb his pride in future. He turned to Hanuman and begged his pardon for having questioned his Lord's ability.

Now Krishna asked Hanuman, "O son of Vayu! I hope you will keep your oath and help Arjuna in the war that is soon to come. You should sit on his pennon and help him in all possible ways without actively participating in the war." Hanuman promised to abide by his promise. Arjuna thanked him and went off to complete his *tapasya* to Shiva, and Hanuman returned to his own cave to perform his evening worship.

The Pandavas finished their exile successfully, but the Kauravas still refused to give them their rightful portion of the kingdom. Yudhistira did his best to avert war, but Duryodana refused to part with even the smallest bit of land. Krishna went as ambassador to the court of the Kurus and tried to prevail upon the elders to reason with Duryodana and make him see reason, but it was all to no avail. At last the two factions met on the field of Kurukshetra, prepared for battle. Krishna went as Arjuna's charioteer and Hanuman, as promised, sat on his pennon and made terrible grimaces and contortions that sent chills down the spines of those who faced him.

Some accounts say that Krishna asked Arjuna to repeat the Hanuman *mantra* a hundred thousand times in order to ensure victory. Thus, Arjuna was the first person to worship Hanuman as a god. Krishna then told Hanuman to accept such worship in the ensuing *yuga* known as Kali.

At the very commencement of the war, Arjuna told Krishna in his role as charioteer to place the chariot in the middle of the two armies so that he could survey the enemy formation. However, when he saw that the opposing army was filled with his teachers and grandsire and cousins, his heart failed him and his bow fell from his nerveless grasp. He refused to fight. The following great advice given by Lord Krishna to Arjuna is known as the Srimad Bhagavad Gita. It is a scripture that gives a practical approach to spirituality and tells us how to deal with any situation, however horrific it might be.

"This is not a war for a kingdom but a war of righteousness in which you should fight without hatred, for the enemy is within yourself. Only the person who conquers his own base nature can be called a hero. Be equal in success and failure, happiness and sorrow, honor and dishonor, and you will incur no sin. Therefore, O Arjuna, arise and fight as a divine instrument."

This advice of Krishna to Arjuna was meant for all posterity and it holds as good today as it did five thousand years ago on the battlefield of the Kurus.

From his perch on Arjuna's flag, Hanuman enjoyed the unique privilege of being the first to hear the complete discourse between Krishna and Arjuna on the battlefield of Kurukshetra that is known as the Sreemad Bhagavad Gita. He was also the sole witness of Krishna's revelation of his cosmic form. Krishna also told Arjuna that the only reason his chariot did not burn with Karna's arrows was because Hanuman was sitting in it. In fact, at the end of the war, when Hanuman descended from his perch, the chariot burst into flames.

> *One who reads this Hanuman Chalisa,*
> *Gains success—Gouri's Lord is witness.*

Hanuman Chalisa by Tulsidas

Aum Sri Hanumathe Namaha!

35

Shubham

Kali Yuga

So sab tava pratapa Raghurai!
Natha na kachu mori prabhutai.

Everything is due to your might, O Lord!
No credit is due to me for the same.

RAMACHARITAMANAS BY TULSIDAS

The Dwapara gave place to the Iron Age of Kali, and Hanuman continued his contemplation of his Lord in the Himalayas.

At this time Shani, son of the sun god and ruler of the planet Saturn, approached him. Hanuman recognized him as he had once released him from Ravana's dungeon. Shani was black, ill-figured, and he had a crooked neck that kept his head bent downward. If ever his glance fell on anyone, he was bound to be doomed. Shani informed him that the age of Dwapara was over and that Lord Krishna had left the earth along with the other celestials that had incarnated with him. Shani had been granted enhanced powers to torment earthly being in the dismal age of Kali. He did this by invading their zodiacal sign for a ruinous seven and a half year cycle. He specially loved to prey on the elderly by afflicting them with lingering and painful bodily afflictions. Exulting in his new powers, Shani announced to Hanuman that now that he was old and his strength greatly reduced, he was going to afflict his body straightaway.

Hanuman did not fear Shani any more than he feared his death-dealing brother Yama. "There is no room in my body for anyone but Rama," he said, "so I advise you to go somewhere else."

Shani laughed and said, "We'll see about that!" Then he outlined his normal plan. He would start with two and a half years on the head to weaken the mind and an equal period in the stomach to destroy the digestion and overall health and finally another two and a half years of crippling the knees and legs, by which time the victim was usually ready to welcome his elder brother Yama!

"Well, better get started," said Hanuman, pointing to his head. "We can see about the stomach and legs later." Shani gleefully clambered on top of Hanuman's head and very soon his scalp began to itch. Hanuman was annoyed, and breaking off a large boulder, he clapped it on his head.

"Hey! What are you doing?" Shani shouted.

"This is how I generally deal with itches and headaches," said Hanuman.

When the itching persisted, he selected a second and larger boulder and slapped it on top of the first. Shani writhed in agony and managed to gasp. "Perhaps we could negotiate. Maybe I'll make an exemption in your case and make it seven and a half weeks or perhaps even days!"

"Oh, that's all right," said Hanuman. "You should get on with your work while I get on with mine!" So saying, he picked up a third and even heavier boulder and piled it on top of the other two.

Shani shrieked and started to vomit blood. "Let me go! Please let me go, and I'll never bother you again," he pleaded.

"I know you!" said Hanuman. "You'll just go and bother someone else!" So saying, he delicately placed another boulder on top of the last.

Shani screamed for mercy and said, "Save me, O Son of Vayu! Release me, O Messenger of Rama! I promise henceforth never to afflict anyone who remembers you!"

Hanuman was pleased especially by the invocation to his Lord and removed the boulders. Shani descended and swore to keep his word.

There is another version to this story, which is worth mentioning here.

One evening Hanuman was meditating at the seaside in one of his favorite haunts, which happened to be the bridge made by the monkeys to Lanka so many eons ago. The inauspicious Shani came ambling along and noticed him. He was feeling particularly good since his powers had become stronger and people everywhere went in terror of him. He was well aware of Hanuman's reputation and thought that if he could get the better of him, his own reputation would go up by leaps and bounds. So he went up to Maruti and shouted, "O Monkey! I am Shani, most powerful of all the planets. Stand up and fight with me instead of pretending to be a great *yogi*!"

Hanuman greeted Shani respectfully and suggested that he go elsewhere to find a more worthy opponent, since he had become very old and was not interested in anything but the remembrance of Rama. Shani replied that once he had selected a victim, he would never let him go until his full cycle of devastation was complete. He stepped closer and seized Hanuman's paw. Hanuman stood up and enlarged his tail, winding it around Shani and binding him from head to toe. Shani did his best to free himself but could hardly get his breath to talk.

Hanuman ignored him and looked at the sinking sun, saying, "I have to do my daily circumambulation of the Lord's bridge!"

So saying, he sprang on to the rough causeway and set out at a brisk trot—two hundred leagues to Lanka and back. Periodically he punctuated his strides by slapping his tail down hard on the jagged rocks. The tail was like adamant and did not suffer from this treatment, but the same could not be said of its unwilling passenger. By the time the journey was complete, Shani was beaten to a pulp and was babbling for mercy. Hanuman stretched himself out leisurely on the sand and said,

"If you promise to stay out of the horoscopes of my worshippers, I will let you off."

Shani could hardly talk, but he nodded his head weakly and was freed. He hobbled away and begged for some *til* oil to rub on his wounds. To this day his worshippers offer him this oil on Saturdays, which happen to be Shani's day.

During the time of Rama, in the Treta Yuga, a woman called Vaishnavi wanted to marry Rama, but he turned her down because he was already married. However, he promised to marry her in Kali Yuga so Vaishnavi decided to do *tapasya* in the Himalayas until the advent of Kali.

One day a sorcerer called Bhairo visited her *ashrama*. As was customary, Vaishnavi offered him food. However, Bhairo was not interested in vegetarian fare and asked for wine, meat, and sex so that he could perform an occult rite.

Vaishnavi, who had sworn herself to Rama, refused to comply with his request and when he tried to use force, she ran away. Of course, he ran after her. Vaishnavi ran over hills and dales for days until she was totally exhausted and thirsty. She begged Rama to help her. At that moment Hanuman appeared before her. He kicked a rock and out sprang a stream of water. He also punched a cave into the hillside. She drank the water and rested in the cave for nine months, performing severe austerities, while Hanuman fought with Bhairo. At the end of this period she shed her human form and emerged as Adi Shakti, the divine Mother, armed with all the eighteen weapons. She raised her trident and beheaded Bhairo.

She thanked Hanuman for his timely assistance and accepted him as the attendant guardian of her shrine. The shrine of Vaishno Devi in the Himalayas has an idol of Hanuman at the gateway.

The great *yogi* known as Matsyendranath once wished to enter the shrine of the goddess and learn occult secrets from her. Hanuman stopped him at the gate and fought with him. He found the *yogi* to be a worthy opponent and let him in. Matsyendranath was so pleased with him that he offered to do whatever he wished. Hanuman decided to test the worth of this *yogi,* so he told him to go to the land peopled only by women (*stree rajya*), and offer them the pleasure of his company! The gods had decreed that any man who entered *stree rajya* would die an instant death.

Matsyendranath was surprised to hear this strange request, so Hanuman told him the story of this place and why he had undertaken to help the women. The event had taken place long ago when he was serving Rama in Ayodhya. Hanuman would take care of Rama's every need, much to Sita's annoyance. To keep him away for a while, she told him, "It's my wish that you father a child. Leave Ayodhya and return only after you have done so." Naturally, her request horrified Hanuman as he had taken a vow of celibacy. Thus, he feared he would never be able to father a child and be able to return to Ayodhya! In despair he wandered over the whole earth singing of Rama's glories.

The women of *stree rajya* heard him sing and such was the potency of his voice that it made them all pregnant. In due course they produced children whom they presented to Hanuman, who returned them to their mothers since he said he was not a *grihastashrami* (householder).

They said, "Now you can return to Ayodhya since you have produced children without breaking your vow of celibacy!"

Hanuman was so pleased with them that he offered them a boon. They promptly asked him to send a man to their land so that they could enjoy the pleasure of male company. Hanuman had promised to do so and Matsyedranath was the chosen man since Hanuman knew that he was the only one who had the power to overcome the curse of the gods! Such was the *yogic* power of this great sage that he was able to go into this strange land and stay in the company of the women for some years and thus keep Hanuman's word to them. The curse of the gods had no power over the sage!

The Tulsidas Ramayana, known as the Ramacharitamanas, is the best known Ramayana after that of Valmiki's. In fact, the popular theory is that Valmiki himself was born as Tulsidas since he felt that he hadn't done enough justice to Hanuman in his own Ramayana. The story of how he saw Hanuman's Ramayana inscribed on rocks has been narrated earlier.

During the time of the Moguls, when Akbar the Great was emperor, he had a very good Hindu minister called Atmarama. His son was called Tulsiram and he was extremely fond of the child. When the boy came of age, he had him married to a very pious girl called Mamta Devi. He then left his wife in the care of his son and taking the emperor's permission, he went to Kashi (Varanasi), in order to mediate on God. Due to his love for Atmarama, Akbar appointed Tulsiram in his father's post. Unfortunately, the young man got into some wild company and his whole character changed. He was always seen drinking and gambling and moving with women of low morals. Hearing this, Atmarama came back and tried his best to advise his son, who turned a deaf ear to his father's exhortations. Atmarama then shifted his whole family from the Mogul capital at Delhi to a small village on the banks of the river Yamuna near the town of Mathura.

Tulsiram now turned his passion toward his own wife and spent his whole time in her company, totally neglecting his work as well as his spiritual duties. His wife kept advising him to return to a normal state of affairs, but the man was so bemused by her beauty that he could think of nothing else but consorting with her. Akbar now sent word asking him to return to the capital as he had some work for him. Tulsiram refused to see the officers who had come to get him. At Mamta's insistence, he decided to go. When he reached Delhi, he was in a fever of impatience to get back since he was craving for his wife. At last, he asked the emperor to give him leave since he had not bid farewell to his mother and wife when he left. He promised to return very soon.

As soon as he got permission, he took a one-horse buggy and started off with all speed to his village even though it was already evening. Very soon the sky darkened and it started to rain. The driver begged him to stop somewhere for the night, but Tulsiram refused to listen to reason and urged him to whip the horse and make it go faster. The storm did not abate and the poor horse carried on in the face of the bitter wind and rain. At last it just could not go any more and collapsed at the outskirts of the village. Tulsiram cursed the driver and the horse and jumped out of the carriage and ran all the way to his house. His mother was astounded to see him standing at the door all wet and bedraggled at two in the morning.

"What's the matter"? she asked. "Why have you come at this time of the night?"

Tulsiram did not even bother to reply to his mother. "Where is my wife?" he demanded. "I must see her immediately."

"She has gone to her own house across the river," said his mother.

Without wasting a moment, Tulsiram ran to the river, which was swollen and rough due to the storm. There was not a boat or boatman in sight. He was afire with the desire to see his wife and without even thinking of how he was risking his life, he jumped into the swirling waters of the Yamuna and started swimming against the strong current. He found that he was not progressing very well. At that moment, as if in answer to a prayer, he saw a log floating down. He caught hold of it thankfully and was taken across the river. He jumped onto the banks and when he turned around to look at the river, there was a sudden burst of lightning and he saw to his horror that the thing that he had thought was a log was actually a corpse!

Without wasting time on unnecessary speculations he dashed to his wife's house and found the gate locked. The walls were quite high and it was impossible for him to get a foothold to jump over it. He shouted and shouted to her to come and open the gate, but the noise of the thunder and the storm drowned his voice. By this time he was crazed with lust and totally devoid of reason. He went round and round the walls like a crazy man and suddenly spied a thick rope hanging down the wall. He grabbed it and somehow or other managed to scrabble to the top of the wall and jump into the compound. He then went and pounded at the door until he woke the whole household. They were all aghast to see his wild condition and wondered how he had managed to cross the river and climb over the wall. He told them that he had hung onto a log and found a rope on the wall. When they went to inspect the rope they found that it was actually a python!

As soon as they reached their bedroom he could contain his lust no longer and grabbed his wife in his arms. She pushed him off in all fury and burst into a tirade of rage and sorrow.

"How can you behave like this? Have you lost all sense of decency and decorum? This body for whose sake you have dared to cross this raging river and climb a wall with the help of a snake is only made of flesh and blood and bones and will decay and become old in no time. If you have half the love for God as you have for me, you would have become a realized saint! If you longed for the vision of Rama as much as you craved for my vision, you would have seen him by now. Actually, it is not love that you have for me but lust for this flesh! You are born in a noble family and you have the possibility to become enlightened in this life. Don't waste this precious life in sexual pleasures. Repeat the name of Rama and attain liberation!"

Tulsiram was stunned when he heard this. Her words made a deep impression on him. It was as if she had given him a blow on his head and something had burst inside. As the dawn appeared in the sky, a light flamed in his head. Without another word, he left the house and went to the city of Kashi to start intense austerities. As much as he had yearned for the sight of his wife, now he yearned to have a sight of his beloved deity Rama. He could not eat or sleep. He went around as one possessed, inquiring for Rama. At last he met someone who told him that the only one who could fulfill his desire was Hanuman.

"Where can I meet Hanuman?" he asked.

"He is always present wherever the story of Rama is told. The Ramayana is being sung at a certain place right now. You will surely find him there. But remember he will not be in his own form. I have often noticed that a Brahmin dressed in tatters is always present at the discourse. He is the first to come and the last to leave. No one knows who he is or where he lives. I suspect that he is indeed Hanuman. Catch hold of him. Never leave him and he will be able to give you the vision of the Lord."

Tulsiram went daily to the discourse and observed the old Brahmin carefully. However, every time he tried to follow him, he found that the old man disappeared instantly. However, nothing could deter his urgency to meet Rama. The same determination that compelled him to risk his life in order to reach the side of his beloved on that stormy night was now directed to meeting the divine beloved! One day he jumped and caught hold of the Brahmin's *dhoti* (cloth worn by men) that was around his waist and tied his hand to it. The old man ran very fast into the dense forest and very soon Tulsiram could not keep up with his speed. But he hung on to the cloth and was dragged over the rough ground until he was torn and bleeding. All the while he kept repeating the *mantra* of Rama. He was determined never to let him go until his wish was fulfilled. At last the Brahmin stopped. Tulsiram grabbed hold of his feet and said.

"My Lord, I know who you are. I will not let you go until you give me a vision of Rama!"

Anjaneya now took his own form and raised him up and said, "Indeed, I am pleased with your devotion. You shall have a vision of the Lord tomorrow!"

Thus saying, he vanished. Tulsiram returned to his abode and spent the night in ecstasy thinking of the joy in store for him in the morning. The next day he cleaned his whole hut and compound and waited anxiously for his Lord to come. However, the only ones who came were two hunters dressed in green and mounted on horseback. That evening he went to the Brahmin and cried loud and long, for he had not got the vision that had been promised.

Hanuman replied, "He did come, but you did not recognize him, for he was dressed as a common hunter! But fear not, tomorrow evening he will give you the *darshan* you are longing for."

The local people heard about this and many were present in Tulsiram's courtyard. The shades of night were falling, and the yard was filled with people all chanting, "Rama! Rama!" Suddenly all of them were thrilled to see Rama approaching with Lakshmana and Sita on either side. Tulsiram fell at Rama's feet and was unable to get up. Rama lifted him up tenderly and told him,"My son, your love alone has brought me here. You are truly blessed. From now on you shall be known as Tulsidas. It is your duty to write the story of the Ramayana in simple language that the common people can understand."

Tulsidas was astounded, "My Lord!" he said. "I am totally incapable of writing on such a great subject. All I know is to chant your name. How can I fulfill your command?"

Rama looked lovingly at him and said, "Fear not. You will be given guidance by Hanuman, who is not only erudite but also filled with devotion. He has been a living witness to the story of my life. He is the best person to guide you."

Thus it happened that Tulsidas started writing the Ramayana in the common man's language, Awadhi, which was a dialect of Hindi. It was written in the year AD 1575. When Valmiki wrote his Ramayana, India was at the peak of its cultural refinement, while Tulsidas produced his work at a time when there was a widespread degradation in moral values. There was rivalry between different faiths and sects. Through the story of Rama, Tulsidas sought to acquaint the masses with all that was best in the Hindu scriptures and to bring about synthesis and concordance among the various schools of religious thought. In North India, it gained instant popularity among laborers, peasants, and householders alike. It came to be known as the Ramacharitamanas.

Many miracles were attributed to Tulsidas. Hearing about these, the Mogul emperor Akbar sent for him and asked him to perform a miracle for him. Tulsidas replied, "I am only a humble servant of Rama. He alone is the worker of miracles."

"Show me your Rama, then," said the emperor.

Tulsidas remained silent. The emperor became angry at his silence and ordered him to be put in jail. It is said that Tulsidas composed the Hanuman Chalisa when he was in prison at Fatepur Sikri, which was Akbar's fortress at the time. During those forty days when he was composing the verses, he prayed to Hanuman to save him from this predicament. At the end of the forty days, the whole of the emperor's fort was swarming with monkeys. They clawed people, tore their clothes, entered houses, and destroyed gardens. At last the emperor realized that this must be the work of the man he had thrown in jail. He ran to him and fell at his feet, begging him to order the monkeys to go away. Tulsidas prayed to Hanuman and immediately the monkeys vanished, but he told the emperor, "You should leave this spot and take up your residence at some other place, for this is Rama's abode and no one should stay here except the monkeys."

Hearing this, the emperor is said to have changed the location of his fortress. Tulsidas died in the year 1624. Two copies of his Ramayana, written in his own handwriting, are said to be in existence. One is preserved at Rajpur, and the other is in the temple of Sita-Rama, which he himself had constructed at Kashi. Although many of the Sanskrit pundits of his time attacked him for having lowered the dignity of his subject by clothing it in vulgar vernacular, the fact remains that his book is found everywhere from the court to the cottage and is read or heard and appreciated by every class of the Hindu community, high and low, rich and poor, young and old.

Says Tulsidas, Hari's constant servant,
"Lord! Make your abode in my heart."

HANUMAN CHALISA BY TULSIDAS

Aum Sri Hanumathe Namaha!

Aum Mangalaaya Namaha!

36

Mangala Murti

The Auspicious Form

Then Sita spoke, greatly pleased,
"Son of the wind, wherever you reside, by my decree,
You will receive abundant offerings.
In villages, fields, cities and cowsheds,
By roadsides, in hamlets and homes.
Forests and forts, on hilltops and in temples,
By rivers and pilgrim places,
By tanks and towns.
In gardens and groves, under fig and banyan trees,
And in sacred sites.
Men will worship your image to assuage their afflictions,
When you are remembered, ghosts, goblins and ghouls
    will flee."

ANANDA RAMAYANA

Sita's blessing to Hanuman proved to be prophetic, since all the blessings she gave him have come to pass over the years. Hanuman's shrines are in keeping with his personality and are rarely elaborate. They are humble structures built by ordinary people without the help of priests. He is often seen in the open, under trees or on the walls of temples, forts, and palaces. His idols are mainly carved out of stone or sometimes out of roots of trees with stubs that vaguely resemble simian features. They are often covered with vermillion or saffron paste and sometimes decorated with silver foil. Images normally show him carrying the mountain of herbs or standing guard in front of a Rama temple holding his mace. It is rare to see him in a meditative posture like a *yogi*.

His images are also seen at the gateways to settlements and villages to keep out malevolent forest spirits or at crossroads, thought to be where ghosts lurk, or at the entrance to forts, palaces, temples, monasteries, and gymnasiums. So in this sense he can be seen as a liminal god, a god who negotiates between different realms or guards the uncertain space between two places. In the famous Krishna shrine of Nathdwara, in Rajasthan, Hanuman stands guard before the four gates to the temple.

In both Jaipur and Vrindavan, there are many Hanuman shrines. During the early twentieth century, many of the little-known shrines to Hanuman that purported to be ancient and self-formed suddenly sprang into prominence. The city of Varanasi, in Uttar Pradesh, claims many such shrines. The small roadside shrines of Nichi Bagh and Kabir Choura are so crowded on Tuesdays and Saturdays that all traffic comes to a grinding halt. A small shrine in a lane behind Assi Ghat in the midst of a *dalit* (low caste) settlement sprang into prominence when the great nationalist leader, Madan Mohan Malaviya, began stopping there for prayers after his morning ablutions in the *ghat* (bathing place on the river). He kept a forty-day vigil to get Hanuman's blessing for establishing the nearby Benaras Hindu University, and naturally, with Maruti's blessings, the world-famous university was established in 1916.

Of course, the most well-known shrine in Varanasi is the huge *murti* (idol) in the Sankat Mochan temple. The story of this is closely connected with Tulsidas. Tulsidas used to pray to a small Hanuman idol under the twisted roots of a peepul tree after his ablutions in the Ganga. This tree was the abode of a tormented spirit who was grateful for the water that Tulsidas used to pour over it daily. In return, he offered Tulsidas a boon. The saint asked for some *darshan* of Rama but, of course, the poor ghost could not arrange this. However, he told him that the only one who could help him was Hanuman himself. He told him that Maruti used to come daily to the *ghat* in the form of an old leper to listen to the narration of the Ramayana. He sat at the back and was always the last to leave. Tulsidas followed the leper, who led him deep into the forest. He fell at his feet and hailed him as "Vayu Putra!" The leper denied vehemently that he was nothing but an old, sick man, but Tulsidas persisted and eventually Hanuman revealed his own glorious form. Raising one hand over his shoulder he pointed southwest and said, "Go to Chitrakut," and placing the other hand over his heart he added, "I promise that you will see Rama." This is supposed to have taken place at the very spot where the Sankata Mochana temple now stands, and the posture of the idol there has the same gestures that are mentioned above.

It is said that Tulsidas entreated Hanuman to stay in that spot for the benefit of his devotees. Maruti agreed but dived into the ground and disappeared. Tulsidas dug frantically into the sand throughout the night and finally, as dawn was breaking, he unearthed a *swayambhu murti* (self-formed idol) with the same posture in which Hanuman had addressed him. He established this *murti* and thus created the first temple to Hanuman. This miracle is supposed to have occurred on the eighth day of the dark fortnight of the month of Margashirsha (November/December) in 1550. The Bara Hanuman or the Great Hanuman is seen in the Hanuman *ghat* of the city.

The very popular temple at Mehndipur is located in Rajasthan and situated in a small valley, five kilometers from the Agra-Jaipur highway. It is said to be the place where Bala (baby) Hanuman was returned to the lap of his mother by the wind god after he had been chastised by Indra for daring to swallow the sun. Hence, Hanuman's childhood is especially regarded in this region and he is known as Balaji. There are many stories connected with this place. It is said that one of the priests had a dream in which he saw the idol of Balaji. Suddenly he saw thousands of flickering lamps approaching from afar. When they came near, he discovered that the lights were being carried by a huge army of men accompanied by horses and elephants. They circumambulated Balaji and the commander came and prostrated himself to him. After this striking performance, all of them disappeared the way they had come. At that very spot the priest saw three *murtis* and heard a voice saying, "Rise up and attend to my *pujas;* I intend to perform many miracles here." When he woke up, the Brahmin started to search and eventually located the site he had seen in his dream. He discovered the three idols and started offering ritualistic worship to them. Very soon, miracles started to occur in the temple and many people began to come. During the time of Muslim rule, the temple fell into decline, and one king even tried to uproot the idol of Balaji, but he could never find its base. He soon realized that the whole mountain was its body! With the passing of time, the temple rose to its present state of fame and glory.

Actually, there are three main deities here. The first is Balaji himself. This idol is carved out of the boulder and covered with *sindoor* (vermilion) and silver foil. In the hall upstairs, there is the idol to Pretaraj, or the king of ghosts. He is sometimes referred to as Yamaraj, or the king of death. Balaji is thought to be a most powerful deity for exorcising people from evil spirits. Petitions are offered to Balaji by those who seem to be possessed of spirits, and healing occurs in many ways. It is said that the afflicted person starts speaking in the voice of the spirit and is exhorted by Balaji and Pretaraj to leave the sufferer in peace.

In Ayodhya, it is said that Rama turned over the city to Hanuman when he left the earth, and thus Hanuman is the present-day king of Ayodhya. His most important temples here are in Hanuman Garhi, which is a cave temple, and Nageshwarnath, which is thought to have been established by one of Lord Rama's sons.

Lucknow is noted for two temples in the Aliganj area. The Sri Hanuman temple is the more renowned, and the Mahavir Mela festival held there every spring is said to attract all the different religious communities. The famous recumbent Hanuman lies near the Triveni Sangam, or triple confluence, where the visible rivers of Ganga and Yamuna meet the invisible Saraswati in the place known as Prayaga, near modern Allahabad. The huge figure, half-buried in the sandy riverbank, is approached by going down a flight of steps. It is said that two hundred years ago, when the idol was being transported down the river by a wealthy merchant, the boat ran aground and the figure tipped over into the sand. All attempts to dislodge it failed and Hanuman revealed in a dream that he wished to remain at this spiritually potent confluence of rivers.

The Hanuman Dhara (Hanuman Stream), about seventy miles south of Allahabad, sits on a hill and is arrived at by climbing several hundred stairs. It looks over the area where Rama, Sita, and Lakshmana are said to have lived for twelve years. The large idol is carved into the back wall of the cliff and over it a stream of water emerges and constantly bathes him, with the thought of helping to cool him off after he had burned Lanka.

In the temple of Lord Jagannath in Puri, Orissa, Hanuman guards all the four gates of the temple in order to prevent the sound of the sea from entering the shrine and disturbing his master. There are many other famous shrines to Maruti in Puri apart from the four that guard the gates. The Dariya Hanuman (Hanuman of the Sea) was installed so that he would protect the city from onslaughts by the ocean. However, Maruti abandoned his post to go and have *darshan* of his Lord. When the citizens complained to Lord Jagannath, he told them to chain him to his post. Since no ordinary chains could bind him, he was secured with a stout chain of gold links on which were inscribed Rama's name.

However, the most famous Hanuman in Orissa is in the village of Siruli on the Puri-Bhuvaneswar road and it is known as Mahavir. It is a black stone idol believed to have emerged from the earth. Its left eye gazes through a small window toward Puri and the right eye stares balefully toward Lanka in the south.

In the very heart of modern Delhi, just behind the bustling circle known as Connaught Place, stands a most vibrant Hanuman temple known as Sri Hanumanji Maharaj. The main statue is fairly recent and is of white marble, but the actual *murti* is on one side and placed at the right side of the statues of Rama and Sita. Normally, the features are hidden by a heavy coating of *sindoor* but now and again this falls off to reveal the original idol. It is a small bas relief of a simian profile with head facing south and bared teeth. One raised fist brandishes a tiny club and the other rests on his heart. He wears a tapering crown and a sacred thread over his right shoulder and he has a loincloth hanging between his short legs. The *murti* is said to have been established by the Pandavas when their capital was in Indraprastha—modern Delhi.

Another important Hanuman temple in Delhi is found in Old Delhi in the place known as Yamuna bazaar, near the river next to the burning *ghats*. It is known as the Marghat Baba Hanuman. The small but busy complex contains a modest shrine, and beyond that lies a dark narrow staircase leading down to the sanctum in which the small figure stands. The descent to this subterranean sanctuary creates a mysterious atmosphere. During the monsoons, the waters of the Yamuna seep into the room, and at times Hanuman stands neck-deep in water, but the temple never closes, as the site is said to be a very powerful place and what is more, is thought to have been founded by Bhima himself, the strongman among the Pandavas. These two Hanuman temples provide a great contrast. They denote the two aspects of Hanuman—*bhakti* and *shakti*.

Maharashtra abounds in Hanuman shrines and they are even said to exceed the Ganesha shrines. In South India, the medieval city of Vijayanagara is supposed to have been the place of the ancient monkey kingdom of Kishkinda. The small hill known as Ajanadri (hill of Anjana) is supposed to mark the birthplace of Hanuman.

One of the most important shrines to Hanuman is found in Suchindram in Tamil Nadu. It has a twenty-foot statue that is said to be growing. Abhishekam, or the ritual bath, has to be done by priests who must climb up ladders. This image is purported to be the form that he took to reassure Sita. There is another shrine to him in Kanyakumari, close to Suchindram, at the tip of the Indian subcontinent.

Another important Hanuman shrine in South India is located at the place known as Namakkal, near Salem. Carved out of a single stone, the imposing and colorful Hanuman idol is plastered with butter on Saturdays, and even on hot days the butter is said to remain without melting until the next morning. The priests make fascinating designs on the butter with leaves and flowers. Hanuman stands facing a temple to Narasimha Murti, the fourth *avatara* of Vishnu. Since Narasimha has no roof over his head, Hanuman also refused to have a cover above him and stands exposed to the elements.

In the famous Krishna temple of Udupi, devotees always have *darshan* of Anjaneya before proceeding to the main temple of Krishna.

In some of the temples in Gujarat, Hanuman is depicted as a stout figure with a handlebar mustache. In Sourashtra, several figures of Maruti are found alongside the one thousand and five hundred steps going up the sacred Girnar Mountain.

Many books contain a list of famous Anjaneya shrines. The list above is far from being complete. It is doubtful that anyone can take an account of the number of shrines and idols dedicated to this amazing being, many of which are said to have miraculous properties. There are speaking and shaking Hanumans and subterranean and submerged Hanumans and those that emerge from boulders and farm furrows like Sita. For those who want to make a pilgrimage to the Hanuman shrines, one safe way is to follow Rama's path in the Ramayana from Ayodhya to Lanka. All along this route are found many of Anjaneya's most important shrines.

As we know, power and devotion, or *shakti* and *bhakti,* are his dual characteristics. As such, Hanuman *murtis* are divided into these two types. Those that denote *bhakti* are known as having *dasa bhava,* and those with a virile mood are known as having *vira bhava.* The former *murtis* should be worshipped with *sattvika,* or pure types of offerings like fruits and nuts, while the other types can be worshipped with *rajasic* (passionate) offerings that might even include alcohol. The latter figures are supposed to denote his form as Rudra, or the incarnation of the eleventh Rudra, and are often just a stone smeared with *sindoor.*

It is commonly noticed that if the right foot is placed to the front, it depicts his mild devotional aspect while the demon-slaying aspect is stressed if the left foot is kept forward. As an embodiment of *shakti*, Hanuman is closely associated with control of the elements and the destructive aspects of creation that are the characteristics of Shiva and his consort Shakti. As an example of *bhakti,* or self-effacing love, he drowns himself in the river of Rama's love.

Hanuman is said to be the *pratyaksha devata,* or most efficient deity of the present age of Kali, since he is still alive. He alone is purported to be capable of bestowing all the four aims of life (*dharma, artha, kama,* and *moksha*), and that is the reason that in this Kali Yuga, more and more temples are being built for him.

High in the Himalayas (abode of snow), on the way to the Hindu holy town of Badrinath near the Tibet border, where sits the famous shrine to Lord Vishnu, one passes through a small village called Pandukeshwara. Above it is the mountain known as Hemakuta (golden mountain). This is the beautiful place where Lakshmana is thought to have done *tapasya* to atone for the sin of having killed Indrajit. Here the Sikhs have built a huge temple by a glacial lake. The area is inaccessible all but four months of the year, when snows melt and wildflowers bloom wildly. The temple, which is called Hemkunt Sahib, is the highest in India. And above even that place, in the towering heights of the golden mountain, is the abode of the Kimpurushas. Here Hanuman still resides and many *yogis* claim to have seen him there.

> *Son of the Wind, banisher of affliction,*
> *Embodiment of auspiciousness,*
> *Dwell in my heart, king of gods,*
> *Together with Rama, Lakshmana, and Sita.*

HANUMAN CHALISA BY TULSIDAS

Aum Sri Hanumathe Namaha!

APPENDIX ONE

Poems on Hanuman

Verses Composed by Vanamali

Hail to Thee O Son of Wind!
Messenger of Rama!
Harbinger of light and life!
Light to Sita,
Life to Lakshmana,
You flew into my heart,
Like a tender bud,
And made it blossom into a full blown lotus.
What did I know about bhakti,
Until you came and took residence in my heart.
What did I know of shakti,
Until you empowered my limbs,
Ah! precious harbinger of hope and love,
Show me your form when you crept into Lanka,
Sweet and small like a baby cat,
The form that enticed Sita,
As you parted the leaves and gazed at her.
As you chanted the tales of her beloved,
Filling her with rapture.
I shudder to think of your enormous frame,
Reducing Lanka to cinders.

O gentle one!
People say you are mighty and impossible to
*   control,*
But I see thee kneeling at Rama's feet. . . .
Vanamali's feet that I cherish in my heart.

O Lordly One!
Terrify me not with thy brooding looks,
And horrific grimaces scattering the demons in
*   fear,*
Let me drown in thy amber eyes,
Piercing me to the depths of my soul,
Filled with compassion,
For this hapless soul,
Floundering in the sea of samsara.

Give me the eyes to perceive thee,
Take me to thy abode.
In the heart of the golden peak,
To the land of the Kimpurushas
Half wild, half-human,
Waft me away in thy arms to the mystic
*   mountain,*
Surrounded by celestial beings.

I shall turn my face to thy father,
And feel his caressing tendrils on my face,
I shall lie near thee on the lap of nature,
And gaze upon the face of god,
For you will be where Rama is,
And Rama is none but my beloved,
Vanamali!
Therefore O Vanara!
Take me to Vanamali!

I have searched for him far and wide,
In thee I have found the perfect vehicle,
My sweet Maruti,
Deny me not this request,
For I am thy eternal servant,
Sent by him to me,
For now I know that thou and he,
Are never two but always one.
Who came first, god or bhakta?
None can tell, for they are united in eternity.

I gaze at the monkeys that flock in my garden,
And wonder if you could be among them,
They destroy the garden like you did,
They eat up the fruits and despoil the pools,
Am I to tolerate their inequities?
They belong to your race.
Tell me, O Divine Vanara!
Why the violence and worry?
Can you not protect me from this?
Am I your servent for nothing?
Teach them to curb their nature,
As indeed you did.
And then I shall love you even more.

My noble Hanuman, help me to understand,
The vagaries of the monkey mind,
Help me to control mine,
Direct me to the source divine,
From which alone your inspiration comes.
Hold me aloft in your hand like the herb
   mountain,
Waft me to Vaikunda, the abode of Vanamali,
O Vanara! Be my messenger to Vanamali!

Whisper in his ear as you did to Rama,
Of the love of Sita for Rama,
Of the love of Devi for Vanamali!

Mantra heenum, kriya heenum,
Bhakti heenum sureshwara,
Yad poojitam maya Deva,
Paripoornam tadastu.

O Lord! I beg of you to accept and make perfect
This *puja* (work) of mine, that is,
Devoid of proper chants, actions, or devotion.

Aum Sri Hanumathe Namaha!

APPENDIX TWO

Names of Hanuman

Anjaneya	Son of Anjana
Bajarangabali	Strong as a thunderbolt
Balaji	Baby Hanuman
Bhaktavatsala	One who is kind to devotees
Bhima	One with a huge form
Daityakulantaka	Destroyer of the rakshasa clan
Hanuman	One who has controlled the mind; one with a broken jaw
Jitendriya	One who has controlled his senses
Kapindra	King of monkeys
Kesari Nandana	Kesari's pet
Kesari Putra	Son of Kesari
Lakshmana Pranadhata	Giver of life to Lakshmana
Lokabandu	Relation of the world
Mahabala	One with extraordinary might
Mahatejasvin	One who is filled with spiritual luster
Mahatman	The noble one

Mahavira	The great hero
Mangala Murti	The form of auspiciousness
Maruti	Son of Marut (wind god)
Pavana putra	Son of the wind god
Pranadeva	Giver of breath (life)
Ramadasa	Rama's servant
Ramaduta	Messenger of Rama
Ramapriyan	Beloved of Rama
Rudrasya-Soonu	Son of Rudra (Shiva)
Sahasravadana	Possessing a thousand faces
Sankata Mochana	Dispeller of sorrow
Shoora	The courageous one
Shubangana	Having auspicious features
Shubham	Auspicious
Sugriva Mitram	Sugriva's friend
Sundara	Beautiful
Tapaswin	One who practices austerities
Uttaman	The noblest one
Vatamaja	Born of wind
Vayu Putra	Son of Vayu (wind god)
Veera	Heroic one
Virupa	Strange-looking one

Names of Other Characters in the Hindu Pantheon

Agastya	Great sage with divine powers
Agni	God of fire
Ahalya	Wife of sage Gautama
Ahiravana	Sorceror; son of Ravana
Akampana	Name of a rakshasa
Aksha Kumara	Ravana's youngest son
Amabalika	Celestial nymph
Anasuya	Wife of sage Atri
Angada	Son of monkey king Vaali
Anjana	Hanuman's mother
Ananta	Celestial serpent on which Vishnu sleeps
Arjuna	The middle sibling among the Pandavas
Aruna	Charioteer of the sun god Surya
Atikaya	One of Kumbhakarna's sons
Atri	Great sage
Ayyappa	Incarnation of Dharma Shasta
Bhadra	Rama's friend

Bharadwaja	Great sage who lived in Prayaga
Bharata	Rama's brother
Brahma	The Creator in the Vedic Trinity
Brihaspati	Preceptor of the gods
Bhima	The strong man of the Pandavas
Dasaratha	Rama's father
Devantaka	One of Kumbhakarna's sons
Devi	Goddess
Dharmashasta	Son of Shiva and Vishnu
Dhumraksha	Ravana's general
Dhushana	Ravana's general
Dundubhi	Buffalo demon
Durvasa	Sage noted for his bad temper
Ganesha	Elephant-headed son of Shiva
Ganga	The holy river
Garuda	Eagle vehicle of Lord Vishnu
Gautama	Great sage; husband of Ahalya
Hanuman	Son of the wind god
Hayagriva	Horse-faced incarnation of Vishnu
Hema	Mandodari's mother
Himavan	King of the Himalayas
Indra	King of the gods
Indrajit	Ravana's eldest son
Jambavan	King of the bears
Jambumali	Son of Ravana's general
Janaka	Sita's father
Janaki	Janaka's daughter Sita

Jatayu	Vulture who was Rama's friend
Jayanta	Indra's son who came in the form of a crow
Kaala	The spirit of Time
Kaali	Horrific aspect of the goddess
Kaikeyi	Dasaratha's wife; Bharata's mother
Kalanemi	Rakshasa who tried to obstruct Hanuman
Kampan	Author of the Ramayana in Tamil
Kartikeya	Shiva's son; general of the gods
Kausalya	Wife of Dasaratha; Rama's mother
Kesari	Hanuman's monkey father
Khara	A rakshasa
Krishna	Supreme incarnation of Vishnu
Kubera	God of wealth; Ravana's stepbrother
Kumbhakarna	Ravana's brother known for his enormous body and appetite
Kunjara	Anjana's father
Kusa	A type of grass; one of the twin sons of Rama
Kuvachana	A man who had insulted his ancestors
Lakshmana	Rama's brother
Lakshmi	Goddess of wealth and auspiciousness
Lankini	Guardian goddess of Lanka
Lava	One of the twin sons of Rama
Madhavi	Goddess of the earth
Madhvacharya	Founder of the Dvaita school of Vedanta
Mahakaala	The great god of death; one of the names of Shiva
Mahakaali	The great Kaali; horrific form of the Devi
Mahaparshava	Ravana's trusted general

Maheswara	The great god; name of Shiva
Mahiravana	Sorcerer son of Ravana; king of the netherworld
Maithili	Sita, princess of Mithila
Makaradwaja	Hanuman's son born of a crocodile
Mandavya	Great sage
Mandodari	Chief wife of Ravana
Manthara	Hunchbacked maid of Kaikeyi
Manu Swayambhu	Progenitor of the world
Maricha	Rakshasa who enticed Sita in the form of a golden deer
Matali	Indra's charioteer
Matanga	Great sage
Mayan	Architect of the demons
Mayavi	Rakshasa who fought with Vaali
Meghanatha	Eldest son of Ravana, later known as Indrajit
Mohini	Alluring form of Vishnu as a woman
Muruga	Another name of Kartikeya, son of Shiva
Nala	Monkey who designed the bridge to Lanka
Nandi	Bull vehicle of Shiva
Narada	Celestial sage noted for his mischief
Narantaka	One of Kumbhakarna's sons
Narayana	The primeval being who slumbers on the waters
Narasimha	Fourth incarnation of Vishnu
Nila	Another monkey who helped to design the bridge
Panavati	Embodiment of baneful astrological influences
Pandavas	Five brothers who were heroes of the Mahabharata
Parashurama	Sixth incarnation of Vishnu

Parvati	Wife of Shiva; daughter of Himavan
Prahastha	Commander in chief of Ravana's army
Prahlada	Demon boy who was a great devotee of Vishnu
Punchikasthala	Celestial nymph who became Hanuman's mother, Anjana
Raghava	Another name of Rama
Raghu	An ancestor of Rama
Rahu	Malignant node of the moon that eclipses the sun
Rama	Seventh incarnation of Vishnu
Ramachandra	Another name for Rama
Ravana	King of Lanka and of the rakshasas
Riksha	The very first vanara (monkey)
Rudra	Fierce aspect of Shiva
Rumi	Wife of Sugriva
Sagara	Name of the monarch of the ocean
Sampati	Vulture brother of Jatayu
Sanat Kumara	One of the four boy sages
Saraswati	Goddess of all arts and sciences
Satabali	White-furred bear
Shabari	Old female ascetic
Shambasaadan	Rakshasa who tried to entice Anjana
Shani	Saturn, the malefic planet
Shatrugna	Rama's brother and Lakshmana's twin
Shilada	A sage
Shilavati	A very chaste woman
Shiva	The destructive aspect of the trinity
Shurpaneka	Ravana's sister

Sita	Rama's wife; princess of Videha
Skanda	Kartikeya; Shiva's son; general of the gods
Suka	Ravana's minister
Sugriva	Monkey king; brother of Vaali
Sulochana	Indrajit's wife
Sumantra	Charioteer of Dasaratha
Sumitra	Mother of Lakshmana and Shatrugna
Surya	Sun god
Sushena	1. Father-in-law of Sugriva; 2. Ravana's court physician
Swaminathan	Another name for Kartikeya
Swayamprabha	Nymph who was guarding the cave
Tara	Vaali's wife
Trijata	Rakshasi who helped Sita
Trisira	One of Kumbhakarna's sons
Tulsidas	Author of Ramacharitamanas
Tulsiram	Previous name of Tulsidas
Ugrati	Leper husband of Shilavati
Vaali	Monkey king; Sugriva's brother
Vaidehi	Sita, princess of Videha
Vaishravas	Ravana's father
Vajradamshtra	Name of a rakshasa
Valmiki	Author of the first Ramayana
Varaha	The second avatara of Vishnu as a boar
Varuna	Lord of the waters
Vasishta	Great sage; guru of clan of Ikshvaku
Vayu	Wind god; Hanuman's father

Vedavati	Name of Sita in a previous incarnation
Vibhishana	Noble rakshasa; half-brother of Ravana
Vinata	Sugriva's general
Virupaksha	One of Ravana's generals
Vishnu	The Preserver in the Vedic Trinity
Vishwakarma	Architect of the gods
Vishwamitra	The royal sage
Vrishakapi	Monkey god mentioned in the Vedas
Vyasa	Author of the Mahabharata and eighteen Puranas; compiler of the Vedas into four books
Yama	God of Death
Yayati	King of Kashi
Yudhistira	Eldest of the Pandavas

Alphabetical List of Mantras

The mantras that open and close every chapter of this book have been listed here in alphabetical order to facilitate location of their translations.

Aum Anjaneyaaya Namaha!	Prostrations to the son of Anjana
Aum Banda-mokshadaaya Namaha!	Prostrations to the one who releases us from bondage
Aum Bhaktavatsalaaya Namaha!	Prostrations to the lover of devotees
Aum Brahmachaarine Namaha!	Prostrations to the celibate
Aum Daityakulanthakaaya Namaha!	Prostrations to the killer of the race of the demons
Aum Dhumraketave Namaha!	Prostrations to the one who is fierce like a comet
Aum Kapishwaraaya Namaha!	Prostrations to the king of monkeys
Aum Kesari Suthaaya Namaha!	Prostrations to the son of Kesari
Aum Lakshmanaprana-dataaya Namaha!	Prostrations to the savior of Lakshmana
Aum Mahakayaaya Namaha!	Prostrations to the one with a huge body

Aum Mahatejase Namaha!	Prostrations to the effulgent one
Aum Mahatmane Namah!	Prostrations to the noble soul
Aum Mahaviraaya Namaha!	Prostrations to the great hero
Aum Mangalaaya Namaha!	Prostrations to the auspicious one
Aum Manojavaaya Namaha!	Prostrations to the one who is as swift as the mind
Aum Marutaatmajaaya Namaha!	Prostrations to the son of wind
Aum Pingalakshaaya Namaha!	Prostrations to the tawny-eyed one
Aum Ramabhaktaaya Namaha!	Prostrations to the devotee of Rama
Aum Ramadhutaaya Namaha!	Prostrations to the messenger of Rama
Aum Ramayana-priyaaya Namaha!	Prostrations to the one who loves the Ramayana
Aum Raudraaya Namaha!	Prostrations to the fierce one
Aum Ravana-maradanaaya Namaha!	Prostrations to the scourge of Ravana
Aum Sahasravadanaaya Namaha!	Prostrations to the one with a thousand faces
Aum Samsara-bhayanashakaaya Namaha!	Prostrations to the one who releases us from fear of rebirth
Aum Sathyavachaaya Namaha!	Prostrations to the one who is ever truthful
Aum Satyasandaaya Namaha!	Prostrations to the one who keeps to the path of truth
Aum Shashwathaaya Namaha!	Prostrations to the eternal one
Aum Sita Shokavinaashakaaya Namaha!	Prostrations to the dispeller of Sita's sorrow
Aum Shooraaya Namaha!	Prostrations to the courageous one

Aum Shubakaraaya Namaha!	Prostrations to the one who does noble deeds
Aum Shubhangaaya Namaha!	Prostrations to the one with auspicious features
Aum Sri Ganeshaaya Namaha!	Prostrations to Lord Ganesha
Aum Sri Hanumathe Namaha!	Prostrations to Sri Hanuman
Aum Sri Ramaaya Namaha!	Prostrations to Sri Rama
Aum Sri Ramachandraaya Namaha!	Prostrations to Ramachandra
Aum Tatwajnanapradaaya Namaha!	Prostrations to the one who gives knowledge of Reality
Aum Uttamaaya Namaha!	Prostrations to the noblest one
Aum Vajrakayaaya Namaha!	Prostrations to the one with a body like a thunderbolt
Aum Vayuputraaya Namaha!	Prostrations to the son of Vayu
Aum Veeraaya Namaha!	Prostrations to the Hero

Glossary
of Sanskrit Terms

abhijit: A favorable star

abhishekam: Ceremonial bath for gods and kings

adharma: Unrighteousness

adi kavi: The first poet (Valmiki)

ahamkara: Ego

amavasya: Night of the new moon

amsa: A part or portion

anga: Limb; individual soul

apana: The outgoing breath

apsara: Heavenly nymph

artha: Wealth

arya: Noble

ashoka: A tree; without sorrow

ashrama: Spiritual sanctuary

ashramite: One who lives in an ashrama

ashwamedha yaga: Horse sacrifice conducted by kings to establish supremacy

astra: Weapon

asura: Demon

atma(n): The divine spirit embodied in the human being; the soul

Aum Namashivaaya: Mantra for Shiva

avatara: Incarnation

Ayurveda: Vedic science of healing

bandar: Monkey

Bhagavad Gita: Song of God

bhajan: Religious song of adoration

bhakta: Devotee

bhakti: Devotion

bhakti yoga: The yoga of devotion

brahmachari: A celibate

brahmacharya: Celibacy

brahmajnana: Integral knowledge of the Supreme Brahman

brahmarishi: A sage who has brahmajnana

brahmastra: The weapon of Brahma

chakora: Bird that is said to drink moonbeams

champaka: Tree with sweet-smelling flowers

chandala: An outcaste

chiranjeevi: Long-lived person

chourie: Yak tail fan

chudamani: A crest jewel for the hair

daitya: Demon

dakshinayana: The six months of the year from July to December

dalit: A low caste

darshan: Auspicious sight of god or a noble being

darshanas: The different schools of Hindu philosophy (six in number)

dasa bhava: Attitude of a servant (male)

dasya bhava: Attitude of a servant (female)

deva, devi: God, goddess; shining one

dharma: Righteousness

dhoti: Cloth worn around the waist by men

dhruva: Type of grass

dwarapalas: Guardians of the gate, especially in temples and palaces

gada: Mace

gandharva: Celestial singer

gayatri mantra: Famous hymn to the sun god

ghat: Bathing place on the river

griha: House; planet

grihastashrami: One who leads a householder's life

gunas: The three strands of nature—*sattva* (harmony), *rajas* (passion), and *tamas* (inertia)

guru: Spiritual preceptor

guru-dakshina: Fee given to the guru

han: To destroy

hanan: To annihilate

hanu: Jaw

hatha yoga: Special branch of yoga in which bodily postures, breathing techniques, and principles of meditation are taught

hatha yogi: One who practices this type of yoga

japa: Repetition of the names of god

jivatma: The embodied spirit; individual spirit

jnana: Wisdom

kaala: Time

kadamba: A type of flower

kalas: The sixty-four art forms, or the classical curriculum of sacred studies

kama: Love

kanda: One portion of a book

kapha: Phlegm

karma: Action

karma sakshi: The witness of all action (god)

karma yogi: One who practices the yoga of action

Kimpurushas: Mystic beings that are half-human and half-animal

kirtan: Spiritual song of praise

kshetrapalas: Guardians of the temple

kund: A lake or pool

kunjara südana: Killer of elephants

kusa: Type of grass used in rituals

lakh: One hundred thousand

langur: Black-faced monkey

laya yogi: One who practices the yoga of immolation, dissolving into the Supreme

lila: Play; game of God

lingam: A stone symbol of Shiva

loka: An astral world

madari: Trainer of monkeys

Mahabharata: The great classical epic poem of Vyasa

man: Mind

manduka: Frog

mantra: Mystic sound

Maryada Purusha: The perfect human being; Rama

maya: Illusion

mohastra: Weapon to banish illusion

moksha: Liberation from mortality

mritasanjivani: Herb that brings the dead to life

munja: Type of coarse grass

murti: Idol

naga: Snake

naga pasha: Rope made of snakes

navagrahas: Nine planets of Hindu cosmology

navami: Ninth day of the lunar calendar

navaratri: Nine days of worship of the goddess

panchamukha: Five-faced

Paramatma: The Supreme spirit

pitta: Bile

Prakriti: Cosmic matter

prana: Life current

pranava mantra: Aum

pranayama: Science of breath control

pratyaksha devata: The god that can be seen by our physical eyes; the sun god

puja: Ritual worship of god

Puranas: An important collection of post-Vedic classical literary texts written in Sanskrit; from "purana" (of ancient times)

puranic: Pertaining to the Puranas

Purusha: Spirit that dwells in the body; person

putrakamesti yaga: Fire sacrifice for getting a son

rajas: One of the three strands of nature; passion

rajasic: Pertaining to rajas; passionate

rakshasa: Malevolent, cannibalistic spirit

rakshasi: Female rakshasa

rakshasic: Having the nature of a rakshasa

Ramacharitamanas: Hindi Ramayan by Tulsidas

Ramayana: Great epic that recounts Rama's journey to save his wife

Rig Veda: Oldest of the Vedas, this is a collection of ancient Sanskrit hymns; from "rig," or praise and "veda," or knowledge

Rigvedic: Pertaining to the Rig Veda

rishi: Great sage

sadhaka: One who does spiritual practices

sadhana: Spiritual practice

sal: Type of ironwood tree

saligrama: Stone symbol of Vishnu

samadhi: Super-conscious state

samana: Equilibrium

samkhya yoga: Yoga of wisdom

sandal: Sandalwood tree

sandhani: Herb capable of joining fractured bones

sandhya: Twilight devotions

sankalpa: Intention

sannyasi(n): One who has renounced the world

sapta rishis: The seven original sages

sari: A five-meter piece of cloth worn by Indian women

sattva: One of the three stands of nature, standing for balance and harmony

sattvika: Harmonious; peaceful

Shaivite: Follower of Shiva

shakti: Power

Shakti: The divine feminine force

Shani: The malefic planet Saturn

shastras: Scriptures

siddhis: Supernormal powers

sindoor: Red powder used to put a dot on forehead of married women

sita: Furrow

soma: Medicinal plant used in Vedic sacrifices

sthitha prajna: One of steady intellect (enlightened one)

stree rajya: Land of women

surya namaskara: A yogic exercise in praise of the sun god

suvarnakarani: Herb that restores the color of a dying person

swarupa: Actual form

swayambhu murti: Self-formed idol

tamas: One of the three strands of Nature, standing for inertia, dullness

Tantras: Scriptures giving rules for esoteric rites

Tantric: Pertaining to the Tantras

tapas; tapasya: Askesis; austerity

til: Sesame

tulsi: Holy basil

tyaga: Renunciation

udana: One of the five breaths

uttarayanam: The six months of the year from January to June

vaal: Tail

vadas: Savory doughnuts

Vaishnavite: Follower of Vishnu

vajra: Thunderbolt

vanara: Monkey

vata: Wind

vayu: Air

Vedas: Oldest sacred texts of Hinduism; from the root "vid," to know

Vedic: Pertaining to the Vedas

vina: Stringed instrument like a lute

vira bhava: Hero's pose

vishalyakarani: Magic herb

Vishnu Sahasranama: Thousand names of Vishnu

vyakarana: Text that explains the meaning of the Vedas

vyana: One of the five vital breaths

yaga; yajna: Fire sacrifice

yajna kund: Hollow in the ground in which fire is kindled for the sacrifice

yajnashala: The place where the (yajna) or sacrifice is conducted

yaksha: Celestial being; guardian of wealth

yantra: Mystic geometric diagram that is meant to convey a concentrated aspect of the divine

yoga: Controlled physical or mental exercises that lead to union with the divine

yogasanas: Physical postures that purify the body and mind

yogi: One who practices yoga; one who is in union with the divine

yojanas: A distance measurement that spans several thousand miles

yogini: A female yogi

yuga: Epoch

Bibliography

Growse, F. S., trans. *Eternal Ramayana: The Ramayana of Tulsi Das.* New Delhi: Interprint, 1983.

Karyalaya, Govind Bhavan, trans. *Translation of the Valmiki Ramayana.* Gorakhpur, India: Gita Press, 1992.

Lutgendorf, Philip. *Hanuman's Tale: The Messages of a Divine Monkey.* New York: Oxford University Press, 2007.

Index

DAVID MUIRHEAD
THE CLAMOUR KING

snowbooks

Proudly Published by Snowbooks in 2008

Snowbooks Ltd.
120 Pentonville Road
London
N1 9JN
Tel: 0207 837 6482
Fax: 0207 837 6348
email: info@snowbooks.com
www.snowbooks.com

British Library Cataloguing in Publication Data
A catalogue record for this book is available from the British
Library.

ISBN 13 978-1905005-74-1

Printed and bound by J. H. Haynes & Co. Ltd., Sparkford

DAVID MUIRHEAD
THE CLAMOUR KING

"We are all slaves of the gods, whatever the gods might be."

Euripides

ONE

"What's on the sandwich, Wankworth?"

Wentworth fiddled with his shoelaces, clenching the slices of bread between his teeth.

"Henut hutter," he mumbled.

"What?" Voaden demanded, cupping a hand to his ear, leaning forward.

"Henut hutter," Wentworth said a little louder.

Voaden pulled a face to show his disgust.

"Get your mum to put something decent on – on the sandwich that is," he said.

The other boys chuckled. They moved in closer.

Wentworth straightened up, but he kept his eyes on his shoes. He wished he'd been paying better attention; he wished he'd got out of the bicycle shed in time. There was nowhere to go. The older boys were blocking all escape routes. Their toothy grins encircled him like the bars of an ivory cage. He took a small bite but didn't swallow, fully expecting a sudden sharp jab in the ribs from Voaden's big fingers.

DAVID MUIRHEAD

"Ask her to try a new spread," Voaden continued amiably. "There's a new one in the shops."

Wentworth looked up briefly. He was careful to avoid eye contact with any of them.

"Durex," Voaden said with a deadpan expression: "Ask your mum for that. It's fucking delicious – isn't it, Root?"

Root didn't laugh at that. None of them did.

"Yeah, fucking delicious," he said with a poker face.

Wentworth swallowed. He felt the piece of sandwich forcing its way down his throat against the strenuous counter-measures of the rest of his terrified little body. He knew if he threw up on Voaden's trousers his small world would end, probably with great violence. His head began to nod. He was surprised when that seemed to be enough. Voaden's head began to nod too. He was actually smiling, satisfied that his sales pitch had worked.

"Remember the name, Wankworth – Durex. Ask your mum tonight."

A wind came up then. It was one of those huge pointless winds that seem to explode straight up out of the earth on hot days. It enveloped the bicycle shed, banging the tin roof like the skin of a pagan drum. The boys had to shut their mouths and eyes to stop the whirling dust. Their blue school ties writhed crazily at their pale throats like water snakes.

Close by, Philip Dryden, the teacher on break duty, was standing by a classroom wall watching. He had to shield his eyes and hold his breath as the raging wind howled past. It was full of dancing dead leaves and pigeon feathers: the waste of living things.

He hadn't heard any of the words in the shed because of the noise in the playground. He was watching the group closely, though, waiting for something physical to happen. He was pleased when nothing did. The wind passed on. Voaden and his friends went in search of another victim, leaving Wentworth alone with his sandwich.

Dryden tapped the tip of his cane rhythmically against the side of his shoe. He looked at his watch. Another eight minutes of break, it told him. A tennis ball bounced off the wall quite close to his head. He pretended not to notice.

***

He was already at the staff room door when the bell rang. All the other teachers were leaving or had already gone back to their classrooms. Only Arthur Tetley was still there. He was listening to the news on the radio.

"Doesn't look as though the Chinks are going to back down," he said. He turned the radio off.

"That bad?" Dryden said disinterestedly.

The sandwich plate was empty apart from a few crumbs. Dryden didn't know why but in his mind's eye he fixated on Kent, the French teacher. He could see him hurriedly stuffing the last two or three cucumber wedges into his fat, bearded face. He could picture him blowing his nose in the revolting ostentatious way he had: a handkerchief full of snot and crumbs.

"There's no doubt now that the ships are carrying troops," Tetley continued importantly.

Dryden nodded.

"You don't seem worried."

"I don't suppose they fancy having the nuclear crap blown out of them either," Dryden said.

Tetley thought about that. He seemed unconvinced.

"They don't think like us," he said.

Dryden shrugged. He took the lid off the teapot and peered in. The situation really didn't worry him, because he didn't

7

think anything would happen.

Tetley was about to say something else, but he was interrupted by a woman's voice blaring from the intercom on the wall near his elbow: "Is Mr Dryden there?"

He pressed the black button: "Yes, Alice."

"Can you ask him to come up to the Headmaster's office? There's a new boarder."

"He's on his way," Tetley said.

Dryden put the teapot down, his cup half filled.

"Shit," he said.

He didn't like being summoned to Bruder's office. It brought back unpleasant memories of visits to the headmaster when he was a schoolboy, not ten years previously. He knew it was silly to be like that, to think like that, but that was how it was.

Bruder was sitting sphinx-like at his desk when Dryden entered his office. Arms outstretched, his manicured hands were laid flat on the polished mahogany, paper-devoid surface in front of him. On the other side, transfixed, sat a woman and a boy.

Dryden didn't listen to the introductions. He was bad like that. The names came and went. He didn't hear them. He shook hands, first with the woman and then with the boy. The woman was very beautiful in an angular kind of way: very early thirties, he guessed, much younger than most. It was the boy who startled him. He had the most perfect complexion and symmetrical features Dryden thought he'd ever seen. He couldn't stop staring. The boy looked back, smiling slightly. His bright eyes searched all over Dryden's face, inspecting each feature, without ever actually meeting his. It wasn't a cocky look, it wasn't insolence, but it was weirdly unsettling.

"… in the Far East," he suddenly heard Bruder saying.

Dryden had no idea what he'd been talking about.

There was an awkward silence. They were waiting for him to speak, perhaps to agree or disagree or to say something soothing or amusing. When he said nothing, Bruder realised he hadn't been listening. He didn't show his annoyance, but he didn't want to go on making idle chitchat either.

"Anyway, I expect you're in a hurry to get back up to London, Mrs Chapman," he said.

Mother and son said their good-byes at the door while Dryden and Bruder stood in the background pretending to be invisible. It was an intensely private moment both had witnessed many times. Then she was gone. Bruder sat down at his desk again. The boy stood obediently by the door.

"I'm putting Peter in School House, Philip," Bruder said. "He's just turned thirteen. We'll start in him in Lower 3B but I'm sure he'll soon work his way up to the A stream – not so, my boy?"

The boy smiled. That seemed to light up the room.

"He's an excellent swimmer and diver according to his report, good enough to make the school team," Bruder added.

Dryden nodded approvingly.

"Wait outside please, Peter. Mr Dryden will be there in a moment to get you sorted out."

When he'd gone Bruder motioned Dryden to sit. He took off his glasses and began polishing them methodically with a small yellow cloth, his big watery eyes fixed but unfocussed on Dryden's face.

"I'm very pleased with the way you've settled in as House Master, Philip. You really seem to have the boys' respect, and that's very important," he said.

"Thank you, sir."

Bruder went on polishing. He looked friendly and even

fragile without the glasses. He reminded Dryden of the tired old men with sticks and baggy pants walking on the seafront promenade, gazing out beyond the waves, seeing dim sepia scenes from their youth. Then the glasses went back on and the illusion, if it was one, disappeared.

"Happy with your accommodation?" Bruder asked.

Dryden thought about his small room, wedged on the landing between Dorms 4 and 5, tucked away in the heart of the convoluted warren that made up the boarders' wing. His one small window looked down on the graveyard of St Mary's Church and all its buried bones.

"Fine, thank you," he lied. He wondered what Bruder was expecting to hear. He wondered why it was a topic at all after three whole months.

The old man nodded solemnly. He took his glasses off again. He'd missed a spot. There was another short silence, more absent-minded polishing.

"There's a bit of a history to this boy, and I want you to keep a special eye on him," he said eventually.

Dryden nodded. He waited. The silence started to feel awkward. It didn't seem as though there was going to be any more. Bruder's mind seemed to be somewhere else.

"What sort of history, sir?" Dryden asked eventually.

"He wasn't expelled from his last school – nothing like that – but there was an incident."

Bruder put his glasses back on for the second time. It was quite disconcerting the way his appearance kept changing back and forth, from granddad to despot.

"What sort of incident, sir?" Dryden asked.

"One of the masters at his last school committed suicide," Bruder said. He let that hang in the air too. He seemed reluctant to get the story out.

Dryden waited politely, but by then he was very curious. He

didn't wait as long.

"I'm sorry, sir, I don't follow? Did this boy witness the suicide or something?"

"No," Bruder said. "I gather he was the cause of it – in a sense at least. Apparently the master kissed him in front of the whole class."

Dryden wasn't expecting that. He immediately wondered whether the classroom kiss was a euphemism for something more. Bruder seemed to read that thought, perhaps predictably.

"These things always leave a sour taste, they're very embarrassing all round but I gather no real harm was done," Bruder said. "To the boy, I mean," he added quickly. "I spoke to the headmaster at his last school and they're not really sure that the two things were even connected anyway. Apparently he had various problems, financial, other things. But there was a lot of chatter, teasing from the other boys. You know how they are, you know the sort of thing. His parents thought it best to move him."

Dryden realised he was sitting with his mouth open, gawping like an idiot.

"I debated whether to tell you any of this," Bruder went on, "but on balance I think you should know. Needless to say, you must keep it to yourself."

"Of course, sir."

There was another short silence. Dryden wondered whether they were both thinking the same thing. The boy outside was astonishingly good looking, ethereally so, but it didn't seem a good time to mention that.

"Anyway, we can't keep him hanging around out there any longer," Bruder said. "I'll leave it to you to get him settled in. Get one or two of the other boys to take him under their wing. Rowell's in his class, I think – he seems a steady sort."

***

Christopher Rowell sat on his bed, watching the new boy unpack. Chapman's sudden arrival meant he'd missed maths, the last lesson of the morning. That was a good thing. It had put him in a good mood.

The two boys were alone in the barn-like dormitory, tucked away in the corner across from the swing doors. It was the biggest dorm in the school. Three rows of eight beds – one against each long wall, and a third one down the centre – stretched away on metal legs to a line of hand basins at the far end. The high windows let in plenty of light, but the only view they had was of clouds and sky. "So the neighbours don't have to look at you changing through their binoculars," Mr Tetley had once explained with enigmatic sarcasm.

"So why did you move schools?" Rowell asked.

Chapman didn't answer straight away. He didn't look round.

"My dad said it was a shithole." He made it sound incidental, as though it didn't matter much anyway.

Rowell nodded dubiously. The parental mind was an unfathomable place: any school was a shithole, whichever way you tried to look at it.

"Are your parents still married?"

Chapman nodded. "Yours?"

"Uh, uh. Divorced, three years ago."

Rowell sat bolt upright when he saw the cigarettes. The pack dropped on to the floor as Chapman took out a pair of socks. Rowell bent down smartly to pick it up.

"Shit! Don't get caught with these," he said. He juggled the pack for a second or two and then thrust it under Chapman's pillow. "You can't leave them there, either."

"Where, then?"

"I don't know – maybe stick them under your mattress. But sheets get changed on Fridays, and Matron comes poking around all the time."

Rowell looked at Chapman with sudden respect. He didn't smoke himself; none of his peers did, excepting maybe Pearce. He said he smoked in the holidays, Gitanes he said, but he was probably lying about it because he always wanted to seem like big stuff. Smoking was something Rowell associated with the older boys. The pack of Embassy was like a passport to a bigger, rougher, altogether more confusing world.

Chapman glanced back at the door and then lifted his pillow and took the pack out again. He put it in his wash bag and stuffed that into the locker by his bed.

"Do you think that'll be safe?" he asked. He didn't seem nervous about it, just curious.

Rowell shrugged. "Should be I suppose," he said. "How long have you been smoking?"

Chapman sat down too because he'd finished unpacking the trunk.

"I don't know – a couple of thousand years," he said.

Rowell nodded. He was impressed, that he couldn't deny, but in a complicated way he didn't understand and couldn't really explain to himself, he also disapproved.

"Have you finished? It'll be lunch soon, but I can still show you around if you like."

"Thanks. Where do I put my trunk?"

"It goes in the storeroom. Let's take it down now," Rowell said.

They set off holding the trunk between them. On the way out, Rowell pointed with his free hand to various beds, naming the boys who slept there and describing what he considered their main characteristics.

"Pearce – he's a complete turd, but don't get into a fight with him; Higgins – him and Pearce are like that. Thornton – a major nerd; Roger Coffin – weirdo, plays with knives all the time; Leomond – a voodoo darkie from Trinidad, also weird…"

The intimidating list of grotesques could have gone on, but it was cut short when the doors to the dorm swung shut behind them.

A bell sounded when they were on the stairs. By the time they reached the ground floor, there were already other boys in the corridor. A corner of the trunk bumped into one of them and he made a fuss about it. He was a bigger boy, about two years older.

"Sorry," Rowell said.

"Look where you're fucking well going," the boy said to Chapman.

"Sorry," Chapman said, smiling.

The other boy stared at him crossly for a moment or two. He went on but he stopped and turned round after a few paces to have another look. He didn't say anything else. He just stared at Chapman until the trunk and the two boys went around the corner.

"That's Gatesford Minor; he's a right prick. His brother's a prefect," Rowell said.

They had to get the key to the storeroom from Matron Abercrombie. She moaned about it. She always had a bit of a moan about everything anyone asked her to do. If one of the boys asked for a button to be sewn on to his shirt she had a big moan about that. It seemed that she was always so busy sitting at her desk down by sickbay that just about anything anyone asked was an interruption of her work. Rowell's stomach had been upset the previous week and he'd been to see her about it because he was practically doubled up with pain and having to run for the toilet every five minutes. She'd given him a spoonful of something, but not before she'd made it clear that Rowell's stomach was an enormous nuisance.

"I was just off to lunch," she said to the boys as they stood in front of her desk with the trunk. "Make sure you lock the door again and bring the key back here – leave it on my desk."

There were lots of trunks in the storeroom, mostly black or grey metal but there were some made of fabric with wooden stays. They all looked as though they were waiting patiently for the last day of term. The trunks were piled four high and in some places there were even five piled one on top of the other. Rowell and Chapman had quite a struggle lifting his trunk onto the top of one of the piles because there wasn't really room for it on the floor.

"How tall are you?" Rowell asked when they'd finally got it up there and made sure it wouldn't fall off when their backs were turned.

"I don't know – five three, I think," Chapman said.

Rowell shook his head.

"I'm five three and I think I'm a bit taller."

He raised his chin and stretched a bit and it would have been fairly clear to anyone else in the room, if there had been anyone else, that he was a shade taller, but not by much.

"What was the food like at your old place?" Rowell asked as he put the key down in the middle of Matron's desk.

"Crap," Chapman said.

"Same as here then," Rowell said.

Rowell asked Chapman a lot of question about his previous school during the next half-hour. The answers made it obvious to him that the boy's dad certainly knew a shithole when he saw one. About Chapman's extraordinary beauty he seemed blissfully unaware.

TWO

Dryden tossed his book onto the bed and stood up to open a window. A startled pigeon flapped abruptly into life on the ledge outside. He watched it glide across the street towards the church. The streetlights were on and the grey, flintstone bulk of St Mary's was bathed in a soft golden glow. The scene was almost pretty. *That's a neat trick*, he thought. In daylight, St Mary's was one of the ugliest churches he'd ever seen.

There must be more to life than this dump. He thought that all the time. It wasn't just the place: it was everything – what he was doing with his life; what Life was doing to him. Becoming a teacher had been a mistake, an easy option, but he couldn't face living in London. He hated cities, he always had. But that's where the money was, the road to fame and fortune. His father told him that every time they met: "Stop farting around with teaching and get a career in the city. *That's* where the money is."

He could hear the level of noise rising steadily outside, the usual evening pandemonium. He looked at his watch. It was time for his rounds.

The racket subsided when he entered Dorm 4. A few of the boys were already in bed; others were fiddling in their lockers. Pearce and Higgins were both sitting cross-legged on the same bed playing cards. Only one boy was still at the basins, bent forward splashing his face. The figure straightened up as Dryden approached and he saw that it was the new boy. He wasn't wearing a top. The elastic waistband of his pyjamas was folded right back on itself, low down below his hips. Half an inch lower and there wouldn't have been much point in having trousers on at all. As Dryden got closer, Chapman saw him. He wasn't flustered; he didn't put on his pyjama top and hurry back to bed as the master expected.

Dryden looked him up and down as he approached. He judged the boy to be about five foot two. He had a slight tan, not a white and pink body like the rest, and he was thin. No, Dryden decided; he was so well formed and proportioned that it wouldn't really be right to call him thin. He was thin, but he was also flawless somehow; perfect, immaculate.

"You're supposed to be ready for bed now," Dryden said. He tried to sound matter-of-fact, not cross or bossy.

"Sorry, sir."

Chapman picked up his wash bag and walked away, back toward his bed in the corner. That had a fluid grace about it, Dryden thought, just the way he moved. But despite the gob-stopping beauty, the soft, luminescent waves and curls of chestnut hair, the startling eyes, there was nothing sissy about him.

Higgins and Pearce started throwing cards at each other. Dryden turned his attention to them, bellowing their names, one after the other. All the boys shut up briefly.

"Lights out in two minutes," he said.

He walked slowly down the next aisle, back towards the door, following the same path as Chapman had. The boy was in bed by the time he got to the end. He was leaning over, reaching into his locker. He still hadn't put on his pyjama top. Rowell was in the next bed lying flat on his back, his arms by his sides, the covers pulled up to his chin.

"You need a haircut, Rowell."

"Yes, sir."

"See Matron about it tomorrow."

"Yes, sir."

Chapman stopped fiddling and lay back, pulling his own covers up.

"Everything alright, Chapman?" Dryden asked.

"Fine thanks, sir."

Dryden hesitated. He wondered whether to tell the boy to put his pyjama top on because that was the rule. He knew he should but he decided not to. It didn't really matter now, he told himself. He turned and walked away towards the door.

"I don't want to hear a peep out of you lot tonight," he said.

He paused and took a last look around before switching off the lights.

"Goodnight," he said. He waited briefly as the chorus of young voices responded.

There was complete silence for a couple of minutes. The boys waited to see whether Dryden was still lurking outside. He did that every now and again. When it seemed safe, the whispering started.

Leomond turned on his torch and started reading a book, ignoring protests from the boys on either side. The bright light reflected in the whites of his eyes. It was a startling sight from some angles. It frightened Thornton in the opposite bed. Higgins tossed something through the semi-darkness and it landed on Pearce.

"Fuck off, Higgins," Pearce said.

Chapman propped himself up on an elbow.

"Are you a nudist, Chapman?" asked a disembodied voice.

A few giggles followed but they were cut short. The gigglers wanted to hear the answer.

"Fucking porno star, if you ask me," Pearce said, breaking the silence.

"Nobody did, Pearce. Well, are you?"

"Piss off, Coffin," Rowell said.

"I bet you're pissing in your bed right now," Coffin said.

Chapman smiled and lay back down again. He stared up at the high window above his head. He could see a few stars, nothing else.

"Don't take any notice of those jerks," Rowell whispered.

He'd hardly got the words out when a body fell heavily across his midriff like a sack of potatoes.

"You were saying, Rowell?"

"Piss off."

The bigger boy slid onto the edge of the bed, fending off a couple of wild swings from Rowell's small fists.

"OK, OK, cut it out. I'm kidding, I'm kidding." Coffin turned his attention back to Chapman, peering through the gloom at him, dodging a last half-hearted swing. "Sorry, no hard feelings. I was only kidding."

"No sweat," Chapman said.

"Shush," Leomond said. He lit them up briefly with his torch.

"Turn that fucking thing off, Leomond -- Drydork will see it," Pearce said.

"Get your fat arse off my hip," Rowell said softly.

Coffin shifted his backside a little.

"Where've you come from then?" he asked.

"Saint Stithians."

"Where's that?"

"Timbuktu, you great fat turd," Rowell said.

Coffin lay back on Rowell's midriff again, squeezing the air out of his lungs, but he sat up again immediately.

"It's near Littlehampton," Chapman said.

"Why did you leave?"

Chapman shrugged. "My parents decided to move me."

Coffin nodded. He sat quietly for a while longer but couldn't think of any more questions. He was nervous about being out of bed anyway. "Better go – Drydork's probably going to poke his head in again. Sleep tight."

"Goodnight."

"Good riddance," Rowell said.

The other whispered conversations soon petered out. The light on the landing went off and only a dim glow from the stairs filtered into the dormitory. On the far side a single blob of faint yellow light showed that Leomond had retreated under his blanket with his torch, still reading.

In the silence Chapman lay on his back looking up at the rectangle of stars. He thought about Jenkins being dead, hanging from a pipe in the boiler room with a skipping rope tied tightly around his neck. He hadn't actually seen that, but he could picture it all too clearly in his mind, even the bulging eyes and the fat purple tongue. It made him shudder and he pushed the image out. Jenkins came back anyway, still alive in his head, wanting to talk to him about stuff, wanting to touch him, fondling his hair, patting his knee. Then he thought about being in Jenkins' bed, and that was really weird, so he pushed it out too.

He loves you, yeah, yeah, yeah
He loves you, yeah, yeah, yeah
With a love like that,
You know you must be bad

Chapman could hear the lines in his head. He could hear Cooper singing them over and over again. He could hear the others joining in. In his mind he could see Ironwood, the science teacher, coming into the class and remembered the fuss he created. The song in his head stopped abruptly just like it had back then. He heard his dad's voice instead and remembered his words exactly: "Don't talk about it, don't think about it. Forget it, Peter. It's a shithole of a school anyway."

There was a soft snort from Rowell in the next bed. Chapman closed his eyes and forced himself to think about something else. He thought about where he was now, going over each detail of the day. It didn't seem that bad. He opened his eyes and looked up at the stars framed in the small window high above. He wondered how many of them there were. He started counting them as though they all belonged to him, like jewels in a chest, each distant shining one. Soon after that, he fell asleep.

THREE

Richardson waited at his desk for the boys to settle down. There was actually more noise coming through the partition from 3A next door. He guessed, correctly, that Dryden was late getting back to his classroom.

He stood up and went around to the front of his desk and leaned against it. It was a short journey, even for a fat man, but the movement was enough to stop the shuffling and put an end to the last few muted conversations.

He picked up a book from the small pile beside him on the desk and held it up.

"You'll be pleased to hear the Headmaster and I have agreed on the choice for the next Dramatic Society play," he announced. "It's the Bacchanals."

If he was expecting applause or any reaction at all he was disappointed. The class stared up at him with blank looks. Then one tentative hand went up.

"Yes, Wentworth?"

"Is that by Shakespeare, sir?"

"No, it's by Euripides."

"Who, sir?"

"Euripides," Richardson repeated. "One of the greatest of the Greek dramatists."

He surveyed the raised faces and saw the lights going out behind them one by one. Where there had been at least idle curiosity there was nothing but bored resignation. It didn't make him angry, as he wasn't really expecting anything else. He opened the book, flicked through the pages and began reading in his loud booming voice:

But she, with foaming lips and eyes that rolled
Wildly, and reckless madness-clouded soul,
Possessed of Bacchus gave no heed to him;
But his left arm she clutched in both her hands,
And set against the wretches' ribs her foot,
And tore his shoulder out – not by her strength,
But the God made it easy to her hands.

He closed the book with a dramatic snap. There was total silence in the class marred only by a muffled wave of laughter from next door. The noise wasn't enough of a distraction from Euripides' grisly words: Richardson's class sat momentarily mesmerised.

"Not quite as dull as you were expecting, perhaps," he said.

He picked up the small pile of books and plonked them down on the first desk he came to. It happened to be Rowell's.

"There aren't enough books to go round so you're going to have to share."

Rowell took one book and passed the rest over his shoulder to Pearce. Then he opened his copy and began flicking through the pages, looking aimlessly for the passage Robertson had just read, wondering whether there were pictures. Chapman leaned over from the neighbouring desk to look too.

"The passage you're looking for is on page thirty four, near the end," Richardson said. "But I want you to spend the next ten minutes reading the introduction – that explains the play."

He waddled back around his desk, sat down and watched as the page flicking went on more or less unabated.

"You've got precisely nine minutes left," he growled.

Wentworth's hand went up again.

"Yes, Wentworth?" Richardson said wearily.

"Half the introduction's been torn out of this one, sir."

"Well, read the other half."

There was silence after that, even from Dryden's classroom. Outside the sun shone. A strong wind blew intermittently, hinting at an overnight change in the weather. Framed in the high classroom window, the heavy foliage of a large chestnut tree heaved ponderously every now and again like a huge green sea. The clock on the classroom wall, its thin black hands impervious to the will of countless schoolboys, measured each long minute with mechanical indifference.

"OK, time's up," Richardson said finally. "What's the play about, Rowell?"

"Me, sir?" Rowell asked, not expecting to be singled out.

Richardson smiled, showing his big white teeth: "No Rowell, I don't think it's about you. Unless you're a Greek god, perchance?"

Rowell blushed. He cursed under his breath and buried his face in the book. He flicked through the pages of the introduction again. He hoped forlornly that in amongst all the long words, the author had somehow managed to squeeze in something that might suddenly pop out and make immediate sense.

Richardson let him open and close his mouth for a few moments before taking pity on him.

"The basic story is about how Dionysus, the son of Zeus, otherwise known as Bacchus, the Greek god of wine, comes to Thebes on a kind of self-promotional tour and runs into Pentheus, the King of Thebes. Pentheus doesn't think much of Dionysus and his drunken ways. He doesn't believe he is a god and has him thrown in jail. That naturally annoys Dionysus and, to cut a long story short, the god – because he really is one – puts a spell on Pentheus' mother and the other women of Thebes so that they end up tearing Pentheus to bits. That's the passage I read just now that you all apparently found quite fascinating. Do you think that's an accurate summary, Rowell?"

Why do you keep picking on me you fat old fart, Rowell said under his breath. "I suppose so sir," he said out loud.

"And do you concur?" Richardson continued, hesitating over the new boy's name. "Chapman, isn't it?"

"Yes, sir."

Richardson looked closely at Chapman for the first time and the boy looked back. For a brief moment Richardson lost his train of thought, not sure which question the boy had answered.

"Well, of course it's a lot more complicated than that – it's a complex play, a long poem really," he continued after a pause.

He was itching to talk about Euripides' lifelong struggle to reconcile the mystery of God and the life of man. He wanted to talk about the conflict between God as the apogee of conscience, of all things good, and the creator of everything in nature, both sublime and terrible; of God's judgment of man and man's judgment of God. But he knew that after about eight seconds, he would be talking to himself. The play wasn't on the syllabus anyway. He'd only really brought it up because he enjoyed it himself. He was also still looking for two Maeniads.

"Who would like to be a Maeniad?" he asked.

There was complete silence and then predictably Wentworth put up his hand again.

Richardson ignored him, guessing what he was going to ask.

"Maeniads are the followers of Dionysus, enraptured women devotees of the god," he said.

There were disgusted murmurs at that. None of them fancied being a wrapped up woman in a school play.

"What – no takers?" Richardson said sarcastically.

All the boys found something to look at on their desks and Richardson smiled. He knew he would have to hunt for Maeniads in the fourth form. He'd expected that anyway.

"Who's playing Pentheus, sir?" Pearce asked when he sensed the danger had passed.

"Chatsworth," Richardson replied.

There were more murmurs.

"Can I play his mum, sir?" Pearce asked with a sly grin.

One or two boys giggled. The rest soon followed, though most didn't have a clue what they were giggling at. It sounded funny anyway, the idea of Pearce being Chatsworth's mum.

"Very droll, Pearce – but at least it shows you were paying attention. Pentheus' mother doesn't actually tear him to bits on the stage. You only hear about it in the speech I read."

Pearce smiled anyway. He looked around at the others, harvesting whatever admiration there might be for his witty comment.

"Well that's all the time we can spend on the Bacchanals. Back to reality. There's just enough time before break for a spelling test," Richardson said.

There was a loud communal groan and much shuffling of books.

"Conceit," he said, "two syllables."

***

The small penknife hit the base of the tree handle-first and glanced off to the side, falling a little way beyond on the gravel. Coffin stooped down and picked it up.

"You're flicking your wrist too much," he said.

He stepped back a couple of paces and threw the knife himself. The tip of the small blade embedded itself in the rough bark momentarily before falling out.

"You're not so great at it yourself," Leomond said.

"It hit a hard patch," Coffin explained. "This isn't really a throwing knife. Try again."

He handed the knife back to Chapman who tossed it at the tree for the third time with more or less the same result.

Rowell wasn't paying much attention. He'd been keeping an eye on Voaden and Root. Every time he looked for them in the playground crowd, they seemed a little closer.

"I don't think I'm ever going to get the hang of it," Chapman said. He was bored stiff with the whole business but he didn't want to hurt Coffin's feelings by saying so.

Leomond bent down and picked up the knife. He held it in his fist and thrust the blade firmly into the bark of the tree.

"There," he said.

"Anyone can do that," Coffin said indignantly, but he did finally get the message. He pulled the knife out, closed the blade back into its handle and put it into his pocket.

Rowell glanced away again to look for Voaden. He was startled to see him heading straight towards them.

"Playing with knives, are we, girls?" Voaden asked sarcastically. "Can I play?"

Coffin started to take the penknife out again.

"Not with that little piece of crap," Voaden said.

He took a thin black cylinder from his jacket pocket and held it out towards Coffin. He pressed a small silver button; there was a distinct click and a three-inch blade shot out. Under other circumstances Coffin would have been drawn to the superb workmanship that had obviously gone into the manufacture of the evil looking switchblade; instead he took an involuntary step back. So did Leomond.

"You can get expelled for having one of those," Rowell said. He kept his eyes on the knife as though it was a snake.

"Really?" Voaden said with mock wonder.

He spun the knife around in his fingers, showing off his confidence and expertise.

"Can I have a look?" Chapman asked. He held out his hand.

Voaden wasn't expecting to be asked that, not by any of them. He hesitated for a moment, looking down at Chapman's outstretched hand. Then he looked down at the knife in his own hand. Root started to say something but Voaden cut him short.

"OK," he said and put the knife down in Chapman's open palm. "Who the fuck are you?"

"His name's Chapman, he's a new boy," Rowell said.

Voaden glared at him, irritated at the interruption, but he didn't say anything.

"He smokes," Rowell added. He regretted it instantly and wondered why he'd blurted it out.

Voaden nodded but he didn't look at Rowell again. He kept his eyes on Chapman.

Chapman turned the knife over this way and that. Then he dragged the blade lightly across the palm of his left hand.

"Ouch, it's sharp," he said. The edge of the knife had grazed the skin. Tiny beads of blood appeared.

"Of course it's sharp, you little dweeb," Voaden said. The words were harsh, but his tone was uncharacteristically gentle.

Coffin edged forward for a closer look. That was too much.

"OK, the fucking show's over," Voaden said, needing to reassert his authority.

He grabbed the knife back, retracted the blade and put it away.

"You owe me a fag," he said to Chapman. He was curious to see whether what Rowell had said was true. It didn't seem very likely.

Chapman licked the palm of his hand before reaching into his jacket pocket and taking out a pack of Embassy. He extracted one of the four cigarettes left in the pack and held it out. Voaden grabbed it and dropped it into the top pocket of his blazer, glancing round to be sure that no one important had been watching.

"Thanks," he said, and that too was unusual.

The little group stood in silence for a moment or two. Chapman licked the palm of his hand again. It had started to sting a little.

Rowell was perplexed by Voaden's strangely compliant behaviour. New boys were fresh meat; he hounded them remorselessly until they cringed whenever he approached. Even that didn't help much, Rowell remembered: the more you cringed, the more Voaden enjoyed beating the crap out of you. He waited for the bully's mood to change back to normal, ready to defend his new charge in whatever modest way he could.

As if on cue, Voaden reached out and grabbed the back of Chapman's slim neck with his powerful fingers, pulling him forward. With his other hand he punched him softly in the stomach. There was no force at all in the blow. Before Rowell could react, he realised with surprise that Voaden was actually being friendly.

"You can join us for a smoke after last lesson," he said.

It was more of a command than an invitation.

"Thanks," Chapman said.

Voaden gave him a friendly tap on the shoulder and walked away. Root followed him. He was no less surprised by what had just happened than the four younger boys.

"Well that's a first," Rowell said when they'd gone.

"You want to stay clear of him," Leomond said to Chapman. "Now he thinks you're a soft touch for free cigarettes. How do you get hold of those things anyway?"

"I nicked these from my mother," Chapman replied. "It's my last packet."

"How can you steal something from your mother like that?" Coffin asked disapprovingly.

Chapman smiled sweetly at him, waving his hand to and fro. "She won't miss them – she gets them duty free. She smokes two packs a day."

"Well that still doesn't make it alright," Coffin said. He wondered what "duty free" meant.

"Is your hand OK?" Rowell asked. "That was a daft thing to do."

Chapman nodded. The blood had stopped, blocked by his spit.

Rowell felt vindicated in telling Voaden that Chapman smoked. It seemed to have given him status and with it some measure of protection. At the same time, deeper down, he knew that really had nothing to do with it; he was sure something else had happened.

"But Leo's right, you should stay clear of him, he's really, really bad news," he said. "He might be friendly now but tomorrow he'll probably shove your head down the toilet."

"The other bloke looks a lot tougher," Chapman said.

"Root? He's as thick as a plank. He won't do anything without Voaden."

The bell went, its shrill tones cutting through the hubbub in the playground. A general drift of bodies back towards the classrooms began immediately.

"Don't you think I should go then?" Chapman asked.

Rowell shrugged because he didn't know the answer. He thought about it as they walked.

"Maybe you should go," he said eventually, contradicting his earlier emphatic advice.

Chapman nodded.

As it turned out he did go and that was just as well because Voaden seemed to be genuinely pleased that he'd come.

"You're a cocky little fucker," he said, and he ruffled Chapman's hair.

FOUR

Reverend Kennedy didn't like to be kept waiting, least of all by one of the boys, but his irritation was focused at that moment on Bruder. Chapman was still only four minutes late, but the new boy had been at the school for over a week before Bruder had seen fit to inform him. There was also the business of the new play. Who in their right mind would choose that irreligious rubbish for a schoolboy cast, he kept asking himself; half the characters were depraved women, and the whole thing seemed to be about the triumph of debauchery.

Winston, his fat old spaniel, snorted on the carpet in front of the cold gas fire grate, dreaming doggy dreams of better, more agile days. He always lay there now, winter and summer. Despite the best efforts of Mrs Summerly, the charlady, the faded old carpet was impregnated with dog hair and old dog smell. Kennedy had long since become inured to it.

Winston raised his head briefly at the sound of footsteps

but laid it down again when there was a knock on the door. He knew it wasn't for him.

"Enter," Kennedy said, glancing at his watch.

Chapman came in, looking a little anxious. He stood by the door waiting for instructions, glancing down at the dog. He involuntarily wrinkled his nose.

"Sit down, Peter," Kennedy said, pointing to one of the upright wooden chairs on the other side of his untidy desk. "I don't want to start by ticking you off but you're six minutes late."

"I'm sorry, sir."

Kennedy nodded, waiting for an excuse, but none was offered. The pause gave him an opportunity to look at Chapman. He could understand the story Bruder had told him now. If he was any judge of pubescent boys, there might well be a problem here too, sooner rather than later, he thought. In his mind's eye he slipped Chapman into a choirboy's cassock and put a white ruff round his slender neck. The resultant image at least sanitised the boy's remarkable beauty, putting it beyond reach, beyond contemplation.

"Well, if you haven't got an excuse I suppose it's at least honest that you haven't made one up," he said, sounding grumpier than he intended.

"I wasn't sure where to come, sir."

That's pretty feeble, Kennedy thought, but he was already regretting having said anything at all. It was not an auspicious start.

"That's understandable, I suppose," he said with a big forced smile. "Well let's forget about it, you're here now, and how are you settling in? Have you made any friends yet – though it's still early days?"

"I'm fine, sir. Everyone seems very nice."

Kennedy put his hands together in an imitation of prayer,

resting the tips of both forefingers on what passed for his chin. He nodded his head back and forth, continuing even when Chapman had finished his short answer. It was as though he had found some unlikely profundity in the stock phrases.

"I understand you're in Mr Dryden's House?"

"Yes, sir."

"And that you're a champion diver."

Chapman smiled for the first time but he didn't reply. Kennedy ascribed his silence to modesty and moved on.

"Well you know what my job is here," he said, tapping his dog collar with a bony finger. "My job is to look after your spiritual well being. If you have any problems, my door is always open. Any kind of problem," he added with special meaning.

"Thank you, sir."

"You haven't been confirmed yet, have you?"

"No sir."

Of course not; I doubt whether you've had your first wet dream, Kennedy thought.

"Is it something your parents have discussed with you?" he asked.

"What sir?"

They looked at each other and Kennedy wondered whether he was really listening. For one unnerving moment the absurd thought occurred to him that the boy might actually be hearing more than he was saying out loud. He felt a little flustered.

"Confirmation," he said.

"No, they haven't, sir."

Kennedy had read in the file that the boy's father was in the Army, stationed somewhere out in the Far East, Malaya he seemed to recall. He wouldn't be able to ring them up. He'd have to write a letter.

"Well there's plenty of time for that. Will they be picking you up at the end of term?"

"I don't know, sir."

The tips of Kennedy's fingers went back to his chin and he started nodding again, massaging his pendulous lower lip with his fingertips.

"I think there's something the matter with your dog, sir."

Kennedy didn't understand at first. His mind was still busy with the problem at hand but he followed the boy's gaze down to Winston, on the carpet. The old spaniel was shuddering slightly and there was a small puddle of froth at his muzzle. As they both watched, he gave one final shudder and then lay absolutely still. Chapman got out of his chair and knelt down by the dog, placing his hand on its side. There was no sign of breathing. He looked up at Kennedy. The old parson was still sitting there, staring down as though hypnotised.

"I think he might be dead, sir."

"Good heavens," Kennedy said in a quirky voice. "Just like that?"

Chapman stood up, not certain what to do next. They stayed like that for what seemed like a very long time to him, the boy on the carpet by the dead dog and Kennedy frozen in his chair.

Finally the parson pulled himself together. There were tears welling in his eyes, and he avoided looking at the boy.

"I think we'd better carry on with our chat a bit later," he said, standing up.

"I'm sorry, sir," the boy said, but Kennedy didn't hear him.

FIVE

Drummond watched Thornton as he threaded his way between the rows of fifth form boys, dodging elbows and expansive gestures. His face was a study in concentration as he balanced and protected the brimming cup of tea. At any moment one of the bigger boys might notice and his precarious journey would come to an abrupt end. But it was Thornton's lucky day. He reached his destination and put the cup down. Chatsworth ignored him. He was too busy holding court at the head of the table to notice.

Drummond carried on watching Thornton with idle interest as he made his way back to the third form benches. He squeezed in beside Rowell and Chapman. Voaden was standing over Chapman, resting both his hands on the younger boy's shoulders, talking directly into his ear.

Drummond felt a tap on his own shoulder and looked up.

"Mr Dryden says he wants to leave at nine fifteen. He says he'll pick you up by the lower gate, and can you make sure

Simpson and Chapman are there too."

"Chapman? Is he a diver?"

"I don't know – I suppose so. That's what Mr Dryden said."

"Thanks."

"Must I tell the other two?"

"No, I'll do it, don't worry – thanks," Drummond said quickly. He raised his six-foot-two frame from the chair. The chatter at the tables died at his approach and resumed in his wake as he strode down between the forms. Voaden saw him coming and quickly moved away. Drummond glowered after him and stopped in his vacated place.

Rowell and Leomond looked up at the Head Prefect apprehensively but he wasn't interested in them.

"Tell me, Thornton, why do you keep carrying cups of tea to Chatsworth?"

"He told me to," Thornton croaked, sinking lower on the bench. His small chin almost touched the table.

"You don't have to fag for him. You know fagging isn't allowed anymore – I'll speak to him."

Drummond didn't believe for a moment that speaking to Chatsworth would lessen Thornton's misery. It would have the opposite effect. But he was intent on impressing the new boy with his power and magnanimity.

"I gather you're coming to diving practice this morning, Chapman," he said, speaking to the top of the boy's head.

Startled, Chapman tried to stand up and turn around. His legs caught between the bench and table and he almost fell against Drummond.

"Yes, sir," he said.

Rowell winced. Drummond didn't like being called "sir". Given his size and every small boy's desire to be as obsequious as possible in any conversation with him, it was an understandable and frequent mistake. Rowell had done it himself – quite often in the beginning. He was surprised when the usual sarcastic quips about the Knights of the Round Table didn't follow.

"Mr Dryden will pick us up at the bottom gate in twenty minutes. Do you know where the bottom gate is?"

"Yes, sir."

"Make sure you're there."

"Yes, sir."

Rowell winced again and again, but there was still no reaction from Drummond. He just stood there looking down into Chapman's upturned face. His own features were set in their usual stone mask. But he actually smiled faintly before walking away to look for Simpson.

"Blimey," Rowell said.

"What?"

"Don't call him 'sir' again. He usually explodes."

"Perhaps he's been knighted by now," Leomond said, "Sir Drummond."

Rowell laughed but Leomond didn't. He chewed on his toast, fixing his big brown eyes on Chapman.

"Or perhaps he just likes you," he added.

Chapman shrugged.

"I'm going for a puff with Nick," he whispered to Rowell. "Are you coming?"

Rowell hesitated briefly and then nodded. The two boys got up from the table and headed out towards the yard, following the route taken by Voaden and Root to the playground toilets.

Rowell had changed his mind by the time they got there, as he'd known he would all along. He knew he wasn't welcome, that the invitation had just been meant for Chapman. It was odd to be tolerated by Voaden, but he hadn't forgotten the countless series of run-ins he'd had with him, the last only ten days ago. They always ended up with him on the floor and Voaden's shoe on his neck or in his crotch. That had changed now with Chapman being Voaden's friend but Rowell didn't kid himself that Voaden actually liked him all of a sudden. It was Chapman that he seemed to like so much and it was really weird.

The thought of smoking actually still scared him a little too. The smell made him feel slightly sick. It conjured up confusing images of an adult world he wasn't quite ready to enter.

"You go in, I'm feeling a bit yuck," he said, stopping at the door.

"Come on!"

"No, really. I think I'm ready to throw up; it's those bloody sausages."

Chapman looked at him, not unkindly.

"Are you sure?"

Rowell nodded. He was beginning to feel a bit sick for real.

"I'll wait for you out here. You'd better be quick though, it's almost five past already."

Rowell did wait, sauntering aimlessly around the yard listening to the gravel crunch under his shoes. He picked up a stone and tossed it in the direction of a solitary pigeon pecking about underneath one of the gnarled old chestnut trees. It missed by a mile so he threw another one. That landed quite close. The bird tried to fly but there was something wrong with one of its wings. It disappeared behind the trunk of the tree in a flurry of lopsided flapping.

After a few minutes, a couple of other boys who had finished breakfast came out into the yard with a football, kicking it to and fro, waiting for others. They waved to Rowell, but he shook his head. Normally he would have been keen to join them, because that's what he did mostly on a Saturday morning, but by then he'd managed to convince himself that he really wasn't well. There was nowhere to sit down, other than on the gravel. He stood swaying gently to and fro on the balls of his feet.

"Shit," Chapman said, reappearing abruptly from the toilets, "Now I'm late."

He bolted off across the yard, skidding on the gravel at the corner. He slowed down as they reached the door to the corridor but not enough to avoid colliding with someone coming out. The force of the collision nearly sent both their bodies flying. A few paces behind, Rowell managed to pull up short and saw with horror that it was Chatsworth.

"What the fuck do you think you're doing, you little prick?" Chatsworth yelled. "You're not allowed to run in here."

"Sorry, sir," Chapman stammered, "I'm late for diving practice."

He tried to move past, but Chatsworth grabbed him by the arm.

"And where the fuck do think you're going now? What's you name?"

"Chapman, sir."

"Drydork's waiting for him, Chatsworth," Rowell said breathlessly.

"Stuff off, Rowell, and it's Mr Dryden to you."

But the mention of Dryden's name did make Chatsworth hesitate. He let go of Chapman's arm, but he still blocked the way.

"And Drummond," Rowell said, pressing his advantage. "They're both waiting for him at the bottom gate."

Chatsworth glowered at him, his eyes full of venom.

"OK, but you're in DT, Chapman," he said.

He stood aside and watched them go. They were still

running, despite what he'd just said. He stayed where he was for a moment, sniffing the air. The smell had already gone, but he knew with a mounting sense of satisfaction that it had been cigarette smoke. It could only have been on Chapman's breath.

Up in the dorm, Chapman rummaged frantically through his locker. He found his swimming costume, grabbed a towel from the bottom of his bed and bolted for the door. He wheeled round before he got there and dashed back to the locker to put the pack of Embassy in his wash bag. He took out a tube of toothpaste and squeezed a great dollop into his mouth, working it around with his tongue.

"Thanks, Chris," he said.

"You've got some on your chin," Rowell said.

"Thanks. See you later."

"Good luck," Rowell yelled after him. "Stop calling the prefects *sir.*"

Dryden, Drummond and Simpson were already sitting in the car by the bottom gate. Dryden looked at his watch for the fifth time in as many minutes.

"You did tell him, didn't you?"

"Yes, sir, less than half an hour ago."

Drummond looked at his watch too.

"You did tell him where to come?"

"Yes, sir," Drummond replied, starting to get irritated.

A back door suddenly flew open and Chapman jumped in beside Simpson.

"Sorry, sir, I couldn't find my costume," he said.

Dryden grunted, but he didn't say anything. He put the car into gear and pulled away. In the rear view mirror, he could see Chapman's face, his pretty mouth open gasping for breath, and he could smell the toothpaste. Drummond and

Simpson smelt it too, but neither of them said anything. It wasn't a particularly promising subject for conversation.

"Where did you learn to dive, Chapman?" Dryden asked when they were out on the main road, breaking the silence.

"My mum taught me, sir – and I was in the team at Saints."

Dryden nodded. He knew that. The answers he wanted were mainly for the others' benefit, to help establish the new boy's credentials.

"You came first in the county finals last year, didn't you?"

"Yes, sir."

"Under fourteen?"

"Yes, sir."

"How old were you then?"

"Twelve and a bit, sir."

"High board?"

"Yes, sir."

Drummond and Dryden nodded in unison, pleased and impressed. Beside him, Simpson prodded him on the leg and mouthed the words *big stuff*. Chapman pulled a face at him but quickly wiped it off when his eyes met Dryden's looking at him again in the rear view mirror. He looked away, out of the window, at the hedgerows racing past.

The journey to the public swimming pool in Worthing took a little under twenty minutes. In the front, Drummond and Dryden talked mostly about university entrance. The two boys in the back listened with only half an ear, lost in their own thoughts. University was a long way off for them, as far away as the moon.

"We've only got half an hour before they open for general swimming," Dryden said as he parked the car, "so don't dilly dally in the change room."

The air inside the building was hot and stifling, and the

stench of chlorine was overpowering. The boys emerged one by one from the change rooms and dived into the pool. Dryden envied them. He wished he could have swum too.

After the first couple of dives from the high board, Drummond spent a lot of time doing lazy backstrokes and treading water. Being in the pool gave him an inconspicuous vantage point to look at Chapman. By the end of the session he had only managed six dives; Chapman and Simpson had done nine each.

Dryden was irritated and perplexed. He knew it was totally unlike Drummond to wallow but he didn't feel he could rebuke him, not in front of the younger boys. He guessed after a while at the cause and smiled wryly, despite his irritation.

"Last dive, Chapman," he said, looking at his watch.

Swimming slowly backwards in the centre of the pool, Drummond watched Chapman climb the ladder. For the tenth time, up on the high board he raised his perfect arms above his perfect, svelte little body. He soared out and down, arching forward and touching his toes with the tips of his fingers in a classic jacknife. Straitening out, he split the surface of the pool with barely a ripple.

"OK, Simpson, last dive," Dryden yelled unnecessarily.

Simpson was halfway up the ladder and he climbed a little faster. His dive was almost as flawless but only Dryden and Chapman were watching.

"Well done, Chapman. That last one was really great," Drummond said, towelling himself off with his back to the pool.

"Thanks, sir," Chapman said.

On the drive back Dryden was careful to praise Simpson as much as he praised Chapman. Simpson was an excellent diver, but beside Chapman's angelic poise on the high board he looked like the village blacksmith. *It's unfair*, Dryden thought, *but that's the way it is.*

About Drummond's uncharacteristic lethargy he said nothing.

SIX

Prefects' Detention began at five o'clock the next day in an Upper 3B classroom. It came as no surprise to Rowell that Chatsworth was in the chair. There were three other boys spread out over the empty classroom, all of them put there by him. Rowell and Chapman sat down at the back.

"It's good of you to join us, Rowell, but I don't recall giving you detention," Chatsworth said.

"I thought…" Rowell stammered.

"Well that's a first. You thought wrong, as usual. Clear off."

Rowell looked confused. He didn't want to be there, but he didn't want to leave Chapman to Chatsworth's tender mercies either.

"He who hesitates is lost, Rowell. If you're not out in five seconds, you can stay for the full hour."

Rowell stood up, torn inside and confused, but he did walk out, pausing in the door to give the prefect's back a two-fingered salute. The other boys sniggered. Chatsworth knew what was going on, but he didn't say anything, continuing to stare down at the book on the desk in front of him. Only when he heard the door close did he look up. He looked straight at Chapman.

"Have I got BO, Chapman?"

"I'm sorry sir?"

"Maybe you just want to sit at the back so you can play with yourself?"

The other three looked at Chapman. One of them giggled.

Chatsworth expected Chapman to be quaking by then but he wasn't. He just smiled. It wasn't the kind of smile he could object to either. There was too much openness and innocence in it.

"Come up to the front," he said.

The boy did as he was told and he began to sit down at one of the desks on the edge of the front row.

"Here," commanded Chatsworth, pointing at the desk straight in front of him.

Once that was all settled, Chapman opened his history book and started reading. The next hour didn't have to be a complete waste of time, he told himself. Tetley had set a test for Monday on the Tudors. Staring up at him from the open pages was a diagram of Henry VIII's unique family tree. Divorced, beheaded, died; divorced, beheaded, survived. Tetley had repeated that at least three times.

The clock ticked on, and Chapman turned the pages. He had read six of them when Chatsworth next spoke.

"Alright, you lot, you can go."

Chapman looked up, shutting the book. *Great, barely fifteen minutes*, he thought.

He started to get up from the desk.

"Not you, Chapman," Chatsworth said.

The other boys hurried to the door without a backward glance, eager to be gone before Chatsworth suddenly changed his mind about them.

Chapman opened his book again, perplexed at the prefect's whims. Try as he might, though, he couldn't get back into reading, conscious in the silence of Chatsworth's eyes boring into him. He looked down at the jumble of type on the pages and tried hard to focus, distracted by a growing sense of injustice.

Chatsworth stared and the fantasies he'd been having about Chapman ever since he'd bumped into him in the corridor filled his head. There was nothing Chapman wouldn't do in Chatsworth's daydreams. He could barely believe that he had him here now, all to himself, not six feet away. His eyes wandered over and over again up the boy's slender neck and across each impeccable, unblemished feature. Everything was perfect, in each part and in the whole. He was so beautiful that it made Chatsworth ache. He uncrossed his legs slowly under the desk to ease the pressure in his crotch. He wanted to speak, but his mouth was dry and he had to work his tongue around a couple of times to make sure that what he said next didn't come out as a hoarse croak.

"Maybe I'm being too hard on you, Chapman."

The boy looked up in surprise. His bright eyes searched Chatsworth's features, seeming to him to caress his face. His mouth was slightly open but he didn't say anything, not really understanding what Chatsworth meant.

"Do you think I'm being too hard on you?" Chatsworth asked.

"I'm not sure, sir."

There was that "sir" again, Chatsworth thought. Unlike Drummond, he liked it.

He pushed his chair back from the table, intending to

47

stand up. He thought better of it when he glanced down and realised that his erection was creating a conspicuous bulge in the crotch of his trousers. Instead he leaned forward, putting his elbows on the table and cupped his chin in his hands.

"Can I go then, sir?" Chapman asked, closing his book hopefully for the second time.

Chatsworth didn't reply. He just went on staring with hard unblinking eyes. It was unnerving. Chapman opened the book again, not sure what to do or where to look. He kept his eyes on Chatsworth's face, letting his gaze wander over the prefect's thin, spotty features. The tip of his tongue peeked out briefly to moisten his lips. For the first time, Chapman was a little frightened.

"Tell me about yourself," Chatsworth said at last. "Do you smoke?"

Chapman thought it was a joke, and perhaps it was but there was something in Chatsworth's tone that denied that. It sounded like a genuine question, as though he was actually about to offer him a cigarette.

"No, sir."

Chatsworth smiled, knowing he was lying.

"Well I do, Chapman, but then I'm seventeen. How old are you?"

"Thirteen, sir."

Chatsworth felt confident enough to stand up then. He came round the table and sat on the desk, inches away, leaning over.

"Life can be very, very miserable here if you upset me, Chapman."

To his surprise Chapman didn't cringe away. He stayed motionless, looking up at him, even when Chatsworth put his fingers on the tie at his throat, moving the knot gently from side to side.

"But you're clever enough to know that, aren't you?"

"Yes, sir."

Chatsworth stopped fiddling with the knot and ran the tips of two fingers slowly up the boy's throat, lifting his chin slightly. Then he put his hand on Chapman's shoulder, massaging it gently. He let the hand rest there and it felt very heavy, but Chapman sat still, clutching the history book.

"Believe it or not, I actually quite like you, Chapman. At least you're not a cry baby."

There was no sensible answer to that, not one that Chapman could think of, anyway. Chatsworth tapped his restless fingers on his shoulder while the boy worried where they might go next.

After what seemed a very long time, Chatsworth stood up again. He went back to his chair and sat down. Chapman let the air slowly out of his lungs.

"OK, you can go."

"Thank you, sir."

Chapman picked up the Tudors and headed for the door, but for the second time in two days, Chatsworth grabbed his arm as he went past.

"We're going to be friends, aren't we, Chapman?" It was less of a question than a statement, and there could only really be one answer.

"Yes, sir."

"And you're going to do whatever I tell you to do from now on – whatever it is?"

Chapman nodded and even managed to smile slightly.

That was enough for Chatsworth. He released his grip so that the boy could finally escape.

SEVEN

As pubs went, it wasn't bad: a bit plastic-rustic, a bit off the beaten track, but then it was good to get out into the country, and there was a nice view over a big bend in the Adur. Dryden wasn't looking at the river. He had his back to it. He had chosen the seat deliberately when they sat down, so that Sarah could enjoy the view. It had seemed the gentlemanly thing to do. All he could see beyond her was the car park, and more than once his eyes had rested on her red MG. Behind it he could just make out the faded boot of his old Hillman. The contrast did little for his mood.

"So when's the interview?" Sarah asked.

Dryden swallowed a mouthful of beer and tried to remember.

"Day after tomorrow, eleven thirty."

"I think you doing the right thing," she lied. "I never really pictured you as a teacher."

I never pictured you as a doctor, Dryden thought, *in fact I still can't.*

His eyes wandered back to the red sports car.

"You've obviously got no regrets," he said.

"Sometimes," she said, "it's not much fun looking up old men's arses. That bit I could do without."

"I'm sure," he said.

Dryden studied her as she picked at the ploughman's lunch, trying to control a wayward pickled onion with her fork. It didn't seem five minutes since they'd both been at Oxford. They'd shared a flat and had great sex back then and huge philosophical conversations that had rambled away in the dark, going nowhere. She hadn't changed much, maybe the hair was a bit different, shorter perhaps, but everything else was still the same. Maybe her eyes had grown a little older and her lips seemed firmer than he remembered, thinner somehow, but she was still very pretty. After a bit of mental arithmetic he realised with a small shock that she was now twenty-seven and so was he.

"So what happens at Grindlay's Bank? What does the job involve?" she asked.

"I haven't got it yet."

"I'm sure you will."

"I'm still not sure I want it even if they do make me an offer."

Still stumbling about trying to find a future, Sarah thought. That had always been his problem. When Oxford ended she had known exactly where she was going; she had always known. Philip had sort of wandered out of the place with a dazed look on his face. That look was still there, only now there was a little bitterness etched in.

"Well assuming they do and assuming you do, what does it involve?"

"Africa, maybe, or India."

"You mean straight away?"

"I bloody well hope not; I assume they'd teach me something about banking first."

Sarah tried hard to visualise him in a pin-striped suit and maybe a pith helmet, counting out rupees or whatever. None of the images worked. It would be another mistake, but she didn't want to say so, doubting that he would ever really go for it anyway. But he didn't look like a schoolteacher either, he never had. That had come out of the blue.

"I don't think much of this cottage pie," he said, "it tastes of soap."

He pushed the plate away and raised his glass, emptying the last few drops of beer. A wasp appeared, buzzing to and fro, homing in on the empty beer mug. Unperturbed by his half-hearted swatting, it settled on the rim. Then it fell in and was embroiled in the froth at the bottom. They both watched it struggle, wondering whether it would be able to extricate itself.

When that didn't seem likely, Dryden picked up the mug and flicked the dregs and the wasp onto the grass.

"I'm glad you ended up down here," he said.

"It's nice."

"It's a big hospital."

She nodded.

"When do you think you'll go into general practice? That's still the plan, isn't it?"

She nodded again, her mouth full of cheese. The cheese was a bit stale too. Maybe it wasn't such a good pub, after all.

"Hopefully in the middle of next year."

The wasp reappeared and settled on the rim of the beer mug again. Dryden was becoming uncomfortably hot in the sun. All the shade from the umbrella was on Sarah's side of the table, and the shade from the big oak tree, which had given him some comfort at the beginning, had now moved away, obeying the sun. He debated with himself whether to move his chair round to her side but decided against it. He wouldn't have given it a second thought two years ago. It was odd how such a relatively short time apart could put such a huge distance between them.

"So you're really fed up at Dotheboys Hall?" she asked, changing the subject.

It was his turn to nod.

"Actually, though, it's not all bad," he said. "It is a bit Dickensian, but I quite enjoy the teaching part. Agreeing to be a House Master was a mistake though. I never get a moment's peace, and the room is bloody awful. I've got a view of this dreary old graveyard and an endless supply of pigeons comes and craps on my windowsill."

"Charming. And how do you get on with the kids?"

He smiled before answering, debating briefly with himself what to say to her.

"They worship the ground I walk on, and they call me Drydork."

"To your face?"

He shot her a reproachful glance, feigning injured pride.

"Sorry," she said.

She thought how close they'd come to having a kid of their own, remembering the long tense wait for the results to come back. After that fright, she'd gone on the pill. Back then, when that happened, she had thought he would make a good father. But she wasn't ready to be a mother then, and she thought now that maybe she never would be.

"There's an interesting new kid," he said after a pause. "He arrived a couple of weeks back, complete with a dark secret."

Sarah raised her eyebrows, exaggerating her real interest.

"Actually I shouldn't be flippant about it," he said, feeling guilty. He regretted having brought it up. It didn't matter here, it had nothing to do with her, but talking about it was still a breach of trust.

"Sounds intriguing," she said.

She was now genuinely interested, and he couldn't drop it, so he told her the story as Bruder had told it to him. He tried to make Bruder a comical focal point but that didn't work. Bruder wasn't at all funny, and having never met the man his foibles were in any event meaningless to her.

"So has he settled in all right?" she asked when he'd finished.

"He seems fine, but he is an odd kid in some ways."

"Odd in what way?"

Dryden thought about how to reply, not sure now what he had meant himself. In any objective sense Chapman was as normal as any boy his age but there was something different about him, apart from the astonishing looks.

"Well for a start, I think the Head Prefect's in love with him."

She laughed at that, choking on a mouthful of wine, trying not to spray it out over the table. Dryden grinned too. Her laughter had always been infectious and the mood it instantly created seemed to transport them back, telescoping the intervening years into irrelevance.

"Sorry, I shouldn't laugh – but that hardly makes the boy odd, does it?" she said, regaining some composure. "It certainly says something about the Head Prefect, though."

"I'm probably being unfair to him," Dryden said. "He's actually a real macho type, captain of the First XV and all that – brilliant swimmer and diver. But at diving practice he didn't seem to be able to take his eyes off Chapman."

"Is that the boy's name?"

"Yes. I shouldn't have told you any of this, but I don't suppose it matters."

"He must be a real beauty."

Dryden pondered about that. It wasn't a term you used to describe a thirteen-year-old boy, least of all to your girlfriend; you might say handsome perhaps, good looking – not beautiful. But Chapman was beautiful, and as he thought about it even that word seemed inadequate. The boy had a seductive, wraithlike quality. In a strange way it both enchanted and disturbed him.

Sarah watched him thinking and was surprised at the lost look on his face. The laughter of a few seconds ago had vanished. He seemed to have drifted far away.

"Hello, I'm still here," she said after a while.

Dryden looked at her blankly for a second or two and then he was himself again, back in the hot sun, smiling.

"Well Drummond obviously thinks he is," he said, picking up the conversation again.

A waitress came to collect their plates. She looked disapprovingly at the remains of the cottage pie but she didn't say anything, perhaps not wanting to invite a complaint that late in her shift. The other tables had thinned out. Only one other couple remained on the terrace and they were getting ready to leave.

"How about a walk on the beach?" Sarah suggested.

They decided to go in her MG and come back for his car. It was obvious she was proud of the MG and eager to show it off. He envied her the car and, more than that, what it represented. She had made the right choices and had got to where she wanted to be. On the narrow roads down to the coast she drove much too fast, but that was part of it too.

There was a cool breeze off the sea and they didn't walk for long before sitting down on the shingles in the lea of a wooden breakwater. It wasn't very comfortable but that didn't seem to matter much to either of them. He put his arm around her waist, and she leaned her head on his shoulder and put her hand on his leg, gently massaging the muscle above his knee. They sat like that for quite a while, not speaking, at ease with each other again. The first real kiss in nearly two years came quite naturally.

A gull landed on the breakwater close by with a small crab in its beak, too intent on its meal to take much notice of them. Before long others came, hoping to share the crab, or better still to steal it all away. Their squabbles rose in intensity. The sharp piercing cries soon grew so loud that they hid the sound of the grey and white pebbles turning over and against each other at the edge of the sea.

"I hope you don't go to Africa," she said quietly, almost to herself.

He smiled at that and kissed the top of her head.

"Maybe it'll be India."

"You know what I mean," she said.

He was happy inside, happier than he had been in a long while, but he did wonder whether he really understood what she meant. He looked away out over the sea at the wide horizon where both Africa and India lay, hidden and very far away.

EIGHT

Halfway up the steep green slope on the Downs, Rowell stopped again. On the path far ahead, near the crest of the ferocious hill, he could see Coffin and Thornton side by side: Winnie-the-Pooh and Piglet. He was annoyed that they were beating him.

"Shit, I hate this," he said, bending forward, putting his hands on his knees, gasping for air.

There was too much air. Invisible oceans of air stretched limitlessly away in every direction. All of it seemed intent on forcing its way in and out of his aching lungs. He felt as though he were being drowned by crisp clean air.

Chapman stopped a few yards ahead. He didn't seem all that puffed. Rowell was grateful that he was lagging behind, keeping him company, but he felt guilty about it at the same time.

"Did you have to do this at Saint Whatsits?" he wheezed.

Chapman nodded, his hands on his hips. He was breathing

hard, but he wasn't breathless.

"What's the point?" Rowell gasped.

He straightened up, already feeling slightly better. The air was starting to form orderly queues; he could manage the two-way traffic again. He started walking and Chapman waited for him, and then they walked together.

It was hot on the Downs. The sun blazed down from a vast blue sky. The only clouds were far off on the southern horizon, out over the deeper blue of the English Channel. If either of the boys had wanted to look, they would have been able to see for miles and miles. They didn't care about that, because they didn't want to be on the hill. The view was irrelevant, not something they had chosen. They were both perspiring, hair sticking to their foreheads and the nape of their necks. They longed for shade.

"Are we still ahead of Leomond?" Rowell asked hopefully. He already knew the answer, but it was nice to be reassured.

"He's miles behind – he stopped running when we went round the first corner," Chapman said.

He turned round and walked backwards for a few paces looking down the steep path to check that what he had said was true. There were about fifteen boys still behind them spaced out at irregular intervals along the thin line of chalk, all the way down to the bottom of the hill. The rotund figure of Leomond was not among them. Chapman smiled, wondering whether he was really going to stroll round the block and wait for the leaders to come past before unobtrusively joining the race again. That had been his plan.

The nearest boys were slowly gaining on them. Chapman started running again and Rowell reluctantly followed suit. Coffin and Thornton had already disappeared over the brow of the hill. There was no one in sight ahead of them any more. Chapman lifted the front of his tee shirt to mop his face as he ran. He felt the cool air on his bare midriff and tugged the shirt right off over his head, stumbling on the loose chalk as he momentarily lost sight of the path.

"You'd better put that on again before we get to the top," Rowell said. He felt the words punch out of him with each impact of his running feet on the hard uneven path. "Tetley might be up there, and he gets hysterical if you strip off. You'll get detention for sure."

Chapman accelerated slightly, pulling a little way ahead, skipping rather than running. He waved the tee shirt high above his head in wild defiance of the invisible Tetley. Rowell looked at him for a while, feeling his own damp shirt sticking to his back. Despite what he'd just said, he threw caution to the wind and pulled his shirt off too. They pranced and danced up the hill shouting and waving their tee shirts like banners, triumphant in their rebellion against the hill and the men who made them run there.

There was a small flock of sheep a little way on up the hill. They had watched the stream of boys running past all afternoon, chewing and raising their heads, unperturbed. They took fright at the sudden commotion, the waving shirts, cantering away down the green slope away from the path.

Rowell was the first to stop. His euphoria quickly ebbed away in the face of the hot sun and the debilitating grasp of the remorseless upward slope. He wiped his face with his damp shirt and then pulled it back down over his head. Chapman danced on a bit longer and when he stopped he still didn't put his tee shirt on, holding it bunched in his hand instead. His eyes were wide and his mouth was open and he looked as though he could run and dance forever.

Rowell glanced back down the slope to measure their progress.

"Oh, shit. Here comes bloody Drummond," he said. "They

must have left half an hour after us – how the hell did they get here so quick?"

The Head Prefect was coming up the path with the inexorable bulk of a locomotive. Four or five other sixth formers were not very far behind. They had already overtaken most of the small stragglers, scattering them to left and right of the narrow path. It was obvious they would soon overtake Rowell and Chapman too.

"I hope he didn't see us," Rowell said, starting to run again, "I really, really don't need another detention."

Chapman ran too, struggling to unravel his bunched tee shirt and get it back over his head. The top of the hill still seemed a long way off but they both ran faster than they had since the start, needing to get to the summit before the young men surging up the hill behind them. Why it was important neither of them really knew. In some vague, indefinable way, the top of the Down seemed to offer sanctuary.

Rowell's legs began to buckle. Every now and again his knees collided with each other, threatening to send him flying, but he kept running. He could hear Drummond behind him getting closer and closer until he imagined hot breath on the back of his neck. Then quite suddenly the big Head Prefect was ahead of him, bearing down on Chapman's fleeing form. As he drew level, Drummond put out a big arm and in one continuous movement scooped up the running boy and slung his slight body over one shoulder. It didn't seem to slow him down, but the added weight must have had some effect, because Rowell started to close the gap. He was soon looking up into Chapman's surprised and grinning face. The taut muscles in Drummond's shoulder dug into the side of the boy's stomach and tickled with each heavy step.

At the top of the hill, Drummond stopped long enough to put him down. He did it with remarkable gentleness for someone so big and in such a hurry.

"Thanks," Chapman said, not really knowing what else to say.

"You're welcome, Chapman, but run faster next time – you can do it," Drummond said between clenched teeth. Then he was gone, hurtling down the hill.

The other sixth formers came past in a tight pack almost immediately, running and breathing hard, their eyes on the ground ahead. They took no notice of the two boys standing off the path to let them pass. Chatsworth was last in the group, his face scarlet and his sharp features bathed in perspiration. He did glance at Chapman but he didn't say anything, saving his breath.

"What the hell was that all about?" Rowell said, holding his side where a stitch had set in. "Bloody show off."

"At least we're at the top," Chapman said.

In all the excitement Rowell had overlooked that fact. The realisation pleased him immensely. It was all down hill or flat from there on in and he felt invigorated enough to start running again.

"I think Leomond's right," Rowell said.

"Right about what?"

"Drummond's got the hots for you – that's the second time he's let you off something, let alone carrying you up this shitting hill."

"No he hasn't, he probably didn't see us," Chapman said.

"He'd have had to be blind."

"Well what's the big deal," Chapman said crossly. "It's a stupid rule anyway."

They ran on in silence for a while. Rowell was jealous that he hadn't been singled out for a lift. He didn't admit it to himself; he didn't really realise that was what it was, but it stabbed at him as insistently as the stitch in his side. Beside him Chapman felt embarrassed by what had happened, by what Rowell had said. He didn't know whether to like or loath Drummond. His feelings oscillated back and forth between indignation and gratitude.

Their bodies seemed lighter, almost airborne as they flew down the steep slope. They started racing in earnest, competing with each other for the first time. They could see Coffin and Thornton again. The other two boys were almost at the bottom, being overtaken by Drummond and his pack, where a wooden gate led out of the fields onto a tar road. There was a man leaning on the gate. As they got closer they could see it was Tetley. He was smoking his pipe and the sun flashed on his glasses as he looked up from his clipboard.

"Have you two been having a picnic up there?" he said as they scrambled over the gate. "You're a good twenty minutes behind the leaders. Get a ruddy move on."

"Yes, sir," they said in unison.

They both stopped running the moment he was out of sight around the first bend.

"Get a ruddy move on," Rowell said in a deep, whiny voice. "I'd like to see his fat arse making it up that hill."

He looked at Chapman when he got no response, regretting what he'd said on the hill. He didn't want the quarrel to grow. He didn't want to believe there was one. The stitch in his side was worse, but the jealousy had mostly gone.

"I was only pulling your leg," he said.

Chapman didn't respond immediately. After an awkward moment or two he grinned and grabbed Rowell around the neck. He locked his right arm in place with his left hand, pushing Rowell down and forward. They staggered on a few paces like that, bound together in mock battle until Rowell managed to wriggle free. The physical contact mended things, rubbed the anger away. They were soon level with the first houses, the start of the town.

"Do you really think he fancies me?" Chapman asked suddenly.

Rowell was cautious about replying, not wanting to rekindle the quarrel. He regretted he'd ever said anything about it. He felt he should be honest.

"It's pretty obvious, but so what," he said. "It's OK if it helps you get away with stuff, isn't it?"

Chapman shrugged. He wasn't actually thinking about Drummond anymore. He was thinking about Chatsworth, his odd stares and wandering hands. Chatsworth was looking at him all the time now, smiling, saying witty things. He wondered whether to say something about that, wondered whether Rowell had noticed it too. He decided to keep it to himself.

"Let's catch up with Pooh and Piglet," he said. He was eager to change the subject, to forget it and move on.

They were only a couple of hundred yards from the school gate when they eventually caught up with Coffin and Thornton. The four of them arrived back together.

NINE

Voaden had been on the run. He had finished an hour earlier and had already visited the big Dorm looking for Chapman. For the second time that afternoon he poked his head through the door. Chapman was sitting on his bed pulling on his socks.

"You took your bloody time," he said. He sat down on the bed beside him.

"Sorry," Chapman said. "I didn't know you were looking for me."

Voaden ruffled his hair and gave his shoulder a soft punch. Every time he saw Chapman he felt the urge to touch him. He didn't know why, and he didn't give it much thought either.

"Do you want to come for a fag?" he asked.

"OK," Chapman said. "But I haven't got any, can I pay you back?"

"No problem."

"If I give you the money, can you get me some next time you go?"

"No problem," Voaden repeated. "I've got something else," he said, lowering his voice. He glanced at the door and then around the room.

There were only two other boys in the dorm. Higgins was lying on his bed reading a letter. Heathfield was over on the far side drawing on a pad.

Voaden took a small piece of folded brown paper from his pocket. He opened it out, hunching over so that his upper body would shield the process from the sparse potential audience. Chapman looked down and saw a couple of small pills. He had barely glimpsed them before Voaden was wrapping them up again, slipping the small packet back into his pocket.

"What are they?" Chapman whispered.

"Purple hearts or something. I got them from a friend. Are you game to try one?"

"What do they do to you?"

"Fucked if I know," Voaden said between his teeth. "I think they give you a big lift, blow your mind, that's all. Come on."

"I said I'd wait for Chris," Chapman said.

Voaden stood up. He was about to say that Rowell was a pain, but he thought better of it. "Root and Ainsworth are waiting for me; we're going down to the fields. We'll see you there," he said.

"Thanks," Chapman said. "I won't be long." He stood up himself, doing up his tie.

Voaden gave him a friendly jab in the midriff and ruffled his hair again. The hair ruffling irritated Chapman much more than the rib tickles and the soft punches, but he grinned anyway.

"So you're really game to give it a try?" Voaden asked, patting his trouser pocket where the pills were.

Chapman nodded.

"Great," Voaden said. "We'll see you there then."

Just like that, he thought. Chapman seemed to be game for anything. It was one of the things he liked about the boy.

On the landing outside, he passed Rowell coming up from the bathrooms, drying his hair. Voaden ignored him. He carried on down the corridor and then took the stairs two at a time to the room in the attic he shared with Root and Ainsworth.

The playing fields were ten minutes' walk from the school, down leafy streets lined with a mixture of free standing and semi-detached houses; a middle class suburb inhabited by middle managers and retired people. It was the only route the under fourteen boys could take alone in the outside world without a chit from one of the masters. There were no shops or other diversions along its entire length.

Rowell hadn't wanted to come when he knew it involved meeting up with Voaden and his friends. He had given in eventually to Chapman's pleading, even though he knew he would probably end up standing under the big tree cooling his heels, kicking acorns. There was always the chance of a game of football, if there was one on the go, but he was already feeling stiff after the run. The thought of playing football wasn't as appealing as it would normally have been. As they walked he kept wishing he'd said no, but he hadn't and that was that.

They said very little on the walk down, what with Rowell lost in his own grumpy thoughts and Chapman feeling guilty that he had pressured him into coming along.

At the fields, no one was playing football; in fact, there was no one there at all. Rowell wondered hopefully whether Voaden had changed his mind. The thought was quickly shattered by a yell from the foliage above.

Even standing directly under the huge oak tree looking up

into the branches, it was difficult to see Voaden, Root and Ainsworth, especially coming in from the bright sunlight. They were well hidden, and that made the tree ideal for smoking. There was no direct way up the massive trunk either. The boys had to climb into a smaller tree, then onto the top of the boundary wall. That in turn was overhung by a branch of the huge oak itself. From there it was relatively easy. There were plenty of perches in the different storeys, some more secure than others.

The two boys clambered up and found a place to sit just below the other three. Ainsworth was highest in the tree, his legs dangling, his left arm wrapped around a thick branch. With his staring brown eyes and broad flat nose he reminded Rowell of a big monkey. Voaden and Root looked a bit like monkeys too. Their legs were at odd and undignified angles so that their feet could get a steady purchase on the branches. When he looked straight up from his perch Rowell found that the top of the tree and the sky beyond were mostly blocked by Root's crotch.

Voaden leaned down holding out an open pack of cigarettes and Chapman took one. So did Rowell when it was offered to him. He was surprised and secretly disappointed that he'd been included.

The first puff made Rowell cough and splutter. The cigarette slipped out of his fingers and fell. It bounced off a branch in a little shower of sparks and disappeared.

"Oh shit," he said.

"Oh shit is right," Voaden said. "I hope you're going down to get that."

"I can't see it," Rowell said, bobbing to and fro on his branch trying to get a view of the ground. *Why the hell did I come*, he muttered to himself for the tenth time.

"Get your fucking arse down there and look for it. That's

all we need: a master to come past and see a smoking fucking cigarette down there," Voaden said.

Rowell had already started to clamber down. He was eager to get away from the angry, reproachful looks of the older boys. Chapman began to follow and then realised he had his own cigarette in his hand. He held it out to Voaden to hold. Voaden shook his head.

"Hang on here, he dropped it, let him find it," he said.

Rowell was in midair, jumping down from the wall, when he saw that there was a man down there. The fright it gave him made him lose concentration and he fell over when he landed, ending up on his backside, breaking twigs.

"Are you alright?" Chapman asked, his voice sounding anxious in the big tree.

Rowell looked up and saw with relief that it wasn't one of the masters. The man had an untidy beard and was wearing a cloth cap. Despite the heat he was dressed in a long tatty overcoat. He was holding a cigarette between very dirty fingers. He grinned at Rowell and the boy was pretty sure that it was his cigarette the man was holding. The end was frayed.

"Got a light?" the man asked.

Chapman appeared up on the wall, looking down anxiously, still holding his own smoking cigarette.

"Are you alright?" he repeated.

"I'm fine," Rowell said, standing up and dusting off the seat of his pants.

"Who's that?" Chapman asked, catching sight of the tramp.

"I don't know but he wants a light," Rowell said.

"Oh," Chapman said, "Here's one." He crouched down, balancing on the top of the wall, holding out the lighted cigarette.

The tramp reached up and took it. He put the other one in his top pocket.

"Thanks, mate," he said and walked away, back towards the road, puffing on Chapman's cigarette.

The two boys watched him go, astonished at first, and then they burst out laughing.

"What the fuck's going on down there?" Voaden growled from high above.

The boys didn't answer, still giggling and watching the tramp. He turned round when he got to the road, snapped to attention and saluted.

"What a jackass," Rowell said.

Chapman clambered back onto the big overhanging branch still giggling. Rowell reluctantly followed, hoping the story of the tramp would deflect the anger of the older boys. Voaden and the others did laugh when they heard what had happened, but the pack of cigarettes didn't get offered round again. Voaden gave the remains of his to Chapman, ignoring Rowell, who was pleased to be ignored this time.

After a few puffs Chapman stubbed out the cigarette and flicked the stub away into the leaves. Voaden eased himself down to sit beside him. He dug into his trouser pocket, steadying himself with his other hand against the massive trunk. With a bit of a struggle he pulled out the small brown packet.

"Still game?" he asked.

"Yes, I suppose so," Chapman said. "What can I swallow it with?"

Rowell was sitting with his back to the rest of them. His mind had drifted away. He hadn't been paying any real attention, but he turned round when he heard that.

"Work up some spit," Voaden said. He opened up the tiny brown parcel. "Don't drop the fucking thing," he said, glancing at Rowell.

Chapman took one of the small pills, holding it gingerly between his thumb and forefinger.

"What the hell are you doing?" Rowell said. He couldn't believe what he was seeing.

"What does it look like?" Ainsworth said, stretching down to kick him lightly on the shoulder. That came as a surprise, and Rowell wobbled on his branch for an instant, but it didn't distract him.

"You're fucking crazy," he said, "We've got to be back for roll call in twenty minutes."

Voaden glared at him. There was the kind of malevolence in his eyes that Rowell had seen all too often in the past.

"Stuff off, Rowell," he said.

"Yeah, stuff off, you stupid little dweeb," Root added.

Chapman hadn't been looking at any of them. It didn't seem as though he had really heard any of them either. He was looking at the pill and there was a wild expression on his face. He was nervous and excited. He put the pill in his mouth and swallowed, putting an abrupt end to the debate.

"Shit," Rowell said.

There was a long silence after that. The other four boys stared at Chapman as though they thought he might explode. They slowly began to relax when nothing happened. A disappointed look crept over Voaden's features; the same look boys have when a firework fails to go off.

"I don't feel anything," Chapman said.

"Maybe it takes a while," Voaden said.

They waited a little longer, but Chapman just smiled, looking back at each of them in turn.

Rowell stood up gingerly on his branch, his head coming up level with Root's crotch.

"We'd better get back," he said and started to climb down.

"Yeah, run along, you little twerp," Root said.

Chapman stood up ready to follow. Voaden wanted to stop him, but he knew that was pushing things too far. He and the others could stay out another hour but the two younger boys had to be back for roll call by six or they'd automatically get DT.

"You owe me five bob for that," he said, wanting to salvage something.

Chapman nodded. "I'll have to owe you; I haven't got it here," he said.

He had to ease past on the branch and he nearly lost his balance and fell against Voaden when he did. He put his hand out instinctively and it landed on Voaden's thigh, slipped down his trousers and ended up pressed against his belly. Voaden winced at the impact but he grabbed Chapman's arm to steady him. They were frozen like that for an instant, their faces inches apart.

"Sorry," Chapman said.

Voaden grunted. He let go and watched him climb down in silence.

Down on the ground, Rowell walked quickly. He was angry that his protest up in the tree had been ignored, angrier still that he'd been persuaded to come along in the first place. Chapman had to run to catch up with him in the street.

"Sorry, I just wanted to know what it was like," he said when he caught up, falling into step.

"And?"

"What?"

"What's it like?"

Chapman shrugged but he was beginning to feel a bit strange after running, as though his legs were walking briskly by themselves. Rowell's voice sounded very clear, like the chimes of a bell. Even the cracks in the pavement seemed more defined, snaking this way and that with a startling clarity and purpose he'd never noticed before. They walked in silence for a while and the strangeness grew.

"I feel really weird," Chapman said after a while.

There was a crazy edge in his voice. It made Rowell stop being angry. He started to get anxious instead.

"God, you're a jerk," he said.

He was startled when Chapman grabbed hold of his right hand. His first instinct was to shake it loose. He did try but something made him stop. In a vague, weird way he felt Chapman maybe needed to be anchored like that. He even returned the grip, hoping they wouldn't be seen by anybody, ready to break loose.

As luck would have it, a policeman walking his beat appeared abruptly from one of the side streets right in front of them. Rowell immediately tried to pull his hand free, but Chapman wouldn't let him. It was pointless to struggle, to make an issue of it. It would only attract more attention, he thought. He avoided looking at the policeman's face as they came towards each other on the pavement.

Chapman saw the policeman too. The buttons on his uniform shone like small suns.

"Evening, boys," the constable said.

"Evening, sir," Rowell mumbled.

Chapman grinned up at him as though he was a long lost friend.

Then he was gone, behind them. They didn't see him stop and turn round. The constable had seen many things but he had never seen two boys that age holding hands. He shook his head slowly from side to side and went on his way.

"I feel as though I've got to do something really stupid," Chapman said.

"You have already, you stupid jerk," Rowell said.

Chapman suddenly let go of Rowell's hand. He put his arms around his neck, hugging him close, trying to kiss him. It took a lot of force to prise him away.

"Get a grip on yourself," Rowell said sternly. As the words came out of his mouth, he could hear his father's voice in them.

"Sorry," Chapman said, but he was laughing, and his eyes were sparkling.

Rowell stared at him, his expression full of reproach. Chapman made a petulant little-boy face and took hold of his hand again. They walked on as they had been before.

"What the hell did Voaden give you?" Rowell asked.

"I don't know," Chapman said.

"He gives you any old shit and you swallow it – you're a complete jerk."

"Sorry," Chapman said again.

"It's your funeral. What are you going to do at roll call? You can't be all weird like this," Rowell said. "Are you going to hug Tetley?"

"Yuck," Chapman said.

Rowell shook his head from side to side. "You're priceless," he said.

There were several boys in the schoolyard playing football. They didn't take any notice of Rowell and Chapman as they walked across. That was just as well, because Rowell had forgotten they were still holding hands; it had already started to seem that natural, like walking with a baby brother. The bell sounded when they were nearly at the door. That woke him up with a start. He twisted his hand to free it from Chapman's grip.

Neither of them noticed Chatsworth watching from a window of the prefect's common room high above. He had been looking out anyway, leaning his elbows on the windowsill. He called Gatesford and Barnes over so that they could look too.

Chapman giggled a lot at roll call. At one stage he unzipped his fly. Rowell thought he was going to piss on the legs of the boy in front but he didn't. He was only pretending. Tetley paused once or twice in reciting the litany of names and looked over the others' heads in their direction, but that was all. He didn't say anything. He just scowled and carried on.

When roll call was over, Chapman went up to the dorm ahead of Rowell. Rowell was fed up with him by then, glad to be rid of him in a way. Part of him didn't care what happened next. *If Chapman did something stupid he could do it on his own,* he thought.

"Has he gone off his rocker?" Coffin asked Rowell on the stairs.

"He's always been off his rocker," Rowell said.

Chapman was standing by his bed when Rowell eventually got up to the dorm. He'd taken his clothes off except for his underpants. They were half off too. Chatsworth and Gatesford were standing there.

"Oh, shit," Rowell said to himself. He stopped inside the door. He had to force his feet to move again by a conscious act of will.

He was surprised to see that the two prefects were grinning. They were obviously not upset or angry. They even grinned at him briefly when they saw him. Rowell went over to Leomond's bed, not wanting to get dragged into whatever was happening.

"How long have they been here?" he whispered to Leomond.

"A few minutes," Leomond said in a low voice. "What's with Chapman?"

"Voaden gave him a pill," Rowell whispered.

"He's being really weird," Leomond said as though he hadn't heard. "Why's he taken his clothes off?"

"I don't know," Rowell said.

Chatsworth and Gatesford didn't stay much longer. Chatsworth ruffled Chapman's hair and then they both walked out still smiling. Chatsworth even gave Rowell a friendly wave. Chapman collapsed onto his bed. He didn't sit down; he just kept his arms by his sides and fell over backwards. Rowell went over and looked down at him.

"That was bloody close," Rowell said. "What did they say to you?"

Chapman didn't answer. He waved his arms to and fro as though he was conducting an invisible orchestra. That made Rowell angry again, being ignored.

"Why did you take your bloody clothes off? It's supper in fifteen minutes."

Leomond came over and sat down on the bed next to Chapman. He bent down and picked his trousers up off the floor. He put them on the bed on top of Chapman's shirt and blazer. Chapman finally sat up.

"Sorry," he said.

Rowell shrugged. "Stop saying that – it's nothing to me," he said. He didn't know what else to say. He was perplexed that Chapman wasn't in deep trouble. He'd expected to see the two prefects march him off to Dryden or Bruder or something. He'd been ready for a really big drama, hoping that it wouldn't include him.

"Get dressed," Leomond said.

"I'm going for a swim," Chapman said.

"No you're not," Leomond said. He picked up the trousers and held them out. "Put them back on."

Chapman hesitated for a moment. Then he obeyed.

"Are you going to be alright at supper?" Rowell asked. "You're not going to do anything daft?"

Chapman shook his head.

"Has it worn off?"

"I think so."

The two of them looked at him and he grinned back. He still looked a bit crazy.

"God, you're a jerk," Rowell repeated.

Chapman pulled a face at him. Then he flopped back down onto the bed again. He pointed up at the window high above his head. In one corner of the dusty glass a spider's web was catching the crimson rays of the evening sun. Beyond that the sky, it seemed to him, was all on fire.

TEN

Dryden woke up with a start when he heard the noise. It sounded like someone missing a step and tripping on the stairs. For a few seconds he debated whether to ignore it, but he knew he shouldn't, and so he climbed wearily out of bed, grabbed his dressing gown and flung open the door. The landing was empty. He stood there, tying up the cord of the gown, listening intently. The cold in the wooden floorboards began to explore the soles of his bare feet. He glanced at his watch. With a surge of anger he saw that it was well after midnight.

He went down the stairs to the next landing and paused again. He still couldn't hear anything but he did catch a faint whiff of cigarette smoke, so he went on down.

In the basement, the door to the bathrooms was slightly open, and the smell of cigarettes was obvious. He could barely believe the cheek of it. The lights were off inside. He fumbled around on the wall, trying to find the switch. He couldn't at first. A faint sound from one of the bath cubicles made him look harder.

The instant the lights came on, there was a distinct noise, and Dryden's hackles rose. Four long strides took him to the cubicle, and he pushed and held the door open on its swing hinges, relishing his moment of sweet revenge. The feeling was short lived, because what he saw made him freeze.

Chapman was on the floor in the narrow damp space between the bath and the wall. He was sitting with his knees pulled up to his chin. His wide, bright eyes looked up at Dryden from beneath a mop of dishevelled hair. He was stark naked. What startled Dryden even more was that there seemed to be something tied around his ankles.

"What on earth are you up to?" he asked.

As the question came out, it seemed ridiculously unanswerable. Chapman didn't reply. He hid his face on his knees. He was shivering, and he looked very small. Dryden took a step forward, letting the door swing shut behind him.

"I can't get the knot undone, sir," Chapman said in a tiny voice.

Dryden looked at the boy's feet. He saw then that it was a school tie. He crouched down and set about trying to undo the knot. It absorbed all his attention for fully half a minute. The knot had been pulled really tight. Dryden's fingers hurt when he finally got it loose.

"Were there other boys down here?" he asked. "Did they do this to you?"

Chapman didn't answer. He kept his head down and his feet together when they were finally free, staying motionless in the same position. Dryden felt acutely embarrassed for him. He put his hand lightly on the boy's shoulder. The little shivers from his skin seemed almost like an electric current.

"It's alright, Peter, you don't need to be embarrassed, up

you get," he said.

Chapman stayed as he was for a few long seconds. Then he lifted his head, and he started to get up. Dryden saw the glistening smears on his face and chin. There was more on his chest and stomach, even on his legs. It was obviously semen.

"Good God – did the other boys do that?" Dryden asked. His voice echoed strangely in a hollow space inside his head.

Chapman nodded. He tried to wipe some of the mess away.

"You'd better get into the bath and wash it off," Dryden said.

The boy obeyed. He got into the bath but then he just stood there in a daze. He didn't seem to know what to do next. Dryden told him to kneel down and turned the tap on for him. He watched the boy washing himself until the intimacy of the scene made him realise what he was doing and he turned away.

"Where are your pyjamas?" he asked.

"I think they're outside somewhere, sir," Chapman said.

Dryden pushed his way out of the cubicle and had a look around. A pair of pyjama pants was lying on the floor in the far corner but there was no sign of a top. When he picked up the pants he found they were wet. He continued searching for the top, wondering whether Chapman had actually been wearing one to start with. He finally found it hanging on the edge of a toilet bowl; it had obviously landed there from being thrown. All but one of the buttons had gone and it was also wet and badly torn.

"Bloody animals," he muttered angrily. He couldn't believe all this had been happening while he'd been soundly sleeping up above.

He waited outside the cubicle with the sopping, torn pyjamas. Then he realised that was hopeless. He looked for a towel but couldn't find one so he took off his dressing gown. The tap had been turned off by then and there was silence from the cubicle. He waited a few more moments. When the boy still didn't come out he went back in. Chapman was still kneeling in the bath. He stood up when the door opened. Dryden was surprised that he wasn't crying and a little shocked when he even smiled briefly. He was still shivering, and the beads and thin rivulets of water on his small, slim body sparkled in the light from the bulb above him, like streams of tiny stars. He kept his eyes on Dryden's face, searching his features in the peculiar way he had.

"Your pyjamas are a lost cause; you'd better put this on," Dryden said.

Chapman climbed out of the bath, took the dressing gown and slipped his willowy arms into the huge sleeves. The gown was long on Dryden, much too long for the boy. The heavy fabric puddled around his feet. As he tried to hitch it up, the top half ballooned out and fell off his shoulders. He might as well have been trying to put on a tent. Dryden did his best to solve the problem, winding the gown round the boy's small frame and tying up the belt. The effect would have been quite funny in different circumstances.

"What are you going to do to me, sir?" Chapman asked.

Dryden didn't know quite how to reply to that. It almost sounded as though the boy thought he might be considering taking up where the others had left off.

"I'm not going to do anything to you, but we can't stay here. We'd better go up to my room and sort this out," he said.

He ushered Chapman ahead of him, clutching the sopping pyjamas in one hand and steadying the boy every time his foot caught in the dressing gown. At the second landing, Dryden picked him up and staggered up the remaining flight of steps and into his room, shutting the door with a backward kick.

He regretted it instantly; the slamming door sounded like a gunshot in the silence.

He was about to put the boy down on the bed but a sense of decorum made him swerve and drop him down into the worn easy chair instead. He sat down on the bed himself, catching his breath.

"Are you alright? You're not hurt – they didn't…? Do you want me to call Matron?"

"No sir – I'm fine, really."

Dryden stared at him and he did seem fine. He looked more relaxed than he felt himself.

"What on earth happened down there? Were you smoking? Did you go down there to smoke a cigarette with the others – is that when they…?" The question trailed away, overwhelmed in his mind by a host of others.

"I think they got a bit carried away, sir."

Dryden nodded. Got a bit carried away, he repeated to himself. That's a very peculiar kind of answer, he thought – a very adult understatement. Is that what happened to you at Saints? The teacher got a bit carried away. Is that what your mother told you happened? The questions tumbled around in his head but he didn't ask them out loud.

"They behaved worse than animals," he said.

Chapman nodded slightly but he said nothing.

Dryden started to stand and then he sat down again. He looked at the boy. The boy looked back at him, searching his face as though trying to read what the teacher was thinking. There was the ghost of another smile. It was hardly there and was gone.

"I think you'd better tell me who they were," Dryden said.

Chapman didn't answer but he kept his eyes on Dryden's face.

"I'll have to report this to the headmaster. Those boys

need to be caned and expelled for this. They raped you, for goodness sake."

The boy stood up abruptly and the dressing gown slipped off his shoulders. His strange calm fell away too.

"No, sir, please don't – please don't do that, sir," he blurted out.

Dryden was taken aback by his vehemence. He wasn't sure what to do or say next. He felt awkward and embarrassed, and he was beginning to get frightened of something stirring in himself. It was coiling around in his guts and he felt nauseous and perplexed that it could even be there.

He tore his eyes from the boy's pleading face and stood up himself. He went to the window to stare out at the dark. The dark and all its unseen eyes seemed to stare back at him. He knew he should barge into the dorms, turn on the lights and shout and threaten until someone owned up. He was equally sure that nobody would; he knew he should go through the motions anyway, not least for his own sake: to show he was doing his job, to show how revolted and angry he was. Instead he just stood there.

"I really don't know what to do if you won't tell me who they were," he said eventually. He didn't turn round, waiting for Chapman to say something, to help him forward, but there was only silence.

"I know something happened to you at Saint Stithians – that's why you changed schools, isn't it, because you were teased about it? I really don't want to put you through all that again. I won't make a fuss if you really don't want me to."

He stayed staring out of the window with his back to the boy. He doubted that he was doing the right thing, the sensible thing, making an offer like that. He dimly sensed a vortex forming somewhere in his own future. He could feel the edges of it spiralling out to draw him in.

"Please don't do anything, sir – I'm OK, really," Chapman said behind him. He did sound calm again.

"You're absolutely, one hundred per cent sure?"

"Yes, sir."

Dryden turned round then. He was surprised to see that the boy hadn't made any attempt to pull the gown back over himself. He was sitting down again, but if anything it had practically fallen off, and the cord had come undone.

What kind of a kid is this, he asked himself; *what the hell really did go on down there?*

"Aren't you angry? Don't you want to see them punished? They aren't worth protecting – leaving you tied up in the dark like that. What on earth were they expecting would happen to you?"

Again he waited for an answer, but Chapman just stared at the carpet.

Dryden looked at his watch. It was nearly a quarter to one. He decided to get him back into bed and try and sort it out in the morning. He'd have had a chance to think it through by then, to come up with a plan, he told himself.

"Do you have another pair of pyjamas in your locker?" he asked.

"I think they're in the laundry, sir."

Dryden picked the wet pyjamas up off the floor where he'd dropped them.

"Well you can't wear these; they're sopping wet. You'll have to sleep as you are."

Only then did he begin to think of the practicalities of getting the boy back into his bed. He didn't want to let him go with his dressing gown; he felt it would be unfair to let him go stark naked. It was dark in the dormitory, but not that dark; any one of the other boys might wake up and see him. That made him think of something else he wanted to know.

"Were any of the other boys from your dorm down there with you?"

"No, sir."

"Not even Rowell?"

"No, sir, he was asleep. I think they all were when I left, sir."

They looked at each other again. They both knew that Chapman had inadvertently given something away, narrowed the possible field of suspects, though not by much. Dryden wasn't surprised at the answer. It hadn't ever seemed likely that any of the younger boys were involved, not with all that mess. Down in the bathroom, he'd immediately thought of Voaden and his over-sexed cronies. He'd seen Voaden with him several times, pawing at him. He'd been on the verge of intervening.

"You really don't want to tell me who they are?" he asked again.

Finally Chapman did pull the dressing gown back up. He held the lapels together at his throat.

"I can't, sir," he said.

"Why not?"

"I can't say, sir."

"Did they force you down there?"

"No, sir, not really."

Again their eyes met.

"But you just went down there for a smoke – that's all, isn't it? Why didn't you shout when they started…?" Dryden asked, letting the question taper away again.

"I don't know, sir. I'm sorry, sir."

He started to shiver.

"OK, that's enough for now," Dryden said. "I want you to come and talk to me tomorrow, but you'd better get back to bed now," he said. "You're sure you're all right – you're quite sure you're not physically hurt in any way?"

The boy nodded. Then he surprised Dryden again by standing up and taking off the dressing gown.

"You can't go back to the dorm with nothing on," he said quickly. "Put it back on. I'll come with you. You can give it back to me when you get into bed."

Chapman did as he was told and Dryden cautiously opened the door.

"Let's keep it quiet and make it quick," he said.

He felt ridiculous tiptoeing after the boy across the landing and down the short flight of steps to the dormitory, but it was all over in a matter of seconds. Chapman took off the dressing gown and handed it to him before slipping quickly into bed.

Dryden hovered for a few seconds and then bent down until his mouth was close to the boy's face, his lips almost touching his forehead.

"I'll dry your pyjamas somehow and bring them in to you before the wake up bell goes," he whispered quietly. "We'll talk about this tomorrow."

He straightened up and was about to go when a small hand shot out of the blankets and grabbed his sleeve.

"Please promise you won't tell anyone, sir – please," Chapman whispered urgently.

"I promise. Try and go to sleep now. Come and see me in my room straight after Chapel."

"Thank you, sir. I'm sorry, sir."

Dryden put his hand on the bed where he thought the boy's shoulder might be.

"Go to sleep," he whispered.

He stopped briefly at the door to listen, staring intently around in the darkness but he heard nothing. All the other boys still seemed to be asleep.

He was as good as his word, and he did manage to dry Chapman's pyjamas, hanging them over a chair in front of his small bar heater. He even rinsed out the top in his basin.

It became insufferably hot in the room and he had to open the door to let a draught through. The pyjamas needed to be turned around often and it took nearly an hour before he was satisfied that they were dry enough. He wondered several times whether it really mattered. Chapman could just get dressed in his normal clothes when he woke up; none of the others were likely to notice that he'd slept naked, he thought. Chapman always seemed to be just about naked in the dormitory anyway, he told himself. By the end he felt really stupid about it, but he'd said he would do it and so he did.

It was after two in the morning when he trod softly into the dormitory again. He was pleased to find that Chapman was asleep, lying on his side facing the wall. He put the folded pyjamas down on the bed behind his bare shoulders, carefully tucking them in under the bedclothes and left.

In the next bed, Rowell lay motionless in the dark, more asleep than awake, and for the second time that night, watched Dryden leave.

ELEVEN

The choir sang the first verse of *All Things Bright and Beautiful* accompanied by a dull drone from the rest of the congregation. Richardson's loud voice, slightly out of key, was the only one distinguishable from the Master's pews.

Keep your lips moving, Dryden reminded himself at the beginning of the second verse. He didn't want to get ticked off by Kennedy again for not singing. The parson said it set a bad example for the boys.

Dryden didn't feel there was anything bright and beautiful about the morning. He'd only managed about three hours sleep. He was feeling it already. He hoped that Kennedy's sermon would be a short one for a change.

He looked through the sea of faces, looking for Chapman, but couldn't find him. Then he started thinking about the tie again. He'd only remembered it when he'd dropped off the boy's pyjamas. He had gone down to fetch it, excitedly thinking that it would be a clue to the identity of the culprits.

It had turned out to be Chapman's own tie, his name neatly spelt out in blue stitched letters on a little white label. He had given it to Chapman in the morning, when the boys were getting up. It had provided an excuse to check up on him. He had even pretended to tick him off about it.

As the hymn ended, Kennedy made his way up to the pulpit. By the time the congregation was seated he was ready. His bald pate shone in a shaft of sunlight coming through one of the arched windows. The effect would have been dramatic on a more robust man, showing cosmic approval of the words he was about to utter. It served instead to show how old and dishevelled the parson actually was.

"He giveth and he taketh away," he began eventually.

Half the minds in the stuffy chapel shut down immediately. The other half had already drifted away to a hundred different places peopled by all kinds of real and imaginary beings. Kennedy droned on in the background of these other worlds, his voice reduced to the kind of dull hum people hear in railway stations: announcements full of messages for someone else.

Bruder sat alone in the front pew staring up intently at the pulpit, his hands resting on his knees. He was wondering whether he had done the right thing, the correct thing. The more he thought about it the more he worried that he hadn't. But it was too late now. They were waiting outside, or should be, ready to come in. He had already sent a note through to Kennedy saying he wanted to make an announcement at the end of the service. That would annoy him, but the intention was good: the old man would see that soon enough. He took his glasses off and blinked his eyes, forcing himself to pay attention to Kennedy's rambling sermon. The parson sometimes asked him questions afterwards, pretending to want to debate some point or other. Bruder knew it was really just a way of checking that he hadn't nodded off.

Voaden shifted uncomfortably on the hard pew. He had scribbled a note too and watched its progress as it went surreptitiously from hand to hand. He lost track of it for a while but picked it up again as it crossed the aisle to a boy near Chapman. He watched intently until it reached its intended destination.

Chapman opened the note and read it. *Meet me after Chapel. Nick*, was all it said.

Chapman looked around until he saw Voaden looking at him from a sea of heads across the way. He mouthed the word *Can't* and then *Dryden*. Voaden looked blank, so he repeated the exercise. It seemed to work then, because Voaden nodded. He leaned back in his seat and looked up at Kennedy. The expression on his face showed that he was disappointed or angry or both. Beside him, Ainsworth blew Chapman a kiss but the boy didn't see that. He crushed the note up into a little ball and slipped it into his jacket pocket.

Beside him in the pew, Rowell couldn't stop wondering what Dryden had been doing with his friend's pyjamas in the middle of the night. He had come very close to asking several times that morning, from the moment they had woken up, in fact, but he hadn't been able to. The question shrivelled in his throat each time he tried. He was afraid of the answer he might get. There could be any number of explanations he kept telling himself, but only one that kept making horrible and pervy sense.

Kennedy suddenly stopped preaching, catching everybody by surprise. He switched the reading light off in the pulpit.

"We will close with Hymn No. 354," he said. "Before you file out the Headmaster has an announcement to make." He was unable to completely hide the irritation in his voice.

Bruder stood up when they began singing the last verse.

He felt ridiculous about what he was going to do, more like the ringmaster in a circus than a headmaster. He positioned himself at the head of the aisle, turning to face the congregation and waited for complete silence. He cleared his throat as the last strains of the organ died away.

"As most of you know Reverend Kennedy's dog Winston died last week. He had a long life and a happy one and he was a good companion who will be sorely missed by all of us at school," he said.

The old parson was standing by the steps to the pulpit, looking bewildered. Bruder turned and addressed the rest of the short speech directly to him.

"No good companion can be replaced, Stanley, but some of the senior boys came to see me the other day. They suggested that we get you another dog. I agreed immediately, and that is exactly what they've done."

Bruder looked back down the aisle like a master magician, expecting to see a couple of the Upper Fifth form boys coming towards him with a puppy. The boys were coming down the aisle but between them was one of the largest black dogs Bruder had ever laid eyes on. The smile abruptly vanished from his face. He immediately thought that he had been set up, that the dog was a practical joke. He stared incredulously as the huge creature padded down the centre of the chapel towards him, pulling the two boys in its wake, its big red tongue hanging out. He glanced at Kennedy, half expecting the old parson to have fainted. Instead he was grinning broadly; he had actually come forward to receive his gift.

The dog seemed to know immediately who its new master was. It ignored Bruder, brushing past him. It took the combined strength of both boys to hold it back. It nearly knocked Kennedy over anyway, making a huge fuss, ecstatically wriggling its whole body, slobbering all over the parson's outstretched hands.

Bruder's face was scarlet with rage. He stared at Drummond, looking for someone to blame.

How in God's name is an old fart like this going to look after a dog like that? he wanted to shout.

Drummond shrugged his big shoulders. He didn't know what had happened. He'd been expecting a spaniel.

Voaden waited on the pavement beyond the chapel gates as the rest of the boys filed out. Root and Ainsworth waited with him.

What had just happened inside the chapel had created a carnival mood among the boys, a sense of release like the last day of term. There was a lot of laughter and light-hearted pushing and shoving. The invisible cage of rules and timetables seemed to have lifted temporarily. The set expressions on the faces of the three boys waiting by the gate set them apart, and they were ignored all the more because of that.

Chapman and Rowell were almost swept past in the general crush but Voaden's sharp eyes caught sight of them. He moved quickly to intercept Chapman, grabbing his elbow and guiding him out of the stream of bodies. Rowell followed a little way behind, not wanting to get too close. Root and Ainsworth moved in behind Voaden, cutting him off anyway.

"Are you OK?" Voaden asked.

Chapman nodded. "I just have to see Dryden, that's all."

"What about?"

The boy looked up at the steeple of St Mary's. It towered into the sky above the tiled roof of the chapel. His elbow was still firmly gripped in Voaden's fingers and when he didn't answer fast enough the grip tightened.

"What about?" Voaden repeated.

"Ow, you're hurting me – I don't know. He told me to come and see him this morning."

"You're not pissed off, are you?"

"No."

Voaden swung him round so that they were facing each other, blocking out the steeple and the sky.

"You're not going to tell him about the pill or anything, are you?"

"No, of course not." Chapman said, and he smiled slightly. "It was really weird, but fun – sort of."

The tense look lifted from Voaden's face. He relaxed. He let go of the boy's arm and ruffled his hair.

"You're a good sport, Pete," he said with a grin, glancing at the other two.

Chapman looked away again, back towards Rowell, who was hovering uncertainly behind Root and Ainsworth. They looked relieved too.

"I've got to go," Chapman said, "Dryden said I must come straight after chapel."

"Fine, good luck. I'll see you later, then."

The three bigger boys stood and watched as Chapman and Rowell crossed the street, hurrying between the slow moving cars belonging to parents picking up their dayboy sons.

"Why don't you just tell that big jerk to fuck off?" Rowell said when they were over the road and safely out of earshot.

Chapman shrugged.

"He's going to end up getting you into real shit."

Chapman shrugged again, but Rowell could see that he was upset. He'd seemed preoccupied and worried all morning. Rowell was convinced it was because Dryden had been fiddling around with him in the night. Still he couldn't bring himself to ask about it.

At the foot of the staircase that led up to Bruder's office, Chapman stopped and stared up as though he were expecting someone to come down. His eyes were suddenly bright with the first flush of tears.

"Are you all right?" Rowell asked, echoing Voaden's words of a few moments before.

Chapman nodded. "I'm fine – no problem."

He sniffed a little and then he turned and gave a big smile, blinking his eyes to clear the tears. He abruptly grabbed Rowell around the neck just like he'd done on the run at the foot of the Downs. It was a hug really, pretending to be something else, and he let go almost immediately.

"You're a real dork," he said.

"I am?" Rowell said with mock indignation. "You're the king of the jerks."

"I know," Chapman said. "Will you wait for me in the dorm? I want to get out, go to the beach or something."

Rowell nodded.

"Good luck with Drydork," he said. He really meant it, more than his friend could know.

TWELVE

Dryden's ribs hurt. He thought he might have injured himself trying to keep the laughter from bursting out when he'd seen Bruder's expression. Apart from the boy escort, the dog had looked like something from a gothic nightmare advancing towards the portly headmaster through the chapel gloom.

He stopped smiling to himself when Chapman knocked softly at his door.

They resumed their positions of the previous night, with Dryden on the bed and the boy in the chair. The moment they sat down, Dryden regretted recreating the same scene like that. Chapman seemed fine though, exploring his face as usual with his remarkable, bright eyes. He smiled slightly, and there was only a hint of awkwardness or embarrassment.

"That was quite a performance in chapel, wasn't it?" Dryden said.

"Yes sir," Chapman replied. The smile even spread a little.

"Reverend Kennedy should be able to ride that dog in the Grand National."

The boy grinned briefly at the incongruous image.

Dryden leaned forward on the bed, bringing his face closer and down to the same level. He looked at the boy's knees, not at his face, wondering where to start, already having forgotten what he had just rehearsed during Kennedy's sermon.

Chapman broke the ice for him. "Thanks for bringing my pyjamas, sir," he said.

"I'm afraid you'll still have to deal with Matron with all those buttons gone," Dryden said.

Chapman nodded. "And for fetching my tie, sir."

Dryden looked up at that, into his face. The tie had been worrying him all morning. It was round his neck now where it should be, but in his mind's eye Dryden could still see it tied tightly around his small ankles. The tips of his fingers hurt slightly from undoing the knot.

"How did your tie come to be down there?" he asked. He was unable to keep a slight note of accusation out of his voice.

"I don't know, sir."

"Did one of the other boys take it?"

"I suppose so sir, I don't know. I think it was hanging on the end of my bed."

Dryden wondered whether Chapman understood why he was asking. The only reason to take the tie like that, in the middle of the night with everyone in pyjamas, was to use it for exactly what it had been used for – at least he couldn't think of any other reason. That meant nothing spontaneous had actually happened, no one had really got carried away, as the boy had so quaintly put it. It had been thought out before hand. He debated with himself whether to say as much but decided against it.

"No after effects? You're definitely not physically hurt?" he asked.

"My ankle hurts a bit, sir, but it's nothing really."

Dryden looked down at his feet. The boy shifted them slightly, conscious of his dirty shoes.

"And you still won't tell me who they were?"

Traces of anxiety and irritation flitted across Chapman's features. He thought that had been settled.

"I can't, sir; I don't want my parents to know," he said.

Dryden nodded. That made sense, he thought. They would inevitably find out if the whole thing did become public, if there were some kind of inquiry – Bruder would probably tell them to cover his own arse. But it wasn't really enough of a reason.

"You're a strange boy, Chapman. If I were you, I would be as angry as hell. I wouldn't care a damn about what happened to the thugs who did something like that to me – if they got kicked out of school, I'd be leading the cheering."

"I'm sorry, sir."

"And if they do it again?" he asked.

That seemed to really startle the boy. Dryden thought for a moment that he'd found a way through but he was soon disappointed. Chapman wrestled with the possibilities for a while, seeming to weigh up things only he could know. Then he shrugged slightly or shivered, Dryden couldn't decide which, and looked at him, searching his face again. He said nothing.

Dryden waited a while longer and then shook his head slowly from side to side.

"You're not leaving me with a lot of options, are you?"

"What do you mean, sir?"

"If it does happen again, or something even worse, if that's possible, and then it comes out that I knew about this and did nothing…"

He let the sentence trail away, regretting having made it sound as though he was more worried about himself than the boy.

"But you promised you wouldn't tell anyone, sir."

There was alarm and even a hint of anger in Chapman's voice. He was beginning to feel cornered. Dryden didn't want to scare him, to make things more difficult, and so he backed down.

"Don't worry, I'll keep my promise. But I want you to realise that it's not an easy one for me to make. I'd like to see those boys punished, I'd like to be able to protect you – that's what I'm here for and that's what I'd like to do – but you're making it well nigh impossible."

"I'd never tell anyone, sir, ever, I promise," Chapman said emphatically.

Dryden nodded. *We've got a pact then,* he thought: *you, me and two or three over-sexed, anonymous yobs who like to tie you up and wank all over you. Let's hope they don't get other ideas.* He seriously considered saying that out loud, but instead he took a different route. He convinced himself that it had some relevance.

"What exactly did happen to you at Saint Stithians? You can tell me that, can't you?"

Chapman didn't answer straight away. He stood up and hesitated briefly before sitting down right next to Dryden on the bed, almost touching. The simple incongruous shift totally changed the dynamics in the room. Dryden wondered why he'd done it. He edged away very slightly on the bed but he didn't get up. He didn't want to seem to rebuff the strangely intimate gesture.

"Mr Jenkins kissed me in class, sir. He'd done it before, it was no big deal."

"What do you mean, he'd done it before?"

"Lots of times and when I had nightmares, sir."

"What kind of nightmares?"

"I don't know, sir. He used to wake me up in the dorm sometimes and whisper that I was having a nightmare and I should come through to his bed for a while."

"And did you?"

"Yes, sir."

"Why on earth did you do that?"

"Because that's what he wanted, sir," Chapman replied.

Dryden opened his mouth, intending to apologise but he decided against it. It was a natural enough question. He didn't know whether he understood the answer.

"Did he get into bed with you?"

Chapman nodded solemnly. Dryden got the impression, rightly or wrongly, that the boy was beginning to enjoy his embarrassment, that he was being punished for asking for the sordid details, that maybe he deserved to be.

"Yes sir. He used to cuddle me for a long time. I didn't like it, sir – I didn't like *him* much." Chapman paused for a moment as though remembering. "Then he would get upset and say I was fine and I must go back to bed. It was really weird."

Dryden nodded again. He had to concentrate to stop himself. The bed under him felt like quicksand and he felt a powerful urge to stand up, but he didn't. He thought it would seem as though the boy repelled him, and that certainly wasn't true. He didn't know what to do or say next.

"Do you think I'm a homo, sir?"

Dryden was startled by the question, but he answered quickly and with conviction.

"No, of course I don't – you're much too young to be thinking things like that. It's utter nonsense; you're only just thirteen, for goodness sake. And you like girls, don't you?"

"Yes sir – except the really fat ones."

"Hardly anyone likes the really fat ones, Chapman."

They smiled at each other briefly over that, discovering something in common.

"Have these other boys been calling you a homo?"

Chapman shrugged and Dryden assumed that meant yes.

"Well don't take any notice of them, they don't know what they're talking about."

The boy nodded, seeming to be satisfied.

"I didn't want to get into Mr Jenkin's bed, sir. I've never told anyone else about it," he said.

Dryden sensed that Chapman thought he was sealing the pact by giving him another secret and maybe it was like that. There had to be some kind of special bond between them after last night, he thought.

"I'm sure you didn't want to. He was obviously a very troubled man," Dryden said.

"What do you mean, sir?"

"He shouldn't have done that," Dryden said. He left it at that. "Did any of the other boys at Saints know about it?"

"I don't think so, sir – maybe Cooper."

Dryden nodded and then he stood up. The boy stood up beside him.

"You've been really good to me about this, sir."

He seemed genuinely sincere, not just buttering him up. Dryden felt his heart swell a little. He felt like hugging him but instead he put out his hand and ruffled the boy's hair, remembering too late that he had seen Voaden doing exactly the same thing.

"I'm glad I've been able to help a bit. I'm glad I found you before anyone else," he said. He wondered what might be happening if it had been someone else. "I could help more – if you'd let me; but let's not go over all that again. If you change your mind, just come and see me, whenever you like, day or night. If they go after you again just shout your head off and run in here, run like hell," he said.

"Thank you, sir. I will, sir, I promise. Can I go now?"

"Yes, but I want one more promise."

Dryden let that hang in the air for a few moments while the boy looked up at him a little apprehensively.

"Absolutely no more smoking – do you understand?"

"Yes, sir."

The boy was halfway out of the door when Dryden stopped him again.

"One last thing. Try and stay away from Voaden and his friends. They're much bigger than you."

The boy looked at him, holding on to the door. He didn't nod or say anything. Dryden didn't know quite what to make of that.

"OK, off you go."

Dryden stood motionless in the middle of the room when the boy had gone, thinking about what had been said and not said and worrying too about his own feelings. He thought it had been really odd, the way Chapman came and sat down so close beside him on the bed. If it had been any other boy that age he would have regarded it as impertinent, but instead he was glad Chapman had done it.

He looked at his watch and got a bit of a start, realising that Sarah would be outside in the car in less than ten minutes.

There were quite a few boys in the dorm when Chapman got back. It was hot and stuffy. Rowell was struggling with the long pole with the hook on the end trying to open one of the high windows. It was a tricky business and more than one window had been broken like that, some because two boys were fighting over who should use the pole. But every broken window was worth four strokes of the cane from Bruder, whether it was an accident or not. He was fed up with the bills from the glazier.

Pearce was lying on his bed watching Rowell, debating whether to sneak up and tickle him under the armpits. He was distracted from that when Chapman came in.

Virtually all of them knew Dryden had summoned him, and they wanted to know why.

"You were a long time," Pearce said loudly. "Was Drydork teaching you how to wank?"

Chapman stooped and picked up a soccer boot from the floor by one of the beds and hurled it hard. Pearce saw it coming, and he curled up and rolled over but the boot hit him in the back, and it must have hurt.

"Fuck you, you stupid shit," Pearce bellowed, nursing his back.

He recovered quickly and charged across the dorm, bouncing over the intervening beds. He knew he could flatten Chapman with ease. He was nearly within reach when he tripped, falling between the last two beds and banging his shoulder on one of the metal frames. Now it was worse; he had been made to look like a complete idiot.

"Fuck you," he said again, rising to his feet, holding his shoulder, knowing with mounting fury that he couldn't press home the attack.

"You're a first class turd, Pearce," Leomond said beside him. "Maybe Drydork will give you wanking lessons if you ask him really nicely."

Pearce didn't reply. He turned away to concentrate on nursing his injury, tears of pain and anger in his eyes. He didn't want to have a confrontation with Leomond; he knew he could sort out Chapman, but Leomond was big. He had always been an unknown quantity.

When he was sure that Pearce was out of action, Leomond turned to Chapman. He was sitting on his bed reaching into his locker, seemingly unconcerned. Rowell was there too, standing by his own bed

"And how *was* the wanking lesson?" Leomond asked in a deadpan voice.

Chapman smiled up at him weakly and pulled a face, feeling exhausted and keyed up at the same time.

"I really, really must have a ciggey," he said.

He found what he was looking for and folded the bank note over once, thrusting it down into his trouser pocket.

"Will you come to the shop with me, Leo? You look sixteen."

"No."

"Please, Leo," Chapman pleaded, putting his hands together.

"What would I get?"

"A Mars bar?" Chapman suggested brightly.

"Two Mars bars – no, a Mars bar and a Bounty," Leomond said.

Chapman quickly agreed. He turned his attention to Rowell, grateful that he'd dropped the pole and come running when Pearce was hurtling towards him. The end of the pole had nearly brained Thornton on the way down.

"Thanks for galloping to my rescue, Chris," he said.

"That's fine, but I doubt he'll just let it pass like that," Rowell said, looking over at Pearce.

He was on his own bed again making a big production out of his injured shoulder. Higgins was with him, glowering over at them every now and again.

"Stuff him. Drydork's a very nice bloke."

Rowell looked at him and wondered what that really meant. He could see a corner of Chapman's folded pyjamas peeking out from under his pillow. Pearce's joke had turned him cold inside, landing like a jagged rock in the pit of his stomach.

"What *did* Dryden want to see you about?" he asked cautiously.

Chapman was bending forward fiddling with his shoe and he seemed to take a long time over it before straightening up. Even then he didn't look directly at Rowell when he answered.

"Nothing really – just how I was and stuff," he said.

He stood up and looked at Leomond and then at Rowell.

"Can we go then?" he said.

"Aren't you going to get a chit?" Leomond asked.

Chapman shook his head.

"We can go to Jessops through the back streets."

"And what if we bump into a prefect or one of the masters?"

Chapman shrugged. "We won't," he said.

Leomond and Rowell looked at each other and then Rowell shrugged too. That seemed to settle it.

"I'm going to get you, you horrible little dweeb," Pearce shouted as they walked out.

Chapman raised two fingers at him then ducked out of the door before the soccer boot had a chance to come back.

THIRTEEN

The red MG was parked in the street right outside the main school gate. A small group of boys was hanging around, looking at it admiringly. Sitting in the driver's seat, Sarah flattered herself that they were also looking admiringly at her.

Dryden felt very self-conscious and emasculated walking around the car to the passenger side. He climbed in quickly, hoping that Sarah would start up and get away as rapidly as possible, but she didn't.

"Would you like to drive?" she asked, understanding that he was feeling awkward about it.

"No, let's get the hell away from here," he said in a low voice.

"Are you sure?"

"Absolutely."

Even then she seemed to take ages to turn the key. When the motor was running and she was ready to pull away, a long procession of other cars suddenly appeared in the street.

They still sat there with the boys gawking at them, waiting for a gap in the traffic.

"Which way?" Sarah asked.

"Back that way, I think, but you better go round the block," he said.

She didn't take his advice though. When there finally was a gap she roared into a U-turn, not quite making it in the narrow street. The front right wheel mounted the kerb, narrowly missing a lamppost. Then she had to brake hard because three boys were crossing the street, not having expected her to come back round like that.

"That's him," Dryden said through clenched teeth.

"Who?"

"Never mind."

Rowell and Chapman had leapt onto the pavement, but Leomond was a little slower, apparently prepared to risk getting run over for the sake of his dignity. But she didn't hit him, and when he was safely out of the way, she drove forward a little, stopping beside them.

"I'm very sorry, boys," she said, trying to sound disarming.

Two of them grinned back but the tubby black boy looked unhappily the other way.

Dryden scowled at the dashboard, wishing he had accepted her offer, willing her to get going again. He didn't realise immediately that Chapman was calling him, trying to get his attention.

He had come forward to the driver's door, leaning into the car.

"Sorry, Miss," he said, giving her a beautiful smile. He immediately turned his attention back to Dryden. "Can we have a chit, sir? We want to go for a walk down to the harbour."

They were already beginning to cause a minor traffic jam. The second car back hooted. Dryden looked at Chapman and then at Sarah. The same car hooted again, a longer blast this time.

"OK, you can go," he said crossly, looking at his watch. "I'll give you a note later. Be back for lunch, one o'clock."

"Thanks very much, sir," Chapman said, grinning broadly. He stepped back onto the pavement. "Sorry, Miss," he repeated.

"You're welcome," she said. She put the car into gear and roared away down the street. They'd gone half a mile before either of them spoke.

"Sorry Philip, I didn't mean to embarrass you like that," she said.

"You didn't, no problem at all. It would have been easier to go round the block, though," he said, stating the obvious.

She accepted the mild reproof, knowing she deserved it.

"Was that him?"

Dryden nodded. He immediately knew what she meant. As things had turned out, she'd been given a really close view.

"He's breathtaking," she said.

He didn't reply, not wanting to get drawn into it again.

"That is the boy you were talking about, isn't it?" she said, not letting him off the hook.

"Yes."

"The Head Prefect's made an excellent choice."

He would have smiled at that normally. She wasn't to know just how tasteless her joke had been. She was surprised when he didn't react at all, staring expressionless at the road ahead. For an instant the thought flitted into her head that he had a crush on the boy too, but she dismissed it quickly, ticking herself off for letting it in. It was obvious that he didn't want to talk about it, though, so she changed the subject.

"So how was the interview in the end?" she asked.

"Bloody horrible. They had a shrink sitting at the back taking notes."

"Blimey."

He thought back to the oak panelled room with the line of three bank managers staring at him with granite faces. They had smiled at the beginning, and all three smiles had vanished at precisely the same instant. Then the grilling started, and it was all hypothetical crap. He could imagine the shrink's pencil going ten to the dozen in the background. That had been mighty distracting.

"What would you do if you were managing a branch of the bank in Utter Pradesh and the whole staff went on strike because the envelope glue had some gunk in it they didn't like?" he asked, adopting a pompous accent.

"Call my mum?"

"That was probably the right answer. Everything I said I'd do seemed to be wrong. In the end I said I'd fire the lot of them. They looked especially glum when I said that."

"So that's that, then?"

"No, funnily enough I don't think so. They phoned me the next day to say how impressed they'd been, and they want me to come up again next week for another grilling."

"Well, that's good," she said, trying to put conviction into her voice.

She knew she'd failed when she saw him looking at her from the corner of her eye.

"Are you really going to cook me lunch?" he asked.

"Why? Don't you trust me?"

He smiled, feeling naughty, thinking back to some of the abominable concoctions she'd come up with in their flat in Oxford.

"I have improved a bit," she said, smiling too.

"I never said anything."

"Well, I'm not actually going to cook anything anyway. Cold meat and salad. I can't stuff that up too badly, can I?"

"Sounds great."

"Liar."

"I'm serious. Hot day, salad, just the thing."

Her flat was on the top floor of a large terraced house in Worthing, two streets back from the seafront. It seemed very spacious to Dryden after his small room, and he recognised the odd piece of furniture and a rug carried over from their Oxford digs. There was a photograph on a small table of them both standing on the Tay Bridge, looking younger, both with much longer hair. He picked it up, pleased that she still had it, trying to remember who had been holding the camera.

"Remember how freezing it was that day?" she said, coming to look over his shoulder.

He nodded and they both stared at the little window into the past for a few moments. He put the frame back down on the table and looked round again.

"I like the flat," he said.

"It's only ten minutes to the hospital."

"That's handy," he said. "I don't even have to get out of bed to be at work."

She put her arms round his waist from behind, hugging him tightly and burying her face in his back, between his shoulder blades. When she spoke, her muffled voice seemed to come from inside him.

"Why don't you give up the house master thing and move out, come and stay here."

"What about Utter Pradesh and the bank managers?" he said.

"Stuff the bank managers."

He didn't reply, enjoying her closeness, but her words started his mind worrying again, about where he was, what he was, about the future. She could feel the tension and let go so he could turn round.

"I'm serious, Philip," she said and she had on her serious face to prove it.

"So you don't think I should become a bank manager?"

"There are banks in England, there's one down on the corner."

He smiled at that, at the absurd contrast – Worthing or Utter Pradesh, it was all the same when it came to counting other people's money.

It was his turn to put his arms around her, and they kissed for a while, seeming to forget briefly about everything else. But after a bit the fire went out and she knew that his mind had kicked in again, asking question, wanting answers.

"I couldn't just walk out in the middle of term anyway," he said.

"Couldn't they get someone else?"

He thought about that, how everyone considered himself indispensable, no matter how tiny his empire.

"I suppose so, but it would be a bit of a shitty thing to do to them."

"They'd recover," she said, not really caring.

He looked over her head at the painting on the wall. It had been in the Oxford flat, and he'd never really taken much notice of it back then. It was a pastoral scene, full of wild flowers, rocks, a profusion of unruly shrubs and bright sunshine. He could see all that, but overlaid somehow in his mind was Peter Chapman's incredibly beautiful face, his bright eyes searching, it seemed to him, into the very depths of his soul.

"No, I really can't this term," he said, looking away from the picture and kissing the top of her head. "There's too much on the go and it wouldn't be fair. Besides I have to give notice."

"Well give them notice now at least. How much longer is it?"

"About five or six weeks still. I suppose I could do that," he said, almost to himself, not sounding very convinced. Then he suddenly realised that he was rebuffing her and he didn't mean or want to hurt her. "Yes," he said much more emphatically, "I could do that."

He hugged her tighter to emphasis his commitment.

"But you still want to go on teaching?" she asked.

"You've put me off banks."

"No I haven't."

"Yes you have."

"You've put yourself off."

"No I haven't."

"So you do want to be a bank manager?"

They started giggling then and he pulled her backwards and they collapsed in a heap onto the couch, kissing in earnest, exploring each other's bodies with impatient hands, forgetting about lunch. They made love on the couch and there was a huge amount of passion in him, more than she remembered. It surprised and exhilarated her to the point of near exhaustion. When it was done he went to the bathroom first to clean up, leaving her on the couch hugging a cushion.

There was a yellow plastic duck on the edge of the bath and he smiled at that, glad she'd kept it too. The red circles around the eyes were mostly rubbed off but it still looked cheerful. He remembered trying to drown it with his toes in the bath back in the flat in Oxford but it kept popping up and righting itself, as it was designed to do, smiling happily. He'd bought the duck and she had teased him endlessly about it when he came back from the shops one day with the duck buried in among the groceries.

"I see you've still got Captain Quack," he said in a loud voice from the bathroom.

She didn't answer, pretending not to hear. She remembered how she'd thrown it out once when it was looking dishevelled and he hadn't bothered returning her calls. She had gone down early in the morning before they collected the rubbish and fished it out of the bin. It was still smiling even after that experience.

She lay on the couch staring at the ceiling, listening to the water falling in the shower. She closed her eyes and started to drift away, waking again when the water stopped.

He came back into the lounge with a towel around his waist, still wet from the shower, his hair standing out as though he'd had a massive electric shock. He bent down over the couch and kissed her gently on the forehead.

"I see you've still got Captain Quack," he repeated.

She nodded, smiling. "He refused to leave."

He straightened up, not quite knowing how to interpret that, but feeling too content to bother with it.

"Are you still going to give me lunch?" he said, pulling off the towel, and then vigorously drying his hair.

"I suppose you've earned it," she said lazily. She stretched her arms, trying to summon the energy to get up.

He dropped the towel and pounced on top of her. He tickled her sides until she giggled and screamed at him to stop.

"OK, OK, you really deserve it," she said breathlessly, getting up and hitting him with the cushion.

He got dressed slowly while she showered, absorbing the room and imagining himself living there with her, doing what they'd just done. His eyes rested on the painting again. The sun, though out of view, seemed to be shining down on that anonymous wilderness with a much greater intensity than the one outside.

He was still looking at the painting when she came out of the shower, drying her own hair.

"Where is that?" he asked.

She looked at the painting too, trying to recall.

"I think it was painted in Greece," she said.

FOURTEEN

The three boys decided to head for the beach instead of the harbour and find a newsagent along the way. They could always say they were going to the harbour if someone challenged them; the routes weren't that different, only towards the end.

They found a shop easily enough but had hung around for a long time outside, trying to work up Leomond's courage. Back in the dorm, he had seemed supremely confident; faced with the reality of being ticked off or worse, he faltered badly. The enticement of an additional Mars bar seemed to have little effect. Chapman and Rowell had to resort to ridicule when nothing else seemed to work. In the end he had gone in, perhaps feeling that the embarrassment he might suffer inside couldn't be any worse.

As things turned out, the shop assistant handed over the pack of cigarettes without a murmur. She didn't really care, having her own cigarette going in an ashtray right then and being barely sixteen herself. The black boy could have been thirty for all she knew, or so she said to herself, discounting the school uniform. But she really understood exactly what was going on. She could see Chapman and Rowell through the window, hanging around on the pavement and they were very obviously under age. She looked several times at Chapman, liking what she saw.

"Have you got any Bountys?" Leomond asked, his confidence restored now that the pack of Embassy was sitting snugly beside his Mars bar on the counter.

"We've run out, they're delivering tomorrow," she said.

Leomond thought for a moment, eyeing the merchandise again. He took a second Mars bar and added it to his collection. He looked up at her, perched higher than he was on a stool behind the counter.

"Is that it?" she asked.

He nodded.

She took the money and rang up the amount on the old fashioned till.

"What's his name?" she asked as she handed Leomond his change.

"Who?"

She gestured with her chin, holding her chewing gum between clenched teeth. Leomond looked out of the window at his two friends.

"Which one?"

"The good looking one," she replied. Her tone suggested it should be obvious.

"You mean Peter?" he asked, beginning to understand.

"That's a nice name," she said thoughtfully and began chewing her gum again.

Leomond picked up the chocolates and the cigarettes, putting them into his jacket pocket and turned to leave.

"Give him this," she said suddenly, handing him a small tube of sweets.

Leomond took them but he didn't put them in his pocket, realising immediately that they were a kind of bouquet. He grinned broadly when he saw that they were Love Hearts. He didn't like them much; they made his mouth sore after half a dozen or so.

When he'd gone she watched to see what would happen. She saw the two smaller boys come up to the chubby black boy immediately. The one she was interested in patted him on the back and took the cigarettes and put them quickly into his own pocket. Then he took the small tube of sweets, his face showing surprise, listening intently to what the black boy said. They both looked back at her through the window and then Chapman smiled and waved. She smiled too and gave a little wave back, half expecting him to run away. Instead he opened the door. He didn't come all the way in.

"Thanks very much," he said.

"You're welcome," she said, feeling embarrassed now, hearing his voice and realising how young he actually was.

They looked at each other briefly but before the silence could get really awkward he stepped back, letting the door close and disappeared after the other two.

"It'll be easy to get ciggeys there," Chapman said when he'd caught up with them.

Leomond looked at him disapprovingly, his mouth full of chocolate and toffee.

"She's very sweet," he said, the words sticking to the roof of his mouth, "and pretty."

"A bit fat," Chapman said.

He opened the tube of sweets and held it out to Rowell who hesitated before taking one. He did though, wrestling it out of the tight packaging. He looked at the message.

I'm all yours, it said.

He showed it to Chapman and Leomond. Leomond glanced

at it and didn't react at all but Chapman smiled, feeling awkward. He was glad when Rowell put the sweet in his mouth and the trite message had gone, dissolving in saliva. He took a sweet out of the tube for himself and popped it into his mouth without looking at what it said.

They carried on walking for a while, following the road down to the sea but after a couple of minutes Leomond stopped. He looked at his watch.

"I'm going back," he said. "Lunch is in half an hour."

"We can be on the beach in five minutes," Chapman protested.

"What's the point? It's twenty minutes back to school from here."

"Ten if you run."

Leomond peered at him over the rim of his glasses and the look said it all.

"Well I'm going on," Chapman said, looking at Rowell.

Rowell nodded, and they parted company with Leomond, watching briefly as he walked away, taking the second Mars bar out of his pocket as he went.

"She didn't look that fat," Rowell said, reminded of the earlier exchange.

"You didn't see her properly, she's a real porker," Chapman said.

There was a lot of cloud about, and the sun kept disappearing, but it was still a warm day, and after a while Chapman undid his tie and put it in his jacket pocket. In another minute or two he took the jacket off as well, slinging it over his shoulder. He unbuttoned his shirt, pulling the tails out of his trousers so that it flapped open.

Rowell said nothing, being used to it now. Chit or no chit, he would get detention if a master or a prefect saw him like that, even on the beach, he thought. Sometimes some busy body would report you, and you might never know who it was.

They weren't really that sure of the way, walking by instinct to where they thought the sea must be, having to turn here and there in the maze of streets but always coming back to the same direction. In the end they were proved right, and the sea came up quite suddenly, held in check by the steep shingle beach. They both ran the last few yards, eager to pick up stones and hurl them into the sea. The game went on for several minutes, random throws at first but then concentrated on a piece of flotsam which appeared and disappeared at the whim of the small waves. Chapman tired of the game first and sat down by a breakwater, out of sight from the road, and took out the pack of cigarettes. He peeled off the cellophane wrapping and let it go so that it danced between his feet, caught by the slightest breeze.

"That's littering," Rowell said, sitting down beside him.

"Sorry," Chapman said, sounding unconvinced, but he picked up the wrapper and stuffed it into his trouser pocket.

He took out a cigarette and put it between his lips. He offered the pack to Rowell but he shook his head.

"It can't fall far," Chapman said with a grin.

"Stuff off."

He'd lit the cigarette and had taken the first drag, holding the smoke in his lungs and looking out to sea when Rowell nudged him in the side. A man had come over the rise from the road. He was walking down to the beach.

"Shit," Chapman said and he hid the cigarette behind his back, ready to stub it out if necessary.

The man was looking the other way but he stopped at the edge of the shingles and his head swung slowly round until he saw them. Somehow the whole thing looked a bit staged, as though he knew they were there already. He stared for a few moments and then gave a small wave. The boys didn't respond, pretending to be absorbed by the stones at their feet. The man sat down on a concrete bench, looking down carefully first to check what he was about to sit on. He was middle aged, too well dressed for the beach. He stared out over the sea or seemed to, but both boys felt he was really looking at them from the corner of his eye. They decided to move, climbing up over the wooden breakwater. Chapman still had the lit cigarette in his hand and the moment they were over and out of sight of the man he took another drag.

"We'd better get back, we're going to have to run some of the way as it is," Rowell said.

"Just a few more puffs."

"Addict."

"Dork."

Smoking fast made Chapman's head swim a little and he soon dropped the half-finished cigarette down on the round stones, trying unsuccessfully to stub it out with his shoe.

As they started to walk up the beach they were alarmed to see that the man was now standing at the top, directly in their path, looking down at them. They paused for an instant but there was no real choice and so they carried on walking over the loose pebbles taking a diagonal path to avoid coming up right in front of him.

"Are you boys from the Grammar School?" the man asked in a loud voice when they were nearly on the grass, about ten yards to his right. "I'm a friend of the headmaster."

There was no point in denying it, not with Rowell's blazer giving the game away.

"Yes, sir," Rowell said. He was dreading the lecture on smoking that he was sure was coming next.

The man walked towards them smiling and they waited. He looked them both up and down but his attention seemed to be focused mainly on Chapman. He had been the one who was smoking, and he still hadn't bothered to do up his shirt. He was holding his blazer so that it touched the ground.

"Do you fancy an ice cream?" the man asked, taking them by surprise, looking directly at Chapman, smiling still.

The boys looked at each other and back up at him. There was a brief moment of awkward silence. Then Chapman abruptly pulled his shirt wide open and gyrated his small hips, doing a poor imitation of a belly dancer, grinning and fluttering his eyelids. He even blew a kiss. The performance only lasted three or four seconds. It was enough time for the man's mouth to drop open.

"No thanks," Chapman said when he stopped. He started laughing. They both did. Then they ran like the wind. They kept running down the streets, retracing their steps, until they were well out of sight of the beach. Even then they kept walking at a brisk pace, breaking into a jog every now and again, glancing back to see whether the man was following. They couldn't know that he was still standing exactly where he had been, staring into space.

"What the shit did you do that for?" Rowell said when they stopped, still grinning nervously.

"That's what he wanted," Chapman said, "and a lot more, I bet."

"Perhaps he really is a friend of Bruder's," Rowell said.

Suddenly none of it seemed at all funny any more.

"Maybe he is; who cares," Chapman said. "He was trying to pick us up."

"You can't know that for certain."

Chapman gave him a pitying look but he didn't answer.

"He could still report us," Rowell said. He was anxious now, worried what might happen.

Chapman shrugged.

"We'd better be back by one," he said. "I don't want to get into trouble with Drydork."

They started running again but the mention of Dryden coupled with what had just happened on the beach finally overwhelmed Rowell's dread of knowing. He asked the question that had been torturing him all morning.

"What was Drydork doing with your pyjamas in the middle of the night?"

Chapman stopped running abruptly.

"How did you know about that?" he asked.

Rowell stopped a couple of yards ahead and turned round. He felt the earth tilt a little under his feet. He wished he hadn't asked.

"I woke up when he came in. I saw him put them in your bed and then he went out again."

Chapman looked at him; his bright eyes danced all over the other boy's worried face. His own complexion seemed to have turned a little redder, but maybe that was just the running. He was smiling slightly still and didn't seem upset.

"I think I left my top in the bathroom," he said, starting to walk again. "Drydork must have found it."

Rowell knew he was lying, but he was only too glad to accept the explanation, to let it ride. It sounded almost plausible if you ignored the fact that Chapman had been wearing Dryden's dressing gown, he thought. He decided he didn't want to delve into it after all. His mind was already disposing of the questions, tucking them away where they couldn't do any more harm.

"You're lucky he didn't give you DT," he said as a compromise.

"He's a really great guy," Chapman said.

Hearing that, the questions paused at the door to the basement in Rowell's mind, but he gave them a nudge and they went in anyway. They went to wait in the dark with all the other restless and uncomfortable thoughts and memories.

"We'd better run," Chapman said, buttoning up his shirt. "I think we're going to be a bit late anyway."

They ran more or less the whole way back, pausing only long enough for Chapman to put his tie and jacket on, but they were still a few minutes late and the lunch bell had already gone. All the other boys were eating.

As bad luck would have it, they bumped into Drummond on the way into the dining hall. He stopped them before they could slip in and sit down. He looked meaningfully up at the big clock on the wall.

"What time is it, Rowell?" he asked

"Ten past," Rowell said in a flat voice.

"And what time are you supposed to be here, Chapman?"

"One o'clock, sir."

"Precisely," Drummond said.

He seemed to debate with himself what to do next, noticing for the first time how damp they both were. They had obviously been running hard for a long time.

"Where have you been exactly?" he asked.

Rowell and Chapman glanced at each other. Drummond immediately thought that was suspicious.

"We went to the harbour. We had a chit from Mr Dryden, sir," Chapman said.

Drummond held out his hand, motioning for the chit with his fingers.

"He said he'd give us the chit later, sir."

Drummond dropped his hand and his eyes narrowed a little. He regretted having made an issue of it. Chapman suddenly looked very vulnerable and he was the last boy on earth he wanted to punish for anything. But there were limits, especially with another boy involved.

"That's a bit lame, isn't it?" he said.

"It's true, sir, honest, he was on his way out with his girlfriend and he was in a hurry. They were already in her car, sir. You can ask him."

The detail sounded convincing. Drummond doubted he would risk concocting a tale like that if it wasn't true. It would be easy enough to check. He was very relieved.

"OK, off you go, but don't be late again. I'll eat you for lunch next time."

Rowell hurried off but Chapman didn't move straight away. He stood for a second or two in front of Drummond smiling up into his face, the sparks back in his eyes again. The Head Prefect smiled back despite himself, disturbed but pleased at the strange unspoken exchange that seemed to be taking place between them. Then Drummond watched Chapman hurry away, weaving through the forms after Rowell. He climbed in next to him on the third form benches.

FIFTEEN

The second play practice wasn't going well. Dionysus hadn't pitched up. His mother had phoned to say that he had the 'flu and wouldn't be able to come. She assured Richardson that he was learning his lines, painting a graphic picture of the noble invalid hard at work in his sick bed. She had seemed genuinely terrified that a dose of the 'flu might get between her son and an outstanding future as a great thespian.

That was the problem with picking Simpson for the part, Richardson thought; he was a dayboy and the dayboy's mothers were always hanging around.

He sat with his head in his hands, listening to the six boys who made up the Chorus drone on and on. It was obvious that none of them had learned a single line since the first rehearsal. They were all still reading from their books, lifting Euripides' words off the page one by one, mangling them into disjointed phrases. It made the great dramatist sound like a half-wit. Some words were sticking obstinately to the page, refusing to come off at all or give up any kind of meaning.

"With pie... piegree... and..."

"Phyrygian!" Richardson bellowed, standing up. "How many times do I have to pronounce it for you?"

The boys lowered their books and looked at him, hoping forlornly that he would finally call it a day. They had been going at it for nearly two hours, from soon after lunch. It hadn't been much fun at the beginning. It was agony now.

Chatsworth was sitting off to the side watching. He had learned his lines, Pentheus' first long speech and a few others at any rate. He had delivered them quite well, better the second time. He kept looking at his watch, seeming nervous and distracted. When Richardson glanced over at him he looked at it again. The teacher followed suit, looking at his own watch and then up at the clock on the gymnasium wall. Both timepieces agreed that it was nearly four o'clock.

The boys in the chorus looked at Richardson hopefully, taking the glances at his watch and the clock as a positive sign.

"We've got four weeks, that's all," Richardson said. "We're never going to get there if you don't learn the lines. I want you all to have learned up to page twenty – *Enter Herdsman* – by Wednesday."

The boys groaned inwardly but they were ready to agree to anything if it meant the teacher would let them go.

"Wednesday, straight after supper, seven thirty sharp," Richardson said.

There was a communal sigh of relief. The hall emptied out quickly. Richardson and Chatsworth were the last to leave.

"That wasn't bad, Philip, but you still need to put a bit more heat into it," Richardson said. "You seem preoccupied – everything all right?"

"Fine, sir," Chatsworth said, blinking in the bright sunlight.

"I'll give you a lift back if you like," Richardson said, fumbling around in his pockets for his car keys.

"It's OK, sir, I'd prefer to walk; I need the fresh air."

The teacher looked at him quizzically, but he didn't say anything; he shrugged his big shoulders and waddled off towards his old Jaguar.

"Pentheus is a very proud man, and you're going to have to get that out right at the start. But you're getting there – keep it up," he said over his shoulder in a loud voice.

Chatsworth watched him drive away. He started walking; he didn't head back towards the school right away, going instead around the corner of the gym building to the playing fields where he could hear boys' voices. There were about a dozen or so playing football on one of the pitches on the far side. One of them had his shirt off. For a brief instant he thought it was Chapman. He soon realised it wasn't; even at that distance he could tell easily. He turned back, heading for the gate.

He thought about the play as he walked, reciting Pentheus' words in his head. He imagined Dionysus responding except it wasn't Simpson's earnest face he conjured up: it was Chapman's, smiling and beguiling.

He dawdled on the way, taking a round-about route so that he could smoke a cigarette. It took him fifteen minutes to get back to school. He went straight to the science labs. The Photographic Society darkroom was wedged between two classrooms. It had been a storeroom originally, and it had no windows to the outside. The door was locked when he tried the handle, so he knocked. He was about to knock again when Barnes opened the door. He stood aside to let Chatsworth in, sticking his head out briefly to check that there was no one else in the corridor. He locked the door again. With the daylight gone, the room turned red. It was moist and hot and stuffy, claustrophobic. It felt like being in something's mouth, Chatsworth thought.

"Only three of them came out properly," Barnes said. "I've only just finished developing them."

"Let's have a look," Chatsworth said.

Barnes pulled the curtain back. The prints were still wet. They were hanging on a line, attached by clothes pegs. There were six in all but three of them looked solid black. Chatsworth wondered why Barnes had bothered to hang them up. He looked at the others, going right up to them, tilting his head this way and that, raising his hand but careful not to touch. His calm matter-of-fact demeanour hid his excitement well. There was bile in this throat, and he felt slightly nauseous, a little giddy, but he was grinning.

"They came out really well," he said.

"Thanks," Barnes said.

"How long before you can take them down?"

Barnes shrugged. "About twenty minutes," he said.

"For God's sake, don't leave them up here," Chatsworth said looking at him.

"I'm not that crazy."

Chatsworth looked back at the photos again. He felt something stir in his stomach, a twinge of remorse perhaps.

"God, he's a pretty little shit," he said.

As he stared at the photos, Pentheus' words from the play popped into his head again: *Away, enjail him in the horses stalls hard by, that he may see but murky gloom.*

SIXTEEN

The note had been pushed under Dryden's door. He stood
on it before he noticed it. As he unfolded the paper he saw
with a sinking feeling that it was a note from Bruder. The
headmaster's spidery scrawl asked that Dryden come and
see him in his office the moment he was back. The time
was printed in next to his initials – ten to six, less than five
minutes ago.

"Damn," he said out loud. "Sunday bloody evening. What
now?"

Maybe Sarah was right, he thought. He should just chuck it
in – tell Bruder that enough was enough. But even as he had
those thoughts he knew he had to go; curiosity was already
getting the better of his anger anyway. He looked at the note
again to check whether Bruder had written "please"; he had.
That mollified him a little too.

Bruder's office door was ajar, and Dryden could hear voices
as he came up the stairs. He knocked once, poking his head

in, and the Headmaster immediately beckoned him to enter. Bruder was dressed very casually, not even wearing a tie, a rare thing in itself. He had obviously been interrupted in his Sunday evening, just like Dryden.

Apart from Bruder, there were two other people in the room: Drummond and a man he didn't know but recognised vaguely. Drummond was standing by Bruder's desk, looking very unhappy. The other man was sitting in one of the easy chairs looking comfortable. He stood up slowly when Dryden came in and smiled at him, holding out his hand. He was middle aged, quite distinguished looking in a smarmy kind of way, Dryden thought.

"Thanks very much for coming, Philip," Bruder said briskly. "We've had search parties out for you."

Dryden looked mystified and he was.

"Let me introduce you," Bruder continued, deferring to the visitor. "This is Philip Dryden, he's the House Master of School House, teaches Maths. Philip, this is Deputy Mayor George Featherstone, and he's come to see us about a very peculiar and disturbing matter."

The two men shook hands, and Featherstone's face, now that it had a name and a title, immediately clicked into place. Dryden had seen it smiling out of the pages of the local newspaper. He vaguely remembered that not all the stories that went with the face were flattering.

Featherstone sat down again, and Bruder gestured to a chair to show that Dryden should do the same. He ignored Drummond, who was still standing by the desk more or less at attention, looking utterly miserable. Dryden had the impression that Drummond was avoiding looking at him in particular, and that made him uneasy. Things had moved too fast for him to have formed even an inkling of what the strange meeting was about, but he knew he probably wouldn't be there if he wasn't about to be blamed for something. Drummond was behaving like the finger man.

"I've been doing a bit of detective work, Philip, trying to find out which of our boys could have been on the beachfront at about half past twelve…"

"Quarter to one," Featherstone interjected.

Bruder looked at him. "At about quarter to one this afternoon; that's just before lunch. The two boys were around twelve or thirteen," he said, looking at Featherstone for confirmation.

The Deputy Mayor nodded, still smiling. Between the smiles and the relaxed posture he really seemed to be enjoying himself.

"I asked Drummond to try and do some checking and he immediately came up with a couple of contenders: Rowell and Chapman. They were late for lunch, and Chapman told him that you had given them a chit to go for a walk down to the harbour?"

Bruder turned the last statement into a question and waited for a response.

Dryden hesitated, wondering what an admission would lead on to but he couldn't lie and as yet there didn't seem to be any point in trying. He was starting to get alarmed though. It had seemed like a parlour game, but the mention of the two boys' names had changed all that.

He looked at Drummond. The Head Prefect was staring into space, obviously embarrassed at being cast in the role of sneak.

"Yes, I did give them permission, but I was in a bit of a hurry at the time, and I didn't give them a chit as such," Dryden said.

"Did they tell you they were going to the harbour, not to the beach front?" Bruder asked.

Dryden sensed that a door was being readied for closure

depending on his answer and he decided to try to keep it open.

"They could have said the harbour or the beach, I can't be absolutely sure," he said. "I can't see any real harm if they went to the one or the other. I would have given them permission for either. And there were actually three of them, Leomond was with them at the time."

The mention of Leomond seemed to derail Bruder's inquisition momentarily but he dealt with it soon enough by dragging Drummond in again. The Head Prefect confirmed that only Chapman and Rowell had been late. Leomond was already eating lunch.

"So we're back to the two boys," Bruder said. "Unfortunately, it's very much to the point as to where they were because we don't want to make a mistake in this. The incident the Deputy Mayor has reported to us took place on the beachfront. If you say you don't know where they went, it seems highly probable now that Rowell and Chapman did go to the beach," Bruder said.

Beach, harbour; harbour, beach − what's the bloody difference, Dryden said to himself.

Bruder turned to Featherstone again. "Perhaps you'd be good enough to repeat your description of the boys and tell Philip exactly what happened."

Featherstone seemed to be only too delighted. His detailed descriptions, particularly of Chapman, left little room for any doubt.

You must have had a very good look, Dryden thought.

"I usually go for a stroll along the front before lunch on a Sunday, and I happened on these two sitting by one of the breakwaters," Featherstone continued. "The one boy had his jacket and tie off and he might as well have had his shirt off too, and I decided to talk to him about it. I know the rules;

I was a pupil here myself many years ago and it doesn't do much good for the school's image, or the town's, to have a boy parading around like that in public. Anyway, at the risk of being a busybody, I called them over." He paused for a moment or two, searching for the right words to describe what happened next.

Dryden sat and listened stone-faced as Featherstone went on to describe Chapman's hip wiggling. In his version it had developed into a virtual striptease. He described how they had run away, yelling something, probably obscene, that he couldn't quite make out.

There was silence when he'd finished and the other three were all looking at Dryden.

He was beginning to find Featherstone thoroughly obnoxious. The Deputy Mayor had seemed to relish telling his sordid little tale, his pompous self-righteousness only serving to highlight the fun he'd obviously had in watching Chapman's antics and in recalling them now. The fact that he was here at all, intent on seeing the boy dragged through the dirt and probably thrashed, compounded his perversity in Dryden's eyes.

Gang raped on Saturday night and doing striptease acts for dirty old men on Sunday afternoon, he thought. He didn't know whether to laugh or cry.

"Well, Philip?" Bruder asked. "From those descriptions, is there any doubt in your mind that it was Rowell and Chapman?"

Dryden tried not to look at Featherstone, barely able to hide his anger and contempt. "It sounds as though it could have been them, but I have a hard time believing it," he said.

The ever-present smile vanished from Featherstone's face but Dryden's response was too ambiguous to risk taking offence. He said nothing.

"Go and fetch them, will you Drummond," Bruder ordered. "That's the only way to settle this."

***

Chapman was crouching by his bed, fiddling with a loose floorboard when Drummond came in to the dorm. He'd discovered it by chance while looking for a dropped coin. The space underneath was an ideal hiding place for cigarettes. He had just put the pack Leomond had bought for him in there, tucking it out of sight. He stood up, dusting off his hands on his trousers and got the fright of his life when he turned round. He looked straight into Drummond's broad chest.

"Where's Rowell?" Drummond asked with a face like an undertaker.

"In the loo, I think, sir."

"Go and get him, the Headmaster wants to see the two of you right now."

That proved unnecessary because Rowell came back in as he was speaking. He immediately saw Drummond towering over Chapman. They both looked at him and he saw the expressions on their faces. He felt like running out again, not knowing what it was about, not wanting to know, but it was too late for that.

Drummond led the way, the trio igniting speculation with their worried looks among all the other boys they passed in the corridor.

Drummond knocked on Bruder's door and then ushered the two boys in. He had to nudge them further forward into the room, away from the relative safety of the door, to get back in himself.

Rowell kept his eyes on the carpet, but Chapman looked round briefly to see who was there. He felt his heart stop when he saw Dryden, thinking immediately that he'd broken his promise. Then he saw the other man and wondered who he was, not recognising him at first. The man smiled at him, and then he understood what was actually happening. He could barely believe it. Despite himself, he smiled in return before following Rowell's example.

"Did you two boys go to the beach front this morning?" Bruder asked without any kind of preamble.

Chapman looked up again immediately, not at Bruder but straight at Dryden.

"Yes sir, we meant to go to the harbour but we got a bit lost," he said, keeping his eyes on Dryden, trying to say sorry.

Bruder ignored the excuse, turning once again to the Deputy Mayor.

"Are these the two, Mr Featherstone?"

Featherstone nodded, staring hard at Chapman, trying to picture him with all his clothes off.

"All right boys, wait outside," Bruder said.

No one was really expecting that, least of all the two boys. Chapman hesitated briefly, seeming to want to say something. Dryden sat forward a little, willing him to speak. He was disappointed when the boy simply shrugged and followed Rowell from the room.

"We'll take it from here, Mr Featherstone," Bruder said, keeping up his brisk pace. "Needless to say you have my most sincere and abject apologies on behalf of the school. You can rest assured that these two will be properly dealt with."

Featherstone seemed taken aback. He'd been hoping for a more protracted show, an opportunity to see the boys squirm and maybe even get caned. With Bruder hovering over him, he had little option but to stand up.

"I don't think you should be too hard on the second boy," he said magnanimously. "He didn't play much of a part in it – obviously led on. It's the other one who needs a good thrashing. I think he may have been smoking to top it all."

Bruder nodded, glancing at Dryden as though it was going to be his job.

Featherstone stopped outside the door where Chapman and Rowell were waiting. Bruder and Dryden were close on his heels.

"I hope you've learned a lesson from all this," he said to Chapman, smiling again, ignoring Rowell.

"Yes, sir. I'm sorry, sir," Chapman said.

"Sorry, sir," Rowell echoed.

Featherstone stayed staring at Chapman's downcast features. It made everyone feel awkward. Only when Bruder took another step forward did he eventually move, disappearing slowly down the stairs.

Bruder waited until he heard the front door open and close below. Then he spoke to the two boys, specifically to Chapman.

"Mr Featherstone is the Deputy Mayor, my boy – you chose the wrong man to insult like that. What on earth got into your head to behave like a Turkish whore?"

Chapman looked up at him, not quite sure how a Turkish whore behaved. It sounded shocking. He seemed to be on the verge of saying something again but thought better of it. He mumbled another apology and looked back down at his shoes.

"I'm going to ask Mr Dryden to punish you. You were out on his chit, and you've let him down badly," Bruder continued. "You've let us all down badly. Now off you go."

Chapman looked at Dryden, his eyes sending one last appeal, before following Rowell down the stairs. Drummond waited to get a nod from Bruder and then he went too.

"I'd like a few more words, Philip, if you don't mind," Bruder said.

He sat down heavily in one of the easy chairs when they were back in his office, looking angry and exhausted. He took his glasses off but didn't polish them, letting them dangle in his fingers and staring up at Dryden.

Dryden readied himself for some kind of lecture. He was worried that his own anger might get the better of him. The whole thing had been a kangaroo court. He was seething about that.

"God, I loathe that man," Bruder said suddenly.

Dryden looked at him uncomprehendingly at first. Then the meaning sank in.

"Featherstone?" he asked. It could only be him.

Bruder nodded.

"You didn't believe him either?"

Bruder shook his head slowly from side to side.

"Some of it, not all of it. I may be sagging at the edges, but that's because I've been round the block a few times. I've a pretty shrewd idea what really happened with those two boys. Featherstone's an elegant piece of dog shit, and you'd know that too if you'd lived in this town as long as I have. But you seemed to get the measure of him quick enough."

Dryden was astonished, not least by the language. He'd never imagined another side of Bruder. It was as though a stone Buddah had burst open, and a lively little dwarf had suddenly emerged into the sunshine, mouthing obscenities.

"Why didn't you give the boys a chance to tell their side, sir?" he asked.

"Not a lot of point in that," Bruder replied. "The sooner we got them in and out the better, shut the whole thing down. Featherstone isn't a politician for nothing. He wouldn't breeze in here if he didn't have a good story. He can't have touched them or propositioned them, nothing like that. But Chapman told him – or showed him – what he was and that obviously infuriated him – that's my guess. He came here to get his own back. But he can do the school a lot of damage, make no mistake about that – and his brother's on the Board of Governors."

Dryden's anger had evaporated. He looked down at the older man with a respect he'd never felt before, embarrassed in himself for having misjudged him so badly, now and perhaps all along.

"But you must punish the boys, Chapman at least – four strokes," Bruder said.

"Is that really fair, sir?" Dryden asked.

"I'm going to have to insist on it, I'm afraid. It may not be entirely fair but we've got to carry this charade through to a proper conclusion. These things have a way of leaking out and I don't want Featherstone to hear that we let him off with a slap on the wrist. Do you understand?"

Dryden nodded obediently but Bruder could see he was only partly convinced.

"Chapman shouldn't have behaved like that and besides they did technically lie to you about where they were going. And they were probably smoking – God knows why Featherstone left that till last," he said.

Dryden kept silent, wondering whether he should say anything. The thought that Chapman had gone straight out after their talk and lit up a cigarette saddened him rather than anything else. He shrugged it off by reminding himself that it wasn't necessarily true.

Bruder put his glasses back on. He heaved himself up out of the easy chair.

"Thanks for your help with this, Philip, and I'm sorry to mess up your evening," he said.

"I'm on duty again from six anyway," Dryden said absently.

"Yes, I thought so; no rest for the wicked, eh?"

On the way back to his room, Dryden thought about the extraordinary contrasts of the past weekend, about Sarah and the future and about Chapman dancing like Delilah at the edge of the sea. He wasn't sure what he was going to do, although Bruder had left him little option.

SEVENTEEN

Supper was a sombre affair, at least for Rowell and Chapman. The two boys picked at their food largely in silence while the others looked on like guests at an impending execution. Every now and again one of them would try to lift the mood with a joke or a smart remark but it inevitably failed, like a flame going out through lack of air.

Given the fact that he'd done nothing wrong, Rowell had been very philosophical about sharing Chapman's fate. He brushed off his apologies with remarkably good grace. In part it was because the experience in Bruder's office had completely convinced him that his friend had been right about Featherstone. The shared sense of injustice at how things had turned out was a powerful new cement in the bond between them. Deep inside, Rowell thought Chapman had been a stupid prick, but in most of his being he was proud to be facing a hostile world beside him.

In marked contrast to their mood, a little way down the table Pearce and Higgins were in high spirits. Their good humour was given an additional boost every time they looked at Chapman.

"Whack, whack," Pearce said, pretending to be a duck.

"Whack, whack, whack, whack," Higgins said, a little louder and started giggling.

Rowell looked down the table at them and pulled a face.

None of the others knew what had really happened but they all knew that an imminent caning was involved. They knew it was serious too, not some minor infringement – probably a six stroke event; Drummond marching them down the corridor to Bruder's office had seen to that.

Higgins pretended to hit Pearce on the bum with an imaginary cane. It was a difficult pantomime to perform given that his friend was sitting on a bench. The intent was clear enough though, especially when Pearce raised his backside a couple of inches and provided sound effects. A few of the other boys smiled but none of them really found it funny, not envying Rowell and Chapman their predicament.

Dryden had told the two of them to come to see him at seven thirty. They both wished he'd done it straight away, not let them worry through supper. It seemed unnecessarily cruel. They had little doubt that he was extra pissed off, having been dragged into Bruder's office because of them. That thought made them worry even more. Dryden had a reputation as a hard hitter, maybe the worst.

Pearce was about to say something else, leering down the table, when he abruptly changed his mind. He turned his full attention back to the plate in front of him.

"Cheer up," Voaden said, approaching from behind and ruffling Chapman's hair.

He squeezed himself onto the bench, sitting backwards and forcing Rowell to edge to his right. That caused a ripple among the other four boys all the way to Thornton on the end.

"What the hell have you been up to?" Voaden asked, resting his elbow lightly on Chapman's shoulder.

"Nothing much," Chapman said. He tried his best to convey a nonchalance he wasn't feeling.

"They didn't catch you having a puff, did they?"

Chapman shook his head. He stabbed at a small piece of fish on his plate, breaking it apart. The fish tasted horrible. He had no intention of eating it.

"You should have stuck with me," Voaden said. "Where were you this morning?"

"We went to buy ciggeys and then on to the beach."

"Somebody catch you?"

"No, we had a chit from Dryden," Chapman said.

Voaden thought about that for a moment.

"So what was it then?"

Chapman sighed and Voaden felt it through his elbow. He seemed very small and fragile and the bigger boy took his arm away. He stayed sitting, pressed against him on the narrow bench.

"Some old fart caught me with my jacket and tie off and reported it to Bruder," Chapman said.

Voaden waited, expecting him to go on but there wasn't any more.

"Is that it? A caning for that? That's crazy," he said.

Chapman really didn't want to tell him about the Turkish whore thing, about Featherstone's offer of an ice cream. He really didn't want to talk to him at all, to anybody. He was beginning to be overwhelmed with everything, with Voaden's body pressed up against his, his breath in his ear again, letting Dryden down, getting caned, Bruder, Pearce, all of it – but above everything else by Chatsworth and Gatesford and their pervy society.

He bit his lip to stop himself crying but a couple of

muffled sobs did shake his body. Voaden felt those too and misunderstood the cause. He stood up and patted the younger boy's shoulder, a little troubled that Chapman was being a bit of a wet about it all.

"It's not so bad, all over in a minute. Don't let it worry you," he said.

Rowell glanced up at him and Voaden glowered back, not caring a toss about him.

Given space, Chapman quickly regained his composure. He stood up too, his eyes a bit brighter. An uncertain smile came and went on his lips.

"I'm fine, it's no big deal," he said. "Come on, Chris, we'd better not be late."

Rowell got up slowly, conscious of all the eyes on him but not really caring anymore. He'd had plenty of strokes before and it hurt, but it was over soon enough; Voaden was right about that. He thought about afterwards when he would get the kind of attention people reserved for survivors, deferential and caring, full of unspoken wonder. That didn't last long either, but it was good while it did.

***

The door of the staff common room was shut when they got there. They had to knock, doing their best to ignore the small audience of curious boys hanging around, pretending to be engrossed in other things. They could hear voices inside the room and hoped there wasn't going to be an audience in there too. There was no response to the first timid knock, and Chapman eventually had to knock again, a little louder.

Dryden opened the door and stood to one side, motioning them to come in. Then he took no notice of them. Inside, Tetley and Richardson were sitting in easy chairs but they stood up as the boys came in and started to get ready to leave, picking up books and papers. It seemed to Rowell and Chapman as though they were clearing the decks for what was about to happen.

The boys stood by the door, feeling shy about being in the master's inner sanctum, let alone being there to get caned. It wasn't a big room, and the furniture certainly wasn't anything special. The dominant piece was a big kitchen table, littered with books and magazines. The room stank of cigarettes, and Richardson had stubbed one out when they came in. He hadn't done it very well; there was still a thin stream of smoke curling up from his stub in the ashtray.

The boys had been surprised when Dryden had told them to come there, expecting him to whack them in his own study by the dorm. At the end of the day though, it didn't really matter where it happened.

Tetley ignored them, but Richardson winked as he went past, as though he were wishing them luck. It was an odd thing for a Master to do in the circumstances. He was probably embarrassed about being there too. When they'd gone and the door was closed, Dryden sat down at one of the upright chairs at the big table. He beckoned them to come and stand in front of him. There was no sign of a cane but that didn't reassure them because it could be waiting anywhere.

Dryden looked at first one and then the other for quite a long time before saying anything. When he did finally speak he looked at Chapman.

"Mr Featherstone said Rowell didn't really play any part in all of this, is that true?" he asked. There was no trace of anger in his voice, none at all. The boys thought that was promising but they didn't relax, still scared that it was the calm before the storm.

"Yes, sir, he didn't do anything," Chapman said.

Dryden shifted his gaze to Rowell, raising his eyebrows to ask for confirmation but Rowell didn't know what to say. He felt oddly offended at being edged out straight away even if it did mean his backside might be spared.

When he didn't respond, Dryden had to prod him.

"Did you take your tie and jacket off?" he asked.

"No, sir."

"And did you do a belly dance for Mr Featherstone?"

Rowell smiled briefly despite himself, having to purse his lips to stop.

"No, sir, and nor did Pete, not really sir," he said.

Dryden looked slightly surprised.

"Are you calling the Deputy Mayor a liar, then?" he asked in the same quiet, almost disinterested voice.

"No, sir," Rowell said.

"But you at least entertain the possibility?" Dryden asked.

"Yes, sir, I mean no, sir. I don't know, sir," Rowell said and it made him cross to be put on the spot like that. *Of course the stupid old fart's a liar*, he thought.

Dryden looked at him quizzically for a bit, watching him go red in the face. Then he turned his attention back to Chapman.

"Do you think it would be fair if Rowell was punished?"

"No, sir," Chapman said emphatically. "He really didn't do anything at all, sir."

Dryden nodded, seeming to weigh up the testimony in his own mind, such as it was. He sat quietly for a long time studying a pencil he was turning around in his fingers. The boys looked at each other briefly and Chapman pulled a face and nodded slightly as if to say that it was looking hopeful.

"OK, Rowell, you can go – count yourself lucky," Dryden said at last.

Chapman grinned briefly, and Rowell should have been

pleased, but he just stood there staring. Dryden had been slowly metamorphosing before his eyes. He had turned into a monster. Rowell suddenly realised that the teacher had been intent on getting rid of him all along. He wanted Chapman to himself. *You want to get me out of here,* he thought; *you want Pete on his own. What were you doing with his pyjamas? What are you going to do to him now?*

"But you can't cane Pete without me," he finally blurted out angrily.

Dryden was shocked. His calm evaporated instantly.

"Don't tell me what I can and can't do, Rowell," he said.

"Sorry, sir," Rowell stammered but his flushed angry face showed all too clearly that he wasn't.

Dryden stared hard at him, his eyes unflinching.

"And don't adopt that tone of voice with me. What on earth's got into you?"

He was angry too now and perplexed. He had fully expected relief and even gratitude, not the hatred that seemed to be bubbling inside the boy, pouring out of his eyes. Solidarity was one thing, he thought, but impertinent bravado certainly wasn't acceptable.

"Sorry sir," Rowell repeated.

"It's good that you stand up for your friend, but don't be stupid about it. I'm not going to eat him," Dryden said.

Those last words gave Rowell another start. They matched up quite closely to one of the many confused and terrifying images rattling around in his head. The banality of the phrase did have a calming effect though and he thought he'd made his point now anyway; he'd made Dryden understand that he knew that something unspeakable was going on. He did start to leave then but he stopped when his hand was on the doorknob, unable to resist a last ditch effort in Chapman's defence.

"That man wasn't telling the truth, sir; he was following us," he said. As the words left his mouth, they sounded hollow and wasted to him. *What the shit does that matter to you anyway – you stupid perve*, he thought.

Dryden nodded, but he didn't say anything else, waiting for him to leave. When Rowell got no other response he did go, slamming the door behind him harder than he actually intended.

Dryden frowned at the closed door for a moment or two. He motioned Chapman to sit down in the chair opposite him. They looked at each other, and the boy smiled awkwardly, still not knowing what to expect.

Dryden shook his head slowly from side to side.

"What in heaven's name was that all about?" he asked.

"I don't know, sir," Chapman replied. He was wondering himself.

Dryden pondered about it for a little while longer and then seemed to shrug it off.

He stood up and went over to one of the easy chairs and picked up the cane that had been leaning against the back of it all along. Chapman's chest closed up when he saw it and he started to get up, anticipating the worst. But Dryden didn't tell him to bend over or look at him at all. He stayed where he was and raised the cane, bringing it down hard on the padded arm of the easy chair. It sounded just like the real thing, so real that Chapman flinched involuntarily. Dryden repeated the action three more times, pausing between each heavy stroke. The boy watched him, half in and half out of his chair, wondering what was happening, whether they were practice strokes or if it was the start of some other dark grown up game. But after the fourth stroke Dryden leaned the cane back against the chair and came and sat down again.

"I've just given you four strokes as the Headmaster told

me to do," he said softly. "I think Rowell and whoever else is listening outside probably heard that, don't you?"

Chapman stared at him. A nervous smile flickered on his lips.

"Yes, sir – I think so," he said.

"Sit down, Chapman," Dryden said in the same near whisper. "If anyone finds out I didn't really cane you, I'll probably get the sack. I hope I can count on you to play along?"

"Yes, sir. Thank you, sir."

"You probably think I've gone soft in the head."

"No, sir," Chapman said quickly, thinking exactly that.

Dryden looked at the boy across the table. He felt heart sore when he saw the fear still dancing in his eyes and in his flickering smile. *You really are so bloody beautiful*, he said to himself. It worried him because that thought was coming into his head too often.

"Why on earth didn't you speak up in Mr Bruder's office?"

"Sorry, sir?" Chapman asked, not realising what he meant.

"You were going to say what really happened on the beach, weren't you?"

As the words sank in, Chapman began to understand the reason behind the strange pantomime. The worry lifted from his face and he smiled properly. Dryden felt he could relax a bit then, too.

"He offered us ice cream, and I'm sure he really wanted to pick us up, like Chris said, sir."

Dryden nodded, showing no surprise at all.

"He's not a very nice man," he said.

Chapman looked at him, expecting him to say more, not knowing that he had already said too much.

"I didn't think Mr Bruder would believe us, sir – I was afraid it would just make things worse," he added when Dryden didn't elaborate.

Dryden thought briefly of Featherstone's last minute accusation that the boy had been smoking. That would have made it worse. He debated briefly whether to bring it up but decided that he didn't want to know or be lied to.

"I think you may be underestimating the Headmaster," he said quietly, almost to himself. He was embarrassed at his own failures in that respect. "But you're also probably right, I'm afraid; it could well have made it worse – he's an important man. It was a pity about the belly dance. That was a daft thing to do."

Chapman's cheeks flushed slightly and Dryden couldn't help smiling.

He looked at his watch. He didn't want to spend too long talking after the fake caning. He didn't want to know too much either, in case he ended up giving away more than he should about Featherstone and about his own conversation with Bruder.

"You'd better go now, but remember to play your part. Don't tell anyone what happened here, not even Rowell – no one, understand, or I'll look like a complete idiot. Pretend your bum hurts, but for goodness sake don't overdo it."

Chapman stood up, grinning like a co-conspirator.

"You're really, really nice, sir, really great again, thanks," he said.

"Don't think I'm a soft touch, Chapman, because I'm not," Dryden said. He picked up a book and opened it. It wasn't one of his but he had to look at something because he was worried that he was being an idiot. It would have been much simpler to have caned him, he thought, but he couldn't after last night; he also couldn't bring himself to give Featherstone the satisfaction, even in absentia. He knew too that the encounter wouldn't have ended like it just had if he had caned the boy. That mattered to him now, much more than he was ready to admit, even to himself.

***

Chapman played his part well. He drew on plenty of practical experience from Saint Stithians. Nobody suspected anything strange had really happened. Back in the dorm he ignored requests from Coffin and one or two others to have a look at the non-existent welts on his backside. No one pressed the point, curious still and disappointed, but respecting his privacy. After a while all the other boys lost interest and forgot about the drama, unable to tease any more vicarious thrills from it. They turned again to their own preoccupations and amusements.

Rowell was a different story. Chapman was surprised and confused at just how strong and vociferous his hatred of Dryden had suddenly become. He had ranted on about him from the moment Chapman had come out of the Masters' common room, only really shutting up when they got back to the dorm. It didn't make any sense, Chapman thought, especially since he'd been let off completely. Dryden could have given him DT, he thought; that would have been fair, even if he did know the real story. Rowell even seemed to be offended when he refused to join in cursing and ridiculing Dryden. He sensed that some of the anger was directed at him when he stuck up for the teacher. He said as much and Rowell went into a sulk.

Later in the evening when they were all getting ready for bed, Chapman changed furtively into his pyjama bottoms, keeping his backside facing the wall. He took out the top and was about to put it on when he saw that all the buttons had gone. The left sleeve was hanging by a thread. He put it quickly back under his pillow and sat down. The terror of the previous night flooded back in one huge nightmarish wave. It made him feel physically sick.

Lying on the next bed Rowell saw it in his face and sat up.

"Did Drydork do that?" he asked quietly, almost in a whisper.

"What?"

"Rip your pyjamas like that."

"Don't be crazy," Chapman said.

"Well he came in with them last night," Rowell said, still angry enough to want to know it all now.

"I told you about that," Chapman said.

Rowell swung his legs off the bed so that they were sitting facing each other, only three feet apart. No one else was taking any notice.

"That was a load of crap. He's fucking around with you, isn't he?" he whispered.

Chapman didn't reply immediately. The reason for Rowell's anger was suddenly all too obvious. He hesitated, not knowing what to say, how to deal with it. Rowell took the silence as confirmation.

"I thought so, the fucking creep," he said. "Why do you let him?"

"I don't let him. Dryden didn't do anything to me," Chapman said indignantly. "He found me last night when it was all finished; he was really great about it."

Rowell's confidence had been buoyed up by self-righteous anger. It started to sink rapidly as he realised that his explanation might be the wrong one – that there was an even bigger horror he didn't know about.

"When what was finished?" he asked cautiously.

"I can't tell you now, I'll tell you tomorrow," Chapman said.

He climbed into bed. He hadn't cleaned his teeth and he wasn't going to. Bed seemed the only really safe place.

He pulled the covers tight around him, up to his ears and rolled over to face the wall. Rowell sat staring at him. He felt as though he was hanging in mid air somehow, holding onto nothing at all. After a moment or two he moved onto Chapman's bed and leaned down to whisper in his ear.

"You've got to tell me something now."

Chapman lay completely still for a few long seconds. Then he rolled and turned his head until he was looking up into Rowell's perplexed and worried face inches from his own.

"Chatsworth and his friends are fucking around with me," he whispered emphatically. "But shut up about it. I'll tell you the whole thing tomorrow. And stop being such a jerk about Dryden, he's really, really great, more than you know."

When he'd finished his little speech he immediately rolled back, pulling the covers up over his head. He lay as still as a rock. Rowell sat where he was for quite a long while feeling foolish. His anger tried to resurface but it was hopelessly swamped by a whole new set of anxieties.

"Sorry, Pete," he eventually whispered to the blanket covering Chapman's head.

When he got no response, he picked up his toilet bag and went to wash his face and clean his teeth. He seemed to float through the bedlam going on around him in the dorm, not really hearing or seeing any of it, his mind in a frightening place.

No one disturbed Chapman, letting him sleep in peace, the kind of honoured rest and quiet reserved for casualties of war. It was a long time before the boy really slept. When he finally did drift away, much later in the night; his pillow was still damp with tears.

EIGHTEEN

Two significant things changed in Voaden's universe on Monday morning, the one good and the other bad. He was at a total loss to explain either. The good news was that Chapman seemed to be all over him, following him around like a puppy. That was good, because he thought he'd frightened him away. The bad news was that Dryden suddenly seemed to be all over him too, but with the kind of attention he would have preferred to do without. He kept popping up and getting on his case – in the hall at breakfast, at break and then in the classroom, where his sarcasm was inescapable and largely unfathomable. For the first time in many months Voaden had been given detention, and it irked him that it should be over something as trivial as not having finished his maths homework.

"What's with that stupid snotbag all of a sudden?" he had asked Root. Root could only shrug because he didn't have an answer either.

It wasn't in Voaden's nature to ponder too deeply about it. He accepted it as just one more piece of crap he had to deal with in a generally hostile world.

Enthroned on the toilet bowl, he took another deep drag on his cigarette and then passed it up to Root who was leaning against the door. Crammed between them, propping up a wall of the cubicle, Chapman waited for his next turn.

"Come on," Voaden said to Chapman for the second time, "let's have a peek."

Chapman hesitated for a while, wanting to say no again. Then he turned his backside slightly from the wall, stuck his thumb in his belt and pulled his trousers down a fraction, showing a little skin before instantly hitching them up again.

"I couldn't see anything," Voaden said.

"There nothing left – it's faded," Chapman said.

Voaden meant that he couldn't see anything of the boy's backside, but he let it pass.

"Well that figures, Drydork's such a wimp. What did he whack you with: his powder puff?"

Root passed on the cigarette and Chapman took another deep drag, glad of the excuse to be doing something rather than having to answer.

"He's given me DT for not doing my homework," Voaden continued, grinning. "Can you believe that? If he thinks I'm pitching up, he can dream on, the stupid fart."

"What happens if you don't?" Chapman asked.

Voaden blew another lung full of smoke into the already overburdened air in the cubicle.

"Fuck all. I'm leaving at the end of term – sixteen, finito, fucking out of here."

"What about your dad?" Root asked.

"Screw him," Voaden replied.

Chapman shook his head when Root passed the cigarette round yet again and Voaden took it. He had one last pull and then stood up and dropped the stub into the toilet bowl where it died with a tiny hiss. The two bigger boys went out first. Chapman was following when Voaden suddenly pushed him back so hard that he sat down involuntarily on the toilet. Before he could figure out what was happening, the door was pushed shut and he heard Kent's voice.

"It looks as though this bloody place is on fire, Voaden, there's smoke billowing out of the window."

"Sorry, sir," Voaden said.

Kent glowered at him, standing with his hands on his hips by the door.

"You're a lost bloody cause – and you Root – but if you must smoke at least get off the school grounds."

"Yes, sir."

Chapman sat stock still on the toilet holding his breath.

"Is it just the two of you? Is there someone else back there?" Kent demanded.

"Just us, sir," Voaden replied.

"Where's Ainsworth?"

Voaden shrugged but Chapman couldn't see that. The terror of being discovered seemed to crawl all over him like a living thing.

"OK, get on to lunch, both of you. If I catch you smoking in here again I'm taking you straight to Mr Bruder. You may be leaving, Voaden, but it'll do you no good to get expelled before that can happen."

"Yes, sir, thank you, sir," Voaden said. He didn't sound very convinced or grateful.

There was silence for the next few minutes but Chapman couldn't be certain that they had all gone. He was scared to come out, terrified that Kent would be standing there quietly waiting, wiping his nose with his handkerchief or maybe having a pee himself.

The toilets suddenly seemed a very hostile and lonely place, reeking of urine and stale cigarette smoke. He hated being there and began to wonder whether he was a lost cause too and what that really meant.

He hadn't taken much notice of the graffiti; waiting alone in the silence and the stench his eyes were drawn to it. Every square inch of the walls was covered with crude messages and obscene drawings. He was startled to find his own name featured in among it all, low down near the bottom on the cubicle door. There was no message, just his name, spelt out in uneven block letters: CHAPMAN. He stared at the name for a long time trying to understand why anyone should write it amongst all that filth. He wondered why they should think his name needed to be there, whether they knew somehow.

In the end he had to come out. He did it cautiously but once out of the cubicle he bolted for the door and out into the fresh air. The sun was shining, and a slight wind was moving a few lost leaves about. The yard was deserted, and he remembered that the lunch bell had gone ages ago, while they were still smoking. He started walking to the dining hall, but his pace slowed as he thought about Drummond. He felt he couldn't risk running into him again so soon and he turned away. He decided to wait out of sight by one of the big chestnut trees. He wasn't really hungry, anyway; the cigarette had taken care of that.

The tree he chose was the same one they'd been using for target practice with Coffin's penknife. He picked up a small twig and leaned against the tree, breaking little pieces off in his fingers and tossing them away. When the one twig was gone, scattered in little pieces, he picked up another and repeated the process, all the while thinking and worrying, faces and words going through his mind in a random procession.

Rowell's face was among them, repeating his questions of the previous night. He hadn't told him yet what had happened, as he'd promised he would. He had actually avoided him all morning, seeking out Voaden at the morning break and again at lunchtime. He didn't know why he'd been so keen to be with him, but he'd been driven by some kind of force the moment he woke up. Rowell faded slowly, still talking. Dryden's face came next, shouting something at Voaden and Root and then glancing at him, his expression angry and disappointed. Then Dryden faded away, leaving him with Voaden and Root, who didn't have much to say, calling the teacher various names and laughing. Then they were both gone too, and his thoughts took him back to Saint Stithians, dwelling on the good mostly, ignoring Jenkins, and then beyond that to his mother sitting by the pool in Kuala Lumpur, smiling up at him with a cigarette between her fingers. She didn't get a chance to speak because Rowell appeared again, only this time he really was there.

"Why did you miss lunch? I've been looking for you all over the place," he said.

Chapman didn't want to go into a long explanation.

"I wasn't hungry," he said. "What was it?"

"Bangers and mash – quite nice for a change," Rowell said.

Chapman shrugged, throwing away a last little piece of twig.

"Did anyone notice I wasn't there?" he asked.

"I don't think so – except Voaden; he asked me where you were when I was leaving to look for you."

"I was having a ciggey with him and Root, that's why I didn't make it."

Rowell looked surprised.

"Well he did, he'd already had lunch when he spoke to me – so had Root, I think."

"I got stuck in the toilet," Chapman said, feeling foolish as he said it.

Rowell laughed.

"What, literally?"

Chapman shook his head, smiling a little.

"Kent came in – he didn't see me, thanks to Nick, but I had to wait in there until I was sure he'd gone. I didn't want to get caught being late by Drummond again."

"What did Kent do to them?"

"Nothing," Chapman said. He was still surprised by that. "He just ticked them off, that's all."

Rowell thought about it, not showing any surprise at all.

"Beyond the pale," he said.

"What?"

"I heard Richardson saying those two were beyond the pale," Rowell said.

"What does that mean?" Chapman asked.

"I don't know. I suppose it means they've given up bothering about them – let them do what they like. Voaden's already turned sixteen – he's leaving at the end of term, isn't he?"

Chapman nodded.

"Kent called him a lost cause in the loo."

"Same thing, I suppose," Rowell said. He was secretly satisfied that Kent was right.

There were more boys out in the yard and Rowell could see Wentworth and a couple of others heading for the side gate. It reminded him that they had a class at two.

"We'd better get going – you haven't forgotten we've got Art, have you?"

"No," Chapman said, although he had really, but he was glad to be reminded. It was better than maths, better than Latin.

Art was a doddle, a nice way to spend a Monday afternoon.

The art teacher's classroom – or studio, as he preferred to hear it described – was above the gymnasium at the playing fields. You could see the smokers' tree out of the window. They were half way there before Rowell brought up the subject, unable to let it stand there in the background any longer, tapping him insistently on the shoulder, gnawing at his guts when he tried to ignore it.

"When are you going to tell me what happened with Chatsworth?" he asked.

"Do you really want to know?" Chapman said, keeping his eyes on the pavement.

Rowell was a little hurt by that, thinking their friendship amounted to more, but he didn't let it distract him.

"Don't you want to tell me now?" he asked.

Chapman didn't reply, wondering how to tell him. It hadn't got any easier since last night. He wished he was more like Voaden. He wouldn't give a stuff about telling and it would never have happened to him anyway; he'd have fucked Chatsworth up, killed him probably with that flick knife; fucked up all three of them, he thought.

Rowell walked on beside him in the silence, wondering what to say next or whether to just wait. They were catching up with Wentworth and the other two, and when they did it would be too late again. They would be at the playing fields soon anyway. He was about to prod when Chapman suddenly spoke up.

"When I was freaked out with that pill, Chatsworth told me I'd been elected to some secret society called the Harvesters or something. When he was there with Gatesford in the dorm that night. He'd told me about it before, but I didn't really know what he was on about."

Rowell nodded.

"They said they'd come and fetch me in the night for a meeting. They said I must keep it secret, not tell anyone. Barnes came and woke me on Friday night – that same night – and he took me down to the bathrooms. I tried to wake you; I kept bumping your bed, but you were snoring like hell."

He paused and gave Rowell a reproachful look.

"Chatsworth was already down there with Gatesford. They were smoking and swigging stuff from a flask. I thought that was pretty cool – like I was in the big league or something."

Chapman stopped talking and Rowell could see in his face that he was finding it difficult to go on. He did though, taking a deep breath before speaking again.

"They started talking some crap about the Harvesters and then said I had to take my pyjamas off because those were the club rules, or some shit like that. Then I knew what was going on. I tried to get out but they grabbed me and pulled my pyjamas off anyway. That's when the top got stuffed up."

"Didn't you yell?" Rowell asked.

"No, I just couldn't, I don't know why – I didn't want anyone else to come," Chapman said.

"I'd have blown the bloody roof off," Rowell said.

Chapman looked at him again. *You weren't there*, the look said.

"They tied my feet up with a tie to stop me kicking – it was my fucking tie; Barnes must have taken it from the end of my bed. Then they took turns kind of sitting on me and wanking and all their horrible bloody shit ended up all over me. They kept shoving their bloody pricks into my face – it was disgusting."

Chapman shook himself and ran his hands over his body from his chest to his hips. It was as though he had ants crawling all over and was trying to brush them off.

Rowell was shocked. His mind struggled to cope with the images being conjured up.

"Then they just left me there and turned the lights out – can you believe that? They were absolute fucking shits. I was covered in their crap and I couldn't get the tie undone – I couldn't see."

His desperation and terror had become immediate, not remembered things; he started sobbing a little, biting his lip.

Rowell hesitated. He put his hand tentatively on Chapman's shoulder and then took it away again, not really knowing how to react.

"Is that when Dryden came along?" he asked.

Chapman nodded, drawing in deep breaths and wiping his eyes with the back of his hand.

"Jesus, I'm sorry," Rowell said. He felt tears beginning to push at the back of his own eyes.

"I never realised… Why didn't you just tell Dryden what happened?"

Chapman stopped as though the real horror of everything had just opened up like a black pit in the path in front of him.

"Because they said they'll really sort me out if I say anything and Barnes had a camera and they took flash pictures with it. They say they'll send them to my mum and dad if I say anything to anyone."

"Jesus," Rowell said.

Chapman looked up at the sky and he smiled weakly, almost seeming as though he was about to laugh. Rowell was glad he didn't because he knew it would sound crazy somehow.

"You know what Gatesford said to me? He said he knew they wouldn't have to send the pictures because he could see I'd really enjoyed it."

"What a fucking shit," Rowell said.

"Why would he say a thing like that?" Chapman asked, his eyes searching Rowell's face for an answer.

"Because he's a fucking shit, that's why," Rowell repeated, knowing it wasn't enough.

They started walking again. They were almost there.

"Maybe you should speak up; maybe there wasn't really any film in the camera; maybe it could still be confiscated," Rowell said.

He heard all the maybes as they were coming out of his mouth and knew there were too many.

Chapman shook his head.

"I think they'll leave me alone now," he said, without explaining why. He didn't sound as though he believed it either. "But you must promise not to say anything – please Chris, I mean it."

"I promise," Rowell said without hesitation.

NINETEEN

They were earlier than most getting up to Turner's classroom; only Wentworth and two others were there before them. The teacher was still busy putting the finishing touches to a pile of fruit in a big bowl on a small white table in the middle of the room. He acknowledged them with a slight nod as they came in but said nothing, too intent on his task to be distracted.

"Great," Rowell whispered, "apples and bloody bananas."

Chapman smiled, already beginning to cheer up in the atmosphere of safe domesticity.

Turner was wearing an apron, and it would have looked ridiculous on any other man, but it somehow looked quite natural on him. It was covered in splotches of different coloured paint.

"What do you think?" Turner said finally, standing back to admire his handiwork.

"Looks nice, sir," Wentworth said immediately.

Turner glanced at him but he wasn't satisfied. He leaned

forward again to change the position of an apple. That seemed to do it. Then he abruptly lost interest in the bowl of fruit and turned his attention to the boys, who were still arriving in ones and twos, telling them to get a move on and sit down.

Leomond was one of them and he came and sat at the desk next to Chapman.

"Where were you at lunch?" he asked in a low voice.

"Having a ciggey," Chapman replied.

Leomond shook his head sadly from side to side.

"You shouldn't miss lunch; you're too skinny," he said.

Before Chapman could say anything in return, Turner clapped his hands to tell them that the lesson had begun.

The boys tried to follow what he was saying for a minute or two, but he used very long words, and after a while it was easier to look out of the window, and easier still – and less risky – to just look at Turner, prancing around the room waving his hands about. He put on a good show, even if he was mostly speaking in another language. He never spoke for very long, and another good trait was that he seldom asked questions. Even when he did, he would usually answer them himself, having much longer words to do it with. The only boy he ever really listened to was Heathfield, because he had some pretty fair sized words of his own, and he could draw like a professional already. Heathfield's apples and bananas would probably look just like the real thing.

"Alright then, pick up your pencils and get started," Turner said when the lecture was over.

When he saw that everyone had done that and that their attention was focused on the bowl of fruit, he remembered he had something urgent to attend to. He left the classroom feeling for his cigarettes and the lighter in his jacket pocket as he went.

It was quite pleasant in his studio, light and airy with the high, big windows. The real world didn't seem to matter much. There was also nothing wrong with trying to draw a banana – it was actually quite absorbing, even for those who thought that Art was a load of cobblers. For that reason the boys stayed quiet even when Turner had left. Only when they'd got something down on paper and had started to glance at each other's efforts would the comments start and then things would soon get out of control. Turner usually came back before that happened.

He would come in quietly, as though entering a cathedral where there was a service going on. He'd stand for a while behind each boy in turn, going slowly round the rough circle of desks. On the first circuit he seldom said anything but the second time around he would lean down and whisper some useful comment or other into each boy's ear. Turner didn't believe in being derogatory. Even if what he saw looked as though a drunken chimpanzee had drawn it, he wouldn't say so. What he said was always constructive.

The boys were allowed twenty minutes to complete their drawings and most were still busy when Turner clapped his hands and told them to put down their pencils. He was standing behind Heathfield when he clapped. He happened to look down and noticed that the boy had actually done two drawings and was slipping the one under the other. The drawing that was now on top was of the bowl of fruit and as usual it was excellent. Turner leaned down and picked it up and underneath was a head and shoulders drawing of a boy. He recognised who it was immediately because Heathfield really was that good. He looked across the circle at Chapman and then down at the drawing again.

"I suppose I should tick you off, Heathfield, but that's actually very good, very good indeed. You've captured his mouth particularly well," he said.

Heathfield's normally pallid face went bright red, almost as red as one of the apples in the bowl. The boys on either side craned over to see what Turner was talking about, knowing it couldn't be about apples and bananas.

"He's drawn Chapman," Wentworth said so that they could all hear, wanting to be first with the news.

Several boys got up then to come round and have a look themselves. Turner didn't stop them. Heathfield went even redder as they craned over his shoulder from either side. He was too embarrassed to look up again, beyond the bowl of fruit at Chapman. His model was still sitting there, having heard his name. He was watching the other boys crowding around Heathfield's desk, still not quite sure what was going on. Rowell had gone round to look but Leomond stayed where he was, surreptitiously taking the opportunity to add a few finishing touches to his own drawing while Turner's attention was distracted.

"That is very good, Heathfield," Rowell said and several other boys murmured in agreement.

They all looked back and forth from the drawing to Chapman and he began to get embarrassed too, feeling as though he was sitting in a shop window.

Turner clapped his hands then and told them all to go back to their desks. He put Heathfield's drawing of the bowl of fruit back down on the desk, covering the portrait.

"He's got you exactly," Rowell said to Chapman as he sat down again.

"Why was he drawing me?" Chapman asked.

"He's done the fruit too, he's really bloody good," Rowell said.

Chapman looked across the circle at Heathfield and their eyes met very briefly but the other boy quickly looked down at his desk. His face was still glowing like a traffic light.

Turner started talking again, commenting on what he'd seen in the boys' drawings, criticizing this and that but not singling out anyone by name. He didn't talk for very long because the time for the lesson was almost up. He told them to remember to write their names in the bottom right hand corner and leave the drawings where they were. Then he told them they could go.

Most of the boys left quickly, eager to get off to change for sports. Heathfield seemed in a hurry to leave too, but before he could Turner came back to his desk and picked up the drawing of Chapman to look at it for a second time. Chapman and Rowell stopped to look as well and Heathfield's face started to go red all over again.

"You can take this with you if you like, I'm not going to mark it," Turner said.

Chapman still hadn't been able to get a proper look and Turner realised that and held it out so that he could.

"It's really very good," Rowell repeated, looking over Chapman's shoulder.

"Yes it is – perhaps you should give him the chance to finish it properly," Turner said, handing the drawing to Heathfield.

Chapman smiled, although in the drawing he wasn't smiling. He looked at Heathfield but the other boy kept his eyes down, slowly rolling up the drawing in his long fingers. They had never said more than two words to each other despite the fact that they were in the same dorm. It was difficult to know what to say now.

"OK, if that's what you want," Chapman said to Heathfield, feeling a little awkward but flattered.

Turner walked away and began picking up the boys' drawings from their desks, going slowly around the circle.

It didn't take long for Heathfield to roll up his portrait, although he did it very slowly. He was half hoping the other two boys would go, but when he'd finished Chapman and Rowell were still standing there.

"Why did you draw me?" Chapman asked.

Heathfield looked at him for the first time, unable to avoid it anymore.

"Because you looked more interesting than that bowl of fruit," he said eventually.

"Thanks," Chapman said, pretending to be indignant. He was smiling still.

From the corner of his eye Turner watched the little group, listening to what was said and to the awkward pauses, smiling to himself. When they left, he stopped picking up the drawings and stared at the wall for quite a long time as though he was remembering something that pleased him.

Down in the street, Heathfield walked quickly, surprised to have Rowell and Chapman walking on either side of him. He fully expected them to have started ignoring him again. He usually walked on his own and it was an odd feeling being part of a group, especially when the other two were rebels. His face wasn't red any more but he still felt embarrassed – as though he had just been caught peeping at Chapman in the showers. But the other two didn't seem to be thinking anything like that, seeming genuinely interested in him all of a sudden.

"Do we have to walk so fucking fast?" Rowell said.

"Sorry," Heathfield said, immediately slowing down.

"Where did you learn to draw like that?"

"I don't know – it's just a knack I suppose."

"Well, you're bloody good," Rowell said.

"Can I have the drawing – to send to my parents?" Chapman asked.

Heathfield glanced sideways at him, feeling flattered himself.

"Yes, of course," he said and he held up the roll of paper.

"Is it finished?"

"No, not really," Heathfield replied cautiously. The idea that Chapman would actually pose for him to finish had been too ridiculous to even contemplate.

"How long would it take you?" Chapman asked.

"Oh shit," Rowell said, stopping suddenly.

The others stopped too, startled by his tone, looking around in alarm.

"It's fucking Chatsworth," Rowell said and he turned and started walking quickly back the way they'd come.

Heathfield started to follow him, not knowing what was going on. They both stopped again when they realised Chapman had stayed where he was.

"Come on, Pete – let's go," Rowell said, gesticulating wildly.

But Chapman shook his head and started walking slowly on. Rowell stared after him for a second or two and then hurried to catch up. Heathfield hurried back too, confused and alarmed, wondering what drama he was suddenly caught up in.

Chatsworth and Barnes were walking down the other side of the street toward the playing fields, deep in conversation. They were both dressed in cricket clothes. They were nearly level before they noticed the three boys. When they did they stopped briefly, seeming to debate what to do before crossing over to intercept them.

"Hello, Chapman – I was hoping I'd run into you," Chatsworth said with a big friendly smile. He blocked the path with his cricket bat. "You seem to be avoiding me."

Rowell clenched his fists at his sides, but there was tepid

water rather than fire in his veins, and he felt helpless and scared. He couldn't bring himself to look directly at either Chatsworth or Barnes. He looked at the cricket bat instead.

Barnes looked away too, down the street, seeming uneasy and not wanting to be part of the encounter.

"Sorry," Chapman mumbled.

"I want you to come and see me tomorrow – straight after supper – alright?" Chatsworth said. His tone exuded fatherly concern.

Chapman glanced at Rowell, his eyes asking for help but Rowell was still staring at the cricket bat and he couldn't give any.

"Where do you want to see me?" he asked in a flat voice.

"In my room," Chatsworth replied harmlessly and started to walk on.

"On your own?" Chapman called after him, looking at Barnes' back.

Chatsworth stopped and turned round. The benign expression vanished from his face for an instant before reappearing just as suddenly.

"Just the two of us – just for a chat," he said, smiling. He turned away again, swinging his bat. He was irritated and disappointed that Chapman wasn't calling him 'sir' anymore.

The three boys continued walking in silence for a while but the cocktail of emotions bubbling inside Rowell was threatening to blow him apart. He wanted to talk to let something out. Heathfield was suddenly a nuisance – not interesting anymore, like a stone in his shoe.

"What was that all about?" Heathfield asked.

"What was what all about?" Rowell countered immediately, sounding cross because he was.

Heathfield regretted having spoken. He knew it was actually none of his business. It wasn't his world, and he didn't understand it. He felt the unlikely friendship beginning to slip away already and that distressed him much more than he felt he had a right to expect.

"Sorry, I didn't mean to be nosy," he said.

"Chatsworth thinks I fancy him," Chapman said with the faintest trace of a smile.

Heathfield looked shocked, and he was a little. It had never occurred to him that Chapman could have such feelings, let alone for an older boy, or even joke about it. It was a new notion, scary but also quite titillating.

The other two didn't seem to notice his reaction at all, thinking in different ways about Chatsworth and intent now on getting back to school.

"Have you got time to finish it now?" Chapman asked when they got to the gate.

"You mean the drawing?"

Chapman nodded. "Do you need to look at me still?" he asked.

It was Heathfield's turn to nod, delighted that he hadn't forgotten about the portrait. "About ten minutes," he said, wishing he'd said twenty.

"Don't you have cricket?" Rowell asked grumpily.

"At four o' clock," Heathfield said.

"I've only got diving practise at four thirty," Chapman said.

"Well, he hasn't got time – we've only got fifteen minutes to change and get back down to the fields," Rowell said. He was irritated that Pete had brought it up at all. He still wanted to talk about Chatsworth but he realised now that his friend was avoiding it again.

"Well, maybe later, then," Chapman said.

But Chapman did come to look briefly at the drawing again when they were in the dorm, sitting down on Heathfield's bed while he changed into his cricket clothes. It was a strange experience to have him there, sitting so close, smiling at the drawing and then at him, seeming so pleased at something he had done. He blushed a little when he thought of the other drawings hidden in his locker not three feet away. Chapman was the subject of those too, virtually naked – as he often was in the dorm. In some of them he had wild flowers in his hair and vines entwined around his slim limbs and exquisite body. In one drawing he wore a crown of laurel leaves, befitting the beautiful young spirit of the woods Heathfield chose to believe he was.

TWENTY

"I've been telling them for weeks," said the superintendent, "but you know how it is."

Dryden didn't know how it was, but he agreed anyway. He was irritated that they should be phoning to tell him so late in the day.

"So how long are you going to be closed?" he asked.

The man at the other end of the line sneezed, and Dryden instinctively held the phone away from his face.

"Sorry, I've got a real summer streamer coming on," said the superintendent; Dryden could hear it in the nasal twang. "Hopefully just the rest of the week."

Dryden nodded and then felt stupid, realising that the man couldn't see him.

"OK, fine," he said. "I'll phone you on Monday to check."

"Sorry about this."

"Can't be helped, I suppose. Goodbye."

Dryden looked at his watch and saw that it was nearly five

past four. He was actually quite glad that swimming was off, because it was his free evening. Now he could get away a little earlier, maybe pick up some flowers for Sarah on the way – she'd always enjoyed that rare treat.

Before he did anything else, though, he'd have to tell the boys. He went off in search of one of them, heading for the dorms as the most likely place to find either Chapman or Simpson.

Chapman was sitting on his bed, alone in the room. Everyone else had already gone off to cricket. He stood up when Dryden came in and looked at his own watch, worried that it might have stopped.

"Diving practice is off, I'm afraid; they've got a problem with the pumps," Dryden said. "Can you find the others and let them know?"

"Yes, sir," Chapman said.

Dryden started to leave immediately, but he changed his mind. He came back when it occurred to him that he had a good opportunity to talk to Chapman in private.

"I'm sorry I was a bit grumpy with you this morning," he said.

The boy was slightly taken aback, not quite sure what he meant.

"When you were with Voaden," Dryden explained. "I was a bit cross that you were with him after what I said to you yesterday. But I'm wrong about him, aren't I?"

"Yes, sir," Chapman said cautiously. He began to worry that Dryden was going to work his way steadily through everyone until he knew the truth.

"I'm not wrong about him being a bad influence, mind you. I was hoping you would see that yourself," Dryden said.

Chapman looked down at his bed, feeling awkward and not wanting to agree or disagree. He wondered whether Dryden was going to call Voaden a lost cause too, and whether the teacher himself was beginning to think that about him as well the other boy.

"Have you got anything organised after Chapel on Sunday?" Dryden asked instead.

The boy looked back up at him then, relieved that he had abruptly changed the subject.

"I don't think so, sir."

"Would you like to come out with me?"

"Sorry, sir?"

"With me and Sarah, the lady who nearly ran over you. I think it would do you good to get a change of scene. You've been having quite a tough time of it these past few weeks."

"Yes, sir, that would be great, sir," Chapman said, and he sounded genuinely pleased.

"Good. Perhaps we can go and have tea somewhere – in the country. I'll think about it."

"Thank you, sir."

Dryden smiled awkwardly. He walked out, puzzled and embarrassed by his own spontaneity. Chapman followed him out to go in search of Drummond and Simpson.

"Thanks very much, sir," he said again. He gave Dryden a big smile before disappearing down the stairs.

I've just asked him out on a date, Dryden said to himself. He laughed out loud at the absurdity of putting it that way, even to himself. He quickly replaced the awkwardness with a fuzzy feeling of how philanthropic he was being. The feeling grew and it was even strong enough to withstand Sarah's look of surprise when he told her later that evening.

She was busy with the flowers he had given her, cutting off the stems over the sink in the flat. She paused in the task when he told her and looked at him.

"Do you think that's a good idea?" she asked.

"The poor little bugger's been going through hell there – it'll do him the world of good to get out for a bit."

"With us?"

Dryden's confidence wavered a little at her tone and he realised he'd taken a lot for granted.

"I'm sorry, I know I should have checked with you first," he said.

"No, I didn't mean that, that's fine – I don't mind, really I don't. I meant do you think he'd really enjoy going on an outing with two old farts like us?"

"Well he seemed pleased enough – we're not that ancient, are we?"

She shrugged and turned back to the sink, snipping away at the last couple of stems. She liked getting flowers because they always cheered the place up, but more than that they proved that he had been thinking about her. She put the vase down on the coffee table, fiddled with the arrangement briefly and then sat down beside him on the couch. She kissed him on the cheek.

"Do you think I've been a bit daft then?" he said. He was miles away, watching an absurd fantasy in his head of himself giving flowers to Chapman.

"No, I think it's a sweet idea. What do you mean about him going through hell?"

For a moment he considered telling her but decided not to again. It was a private thing now, between him and the boy. He didn't want to be judged on how he'd handled it. He was a little scared that she wouldn't approve. He knew that none of his colleagues would, least of all Bruder.

"Some of the bigger boys are picking on him a bit, and I think he's falling in with a rather bad crowd," he said. He was pleased that he was telling some of the truth.

She put her hand on his knee, stroking the fabric of his

trousers with her slender fingers and looking at the flowers, enjoying their delicate beauty. It didn't sound like hell exactly, she thought. She sensed that there was something more that he wasn't telling her.

"But is it going to help if they think he's a teacher's pet – if you single him out for special treatment, I mean?" she asked.

He was startled by the question – by the obvious common sense in it. He hadn't really stopped to think about that at all, and he knew immediately that she was right.

"Do you think we should include one of his friends, then?" he asked.

"I don't know – you want him on his own, don't you?"

Dryden wondered why she had put it like that. He was vaguely disturbed by the positive answer that came into his head. It had already occurred to him to include Rowell – soon after he had spoken to Chapman in fact – but he had immediately trampled on the idea.

"I thought it would be a good idea for you to have a look at him, give your professional opinion, so to speak," he said, trying to offer something that made sense.

But it obviously didn't and she turned her head to look up into his face.

"If you think he's got some kind of mental problem, I'm not remotely qualified to judge. I haven't done anything at all in that area."

"No, no – he's right as rain in the head," he said quickly. "I just thought you could help me decide what makes him tick, that's all."

He was beginning to feel embarrassed about it. She saw that in his face and looked away again at the flowers. They really were beautiful, just like the boy, and they must have been very expensive, she thought.

"Perhaps it would be better to invite a friend along," she

said. "He'd probably feel more comfortable with that – maybe we all would."

He nodded. He felt strangely deflated.

"I'll invite Rowell as well then; he seems to be his best friend," he said.

They sat in silence for a while, thinking their own thoughts. Chapman seemed to be between them somehow, as though he was there on the couch, smiling at first one and then the other, linking them and keeping them apart.

"Where do you think we should take them?" Dryden asked eventually, wanting to get through it now and move on.

"What about the zoo?" she suggested.

"I think they're a bit old for that – Chapman smokes."

"What, at twelve? How do you know – have you caught him?" she asked.

"He's thirteen – just. He admitted as much," he replied.

"Well, perhaps the zoo would be a bit tame," she said. "Maybe we should take them for a pint at the Dog and Duck."

He grinned, thinking how much they'd probably like that.

"I think not," he said. "Anyway, we don't have to decide anything now. What would you like to do this evening?" he asked. He was sorry in some ways that Chapman had become an issue at all.

"I thought we were going to the cinema."

"Can do – I'd like to take you to supper first, though."

He put his arm around her shoulders and gave her a hug.

"Do you like the flowers?"

"Very much," she said.

She put her hand back on his knee. She was about to ask whether he'd told Bruder that he wanted to quit being a House Master but she decided against it. She didn't want to get into all that again right then.

"You really like this boy, don't you?" she said after a bit.

Dryden didn't reply immediately, thinking about what to say.

"He reminds me of Captain Quack," he said.

She smiled, looking up into his face again.

"Why?"

"I don't know – if he's pushed down he always seems to bob up smiling somehow. He's got great spirit, plenty of guts."

"He's not shy either, is he?" she asked, remembering how Chapman had leaned into the car, asking for a chit.

"No, he certainly isn't," Dryden said. He thought about him standing in the bath and the streams of tiny stars.

TWENTY-ONE

Gladstone whined hopefully when Kennedy stood up and came round his desk, but once again he was disappointed. The old parson stretched, made a half-hearted attempt to touch his toes and then went and sat down again.

"You want walkies, is that it?" he asked.

The dog tilted his big head, trying to anticipate his master's next move, trying to make sense of the noises coming out of his mouth. Then there was a knock on the door. The dog abruptly lost interest in him, rushing up to see who it was, sniffing around the door frame.

"Enter," Kennedy said.

Drummond came in, and the dog immediately started to make a huge fuss, banging into his legs and threatening to jump up.

"I've prepared a roster, sir," Drummond said. He held up a piece of paper with one hand and fended off the dog with the other so that he could get over to the desk.

"Excellent," Kennedy said, leaning across to take the paper. "You didn't force any of them into this, did you?"

"No, they're all delighted to do it, sir," Drummond lied. He hadn't spoken to a single boy on the list but he doubted there would be a problem.

Kennedy smiled, looking down at the names of the volunteers and muttering them under his breath.

"Chapman and Rowell," he said thoughtfully, looking up at Drummond. "Chapman was here with me when old Winston passed away. I'm glad he's volunteered."

Drummond smiled amiably, trying to keep the dog's nose out of his crotch.

"But wasn't there some problem with those two yesterday – I heard they were caned?"

The young man's smile vanished abruptly.

"Chapman was, sir," he said.

"What for?"

Drummond squirmed a little, remembering his ignominious role. Then he told Kennedy about Featherstone and all that had happened. Kennedy's eyes widened when he got to the bit about the Turkish whore.

"Good grief. He's a strange little lad," Kennedy said when he'd finished. "Do you think he should be allowed out so soon?"

"They're only on the roster to take Gladstone down to the playing fields, sir."

Kennedy nodded. "Can't get into much mischief doing that, can they?" he said.

It was a rhetorical question, and Drummond merely nodded in agreement.

"I never did finish my chat with him," Kennedy said and he rummaged around on his desk, looking for his diary.

"Ask him to come and see me at five thirty on Thursday, will you?"

"Yes, sir."

Drummond turned his full attention back to the dog. He bent forward, cradling the huge head in both hands. Gladstone promptly reared up, trying to get his big front paws onto the young man's chest, nearly knocking him over. He was going to prove a handful even for two boys.

"Why did you call him Gladstone, sir?" he asked.

Kennedy had picked up the list again but he put it down and stood up, coming round to pat the dog.

"I don't know. Don't you like it?" he asked.

"No, it's a great name, sir," Drummond said.

"His name was Zeus, apparently, but I didn't think it would be very appropriate for a parson to be bellowing that out in public."

Drummond nodded, thinking that it wouldn't sound much better to be yelling the name of a dead prime minister either. But he could sense a kind of tortuous logic in the choice of name, following on Winston as it did.

"I'll take him today, sir – kind of a trial run," he said.

"Are you sure?" Kennedy asked. "Can you manage by yourself?"

Drummond grinned at that.

"I think so, sir," he said.

Out in the street with Gladstone pulling at the lead like a team of huskies, he didn't feel quite so cocky, but he was very strong and never really in danger of losing control. He started worrying what might happen with the smaller boys though, thinking it had maybe been foolish to include third formers like Rowell and Chapman on the roster. But Gladstone calmed down pretty quickly and was soon insisting on stopping to smell each tree and gatepost. After a few minutes, Drummond had to do some of the dragging.

They walked down Connaught Avenue in stops and starts

towards the playing fields. There were already some boys coming back from cricket. Gladstone greeted each small group with a lot of body wagging and they in turn made a big fuss of him.

Pearce and Higgins were in the third group they passed and Drummond told them that they were on the roster to take Gladstone for tomorrow's walk.

"Great," they both said, genuinely delighted.

"Are you sure you can handle him?" Drummond asked.

They nodded enthusiastically. Pearce crouched down so that his head was level with the dog's and reached out to pet him. Gladstone launched forward and licked him on the face with his huge tongue. Pearce promptly fell backwards onto his bum. Drummond pulled the lead tight, dragging the dog back.

"It doesn't look like it," he said with mild alarm.

Pearce jumped to his feet and took the lead so that they were both holding it for a moment. Then Drummond apprehensively let go, getting ready to lunge after the dog if necessary. In the event, Pearce seemed quite capable of holding Gladstone in check. Even when the next group of boys came up and the dog pulled and tugged to get at them, he seemed fine. Higgins didn't even have to lend a hand.

Rowell was in the next group and Drummond told him that he was on the roster with Chapman for Friday. He was pleased that he was making such a good start on the list so quickly. Coffin was in the group too. He said he was disappointed that his name wasn't included.

"I've got a dog like this at home – I think he's got some Great Dane in him," he told Drummond.

"I'm sure we can make a plan," Drummond said, delighted that it was all working out so well.

There were a couple of cricket games still on the go and

he decided to walk on past the playing fields down to the river thinking he might let the dog off the lead there so that it could have a proper run. Once past the distraction of the boys, Gladstone trotted along quite happily beside him, less interested in doggy smells, so they were able to make good progress. On the river bank, Drummond let him off with a silent prayer, hoping earnestly that he wouldn't bolt. That didn't happen and he soon began to relax, enjoying the walk himself and going further than he intended. Only when he turned for home did there seem to be a problem. The dog was quite far ahead of him by then and seemed not to hear his calls. He felt a complete prat yelling *Gladstone* at the top of his lungs. In the end he decided to try the dog's original name.

"Zeus," he bellowed.

The dog came immediately, flying over the intervening distance towards him, seeming to grow huge, like a big black gust of wind.

TWENTY-TWO

It was Chapman's first visit to the prefect's wing. He didn't know which was Chatsworth's room. That made things worse. He hovered around on the landing, scared to knock on any of the doors in case it was the wrong one. He was still standing there, undecided, when two prefects came up the stairs – Vaughn and Johnston. Chapman had never been spoken to directly by either of them before. At first it seemed as though they were going to ignore him now, but then one of them stopped.

"What are you doing here?" Vaughn asked.

"I've come to see Chatsworth, sir."

"What, here – in his room?"

Chapman nodded and the two prefects looked at each other, their eyes widening in surprise. The silent exchange made him feel even more uncomfortable.

"Isn't he in?" Vaughn asked.

"I don't know which room," Chapman replied.

"You're standing right outside it," Vaughn said. He smiled for the first time and took a step forward. He knocked on the door. "You've got a visitor, Chatsworth," he called loudly, "and she's pretty."

The two of them sniggered at that. Chapman felt a strong urge to bolt for the stairs right then but before he could the door opened. Chatsworth glanced at him briefly, standing to one side and gestured for him to come in. His attention was mainly focused on Vaughn and Johnston.

"Why don't you two grow up," he said to them, slamming the door behind him.

The room was much smaller than Dryden's. The moment the door was closed, it was immediately claustrophobic. The bed, a desk and a big easy chair took up most of the floor space. The one small window looked down onto the playground but the curtains were half drawn, adding to the gloom. The most dominant feature was a huge poster up on the wall above the bed of Jimi Hendrix.

Chapman stood uncertainly by the big chair, unable to put any useful distance between himself and Chatsworth.

"If you touch me, I'm going to scream my head off," he said, remembering what Rowell had suggested for openers.

Chatsworth looked at him in apparent surprise. Then he went and lay down on the bed, putting his hands behind his head and stared at the ceiling. Chapman's brave opening remark hung in the air like the smoke from a spent canon, slowly fading away and losing power. After a minute or two Chatsworth indicated with a gesture of exaggerated chivalry that Chapman could sit in the chair.

"Would you like a cigarette?" he asked. He propped himself up on the bed on one elbow and held out a pack of Dunhill's.

Chapman remembered the first time he had said something

like that, thinking then that it had been a trap. He looked at the cigarettes and hesitated for a moment, longing to take one. Then he shook his head, not wanting to owe him anything.

Chatsworth didn't take one either. He lay back down again, closing his eyes.

"Why did you want to see me?" Chapman asked after another minute had ticked away. He sat on the edge of the chair feeling more and more uncomfortable in the silence.

Chatsworth made him wait a while longer. When he did speak he still had his eyes closed.

"Why do you play so hard to get, Chapman?" he asked.

Chapman didn't understand what he meant. He rummaged in his head for some kind of reply but he couldn't find one and so he said nothing. He watched a thin smile appearing slowly on Chatsworth's lips. He thought how ugly he was lying there with his white face and pimples.

"I've got the photos. Would you like to see them?" Chatsworth asked casually.

Chapman started in the chair as though he'd had an electric shock. What little courage he had left ebbed away. Stay angry, Rowell had told him. But he couldn't be angry any more; he felt too scared and helpless knowing the photos were real.

"Did you know that Barnes is the honorary secretary of the Photographic Society? He's really very good – especially in the dark room," Chatsworth said in the same matter-of-fact voice.

"Why are you being so nasty to me?" Chapman said. The words tumbled out, tripping over each other in his throat.

Chatsworth didn't reply immediately. He sat up and swung his feet off the bed.

"If you touch me, I'm going to scream my head off," he said in a whiny imitation of Chapman's first words.

The boy began to stand up and then sat down again. He

was thoroughly miserable and close to tears but he didn't want to cry in front of Chatsworth. He was determined to somehow keep that pleasure from him.

"You're being really shitty to me, and I've done nothing to you," he said.

Chatsworth stared at him like he'd done in DT, ignoring the pleas in the fragile small-boy voice.

"What do you think your mum would make of those pictures?" he asked. "I expect she opens her mail at breakfast with Daddy Chapman sitting on the other side of the table eating his boiled egg. My, my, here's little Peter and he's playing with himself in the bathroom. What's all that stuff on his face – it looks like …"

Chapman snapped. He launched himself at Chatsworth before he could finish. The young man grabbed both his arms, bringing up his knee to protect his crotch. He rapidly adjusted his grip to get the boy in a bear hug and rolled back down onto the bed with him, squeezing the air out of his lungs. It was an unequal contest and in an instant Chatsworth was on top, pining Chapman's arms to the bed. The boy struggled, arching his back and wriggling his body under the heavy weight. Eventually he gave up and lay still, his head to one side, looking at the wall, fighting back the tears.

"I'd already forgotten what a lively little sod you are," Chatsworth said breathlessly. He tentatively loosened his grip but immediately tightened it again when Chapman seemed ready to resume the struggle. They stayed like that for a couple of minutes and Chatsworth could feel the boy's laboured breathing through his inner thighs.

"Are you going to behave if I let you up?" he said eventually.

Chapman kept silent, lying there motionless. After a while he nodded imperceptibly. Chatsworth started to let him up, cautiously at first. He backed off the bed looking down at the boy, smiling broadly. An obvious bulge in the crotch of his trousers showed how exciting he'd found the tussle. Chapman saw that as he sat up. He pulled his knees up under his chin, trying to make himself into a tight ball on the bed.

"I haven't told anyone anything; why don't you just leave me alone?" he said.

Before Chatsworth could say anything, there was a loud knock on the door. His whole demeanour changed instantly.

"Just a minute," he said loudly. He glanced quickly around the room looking for anything out of place. He grabbed Chapman by the arm and pulled him up off the bed, cursing himself for not having locked the door.

"Sit in the chair," he hissed between clenched teeth.

Chapman did as he was told but he moved slowly, trying not to cooperate, delighted at his tormentor's panic.

There was another knock, louder and more insistent. The handle turned and the door started to open from outside. Drummond's head and shoulders loomed through the opening. He stared in without saying anything, still holding onto the door handle, looking first at Chatsworth and then beyond him at Chapman huddled in the chair. He saw that the boy's hair was dishevelled and that his tie was skewed around in his collar.

Chapman grinned up at him, relieved to be rescued.

"This won't do," Drummond said, misinterpreting the grin. "You know I don't like third formers being up in our rooms. What's he doing here?"

"I was about to send him packing," Chatsworth replied quickly and with astonishing composure. He glanced down at Chapman. "He came to see me about a personal problem."

Chapman stood up when he heard that. Drummond saw that his shirt-tails were hanging out of his pants too. The grin had gone and he looked wild eyed and alarmed, like someone caught doing something they weren't proud of.

"Next time I'd appreciate it you could wait for me to open the door," Chatsworth said, going on the offensive.

Drummond seemed to ignore the rebuke, staring at Chapman and trying to understand what was happening. He didn't want to believe what he thought he was seeing. He could hear Featherstone's smooth voice in his head and then Bruder's: *What on earth possessed you... like a Turkish whore.* The disappointment made him feel physically sick. He stepped back without another word, and Chatsworth closed the door, putting his finger to his lips when he saw that Chapman was about to blurt out something.

They stared at each other, frozen in place. The boy's mouth was open and he still looked as though he was about to call out. Chatsworth raised both his hands to his face and pretended to take his picture. When Chapman saw that, the fire kindled by fresh hope went out abruptly. He slumped back down into the chair and looked up at Chatsworth with a blank, exhausted face.

Chatsworth breathed more easily, beginning to recover from the fright he'd had. He actually began to feel sorry for Chapman, wondering now why he was being such a shit. He hadn't meant it to be like that, not really. It had all started badly with Vaughn's snide crack and then Chapman's own belligerent opening line. He'd intended apologising, hoping to win the boy over. Except that there was a part of him that just wanted to go on hurting him, grinding his beautiful face into the dirt. That part was muted now, even frightened, recoiling into his guts with its power spent.

"I'm sorry, Chapman," he said. He went and sat down on the chair by his desk. He picked up a pencil and fiddled with it in his fingers, waiting for a reaction, not sure what to do or say next. It was as though he had been somewhere else and had just come in.

Chapman sat stock still, looking dazed. He said nothing, not seeming to hear Chatsworth's apology. He was wondering why Drummond had just gone out and left him like that.

"You'd better go now," Chatsworth said finally, unable to decide on anything else.

Chapman stood up immediately. He tucked his shirt back into his trousers. Chatsworth leaned forward and adjusted his tie. He did it gently, like a mother getting her child ready for school. Chapman let him.

"I'd like to be friends," Chatsworth said, dropping his hands onto his knees. "I really would."

Chapman nodded. He seemed to understand that the monster wasn't there any more – that it had gone back to its own dark place with the pictures. But he left without saying anything, opening and closing the door behind him without looking at Chatsworth again.

Drummond was still on the landing talking to Vaughn. They stopped talking when the door opened and Chapman came out. The boy was aware of them but he didn't look in their direction. He walked quickly towards the stairs, anxious to get right away.

"Just a second, Peter," Drummond said.

Chapman stopped at the head of the stairs, his hand on the bannister.

"Are you alright?" Drummond asked, coming over.

Vaughn lingered in the background. His expression showed curiosity rather than concern.

"I'm fine, thanks," Chapman said, trying to smile.

"Are you sure?" Drummond persisted, looking him up and down for signs of physical damage, noting that his clothes had been sorted out.

The boy seemed to sigh then, taking a deep breath. He looked up into Drummond's face for the first time and nodded.

"Why did you come up here – did Chatsworth ask you to come?" Drummond asked.

Chapman nodded again, still clutching the head of the bannister, wanting to put his foot down on the first step and go.

Drummond stared down at him, struggling in his own mind for the next question. One came out anyway, not waiting for approval.

"Did you want to come up here?"

Chapman didn't seem to understand the question at first, knowing he'd had no choice in it. Then the real meaning hit him and his expression abruptly changed to one of surprise and indignation.

Drummond was pleased when he saw that, but the pleasure was short lived.

"I really don't mind; it's fine," Chapman said. He glanced towards Chatsworth's door, thinking about the photographs and the breakfast table in Kuala Lumpur.

"You don't mind what?"

"Nothing, sir. Can I go now – please?"

Drummond thought for a little. He seemed on the verge of saying something else but he just nodded. He watched Chapman go, leaping down the stairs two at a time.

"I think that little tart actually enjoys it – but why Chatsworth of all people?" Vaughn said when he'd gone.

Drummond glowered at him and at Chatsworth's door. He clenched his big fists and seemed ready to stride over and knock them both flat.

"How can you possibly know that, you stupid jerk," he said

instead. He went back into his own room, slamming the door hard enough to make the floor shake.

TWENTY-THREE

There was a strange atmosphere in the dorm when Chapman got back. He headed straight for his hiding place to fish out a cigarette, not taking much notice. The rest of the boys were clustered in a group by the washbasins, and there seemed to be some kind of conference going on. Rowell was there too, but he broke away when he saw Chapman and came over.

"What did Chatsworth want?" he asked in a low voice.

"What do you think," Chapman said, lifting up the floorboard. "I'm going for a ciggey – do you want to come?"

"We've only got twenty minutes," Rowell said, torn between wanting to hear more and wanting to be part of the meeting.

"What's happening over there?" Chapman asked.

"There's going to be a dorm raid tonight," Rowell said. "They're all discussing what to do."

Chapman paused for a moment and looked over at the group by the washbasins.

"Stuff that," he said, putting the pack of cigarettes into his inside jacket pocket. "Are you coming or not?"

"What did he say?" Rowell asked. He really wanted to know but he was also keeping half an eye on the others, not wanting to miss out on anything there either.

"Nothing much," Chapman lied, wishing he could remember it as that. "He said he was sorry."

"Really?" Rowell said in disbelief.

"Well, sort of, after he'd fucked me up a bit – I really don't want to talk about it. Drummond came in and that was the end of it."

Rowell's eyes opened wider, sensing a major drama, but he was still distracted.

"Are you coming with me, then?" Chapman asked again.

Rowell hesitated, trying to gauge whether Chapman was all right. Then he decided that their friendship was more important than the dorm battle plan anyway.

"OK," he said with a last glance at the others.

Pearce and a couple of other boys yelled something after them but they pretended not to hear.

Outside it was twilight, and a small wind was moving the leaves of the trees to and fro, making them sing softly, like a far away choir. Two or three stars were already pricking their way through the darkening sky. In the distance, down towards the river, a dog was barking.

The boys hurried across the schoolyard, heading for the toilets. Chapman changed his mind before they got there, and they went around to the narrow passage at the back of the Upper Second classrooms instead. They would be invisible from the main buildings, and it was very unlikely anyone would come down that way so late. The lights were out inside and the windows of the classrooms looked like square black holes. They sat down on the gravel, with their backs to the flint stone boundary wall, but with the clear sky directly overhead they felt surprisingly free.

Rowell sucked at his cigarette, but he was careful not to inhale the smoke. Even then it made him want to cough, but he managed to stifle the urge. He pretended he was enjoying it, holding the cigarette well away when he wasn't actually sucking so that the smoke didn't trouble his eyes. Beside him, Chapman smiled to himself, pretending not to notice.

"Did he really say sorry?" Rowell asked.

Chapman nodded, relaxing as the nicotine did its work.

"He's really creepy, apart from everything else," he said.

"But why did he want to see you – just to have another… you know?"

"Fuck?" Chapman suggested, almost smiling.

Rowell blushed, but it was invisible in the fading light.

"He says he's got the pictures of me – he was a real shit about that," Chapman said.

Rowell didn't know what to say about the pictures anymore – it seemed to be an insoluble problem.

"So what happened when Drummond barged in?"

"He just said 'this won't do' and fucked off again," Chapman replied, imitating Drummond's deep voice. "I think you were right about him."

"Right about what?"

"Nothing. Let's talk about something else," Chapman said, flicking the ash off the end of his cigarette. He stared at the glowing red tip, imagining that it was a tiny world on fire.

"We're supposed to be raided by the blokes from Dorm 6 and 7 tonight. They've got an alliance," Rowell said.

"What – they just come in and hit us with pillows and stuff?" Chapman asked. Somebody always ended up with a bloody nose in dorm fights, and he hoped it wasn't going to be him.

"No, they try and take a hostage — Pearce thinks they're after Thornton again."

"And then what?"

"We have to pay ten bob to get him back."

"Ten bob?" Chapman asked incredulously. "What if we don't?"

Rowell shrugged, feeling a bit foolish explaining it, because it sounded foolish, sitting out there under the stars, smoking a cigarette.

"Those are the rules," he said.

"What about Dryden?"

"That's the whole point — he's off tonight. Kent's on duty and he always clears off soon after lights out."

"Well I'm just going to dive under my bed," Chapman said, blowing a lung full of smoke up into the night sky.

Rowell thought about that and decided it sounded sensible enough in principle.

"Pearce has got a whole plan worked out. We're all supposed to have positions, and him and Higgins are the last line of defence. They're planning to have Thornton stuffed under the basins in the corner."

Chapman started giggling. "What's our position, apart from being under the bed?"

Rowell smiled despite himself, trying to take it seriously because he knew it would get rough, although it sounded funny talking about it out there, with Chapman taking the piss.

"We're supposed to be on the right side. The heavy blokes like Leomond and Coffin are supposed to be in the centre, kind of fighting off the main attack."

Chapman really began giggling then and he started choking on the smoke.

"It's not that funny," Rowell said. "There are some really

big blokes in Dorm 7 – Gatesford's brother for a start."

Hearing the name, Chapman stopped laughing abruptly, but he went on coughing, choking in earnest now. Rowell tried to pat him on the back, but Chapman brushed his arm away. He recovered quickly and stubbed the cigarette out, tossing the butt over the wall behind him. Rowell stubbed his out too, even though it was only half finished.

"Then I'm really going to hide under the bed," Chapman said. There was no laughter in his voice any more.

"Just stick with Leomond – he's bigger than most of them, and they're all shit scared of him," Rowell suggested.

Chapman nodded and then stood up. He breathed in and out, big breaths to get the last of the smoke and the smell out of his lungs. Rowell followed his example.

"I must get some mints," Chapman said.

"Maybe we should just stop smoking," Rowell said.

"You sound like Leomond."

"Maybe he's right."

"Dork."

"Jackass."

"Drydork's asked me out on Sunday," Chapman said, suddenly remembering.

"What do you mean?"

"For an outing – with his girlfriend."

"What – just you? Isn't that a bit weird?" Rowell said.

"Why?" Chapman asked. He was mildly irritated that Rowell was pricking his balloon.

"I don't know, it just seems a bit weird, that's all."

"I don't think it's weird – I think it's very nice of him."

Rowell shrugged. Then he saw that Chapman was starting to get upset with him and he tried to think of a way of undoing the damage.

"Maybe he feels guilty for caning you – I think he knew

Featherstone really was a… you know."

Chapman said nothing, but Rowell's theory seemed to mollify him, and they left it at that.

Back in the dorm, the war plans seemed to have been finalized. All the other boys were going about their usual routine, getting ready for bed. The atmosphere was a lot more tense than usual, though, and nobody was talking much. A couple of the more timid boys were already in bed pretending to be fast asleep, hoping the invading force would ignore them if they did that. Pearce was standing on his bed surveying the impending field of battle like a five-star general. He immediately spotted Rowell and Chapman as they came in. He jumped down and came over to their corner.

"Where did you two fuck off to?" he demanded.

"None of your bloody business," Rowell said.

Pearce didn't respond in kind, taking his responsibilities seriously. He didn't want to sow any further discord amongst his modest forces. His dislike of Chapman and his determination to get even were still very much intact, but there was a time and place for everything, and right now he needed everyone to stand together. He knew too that Rowell and Chapman were not gutless wonders, and that was important. He sat down on Rowell's bed.

"We're guessing they're going to come between ten and ten fifteen," he said, getting right to the point. "They won't risk making it any later because Drydork usually gets back at about eleven but he sometimes comes in earlier than that. And I don't think they'll come earlier, because they'll be hoping some of us will be asleep."

Chapman sat down on his bed, wanting to put his cigarettes back under the floorboard but he didn't want to do it right in front of Pearce. Then he thought briefly about taking the piss but Pearce's earnestness was infectious, and so he just sat there listening.

"There are twelve of them in six and ten in seven," Pearce said. He paused briefly in case he was getting the numbers muddled. Satisfied that he wasn't, he went on. "If you subtract the wets, that means there'll probably be about sixteen of them coming through that door. If you take off our own wets that means it's pretty well one on one, though there are some really big fuckers in amongst their lot. But we just have to keep them away from Thornton for about five minutes, and I'm sure they'll chicken out."

He paused again and looked at Rowell and Chapman in turn, to make sure they were both following him so far. Both boys nodded.

"The first line of defence of course is the door, and we must try and hold them there as long as we can. They'll have to bunch up, but once they're through, they'll be all over us. Leomond, Coffin and Jones are best for the door, but with the exception of Coffin, they're pretty bloody slow, so the moment you get the alarm, I want you two to get to that door and help try and keep them out. Can you do that?"

Rowell and Chapman nodded solemnly.

"They won't know where Thornton is, but they'll be expecting him to be in bed. That's where they'll head once they are through, down that side, and it's important that we delay them as long as we can, bed by bed. Don't spread out, stay on that side so they think we're trying to keep them away from Thornton's bed, OK? The longer they're in here the more chicken they'll get, worrying about Drydork or prefects pitching up. We'll only have to keep it up for a few minutes. Thornton's going to be under the basins in that corner, and that's our fall back position. Once they find he's not in his own bed I want everyone into that corner to form a solid wall around him. That's our last stand – once they've got their hands on him, it's all over. All clear?"

The boys nodded again though neither of them really believed it would work out like that at all. It would be total chaos, and they would get flattened, but it was good to have a plan anyway and make a kind of game of it.

"Are you sure they're after Thornton?" Rowell asked.

"That's what I've heard," Pearce replied as though that should be enough.

Rowell shrugged, thinking it probably was true. He was the smallest dweeb in the dorm. They'd gone after him last time and got him. It had only been the boys from Dorm 6, and even then it had been a pushover for them.

Pearce got up and swaggered away, pausing to say a few words here and there. Chapman smiled as he watched him go, resisting the impulse to stand at attention and salute.

"I think we should just tell Thornton to sit by the door with ten bob in his hand and then we can all get some sleep," he said.

"Why didn't you suggest that?" Rowell said with a hint of petulance in his voice.

Chapman didn't reply, not wanting to sound even more of a spoilsport. He got changed into his pyjamas, putting the top on and then taking it off again. It didn't hold the same horrors as it had the previous night but there wasn't a lot of point with the sleeve hanging off still and no buttons. It would be another two days before he got his other pair of pyjamas and he preferred sleeping without a top anyway, so it didn't really matter. He folded the waist elastic down over itself so that his pyjama pants hung well below his hips.

"Why do you always do that?" Rowell asked.

"What?"

"Fold the elastic down like that."

"I don't know – it's more comfortable."

"It looks as though you're wearing a bikini."

Chapman put his hands on his hips and wiggled his body, doing the same little belly dance he'd done for Featherstone.

"Very funny," Rowell said, turning away to get his own pyjamas out from under his pillow.

Chapman went to the basins and washed his face and neck. While he was cleaning his teeth, he looked into the mirror and noticed Heathfield lying on his bed looking at him. He gave a little wave without turning round. Heathfield immediately looked down at the book in his lap, pretending not to notice. Chapman spat out the toothpaste, rinsed his mouth with water and then went over to the bed and sat down beside him. Heathfield looked up from the book, seeming surprised to see him, looking awkward again.

"Can you finish the drawing tomorrow?" Chapman asked.

"Yes, if you like."

Chapman took the towel from around his neck and gave his face another wipe. When he'd finished he held the towel in his lap and looked at Heathfield, his eyes wandering over the other boy's face, randomly inspecting each feature.

"Why did you draw me – really?" he asked.

Heathfield closed the book, keeping his finger in between the pages to hold his place.

"I told you," he said, going a little red again. He wanted to tell the truth. He longed more than anything in the world to reach out over those few inches and touch him.

Chapman studied his face a little longer and then abruptly looked away towards the door, where Kent had just come in, barking orders. He stood up then but stayed standing beside the bed for a few moments longer. Heathfield looked up surreptitiously at his slender figure; needing desperately to tell him how beautiful he was, saying the words like an incantation over and over in his own head.

"I hope we don't get too stuffed up tonight," Chapman said, unknowingly breaking the spell. He walked away towards his own bed.

Heathfield opened the book again, but he didn't look at it. His eyes followed Chapman's progress back across the dorm instead, oblivious to everything else.

Kent turned the lights out five minutes early, but by then everyone was in bed and quiet, anticipating the coming battle with varying mixtures of dread and excitement, so nobody moaned about it.

Leomond switched on his torch as usual, but after a minute or so he turned it off again, not able to concentrate on reading.

Thornton seemed extraordinarily happy, pleased in a confused way to be the object of such concentrated attention – to have some value, even if it was only ten shillings. He lay in bed, smiling happily up at the ceiling, his small thin body as rigid as a pole, ready for action and waiting for instructions from Pearce. He was glad to be under the protection of such a powerful figure – albeit someone who usually called him derogatory names or ignored him entirely.

Chapman leaned down, out of his bed, feeling around with the tips of his fingers trying to find the loose floorboard. When he had, he dropped the packet of cigarettes into the hole and let the board softly down again.

"Are you still going to hide under the bed?" Rowell whispered.

"No."

"Good."

Chapman lay down on his back, trying to fluff up the thin pillow behind his head. It didn't make much difference. He gave up and lay staring at the small window, counting stars.

"How many stars do you think there are?" he whispered

after a few minutes.

Rowell looked up at the window and started counting himself.

"Where?" he asked when he realised that it might take longer than he thought.

"On your bum, you dork – in the sky."

"Zillions."

"How many's that?"

"Oh piss off – how the hell should I know?" Rowell whispered.

Somebody scampered through the darkness and took up a position with their back to the wall by the doors. The shadowy figure peeped out through the glass panels. It was the first of Pearce's lookouts, moving much too early. Lights out in Dorms 6 and 7 wouldn't happen for at least another ten minutes and they were hardly going to trample over Kent. Nobody said anything, though, enjoying the drama of it all.

"Tell us a story, Leomond," Pearce said in a loud whisper, wanting to get the minds of his troops onto something else.

The only reaction was a very long silence. He was about to ask again when Leomond's deep, lyrical whisper startled them all.

"Once upon a time," he said, "in the land of the living dead, there was a zombie called Pearce and an even dumber zombie called Higgins…"

"Tell us a proper story," Pearce interrupted, ignoring the giggles.

Leomond kept them waiting again, though not as long. He put the torch under his chin, opened his mouth wide to show his teeth and switched it on. There were more giggles, but they were not quite the same, containing a tiny hint of fear in them. He turned the torch off after a few seconds, not wanting to waste the batteries.

Then he did begin to tell them a story, and it was mostly about the living dead. Before long, several heads disappeared entirely under their blankets. A few boys even began to imagine that the raiders from Dorms 6 and 7 wouldn't come at all, but that something else would, much later, shambling up the stairs from the basement, leaving a slimy trail full of small twitching body parts. It didn't seem then, lying there in the dark, that it would be satisfied with just taking Thornton or that it would be at all interested in a ten shilling note. The lookout by the door sneaked unobtrusively back to his bed after a while, not wanting to be the first to see whatever might be oozing up from the school basement.

It was a long, rambling story, and when Leomond eventually stopped many of the boys had forgotten about the impending raid. They were listening intently for other things in the silence, hoping not to hear them.

"What a load of crap," Pearce said, bringing some reality back. He sounded far less sure about it than his words suggested.

He hadn't noticed the lookout's desertion, being fairly well down in his own bed by then. Rowell had. He climbed out and went to replace him but he was already too late. As he got there the doors burst open and an avalanche of bodies came pouring through carrying him away like a cork. Chapman jumped up immediately. He launched himself from the end of his bed onto the nearest invader trying to force him down onto the floor. The other boy was too big and it didn't work. He felt someone grab one of his legs from behind and in an instant he was on the floor himself, and there were several pairs of hands grabbing at him.

"Positions!" Pearce yelled, shooting out of his blankets, but it was much too late for that already. They were all over the place, pounding away with pillows and towels and tipping up mattresses with and without their occupants.

Thornton was still frozen in his bed, undecided as to whether this was the raid or a visitation from another kind of hell entirely. Pearce yanked him out by the arm, wanting to get him to the basins, furiously intent on seeing at least that part of his plan put into action. They were both brought down before they'd gone three paces. All he could do was grab Thornton around the waist and roll over on top of him and try to worm under the nearest bed. Higgins stood over them, wildly swinging a pillow from side to side but he went down too, grabbed around the neck and thrown to the floor like a rag doll.

The only counter action that really worked began around Leomond's bed. Coffin and Jones immediately joined him. They pounded their way steadily towards the door, pushing and shoving half a dozen of the raiders before them. Pretty soon they were at the door, and it suddenly seemed to be all over. A couple of retreating stragglers pushed their way past, one of them getting a solid clap on the back of the head from Leomond's big black hand. The rest had already gone and calm descended abruptly. One or two boys were sobbing but other than that there was a strange quiet.

Pearce let go of Thornton and stood up slowly, sensing a victory. He could taste blood in his mouth and when he explored with his tongue he found one of his teeth was wobbling but it didn't worry him unduly.

"They didn't get him," he said triumphantly, and the news was greeted with a ragged little cheer.

Rowell had nearly been knocked cold by the first charge through the doors, banging his head on the floor as he was bowled over. Then he had been stepped on several times in the ensuing milieu. He stayed on his hands and knees for a while, trying to work out if anything was seriously damaged.

When he was pretty sure nothing was, he stood up unsteadily and looked around. Even in the dim light from the landing he could see that the dorm was in chaos. Beds had been pushed at odd angles and several had their mattresses gone. Sheets, pillows and blankets were all over the place. It had been much more savage than last time. Chapman's flippancy earlier in the evening now seemed to ring very hollow.

One of the doors opened a little and someone poked his head in cautiously, ready to pull back.

"We've got Chapman," the emissary said quickly. He threw something into the dorm and disappeared.

Leomond bent down and picked up the small bundle. When he held it up they could all see it was a pair of pyjama pants.

"Shit," Pearce said. He kicked out and in his exasperation and anger he almost kicked Thornton who was still sitting on the floor at his feet. His foot hit the metal leg of a bed instead, and that hurt like hell.

"It's not fair," Higgins said and there were many murmurs of agreement.

"Shit and fuck," Pearce said, hopping on one foot.

Nobody seemed to know what to do next. After a while Leomond spoke up.

"I'll go and get him," he said and he went to get ten shillings from his locker.

"I'll come too," Rowell said.

"OK," Pearce said wearily, nursing his foot. "We'd better get things sorted here. We'll square things up with you in the morning."

Leomond wasn't really expecting any trouble. He thought the exchange would be a formality. He was fed up though, and by the time he got to the door of Dorm 6 with Rowell in tow he was in no mood to be cautious. He simply barged through and stood staring into the gloom.

"He's not here, they took him up to seven," a voice said. "You better hurry because they're being real shits to him."

Leomond did hurry then, with Rowell scampering behind watching his back like a pet monkey. Again he didn't pause at the door. He pushed it open and strode in. It was difficult to see coming in from the light of the passage but he could hear and sense people moving about.

"Where's Chapman?" he said, peering around the room.

"I'm here," said a muffled voice from the corner.

A torch came on suddenly, right in front of him, pointed straight at his face.

"It's the bloody gollywog," someone said.

Leomond put a hand up to shield his eyes. He lunged forward trying to grab the torch or knock it away. In the same instant the lights came on because Rowell had found the switch by the door. The boy with the torch backed away quickly, his advantage gone. Over in the corner, three other boys jumped up from one of the beds. Leomond could see Chapman lying there on his stomach with his face in a pillow. He started to get up, and then the lights went off again. There were strangled noises from Rowell as his neck was squeezed in the crook of a bigger boy's arm.

Leomond went forward, towards the bed and soon bumped up against two or three dim bodies blocking his path. He was a little frightened, but also getting very angry, and he launched himself forward with a loud roar, swinging his big arms like clubs. One boy was knocked flat on his back, and the others gave way immediately, startled by his power and ferocity. He was still swinging when he bumped up against the bed.

The lights came on again then, because Rowell had managed to stretch out to the switch, despite being throttled.

"OK, that's enough – cut it out," one of the bigger boys said in a loud voice. In the bright light that seemed to stop everything very suddenly.

The boy who was strangling Rowell let go of his neck and stood back, looking dazed himself.

Chapman was sitting on the side of the bed stark naked, and that made Leomond remember the pyjama pants still clutched in his hand.

"Thanks, Leo," Chapman said when he took them.

He stood up and pulled the pants on, not looking at anyone, though everyone was looking at him. He seemed strangely calm in the circumstances. He even took time to methodically fold down the elastic waistband.

"You stupid little faggot," a boy said. It was Gatesford Minor, the boy who had been on top of him moments before, holding his arms back and forcing his face into the pillow.

Chapman smiled at him and then blew him a kiss.

Leomond was astonished and irritated by that. He grabbed Chapman by the arm and pushed him towards the door, worried things were going to start getting crazy again.

"Go," he said. He held up the ten shilling note and then dropped it onto the bed.

"Yeah, run along you little whore – kiss, kiss," another boy said.

Chapman paused briefly at the door holding up his hands like a victorious boxer. Without turning round he pulled two zap signs at the boys behind him before scampering down the stairs after Rowell.

"Stuff you – you little prick," a voice said. Something thudded into the door as it swung shut behind Leomond.

None of them said anything on the way down. They were all a bit shocked by the nasty confrontation and anxious to get back to the dorm before they ran into anyone. Leomond was puzzled by the fact that no prefects had appeared, given the din the raid must have caused. He rightly assumed that Kent had long since gone, heading straight for the pub after lights out as he always did on his duty nights. But there was supposed to be at least one prefect on duty making regular patrols until after ten.

Back in the dorm, they'd made a lot of progress in restoring things. Most of the other boys were already in bed, nursing bruises and glad it was all over. Pearce and Higgins were still up waiting by the door.

"Are you OK?" Pearce asked, seeing that Chapman was limping a bit.

"Fine," he said.

"Why the shit did they grab you?"

"I don't know – what's the difference?" Chapman said.

"And why did they pull your bloody pants off?" Pearce persisted.

Chapman hesitated, wanting to get back to bed, not knowing how to answer anyway.

"They just wanted to kiss his bum," Leomond said.

Pearce and Higgins laughed uneasily at that, taking it as a joke but knowing that in some way perhaps it wasn't. Leomond's quip stopped their questions though and they went off to their own beds, fed up with the whole business now.

"Thanks, Leo, you were bloody fantastic," Chapman said.

He put out his small hand, and Leomond looked at it for a moment before shaking it up and down.

"And you're really weird," he said.

Rowell had gone straight to his bed, not pausing at the door. His head was throbbing, and he was anxious to lie down.

"Are you alright, Chris?" Chapman whispered as he climbed between his sheets.

"I think my skull's cracked," Rowell said.

"Are you serious?"

"Not really."

Chapman hesitated a little before lying down.

"Goodnight then – and thanks for coming," he said.

"What was Gatesford doing to you?" Rowell asked, keeping his head dead still on the pillow.

"He's just like his fucking brother," Chapman said.

He didn't elaborate, and Rowell's head was aching too much to ask anything else.

Rowell was already asleep twenty minutes later when Dryden turned the key in the lock and opened and closed the door to his room. Chapman heard him, but it was a while longer before he closed his own eyes and went to sleep. Even then, when the dreams came, there were still wild creatures with strange distorted features reaching out their hands and calling his name, dancing all around him in the dark.

TWENTY-FOUR

A lot of people were looking up and watching when the small aircraft's engine spluttered, caught again briefly and then died away completely. It hung in the air a moment longer like a child's toy suspended by invisible thread. Then its nose dipped forward, and it dropped like a stone.

The woman at No. 14 was hanging out her washing in the back garden. She told the firemen, and anyone else who would listen, that she had seen the faces of the two men through the windshield moments before impact. She said that the expressions on their faces would haunt her until the day she died.

"Today nearly was that day, luv," a police constable told her.

He was right too, because the small plane had landed with an ear-splitting bang in the small front garden of her terraced house. A couple of parked cars and two big trees on the pavement had sustained serious damage, but the house, apart from broken windows, was peculiarly unscathed. There was nothing discernable left of the two men, and it was difficult to see that the pile of mangled metal had been a plane at all. Even the tail was crumpled and broken beyond easy recognition. The absence of an explosion or even much of a fire immediately suggested to the firemen on the scene that the plane had probably run out of fuel, but it would be many weeks before that could be confirmed. The experts would have to sort through all the bits first.

A crowd had gathered quickly in the street. Among the people watching were several boys from the Grammar School. The policemen kept shooing everyone away, but they drifted back again, edging closer for a better look.

They took the woman from No. 14 away in the back of an ambulance, but the crowd soon knew that she wasn't injured, that it was just a precaution.

"Just the shock of it," one neighbour said to another, and the news was passed on quickly.

An old man from two houses down was taken off in an ambulance too, and the crowd soon learnt that he had suffered a heart attack but would probably be alright.

Chapman and Rowell stood gawking and listening with everyone else. Gladstone waited patiently beside them, twitching his big nose at the strange smells coming from all the people and from the pile of twisted, smoking metal.

After a while the police got really impatient. One of them jumped up on a low wall and spoke to the crowd sternly through a megaphone.

"Clear the street," he shouted. "Anyone who doesn't live in this street must leave immediately, and those of you who do must please return to your homes and stay indoors. There's nothing to see here, so please move along now and let the emergency services get on with their job."

He was wrong about there being nothing to see, but that was exactly what policemen always said at the scene of a disaster. It was as if by saying that, it somehow became true.

People did move away, though, with looks of perplexed wonder on their faces, many of them talking to complete strangers as though they'd known them for years.

The two boys lingered longer than most, craning their necks for a better view. Eventually a policeman came walking over to them to repeat what the man with the megaphone had just said, only less politely.

"Hop it, you two," he said.

Chapman tugged at Gladstone's lead, and he came willingly enough.

The policeman watched the two boys and the huge dog walking off down the street. He had recognised them both immediately from his beat, only the last time he had seen them there had been no dog and they had been holding hands. He smiled when Chapman nearly walked into a lamp post, still staring back over his shoulder. The big dog pulled him to one side at the last moment.

"Blimey," Rowell said. "That's not something you see every day."

"What a mess," Chapman said.

"Do you think the engine just conked out?"

"I think it ran out of petrol," Chapman said, repeating what he'd overheard a man next to him say.

"How dumb can you get?" Rowell said.

They were soon back at Connaught Avenue and turned right, heading for the playing fields again. They'd just started out from the school with Gladstone when they had seen the plane coming down. When they heard the bang they went straight there, along with some of the other boys.

"We've got a good excuse if we're late back," Chapman said.

"A plane nearly fell on us, sir," Rowell said, pretending to be talking to Kennedy.

"Imagine if it had fallen on the school," Chapman said.

"Imagine," Rowell repeated.

They did exactly that then, beginning seriously by constructing a variety of grim scenarios. It wasn't long before the plane was coming down on the heads of people they didn't like. The more grotesque and bloodthirsty the fantasies they conjured up, the more they began to enjoy them. By the time they got to the fields, Bruder, Kent, Tetley, Chatsworth, Gatesford and a whole host of others had been decapitated, incinerated or blown to bits. They were giggling non-stop. Gladstone was glancing up at them, wondering whether to bark.

"Can you hold Gladstone while I nip up the tree for a quick ciggey?" Chapman asked when they'd gone through the gates.

Rowell looked at him dubiously. "What am I supposed to do if someone comes along – there are supposed to be two of us."

"Say I've gone for a piss."

"What – up in the tree?"

"Say what you like," Chapman said holding out the lead.

Rowell took it reluctantly, looking around to see if anyone was watching. There were some boys playing football a couple of fields away, but other than that, the coast was clear. When Chapman started climbing, Gladstone pulled Rowell under the tree and looked up anxiously, starting to whine a little. Rowell patted him on the top of his gigantic head, but that had no effect. After a bit he let out one of his thunderous barks.

"Shut him up," Chapman hissed from high above.

"How?"

"I don't know."

"Why don't you piss on him – that should do it," Rowell said.

"Fuck off."

Gladstone barked again and although they were quite far away some of the boys playing football stopped and looked over. The dog pulled Rowell further under the tree to try a new angle, trying to catch sight of the boy in the branches.

"Come down," Rowell said.

"I've only had one puff."

"He doesn't like you being up there."

"What? – did he tell you that?"

"It's obvious."

"OK," Chapman said reluctantly.

Rowell began to relax again. He tried pulling Gladstone back out from under the tree, but he wouldn't budge and that was that. So they both stood there waiting and looking up into the branches. When there was still no sign of him after a while, Rowell called up again.

"Hang on a minute," Chapman said.

A wind came up then and the big oak murmured, its high branches waving slowly back and forth. A few loose leaves and twigs rained down and Rowell lowered his eyes so that nothing would fall into them.

When Chapman did reappear, jumping off the wall, Gladstone pulled Rowell over and made his usual big fuss, prodding his muzzle into the boy's legs and body.

"You took your bloody time," Rowell said grumpily.

"They're rehearsing that play – I could see them through the window," Chapman said.

"What were they doing?" Rowell asked.

"Nothing much – just standing around like a lot of dorks. Chatsworth's there and Richardson's waving his arms around a lot."

They started to walk off then to do a circuit of the playing fields as they'd been told to do. They hadn't gone far when Chapman stopped.

"Actually I really do want a piss now," he said. "I won't be long – sorry."

Rowell sighed in exasperation, but he didn't say anything. He allowed Gladstone to pull him along until they got to the door to the gym. He didn't follow Chapman inside, pulling hard at the lead to stop the dog. He had to dig his heels in to do that, but the dog did stop at the door, looking back up at him anxiously. At least standing there it didn't matter if anyone came along, he thought, seeing as how his co-dog-walker really had gone for a pee, and no one could blame him for that.

Inside, Chapman could hear Richardson's voice as he walked across the lobby towards the toilets. One of the doors into the hall was ajar, and he paused briefly to peep in, trying not to be seen. Several boys were standing in a semi-circle around Richardson listening intently as he prattled on. One of them glanced over at the door. Chapman immediately pulled back and carried on to the toilet, thinking that it was probably going to be a very boring play even if someone did get torn to bits at the end.

Standing at the urinal, he had a bit of a problem with his zip. He got it loose eventually and had started to pee when the door opened and closed behind him. Nobody came up to take a leak, but he was suddenly startled by Chatsworth's voice. He nearly splashed his trousers looking round.

"No wrestler thou, as show thy flowing locks,
Down thy cheeks floating, fraught with all desire;
And white, from heedful tendance, is thy skin,
Smit by no sun-shafts, but made wan by shade,
While thou dost hunt desire with beauty's lure."

Chatsworth delivered the lines leaning against the doorframe with his arms folded. He stayed there, smiling and staring.

Chapman had finished by then – in fact the pee had dried up abruptly when Chatsworth started speaking. He had zipped up his trousers quickly.

"That's what Pentheus says when he first meets Dionysus," Chatsworth said.

Chapman stood by the urinal, waiting for him to move away from the door, not really understanding the lines; not sure whether they were meant to flatter or insult.

"Give me a break Chapman – I really don't want us to be enemies any more," Chatsworth said.

The boy just stood there staring at him, saying nothing. When he still got no response, Chatsworth moved away from the door.

Chapman hesitated for a moment, as though he was about to speak. Before he could there was a big commotion on the other side of the door and it flew open. Gladstone burst in, towing Rowell on the other end of the lead.

"I can't hold the fuck…" Rowell said. He shut up immediately when he caught sight of Chatsworth.

Gladstone stopped pulling once he was in and looked around eagerly, his big nose overwhelmed by the odours. Chapman grabbed his collar and then put his hands on the dog's huge rump and started shoving him back towards the door. Rowell pulled hard on the lead.

"Come on, Gladstone, you great fat turd, move it," Rowell said.

"His name's really Zeus," Chatsworth said.

The dog looked up at him briefly when he heard the name. So did the two boys.

"Well it was, anyway," Chatsworth added. He looked quite

sad and dejected somehow.

He turned away and walked over to the urinal.

Rowell backed out of the door first, tugging hard. Gladstone suddenly gave up the struggle and went out too, his abrupt change of heart nearly causing the boy to fall over backwards. Chapman was halfway out when he stopped. He looked at Chatsworth's back.

"If that's what you want, it's OK," he said quietly, and closed the door.

Outside, the wind had come up in earnest. Small clouds were scudding rapidly across the sky from the southwest, the advance guard of a thunderstorm. The groaning branches of the big oak trees heaved up and down, seeming ready to snap. The football game had ended. The players were being blown along, hurrying anyway towards the gate, intent on getting back to school and shelter before the first big drops came down.

"We'd better get back too," Rowell shouted against the wind.

Chapman grinned at him, a grin full of mischief. Then he shook his head. He ran full tilt into the fields instead, leaping and punching the air every few yards as though urging the wind to lift him up and make him fly. Despite Rowell's best efforts, Gladstone took off after him, wrenching the lead out of his aching hands.

Chapman lay down on his back when he reached the middle of the fields, stretching his arms and legs wide. He shouted something at the sky but the words were immediately whipped away by the high wind. Gladstone towered over him, his deep excited barks seeming to roll away under the darkening sky like a strange unnatural thunder.

The first heavy drops burst on the grass and on Chapman's limbs and body, wetting the front of his shirt and trousers.

He just lay there laughing.

Rowell caught up and made a half-hearted attempt to catch hold of Gladstone's wildly flailing lead.

"You're a raving loony," he screamed. "We'll get soaked."

An instant later he found himself down on the wet grass too, his legs knocked from under him by Gladstone.

"You stupid bloody flea bag," he bellowed. But despite his real anger and the slight pain in his hip from falling, he found himself giggling too.

He jumped on top of Chapman. They wrestled on the grass in the pouring rain, rolling over and over while the big dog raced around them, barking and darting back and forth, seeming to egg them on.

Then the water came out of the sky in solid sheets, like the heavens had emptied a bath. They started to run for shelter then, but it soon seemed that there wasn't a lot of point. It was impossible to get any wetter. They both stopped. Gladstone walked beside them. The madness had gone out of him too. It wasn't really necessary to hold his lead, but Rowell picked it up anyway.

"It's your turn," he said and held it out for Chapman to take.

The heart of the storm had passed when they got back to the gym, the hard rain subsiding into steady drizzle. The boys debated whether to shelter there or go on anyway back to the school. In the end, they decided to carry on, not wanting to bump into Chatsworth again or perhaps even Richardson. The teacher's ancient Jag was still parked there, covered in leaves and twigs now, so they knew the rehearsal must still be going on.

"What was Chatsworth's story this time?" Rowell asked after a while.

"I don't know – he was saying lines from that stupid play.

He says he wants to be friends."

Rowell thought about that for a moment or two.

"Maybe you should ask him to give you those pictures, then."

"He won't," Chapman said.

They had forgotten about the plane crash, but it all came flooding back again when they saw the police car blocking the side road where the crash had been. They stopped there to stare down the road, but it was too far away to see anything, especially with the drizzle coming down.

A policeman was sitting in the car, and he wound down the window a few inches, thinking that the boys might be considering going down the street.

"You're not allowed down there boys, move along – nothing to see," he shouted.

Chapman had to give Gladstone's lead a strong pull to get him moving again.

"I wonder whether they've got the bodies out yet," he said as they walked on.

Rowell didn't know the answer, so he didn't say anything, wishing now that the rain would stop, but it was still raining when they knocked on Kennedy's door.

"Good grief, look at the state of you two," the old parson said. "You look like a couple of drowned rats."

He sounded embarrassed about it, though, as they were like that because they'd been walking his dog. He took the lead, and Gladstone went in willingly enough, glad to be out of the rain. The moment he was in the hallway, he shook himself vigorously, splattering the walls and the parson's trousers.

"Did you hear about the plane crash, sir?" Chapman asked.

"Yes, I did – it was on the radio news," Kennedy said. "It's a very sad thing."

"We saw it crash," Rowell said. "It happened when we were

walking down to the fields with Gladstone."

"Really?" Kennedy said.

He didn't sound that interested, because he was preoccupied with the dog and the mess its muddy paws were making on the hall carpet. The boys were making a mess too.

"You better run along and get out of those wet clothes," he said.

"It was pretty close," Rowell continued, wanting him to be impressed.

Kennedy nodded, but it was obvious he wasn't really paying any attention.

"Thank you very much, boys. Make sure you have a hot bath and change straight away," he said.

"Thank you, sir," they both said. They ran off over the road back to the school, wondering whether the plane crash had been such a really big deal after all.

TWENTY-FIVE

Only Heathfield and Thornton were in the dorm when they got back up from the bathrooms. Heathfield was sitting on his bed drawing something on a pad, and that immediately reminded Chapman about the portrait. He felt guilty then, because he hadn't spoken to him at all for the past four days, not since before the dorm raid, and before that he knew he'd been a bit of a pest about it. But he hadn't lost interest in the drawing, just forgotten. He really did want to have it finished so that he could send it to his mother, sure that she would like it. He decided to go over and ask him because it seemed like a good time, with half an hour still until supper and no one much around.

He picked up the clean shirt he'd taken from his locker, meaning to put it on, but changed his mind and dropped it back onto his bed. Matron had taken his wet clothes and Rowell's, moaning like a drain about it, saying they wouldn't be dry until the morning. He took his spare trousers out of his locker, but he decided to put them on later too and went over with just his towel wrapped around him.

Heathfield stopped drawing and closed the pad when he saw Chapman coming. He stood up, looking as though he'd just remembered something and was about to leave.

"Did you hear about the plane?" Chapman asked.

"Yes, everyone's been talking about it – especially Pearce. He said he was there soon after it happened," Heathfield said.

"We saw it crash," Chapman said. He couldn't keep a little pride out of his voice, although he tried to sound nonchalant.

"What, actually hitting the ground?"

"No – but almost. It was only a couple of streets away – we were taking Gladstone for a walk."

"Wow, that's close," Heathfield said.

Chapman nodded, pleased that he was more impressed than Kennedy had been.

"Are you still happy to finish that drawing of me?" he asked.

Heathfield nodded, sitting down again.

"What about now?" Chapman asked.

"OK, if you like."

He reached down into his locker to get the drawing out, being careful to ensure that none of the others came out with it.

"Do you want me to put a shirt on and a tie?" Chapman asked when he saw the drawing again.

"No, that's alright, that bit's done already," Heathfield said.

Chapman sat on the next bed and tried to look serious. He couldn't keep a straight face for very long and he started to smile, making a conscious effort not to, but the smile kept coming back. It didn't seem to worry Heathfield, so in the end he let it stay.

"Do you think I've got white skin?" he asked, looking askew at his own shoulder and down at his tummy.

Heathfield shook his head.

"You've got a bit of a tan," he said.

Chapman tried to remember other words from the lines Chatsworth had spoken in the gym toilets but he had been too surprised to really listen so nothing else came back.

"Do you like drawing people?" he asked.

"Not usually."

"Why did you draw me, then?"

Heathfield stopped sketching for a moment and he opened his mouth to say something, but no words came out at first.

"That's the third time you've asked me," he said eventually, smiling despite himself at the simplicity of the trap.

Chapman nodded and his smile broadened a little too.

"So why won't you tell me?"

Heathfield looked beyond him at Rowell and then at Thornton, but neither of them were listening.

"Because you'll think I'm weird," he said. He was blushing again like he'd done in Turner's art class.

"No I won't," Chapman said.

Heathfield took a deep breath then like someone about to jump from a very high place, not sure where or how the coming fall would end.

"OK then — because you're the most beautiful person I've ever seen," he said, mumbling the words quickly, as though he was eager to be rid of them. He kept his eyes down on the paper, watching the pencil moving rapidly to and fro in his fingers; waiting for Chapman to laugh or get up and go away. When neither happened he looked up cautiously, ready to hide his eyes in the portrait again.

Chapman was still smiling, his head held slightly to one side trying to get a better view of the upside-down sketch.

"I wonder how I can post it," he said. "It would be a pity to fold it."

Heathfield was surprised at that, at something so mundane. He was fully expecting ridicule, denial or some sort of protest.

"You can roll it up and post it like a tube," he said.

Chapman nodded and then flopped back down over the narrow bed. He stretched his arms out and tilted his head way back to look at the room upside down, exposing his delicate throat. He stayed like that – like a sacrifice on some pagan altar – for about twenty seconds and then sat up again feeling slightly dizzy.

"Is it finished yet?" he asked.

"A couple more minutes," Heathfield said.

The drawing was finished, as much as it could ever be, but he kept moving the pencil. He knew that the moment it stopped Chapman would get up and go, and that would be the end of it. Looking from his exquisite face to the portrait and back again, he wondered why there hadn't been any reaction at all when he'd called him beautiful. His fear of ridicule gave way gradually to a feeling of disappointment. He was sad that something wrenched from such a private part of him seemed to be so irrelevant.

"There," he said finally, holding up the sketch and turning it around so that his model could see it.

"That's great, thanks very much," Chapman said, standing up. "Can I take it now?"

"All yours," Heathfield said and he handed it over.

Chapman studied the drawing but instead of walking away he sat down beside him, still looking at it and smiling. He sat very close so that there was no space between them at all. Normally Heathfield would have moved if someone sat next to him like that, touching him. But he didn't move and he didn't really breathe much either, wishing that it could stay like that for a very long time.

"Do you like it?" he asked.

"Very much – I think my mum will love it," Chapman said. "I wish I could give you something for doing it."

"You don't have to give me anything – I really enjoyed doing it," Heathfield said.

Chapman looked at him then and their faces were only inches apart. Normally people got uglier up close, but to Heathfield his skin was like a soft mist and he looked even more beautiful.

"You'll probably be famous one day," Chapman said.

"I doubt it," Heathfield said truthfully.

Chapman stood up and carefully rolled up the drawing as Heathfield had suggested. He was obviously getting ready to leave, and he had to leave because things couldn't stay like that forever. Heathfield felt an overwhelming surge of despair.

"Can I draw you again?" he blurted out.

Chapman seemed to be a bit taken aback, but it was only momentary. He grinned and sat down again though not quite as close. But he didn't have a chance to answer because Rowell called to him from the other side of the dormitory and then came over.

"Has he finished it – can I see?" he asked.

Chapman unrolled the paper again and held it out. Rowell looked at it critically, holding his head first this way and then that.

"I think it was more like you before," he said.

Heathfield's face fell and Rowell immediately felt bad about that.

"But it's still very good," he added quickly and handed the paper back.

Chapman stood up, adjusting the towel around his waist because it had started to slip off.

"I think it's really great. Thanks, Simon," he said.

Heathfield watched the two of them walk away. He wondered whether Chapman would tell Rowell what he'd said, half expecting them to start laughing and for Rowell to look back at him when they did. He felt foolish and awkward about sounding so desperate in wanting to draw him again. It must have seemed odd and Chapman had probably guessed now how he really felt. But they didn't look at him, and after a while he realised that he might never get an answer. That depressed him too, because he knew he would be too embarrassed to ever ask again.

Chapman got dressed and was putting on his damp tie when the doors of the dorm swung open and Voaden walked in. He came straight over, immediately grabbing his small friend, squeezing his shoulders and ruffling his hair. He seemed to be in an exuberant mood, and the reason was soon obvious in the smell of beer on his breath.

"So what have you been up to, my little mate," he said, falling down onto the bed and bringing Chapman down with him.

"We took Kennedy's dog for a walk, and we saw that plane crash – did you hear about it?" Chapman asked, trying to wriggle out from under his arm and stand up again.

Voaden just hugged him closer and so he gave up trying to escape, not wanting to seem unfriendly. Voaden's boozy breath hit him in the face at point blank range.

"Yeah – splat. You know who was in it?" Voaden said.

Chapman shook his head. Rowell pricked up his ears, eager to know himself.

"Featherwhatsit, the bloke who got you into the shit – him and some other bloke, bloody jam sandwich now," Voaden said happily.

"You're kidding?"

"No – nice one, not so?" He finally let go of Chapman and stood up himself. "Come and join Root and me after supper – we're going back over for a few toots at Johno's – his folks are away tonight. OK?"

Chapman nodded, wondering who Johno was but mostly still thinking about Featherstone and how his prim and orderly life had fallen out of the sky and been smashed to bits while he had been watching and not knowing.

Voaden left then and such was his good mood that he even gave Rowell a friendly jab in the ribs on the way past.

"That's unbelievable," Chapman said, his voice full of awe and wonder.

"Weird," Rowell said.

They looked at each other and neither of them knew how they should react, whether to laugh and gloat or be solemn about it. Because the indecision made them nervous they both started smiling.

"He was a real turd," Rowell said.

Chapman nodded and he looked for his jacket momentarily before remembering that it was downstairs with Matron and would only be dry in the morning. They left then to go down to supper. Heathfield was also going, and they went together, dropping down the stairs in a series of big hops and leaps. When they reached the ground floor, Rowell was well ahead and Heathfield was lagging well behind, so Chapman waited for him at the foot of the stairs.

"I really do like the drawing," he said when Heathfield caught up.

"I think maybe Rowell's right – the first sketch was better," Heathfield said.

"I think it's great, but you can draw me again whenever you like – starkers, if you like," Chapman said with a grin.

"Thanks," Heathfield said, not really sure that he had

actually heard the last bit and if he had whether it had been meant as a joke.

They didn't speak again and parted company anyway in the dining hall, queuing for their food. Then they went to their different places. Chapman ignored the usual jibes from Gatesford Minor and his friends on the Upper Fourth benches as he hurried past. He squeezed in between Rowell and Leomond.

"Are you going to go for a few toots?" Rowell asked, the moment Drummond had said grace. He emphasized the last word because it was a strange one, and he hadn't used it before.

"I think so – can you cover for me if I'm late back?" Chapman said.

Rowell could think of any number of good reasons for him not to go and that was one of them but he didn't want to sound like a wet so he kept them to himself.

"How late do you think you're going to be?" he asked.

Chapman shrugged because he didn't know. He didn't really know who Johno was or where he lived, or how they were supposed to get there, or what would happen when they did. He knew toots were drinks – that much was obvious anyway from Voaden's breath, and he'd heard his dad use the word once or twice. He was game to try that, to see what it was like.

"I can't cover for you at lights out – you'll be back before then, won't you?" Rowell said anxiously.

"Can't you say I'm in the loo?"

The thought that Chapman could even contemplate still being out there in some unknown place having toots with someone like Voaden when everyone else was safe in bed worried and perplexed Rowell, and it showed in his face. He didn't reply and Chapman saw his confused expression.

"I'm sure I'll be back in time – no big deal," he said.

"What are toots?" Leomond asked, not knowing what they were talking about.

"Booze," Chapman said.

Leomond nodded and it only registered after a couple of seconds that Chapman was planning to go out drinking. Then he stopped nodding and started shaking his head from side to side, but he didn't say anything. He carried on eating.

Higgins stopped behind Rowell on his way past carrying his pudding and tapped him on the top of the head with a spoon. Rowell swung round ready to hit him but Higgins backed away out of range, bumping into the back of a boy in the next form and nearly getting into trouble there too.

"Dryden was looking for you – he wants to see you after supper in his room," Higgins said.

"When did he tell you that?" Rowell snapped.

"Just now," Higgins said, and he scampered on to his own place a little further up the table.

"Stupid jerk," Rowell said; the spoon had hurt even though it had only been a light tap.

"I wonder why he wants to see you," Chapman said.

Rowell was thinking about that too, rubbing the top of his head and running through a whole host of possibilities in his mind. Nothing alarming leapt out, at least nothing that didn't involve Chapman as well – and he hadn't been summoned. It was enough to spoil his appetite, though, because there was virtually no possibility that it could be about something good. He looked at the pudding Leomond was finishing off and decided not to bother with it and go straight away to get Dryden over with.

He stood up and leaned down to deliver a last word of warning in Chapman's ear.

"Watch yourself, Pete, and don't let that big jerk drag you into something really daft," he said softly.

"Thanks, I won't. You will cover for me if Drydork asks where I am?"

Rowell nodded. He extricated himself from the bench and left. He didn't have to go all the way because he caught up with Dryden going up the second flight of stairs.

"Higgins said you wanted to see me, sir," he said.

"Yes, thanks for being so prompt," Dryden said, caught off guard.

Rowell breathed a sigh of relief hearing that, because it couldn't be something serious if Drydork was being polite about it.

"I've invited Chapman on an outing on Sunday, and I wondered whether you'd like to come along too," Dryden said.

Rowell's look of complete surprise was comical, and Dryden couldn't help smiling.

"Yes, sir – that would be very nice, sir – thank you, sir," he stammered.

A couple of other boys came up the stairs and they stood aside to let them pass.

"Good – let's go up to my room, I want to have a chat with you anyway," Dryden said.

Rowell followed him up the stairs, remembering how weird he'd said it was to Chapman – Dryden inviting him on an outing – and now suddenly he was going too and that was also weird, but in a different way. There was no reason he could think of that Dryden should be rewarding either of them. He knew it was something else, not just about having fun.

When they got to his room, Dryden sat down at his desk, and he told the boy to sit in the chair. Rowell sat down cautiously, as though there might be thorns there.

"How many times have you been in DT this year?" Dryden asked but in a friendly kind of voice.

The boy had to do a bit of counting in his head. When he

came up with a number it didn't sound that bad.

"Four – I think, sir," he said. He wondered whether the number of DTs influenced being invited on an outing.

Dryden nodded.

"I thought it was six or seven, but never mind," he said. "What I really wanted to say to you is that I'm very impressed by the way you've taken Chapman under your wing and how you stand up for him all the time. I don't think it's been easy for him settling in here – or easy for you – and you've proved to be a very good friend – almost too good."

Rowell was beginning to puff up listening to Dryden's praise, but the sting in the tail abruptly deflated the feeling. He remembered how he'd behaved when Chapman was caned and started worrying again about what might be coming next.

"Chapman's a bit wild, isn't he?" Dryden said looking him straight in the eyes.

The boy opened his mouth but didn't know how to answer. Dryden knew it was an unfair question so he didn't let it hang in the air.

"I know he's a bit wild and that's why I've asked him on an outing," he said.

Rowell couldn't really follow the sense in that but he assumed it must be a grown up thing; maybe outings were a way of controlling wild things, calming them down, like taking Gladstone for a long walk.

"We're both looking out for him – it's my job as House Master, and you're his best friend – and it's obviously best if we work together, so to speak."

The boy was completely lost now, not really understanding what he was on about, but he nodded anyway, knowing that it was expected of him.

"I'm not asking you to be a sneak but I can't help much if I don't know what's really going on," Dryden continued.

At first the words were just more noises coming out of his mouth, but then they abruptly fitted together and Rowell thought he understood exactly what he was saying. It was all about that disgusting night with Chatsworth and co. Dryden was just looking at him as though it was his turn to say something. He wondered what he was expecting him to say and how much else he knew or was guessing at – and why he cared so much about Chapman for that matter. In between it all he was a little miffed that his invitation seemed to be a kind of afterthought, dependent on his being Chapman's friend, just like it was with Voaden.

"He's fine, sir," he said.

"Is he – really?" Dryden said.

Rowell thought about Voaden and the pill and now the toots and all the smoking and Chatsworth not wanting to be enemies, just wanting another… you know, and the dorm raid and what happened after that. It was quite a long list of things that weren't really that fine and some of them were downright scary. But Dryden said he wasn't asking him to be a sneak so it was difficult to know exactly what he was expecting to hear.

"I think so sir," he said.

"Good," Dryden said doubtfully. "But you will tell me if you feel there's something I should know, won't you? You won't just keep quiet if Chapman really starts to get involved in something stupid?"

Rowell squirmed inwardly, wondering whether he somehow knew about the toots. His own advice of a few minutes earlier bounced back at him, but he nodded solemnly. He wondered whether going for toots with Voaden was stupid enough to spill the beans about.

But Dryden gave up then and rocked back in his chair. It

had been a long shot anyway, and he hadn't really expected Rowell to tell him anything. Nevertheless, he was a bit disappointed, hoping something would slip out.

"And how are you – any problems?" he asked. "You seem to be coping a bit better in maths this term – forty eight per cent in the last test," he said.

"I'm fine, sir. I think I'm starting to get the hang of it now," Rowell said.

"Brave words – let's hope you're right."

The boy smiled, enjoying the thought that he was being brave.

There was an awkward silence then while Dryden searched around for something else to say. He felt a bit embarrassed that the whole thing had really been about Chapman.

"Did you hear about the plane crash, sir?" Rowell asked.

"Yes – very nasty."

"We saw it – Pete and me, we were taking Gladstone for a walk. We got there a few minutes afterwards."

"So you saw the whole thing?"

"Yes, sir."

"Good heavens – it must have been a bit gruesome."

Rowell nodded, although it hadn't been really, just a big mess.

"Did you know that man was in it, sir – Mr Featherstone?"

"Really? No, I hadn't heard that," Dryden said. He was quite shocked at the coincidence, like the boys had been.

Rowell couldn't help smiling a little, and although he bit his lip as soon the smile appeared, Dryden still noticed.

"It's not a very nice way for anyone to die," he said. He tried not to make it sound like a rebuke, but it came out like that anyway.

He stood up, and Rowell stood up too, knowing the talk was over.

"Where are you taking us on Sunday, sir?" he asked at the door.

"I haven't decided yet. It'll have to be a surprise," Dryden said. "Thanks for the chat, Rowell – and you will think about what I've said?"

"Yes, sir," Rowell said, and he knew at least that much was true.

TWENTY-SIX

In the end it was only Voaden and Chapman who went off to Johno's, because Root had decided he wasn't feeling well. Voaden had sobered up by the time they went over the wall behind the science lab, and he wasn't in such a jovial mood anymore. They went over the wall in deference to the fact that Chapman wasn't allowed out at all after supper. Voaden wasn't really allowed out either without a chit, but that was largely a technicality. No one would have challenged him, not before nine or so – Bruder or Dryden maybe, but no one else.

It was still light, but the afternoon storm had left a chill in the air. Chapman wished Voaden had been prepared to wait while he went and fetched a jersey, having just his shirt on and no jacket, but he hadn't and that was that. It wasn't a long walk to Johno's house, Voaden had said, only a couple of streets away from where the plane had crashed, but they didn't take a direct route because he wanted to stop off and buy some cigarettes. He bought a pack for Chapman too, saying he could pay him back later. He also bought a packet of crisps and ate them noisily as the two of them walked along, offering the packet to Chapman a couple of times, but he didn't take any.

"What's all this crap between you and Gatesford?" Voaden asked out of the blue, crumpling the empty packet and tossing it over a hedge into someone's front garden.

Chapman was alarmed by the question, not knowing which of the brothers he was talking about.

"He's telling everyone you're a fairy," Voaden continued when he didn't get an answer immediately.

"Which Gatesford?" Chapman asked.

Voaden glanced at him, surprised that he didn't know and that the bigger Gatesford should even figure as a possibility at all. That thought hadn't even crossed his mind.

"Minor," he said.

"He's a complete jerk," Chapman said.

"Of course he's a jerk, but why's he saying that?"

Chapman was feeling very uncomfortable, thinking about Gatesford pulling his pants off after the dorm raid and sitting on his back on the bed rocking back and forth, working himself up, forcing his face into the pillow. He didn't want Voaden to know how helpless he'd been and think him a sissy because of it. Things like that didn't happen to Voaden, and he couldn't believe they ever had, even when he was smaller.

They passed an old couple who were waiting for their Maltese poodle to finish crapping on the pavement. Chapman didn't want to say anything while they could hear. The little dog stared up at him as they went past, seeming to be embarrassed too. The old lady said good evening, and Chapman mumbled a reply, but Voaden ignored her.

"Well?" Voaden said.

"How should I know – maybe he wishes I was," Chapman said when they were out of earshot.

Voaden laughed a little, but Chapman's words touched a raw nerve, stirring up uncomfortable recollections of his own confusing dreams, and the laugh had a hollow ring.

"Well, fuck him," he said. He decided to let the subject drop. He didn't like it, though. He knew there'd lately been murmurs about his friendship with Chapman, and it was a bit weird when you thought about it, with Chapman being so much younger. He'd already made up his mind to sort Gatesford out anyway, to put a stop to it.

They could hear music from inside while they were waiting on the porch of Johno's house. It was a big place, covered in ivy, probably the biggest house in the street. Voaden had to ring the doorbell three times before there was any response.

It was finally opened by a girl, and Chapman was a bit startled to see how grown up she looked. He suddenly felt a bit silly in his school tie and scuffed dirty shoes. She gave Voaden a big hug and then pulled him in through the doorway. It was obvious right away that she was a little pissed. She didn't see Chapman at first, and then she did a kind of double take and looked very surprised.

"This is Pete," Voaden said.

"Hi, Pete," she said, and she gave him a nice smile. It vanished very quickly, only coming back when she looked at Voaden again.

Chapman followed them into the lounge. There were eight other people there, sitting in chairs or on the floor. Three of them were girls, and all of them looked about seventeen or eighteen, older than Voaden even. The air was thick with cigarette smoke, and there were plenty of beer cans littering the small tables. A half-empty bottle of vodka and a couple of liqueur bottles filched from Johno's dad's liquor cabinet stood on the coffee table. The music was very loud, blaring out from an expensive looking stereo system in one corner.

Chapman hovered behind Voaden and the girl, feeling awkward and out of place. The only ones in school uniform were the two of them, but somehow it didn't seem to matter with Voaden. He'd taken his jacket and tie off now anyway, throwing them over the back of a chair. Chapman took his own tie off and stuffed it into his trouser pocket. He felt a little better when he'd done that, but still awkward, not quite sure what to do except hover in Voaden's shadow.

Johno turned out to be as thin as a rake and over six feet tall.

He gave Voaden a beer and then stood gawping down at Chapman with big round eyes.

"Christ, Nick, how old is he?" he said in a loud voice so that he could be heard above the music.

Voaden glanced down at Chapman almost as though he'd forgotten he'd brought him along. Then he reached out and ruffled the boy's hair and gave his shoulder a punch.

"What the fuck does that matter – he's game for anything," he said and promptly turned away again, back to the girl.

"Want a drink?" Johno said doubtfully, still staring.

"Thanks," Chapman replied, resisting the temptation to nod like the young boy he was.

Johno thought for a moment or two, debating what to give him. Before he could decide one of the girls leaned up from the sofa and tugged at Chapman's shirtsleeve.

"Come sit here," she said, patting the cushion beside her.

He went immediately, glad to have somewhere to go and not to have to stand and look like a dork anymore. The girl gave him a liqueur glass filled to the brim with Crème de Menthe, and he took a big sip.

"I'm Clara," she said.

"Pete," he said and took another sip, liking the taste and the warm afterglow.

"How old are you?"

"Nearly fourteen," he lied.

She smiled at that, but not in a nasty way, and he started to relax then, immediately comfortable in her company. She looked about eighteen herself. She was very pretty and had short blond hair.

"So you're obviously at the Grammar too," she said.

"Yes, I've only just started," he said.

She looked a bit puzzled by that, but she didn't say anything about it.

"Are you a boarder like Nick?"

Chapman nodded.

"What time are you supposed to be in bed, then?"

He felt a bit awkward answering, feeling the big gap between them and knowing that the question was triggered by his age. She was old enough to be out as long as she liked – all night, if that's what she fancied.

"About ten," he said, and it sounded really lame, even adding on an hour.

Johno collapsed onto the sofa on the other side of him with a bottle of beer, taking a long swig on the way down.

"So how come you're a friend of Nick's?" he asked, leaning towards Chapman's right ear so that he didn't have to shout.

"I don't know – we both like smoking I suppose."

"Naughty, naughty," Johno said, shaking his head solemnly from side to side.

He had barely rested his head against the back of the sofa when the music stopped. He had to get up again to go and sort it out. He nearly tripped on the way over, already a bit unsteady on his feet with five beers sloshing around in his thin frame.

Chapman took another swig from his glass, and after that the drink was almost gone.

"Blimey, you're knocking that back quickly," Clara said to him. She leaned forward anyway to get the bottle from the coffee table and refill his glass.

He grinned at her, already beginning to float a little. Then he took out the packet of cigarettes Voaden had bought for him and offered her one but she shook her head.

People came and went in the space beside him, but he stayed on the couch the whole time, talking to the girl, answering her questions and drinking Crème de Menthe. He had a couple of swigs of Johno's beer too during his short visits. After all the drink and about four cigarettes he was beginning to feel ill, but the feeling was mostly kept at bay by the effects of the booze. Clara didn't drink much at all, and she started to stroke his hair gently at one point, but in an affectionate motherly kind of a way and wasn't really meaning anything by it. Her boyfriend saw her doing it though. He came and sat down heavily beside Chapman, burping loudly.

"Isn't it past your bedtime?" he said, meaning it more for her ears.

"Oh stuff off, Alec – you're bloody revolting," she said.

He just lay there for a while with his eyes closed and his head resting against the back of the settee. Then he stood up and looked back down at both of them, swaying slightly and looking with rather bleary eyes from one to the other, nodding his head.

"No doubt about it," he said, "he's definitely prettier than you; I'm going to date him from now on."

She kicked his leg and he nearly fell over onto the coffee table. He recovered in time and bent forward putting out his arm and resting his hand on the back of the sofa between the two of them. He puckered his mouth for a kiss, and she did kiss him briefly before pushing him away, but she was smiling and it was obvious she wasn't really upset.

"He's drunk," she said to Chapman when he'd gone away.

"Is that your boyfriend?" he asked.

She smiled when she heard the disappointment in his voice. She gave him a quick peck on the cheek.

"Sort of," she said, "when he's not being a complete jerk."

They went on to other things then, and Chapman told her about Kuala Lumpur because she seemed to be really interested in that. She told him how much she envied him seeing something of the world and how much she longed to travel. That made him proud and want to tell her more.

After an hour or so, he'd had enough to drink and didn't want any more, but Voaden sat down beside him and held out a bottle of beer. He felt obliged to have a couple of swigs.

"You're going to have to piss off now, mate, it's nearly nine," Voaden said when he took the bottle back. "We're all going out to a club now anyway."

"Aren't you coming back?" Chapman said. He was surprised; he'd assumed all along that they would go back together.

"Don't have to – no bloody Drydorks to turn my fucking lights off. You can find your way back, can't you? – it's easy from here. You'll be OK. Go through the window I showed you."

Chapman was feeling pissed enough not to really be bothered or complain, and he stood up.

"I'll be fine," he said.

Clara stood up too, looking a little worried because she knew how much Crème de Menthe he'd swallowed, and just how young and innocent he really was.

"Don't you think you should take him?" she asked.

"I'll be really fine, honest," Chapman said again, and he did feel confident.

"Of course you will," Voaden said, watching him closely to see whether he was going to fall over.

He didn't, though, and he said goodbye to Clara and headed for the front door, wobbling a bit, but not too badly. They both followed and Johno came over to say goodbye too, shaking him solemnly by the hand and then pulling him in for a quick hug.

"You're a cute kid, Pete," he said. "Come again any time."

Clara gave him a big hug too and a kiss on the cheek at the door. Voaden ruffled his hair, and then the door closed and he was suddenly alone in the dark.

He started walking and was laughing to himself at first, looking up at the night sky and running his fingers along the rough bark of the pavement trees as he went past them. Once or twice he nearly fell over when he weaved too close to the kerb, but on the whole he managed well. Only when he turned into Connaught Avenue did he remember what lay ahead. He started thinking in a befuddled way about the dangers of getting back in and up to the dorm undetected. He hoped Rowell had managed to cover for him earlier on. Then he looked at his watch and realised that he would be too late for lights out anyway and he wondered whether Rowell would be able to convince Drydork he was still in the toilet. A large part of him, the part with the booze in, didn't really care.

There was very little traffic, and he hadn't taken any notice of the few cars which went past, but then one stopped by the side of the road a couple of dozen yards ahead. Its rear tail lights shone in the dark like two red eyes. He hesitated but then walked on, hoping that the car stopping had nothing to do with him. As he drew level, the driver leaned over the passenger seat and called out to him through the window.

"Can you help me, please – I'm a bit lost – I'm looking for the Brighton road."

Chapman stopped, and he went a bit closer to the window, bending down a little to look in. The passenger door swung wide open then.

"You look as though you need a lift anyway," the man said. "Maybe we can help each other. I'll give you ten quid – hop in."

Chapman didn't have a chance to say anything because a dog suddenly appeared between him and the car, and in the night it seemed truly gigantic, as big as the car itself. It let out a huge bark, loud enough to wake even Leomond's living dead. The man in the car pulled the door shut, having to lay virtually flat across the passenger seat to grab the handle. He did it extraordinarily quickly, and he didn't hesitate one second before roaring away. It was as though he thought the dog was straight from hell and had come for his soul.

"Shit, Gladstone, what are you doing here?" Chapman said when he'd recovered from his own fright and saw what dog it was.

Then he finally did fall over, because the dog jumped up and flattened him. He had to struggle to get to his feet, grabbing onto the collar. Gladstone's big tongue washed his face and sobered him up a little as he did it.

"How the fuck did you get out?" Chapman said. The dog whined in reply, still waggling his enormous muscular body to demonstrate his boundless delight.

"Shit," Chapman said again and he stroked Gladstone's big head, trying to calm him down. "I better take you back, you big jerk."

They went off together, and it was difficult holding onto the collar, because he had no real control, and he was pretty wobbly on his own legs anyway. They bounced against each other in the beginning, and Chapman would have fallen over several times if he hadn't been holding on to the collar. But

Gladstone soon calmed down, and after a little while, the boy just had to rest his fingers on the dog's head every now and again to let him know who was boss.

They stood outside Kennedy's front door while he pondered what to do. He wondered how Gladstone had got out in the first place. There was no obvious way at the front, because the windows were all closed, and so he went round to the back, taking the dog with him. One of the sash windows there was open slightly, but the gap was not nearly big enough for a dog Gladstone's size. He tried to pull it up further but it wouldn't budge. He sat down then, feeling very fuzzy headed and the dog lay down next to him.

"Fuck you, Gladstone," he whispered to the dog. "Now you're going to get me into all kinds of deep shit. Why don't you just stay at home?"

The dog looked at him quizzically and then put his big head down on his big paws.

They stayed like that for a few minutes while Chapman tried to figure out what to do. The Crème de Menthe and beer came and went in his throat, threatening to come all the way up once or twice. In the end there didn't seem to be any choice, and he went back round to the front door and knocked. He had to knock a couple of times before the light went on inside. Gladstone stood quietly beside him, but when the door started to open he let out one of his big barks and leapt forward, forcing the door and bowling Kennedy back into the house. The boy stood frozen for a brief instant. He suddenly realised he could escape undetected and he did just that, darting back through the gate and crouching down behind the low flint stone garden wall.

Kennedy peered out after a few seconds, keeping the door mostly shut so that Gladstone couldn't escape again.

"Hello?" he called once and then again. When there was no

answer, he closed the door.

Chapman sat on the pavement with his back to the wall, feeling mighty pleased with himself. Then the booze came back up his throat some of the way, and he felt really bad. He got to his feet and went over the road to the school, figuring he could risk going through the main gate and then circle round to the bathroom windows.

TWENTY-SEVEN

Dryden had been preoccupied what with one thing and another. He was a few minutes late coming to do his rounds and turn out the dorm lights. When he did come to Dorm 4, all the boys were in bed, as far as he could see at a glance. He decided not to do his usual circuit. He just stood inside the door for a few moments and looked around. He had actually said goodnight and turned the lights off when it occurred to him that the corner bed might have been empty. He turned some of the lights on again almost immediately for another look. Sure enough there was a bit of a lump in the bed, but it wasn't big enough to be Chapman or anyone else.

"Where's Chapman?" he asked.

"In the loo, sir," Rowell immediately chirped up from his bed. "He's got a bit of a wobbly tummy."

Dryden took a few paces into the dorm. Then he stopped, seeming undecided. He stared at the empty bed for a few seconds, and then walked out again, turning the lights off without saying anything else. He went straight down the stairs to the toilets and soon discovered that all the cubicles were empty.

"Shit," he said. He was thinking of Sunday more than anything else.

He went back up the stairs two at a time, but at the last moment he veered away from striding back into the big dorm. He went on to the other dorm instead and vented his anger on the laggards there. He turned their lights out five minutes early. Then he went back to his room to wait, leaving his door ajar.

He sat on the bed because he had a clear view of the doors to Chapman's dorm from there. He leaned his head against the wall. After a few minutes he started to feel uncomfortable and ridiculous, so he stood up. He went to haul Rowell out of bed, but he changed his mind again on the landing, thinking it was unfair on the others to start a commotion when they were all just getting off to sleep. He knew he'd hear the doors anyway, so he lay down on his bed instead and picked up a book. It was one he'd taken out of the library. It was called *The Great Escape*. Despite his anger he had to smile a little at that.

Twenty minutes ticked past. His anger had all gone, replaced by anxiety. He was again on the verge of going to wake up Rowell when he finally heard a creak on the stairs. He leapt up and flew out of the door in one continuous movement. Chapman was frozen on the top step. He was not in his pyjamas. Dryden didn't say anything. He beckoned to him with a crooked finger and went back into his room and sat down at his desk.

Chapman came in. His face was as white as a sheet. There were brown stains on the front of his shirt where he'd scraped against the bathroom window ledge.

"Where on earth have you been?" Dryden said, enunciating each word.

Chapman looked at him but he didn't reply. He was swaying a bit and at first Dryden thought he really was sick but then he caught a whiff of alcohol. He got up and went a bit closer, and the smell of booze was overpowering.

"Don't tell me you've been drinking?" he said in disbelief.

"Sorry, sir," Chapman said.

"'Sorry, sir'? God, I want to cry, boy. What the hell is it with you?"

"I think I'm going to throw up, sir," Chapman said.

Dryden steered him to the basin in the corner. He turned on the tap and watched the boy's green vomit circle round the basin and slowly disappear.

He really did feel like crying then. He went back to his desk, shaking his head from side to side.

Chapman hovered over the basin for a while longer. He turned round, wiping his chin with the back of his hand. He turned the tap off. His face was still white, but not quite as ghostly as it had been when he'd come in.

"You'll get expelled for this," Dryden said in a flat voice. "It really makes me want to weep. I really, really liked you, Chapman, I really did – you know that. And you've got Rowell into trouble now too."

"I'm sorry, sir," the boy said again. He sounded as though he was about to start crying himself.

Dryden looked at him, trying to harden his heart. He felt it crack under the strain. He wanted to scream at Chapman and he wanted to hug him too, but he knew that couldn't be.

"Go to bed. Right now," he said in a doom-laden voice.

The boy went straight out without looking at him again. He closed the door softly.

Dryden went to the window. He pounded both his fists down

on the window ledge several times. He actually did start to cry a little, blinking the tears back and taking deep breaths to get control of himself. Then he remembered the half jack of whiskey in his cupboard. He took it out and poured a stiff measure into a glass, swallowing it down in a couple of big gulps, more whiskey than he'd had in the past three months. He lay on the bed, picked the pillow out from behind his head and pressed it down on his face. It smothered a silent scream that no one would have heard anyway.

After a couple of minutes the whiskey started to have an effect. He calmed down and sat up again, tossing the pillow back where it belonged. He felt suddenly foolish, even though he was alone in the room. He was shocked by the intensity of his own reaction, shaken by the realisation of how he actually felt about Chapman, how much he would hate to lose him.

He poured another generous measure, but this time he sipped the drink, sitting at his desk. He opened the first of a pile of exercise books. Maths was a consolation, even the inscrutably bad maths of Lower 4B. He went through the first few books mechanically, marking the answers with a red pen and sipping the whiskey. After the sixth book he'd had enough. The drink was beginning to cloud his head a little, anyway.

He turned the radio on and tuned the dial until he found a station playing soft music. Then he filled his glass again and sat down in the easy chair and stared at the wall, listening to the music and sipping the drink.

That's the end of Sunday, he thought. For some odd reason, that upset him more than anything else. He knew he would have to speak to Bruder. What followed from that was inevitable; smoking was bad enough, alcohol was beyond redemption. He shook his head from side to side and looked at the glass in his hand. The irony of what he was doing was not lost on him.

He'd only been drunk a few times in his life, mostly while he was at Oxford, but he felt like getting drunk now. He swallowed the last of the whiskey in his glass and looked over at the bottle on the desk. He stared at the bottle for a long time, listening to the music wafting around. In the end he reached over and poured himself another measure, regretting it the moment he'd done it. But he sipped it anyway, wondering what would happen if there was an emergency and he had to roll out of his room to rescue Chapman – in a fire, say – and was reeking of booze himself. Then he started to think about Sarah. He half-toyed with the idea of going downstairs to the staff room to phone her but he decided that would be a bad idea in many different ways. There was nothing he felt he wanted to say anyway right then.

The music ended eventually and someone started talking on the radio. It sounded as though they were going to go on talking, so he got up and turned it off. He felt unsteady as he did that, and went over to the basin to splash his face. He could picture Chapman's vomit going around the bowl in the running water. He found himself smiling at that for some reason, and he let the water run for a while, watching it swirl away in a useless waste, like love and life. Then he splashed his face, but it didn't have much effect. He was feeling very unsteady and happy and miserable at the same time, thinking of Chapman and then of Sarah, one after the other, back and forth.

He cleaned his teeth and then lurched over to his bed and started to change into his pyjamas. He found that a surprisingly complicated thing to do. He did manage to fold his trousers over the back of the chair before flopping down onto the bed but he left his shirt on the floor. It was very unlike him to be untidy like that. Getting into bed was a challenge too. He nearly fell off the bed, fighting with the tightly tucked sheet and the blanket, trying to get them over his toes so that he could push his feet down where they belonged. When that had finally been accomplished, he lay staring up at the ceiling. Only then did he realise that he'd left the main light on. He struggled up again to turn it off, at least remembering to turn on the bedside light first, though he nearly knocked that off the table.

He got back into bed more easily the second time because his bedding had given up the struggle. The room started to swim gently around him as he lay there, stopping briefly when he shut his eyes but resuming the slow dance when he opened them again. He turned off the bedside light, but he could sense the room still dancing slowly in the dark. He swayed with it for a time, wondering whether he was going to fall out of bed, but eventually he fell asleep.

Some time later he heard a small voice. He couldn't work out where he was or what time it was and he was too confused to think of the bedside light so that he could look at his watch. He didn't really remember about the watch either.

"Sir," the voice whispered urgently. "I can't sleep, sir, I'm having nightmares. Can I stay here with you for a bit – please, sir?"

He knew it was Chapman, and he knew it was a dream, so he said yes. He even held the blanket up so that the boy could get into the bed with him. It seemed in his dream that Chapman did get in, and that when he lowered his hand to let the blanket down again it touched the boy's skin and that was like touching soft silk. His last thought in the dream was that Chapman wouldn't like the smell of whiskey on his breath so he decided he'd better keep his face to the wall.

He woke up properly when the first grey dawn light started to filter into the room but he didn't move, feeling cramped and very fragile. He knew if he lifted his head his brains would probably fall out and so he kept it down on the pillow. A distant bossy voice that sounded like his own started telling him what a jackass he'd been. When he opened his eyes, he saw that the wall was only a couple of inches from his nose. He realised he was lying like that, all squashed up, because he wasn't alone in the bed.

He was very wide-awake then, but he didn't move at all at first; his body was frozen with shock. Then he started to squirm his way round inch-by-inch like a contortionist. He got right round somehow without really disturbing the bedding much or the body next to him.

Chapman was still sound asleep. In the faint light, he looked at the boy's beautiful face a hand's breadth from his own on the pillow. He felt as though all the happiness and despair in the world had flooded his soul like a boiling sea. He lay looking for quite a long time. Then he whispered Chapman's name a couple of times. He put his hand on the boy's small bare shoulder under the blanket and shook it very gently.

Chapman opened his eyes a little and smiled sleepily.

"Sorry, sir," he mumbled.

"Time to get up. You must get back to your own bed – now."

The boy woke up properly then. His eyes opened a lot wider. He lifted his head from the pillow trying to get orientated.

"Shit, sorry, sir – I was having a nightmare," he said.

Dryden sat up. He climbed over the boy and out of bed. His head hurt like hell as he did. The near empty bottle of whiskey on the sideboard reminded him why. He picked up his watch and saw that it was a quarter to six, fifteen minutes before the wake up bell. He was very relieved at that.

"Come on, up you get," he said softly, "back to your own bed before the bell goes."

Chapman extricated his legs from the covers and stood up,

looking a bit sheepish. Dryden realised that he might have a bit of a hangover too.

"I'm really sorry, sir," he said and he was obviously embarrassed now.

Dryden put his hands on the boy's shoulders and then he hugged him because it seemed the only thing to do. He really couldn't stop himself anymore.

"We were both idiots last night, but thanks for trusting me like that," he said.

"Trusting you like what, sir?" the boy asked.

"Trusting me to save you from nightmares," he said. He hugged a little harder. He knew it was more than that.

"Am I still going to get expelled, sir?" Chapman asked when he let go.

"No – that would be a bit unfair, now wouldn't it," Dryden said. He couldn't really think of anything to add. He wasn't going to cane him or pretend to cane him – he wasn't going to do anything. He couldn't now, anyway.

"Please don't do anything to Chris, sir."

"No, I won't."

Chapman looked up at him, studying his face as though checking that he meant what he said. Then he remembered the bell and went to the door. He paused in the doorway and looked back.

"You won't tell anyone I slept here with you, will you, sir?" he whispered anxiously.

Dryden shook his head.

"Thanks, sir." He started to close the door but peeped back in again. "You snore like hell, sir," he said softly with a slight smile and then he was gone.

Dryden smiled too and then went straight to the basin and drank two big glasses of water. He swallowed a couple of aspirins with the second one, and he started to feel a bit better after that. By the time the bell went, he was already dressed and on his way downstairs to get coffee. Despite the hangover, he was feeling strangely elated.

It was only a little later at breakfast that the doubts crept into his mind like uninvited guests. He thought about Saint Stithians and the teacher there and wondered whether there really had ever been any nightmares, then or last night. And if there were nightmares, the voices in his head said, they must have been truly terrible to drive a boy that age to do something like that – either that or he was really drunk; or he thought sleeping with Dryden would get him out of trouble. That had certainly worked, the voices agreed. At first he worried about it all but in the end he decided that he didn't care, that it really didn't matter.

Leomond and a couple of other boys were awake when Chapman got back to the dorm, but they didn't look at him, assuming he'd been to the loo or the bathroom if they actually noticed him come in at all. Rowell was still curled up in bed asleep, with the blanket pulled over his head.

There was no point in getting back into bed, so Chapman got dressed. He sat on his bed, waiting for the bell that would wake everyone up. He wondered what he was going to say to Rowell, feeling bad about putting him in a spot and getting him into trouble. He didn't know how he was going to explain how he'd got him out of trouble either.

Leomond was already up, standing at the basins washing his face. When he'd finished, he saw Chapman sitting on his bed all dressed and didn't go back to his own bed, coming over to sit beside him instead.

"How were the toots?" he whispered.

The bell went before Chapman could reply. It sounded incredibly loud. Everyone started to stir, mostly sitting up and yawning, though Pearce and one or two others jumped straight up as though they'd been wide awake all the time. Rowell rolled over but he didn't open his eyes. He just lay there wishing it was Sunday and moaning softly.

"It was good fun – I met a really nice girl," Chapman said to Leomond, not having to whisper any more.

Rowell opened his eyes when he heard that but he kept his head on the pillow.

"And what was Johno like?" he asked in a sleepy voice.

"Very nice – they all were – a bit old and a bit pissed, though."

"What time did you get back?" Leomond asked.

"About ten, I think. I ran into Gladstone running around in the street."

Rowell sat up and swung his legs out of bed as though they were made of lead.

"Drydork saw you weren't in bed at lights out – I said you were in the loo."

"Thanks," Chapman said, feeling anxious about what was coming next.

"He didn't look as though he believed me – but he didn't say anything," Rowell added.

"I had to take Gladstone back to Kennedy's," he said, wanting to get away from the subject. "I got him inside, but Kennedy didn't see me – I ducked behind the wall."

"That was lucky," was all Leomond said.

"Drydork's invited me tomorrow as well now," Rowell said, not seeming to be interested in Gladstone.

"That's great," Chapman said. He was pleased, and it was obvious in his voice.

Rowell smiled because it was always nice to be wanted.

"Maybe I need to get caned," Leomond said.

"You wouldn't feel a thing on your fat arse," Rowell said.

Leomond looked at him glumly, but he didn't say anything. Rowell felt a bit mean saying something like that. He leaned across and prodded Leomond's knee to show that it was a joke.

"What was the girl's name?" he asked, not wanting to talk about the outing in front of Leomond anymore.

"Clara – she was about eighteen."

"Blimey," Rowell said.

"She had a boyfriend there – he was a bit of a dork," Chapman said.

"You're bloody lucky you weren't caught," Rowell said. There was a hint of sour grapes in his tone, but not enough to get worked up about, really.

"You lead a charmed life," Leomond said, forgetting about the caning and the dorm raid and not really knowing about any of the other stuff.

Chapman bent down and fiddled with the floorboard, trying to lift it up, not wanting to lie or say anything about luck.

"No smoking before breakfast," Leomond said.

"Maybe you're right – I feel a bit yuck anyway," Chapman said.

"How many toots did you have, then?" Rowell asked.

"Lots – Clara kept filling my glass with this green stuff – crème de something," Chapman said.

"Crème de Menthe – my mum drinks it sometimes," Rowell said.

Leomond looked at Chapman in a disapproving kind of way. "You didn't have to keep drinking it," he said. Then he got up and went back to his own bed to get changed.

Rowell stood up too and took his wash bag off the top of the locker.

"Do you know where Dryden's taking us?" Chapman asked.

"He said it'd be a surprise."

"Maybe he'll change his mind anyway."

"Why?"

Chapman shrugged but he thought to himself that it might well happen after last night.

Rowell looked at him for a while, waiting for Chapman to say something else. When he didn't, Rowell went off to the washbasins.

TWENTY-EIGHT

"I still don't understand why I'm such a bastard, sir," Simpson said.

Richardson put the book down. He didn't really need it anymore; he knew the lines off by heart. It was more of a prop than anything else.

"Because you're a god, Simpson."

"A pretty nasty one, sir."

"Maybe; not really – but in a sense, that's the whole point."

Simpson shrugged.

"*I am a god: ye did despite to me,*" he repeated in an angry voice. It still didn't sound very terrifying, only as though he was a bit pissed off about something quite trivial, like somebody barging ahead of him in the queue at the supermarket.

Richardson doubted he was going to get anything more cosmic out of Simpson, so he said it sounded fine, that he'd got it at last.

"But what does that actually mean, sir?" Simpson asked.

"You questioned my divinity, you insulted me; now you must suffer the consequences," Richardson said.

Simpson still looked puzzled.

"In his own mind, Euripides couldn't reconcile the notion that the gods could be capricious and at the same time be omnipotent," Richardson continued. "Dionysus is a god, with all the unlimited power that presupposes and yet he seems to behave like a drunken, self-indulgent party animal. He's the Clamour-king, the embodiment of nature itself. He's the wind in the trees, the beauty and bounty and order of the natural world but also its unpredictable savagery, the blood and the guts and the lust – they're all part and parcel of the same divine mystery, different sides of the same impenetrable coin."

The boys in the chorus looked at him as though he'd started talking Chinese.

"Dionysus is saying that Pentheus should have accepted him for what he is – a god. If he'd done that, everything would be fine; because he didn't, he and his family must suffer the consequences."

"That seems a bit harsh sir," Simpson persisted.

Richardson was beginning to get irritated. He had to remind himself that it was a fair and reasonable comment.

"Euripides agrees with you – but who are you or I or even him to question the will of the gods?" he said with a forced smile.

That seemed to please Simpson – having Euripides nodding wisely at him in his mind's eye. He grinned broadly. "*I am a god, ye did despite to me,*" he repeated for the third time.

"Excellent," Richardson said loudly. *Pathetic,* he said to himself.

Chatsworth looked at Simpson. He studied his aquiline

features. What a jerk, he thought. He was making Dionysus look and sound like he should be wearing a bowler hat and carrying an umbrella. He was the kind of Dionysus you saw waiting for the bus, worried that he was going to be late for work. There was no passion, no mystery, no dark side at all.

"OK, that's it for today," Richardson said. "I'm pleased with the way you're all getting on with your lines – well, most of you. I want you all to be word perfect by next week; that's the last chance before the full dress rehearsal. Don't let me down."

Chatsworth started for the door along with the others, but Richardson called out to him, asking him to wait.

"Did that all sound like gobbledygook, Philip?" he asked.

"No sir, it made a lot of sense," Chatsworth replied.

"I'm glad to hear it. I sometimes wonder whether the play makes sense myself – I suppose that's why it intrigues me so much," Richardson said.

Chatsworth smiled slightly. "Life doesn't make much sense either, does it, sir?"

Richardson raised his eyebrows. "That's very profound; rather cynical for one so young, mind you. Why do you say that?"

Chatsworth was flattered that Richardson had singled him out to share his thoughts, pleased that he seemed interested in what he had to say. His smile broadened a little. "It's just strange how we do things we regret, sir."

Richardson nodded thoughtfully. He wondered what Chatsworth meant, whether he was about to admit to some transgression, to unburden himself. It wouldn't have really surprised him, because Chatsworth had seemed preoccupied for a couple of weeks. In a way, the brooding had improved his performance, adding a touch of melancholy. He prepared himself for the role of confidant or confessor, pleased that

Chatsworth was prepared to give that role to him. "Deeper and deeper, Philip. What do you mean exactly?" he asked.

The smile on Chatsworth's lips disappeared. "It's nothing, sir. It's just that the play makes me wonder whether some things are meant to happen – you know, we make them happen because we have to, we can't stop it – things we regret."

"It sounds as though you're about to confess to a murder," Richardson said with a chuckle. He was faintly alarmed when Chatsworth blushed.

"Not that I know of, sir," Chatsworth said. He smiled again briefly at the joke. "I just feel Pentheus is doomed from the start, that what happens to him is inevitable."

Richardson nodded again. "We are all slaves of the gods, whatever the gods might be," he said.

"That isn't from the play, is it, sir?" Chatsworth asked doubtfully.

"No, but it is a quote from Euripides," Richardson said. "Is this just about the play, Philip, or is there something else worrying you?"

Chatsworth shook his head. "No, sir, nothing really," he said.

Richardson knew that wasn't true, but he didn't press the point.

TWENTY-NINE

It was obvious Sunday was going to be a beautiful day the moment the sun came up, blazing at the edge of the earth and rapidly gobbling up the long shadows. By nine it was already hot, and by the time Chapel was over, it was a real scorcher.

Rowell and Chapman waited at the bottom gate with their swimming costumes and towels. They'd changed quickly, and it felt good to be out of school uniform, adding to the sense of freedom. Now they were eager to get away, very conscious of being given a treat when none of the others were and not really deserving it. There had already been a few jibes at breakfast and afterwards, when the others had started to find out. Pearce had been particularly ticked off about it, probably because he always came top in maths.

Dryden pulled up in his Hillman, and they were mildly disappointed by that, having half hoped that he would somehow have got hold of his girlfriend's MG. But they climbed in eagerly enough after a bit of confusion between them as to who should sit in the front. Dryden didn't say anything, leaving them to sort it out. In the end Rowell sat in front because Chapman was a bit more forceful about being polite.

They went to pick up Sarah at her flat first and then they headed back along the coast road towards Brighton. Both boys were in the back then. At first it all seemed a bit awkward, with Dryden concentrating on driving and Sarah having to crane her neck round every time she wanted to say something or to show that she was listening when one of the boys spoke. So there wasn't a lot of conversation at first, just a few short questions and even shorter answers.

Chapman was fairly dumb struck anyway, because he was impressed with Sarah. He thought she was very pretty and now Dryden had told them that she was a doctor. She looked very young to be that, even to him.

After a bit of a debate between Sarah and Dryden, they decided to stop at the beach in Brighton for a swim and then go on to have lunch in the country. It really was very hot outside and even hotter in the car. The boys were very much in agreement, because their legs were already sticking to the plastic seats of the Hillman.

Sarah and Chapman were the first to get changed on the beach. She had a blue bikini on under her dress; she pulled the dress off over her head and there it was. Chapman didn't bother with his towel, just taking his shorts and underpants off and pulling his costume on, not minding who saw him.

Dryden and Rowell struggled with towels wrapped around their waists, trying to balance on the loose stones, in constant danger of falling over. Dryden finally had the sense to balance against the breakwater with one hand, but it still took him a while because he didn't seem to trust the fold in the towel. He tried to keep hold of it with his other hand and it was difficult to make much progress like that. Rowell eventually did fall over but by then he had his costume around his ankles and it was a quick thing to pull it up. When the two of them were finally ready Sarah and Chapman already had their feet in the cold green sea.

"Ouch, it's bloody freezing," Sarah said.

Chapman grinned up at her and then dived in over the next small wave. His head popped up and he immediately splashed her. She screamed and dived in too so that he couldn't do it again. She swam straight out and the boy swam with her and very soon they were twenty yards out, treading water. They looked back at Dryden and Rowell wobbling down the steep beach over the loose stones.

"It's freezing," Sarah yelled.

Dryden waved. He only glanced up briefly because his feet needed all his attention. He was determined not to hurt his toes or fall over and look like an idiot. Rowell got to the sea before him being much lighter and having smaller feet. When he touched the water he held his thin arms straight out sideways and pulled a face with the shock of it. He jumped in anyway, not wanting to stand on the edge like a prat, and swam out to join the other two.

Despite all his precautions Dryden did fall over, but by then he was knee deep in the sea, and it didn't much matter except to him. It took him quite a few seconds to get his breathing going again properly, the cold was that intense.

Chapman swam out further and the others followed, and by the time they stopped they were the furthest out of all the heads bobbing about in the sea.

"Can you believe how cold it is?" Dryden said, and he could already feel his teeth starting to chatter a little.

Rowell's teeth were going like castanets but Chapman and Sarah seemed alright, smiling happily. Chapman kept disappearing under the water as they floated there in a little circle, just dropping straight down and then popping up like a cork.

"Can you touch the bottom?" Sarah asked him.

He disappeared again and was gone for longer than before and when he came up he was behind Dryden. He held up a small pebble and then swam the short distance to give it to her. She took it from him and kept it in her hand, not wanting to let it go so that it could sink to the bottom again.

"Thank you very much," she said.

"It's quite deep," he said.

Dryden moaned about the cold again. He said he wasn't prepared to be any kind of hero and swam back to the beach. Rowell followed him, his clattering teeth making it obvious that he'd had enough already.

"You're a wonderful swimmer," Sarah said.

"Thanks, miss," Chapman said, grinning.

"I'll race you back," she said.

"OK," he said and manoeuvred round so that he was next to her facing the beach.

"Ready, steady – go," she said.

He immediately plunged forward, but she stayed where she was, treading water and smiling at how young and trusting he was.

He was half way back when he stopped, realising she wasn't racing after all. But she did start swimming when he looked back at her, feeling the cold too now. They got to the beach together, clambering through the shallows over the restless stones.

"Why didn't you race, miss?" he asked.

"Because I always like winning," she said.

"Maybe you would have."

"Against you? – I doubt it."

He grinned proudly hearing that, all the more so because

he'd seen that she was a good swimmer too.

Dryden was splayed out on his towel, trying to expose as much of his skin as possible to the sun's rays. He was already beginning to thaw out, as it was a very hot day. Out of the sea, the sun was king.

"You'll get burned to a crisp," Sarah said.

"I'll have to melt first," he said without opening his eyes. The sun was shining through his eyelids, and his whole world had turned blood red, flecked with blue and white sparks.

She put her towel down next to his and lay down gingerly herself. It wasn't very comfortable because the stones underneath grumbled and shifted, not really prepared to compromise. It was their beach.

Rowell was huddled up in his towel, but his teeth had finally stopped banging together. They were steady in his mouth again.

"That water's like ice," he said when Chapman came up next to him.

"It's pretty cold," Chapman said, and the skin on his arms had goose bumps to prove it. He spread his towel out and lay down on his stomach, leaning on his elbows. The stones underneath easily found their own places in the contours of his light body.

They all stayed quiet for a while, enjoying the warmth of the sun and listening to the chatter of the other people on the beach. More people were arriving all the time, driven there by the sun, and it was already pretty crowded. A toddler came waddling over and stared down at Chapman with big round eyes and snot on his lip. He was holding a small plastic spade, but that wasn't much use on a beach made of stones. The boy looked up at him and smiled and the toddler seemed to get a fright at that and quickly waddled away.

"I thought we'd go and have a look at the Long Man of

Wilmington, have lunch there," Dryden said, sitting up and meaning them all to hear.

"Sounds great, sir," Rowell said, standing up.

"There's no hurry – you can still go for another swim if you like," Dryden said.

Rowell sat down again, keeping the towel around his shoulders, though now it was more to keep the sun out than the warmth of his body in. But he didn't fancy going into the sea again; it was just too cold.

Chapman got up and went to sit next to Dryden on the other side from Sarah, leaving his towel where it was.

"Thanks for taking us, sir – it's really great," he said, sitting down close beside him, a bit in front.

"You're very welcome, my boy. Don't you want to swim again?"

"Maybe in a minute."

Sarah sat up then, not really able to get comfortable anyway. She was still clutching the small pebble Chapman had fetched from the bottom of the sea. She dropped it into her bag without really thinking why. She looked across at the boy, who was looking at the sea and smiling at the antics of the people in the water. Then she looked at Philip and he was looking at the sea and smiling too, glancing down at Chapman now and again. She took a bottle of sun lotion from her bag and put some on her shoulders, massaging it in with her long fingers. Then she nudged Philip's arm and held up the bottle.

"No thanks," he said.

"Peter?"

Chapman looked round at her and saw the bottle of lotion and shook his head.

"No thanks, miss," he said.

"You'll burn," she warned but he just smiled at her and

looked back at the sea again.

She offered lotion to Rowell but he shook his head too and had already put his shirt back on, anyway.

She went on studying Chapman surreptitiously as he sat with his knees up and his chin resting lightly on his slender arms, and she envied his astonishing beauty and his immaculate skin. She saw Dryden put his hand on the boy's shoulder once, resting it there briefly before brushing something away. She didn't see anything fall but assumed it must have been a small speck of seaweed or something. Chapman didn't react to the touch at all, and that surprised her.

In the end Chapman was the only one who went for another swim, and he was in and out quite quickly, partly because it really was very cold and partly because he didn't want to hold things up for the others.

After ten minutes in the car, the other three were all wishing they had gone a second time as well.

"It must be knocking eighty degrees," Dryden said.

Their hair was blowing all over the place because the windows of the car were down, but the wind itself was hot and didn't give much relief. Sarah tried to put a scarf over her head, but she gave up eventually.

They caught glimpses of the giant figure cut into the chalk as they drove through the narrow lanes to the pub, and they had a good view of it from the pub garden where they stopped to have lunch. It took up half the hillside.

Dryden had thought twice about having lunch at a pub, remembering how he and Sarah had joked about it, but it was harmless enough out in the garden and it was a very pretty spot. He was pleased to find that there were other smaller kids there too.

Sarah had a glass of white wine, but he had a soft drink himself because he was driving and also because he didn't want Chapman to think that he hit the bottle every time one hove in sight.

"Who's that giant supposed to be, sir?" Rowell asked.

"I think it's supposed to be Hercules – though nobody really seems to know," Dryden said. "It's very old, over a thousand years or more."

"Can we go up and have a closer look after lunch?"

"Yes – if you like. It looks like a long slog up that hill, though. How do you feel, Sarah?"

"Long slog up the Long Man – if I faint with the heat, you three can carry me up," she said.

Before their food came, she took her lotion out again and insisted the boys put some on their faces and arms because they didn't have hats and the umbrella didn't give much shade. They both obeyed, not having any option, as she looked pretty determined about it, not like on the beach. Dryden put up a bit of a fight, but he lost in the end when she started talking about skin cancer and the things she'd seen at medical school. Rowell asked for a bit more after hearing all that. Chapman still had a small blob on his forehead when he thought he'd finished putting it on. Sarah was about to say something, but Dryden leaned over and smeared it away.

Rowell was the first to see the two small figures climbing slowly up towards the Long Man, because he was facing directly that way. They were carrying a log between them, and it must have been a big one judging by their slow progress, a tree trunk maybe, though it looked tiny like the men themselves from the pub garden. It was obvious what the two small figures were meaning to do with the log when they started up the Long Man's right leg. They stopped every now and again to take a breather, because the thing they were carrying must have been really heavy.

"Probably a couple of students," Dryden said.

He was trying not to smile but Sarah was grinning and so were the two boys, and so he let himself smile too a little and kept glancing back at the Long Man, though he felt they shouldn't really be taking any notice. He started to feel a bit cross with Sarah eventually because she wouldn't let it go. She just kept staring and grinning and when the two tiny figures got the log to where they wanted it to be, she burst out laughing because it looked so ridiculously small. The two tiny figures came a little way down the Long Man's leg and then went back up again and moved the log round a hundred and eighty degrees but that didn't make much difference from a long way off. The Long Man still looked as though he would be mighty embarrassed to take a communal shower.

Rowell looked embarrassed too, but Chapman still seemed to be enjoying the small drama, grinning broadly and looking to and fro, from Sarah giggling to the Long Man.

"Bloody idiots," Dryden said, meaning the two tiny figures, but his comment was enough to wipe the smile off Chapman's face.

Sarah was still giggling when the food came, and there were tears in her eyes by then. She had to take out a tissue to wipe them away.

"Sorry," she said, trying to get a grip on herself.

Dryden was looking quite glum, almost angry, and the two boys took their cue from that and didn't take any more notice of the Long Man or his new appendage other than stealing the odd glance when they thought he wasn't likely to see them do it.

"All of them were originally something to do with fertility cults, I think," Sarah said. "There's one at Cerne – and he's got all his own equipment."

She'd got over the giggles and was getting mildly irritated by Dryden's prudishness. The Cerne giant had a massive hard on and balls the size of helicopter pads and any child going past would see that – and had done for hundreds of years – so she didn't see why he was getting so miffed about the Long Man's little winkie.

"But the Long Man's a national monument – they should respect that and leave it be," he said defensively, guessing more or less what she was thinking.

Somebody obviously agreed with him and had phoned the cops, because a Panda car went by in the direction of the Long Man just as he finished speaking. The blue light was flashing on its roof but there was no siren because the cops inside were trying to sneak up on the culprits unawares.

"This should be interesting," Dryden said with a little note of triumph in his voice.

"Spoilsports," Sarah said.

The boys concentrated on their food, worrying that the dispute might develop into a full-blown row. Neither of them wanted to be in the middle of that. But Dryden smiled and then he actually laughed a little, and that brought everything back to normal.

They all had permission to look then, and they did just that in between mouthfuls. It wasn't very long before four little figures were walking up the Long Man's right leg and even at that distance you could make out that the two in the rear were wearing uniforms. When they came down the two in uniforms were still bringing up the rear. The other two were struggling with the big log.

"There," Sarah said, "They've neutered him again."

"What do you mean – again?" Dryden asked.

"I bet they grassed over the naughty bits back in Victorian times – he looks a right ponce now with his two big poles," she replied.

Chapman had just taken a big swing of orange juice and

he sprayed it all out again, unable to stop the giggles. A little of the spray hit Dryden's trousers but most of it ended up harmlessly on the grass between them

"Sorry, sir," he said.

"That's all right – I'm not surprised you're choking listening to all that cobblers," Dryden said. He smiled slyly at Sarah and wiped his trousers with a paper serviette.

"It's not cobblers. Go and poke about a bit in the turf with a stick," she said.

"Pardon?" he said looking at her with an expression of mock horror on his face.

"You'd probably get arrested too, sir," Rowell said and promptly went bright red.

"Probably," Dryden said.

Sarah smiled but she could see he was actually beginning to feel awkward about it again, and so she changed the subject.

"Philip says you two saw that plane crash," she said.

"Yes miss, we were right there with Gladstone," Chapman said.

"Weren't you scared?"

"Not really – but there was a hell of a bang."

"There was nothing left of it," Rowell said.

They talked about the plane crash and then plane crashes in general for quite a while, and the boys were pleased that she was so interested in what they'd seen and thought about it all.

After lunch they did go for a closer look at the Long Man, but none of them really wanted to slog up the hill with full stomachs in that heat, least of all Sarah. They just stared up from the gate at the bottom for a while.

The Long Man didn't seem to have been upset in any way by his recent experience. He'd probably been through it many times before.

Sarah thought about him standing there between his poles long before she was born and how he would be there after she was dead and buried, centuries from now when no one remembered that she had ever mattered or existed at all. It made her shiver slightly to think of that, of the pointlessly huge expanse of it all.

She was thoroughly wrapped up in her morbid thoughts and got quite a start when Chapman put his hand lightly on her arm. He had a tiny bunch of flowers he'd picked from the verge, buttercups and daisies mostly, and he held them up to her.

"For you, miss," he said solemnly.

"That's very sweet of you, Peter, thank you," she said and she bit her lower lip because she suddenly felt like crying.

Dryden could see the sorrow in her face and put his arm around her shoulders and gave her a hug.

THIRTY

Dryden dropped the two boys off at the front gate and drove off again immediately to take Sarah home. By then it was after five, and the shadows were coming back at the edges of everything, creeping unobtrusively out of their hiding places. But it was still a hot, bright day, and Rowell suggested they go down to the fields and maybe try to join a game of football rather than hanging around school. Just walking into the gloomy front hall was depressing. Chapman agreed straight away, because he was gasping for a ciggey anyway, and he didn't fancy doing that in the outside toilets any more.

There wasn't anyone much about because they were mostly out on chits or down at the fields. They only ran into the first group of boys in the corridor outside the dining hall. They were younger boys, and Rowell and Chapman ignored them, but they looked quite startled when they saw Chapman, and they started giggling when he'd gone past. Rowell glanced back but Chapman didn't seem to notice.

Going up the first flight of stairs, they bumped into Gatesford Minor and a couple of his friends, and they all grinned immediately when they saw Chapman and blocked the way up.

"You look absolutely gorgeous," Gatesford said with an exaggerated lisp. "I really like the flowers."

"Stuff off," Chapman muttered, not knowing what the hell he was talking about.

He tried to squeeze past against the bannister and it seemed at first that Gatesford wasn't going to let that happen, but then he suddenly relented. He puckered his lips as Chapman went by, giving him the smallest of gaps to squeeze past and leaned forward as though expecting a kiss. Then all three of them burst out laughing.

"Shit, I hate that bloody perv," Chapman said when Rowell had caught up on the landing.

"Ignore him."

"That's easy to say."

"What did he mean about flowers?" Rowell asked.

"How the shit should I know?" Chapman replied, but he had an uneasy feeling about that because it obviously meant something.

The dorm was empty when they got there and they changed quickly, eager to get out of school again even if it was only down to the fields. Chapman took his cigarettes out of their hiding place and then they left.

On the walk down they passed a small group of boys coming back from the fields. Their faces were burned red because they'd been out in the hot afternoon sun too long. One of the group, a fifth form boy they knew vaguely through Voaden, gave a wolf whistle from the other side of the road and then struck up an exaggerated pose, like a spearman or a dancer, throwing his head back and stretching out an arm, pointing ahead. It was obvious his antics were intended for Chapman's benefit, and when the group walked on everyone was laughing.

"What the shit's going on?" Chapman asked anxiously.

"Weird," Rowell said.

They were both feeling very uneasy after that and wondered whether it had something to do with going on an outing with Dryden, but that didn't make any sense, so they couldn't really understand it at all. It occurred to Chapman that Chatsworth had been showing the photos of him around, and he felt really sick in his stomach, but it didn't seem to fit either, not with flowers and pointing. He didn't say anything to Rowell, afraid he might come up with a good reason that it might be that.

"Sex-ie," a fourth form boy said, grinning at Chapman as they went through the gate.

"Stuff this," Chapman said and he was starting to feel really upset and a little frightened being the butt of a joke he knew nothing about. He looked around for someone familiar, wanting to know now what was going on.

The first familiar face belonged to Drummond and they bumped into him going round the corner of the gym building. He was with Gatesford Senior, Vaughn and Johnson, and the four of them had obviously been running or training or something because they were all sweating heavily and their faces were red with the sun and the physical effort.

Chapman kept his eyes averted and wanted to get past without being spoken to or having to say anything, but Drummond put out a hand and stopped him.

"Where have you been all day?" he asked as though he'd been looking for him all over.

"Mr Dryden took us on an outing to the beach and then for

lunch, sir," Chapman said.

"Don't call me 'sir', Chapman; I'm not one of the masters," Drummond snapped.

The other three prefects were grinning at him, and they seemed like knowing grins rather than friendly ones. Gatesford looked away quite quickly but the other two went on staring at him, looking him up and down as though trying to get the measure of him. Drummond wasn't smiling at all, and he actually looked quite cross.

"Sorry," Chapman said.

"I'm pleased to see you've got some clothes on for a change," Drummond said in a deadpan voice, and he walked on without elaborating. Gatesford was the only one who looked back briefly and he gave a little wave behind his back, hiding it so that the others wouldn't see.

Chapman stood staring after them, and when they'd disappeared round the corner he still stood there for a bit trying to work out what Drummond had meant.

"I don't think he likes you so much anymore," Rowell said.

"Good," Chapman said, but he didn't really mean it. The sudden rebuke had hurt, especially coming now.

Most of the other boys had played enough football and the games were petering out. Rowell and Chapman tried to join in with one group, but the whole thing soon collapsed, and they were left with only two others kicking the ball to and fro aimlessly. One of the other boys missed a kick because he kept sniggering and couldn't concentrate. He fell down after missing the ball and sat giggling on the grass and Chapman went over to ask what was so funny.

"You – darling," the boy said and he scrambled up and ran off before Chapman could hit him or say anything else. The other boy ran off after him, taking the ball.

"I feel like an absolute prick," Chapman said. "Why are they all laughing at me?"

Rowell shook his head from side to side.

"You don't think it's Chatsworth and those bloody photos or something, do you?" he asked.

"No – why would he do that all of a sudden?" Chapman said, but the hollow feeling in his stomach came back, just in case it was.

They heard a bark then and looked over in that direction and saw Gladstone tugging at his lead far away on the edge of the fields. Pearce was holding the lead and being pulled along, and Higgins was beside him wanting to help. Chapman was relieved to see them for a change, because he knew they would enjoy telling him why everyone suddenly thought he was some kind of ballerina or nude dancer or something.

Gladstone pulled a great deal harder when he recognised Chapman and Rowell walking towards him, and Pearce was too busy trying to stay on his feet to think of something smart to say.

"Why don't you just let him go?" Chapman said loudly when they were still a few yards off.

"Are you going to chase after him, then?" Pearce said angrily. He was thoroughly fed up with having his arms yanked out of their sockets. He didn't trust Higgins to hold the lead, so he held it all the time.

"We let him go – he won't run, I promise," Chapman said.

Pearce didn't say anything but after a moment he did let go and Gladstone bounded over to Chapman and Rowell. He made a big fuss, but he settled down after a few pats and then wandered off, but not very far. Pearce watched him warily, ready to snap at Chapman if he showed any sign of bolting.

"Do you know why everyone's being so weird to me?" Chapman asked.

Pearce and Higgins looked at each other, and then they

started grinning, forgetting about Gladstone.

"You haven't heard about the drawings?" Pearce said.

"What drawings?"

"Someone plastered them up all over the place – even on the main notice board."

"Drawings of what?"

"You, you prick – without any clothes on, or fuck all anyway – you know, like normal. Well, not quite like normal. Why do you let Heathfield draw you like that? I know you're a perv, but, shit, I wouldn't let that fucking freak draw me if you paid me – let alone like that."

"But he only drew my face," Chapman said and he blushed a little remembering what he'd said to Heathfield at the bottom of the stairs.

"Yeah, yeah – we all believe that," Pearce said, enjoying the look on Chapman's face. The malice didn't go very deep, though, because he saw Chapman's beautiful face and the rest of him a bit differently now, after the drawings. He was secretly quite keen to mend fences.

"Is that what everyone thinks – how are they so sure it's me?" Chapman asked.

Pearce shrugged. "It's you alright – he may be a perv, but he's fucking good."

Pearce knew it wasn't really true that Chapman had posed for the drawings. He might be a bit of a jerk most of the time, but he couldn't imagine him standing or lying around like that for ages while Heathfield wanked with his pencil.

"You shouldn't have let that nutter draw you in the first place," he said.

Chapman thought about the art class and knew that he'd had no option, but he didn't say anything about that.

"Do you know who put the drawings up all over?" Rowell asked.

"I haven't got the foggiest – but they were up at lunchtime. Richardson went round taking them down. I think he's got them now."

"How many were there, then?" Chapman asked.

"About four or five – at least. He must really love drawing you," Pearce said, shaking his head. He suddenly remembered Gladstone and looked around in alarm, relaxing again when he saw the dog over by the wall sniffing at something. He turned his attention back to Chapman.

"I'd knock his fucking head in if I were you," he suggested.

"He didn't put them up though, did he?" Chapman asked, not believing it was possible anyway, unless he'd gone really bonkers.

"No – he was crying his fucking eyes out, having a complete bloody fit – Richardson took him off to Matron. Someone must have taken them from his locker."

"How did they know about them?" Rowell asked.

"How the fuck should I know?" Pearce said.

Rowell couldn't think of any more questions, and he looked at Chapman and was surprised to see him smiling a little.

"Thanks, Pearce," Chapman said.

"Stuff him up first chance you get – that's your best plan," Pearce said, and he turned away, calling to Gladstone, who ignored him until he let out a shrill whistle.

"I really need a ciggey," Chapman said. He started walking towards the trees at the far side of the fields rather than back towards the gate, because there were too many people still milling around down there by the big tree. Rowell hesitated momentarily and then followed him.

"I wonder what he's got me doing," Chapman said.

"All kinds of pervy stuff, by the sound of it," Rowell said.

Chapman grinned at that, and Rowell was quite shocked,

expecting him to be in a rage about it, not finding it funny. He seemed to be very relaxed again now that he knew why everyone was making fun of him, but knowing wasn't going to stop it.

"What are you going to do?" he asked, thinking about Pearce's advice and how it made sense.

Chapman shrugged, but he was still smiling.

"There's not much I can do really, is there?" he said.

The trees at the far side all had straight tall trunks with no low branches, and it wasn't really possible to climb up. But there was a shallow ditch next to the wall, and they went down into that and lay on their backs so that they would be invisible from the fields. If someone looked over the wall from the pavement on the other side they'd be seen easily enough, but it wasn't likely to be anyone from the school. It didn't seem to matter much right then, anyway. Chapman took out the cigarettes and offered the pack to Rowell, and he took one but then changed his mind and gave it back. Chapman lit up and had a couple of drags before rolling over towards Rowell and propping himself up on his elbows.

"Why do you think he likes drawing me so much?" he asked.

Rowell tried to remember what Heathfield had said in Turner's classroom, but he hadn't been listening really so he couldn't give the same answer.

"He obviously fancies you," he said.

"Do you think that's all it is?"

"Isn't that screwy enough?"

Chapman didn't answer and he rolled onto his back again and stared up at the sky. They lay there quietly for a while thinking their own thoughts. A flock of geese flew over in ragged formation, heading in the direction of the river, but they were soon out of sight behind a crown of trees. There were birds in the branches above them too, and they could hear a crow calling every now and again, its raucous voice full of anger and complaint.

"It's funny, isn't it?" Chapman said.

"What?"

"How things happen."

Rowell sat up and looked across the fields. They were empty now, and he thought they should be getting back soon too.

"How what things happen?" he asked.

"Heathfield's never done anything to me – he was just trying to be nice," Chapman said.

"I don't think it's nice what he did," Rowell said.

Chapman looked at him and shrugged, smiling slightly. He stood up and flicked the butt of his cigarette against the wall. The evening sun breaking through a gap in the trees lit his face and it seemed to glow like a mask of gold.

"Let's go back," he said.

THIRTY-ONE

Richardson hadn't really been sure what to do with the drawings. In the end he'd put them in a cupboard in the Masters' common room. He'd been back since lunchtime to look through them again. He was back for a second time.

There were five in all, and he was astonished at Heathfield's talent and even more disturbed by the fact that the drawings so easily replaced his own mental image of Dionysus. Whenever he'd tried to picture the god in his mind, he always conjured up a fuzzy, rather muscular, figure, but not any more. Chapman seemed to fit perfectly, dressed in vines and flowers and nothing else, even if he was too young and on the skinny side. He got thoroughly muddled up in his mind thinking about art imitating nature and vice versa. Then he realised what an absurd load of bizarre crap he was dishing up to himself. He laughed and tried shrugging off the weirdness but he couldn't get it completely out of his head. He knew he'd never really be able to look at Chapman again without the nonsense coming back.

He picked up one of the drawings and studied it. His eyes worked their way up along each graceful line, from the feet to the crown of flowers. There was nothing actually obscene about the pictures but it was also impossible to pretend that they weren't erotic. They exuded provocative sensuality. It was obvious that Chapman was in the drawings to fulfil some kind of promise Heathfield had made to himself in his fevered, lovesick mind.

He got quite a start when the door opened. Tetley came in looking for yesterday's newspaper. He immediately saw the drawings spread out on the table.

"Good God," he said.

"Dionysus actually," Richardson said with a wry smile.

Tetley picked up one of the drawings for a closer look.

"You're not planning to kit him out like that, are you?" he asked in disbelief.

"It's nothing to do with the play."

Tetley put the drawing down and picked up another one.

"I recognise him – this is Chapman, isn't it?" he said.

Richardson nodded.

"Who's the artist?"

"Heathfield."

Tetley shook his head slowly from side to side.

"He's bloody good. Did Chapman pose for him – like that?"

"I don't know, but I doubt it," Richardson said.

"That's even more remarkable – they're good enough to hang in a gallery. Where did you get hold of them?" Tetley asked.

"They were plastered up all over the school – two of them on the main notice board."

Tetley looked at him incredulously.

"Heathfield didn't put them up – the poor little bastard's practically having a nervous breakdown about it. They were nicked from his locker."

"That was a shitty thing to do," Tetley said.

"Don't tell me," Richardson said.

"What about Chapman? He must be pretty put out too."

"I haven't seen him yet. He's been on some sort of outing with Philip Dryden all day."

"What a homecoming," Tetley said and he shook his head again.

Richardson gathered the pictures together and put them back in the cupboard. They both stood there for a moment looking at the cupboard door.

"Are you going to speak to the Old Man about it?" Tetley asked.

Richardson shrugged. He'd asked himself the same question several times but was still waiting for an answer.

"I'll give them back to Heathfield when he's calmed down," he said.

"Maybe you should speak to Kennedy – looks like it might be his department," Tetley said.

Richardson dismissed that idea immediately. He knew Kennedy disapproved of the choice of play and he didn't want to give the old parson any ammunition, even if the drawings had nothing to do with it. He would be bound to dream up some connection – he had himself, stupid as it might be.

"I'll have a chat with Heathfield and take it from there," he said. "I'd better put Philip in the picture, though."

Tetley smiled at that and Richardson realised he'd made a gaff and smiled briefly too.

"Have you seen yesterday's paper?" Tetley asked, wanting to get on with his own life.

Richardson shook his head.

"No – sorry," he said.

He looked at his watch and saw that it was nearly six.

"I think I'll go and have a look for Philip – he should be back by now," he said.

When his knock wasn't answered immediately, Richardson started to turn away, but then Dryden barked at him from the other side of the door telling him to wait. He was still tucking his shirt into his trousers, and his feet were bare when he opened the door.

"Sorry, Tony, I thought it was one of the boys," he said.

"No problem – I'm sorry to bother you, but I'm off home soon, and we need to have a chat. Can I come in for a second?"

He looked briefly around the small room, thanking his lucky stars he had a wife and a proper home to go to. Living in one small room hemmed in day and night by the boys would drive him dilly, he thought. Dryden indicated the worn easy chair and he sat down and got straight to the point.

"Have you heard about these drawings?"

Dryden was visibly startled. Richardson wondered why he should be; he'd been very relaxed when he'd opened the door, but he suddenly looked tense, almost guilty of something.

"What drawings?" he asked.

Richardson told him the whole story. Dryden seemed to relax again as he spoke, and by the end he was even smiling.

"Do you think Chapman posed for him?" Richardson asked.

Dryden chuckled at the absurdity of that idea.

"No, I don't. I think it's just a monumental crush and Heathfield's got the talent to put his fantasies down on paper," he said.

Richardson nodded, because that's what he thought too.

"How do you think he'll handle it?" he asked.

"You mean Chapman?"

"Yes."

"I expect he'll shrug it off. I don't think we should make a big deal out of it either – that'll just attract more attention," Dryden said.

"Brian thought we should mention it to Bruder."

"No, I don't think that's necessary," Dryden said quickly. "That'll really blow it up out of all proportion."

"Well it is fairly serious," Richardson said dubiously. "Someone stole the drawings from Heathfield's locker, and he's pretty broken up about it all. He was hysterical. I practically had to carry him down to Matron."

Dryden looked at him while he considered that, his face showing irritation rather than sympathy or concern.

"I'll go down and have a word with him. He'll just have to pull himself together and brazen it out. What choice does he really have? It was pretty damned daft of him to leave drawings like that around in his locker anyway. I'll speak to Chapman too."

Richardson was a little perplexed by Dryden's no-nonsense attitude. It wasn't a huge calamity, he thought, but it seemed to have come pretty close to being the end of the world for Heathfield.

"I've put the drawings away in a cupboard in the common room," he said after a bit of a pause.

"You say there were five altogether?" Dryden asked.

Richardson nodded. "You should have a look at them – they're really quite remarkable," he said.

"Chapman's quite a remarkable little chap," Dryden said.

It was Richardson's turn to look surprised. He'd been thinking about the artist, not the model. He couldn't argue with Dryden's sentiment though, considering he'd been fantasizing during the afternoon about Chapman's place in the pantheon of Greek deities.

"I was going to see how Heathfield's getting on, but perhaps I can leave it all in your capable hands now, Philip," he said, standing up. He was secretly quite glad to be escaping back to the normal world of carpet slippers, reheated supper and TV.

When he'd gone, Dryden sat where he was for a while, pulling on his socks and then putting on his shoes and tying the laces. Only when he'd finished getting dressed did he open the drawer of his desk and take the picture out. It had been shoved under his door like Bruder's note. He'd found it there on the floor when he'd walked in. He knew he should have spoken up about it to Richardson, but he was glad he hadn't. The drawing didn't begin to do the boy real justice, but it was a fair likeness and he wanted to keep it. Chapman was sprawled out suggestively across an altar of some kind in the drawing and there was also a short message written across the bottom of the page: *To Mr. Drydork, love and kisses. Peter Chapman.* That was another good reason he'd decided to keep it hidden.

THIRTY-TWO

The usual loud hubbub died away when Chapman and Rowell came into the hall for dinner. The two boys wavered briefly at the door when they saw all the heads swivelling in their direction, but it was impossible then not to go on. The unnatural silence was broken by a solitary wolf whistle. Then the whole hall erupted with whistles and yells. They were soon followed by the deafening clatter and clamour of cutlery and plates on the wooden tables. Several boys stood up on benches and a brave few even clambered onto the tables themselves to get a better view. Drummond and the other prefects had to bellow very loudly but at first it was hopeless, just adding to the noise.

Rowell kept his eyes down and wished the cracks in the floorboards would open wider because he didn't believe they could lead down to a deeper or more terrible hell. A couple of paces in front, Chapman seemed cheerful by contrast, almost as though the long walk to the Lower Third benches was a kind of triumphal procession. He held his head high, smiling broadly and stretched his arms above his head, fluttering his fingers. One boy bowed low as he went passed and others around him and further on against the benches copied the grandiose gesture. It wasn't easy to tell whether the whole vast cacophony was inspired by ridicule or adulation. In the confusion many of the boys couldn't really make up their mind about that themselves.

Chapman only lowered his arms when he got to his place. By then, Drummond's hoarse and cracking voice was audible above the general din. The racket began to slowly peter out.

The deafening noise had brought the cook and his two assistants out of the kitchen. Dryden and Tetley had appeared in the doorway. They stood side by side like the last knights left standing in the primal battle between light and order and the immense dark hordes of total chaos.

"Silence," Dryden bellowed. His deep angry shout seemed to lift the roof, instantly snuffing out the last few yelps and whistles.

He waited for them all to sit and for the shuffling to stop. He looked across the sea of heads at the cook. The cook looked back at him with a worried expression, holding a huge ladle in his hand.

"I've never heard such bedlam," Dryden shouted angrily. "You'll all be silent for the rest of the meal – no talking, no whispering, nothing. The first one to utter a sound will get DT for the rest of the term."

Drummond, Chatsworth and a couple of the other prefects came over to stand beside Dryden and Tetley in a show of solidarity. They were all furious that things had got so out of control while they'd been responsible. Standing there beside the masters was a good way to get a little credibility back. They tried to look as ferocious as possible.

"Now go and fetch your meals in the usual order," Dryden continued in a loud voice. "Not one word from a single one of you."

No one moved for a few moments. Then one of the boys from the Upper Fifth stood up. The others soon followed him, filing away to get served by the cook's nervous assistants.

Dryden turned to Drummond. "What on earth was that all about?" he asked.

"They were making fun of Chapman, sir – you know, about the nude drawings of him."

"You mean all that was for Chapman's benefit?" Dryden said incredulously. He felt hollow inside, thinking how he'd been down playing the whole business to Richardson not fifteen minutes previously.

"Yes, sir," Drummond replied.

"Have you seen these things, Philip? They were up on the main board at lunchtime – I think the whole damned school's seen them," Tetley said.

"Tony gave me a pretty good idea," Dryden said. He tried not to remember the one in his desk drawer. "But it's nothing to do with Chapman – he didn't know Heathfield was drawing him like that."

The others stared at Dryden, wondering how he could be so certain, but he didn't notice; he was looking anxiously back into the hall, searching around for Chapman on the lower third benches. He breathed a sigh of relief when he spotted him, half expecting the boy to have been torn to pieces.

"What a storm in a teacup," he muttered.

"Heathfield was in a pretty bad way, sir," Drummond said cautiously. "I think he's still down in sickbay."

Dryden felt heartless and a bit foolish being reminded of that.

"I know – I was on my way there when I heard the racket,"

he said. It was more or less true, because he had meant to go down there after supper.

He didn't know quite what to do or say next. Drummond's comment made him feel as though he'd suddenly been caught offside. His legs made up his mind for him. He strode into the hall and down between the forms until he reached Chapman. The boy saw him coming, alerted by the looks on other faces. He began to stand up but Dryden pushed him gently back down into his seat and bent down himself.

"Are you alright?" he asked in a half whisper.

Even the cook's assistants heard the question. Everyone did: they were waiting with their ears open for just that purpose.

Chapman nodded and Dryden gave him a little pat on the shoulder before straightening up and glowering around at the upturned faces.

"I'm appalled that your behaviour just now had to do with the drawings of this boy which some idiot put up on the notice board," he said in a loud voice, almost shouting. "I don't believe for a moment that Chapman was even aware that he was being drawn. For two hundred of you brave souls to turn on him and tease him like that is totally unacceptable and unforgivable. It stops – right now."

He glanced around the hall, fixing his eyes momentarily on boys at random, allowing time for his last words to sink in.

"Heathfield's down in sick bay. He's ill because he was terrified that his private drawings would get exactly this kind of moronic reaction. That must make you all feel immensely proud too. He's an outstanding artist, something you've all apparently seen for yourselves now. Drawing the human form is part and parcel of artistic tradition and has been for thousands of years. So leave him alone. Respect his privacy as much as you'd like your own to be respected."

Dryden paused again briefly.

"This whole business ends now. No more snide cracks, no whispering – leave it be. And to the lout or louts who stole the drawings from Heathfield's locker, be warned: what you did was cowardly and despicable and I fully intend to find out who you are."

Dryden gave Chapman's shoulder another quick pat and then strode back towards the door.

"Excellent, Philip," Tetley said quietly. Then to Dryden's astonishment he started clapping.

Drummond immediately joined in and then everyone was clapping, even the cook. Dryden felt he could really have done without that unnecessary piece of theatre. He knew the boys' applause wasn't sincere. It wasn't the kind of applause you acknowledged either, and he didn't. He gave instructions to Drummond about enforcing the silence and then walked out and went straight down to sick bay.

There was no sign of Mrs Abercrombie – she wasn't in her office and she didn't appear when he called her name. He assumed that she had gone off for her own supper in the staff dining room. That's where he'd been headed himself before the boys erupted.

There were only two beds in sickbay, and one of them was empty. Heathfield was in the other one, and he seemed to be asleep. Dryden stood for a short while looking down at him. He was about to leave when the boy suddenly opened his eyes.

"I'm sorry, I didn't mean to wake you," Dryden said.

Heathfield just lay there staring up at him, not moving a muscle.

"How are you feeling?" Dryden asked. He looked around for something to sit on. There was a wooden chair at the foot of the bed, but he decided to stay standing.

Heathfield closed his eyes again without uttering a word.

Dryden was a little disconcerted by that and he dithered there, wondering whether to wake him up properly. Then he decided that Matron must have given him a sedative and that it would be better to come back a bit later. He didn't feel he could leave without saying anything, because he was sure the boy could hear him.

"We've got all your drawings back," he said softly. "They're quite safe now, and no one's going to tease you about it from now on, I can promise you that."

He waited a little longer for some sort of reaction but there was none and so he left.

Dinner would have been over quicker than usual, but Drummond decided to keep everyone sitting there in silence for fifteen minutes after dessert. It was his way of getting revenge for the humiliation he'd suffered. They all understood and accepted that. When he finally announced they could go the boys filed out without talking much. Everyone seemed to avoid even looking at Chapman and most gave him a wide berth. Being conspicuously ignored was almost worse than being laughed at. Even Leomond and the others seemed to hang back. When Chapman walked out with Rowell there was always space around them. It was as though they were the source of some contagious disease.

"I never realised you had such great legs," Voaden said in a loud voice, appearing behind them at the door. He put his arm around Chapman's shoulders.

"Thanks," he said doubtfully, but for once he was actually glad to have Voaden touch him.

They went out like that, with Voaden hugging him, grinning with amiable menace at anyone who had the temerity to glance in their direction.

"I've got another little surprise for you," he whispered into Chapman's ear.

He took his arm away and Chapman looked up at him. He was about to ask what it was, but Voaden shook his head. Someone else tapped him on the shoulder and he turned round to see who it was.

"I want to apologise for being so brusque with you earlier on, Chapman," Drummond said, ignoring both Rowell and Voaden. "I didn't realise you hadn't posed for those drawings. I'm sorry I snapped at you."

"That's OK, thanks, sir," Chapman said.

Drummond smiled when he heard the "sir" and put out his big right hand. When they shook hands, it seemed to go on for an unnecessarily long time.

"What a giant prat," Voaden said when he'd gone.

"He's not so bad," Chapman said. "What's the surprise?"

"Weed – good stuff," Voaden whispered.

Rowell groaned inwardly. He immediately decided he didn't want to be part of another of Voaden's chemical experiments. He was suffering from battle fatigue anyway. He waited to see what Chapman would do, hoping he'd make some excuse.

Chapman did seem to hesitate for a moment, but the same excited look was back in his eyes, the one that had been there when he took the pill. Rowell knew before he spoke that he was going to go along.

"You mean hash?"

Voaden nodded. He put his finger to his lips. There was no one left in the corridor, but it was just as well to be cautious.

"I can't go over the wall – I can't be late again," Chapman said.

"We'll just have a quick puff 'round the back."

"OK."

Rowell shook his head and started to walk away towards the stairs.

"Hang on, Chris, don't you want to come?" Chapman called after him.

"No thanks – and haven't you got into enough shit lately?" he said.

Chapman shrugged and smiled rather sheepishly. He didn't say anything, so Rowell carried on walking without looking back again. He took the stairs two at a time up towards the dorm.

"Stuff him," Voaden said.

He led the way to the narrow cul de sac by the coal chute. There were high windowless walls there, and it was one of his least favourite places, because everything was covered in coal dust. It was impossible to sit down anywhere without picking up a black backside. But it was secure, and they would be practically invisible, especially on a Sunday evening. He didn't like smoking pot in the toilets, because there was no fun in getting high sitting on the john in the midst of all the pee smell, not to mention the added risk. With cigarettes it didn't matter.

"Have you ever smoked this before?" Voaden asked.

"I had a couple of puffs at a party once – at least I think it was hash; they said it was."

"There's weed, and then there's weed," Voaden said knowledgeably.

He took the joint out of his jacket pocket and rolled it appreciatively between his fingers before lighting up and taking a deep drag.

They smoked the joint in silence, and it was half gone before either of them spoke again.

"Good, eh?" Voaden said.

"Great, thanks," Chapman said, and he did feel good.

Being the focus of a riot at dinner didn't seem that important any more. He thought about Dryden and what a big hero he'd been and how loudly he snored when he wasn't awake.

"Who do you think nicked Heathfield's drawings, then?" Voaden asked.

Chapman shrugged. He stretched his arms lazily and spread his fingers, feeling the warmth of his own blood in them. "Who cares," he said.

Voaden studied his face for a while. He felt pretty relaxed himself – it was good stuff, not like the last shit Ainsworth had got hold of.

"You're a weird little bugger," he said.

"Why?"

"If I told you to jump off a cliff, would you do that?"

"Sure – if I could fly," Chapman said, and he giggled a little at his own wit.

Voaden smiled too when he thought he'd got the joke.

"I'm thinking of going down to Newquay when I leave – learn to surf," he said.

"That sounds great."

"I'll get some kind of job. Johno's been down there. He saves up a bit and goes to North Africa for the winter."

Chapman tried to picture Johno's stick figure on a surfboard or a camel. "I can surf," he said.

"Really?"

"That's what I mostly do when I go home for the holidays – I surf all the time; it's really great."

Voaden envied him that. He thought about his own long string of unhappy holidays, stuck around the house with no money and his dad telling him what a waste of space he was morning and night.

They went for a walk around the school yard when they'd finished the joint, talking about big issues like surfing and the future, looking up at the Chestnut trees and listening to the soft evening breeze in the leaves. It was a good way to make sure that the last of the smell was off their breath before going back in, but both of them wanted to do it anyway.

"It's only two weeks to the end of term," Voaden said. "We must try and keep in touch when I leave."

"Yes, we must," Chapman said. He didn't stop and think how they would do that with Voaden in Newquay. He wasn't sure where Newquay was, even, but it didn't seem a big problem; nothing did, really.

"This is where I first met you – remember?" Voaden said, stopping by one of the trees. "I don't think it's weird that we're such good friends, do you?"

"No, I think it's great," Chapman said. He looked at the tree as though it was an old friend too – the one who had introduced them originally.

Voaden patted the rough trunk as though he were thinking the same thing.

"If I'd had a younger brother, I would have liked him to be you," Voaden said, and he really meant it. "I wish I could take you with me to Newquay."

"I wish I could come," Chapman said. He wondered what the surf was like there and whether the sea was as cold as it had been that morning.

They didn't pay any attention to the ambulance, although it made a hell of a racket going up Pond Road. The light was flashing on the roof, and the driver was really gunning it. He nearly hit a parked car turning the corner to get to the front of the school. He swore at the owner of the car even though he wasn't there, calling him an arsehole for parking so close to the intersection.

The sun had almost gone down and the shadows had all merged into twilight, settling down over everything like a soft carpet. Voaden and Chapman carried on with their philosophical walk, but they hadn't gone much further when a couple of boys came running like mad over from the school buildings towards them. One of them was Rowell and the other was Pearce. It was obvious they were bringing urgent news, from the looks on their faces.

"Heathfield jumped out of a fucking window," Rowell said breathlessly when he reached them.

"From the landing outside dorm two – splat," Pearce said.

"Is he dead?" Voaden asked.

"I think so," Rowell said.

"Well fuck a duck," Voaden said.

They all looked at Chapman, waiting for him to say something. He just looked back at them with his mouth open.

"Matron's lost her marbles – it's bloody awful," Rowell said. He studied Chapman's face to see if he was totally spaced out or just shocked.

"When did it happen?" Voaden asked.

"Just now – about five minutes ago. He nearly landed on some old geezer taking his dog for a walk on the pavement," Pearce said.

More boys had come out of the school buildings. They were milling around the playground in ones and twos and small groups. It was like someone had dropped a lit match into an ant hill.

"That's horrible," Chapman said finally.

The school siren started up then. It began with a low tortured moan as it cranked itself up, rising quickly to an insistent ear-splitting screech. The neighbours all hated school fire practise for that reason. The older ones felt especially upset because it sounded as though the German bombers were coming over again, droning high over the coast with their bellies full of death.

The siren was a signal for the boys to form up in the

playground according to dorms. Many of them had already begun to do that, and virtually all the prefects were there and a couple of masters as well.

"We'd better get formed up," Pearce said excitedly. He was enjoying the drama of it all.

"Come on, Pete," Rowell said.

Chapman looked at Voaden, and the bigger boy nodded solemnly, not knowing what to say any more.

"Thanks for the weed," Chapman said.

A different prefect called the roll for each dorm. Vaughn was the one who called out the names for Dorm 4. He called out Heathfield's name and looked up when there was no answer. It was a second or two before he realised what a huge gaff he'd made, and then he went bright red. The boys could tell, even though it was now quite dark. Nobody said anything, but Pearce muttered "Dead – you dork," under his breath.

Kennedy had appeared on the scene by then, and not long after that Bruder arrived. The two of them spent a long time huddled in a small group with Tetley and Drummond. They were still talking long after all the prefects had finished calling the rolls and the last two or three stragglers had been accounted for. Finally they stopped talking and Bruder came forward to address everyone.

"Good evening, boys," he said.

He waited while they all murmured a reply. The playground lights came on suddenly, which was just as well because they kept the darkness at bay, and it looked as though it was going to be a very dark night with no moon on the rise.

"This isn't a regular fire drill, as I think most of you know, but we'll treat it as such and I'm glad to see that you've all responded quickly and properly. The reason we've brought you all together so suddenly is because there's been a terrible accident involving Heathfield. I know there are already all kinds of silly rumours flying around, especially in the light of what apparently happened earlier today, but for the moment this is simply a tragic accident. Heathfield fell from one of the upper storey windows and he's been seriously injured and taken off to hospital. Mr Dryden has gone with him and we'll let you all know in the morning how he's progressing. I know some of you will want to visit him there in due course and we'll arrange for that. In the meantime I want you all to get back to your normal routine and don't speculate unnecessarily about what happened. It serves no purpose and can end up doing a great deal of unintentional harm. If any of you have been especially upset by this terrible accident or if you feel you can shed some useful light on what happened, my door will be open until lights out. The same goes for Reverend Kennedy, and you can go and see him in the Masters' common room. That's all I have to say for now. Before you disperse, Reverend Kennedy will lead us all in a prayer for Heathfield's speedy recovery."

"He's not dead," Chapman whispered to Rowell.

"I thought he was – he must be pretty smashed up though," Rowell whispered back defensively.

Kennedy was visibly upset by it all. They could hear it in his voice too, and his prayer was short and to the point for a change.

When he'd finished, the boys started to move back inside and Rowell and Chapman moved with them, no longer shunned or even particularly noticed, because Chapman's passive role had been overshadowed by the bigger unfolding drama. That got another huge lift when two uniformed policemen were discovered waiting patiently in the hallway.

THIRTY-THREE

A continuous procession of masters and prefects passed through the dorm in the half hour before lights out. They all had solemn faces, but they were also being especially nice to everyone. Drummond even picked Higgin's towel up off the floor and hung it over the end of his bed without shouting at him or even saying anything. It was pretty obvious they didn't want any more of the younger boys to get pissed off and jump out of a window.

It was quite pleasing in some ways to get so much concentrated care and attention all of a sudden, but it was also mighty inhibiting. No one talked much or clowned around.

"I wish they'd all clear off," Chapman said to Leomond at the basins.

Leomond had his mouth full of toothpaste, but he rolled his eyes to show that he agreed.

Pearce flicked his towel at Chapman's bum as he went past.

It was a half-hearted attempt, and his aim wasn't good. He was keeping an eye open for one of the prefects or masters, not sure how far their new-found tolerance and bon hommie would stretch. The flick missed, and Chapman didn't notice anyway.

The effects of the joint hadn't lasted very long, but Chapman was still floating slightly, feeling more like a spectator than a participant in what was going on. He knew he was being watched and studied surreptitiously, not by the other boys in the dorm so much as by the masters and prefects as they wandered through. On the face of it, everything was normal and nobody had made any cracks at all since dinner, not even Pearce. What had happened to Heathfield seemed to have underlined Dryden's words like a thick red pencil.

All the boys got into bed earlier than they would usually have done, what with the regular patrols going through, and Chapman was no exception. He leaned into his locker and rummaged around and took his diary out. He started scribbling in it, pausing every now and again while he thought what to write. He hadn't written anything for over a month, but it suddenly seemed important to get something down. He wrote about Voaden and the pill and about the plane crash on different dates and about Clara and the Long Man and Sarah and then about Heathfield jumping out of the window.

He was very absorbed in it all and didn't see Richardson come in. He was standing right by his bed when he eventually did notice him. Bruder had phoned him, and he'd been happy to come back and lend a hand with the saturation patrols, or so he'd said on the phone. He sat down on the end of the bed, and it creaked ominously under the heavy load. Chapman was a bit flustered, being caught like that with his diary. He quickly put it away again in his locker.

Richardson found himself wondering whether Dionysus

kept a diary. If he'd been able to get out of his fat body he would have kicked himself in the arse for that. The silly thoughts kept flitting back into his head – flapping around like agitated birds trapped in a small room, crapping on the antique furniture. He also wondered why he'd sat down at all, because he couldn't really think of anything much to say.

"From what I hear, you've handled yourself very well through all of this," he said eventually because both Chapman and Rowell were looking at him and waiting.

"Thank you, sir," Chapman said.

Richardson glanced at Rowell, not enjoying having an audience, and Rowell quickly looked back down at the book he was reading.

"Poor old Heathfield," Richardson said. *Driven mad by your beauty and the terrifying mystery of it all*, he added to himself.

Chapman nodded sympathetically.

"You should think of joining the Dramatic Society," Richardson said after another long pause.

Chapman was looking over his face again in that same unsettling, weirdly familiar way he had. He didn't respond to the suggestion, and it was an odd one, coming out of the blue like that.

"If you were a bit bigger, you would have made a good Dionysus," Richardson explained.

Chapman grinned and glanced across at Rowell to check that he'd heard. It was more impressive than being asked to be a wrapped up woman, whatever that was.

"Thanks, sir," he said.

"Sleep tight," Richardson said eventually and he heaved himself up and went away.

Bruder walked in a couple of minutes later with Kennedy in tow. They did a circuit of the dormitory and also ended up at the foot of Chapman's bed.

"How are you, Peter?" Bruder asked.

"Fine, sir," Chapman said.

"Good, good," Bruder said. He hovered there for a while and Kennedy hovered alongside him, but then they walked away, pausing in the doorway to say goodnight to everyone.

Drummond turned the lights off shortly afterwards, and it seemed as though things were going to get back to normal, but that didn't happen. The visits to Chapman's bed carried on in the dark. Drummond came over right away. He sat down and asked Chapman how he was, and when he said he was fine, the older boy just went on sitting there in the dark saying nothing. It was impossible to tell what he was thinking or what he was looking at. He stood up eventually and said goodnight again and then went out.

Chatsworth came next, about five minutes later. Chapman wasn't expecting to see him at all, and he didn't recognise him in the dark until he spoke.

"Shift up a bit," Chatsworth whispered and he sat down right beside him, not like the others had, at the bottom of the bed.

Rowell got a bit of a fright when he realised who it was. He made a big show of turning over in his bed just to remind everyone that he was only four feet away.

"Are you alright?" Chatsworth asked in a soft voice.

Chapman said he was fine, although he was getting pretty fed up with saying it by then.

"I've brought you a peace offering," Chatsworth whispered.

He slipped his hand under the blanket and Chapman's body went very rigid. He got ready to jump up but then Chatsworth took his hand out again. Chapman felt around a bit and found a small box and he felt the cellophane and realised pretty quickly without having to look that it was a pack of cigarettes.

"Thanks," he said.

"You're welcome," Chatsworth said. Then he just sat there in the dark without saying anything just like Drummond had done, except he was sitting much closer. He bent down after a minute or so and leaned his face very close. Chapman was scared he was going to kiss him again. He tried to pull the sheet and blanket up but it was firmly stuck under the prefect's backside.

"The photos are in a very safe place," Chatsworth whispered very softly in his ear.

Chapman didn't know what to say because he didn't feel like thanking him about it, so he just nodded. Chatsworth saw the nod even in the dark. He put his hand on the blanket and patted Chapman's thigh, and then he ran his hand up slowly over the blanket and patted his hip too, and he might have gone on from there, but Chapman brought his knees up to show that he didn't like it. Chatsworth stood up then using Chapman's knees to steady himself, though it wasn't really necessary. Then he left.

"Are you alright, Chapman, are you alright, are you alright," Pearce said in a loud whisper. He sounded like a demented parrot.

"Fine thanks, Pearce — thanks for asking," Chapman whispered back.

"Stuff off."

Leomond's torch went on, glowing under his blanket, but it went off again almost immediately because he thought better of it, worried about the patrols. He didn't want to have the torch confiscated.

"I wonder whether Heathfield's dead yet?" Pearce whispered speculatively.

There was no answer because everyone was trying to get

off to sleep. They didn't want to think about dead people on the edge of that abyss. The two boys lying on either side of Heathfield's empty bed felt particularly uncomfortable about it, especially the one who had tipped Gatesford Minor off about the drawings of Chapman. He'd never imagined what would happen as a result of that. He didn't want Heathfield coming back without a proper body to stare at him accusingly. He pulled the covers right up over his head in case it was about to happen.

"I'm sure he'll be OK," Chapman said.

They were all pleased to hear that. It seemed to have some real authority somehow coming from Chapman, as though he should know if anyone could.

The next two visitors were a couple of smaller boys from Dorm 2. They darted in very furtively, because they weren't supposed to be up and out of bed. It was obvious they weren't planning to come for a protracted stay because they didn't sit down on Chapman's bed.

"Are you alright," one of them whispered urgently, bending down so low in the dark that his face nearly bumped into Chapman's.

"I'm fine."

"We brought you something," the boy whispered and he put it down on the top of the locker.

"Thanks very much," Chapman said, and he sat up to see what it was.

"It's just some chocolate," the boy said.

"Thanks."

"We think you were really brave at dinner," the boy said.

He was obviously the senior partner and the spokesmen for both of them, because the other one just did a lot of nodding in the dark.

"See you tomorrow," the boy said and they both scampered

out, pausing in the doorway to check that the coast was clear.

Chapman picked up the chocolate bar and was pleased to find that it was one of the bigger ones.

"Do you want some chocolate?" he whispered to Rowell.

"Thanks," Rowell said.

"How come he's so lucky?" Pearce said.

"Come and get some if you want," Chapman said.

Pearce hesitated, though not for long; he jumped out of bed and came over. He arrived at more or less the same time as Leomond. The four of them polished off the chocolate bar quite quickly.

There weren't any more visitors or gifts after that. Drummond came round again, but they all pretended to be asleep so he didn't stay long.

THIRTY-FOUR

Dryden got back at quarter to eleven. He'd phoned Bruder from the hospital to give him the score, and it didn't look good. Heathfield had come down three stories onto a concrete pavement, and it seemed pretty certain that he'd broken his neck, not to mention a few other important bones. The doctors didn't think he was going to die, but they had grim faces and muttered darkly about permanent paralysis.

He'd also phoned Sarah and told her the whole story. They'd had quite a long chat about it because she was really interested and sympathetic, being both a doctor and a caring sort of person. He didn't tell her that he'd kept one of the drawings; he wasn't going to tell anyone that.

"How is Peter now?" she asked.

"He doesn't seem to have been that fazed by it. It must have been horrible for him walking into the dining hall, though," he replied.

"I really like him – he's such a sweet boy," she said. "Give him my love."

His coins ran out shortly afterwards, and the call ended. He would have liked to have gone on talking, because it was pretty lonely sitting there in the waiting room with the bright light and all the hospital smells.

Bruder told Dryden that he'd phoned Heathfield's parents with the grim news. They ran a small hotel in Newquay, and Heathfield's dad was driving up through the night to be with his son, but his mum had to stay behind, since they couldn't both leave the hotel on a moment's notice.

Dryden didn't think he could sleep because he was feeling pretty fed up with himself about the way he'd behaved and handled things. Nobody was pointing a finger at him; in fact, Bruder had heard about his little speech in the dining hall and had commended him for it on the phone, but Dryden knew how it really was. Chapman had been the only one who had mattered to him. He'd actually been quite angry at Heathfield, not really caring how he'd felt about his pictures going on display. He thought it had been wimpish of him to go blubbering off to sickbay, leaving Chapman to face the music.

When he got back to school, he went straight to the staff common room to look at the rest of the drawings, but they'd gone by then, locked away in a drawer in Bruder's desk, so he headed for the dormitories.

He ran into Drummond on the way up the stairs.

"How's everything here?" he asked in a low voice.

"No problems, I've just been up to check again, sir. It all seems fine – they're all asleep. How's Heathfield?"

Dryden shook his head.

"In a very bad way – they say he'll survive, but it looks pretty bad."

"I'm sorry, sir," Drummond said.

"We all are – what a terrible business."

Dryden went into Dorm 4 first, treading carefully and trying hard not to make any noise. He walked down to the basins and then up the other aisle like everyone else had, ending up at the foot of Chapman's bed. The boy seemed to be asleep like the rest of them. He resisted the urge to make sure but stood there for quite a while looking down at his dim outline under the blanket. Then he went out and poked his head into a couple of the other dorms. He didn't go into either of them. They all seemed to be asleep there too.

He considered going out for a walk but decided that was a bit daft so late in the evening and so he went to his room and took out the bottle of scotch. He poured himself a small measure, topping up the glass with water. There wasn't much left in the bottle, not nearly enough to get drunk again, so he felt pretty safe about having just one drink. Then he looked at the drawer where the picture was hidden and started to worry about having kept it.

He'd taken one of his shoes off and was busy with the laces of the other one when the door opened slowly. Chapman came in, and if he'd knocked Dryden hadn't heard it. He only had his pyjama pants on and the elastic was folded right down as usual.

"What are you doing up – you should be asleep," Dryden said, trying to sound stern but he was secretly pleased he'd come.

"I just wanted to know how Heathfield is, sir," Chapman said.

"I'm sure he'll be fine, but he's pretty badly hurt."

Chapman lingered uncertainly in the doorway.

"It's not my fault, is it, sir?" he asked after a short pause.

"Why on earth would it be your fault? No – it's not your fault – none of it was your fault."

"But I said he could draw me, sir."

Dryden felt as though he'd been punched in the guts hearing that. He stared up at the boy in disbelief.

"What do you mean?"

"He drew me in art class, then in the dorm."

"Why?"

Chapman shrugged.

"Because he wanted to, sir – and I wanted the picture to send to my mum."

Dryden was astonished at that idea – that he'd want his mother to see him like that. Then he realised that they had to be talking about different things.

"You haven't seen the drawings have you, the ones on the notice board," he said.

"No – not those other ones, sir. He only drew my face," Chapman replied with a hint of indignation.

Dryden smiled, and he couldn't help glancing at the desk drawer.

"He drew a lot more than that when you weren't looking," he said.

"Have you seen them, sir?"

"I've seen one of them."

Chapman smiled too then, and he didn't really seem to be embarrassed about it at all. Then the smile vanished abruptly and the concern showed in his face again.

"I actually said he could draw me starkers, sir. I was only joking, but I feel a bit of a shit about it now."

Dryden raised his eyebrows a little. "Maybe that was a bit silly – but it still doesn't mean any of it was your fault."

Chapman nodded, but he didn't look that convinced.

"Have you told anyone else you said that to him?"

"No, sir."

"Well I think it's best if you keep it to yourself. It doesn't matter, but these things have a way of getting twisted around – just shut up about it."

Chapman nodded and he came a little further into the room, looking at the chair as though he wanted to sit down.

"You'd better get back to bed," Dryden said.

"Can't I stay for a bit, sir – I can't sleep."

Dryden thought about it for a moment or two.

"OK, you can stay for a little while," he said.

Chapman grinned and quickly sat down in the chair. Dryden took his other shoe off because he felt a bit unbalanced sitting there with only one on, but he ignored the whiskey.

"Thanks for today, sir, I really enjoyed it. Lunch was great, and that was very funny what they did to the Long Man. You've got a fantastic girlfriend, sir, she's really nice," Chapman said, trying to get several topics out to justify sitting down.

"I'm glad you liked it. It seems quite long ago already – it's been a long, strange day," Dryden said. He was thinking about Heathfield mostly.

Chapman nodded and he put on a solemn expression to match the one on Dryden's face.

"Why did you take me and Chris, sir?"

Dryden wasn't expecting him to ask that. He didn't quite know how to reply, because he'd never really given himself a proper answer. He'd just wanted to be with him but that wasn't the answer he felt he could give to himself or anyone else.

"I thought it would do you both good to get out," he said.

"Well, I really enjoyed it – Chris did too, even the cold sea."

"It was cold, wasn't it – aren't you getting cold sitting there like that?" Dryden asked.

"I'm fine, sir."

Chapman folded his slender arms across his waist and sat forward a little.

"You don't think I'm weird or a sissy because I came to sleep with you, do you, sir?"

"No – if that worried me, I wouldn't have taken you on an outing," Dryden said. He felt a bit awkward about it and wished the boy hadn't brought it up.

"It's just that I was having a really bad nightmare – I have it all the time."

Dryden thought about saying that he'd probably still been a bit drunk, but he decided not to, recalling how motherless he'd been himself. In the corner of his eye, the glass of whiskey seemed to wink at him.

"What – every night?" he asked.

"No sir, but quite often – some times are worse than others."

"What's it about?"

"I don't really know sir. There are just all these weird people all around me and their faces keep changing, you know, really fast – kind of stretching and stuff, like rubber only different, and they get bigger – huge sometimes – and then tiny. They're smiling and sometimes they're angry or frightened, but all at the same time somehow. They never say anything, but they try to touch me, and it's as though they all want something from me, sir, but I don't know what it is. It's like thousands of people – really weird. Then there's this old guy but I never see him, I just know he's there, and he's really, really old, but not wrinkled or grey hair and a long beard or anything – just very, very old, older than everything. It's hard to explain, sir."

"Dreams usually are. Do the people do anything to you?" Dryden asked.

Chapman shook his head, and then he grinned suddenly.

"They scare the shit out of me, sir," he said.

Dryden wondered momentarily whether Chapman was pulling his leg, but the grin quickly vanished, and he knew then that he wasn't.

"I have some pretty freaky dreams too sometimes – everyone does. It's just your head getting things sorted out for tomorrow," he said.

Chapman hugged himself a little and then seemed to relax and sat up straight again.

"I'd better go to bed," he said, but he didn't get up.

Dryden nodded.

"I wonder whether Heathfield has nightmares, sir."

"I'm sure he does sometimes," Dryden said.

Chapman considered that seriously, as though it was important.

"He said I was very beautiful – he said that's why he liked drawing me so much."

"He's an artist, he's got a very good eye," Dryden said.

The boy looked at him, and then he smiled and Dryden smiled a bit awkwardly too.

"I'd better go," Chapman said.

Dryden nodded again and he watched him get up and go to the door.

"Sarah sends her love," he said.

Chapman grinned.

"She really seemed to like my flowers," he said.

"She said they were the prettiest flowers she's ever had," Dryden said.

THIRTY-FIVE

What with the drawings and everything, Voaden felt it was high time for his show down with Gatesford Minor, and he got right down to it in the showers on Monday morning. He suggested Gatesford have a good look at his own arse hole because that's where his head would be going if he didn't quit spreading crap about Chapman being a fairy.

Gatesford was only a year younger, and he was big for his age, almost as tall as Voaden himself, but he was a fair bit lighter, and he probably cared more about avoiding pain. He was no coward though, and he felt pretty confident about life in general, having a big brother who was a school prefect, so he told Voaden what he could do with his advice.

"Go screw yourself — and your little boyfriend," he said.

They were brave words, but it was apparent by the expression on his face that Gatesford thought he'd gone much too far almost as soon as he'd uttered them.

Voaden smiled at him, and it looked for a moment as though

he wasn't going to do anything serious. Then he hit Gatesford in the stomach. It was a lightning blow and a really hard one. Gatesford doubled up and Voaden hit him on the back of the neck too and brought his knee up so that it collided with Gatesford's face. It didn't break his nose, but it did split his lip. A fair few drops of blood immediately started appearing on the concrete floor.

A couple of Gatesford's friends tried to stop it then, but neither of them wanted to fight Voaden, so they just yelled a lot and waved their arms about, but Voaden didn't take any notice of them. He kicked Gatesford in the crotch, bringing his foot up between his legs, and the impact seemed to almost lift the other boy off the ground.

The whole thing only took a few seconds. At the end of it, Gatesford's towel had fallen off his waist and he was curled up, naked, hugging his crotch on the shower room floor.

Voaden was quite happy to kick him again, but two of the other boys managed to get between him and Gatesford's prostrate body. A third one risked a lot by putting his hands on Voaden's shoulders, trying to pull him back. Voaden shook him off and walked out. He looked surprisingly calm, not that keyed up about it at all.

At breakfast Gatesford had a very swollen lip, and he looked quite ridiculous. He was obviously still very upset about what had happened and didn't feel like eating. He got up after a short while and left because he didn't like people looking at him and whispering. One of his closest friends got up and went after him, still trying to shove a piece of toast into his own mouth.

Voaden ate quite a big breakfast; whatever was going on, he always ate a good meal. Even when he'd had quite a few toots or was worried about something, he could still tuck it away. He hadn't seen any sign of Gatesford Senior, and he knew that was coming, but it didn't worry him unduly. The bigger Gatesford was just that, a lot bigger; he wouldn't be a push-over like his foul-mouthed younger brother, but Voaden was still confident he could handle things if it came to that. He wasn't sure it would come to another fight because Gatesford Senior liked being a prefect, and he wouldn't carry on being one for very long if he was caught fighting.

The fight was big news at breakfast, but Heathfield jumping out of the window was still a much bigger story. By the time breakfast was over most of the boys had started to put the fight on the back burner, and they were again wondering how Heathfield was getting on and discussing what the likely extent of his injuries might be and whether he was even still alive.

Chapman was a part of both dramas because the reports on the fight in the shower included Gatesford's unwise comment about him being Voaden's boyfriend. Many of the boys kept looking at him surreptitiously. None of them wanted to look too obviously or appear too curious because they weren't keen on Voaden getting the wrong idea.

Chapman had heard about the fight, of course. He was happy that Gatesford Minor had been hammered because he deserved to be, but he was also angry with Voaden because it looked now as though he couldn't stand up for himself. He thought everyone would think him a bit of a wimp if he had to rely on someone else to fight his battles for him. He wished Voaden had just beaten up Gatesford for his own reasons and not dragged his name into it. He said as much to Rowell and Leomond and they agreed with him.

"It does make you seem a bit of a … you know," Rowell said and that didn't help.

It was about then, during breakfast, that someone

commented on the things that seemed to befall people who got on the wrong side of Chapman. No one else had really thought much about Featherstone and the plane crash, because his name didn't mean anything to them. Most didn't even know there was a connection with Chapman until it was pointed out to them. Featherstone had got Chapman caned, and then look what happened, the rumours said; Heathfield had drawn dirty pictures of him, and look what happened as a result. The theory began like that and started to circulate quite widely, and it wasn't long before the Gatesford connection was uncovered: Gatesford had been the one who pulled Chapman's pants off during the dorm raid and had given him a hard time, and look what had just happened to him.

Pearce was irritated when he heard the story, because it made Chapman sound really special, like some kind of wizard or something.

"What a load of crap," he said to the boy who told him.

"You must admit it's a bit weird," the boy said.

"I've never *heard* such a load of crap," Pearce said, but he couldn't help thinking about it despite dismissing it so convincingly.

By then they were sitting in the hall, waiting for Bruder to appear at the podium for Monday morning assembly. All the teachers were already there, sitting on either side of the dais, facing the rows of boys. Bruder always liked to come in last because it was more dramatic that way, and it showed that he had better things to do than just lounge around at the podium, waiting for everyone else to get settled.

When he did eventually appear, he wasn't wearing his academic gown like the rest of the masters because he'd come straight from the hospital. He looked very tired and very old standing at the podium. Everyone listened to what he had to say in complete silence. There were none of the usual coughs and sneezes or the noises which things like books and pencils make when people drop them. There was only total silence.

Bruder didn't talk about good news or bad news; he just gave them the facts about Heathfield. The doctors were pretty certain that he would never be coming back to school, because he would be paralysed from the neck down for the rest of his life. He explained that Heathfield would probably never be able to walk again or do the normal things a boy his age could do without even stopping to think about it. He would never be able to use his hands either, Bruder said, and that meant he would never again be able to paint or draw.

Bruder paused for quite a long time when he'd said that, because he knew it had a special significance and also because he was finding it difficult to control his own voice.

Turner seized the moment to get up and quickly leave the hall, not being as strong willed as Bruder or the other masters and less able to control the emotions welling up inside him. Tears were streaming down his cheeks. The boys would have found that hilarious under any other circumstances, but most of them watched him go with sympathetic eyes.

"There are many lessons all of us can draw from this tragedy," Bruder continued when he was sure his voice was going to behave itself. "I'm not going to dwell on them now because our thoughts and prayers should all be with Simon and with his parents in their time of immense trial. Suffice it to say that we must all learn to be a lot more caring and more thoughtful for the feelings and vulnerabilities of others."

Bruder changed the subject abruptly then and went on to talk about other school business and the shuffling and coughing started up almost immediately. Assembly ended as usual with the singing of the school song. The song's trite and hackneyed message about comradeship and fortitude in the face of life's adversities seemed to take on an unlikely poignancy.

Chapman had added cause to dwell on the words of the song a couple of minutes later when Gatesford Senior stopped him in the corridor and gave him Prefect's DT for talking in Assembly. He walked away without giving him a chance to protest or say anything.

"Oh, shit," Rowell said.

THIRTY-SIX

Bruder was wrong about some boys being keen to go and visit Heathfield in hospital. Nobody wanted to go. He didn't really have any friends in the usual sense, and the thought of standing by a hospital bed trying to make polite chit chat to a live head with a dead body was more than any of them could handle. Just about everyone had a hard time imagining what kinds of things they could think of to say in those circumstances, especially to someone they didn't know that well and had been teasing the shit out of a short while previously.

Even the boys who took their Christianity quite seriously or sang in the choir, not that the two things necessarily went hand in hand, but even those boys didn't come forward to volunteer for a trip to the hospital.

By Tuesday, Heathfield had still not had any visitors from the school other than teachers, and that was why Bruder summoned Chapman and Pearce to his office after lunch.

He called on Pearce because he'd got him muddled up with Rowell. He only realised it when the two boys were standing in front of him. By then it was too late, and they just had to live with the oddness of it.

He wanted Chapman to go because he thought it would do Heathfield the world of good to see his idol at his bedside, and he'd convinced himself that in some way it would be good for Chapman too.

Bruder was quite clever in making it sound as though he knew they were keen to go and visit Heathfield and had only been prevented from coming forward because they were shy about asking. He explained that he was going over to the hospital himself later that afternoon and would be glad to take them along. It was the kind of offer that was impossible to refuse.

"I think Rowell wants to come as well, sir," Chapman said.

Bruder smiled and he said it would be no problem at all. He was privately very pleased about it, because he knew how happy it would make Heathfield's dad to see three boys coming to visit his injured son, if he happened to be there.

"And Higgins, sir," Pearce said.

Bruder was really beaming. Four was even better.

"Meet me in the hallway at five o' clock," he said.

Chapman and Pearce went in search of their respective friends to give them the good news.

"What? Fuck that!" Rowell said when Chapman told him.

"You don't have any choice," Chapman said.

"Why me?"

Chapman shrugged and he smiled a little inside, thinking how he'd dragged him into it, but he didn't feel guilty. It was all in a good cause, he told himself.

"Don't you feel a bit sorry for him?" he asked.

Rowell looked up at the sky, as though he'd find the right

response up there.

"Not really. He didn't have to jump out of the window."

"He didn't have to have his drawings nicked," Chapman said.

"He didn't have to have any drawings to start with," Rowell countered. "I don't know why you care all of a sudden – of all bloody people."

"I didn't want to go either," Chapman said.

That seemed to mollify Rowell a bit, being reminded that he wasn't the only one being singled out, but he was still ticked off about it.

"What are we supposed to say to him?" he asked.

Chapman shrugged because he hadn't even thought about it.

"And haven't you got DT this evening?" Rowell asked, suddenly remembering.

"Oh shit – yes," Chapman said. It gave him a bit of a start remembering that; he'd forgotten all about it.

"Maybe you won't be back in time – Gatesford can't do anything if you're with Bruder. Maybe you should say something to him – there's your chance," Rowell said.

"I don't think it would help – Gatesford would just get more pissed off at me," Chapman said.

"He hasn't done a damned thing to Voaden – nothing," Rowell said.

"He's probably shit-scared of him."

"Well I think you're daft. It was really unfair. You weren't talking, and I don't mind saying that to Bruder," Rowell said.

"Would you? Really?"

Rowell nodded, but the note of surprise in Chapman's voice made him feel immediately uneasy about it. He regretted having stuck his neck out quite so far. He was relieved in a way when Chapman shook his head.

"Bruder would believe him, not us. I'm not going to say anything."

They were waiting in the hall just before five. Pearce and Higgins joined them there. Pearce was scowling and Higgins looked bewildered.

"What a crock of shit this is," Pearce said under his breath, glancing around to check that Bruder wasn't sneaking up on him.

The other three didn't agree or disagree, but they weren't looking forward to it either.

Bruder came down the stairs from his office a couple of minutes later with his car keys in his hand. He smiled at the boys when he saw them. It wasn't a long drive to the hospital, and nobody said anything much, sitting in the big Humber on the way there. Bruder wasn't the kind of person who needed the air around him to be filled with idle chatter.

Heathfield had been given his own room. His dad was quite well off, and he didn't fancy sitting around in a draughty ward with all kinds of other cripples and sick people coming and going. He also thought it would be best for his son to be out of the public gaze. His solicitor had told him that the school would probably end up having to foot the bill anyway, so the money didn't matter.

He was sitting at the bedside, reading the evening newspaper, but he stood up and came out into the corridor when the nurse popped her head in to say that there were visitors for Simon.

"Only two at a time, please," the nurse said to Bruder and the boys. Then she looked at her watch and went away.

The remark sounded odd to Pearce, almost as though they were queuing up for a ride at the funfair, but even that wasn't enough to make him smile. He hated hospitals with a vengeance, because nothing good had happened in or around one in all his life.

Bruder introduced the boys to Heathfield's dad one by one and they all shook hands with him.

He didn't look like the father of a sensitive artist, and he didn't look much like a hotel manager either. He looked more like the kind of bloke who could shovel coal into a boiler for eight hours at a stretch and not be unduly bothered about it. The boys didn't dwell on it, but it was pretty obvious looking at him that Heathfield's artistic talents must have been a gift of the gods or been handed down from some other part of the family.

Pearce and Higgins went in first, ordered in by Bruder because they happened to be standing closest to the door. Chapman and Rowell felt a bit awkward standing there in the corridor. They were pleased when Bruder and Heathfield's dad went off to find a quiet corner somewhere so that they could sit down and have a private chat.

Heathfield was laid out flat on his back, and he didn't even have a pillow. His neck was in a thick padded brace, and his whole body looked as though it was being held rigid by some other kind of contraption. His left leg was in plaster from the hip down and his left arm was plastered too, but the right arm was lying straight out by his side, seemingly unscathed. His pyjamas had been cut to ribbons so that they could be fitted on somehow. They added to the impression that he had just been through a threshing machine.

All he did when the two boys came in was continue staring at the ceiling.

Pearce went straight up to the side of the bed and surveyed the damage.

"Hi, Simon," he said, "How's it going?"

Heathfield's eyes moved from the ceiling to Pearce's face, and he smiled slightly.

"Not good," he said quietly.

"What a bummer, eh?"

"Yes," Heathfield said, almost in a whisper.

Higgins was hovering behind Pearce, but he peeped round his shoulder and gave a little wave. Heathfield smiled slightly at that too.

"Chapman and Rowell are outside – they're next," Pearce said.

He could see all kinds of things happening on Heathfield's face then and couldn't quite work out whether he was terrified or delighted. It seemed to be a bit of both.

"How do you eat and stuff?" he said, wanting to change the subject.

Heathfield didn't reply straight away. He went back to staring at the ceiling for a bit.

"I haven't eaten much – the nurse does it," he said eventually.

Pearce nodded and it hit home for the first time that Heathfield couldn't even nod his head up and down. It was quite a shock to realise that someone could be in such a bad way that they couldn't even do something as simple as that.

"At least you'll miss exams," he said.

"That's something, I suppose," Heathfield said and he looked at Pearce again and smiled weakly.

"They start in less than a week," Pearce said.

Heathfield didn't respond to that news at all and his eyes went back to the ceiling.

Pearce wondered whether he should say something about the drawings. He was about to blurt out that they were very good, if a bit pervy, but decided not to. He couldn't think of anything else sensible to say, and he was feeling really unsettled about being there. He promised to come and visit again and then he said goodbye. Higgins gave another of his little waves and followed him out without saying anything at all.

Bruder and Heathfield's dad were still not back from their private chat, so only Rowell and Chapman were waiting in the corridor. They were leaning with their backs against the wall.

"Waste of bloody time, you were," Pearce said to Higgins.

"I couldn't think of anything to say," Higgins said, and he did feel a bit useless.

"Your turn," Pearce said to Chapman.

"How is he?" Chapman asked.

Pearce shrugged. "Bloody awful – he can't even nod, poor shit. Fuck knows how he has a crap or anything," he said quietly, almost in a whisper.

Rowell and Chapman took a deep breath and went in cautiously. Once inside, they managed to resist an impulse to stop and stare, and both of them were wearing cheerful smiles when they got to the side of the bed. Heathfield smiled back, and he kept his eyes on Chapman's face at first, only looking briefly at Rowell.

"Hi," Chapman said.

"Thanks for coming," Heathfield said, blinking his eyes.

"No problem," they both said, almost simultaneously.

"Did Bruder make you come?"

"No – of course not," they both chimed up in unison.

"I'm sure he made Pearce come," Heathfield said.

"We wanted to come," Rowell said and he felt like the world's biggest liar.

"Thanks," Heathfield said.

"Does it still hurt much?" Chapman asked.

"Not really – they keep giving me pills and injections and

stuff," Heathfield said. "I can't feel anything, really."

Chapman and Rowell glanced at each other, because they both wondered whether he knew how bad it really was.

"Pete likes taking pills too," Rowell said with a smirk.

"Piss off," Chapman said and he glanced back at the door to check that no one had heard.

Heathfield grinned properly for the first time, and they were glad that they seemed to be cheering him up a bit.

"Give him any kind of shit, and he'll smoke it or swallow it," Rowell said, warming to the theme.

Chapman punched him on the arm. It was a friendly blow, but he was actually starting to get a little cross with Rowell, so there was some force in it.

"Ow," Rowell said and he bumped the bed quite hard moving back.

"God, you're a dork," Chapman said.

"Sorry," Rowell said to Heathfield about bumping the bed.

Heathfield didn't seem to mind though. He was still grinning and his eyes were turned hard over in their sockets to keep the two of them in sight.

"Who else has been to see you, apart from your dad and Bruder?" Rowell asked.

"Dryden came yesterday, and Robinson and Turner came this morning," Heathfield said.

"That's nice," Rowell said.

The two boys looked up and down at Heathfield's bandaged limbs and then around the room. It was pretty sparse, with only one chair and a basin in the corner. The only picture on the wall was of a green vase filled with lifeless looking flowers. There was a small window and Rowell wandered over to it and looked out at the view. It was still quite sunny outside and he could see parts of the harbour far away in the gaps between the buildings, bits of big ships and tall quayside cranes pointing their metal arms at the sky. Chapman followed him over to the window and neither of them realised that Heathfield couldn't see them then.

"Do you mind if I speak to Pete on his own for a bit?" Heathfield asked after a short while.

"Sure – no problem," Rowell said, turning away from the window. He knew what it was going to be about, so he really didn't mind being booted out. It was actually a relief. He said goodbye on the way, not wanting to have to come in again to do that.

Chapman came back and put his hands on the bed's metal restraining bar, looking down directly into Heathfield face.

"I'm really, really sorry about the drawings," Heathfield said when Rowell had gone.

"Don't worry about it," Chapman said cheerfully. "I don't mind, really I don't – I said you could draw me, didn't I?"

"Not like that."

"Whatever – it doesn't matter – forget about it. You've made me famous," he said with a big grin.

"Have you seen them?"

"No – Robinson took them all down, and I don't know what's happened to them," Chapman said and he didn't really care.

"Bruder's got them – he told me I can have them back when I get out of here," Heathfield said.

Chapman nodded, and wondered why he'd still want them after what had happened and whether he ever really was going to get out of hospital.

"They're not pervy, not really," Heathfield said.

Chapman felt awkward then, because everyone else seemed to think they were, even Dryden did, so he wasn't sure what to say. He thought briefly about asking why Heathfield had jumped out of a window and tried to kill himself if the drawings weren't at least a bit weird.

"Don't worry about it," he said in the end.

"Is everyone giving you a hard time?"

"Not really – they did at first, but Drydork told them all to drop it at supper on Sunday and they have mostly."

"That's good."

"Voaden beat up Gatesford Minor yesterday."

"That's probably good too, isn't it – was he taking the piss out of you?"

"Yes – but before that too, all the time. He's a complete jerk," Chapman said.

Heathfield shut his eyes then; they were beginning to ache a little. He didn't keep them shut for long, in case Chapman thought he was sleepy and decided to leave. When he opened them they had an intensity that hadn't been there before, and his expression had changed a little too, as though he was in pain. But he was smiling, and in a strange way he looked quite happy.

"I think you're the most beautiful person that ever existed," he said.

Chapman frowned and he tried not to smile, but he did anyway, unable to stop himself.

"You've said that before."

"Well it's true, and I think you're beautiful inside too," Heathfield said. "Anyone else would hate me for what happened."

"Well I don't hate you," Chapman said.

"That's what I mean," Heathfield said and he closed his eyes again.

Chapman surveyed Heathfield's broken body from his feet to his neck, and he shivered slightly at the thought of lying there himself like that. He didn't think he could, that he would rather be dead, and thinking that made him remember

Heathfield had meant to die too.

"Would you kiss me if I asked you to?" Heathfield asked suddenly, opening his eyes.

Chapman wasn't expecting to hear anything like that, and it startled him quite a bit, but he grinned anyway and tried to treat it as a joke.

"They're giving you too many pills," he said.

"Would you – please?" Heathfield said and it was obvious from his tone that it wasn't a joke.

"Why?"

"Because I think it would make me better," Heathfield said.

Chapman looked away at the window, and he had a perplexed expression on his face, but he was still smiling slightly. He looked at the window while he wondered what to say.

"How could it make you better?" he asked.

"I don't know – I just think it would."

Chapman looked down at him. The smile came and went on his mouth like the breeze on a butterfly's wings.

"I'd better go now – but I'll come and see you again," he said finally.

"I'm sorry," Heathfield said anxiously. "Have I screwed up again? It really means everything to me that you came, and I'm so sorry if I've screwed it all up again by asking that."

"You haven't screwed anything up, there's nothing to screw up – don't worry so much," Chapman said. "I'll come and see you again soon, I promise. But I'd better go now."

He meant to leave. He was almost at the door when he stopped and stood uncertainly for a few seconds before coming back to stand beside the bed again. There were tears in Heathfield's eyes and on his cheeks. They would dry there because he couldn't wipe them away anymore. Chapman looked down at him without saying anything for a while. Then he put his hand out and gently brushed the hair away from his forehead. He bent down quickly and kissed him lightly on the mouth and then on the cheek. He could taste the salt from Heathfield's tears.

"I hope it makes you better," he said.

"Thanks Pete – I love you more than anything," Heathfield said.

"No, you don't – don't talk crap," Chapman said. "I'll see you soon."

When he straightened up and turned around, he got quite a fright because Heathfield's dad was standing in the doorway staring at him with big round eyes. Chapman froze solid for an instant, wondering how long he'd been there and what he'd seen and heard.

James Heathfield seemed to shake himself out of a trance. He stopped staring and came on into the room.

"The others are waiting for you at the main entrance," he said quietly.

"Thanks, sir," Chapman said.

He put a hand out as the boy went passed and caught him gently by the arm.

"Thanks very much for coming," he said softly. "I know it means the world to Simon. It means a lot to me and his mum too. She'll be here later this evening."

Chapman nodded, but he couldn't smile right then, and he didn't know how to reply.

THIRTY-SEVEN

Dryden crashed his car on the way over to see Sarah on Tuesday evening. By the time he got to her place he was even more depressed than when he'd left the school. It was just a bad fender-bender, that was all it was, but the old guy in the other car turned it into a major drama and insisted on calling the cops. He said his wife had got whiplash when Dryden slammed into the back of them at the traffic lights. That didn't really seem to be true, but it reminded Dryden of the big collar around Heathfield's neck.

When the cops came, the old man said right away that Dryden was probably drunk. He denied it vehemently and it was fairly obvious that he wasn't. The cops weren't actually that interested, seeing as no one was injured; they could tell the old man was a troublemaker from a mile away. They didn't charge Dryden with anything, just scribbled down most of the things the old man had to say, looking pretty bored about it, and then they wrote down what Dryden had to say too. By then they were yawning, and they told Dryden to be more careful and got back into their Panda car and drove away.

There was nothing wrong with the old man's car, because it was a big Mercedes. Dryden's Hillman had just bounced off the rear bumper, leaving a bit of a dent but not even smashing the brake lights. Dryden's car was another story. The front end had disintegrated, raining down orange rust onto the tarmac. The radiator was punctured and one of the headlamps was smashed to bits, so he couldn't drive the car any more.

When the cops had gone, the old man climbed back into his Mercedes, still muttering to himself. His wife smiled sweetly at Dryden as they started to drive off and then made a face to let him know that she thought her husband had over reacted. The old man was obviously still pretty upset because the Merc nearly collided with a bakery van pulling back onto the road.

When they'd gone, Dryden told the tow truck driver that if the old fart hadn't fallen asleep at the traffic light, the accident would probably never have happened.

"The light was green, for goodness sake, and he just sat there," he added.

"They should take these old geezers off the bloody road – they're a menace," the tow truck driver said. He offered Dryden a lift to the garage in his huge truck.

Dryden got to Sarah's flat just before seven. He really felt as though he was coming apart at the seams by then. The last straw was fighting with the taxi driver because he thought he was getting ripped off.

Sarah was really good when she heard what had happened and saw how unhappy and upset he was. She sat him down on the couch, tucking cushions around him, as though to insulate him from any further harm. She opened a bottle of red wine herself, not asking him to do it, and brought him a glass, making sure the small side table was well within reach, should he want it.

"I'm not hurt," he said, sipping the wine.

"Yes you are, my darling; you're hurting inside, and we can't have that," she said soothingly, but it also sounded as though she was taking the piss a little to try and cheer him up.

"I've only got third party insurance," he said glumly. "I bet it costs more to fix than the car's worth – the panelbeaters are a real rip off."

"It's often worse than it looks," she said.

"Thanks," he said unhappily.

"I mean it's often not as bad as it looks," she corrected herself.

He did smile briefly at that, thinking she should know because she'd had a fair few bumps herself and had completely totalled a Morris Minor.

"You can borrow my car for the next few days. I can take the bus or get a lift easily," she said.

"I can't borrow your car," he said, but the look on his face told her that he was pleased she'd offered.

"Why not?"

"I might prang that too – there are too many old farts on the road," he said, but he really felt that it would be like stealing something she'd worked so hard to own.

"It's fully insured."

"For Drydorks?" he asked, trying to sound miserable and pathetic and succeeding pretty well.

She sat down on the couch and snuggled up beside him, leaning across to put her glass of wine on the side table. She lifted his arm and let it down across her shoulders

"Even for you," she said.

He kissed her then, and he really did love her at that

moment, to the exclusion of everything else.

She was the kindest person he had ever known.

"Thanks very much, but I'll be fine, I don't really need a car except at the weekend. But I could do with a lift back to school this evening," he said.

"Take the ruddy car," she said.

They tossed it back and forth for a while longer, but in the end she gave up, because she knew that what he said made more sense.

"It's been a really horrible week and it's only halfway through," he said, getting back to feeling sorry for himself.

"What's the latest news on the boy who was injured?" she asked. She'd forgotten his name.

"You mean Heathfield?"

She nodded, and he could see that she was serious now and had stopped trying to be cheerful.

"Same as before – no change. The poor little bugger is almost certainly going to be completely paralysed."

"It's sometimes difficult to tell so early on," she said.

"Well, barring a miracle he is, according to the doctors there. It's a pity the fall didn't kill him."

Dryden knew he shouldn't have said it, because the words sounded so heartless and he didn't really mean it like it might have sounded. He took a big sip of wine, waiting for her to tick him off but she didn't; she knew exactly what he meant.

"I feel such an almighty shit about it," he said.

"You couldn't have known how upset he really was."

He knew that was true, and he was glad it was, but it didn't make him feel any better, not really. Whichever way he looked at it, Heathfield had been his charge and he'd let him down.

"And how's Peter?" she asked.

"As beautiful as ever," he said. There was a resigned and wistful tone in his voice that made her smile.

She looked up at him but he was staring into space and didn't look down at her.

"I think you're in love with him," she said, smiling still.

He didn't answer right away, and he didn't get angry and deny it or grin and try and make a joke of it. He felt defeated by it. Right then he felt he couldn't really do anything else but let the truth win.

"In the right kind of way, I hope," he said.

"I hope so too – he's a sweet boy," she said. There was an edge in her voice because she'd meant the comment as a joke. She didn't want to think that there could even be another way to love him.

Dryden picked up the tone, and it stung him out of his melancholy. He cursed himself for being so honest. He put his wine down and gave her shoulders a squeeze. He knew he had to shut the door he'd opened a crack. There was something very nasty trying to squeeze through, and it was eager to destroy everything.

"He's not as thoroughly sweet as you think he is," he said.
"Why?"
"Smokes, drinks and God knows what else," he said.
"Drinks?"
"He came rolling in pissed as a newt on Friday night, well after lights out and threw up in my basin."

"Last Friday? Sweet little Peter? – I don't believe it," she said, sitting up straight. "Surely he'd get expelled for something like that?"

He took his arm away because it felt silly now that she was sitting bolt upright beside him on the couch.

"Yes, he would – but I didn't tell anyone. I let him get away with murder, really," he said. He felt the thing at the door push a little harder.

"How could you keep it quiet – didn't any of the other boys know?"

"They were all asleep."

"But why on earth didn't you do anything about it?" she asked.

He took a sip of wine. *Because you got as drunk as a skunk and he came and climbed into bed with you,* a voice in his head said.

"I don't know – he's so bloody bewitching," he said.

She stood up and walked over to the kitchen counter as though she'd gone to fetch something, but then she just stood there.

"You're not doing him any favours in the long run," she said. Her whole mood had changed. She was angry because she'd seen the consequences of teenage drinking, and it wasn't pretty later on. More than that, though, she felt confused and a little jealous.

"Please don't lecture me," he said and he was getting angry too.

They looked at each other rather stonily for a while. They both knew that they were suddenly on different sides of a chasm. It was frightening that it could appear so quickly like that, straight out of nowhere. Moments before it had all been kindness and love and friendship and even laughter. Now they were looking at each other through a pulsating darkness.

"I was going to punish him – I told him that. I was going to report it to Bruder in the morning and then he almost certainly would have been expelled, but I just couldn't do it," he said.

"But you should have done something, surely – not just taken him out to lunch," she said. She didn't mean it to sound quite so accusatory, but it did.

"What the hell would you have done, then?" he asked angrily.

"I don't know, I'm not a teacher – given him six of the best or something," she said. That sounded ridiculous coming from her, but it was an unfair question anyway.

"Well I just got drunk," he said. He felt really miserable sitting on the couch knowing he couldn't even go down to his car and drive away any more. He really did feel like getting up right then and leaving, leaving it all behind and going to lose himself in Africa. The door was wide open in his head, banging back and forth on the hinges of his mind. The creature that had finally come through so triumphantly had his own distorted features.

Sarah picked up the bottle of wine, but she put it down again because it didn't seem to be so full of joy any more, only confusion and sorrow. She lingered at the counter for a while longer, looking at him. Then she started to feel bad about getting so worked up, seeing how sad and dejected and angry he was. She didn't want it to end like that and so she forced herself to come back and sit on the couch again.

"I'm sorry," she said. "I didn't mean to get up on a high horse – it really must be very difficult for you at times."

He put his hands up to his face and massaged his temples. Then he flopped his head onto the back of the couch and stared up at the ceiling.

"I haven't started fancying little boys – please don't believe that," he said.

She thought back to the beach and she could see him sitting there resting his hand lightly on Chapman's shoulder; she remembered the expression on his face when he was looking at the boy. But there was nothing really carnal or corrupt in any of it; she thought he really did love him for something else.

"I don't think that at all," she said and she put her hand on his leg and began to massage the taut muscles above his knee.

"He climbed into bed with me because he was having

nightmares and he slept there the whole night, but I was too plastered to really notice," Dryden said.

The way he said it sounded like a challenge almost, a kind of test to see whether she really meant what she'd just said. But Sarah kept silent; she kept her hand on his knee, and if she was shocked, she didn't show it in any way.

"I couldn't punish him after that — I didn't want to anyway."

He waited for a while, but she didn't move away or say anything. He put his hand around her shoulders again and gave her a hug, because he hoped her presence and her silence proved that she did believe him.

"Why on earth did you get so drunk?" she asked eventually.

"I really don't know — I just got incredibly upset about it somehow. I've never got pissed like that before — not since Oxford, and even then not like that," he said.

"He is bewitching," she said after a while. "He's probably the most beautiful human being I think I've ever seen."

"Tetley says Robinson thinks he's Dionysus," he said.

She smiled slightly at that, because it sounded almost ridiculous enough to be true.

"He's just joking. Robinson's all wrapped up in this Greek play he's doing — that's where it comes from," Dryden said.

They sat in silence for a while to let the last of the anger and the hurt ebb away and it did seem to mostly, like the tide going out on a rocky shore.

"Do you think he got into bed with you so you'd let him off?" she asked after a while.

Dryden didn't answer straight away. His thoughts went back to the arguments he'd had with himself about it.

"I hope not, I hope that's not what he thinks of me. And I think he really does have nightmares," he said. "He told me about them, and they sounded pretty bad. I'm sure it was that – that and the effects of the booze. I can't possibly believe he could ever be so cynical and scheming. He's only just thirteen, for Christ's sake."

She thought about swimming in the sea with Peter and how she'd tricked him into racing for the beach. She thought about the little bunch of flowers and the pebble that was still in her bag, and she couldn't believe it either.

"Maybe it really is time for you to chuck it in. It's getting to you far too much," she said.

"I really do love him though," Dryden said as though he hadn't heard her. "If I had a son, I would want him to be just like that. He's so alive and brave and vibrant somehow."

She looked up at him then. There was relief in her face, and the last traces of suspicion had fallen away.

"Is that how you see him?"

Dryden nodded, and he kissed her gently on the forehead.

"But you're right, I'm not really cut out for it. I'm going to speak to Bruder tomorrow," he said.

He had made the decision as he was speaking, and just saying it was a way of making it come true.

THIRTY-EIGHT

There wasn't any Prefects' DT on Tuesday evening, because Gatesford heard that Chapman had gone to the hospital with Bruder, and he was the only boy booked in for it. Chapman was back in time anyway, but Gatesford had left a message to tell him that DT had been postponed to five on Wednesday. Then he sent another message on Wednesday morning to say that it wouldn't be the usual kind of DT. Gatesford wanted Chapman to sweep out the cricket pavilion and clean the pads, and he would be there to check up on him, the second message said.

"You should have spoken to Bruder when you had the chance," Rowell told him.

Chapman didn't say anything, because he'd convinced himself that it would have been a waste of time, and he still thought he was probably right.

He wasn't unduly worried about cleaning out the cricket pavilion, as that was better than sitting in a classroom being stared at by Gatesford. He also knew there would be plenty of other boys around at five o' clock on a Wednesday evening, down at the playing fields because there was a match on. It was hardly likely in those circumstances that Gatesford would try anything.

He was more preoccupied right then with the big box of chocolates Mrs Heathfield had sent him. It had arrived at lunchtime, and he'd been summoned to fetch it by Alice, Bruder's secretary.

"You're a very lucky boy," Alice had said. She was glad to get the big parcel off her desk.

It wasn't a box of Black Magic or Dairy Box or one of those boxes that people give to their girlfriends, but more of a hamper really. According to the label it had lots of different kinds of chocolates and sweets inside. It was so big that it wouldn't fit into his locker without taking other stuff out. He didn't want to do that, so he just had to shove it under his bed.

There was a note stuck to the box in a small blue envelope. In the note, Mrs Heathfield thanked him for being such a special friend to her son and apologised in a long-winded and round about way for the inconvenience he'd been caused by the drawings. She'd actually used that word – inconvenience – and it sounded quite odd, like Chapman was some kind of businessman or something and that Heathfield had taken his umbrella by mistake.

He didn't like being described as a special friend either because he didn't think of himself as a friend of Heathfield's at all, not in the usual sense at least. He was a bit embarrassed about getting such a big gift under false pretences. He also wondered whether Heathfield's dad had seen him kiss his son in the hospital and whether he'd told Mrs Heathfield about it. The thought of that was embarrassing too, and he was a bit confused about why she felt he still deserved a big box of chocolates if she did know.

"Aren't you going to open it now?" Rowell asked.

"I'll open it tonight," Chapman said. "Are you going to come down to the fields with me?"

"I will if you like, but I don't want to end up cleaning out the pavilion."

"Neither do I," Chapman said

"You should have spoken up," Rowell said for about the fifth time.

"Will you just sort of hang around then?" Chapman said.

Rowell nodded. He was disappointed that Chapman was only going to open the box later, because he felt like some chocolate right about then.

"Are you scared Gatesford's going to try something again?" he asked.

Chapman shook his head.

"I just wish Nick had left me out of it, that's all," he said.

They left for the playing fields a bit early because Chapman wanted to have a ciggey on the way. He'd discovered a twitten between a couple of houses in one of the side streets and it looked safe from prying eyes. It was off the same street that the plane had crashed into, and that was when he'd first noticed it, when they'd been down there gawking.

There was a dog in the garden of one of the houses that backed onto the twitten. It started barking at them just as Chapman lit up, running up and down on the other side of the diamond mesh fence and yapping its head off. Rowell immediately thought that it wasn't such a great place after all. Chapman went up to the fence and blew a lungful of smoke into the dog's face. He told it to shut up and it did, to their surprise, more or less immediately.

They had to run the last few hundred yards to the playing

fields because Chapman's ciggey took longer to smoke than they'd estimated and he didn't want to be late. He was sure Gatesford would be standing there with a broom looking for any excuse to double the DT or something. As it turned out, he wasn't there and the fields were pretty empty because the cricket match had been switched to an away game the day before. There were a couple of boys in the nets and a small group was playing football far away on the other side but that was all.

Rowell went into the pavilion with Chapman, but he didn't want to hang around too long in case Gatesford arrived and maybe assumed he'd got DT too and gave him a broom or a mop.

"I don't know why they call this a pavilion," Rowell said.

He'd been on an outing with his parents to the Brighton Pavilion, and it did seem a bit ridiculous if you put the two of them together side by side in your mind's eye. The cricket pavilion was more like a potting shed really, just two rooms and a rather ramshackle veranda. There was a small room upstairs for the scorekeeper, more of a platform really, but that was it. The floor was filthy and cricket gear – pads and gloves and old worn bats, mostly – was lying all over the place in one of the rooms. The big wooden chest the equipment was supposed to be in was almost empty. The other room was for the visiting team to change in, and there were benches around it and hooks on the walls.

"Shit, what a mess," Chapman said.

He took his jacket off and hung it on one of the hooks. Then he looked around for a broom and there was one leaning up against a wall, but the bristles were worn down almost to the wood. He started picking up the pads and tossing them into the big chest, and dust began flying around almost immediately. It stank in the pavilion too, of mildew, rotting wood and stale sweat among other things.

"What a horrible pong," Rowell said.

He stood by the door, and he was quite eager to go and hang around somewhere else, but he didn't want to leave Chapman on his own right away. He considered helping pick up the pads but decided not to, in case Gatesford came in and saw him at work and got the wrong idea entirely.

"Aren't you going to help?" Chapman asked.

Rowell reluctantly came in a little further and picked up a glove between his thumb and forefinger. He threw that at the chest, but it hit the side and didn't go in. He stepped back to the doorway immediately.

"Thanks," Chapman said sarcastically.

"You should have spoken up," Rowell said.

"You sound like a stuck record," Chapman said.

He dusted his hands against his trousers, and they became immediately filthy because a lot of the grey dust was made of decayed Blanco from the pads.

"Yuck," Chapman said.

He picked up the broom and started sweeping. He had to go over each small section three or four times before it made any real impression.

"Can't you at least see if you can find another broom?" he said.

Rowell stuck his head back out of the doorway and looked left and right for any sign of Gatesford. Then he went into the other room to hunt around.

"Here's one, but it's not much better," he said when he reappeared.

Chapman took it and tried it out, but Rowell's assessment had been correct.

"I'm going, then," Rowell said.

"What? – you're just going to leave me here?"

Rowell squirmed a bit and looked guilty, and Chapman was glad to see that.

"It's fine – piss off," he said. "But please come back now and again in case Gatesford decides to murder me."

"Maybe he won't show up at all."

"I hope so," Chapman said, and he gave an extra big push with the broom and was promptly enveloped in fine dust. The millions of tiny specks floated and sparkled in a shaft of evening sunshine coming through a window, like the stars of the Milky Way.

Rowell hovered for a few moments longer but then he did go, promising to come back every ten minutes.

Chapman went on sweeping and picking up pads and bats and after about five minutes the room was beginning to look a little better, though he was covered in dust from head to toe. He couldn't get the lid of the big wooden chest to shut because there was simply too much crap and something stuck out whichever way he tried to arrange it. He gave up in the end and went back to sweeping, and it seemed as though the floorboards themselves were turning to dust because it never ended.

Rowell came back after about ten minutes. He was breathless because he'd suddenly remembered his promise and run over from the football game on the far side.

"How's it going?" he said popping his head through the door.

"Fine – if you like this kind of shit," Chapman said.

"No sign of Gatesford yet?"

"No, thank goodness."

"I'll be back in another ten or fifteen minutes," Rowell said and he ran off again.

Chapman swept on and on. By then he'd taken his tie off and hung it over the doorknob so he wouldn't forget it when the time came to leave. He wanted to take his shirt off but he decided not to, because he didn't want Gatesford to arrive and see him without it. He wasn't exactly enjoying himself, but he did begin to take a certain amount of pride in his work because he could see that his efforts were bringing some order to the chaos, and that was pleasing in itself.

"I see you've started without me," Gatesford said suddenly from the doorway and he was holding Chapman's tie in his hand.

"I was here at five," Chapman said quickly.

"I can see that – you've done quite a bit," Gatesford said. He sounded genuinely impressed.

He walked around the room looking at this and that. He lifted the lid of the wooden chest and let it fall back down onto the untidy pile of pads. Then he sat down on a bench and fiddled with Chapman's tie, drawing it through his fingers from one hand to the other and back again. Chapman didn't like that, and he stood in the middle of the room with his brush watching and waiting for him to say or do something else.

"Well, don't let me interrupt you – get on with it," Gatesford said finally.

Chapman immediately went through to the other room and began sweeping there, but Gatesford followed him after a moment or two and sat down on another bench, still playing with the tie and looking at him.

"Your clothes are getting absolutely filthy," he said.

Chapman stopped sweeping, and he guessed exactly what was coming next.

"I think you should take them off," Gatesford said with a grin.

"I'm fine, thanks – Rowell's coming back in a minute," Chapman said, trying to sound nonchalant. He started sweeping again and he glanced at the door to work out if he could get there before Gatesford. He felt pretty sick in his stomach, because he'd hoped Gatesford wouldn't try anything.

Gatesford stood up and walked out onto the veranda. He stood out there for a few moments looking around before coming back and standing just inside the door, still fiddling with Chapman's tie.

"No sign of him," he said smugly.

Chapman just kept sweeping because now he couldn't get out and it seemed like it was the only thing he could do, just sweep and sweep and hope that Gatesford would somehow get swept away with all the other crap.

"You really are a pretty little shit, even when you're covered in dust," Gatesford said.

There was an awful lot of dust floating in the air and lots of it was on Chapman, but he'd got together quite a big pile of it on the floor too by then. It was mixed up with dead grass, sweet papers and the tiny clods of earth people carried in on the spikes of their cricket shoes.

Come on, Chris, Chapman whispered urgently under his breath, *come on back – please.*

There was a noise on the veranda then and Chapman stopped sweeping and looked up eagerly thinking it had to be Rowell. Instead Gatesford's younger brother appeared in the doorway, and Chapman could see two of his grinning friends behind him. The younger Gatesford's lip was still a bit swollen, but he didn't look like a freak any more, just plain nasty.

"My, my, it's still got its clothes on – that makes a change," he said.

There wasn't much point in going on sweeping then so Chapman stopped, but he kept a tight hold on the broom because he thought it might still be useful.

"I've got to go now, Chapman," the big Gatesford said, as though the whole situation was normal and under control. "I'll be back at six, so make sure you've finished off properly."

But he didn't go right away because he was quite enjoying standing there, looking at Chapman and seeing how vulnerable and frightened he was. It turned him on. He hung around in the doorway for a fair while and everyone else just stood there because of that, not wanting to do whatever it was they were planning. But finally he did turn and go out, and the others immediately came all the way in and they closed the door behind them.

"We've brought you a change of clothes – put it on," Gatesford said.

He threw what looked like a bundle of leaves at first but as it flew through the air, it unravelled into a long strand of ivy. He had probably pulled it off the wall or off one of the trees growing by the gate, where it grew in masses. Some of the trees looked as though their trunks were made entirely of ivy.

Gatesford and his two friends weren't grinning any longer, and they looked very keyed up as they waited to see what Chapman would do. The broom worried one of them a bit and he tried to work out the best way to get in and grab Chapman without getting clobbered on the side of the head by it.

"Rowell's coming back any minute," Chapman said.

"Put it on," Gatesford said.

Chapman stared at the ivy for a little longer. Then he bent down and picked it up but he didn't let go of the broom. He hung the ivy around his neck and then looked at the three of them and even managed to smile a little.

That was too much for Gatesford. He lurched forward, but

Chapman scampered back and jumped up onto one of the benches.

"OK, I'll do it, I'll do it," he said quickly because he didn't want to have the crap beaten out of him. He let the broom drop.

The three of them stood in the middle of the room and looked up at him as he began to unbutton his shirt. When he'd done that he pulled the tails out and then undid his trouser belt. He did everything very slowly and methodically, hoping all the time that Rowell would open the door or start shouting from outside but there was still no sign of him by the time he'd taken off both his shoes.

Gatesford soon got fed up with the slow striptease. He leaned up, grabbed hold of Chapman's wrist and pulled him down off the bench. It didn't take ten seconds for the three of them to get all his clothes off because one of them alone could lift him clear of the ground quite easily. They even pulled off his socks, and when he was completely naked they backed off and grinned at his humiliation.

Gatesford bent down and picked up the ivy.

"Put it on," he said. His voice had turned a bit hoarse with the excitement of it all, with the sight of Chapman's sweet limbs, the touch of his silken skin and the thought of what he was still going to do to him.

"I don't know how to," Chapman said and he was very close to tears by then.

"Yes you do, you fucking little faggot," Gatesford said. "You did it for Heathfield."

Chapman blinked his eyes, and he took the ivy again and wrapped the vine around his hips.

A weird thing happened when the leaves touched his skin; the vine seemed to know where to go from there, only lightly guided by his fingers. He managed to look as though he were properly dressed, as though he was meant to look like that. He suddenly didn't seem so vulnerable any more. The dust and decay didn't seem to touch him at all, because his beauty was truly awesome.

It looked like that to Gatesford's two friends anyway, and they'd been ready to laugh, but they felt something inside them shrivel. In a strange way, they were ashamed and a little afraid. One of them stooped down to pick up Chapman's trousers.

The door opened then, and Rowell was there, at long last.

"Leave him alone," he yelled after just one look.

He shouted it loudly, just as he said he would in such circumstances. It was actually more of a scream, and there was no doubt that anyone within a quarter mile radius would have heard it quite clearly. Gatesford Senior certainly heard it as he was walking back towards the pavilion, and it stopped him in his tracks. Vaughn heard it jogging at the edge of the field. So did two policemen who were sitting in their patrol car in the street having a quiet smoke, hoping no one would notice.

"It doesn't end here," Gatesford hissed and he and his two friends pushed Rowell out of the way and ran for it.

"Where the hell did you learn to yell like that?" Chapman asked. He pulled the ivy off and let it drop to the floor.

Rowell shrugged, as he was a little perplexed himself that he had managed to produce such a huge amount of sound.

Vaughn and the cops got to the pavilion at about the same time. When they burst in, Chapman was still stark naked, trying to shake the dust out of his underpants. He put them on quickly when he saw the uniforms.

The cops didn't know quite what to make of it all, but they could see that there were no adults lurking around. It was just the two boys. They weren't that fazed by the fact that

Chapman was naked either, because he was standing in the middle of a changing room, albeit a dirty one.

"Is this just a lark then?" one of them asked. He was already beginning to feel like a jackass for leaping over the fence and running so hard across the field. "It sounded like someone was being murdered."

"Sorry, sir," Rowell said.

"You've probably given half the neighbours a heart attack," the cop said.

"Sorry, sir," Rowell repeated.

"Are you both OK then?"

"We're fine, sir – sorry," Chapman said before Rowell could say anything else.

"And who are you?" the cop said, turning to Vaughn.

"I'm a prefect," Vaughn said.

The cop nodded and he took his cap off and wiped his forehead with the back of his hand before putting it back on again.

"Well you'd better sort this out, then," he said.

"I hope you're Everton supporters with lungs like that," the other cop said with a smile.

The two of them left then. The one who had asked all the questions was still muttering to his smiling colleague as they walked away.

"What has been going on here?" Vaughn asked.

"I'm cleaning the pavilion for DT," Chapman said.

He pulled on his trousers, which were really filthy from being dropped on the floor. So was his shirt when he picked that up.

"Why did you yell out like that?" Vaughn asked.

"They were making him dress up in ivy," Rowell said.

"Who was?"

"No one – it's fine, really, it was just a joke," Chapman said.

A pretty tasteless one, Vaughn thought. He thought about the drawings. He knew it wasn't really a joke, because no one took all their clothes off and dropped them in that filth just for a laugh.

"Who gave you DT?" he asked.

"Gatesford," Chapman said.

Gatesford heard his name as he stepped onto the veranda. He'd dithered until he saw the cops leave, but he'd decided it would have looked odd not to come back.

"What's going on?" he asked.

"Ask them," Vaughn said. He left immediately, thinking it wasn't his problem and he didn't really want to be a part of it.

Chapman was sitting on a bench putting his shoes back on, and Gatesford looked at him and then at his watch.

"You've still got another fifteen minutes of DT, Chapman," he said as though nothing had happened. "You might as well get hold of a broom too, Rowell, seeing as how you seem to like it here so much."

THIRTY-NINE

Dryden went up to Bruder's office at the beginning of the lunch break on Wednesday and told him that he'd decided to resign. He didn't give a long-winded explanation. He just said that he felt it was time to move on. He said that he was considering going into banking and maybe going overseas. Bruder nodded, and he didn't look particularly upset or surprised, only raising his eyebrows a little when Dryden said he wanted to leave at the end of term. They both knew he was contracted to give a full term's notice. He didn't say anything for quite a long time after Dryden had finished, just stared into space.

"I hope this hasn't been triggered by what happened to Heathfield," he said eventually. "You can't blame yourself in any way – I've told you that."

"That's not the reason, but it hasn't helped," Dryden said.

Bruder studied his face, as though trying to decide whether he was being honest. Then he pulled open the top drawer of his desk and took out an envelope.

"I was actually on the verge of asking you to come and see me," he said. "I'm afraid there's something we need to get out of the way. It's not very pleasant, and I don't want you to get unduly upset about it because I know it's simply a piece of mischief."

He took a single sheet of paper out of the envelope, unfolded it and held it out. It was ordinary lined letter paper and there was a short message written in block capitals.

Dryden felt his heart stop as he read the words. His face went as white as chalk.

Mr Dryden is messing with (sex) Peter Chapman and he is scared to own up, the note said.

"I'm sorry to spring it on you out of the blue," Bruder said. "My first inclination is to tear something like this up immediately because I know it's utter rubbish. It's not the first anonymous note I've had along these lines while I've been a headmaster. It probably won't be the last. I have to raise it with you, though."

"It's absolutely outrageous," Dryden said, but he couldn't take his eyes away from the words, reading them over and over again.

Bruder nodded sympathetically.

"Alice found the envelope pushed under the door this morning," he said.

Dryden put the note down on the desk, shaking his head slowly from side to side.

"Of course you're not having any kind of improper relations with Chapman," Bruder said. It was a statement rather than a question, his tone dismissive, almost apologetic, but he didn't smile and his eyes stayed fixed on Dryden's face.

"Of course not," Dryden said. His shock rapidly gave way to fury: "What kind of a little shit would send a note like that?"

He wasn't really expecting an answer. Bruder didn't say anything straight away. He just carried on staring. Then he picked up the note and looked at it again himself.

"My guess is that it comes from one of the boys in the fourth or fifth forms, probably no lower than that, judging by the writing. It's difficult to tell," he said.

He stared at the note a little longer, caressing the paper with his old, creased fingers. Then he tore it in half and crumpled the pieces into a small ball. He dropped it into the waste paper basket.

Despite his indignation, Dryden felt a surge of relief because the action showed immediately that Bruder wasn't taking the note seriously, though it did little to lessen his anger.

"Aren't you going to ask Peter about it?" he said, staring at the basket.

"I hadn't planned to. What purpose would that serve?"

Bruder was a little surprised that Dryden had used Chapman's first name, especially in the circumstances. He glanced down briefly at the basket too.

"He's named in the note, perhaps he has a right to know," Dryden said. He already wished that he'd just let it drop.

Bruder shook his head.

"I don't think he needs to know, and I'm not going to talk to him about it. It would simply upset him unnecessarily, as far as I can see," he said.

Dryden kept his mouth shut then and was worried where the conversation would go. The expression on Bruder's face was difficult to read. There was surprise there, certainly, and a shadow of doubt.

"I understand you took him out for the day last Sunday?"

"Yes, him and Rowell – I thought they needed a break," Dryden said. He felt the flush in his cheeks and cursed himself for it.

Bruder nodded, but it didn't look as though he thought the answer made much sense.

"You haven't got involved with him in some way, have you?" he asked suddenly and it was obvious then that he was having doubts.

"Certainly not," Dryden said indignantly. He was really cursing himself. It all seemed to be running out of control again, just like it had with Sarah.

Bruder went on looking at him and it was impossible to tell what he was thinking. Then he smiled slightly and took off his glasses. He put them down on the desk and massaged his eyes. When he lowered his hands his expression had softened.

"We're all under Chapman's spell to some degree," he said. "He's the most astonishingly beautiful boy I've ever seen, and I've had a long career."

Bruder could see the surprise on Dryden's face even though it was now a little out of focus.

"It's a pity his beauty is proving so devastating," he added.

"What do you mean, sir?" Dryden asked cautiously. He realised that it was the first time he'd called him 'sir' since he'd come in.

"Heathfield," Bruder said, "and the teacher at Saint Stithians – I don't believe I ever knew his name. They both fell in love with the beauty, not the boy, I suspect."

"Aren't the two one and the same?"

Bruder shrugged. He picked up his glasses but he didn't put them back on again.

"I don't know. I suppose that's up to the boy," he said enigmatically.

They sat in silence for a while, and Dryden tried to work out what he meant by that, thinking after a bit that he did understand. The lunch bell rang outside, but neither of them took any notice.

"I'm beginning to suspect Chapman's formidable beauty is ending a very promising teaching career," Bruder said.

"That's absolutely ridiculous," Dryden said immediately. He tried to sound offended, but he could hear his own voice through the bones in his ears and thought he'd failed miserably.

"If that really is the case, I think you should stick with it. I think you're an excellent teacher, and you'll probably make an outstanding headmaster one day."

Dryden smiled very briefly at the praise because it would have been rude and churlish not to, but he wondered how serious Bruder really was.

"Of course, you'd have to do something about your time keeping," Bruder added. "I've never met a mathematician with less interest in punctuality."

Dryden smiled slightly at that, and he felt the praise and humour sweeping him into a corner, albeit a fairly comfortable one. But he still remembered why he was there. He thought of the conversation with Sarah and then the note in the waste paper basket, lying crumpled up at the edge of a dark and hidden truth.

"I suppose I am getting a little obsessive about Chapman," he said. "I suppose that has played a part in my decision. I think he has great spirit and I am very, very fond of him."

He stopped there wondering whether to go on. Bruder nodded encouragingly.

"The problem is that I don't think I'm cut out for teaching, perhaps I never was. I'm not impartial anymore. Chapman's not exactly an angel, and I let him get away with far too much. That horrible little note proves that at least one of the other boys has already decided what that means."

Bruder put his glasses back on, and Dryden suddenly wondered whether it had all been a ruse to get him to own up to something. It angered him all over again because he felt there really was nothing to admit to except his own fears and self-doubt.

"I'd forget about the note," Bruder said. "It's just an obnoxious little piece of pubescent poison. I think it's probably aimed more at Chapman than you anyway. It's not as though there's any likelihood of you jumping into bed with him."

Dryden smiled inwardly at the irony of that.

"If you think there's a problem, surely that's a solution in itself," Bruder continued. "We all have our favourites – it's part of human nature, inevitable. Some teachers are better than others at managing it. But you don't want to go to the other extreme either. You can't punish a boy – or run away from him – because you're fond of him."

Dryden nodded, although he didn't agree. He wasn't fond of Chapman – he loved him. He'd given up trying to hide that from himself.

"It's not just the Chapman issue. I really think my decision will be for the best in the end," he said.

Bruder nodded gravely and it seemed then as though he'd accepted that Dryden's mind was truly made up. He opened his desk drawer again and took out a couple of Heathfield's drawings.

"Have you seen these?" he asked.

Dryden shook his head and he wondered why on earth Bruder was suddenly bringing that up. He leaned forward anyway to look.

"They're really remarkable," Dryden said.

"Yes, they certainly are. Heathfield has enormous talent. I suspect that even the greatest of the old masters would have been hard pressed to really capture Chapman's rare beauty. It seems to belong to a more perfect world somehow, and it's a tribute to Heathfield that he saw that too."

Bruder's tone was wistful, very uncharacteristic of the man Dryden knew. He thought he was being allowed to see a softer side of him now that he was leaving.

"Brian told me about your speech in the dining hall. He was very impressed by that and so was I – I think I told you that on the phone. Chapman's very vulnerable and he really does need protecting," Bruder said.

Dryden stared down at Chapman's naked and beguiling form in the drawing, and he felt his hackles rise at the thought that Bruder seemed to be somehow offering the boy up as a kind of prize in an effort to persuade him to stay. I don't mind if you screw one or two of the boys – take this boy, he imagined him saying – as long as I don't have the bother of looking for another House Master. The thought passed quickly because he knew it was absurd and unfair, and it troubled him immediately that he was so debased in himself that he could even think it.

"He seems to be able to take care of himself quite well," he responded.

Bruder looked at him as though expecting him to elaborate. When Dryden didn't say anything else, he dropped the subject.

"I told Heathfield that he could have these back," he said. "I'm a bit concerned about that now though – about how his parents will feel if they see them."

"Do they know about them, sir?" Dryden asked.

"Yes, but I didn't go into graphic detail."

"I don't think they're anything to be ashamed about."

Bruder considered that while he studied the drawing. He thought to himself that he would be a bit embarrassed about it if that was his son standing there with his hips sticking out and just a smile and a few leaves on.

"You're right, of course, you're absolutely right," he said. He picked the drawings up and put them back in his desk drawer.

His mood seemed to change then and the old familiar Bruder was suddenly back, fixing Dryden with an unblinking stare.

"I want you to think about your decision for another week. If you haven't had a change of heart by then, I'll reluctantly accept your resignation," he said.

Dryden nodded and knew it was time to go, so he thanked Bruder and stood up to leave.

"You've no idea what happened to the sixth drawing, have you?" Bruder asked.

"I thought you had all of them," Dryden said and he felt his heart stop for the second time.

"Heathfield told me there were six in all, and Robinson says he only collected five."

"I don't know – I'm sorry," Dryden said.

Bruder nodded and then he picked up the envelope the note had come in and screwed that up, dropping it into the waste paper basket.

FORTY

Things seemed to get a little better for Chapman over the next week or so. He thought it was because the cops pitching up in the pavilion had scared the shit out of both Gatesfords. The jibes mostly stopped at meal times and Gatesford Minor's many friends seemed to be making an effort to ignore him; one or two were almost friendly. Gatesford Minor still glowered at him, but it seemed the other boys didn't want to be part of it anymore, especially the two who had been there with the ivy.

Gatesford Senior had felt through Chapman's blazer when it was hanging on the hook in the pavilion and had found his cigarettes. Ironically, it was the pack that Chatsworth had given him as a peace offering, but he didn't say anything about it, just held it up briefly to show that he'd seen them and before putting it back. He'd let both boys go shortly after that, not waiting for the full hour to be up. He hadn't done or said anything since, and that really showed he'd had a change of heart, Chapman thought.

Chatsworth was also still being especially friendly, and Chapman had nearly collided with him in the corridor again, running to one of the classes because he was late. Chatsworth had just caught hold of him and dusted him off and smiled without saying anything. He was all smiles whenever they encountered each other. Chapman had decided to ask him for the photos or at least to ask him to tear them up.

"I wouldn't trust him with a barge pole," Rowell said when Chapman told him about it. What he meant was quite clear, even if the words themselves sounded a bit strange.

Voaden also seemed different, and Chapman had only seen him once that week when they'd shared a ciggey down at the fields on Thursday afternoon. He wasn't unfriendly, but he just seemed a lot quieter and more withdrawn than normal, as though he were thinking about something all the time. He didn't say much unless he was asked a direct question. Chapman thought Voaden was worried about the exams, although that didn't seem very likely. He didn't want to risk pissing off Voaden by actually asking what the problem was.

Thornton delivered the invitation on Saturday morning, and although it was just written on ordinary lined letter paper, not on a gold rimmed card or anything, the language was still quite flowery. "I, Derek Arthur Chatsworth, do humbly beg the forgiveness of Peter Chapman," it began, and it went on to invite him to afternoon tea.

"I wouldn't trust him with a bargepole," Rowell repeated. "Tell him to get stuffed."

"As far as I could throw him," Leomond said.

"What?" Rowell asked.

"I wouldn't trust him as far as I could throw him," Leomond said.

"Whatever," Rowell said. "You're not going to go, are you?"

Chapman flopped down onto his bed and stared up at the ceiling.

"Maybe he'll give me the photos," he said.

"Maybe he'll take some more," Rowell said.

"What photos?" Leomond asked.

"Nothing," Chapman said.

Leomond looked from the one to the other, but they avoided catching his eye.

"He couldn't, anyway," Chapman said.

"Couldn't what?" Leomond asked.

"Nothing, it doesn't matter, Leo," Chapman said.

"You need your head examined if you go," Rowell said.

"He says to meet him after play rehearsals at the gym," Chapman said.

"You really are thinking of going aren't you? – you're a complete idiot," Rowell said.

"What are you two on about," Leomond said.

"Never mind, Leo – it doesn't matter," Chapman said.

Leomond got up, shaking his head and walked off to his own bed.

"Why don't you come too," Chapman said.

"I didn't get an invitation, thank God."

"I'll say I'm not going unless you come too."

Rowell thought about that for a while. It didn't seem such a bad plan; he thought Chatsworth would end up telling them both to get stuffed or make some excuse.

"OK," he said in the end.

Richardson was sitting in his old Jag when they went through the gate at the fields an hour later. Chatsworth was standing by the driver's window. Rowell and Chapman walked over to the big tree and hung around, waiting for Richardson to drive off. He eventually did, giving them a friendly wave as he went past. Chatsworth walked over, and he didn't look annoyed or even surprised to see Rowell there too.

"Thanks for coming," he said.

"Do you mind if Chris comes along?" Chapman asked.

Chatsworth smiled and shook his head.

"That's fine – I understand," he said.

Rowell felt awkward then, because Chatsworth seemed anything but threatening. Even his face was a bit different, softer somehow and not so full of angry pimples.

Chatsworth took an envelope out of his jacket pocket and held it out to Chapman. Both boys realised immediately that it was the photos. Chapman opened the envelope to have a look, taking a couple of steps back to make sure Rowell couldn't see. The first one was just solid black and when he looked at the other two he saw that they were all black too.

"Half of them didn't come out. Gatesford has torn up the others," Chatsworth said.

Chapman looked perplexed at first and even a little disappointed but then he smiled and showed the photos to Rowell, flicking through them as though they were bad holiday snaps.

"I'm sorry I was such a shit – I really am," Chatsworth said with a faint smile.

Rowell felt embarrassed being there now, because things were very different from what he'd expected. It was all kind of personal and didn't really involve him anymore.

"I've actually got to get back to school," he said suddenly, and he started to walk away towards the gate.

Chapman tried to call him back, but he just waved and walked a little faster and he soon disappeared into the street.

"You don't have to come to tea with me – I'd like it if you did, but you don't have to," Chatsworth said.

Chapman shrugged and felt a bit vulnerable again on his own.

"You don't have to take me," he said.

That seemed to create an impasse, and they both stood looking at each other. A breeze moved around and between them.

"Do you want to come?" Chatsworth asked.

"I don't know," Chapman said doubtfully. The question reminded him of the one Drummond had asked at the top of the stairs.

"Maybe we should leave it then," Chatsworth said.

Chapman saw the disappointment in his face and felt a bit of a shit about it, because the older boy was trying so hard to make up and be nice.

"No, it's OK – I'd like to come," he said.

"Really?"

Chapman shrugged.

"Yes," he said.

They walked into town, and Chatsworth bought Chapman tea and a slice of cake in a small café off the high street. He had a cup of coffee himself and smoked a cigarette. The only other people in the café were a couple with a small baby in a pram, but they were absorbed in their own world. Chapman took out a ciggey when he'd finished the cake and had put it between his lips. He was about to light up when Chatsworth stopped him, shaking his head and glancing at the back of the café where the old woman who ran the place came and went.

"Don't smoke here – you can smoke up in my room when we get back," he said.

Chapman didn't like the sound of that, the way Chatsworth just assumed he was going to come up to his room when they got back to school. The young man saw the look on his face immediately.

"You don't have to," he said quickly. "But you can if you like – I owe you that at least. I've got some Johnnie Walker whiskey too – have you ever tried that?" he added with a grin.

Chapman put the ciggey away and looked over at the couple with the baby. The woman had taken it out of the pram and was bouncing it on her knee. Her husband was grinning like the village idiot.

"No, it sounds nice – thanks," Chapman said. But he still felt very uneasy about it because the mention of booze sounded like the bait in a trap.

Chatsworth talked a lot about the play on the walk back and in particular about what a load of crap Simpson was as Dionysus. He was actually very funny about it, doing an imitation of Simpson and then of Richardson and some of the others. There was no doubt he was a good actor, and a good mimic and comedian when he wanted to be. Chapman giggled and then he laughed, and he was feeling very relaxed with Chatsworth by the time they got back to school.

"Do you want to come up for a cigarette?" Chatsworth asked when they'd gone through the bottom gate.

Chapman was still giggling a little from Chatsworth's last performance, but he stopped then.

"What about Drummond?" he asked.

"You don't need to worry about him; he's away this weekend for interviews, anyway," Chatsworth said.

Chapman hesitated. He looked up at the main school building, and it looked like a fortress. He could see the window of Chatsworth's room. It was open and a curtain was flapping in the breeze.

"It's up to you – you don't have to," Chatsworth said.

"OK, just for a quick ciggey," Chapman said nervously.

"And a quick scotch?" Chatsworth said with a grin.

"OK," Chapman said, and he smiled a little too.

What happened in the room was very weird, and Chapman was too embarrassed to talk about it at first. He eventually told Rowell because the other boy knew everything else that had happened anyway.

Chatsworth had been fine at first, Chapman said, and he'd given him a whiskey and it tasted bloody awful, but he'd had a few swigs anyway and the taste did seem to get a bit better. Chatsworth had some too, but not really that much. Then he'd suddenly started talking a lot of stuff about how much he loved Chapman and how Chapman might as well tear his heart out right then because he'd stolen it already. Then he started crying and he'd got down on his knees, Chapman said, and he said he'd cut his own dick off if Chapman wanted him to, because of what he'd done to him.

"That was a bit much," Chapman said.

"Bloody hell," Rowell said and he didn't quite know whether to laugh or faint at the thought of it.

He giggled a bit, though and then Chapman did too. They couldn't stop for quite a while and several boys looked over at their corner of the dorm wondering what was so funny.

"You were really daft to go up there," Rowell said when they'd calmed down again.

Chapman just shrugged.

Dryden came into the dorm then and they both climbed into their beds. Chapman wasn't at all tired because of the whiskey, and neither was Rowell, because of what Chapman had just told him.

Dryden didn't do his usual circuit; he just came straight over and sat down on Chapman's bed. He looked pretty serious and didn't even yell at anyone on the way over, although there was quite a bit of noise.

"Hi, sir," Chapman said cheerfully, sitting up.

Dryden just nodded slightly because his mind was somewhere else.

"Voaden's gone; he's left the school — he's been gone since early this morning," he said softly.

"Gone where, sir?" Chapman asked, quite shocked at the news.

Dryden looked at him, or rather through him; he seemed to be seeing something else far away, in another world entirely.

"He went home and apparently had a big row with his dad and then he left, and nobody knows where he is now," he said. "I wondered whether you might have an idea. His dad is worried sick."

Chapman and Rowell just stared at Dryden with their mouths open.

"No ideas?" Dryden asked after a bit.

"No, sir, I really don't know," Chapman said.

Dryden nodded his head slowly and then said goodnight and stood up. He stayed for a moment, looking sad and worried, and then he walked off round the dorm without saying anything to anybody, just stopping at the door to say goodnight and turn off the lights.

"I bet he's gone to Newquay," Chapman whispered after a while.

"Where?"

"Newquay — he wants to learn how to surf."

"Why didn't you say?"

Chapman didn't answer right away. He looked up at the small rectangle of stars and wondered whether Nick could see them too right then. He thought how suddenly free Voaden now was, of school and exams and everything, as free as the wind.

"I just thought of it. Maybe he doesn't want anyone to know, anyway," he said.

FORTY-ONE

Johno's folks were asleep when Voaden arrived at his house. Johno let him in. There wasn't any beer in the house so they drank coffee.

"I'm going to get Pete, take him with me," Voaden said when they'd got through all the other stuff, the row with his dad and so on.

Johno didn't remember who Pete was. He had to ask: "Pete who?"

"Pete Chapman, the kid who was here a couple of weeks back," Voaden said.

Johno remembered then, but he didn't understand.

"Why the shit do you want to take him? He's only twelve, isn't he?"

Voaden nodded. "Thirteen," he said. He stubbed out his cigarette. He'd gone through a pack and a half since breakfast and was getting fed up with them. His tongue felt like the hall carpet. "He wants to come," he said.

Johno pulled a face. He was surprised, not that Chapman wanted to come but that Nick wanted to be saddled with him.

"They'll come after you for sure if you take him," he said.

"Fuck them," Voaden said.

He swallowed the last of his coffee and carried his mug over to the sink. He didn't rinse it out. He just put it down under the tap.

"Have you got that two quid you owe me?" he asked.

Johno was pretty sure he'd paid him the two quid already, but he didn't mind paying again, not in the circumstances. He took his wallet out. A couple of quid wouldn't go very far, but every bit helped. He gave Voaden two one pound notes. They were crisp and clean.

"I don't think you should take Pete with you. It's daft," he said.

Voaden shrugged. He took his own wallet out and put the notes in with the others. There weren't very many, about twelve pounds altogether. It wasn't much to start a new life on.

"If he wants to come, he can come. He's not like the others," he said.

Johno wondered what he meant by that but he didn't ask. In a strange way, at the back of his mind somewhere, he thought he knew the answer.

Voaden left soon afterwards. He didn't go straight to the school because it was still a bit early. He walked aimlessly around and sat down on a low wall for a while and looked up at the stars. There was a quarter moon up but it was still pretty dark, and the stars shone brightly in the clear night sky. He could see Orion low down on the horizon, the only constellation he could name.

It was shortly after eleven when he climbed through one of

the bathroom windows. He made his way cautiously up the stairs, wondering what he would do if he bumped into one of the prefects or even Dryden. He decided he'd just tell them to fuck off and he felt invincible, so he believed they would, that they would just turn away and leave him alone. He didn't have to put his confidence to the test because he didn't run in to anyone.

In the past four years he had been up and down the same corridors and stairs a thousand times, but they seemed strange now: familiar, yet alien, like the pathways in a dream.

Chapman was sound asleep, and he had to shake him quite hard before he woke up.

"Do you still want to come to Newquay with me?" he whispered.

Chapman sat up, and although he was a bit disoriented he heard the question, and he quickly realised who it was by his bed in the night.

"OK," he said and he pulled his legs up out of the covers.

Rowell woke up as Chapman was rummaging in his locker for clothes, and he sat up too, wondering what was going on. His first thought was that it was a fire drill but he couldn't hear a siren. Then he realised that the other dim form was Voaden, and that gave him quite a start.

"What's going on?" he whispered.

"I'm going with Nick," Chapman whispered back, and he was getting dressed by then, pulling a jumper over his head.

"Where are you going?" Rowell asked.

"Surfing," Chapman whispered.

Rowell thought he was dreaming then, because it sounded like something someone would say in a dream. It was just the kind of crazy crap dream people came out with. He lay back down again, but he didn't close his eyes.

Voaden didn't say anything. He just sat on the end of

Chapman's bed, waiting. Chapman put the stuff he wanted to take on his bed and he only realised then that he had nothing to pack them into. Voaden saw him pause, and he lifted his small haversack onto the bed. It was really bulging by the time the two of them had stuffed in Chapman's few clothes and his toilet bag. The last thing he did was bend down to take his ciggeys out from under the floorboard.

"Ready?" Voaden whispered.

"Bye, Chris, I'll see you," Chapman whispered.

"Bye," Rowell said.

The two boys tiptoed out and they were nearly at the door when Leomond's torch came on. He shone it at them and they froze. Leomond quickly switched it off when he saw who it was. Then they were gone, and it was as though they had never been there.

Rowell lay on his back, staring up at the ceiling for a long time. He closed his eyes and opened them again, and he couldn't work out whether he was really awake or asleep. He didn't want to look over at Chapman's bed because he was afraid it would be empty. He just lay there thinking about Chapman surfing in the night and the moon shining on the breaking waves. The waves seemed very white, like rows of teeth in a huge face.

After a while Leomond got up and he came over to the corner and sat down on Rowell's bed.

"That's not good," he whispered.

Rowell sat up and he understood now that none of it had been a dream, not with Leomond sitting there saying something sensible like that.

"He's fucking crazy," Rowell said.

"You have to tell Dryden," Leomond said.

Rowell didn't say anything else straight away. He just stared at the door as though he was wondering what lay beyond it, where it led.

"You must go and wake him up now and tell him," Leomond said and he prodded Rowell's leg through the blanket to get him moving.

"Why don't you?" Rowell said.

"Because you have to do it," Leomond said.

Rowell didn't want to be a sneak, but he knew Leomond was right. He was right about more than just the things he said. He was a bit spooky like that. Rowell threw off his covers and swung his legs over the side of the bed. He sat there for a bit, staring at the door before finally standing up. Leomond stayed where he was, looking up at him. Other boys were beginning to stir in their beds; one or two were sitting up and looking in their direction.

"Pete's going to hate me," Rowell whispered.

"No he won't," Leomond said with complete certitude.

"Voaden will probably beat the living shit out of me," Rowell said.

"Voaden's gone," Leomond said.

That was true, but he had come back, and there was nothing to stop it happening again. Rowell pictured himself waking up to find Voaden's knife poised at his throat. He was on the verge of jumping back into bed, but Leomond prodded him in the leg again.

"Quit doing that," Rowell snapped, "I'm going."

Rowell had to knock quite hard before there was a muffled response from Dryden. He blurted out his story straight away, and Dryden looked dazed at first, blinking up at him in the glare of the bedside light. Then he was wide-awake, and he shot out of bed like a rocket, pulling on his trousers before Rowell had even finished speaking.

"Newquay? Are they planning to hitch?" Dryden demanded, balancing on one foot as he struggled with his shoe.

"I don't know, I suppose so, sir," Rowell said.

"Damn," Dryden said.

He didn't even thank Rowell, and he nearly fell down the stairs in his haste to get to his car. It had come back from the panelbeaters that afternoon, and he hadn't driven it at night. When he turned on the headlights, the left one lit up the leaves of the trees on the pavement.

"Shit," he said.

He turned on the engine and then sat staring through the windshield trying to figure out which way to go, beginning to panic. Blue smoke belched out of the exhaust, curling up to the street lamp like a stream of lost souls. He finally decided to head for the intersection with the main Worthing road, guessing that the boys would go there as the best place to hitch. As he drove, he prayed earnestly that no one would pick them up, that there would be no cars, no trucks, nothing at all.

There was no sign of them at the intersection and he sat there too for a while wondering whether they might have gone the other way, down to the coast road. The indecision drove him mad. He could feel his heart pounding and despair enveloped him like a dense fog.

"Get a fucking grip on yourself," he yelled out loud.

He turned left onto the main road and he knew then that all he could do was go on driving down that road towards the west. He knew he would drive all the way if necessary, all night, that he would never stop. He would drive to hell if he had to, he told himself.

There were not many cars and the few coming the other way flashed at him to tell him to dip his headlights. He tried it once and the left light shone straight up into the sky like a searchlight.

A short while later he knew it was hopeless, that he had gone far beyond the point that the boys could ever have reached on foot. That had happened long ago, miles back. He knew that they must have gone on another route or were already in someone else's car, anonymous in the dark, rumbling towards Newquay. He could overtake them and never know it, and the realisation of that made him slow down a little, but he didn't stop. He had to go on to keep faith with himself, with Chapman.

He saw the car in the lay-by before he saw the two figures standing near it. If his lights had been working properly, he would probably not have seen them at all. He felt like screaming with joy when he recognised Chapman.

The two boys put their hands up to their faces to shield their eyes from the glare of Dryden's headlamps. It looked as though they were about to run for it but they stopped when he yelled out, telling them who he was as he got out of the car. Then he turned his attention to the other car. He went over to the passenger window to lean in and tell the driver to clear off, that the boys belonged to him. He couldn't see clearly who was at the wheel but as he looked in the car's engine started.

"That shit knifed me," the driver shouted.

The car pulled away then, its rear tyres spinning briefly on the loose gravel in the lay-by. Dryden jumped back and watched it roar away. He turned to the two boys standing side by side in the bright light of his headlamps.

"What did he mean by that?" he said. He was still too delighted at having caught up with them, with Chapman, to really care. He was grinning and that was ridiculous in the circumstances, faintly crazy.

Neither of the boys answered him and in the silence the driver's words penetrated Dryden's euphoria. He saw that Chapman looked really frightened and he sensed immediately that it wasn't because he'd been caught.

"What happened?" he asked

"He gave us a lift, and I think he was drunk, sir," Chapman said.

Dryden nodded.

"He kept trying to put his hand in my trousers, sir," Chapman blurted out.

Dryden just kept nodding.

"He stopped here, and he was like a loony, sir. He kept trying to kiss me and stuff. I thought he was going to kill me. Nick hit him from the back with his knife and got me away, sir."

Dryden looked properly at Voaden for the first time.

"Well, that's fine," he said and it sounded ludicrous.

"I think he was bleeding, sir."

Dryden nodded again.

"It sounds as though he got what he deserved," he said.

A passing car slowed down so that the occupants could get a better look at the strange tableau lit up in the lay-by: a man, a youth and a boy, facing each other on an open air stage, frozen in the middle of some ancient drama. The car didn't stop, though, because it didn't look like the kind of situation it would be good to get involved in, not so late in the night.

Dryden went to his car and switched the motor and the main lights off. When he came back Voaden was walking away.

"Hold on, Nick," Dryden said.

"He's afraid you're going to report him to the cops, sir," Chapman said quickly. He was really keyed up, more excited than Dryden had ever seen him.

"I'm not going to call the cops. I won't give you a medal but I'm not going to call the cops," Dryden said.

Voaden stopped when he heard that, but he didn't come back.

"Your dad is worried sick about you, Nick," Dryden said. "I

think you should go home."

He didn't even suggest that Voaden should come back to school because he knew he wouldn't. He was beyond school, beyond help; he had been for a long time. Dryden was grateful that Voaden had saved Chapman, but he was also angry with the youth because he was the reason the boy needed to be saved in the first place. He disliked Voaden intensely for that, for taking Chapman away, corrupting him. Voaden was beyond redemption. Dryden didn't really care what happened to him.

"I'll drop you off at home right now if you like," he said.

Voaden shook his head. He stood for a while longer holding his haversack and then he started walking away again. Chapman looked from one to the other and he seemed ready to follow Voaden into the darkness. Dryden reached out and took hold of his arm. He held him gently but he wouldn't let go, not until the danger had passed.

"You're being really stupid, Nick," he said, raising his voice. "For heaven's sake go home and sort things out."

His words seemed to hang in the night air for a while, as though there were an echo. There couldn't be, not in that flat invisible landscape, but Dryden pulled Chapman a little closer. He imagined unseen bodies moving in, shadowy figures on tiptoe dancing around them in the dark. They stood like that for a couple of minutes. It was soon obvious that Voaden wasn't coming back. He had gone forever, in the company of demons, beyond the pale.

"We'd better get back to school," Dryden said softly. "He'll be alright; he's a tough customer."

He guided Chapman back to the car and opened the front passenger door. He only let go of the boy's arm when he was sitting in the car. He closed the door and went quickly round to the driver's side, not wanting to be more than a foot away from Chapman, not for a second.

"Are you sure he'll be alright, sir?" Chapman asked anxiously.

"He'll be fine. He's as tough as nails. I'm sure he'll come to his senses and go home," Dryden said. He didn't believe it, but he knew it was what the boy wanted to hear.

"I'm sorry, sir," Chapman said.

"Don't worry about it. I'm glad I got you back," Dryden said.

They drove in silence for quite a while, and Dryden was amazed at the distance he'd covered, how far from school they'd gone. He worked out that they must have been close to Arundel. He shivered at the thought of how tenuous the thread had been, how lucky he was to have found them.

"Will I get caned, sir?" Chapman asked suddenly.

Dryden didn't answer straight away. An oncoming car flashed furiously. They both heard the driver yelling obscenities as he sped past.

"No, you won't," Dryden said. "I'll never let anything like that happen to you."

He could sense Chapman looking at him in the dark confines of the car, wondering what he meant.

"What will happen to me, sir?" he asked.

"Nothing will happen to you. You must learn your own lesson from this," Dryden replied. It sounded quite wise as he said it. He hoped the boy accepted it as wisdom and not for what it really was. No harm could come to Chapman, none at all, not through him.

They drove on in silence for a while, and then Chapman suddenly sat bolt upright.

"He's got my stuff, sir," he said in alarm.

"What stuff?"

"My clothes and wash bag and stuff."

"That doesn't matter, I'll buy you some other things."

Chapman looked at him again in the dark, and Dryden knew the boy was wondering why he was being so kind and thoughtful.

"You don't have to do that, sir," he said.

"I don't mind doing it. Forget about it; it doesn't matter," Dryden said.

It was well after midnight when they got back to school. Dryden parked the car, but he didn't get out right away. He put his hand on Chapman's shoulder to stop him getting out.

"Why did you run off with Nick Voaden like that? Are you really that unhappy? Are those other boys still after you?" he asked.

Chapman shrugged. He didn't look at Dryden. He looked straight ahead.

"Did you go just for kicks?" Dryden persisted.

"I don't know, sir. It's what Nick wanted, sir," Chapman said eventually.

Dryden smiled despite himself, despite the circumstances.

"I really want you to stay out of trouble. Will you do that for me?"

Chapman nodded and he looked up into Dryden's face and smiled briefly too.

"The less you say about this the better, the better for Nick too," Dryden said. "Don't blab to the others. Just say I caught up with you and that's that. OK?"

Chapman studied his face, searching his features, wanting answers but struggling to frame the questions.

"Do you think that man will die, sir?" he asked.

"I doubt it. He seemed fine. He could drive all right. He was a stupid shit. Forget about him, it's not worth remembering."

"But don't you think he'll report us to the police, sir?"

"No I don't, not after what he tried," Dryden said.

It was half past twelve when Chapman got back into bed. Rowell heard him and sat up briefly.

"Are you OK?" he asked.

"Fine," Chapman said.

Rowell didn't ask anything else. He wasn't fully awake anyway. He lay down again, turned over in his bed and went back to sleep.

Chapman had to face a lot of questions the next morning, but he didn't say much. He just said that they hadn't gone far when Dryden came along with his headlights all askew. He said Voaden had gone on to Newquay, He'd finished with school and there was nothing Dryden or Bruder or anybody else could do about it, he told them.

Pretty soon people were talking about exams. They started on Monday, having loomed up out of nowhere. Everyone was preoccupied with that, and after a while they didn't really bother pressing Chapman or wonder unduly why he wasn't being punished in any way. Some of them thought he'd been let off because of the drawings and the whole Heathfield thing; he was being given a lot of slack because of that. That was Leomond's theory originally, an easy one to accept when your mind was on other things, like getting through Geography and Latin. Pearce had a theory of his own, but he only shared it with Higgins.

"I think Drydork wants to marry him," he said.

Higgins giggled like a girl.

FORTY-TWO

Heathfield got much better, but he didn't tell anyone it was because Chapman had kissed him. He didn't want anyone to know, and he thought they wouldn't believe it, anyway. After ten days he could move his good arm, and he could move the fingers in both hands.

The doctors were pretty relaxed about being proved wrong because they weren't heartless and didn't always need to be right.

"It's a minor miracle," one of them said to Mrs Heathfield. She looked at him rather sharply; there was nothing minor about it, as far as she was concerned.

The doctors were half right about the paralysis in the end, because Heathfield's legs were still useless. It looked as though they were going to stay that way permanently. The doctors didn't say so with quite the same gloomy dogmatism as they'd used before, but they were pretty sure nevertheless.

Chapman hadn't come back to visit him, but he wasn't

surprised, and he wasn't really that disappointed because he didn't expect it.

The whole choir came one Saturday morning, all ten choristers, led by Kennedy. By then Heathfield was sitting up. Mrs Heathfield was delighted to be at the back of the queue.

All in all, everyone at the hospital, and those at school who'd heard the good news, were impressed and quite touched, given the circumstances, by just how well he seemed to be getting along. Later on, thinking back on it, one of the choirboys said that he had been surprised at how incredibly happy Heathfield seemed to be on that day before he died.

Bruder had been especially relieved to hear that Heathfield was getting much better, because a reporter from the Gazette had phoned and asked if a naked thirteen-year-old boy had jumped out of a window and tried to kill himself. No matter how many times Bruder said he'd had his clothes on and that it was a private matter and nobody's business, the reporter just didn't seem to want to hear any of it.

The article had appeared on page two of the Gazette the next day. It wasn't a long piece, but it was enough to catch the eye of a woman from *The News of the World*. She phoned at eight o'clock on Sunday morning. She'd got hold of Bruder's home number somehow and the cheek of that irritated him. Bruder told her that the boy was getting a lot better, and that it wouldn't help matters at all if *The News of the World* took an interest. He told her to mind her own business and go and look for smut somewhere else.

He had barely put the phone down when Doctor Oakwood rang. He told Bruder without any kind of a preamble that Heathfield had taken a sudden turn for the worse and died. He used the word embolism at some point, but Bruder didn't really pay much attention to that part.

He thanked the doctor for phoning and then he went for a walk and he ended up, as he'd unconsciously intended to, at the chapel. He sat in one of the pews near the back and stared up at the stained glass window above the altar. Jesus was in it, holding his arms out and looking thoughtful and compassionate. Bruder didn't kneel down, but he did pray, and it was a good ten minutes before he came out again. Dryden was waiting for him when he got back to his office.

"Heathfield passed away early this morning," Bruder told him.

Dryden was stunned.

"I thought he was on the mend," he said.

"He was getting better," Bruder said. He didn't go into his office; he sat down heavily in one of the two easy chairs outside.

"What a tragic waste," Dryden said, and it was, he thought, a horrible, pointless waste.

He stood looking down at Bruder and neither of them said anything else for a while. They could both hear the clock ticking on the wall behind Alice's desk.

"Did you want to see me about something?" Bruder asked when the silence started to get awkward.

"It's about Voaden, sir," Dryden said.

"Has he turned up?" Bruder asked.

"He's hitching to Newquay," Dryden said.

Bruder didn't look surprised. It was as though he'd expected to hear something like that.

"He came into the dorms late last night and tried to persuade Chapman to go with him, but I put a stop to that. I couldn't keep Voaden from going, though," Dryden continued. He waited for Bruder to ask for more details, to ask about Chapman, but he just stared into space. He didn't seem to be that interested. Dryden was relieved. *The fewer questions the better*, he thought.

"Does his father know?" Bruder asked eventually.

"I phoned him late last night and told him," Dryden said.

"He's a stupid boy," Bruder said. "He was leaving anyway at the end of term, only a few days to go."

Dryden nodded. He was a stupid boy, he thought, the kind of boy who would be dead or in jail by twenty.

Bruder stood up.

"Have you made up your mind what you want to do?" he asked.

Dryden didn't understand at first. He'd forgotten all about his resignation, about leaving.

"I've changed my mind. I'd like to stay on," he said.

Bruder nodded, and he smiled briefly.

"Good," he said. "I think you're making the right decision. Can I leave it to you to get the word out about Heathfield?"

"Of course, sir."

"I'll talk to Kennedy. He'll need to say something at the morning service. It's probably best if everyone knows beforehand, though, including the boys, don't you think?"

Dryden nodded solemnly. He didn't know what to think.

"What an almighty shame," Bruder said, and he went into his office.

By lunchtime just about everyone knew that Heathfield had died. Dryden only had to tell a couple of the older boys and the news went around like wildfire, so most people had heard by the time Kennedy talked about it in chapel.

One of the last to hear was Richardson. He didn't go to chapel, and he only heard about it from a boy at rehearsals, after lunch. He just stood there like a big round boulder on the edge of a hill for a long, long time, and then he cancelled the play without waiting to talk to Bruder first about it or anything. He just said that the play was cancelled and that was that. The boys were rather flummoxed because they'd learned most of their lines by then, and they couldn't understand why Richardson was cancelling seeing as how Heathfield wasn't even in the play. One of the boys pointed that out to him.

"He is in it – we're all in it," Richardson said cryptically before stalking out. The door swung shut on its big hinges behind him.

"What the shit does he mean by that?" one of the boys asked.

The others just shrugged their shoulders and stared at the closed door.

"The great play of life," Chatsworth said.

They all stared at him then, but none of them left right away. They sat around talking about it amongst themselves, and that was just as well because Richardson came back in after a few minutes. He carried on as though nothing had happened. It was as though he had just gone out to the toilet and had never said anything about cancelling the play at all. He simply carried on. The boys looked at each other, but none of them said anything about it either. In a way they were quite relieved even though none of them really wanted to be in the play anymore; they hadn't wanted to be in it for some time, not even Chatsworth.

FORTY-THREE

Kennedy didn't see it at first although it was a big print, bigger than the usual snapshot, as big as a book. The light wasn't that good in the chapel, and his eyesight wasn't that good anymore either. It was only when he was standing right at the altar that he saw it lying there, laid square in front of the crucifix like some kind of offering. It was a photograph of Chapman. He put on his glasses and stared at it for a long time, taking in every detail. The boy was naked, stretched taut, his arms over his head. His hands were out of the scope of the picture but it didn't occur to Kennedy that someone was holding them. Not even the hand pressing down on the boy's thigh was enough of a clue for that. Chapman's ribs showed and his hips were sticking out on either side of his small flat belly. There were glistening smears and small white puddles on his chest, on his neck and on his face. Kennedy knew immediately what they were. They reflected the camera's flash like dribbles of coagulated milk.

"Good God," he said out loud.

The boy's astonishing face seemed to grin at Kennedy from the picture, his wide excited eyes enticing him to look. That made it all worse: more sacrilegious, more satanic, more demeaning. *How can you enjoy it*, Kennedy thought. *How can you lie like that on the floor, stretch like that, revel in that? How can you be so debased?*

He turned the picture over, face down on the altar cloth. Then he saw the writing: *"To Mr Dryden. Love and kisses. Peter Chapman,"* the words said.

"Good God," he repeated. His legs gave up then, so he had to sit down on the altar steps, panting for breath, clutching the picture. He sat there for a full five minutes.

All in all Bruder was delighted, able to relax. Exams were virtually over; the end of term was a mere two days away. He was looking forward to visiting his sister in Torquay, even though that meant putting up with her irritating drunk of a husband.

He had really enjoyed the play. It had gone much better than he'd expected, better than Richardson had led him to expect. Hardly any lines were lost and the applause from the parents was genuine; he was convinced of that. They weren't just clapping because they had to; most of them had actually enjoyed it.

Chatsworth had given an extraordinary performance. He'd really come alive in the part. Simpson had drawn on some hidden talent too, confounding Richardson's gloomy expectations. He had managed to make Dionysus seem majestic and aloof rather than stiff and pompous. Even the boys in the Chorus had muddled through passably well.

The weather had helped with a performance of its own. The wind had been building all day, and there was a howling gale outside. The fury in the storm constantly rattled the high gymnasium windows, searching for a way in, resonating with the words of the boys on the stage. It was still out there now, hysterical with rage, tearing at the branches of the big oaks, desperate to cast them down.

Boys were milling about in the lobby, and there were still a few parents who had stayed for tea and cake. Bruder mingled amiably among them, chatting for a moment here and there, giving praise and receiving it.

Dryden was there with Sarah and he introduced her when Bruder stopped beside them.

"Philip's told me a lot about you," she said.

"I'm sure he has," Bruder said with a smile. "I hope I'm not as bad in the flesh."

Sarah laughed and Dryden grinned to hide his embarrassment. Bruder kept surprising him, in mostly good ways.

A door suddenly flew wide open, its handle wrenched from someone's grasp. The wind rushed in and hungrily picked up a pile of unused programmes from a small table by the wall, creating an instant maelstrom. Kennedy was standing in the midst of it, the sparse ring of hair around his bald pate blasted into a white frizz. He looked anxiously around, craning his thin neck, oblivious of the chaos he'd caused. One of the boys leaned on the door behind him, forcing it shut. The programmes settled to the floor like giant dandruff.

Kennedy ignored the mess, ignored everybody, searching the room for Bruder. When he spotted him he came striding straight over.

"I have to speak to you very urgently," he said.

"Right now?" Bruder asked, irritated by the apparition.

"Yes – in private," Kennedy said, glancing at Dryden, ignoring Sarah. The glance was full of fear and jealous loathing. Kennedy put his hand to his chest, where the naked, soiled image of Chapman was pressed against his heart. He was afraid that the photograph might somehow slip from his pocket, that everyone would see it, that they would know he had touched it and hidden it away.

Bruder was on the verge of protesting, but Kennedy looked wild-eyed, as though he'd been chased in by the Devil himself, so he decided against it.

"I suppose we'd better go up to Turner's classroom," he said.

Bruder sat down at a boy's desk with the photograph in his hand. He stared at it in horror and then prompted by Kennedy he turned it over and read the words on the back.

"They put it on the altar," Kennedy said, his voice cracking. "On the altar," he repeated.

Bruder looked up beyond Kennedy at the paintings on the walls. They were full of sunshine and fruit, apples and bananas: harmless seeds, natural bounty. He looked down at the photograph again, and he wanted to weep.

"He looks absolutely terrified," he said.

The words stunned Kennedy. It took him a moment to deal with the enormity of his mistake: the simple denial of what he'd chosen to see, what he thought he could still see.

"We've got to get Philip into this; it's completely out of control," Bruder said.

"What do you mean? Why Philip? He's obviously involved in the whole disgusting business," Kennedy said angrily.

Bruder stared at him in disbelief.

"Don't talk rubbish."

"Why on earth would they scrawl something like that on the back? They're trying to tell us – to warn us what's going on," Kennedy said.

Bruder shook his head from side to side. He put the photograph down on the desk.

"I'm surprised you should think that – astonished, in fact."

"What am I suppose to think? Why would they write that?" Kennedy said, almost shouting.

He was on the verge of hysteria.

"Philip's got a big soft spot for Chapman, and a lot of the boys know it. He hasn't been very good at keeping it under wraps."

"A big soft spot?" Kennedy repeated incredulously. The words instantly prompted an obscene image in his mind: Dryden doing disgusting things to Chapman's naked, writhing body.

There was laughter on the stairs, and a couple of fourth form boys burst through the door, giggling. They stopped abruptly when they saw the two men, expecting the place to be empty.

"Sorry, sir," they stammered and started to back out again.

"Hold on," Bruder said.

The boys stopped, their laughter all gone, replaced by fear.

"Ask Mr Dryden to join us up here for a moment, will you, please," Bruder said.

"Yes, sir," one of them said and they bolted.

When Dryden came in, Kennedy was standing, staring at a picture on the wall with his back to the door. He didn't turn round, not ready to confront him, not wanting him there. Bruder stood up and held out the photograph without saying anything.

"Good lord," Dryden said, and he felt dizzy immediately.

"Look at the back," Bruder said.

Dryden turned it over and read what was there.

"Not again, for God's sake," he said.

Kennedy did turn round then, seizing on the blasphemy and taking the words as some sort of admission.

"What do you mean by that?" he demanded.

Dryden looked at him, his own anger rising. He hadn't missed the poison in Kennedy's stare when he'd so rudely interrupted them in the lobby. He was about to speak but Bruder raised his hand, cutting him off. He told Kennedy about the note, once again dismissing it as rubbish.

"I should have told you about it before, but I never imagined it went as deep as this," he concluded.

"What is going on between you and this boy," Kennedy demanded of Dryden, hearing Bruder's apology, drawing righteous strength from it.

"What are you implying?" Dryden said.

"I'm not implying anything: the boys are," Kennedy snapped.

Dryden held the photograph up, thrusting it at the parson's face.

"You think I'm a part of this – that I'd do something like that?" he shouted.

Bruder raised both his hands. He felt sick, about to keel over, but he knew he had to get control again.

"That's enough," he commanded.

The two men stared hard at each other for a moment longer and then Kennedy turned away again. Dryden put the photograph down on the desk in front of him.

"I knew something like this had happened to Peter," he said quietly. "I found him in the bathrooms late at night, shortly after he'd been assaulted, a few weeks ago, but he begged me to keep it quiet. I can see why now – I'd no idea they'd taken photographs; he never told me that."

Kennedy's shoulders sagged slightly and he uncrossed his arms and turned round to face them both again. He put his hand up to his chin, pinching it between his fingers. His face was the colour of white ash.

"It was obviously a bad error of judgement on my part – to keep it quiet, I mean," Dryden said. "But I really thought it was for the best – in Peter's best interests – after what had happened to him at Saint Stithians."

Bruder sat down and he picked up the photograph again, looking at it and shaking his head sadly from side to side.

"Well, we've obviously got to get to the bottom of it now, find out who's responsible for this. I'm not having sick animals like this in my school," he said.

"He doesn't want his parents to know," Dryden said. "He doesn't want anyone to know."

Bruder looked at him and resisted being drawn into the conundrum.

"It won't be difficult to find out," he said, ignoring the plea. "You won't get a picture like this developed at Boots the Chemist. It was obviously done in the school's dark room. Only a handful have access to that, or the knowledge – Bates for one, he's the secretary, the keyholder."

"Chapman will have to own up," Kennedy said.

"Own up?" Dryden repeated angrily. "Own up to what, for God's sake? He was the one who was raped. He didn't want this. He didn't ask for it. Look at his face."

Kennedy took a step back, crossing and uncrossing his hands. He thought about mentioning Featherstone and even Heathfield's drawings, throwing all that in as proof of the boy's debauchery.

"OK, Philip, calm down. I understand what you're saying, but we can't just carry on and ignore a photograph like this," Bruder said.

"They put it on the altar," Kennedy said. As the words left his mouth it occurred to him for the first time that the photo was meant for him, that he'd been meant to find it. He started to wonder why and the answers unnerved him. He pictured the boys laughing behind his back, somehow knowing, joking about the demons he wrestled with, finding them funny.

He only half listened to Bruder as he told them to leave the matter with him. Bruder said he would work out what to do, who to question; that he would get to the bottom of it as discreetly as possible.

Dryden nodded, accepting the assurance that Chapman would be protected. None of it would become public, Bruder said, he would make sure of that. Chapman's parents would never need to know.

"I'm afraid my resignation still stands," Dryden said when he'd finished. "I can't continue under these circumstances." He didn't look at Kennedy as he spoke but it was obvious that the Parson's attitude had been the last straw. He said the words quietly, without anger or bitterness because he felt he was tainted. In some way, in a way they could never know or understand, he felt he deserved to be.

Sarah was one of the few people left when he got back down to the lobby. Her happy mood had long since evaporated, and she had started to think about leaving without waiting for him to reappear.

"What was all that about?" she asked grumpily.

He told her everything in the car, all that had happened, all the things he had kept secret for Chapman's sake. They were still talking about it when they got back to her flat.

"He's a strange boy; you said that at the beginning," she said.

He slept with her that night, cuddling up close, but they didn't make love. Passion seemed to be too far removed from love for him, a distorted, unclean parody.

In the morning he told her that he was leaving, not just the school but England. He was going to go to Africa for a while. He tried to persuade her to come with him. It was a half-hearted effort, and she knew that. She knew it was hopeless anyway. She didn't want to go to Africa, its blue metal skies held no promise for her.

He left after breakfast and went back to school. He got through the day, the last full day of term, with mechanical indifference, like the clock on the wall, doing his job.

He went into the dorm half an hour before lights out, looking for Chapman. He was sitting on his bed, and Dryden beckoned to him, not going all the way in. Chapman followed him out. He didn't have his pyjama top on and he folded the elastic down on his pants, adjusting it as he went. Some of the others watched him go. No one said anything, not even Pearce.

They had their last talk in Dryden's room, both sitting on the bed they'd shared that once. Dryden told him about the photograph, that Bruder knew everything and that he would find the boys who'd assaulted him. They would be punished, he said. He told him that he could trust Bruder, that he was a good man, fair and just. There wouldn't be an undue fuss; his parents would never know; it would still be kept secret.

Then he said he was leaving, going to Africa.

"Why, sir?" Chapman asked.

"Why am I going to Africa?"

"No, why are you leaving the school, sir?"

"Because I can't stay any more. It's impossible," he said.

"It's because of me, isn't it, sir?" Chapman said.

Dryden didn't reply straight away. He looked down at the boy beside him, and the boy looked back up at him.

"No, it's not because of you – it's because of me. I think I love you too much, Peter. That's not supposed to happen, and

I don't know what it means anymore, but I know it's nothing bad, I promise you that. I don't want to embarrass you by it. I shouldn't have told you, but I don't think I can leave without you knowing," he said.

Chapman studied his face, searching him inside like he'd done on that first day in Bruder's office.

Dryden felt despair plucking at his spine, taking away bits of him, leaving him hollow.

"You don't have to leave because of that, sir," Chapman said.

"Yes, I do," he said.

"I'll come with you."

Dryden grinned, but he was ready to cry. "Don't be ridiculous. To Africa? Why?"

"Isn't that what you want, sir?"

"No, what I want is for you to be happy," he said. "I want you to grow up and date girls, marry one eventually. I want you to always love life as much as you do now, to go on kicking the shit out of it. Just stop smoking – it's bad for your health."

Chapman smiled at that, trying to understand what he'd meant by everything else he'd said. He'd smoked a ciggey less than twenty minutes ago, and was suddenly worried that Dryden had smelled it on his breath.

"Are you going to marry Sarah, sir?" he asked.

Dryden ignored the impertinence, the familiarity. It didn't matter. He'd said everything. There were no more secrets.

"I hope so, one day; not now. Maybe when I come back from Africa – if she still wants to marry me by then. It's none of your business."

Chapman grinned.

"You should marry her now, sir. You shouldn't go to Africa."

Dryden was a bit startled by that. He ruffled the boy's hair, pretending to push him away.

"You're too wise for your years," he said, smiling. "You'd better get to bed now."

Chapman stayed where he was, and Dryden wondered whether he was expecting something else to happen. Then the boy stood up and he went to the door. He paused there, and they looked at each other. His skin seemed to shine from within, to glow like pale gold, even in that weak light. The window rattled in the silence, buffeted by a wind that showed no sign of abating. It had blown hard all day. It seemed set to howl forever.

"Thanks for everything, sir," Chapman said.

Dryden nodded. He stood up and went over to the window, turning his face away so that Chapman couldn't see how sad he was.

"Lights out in ten minutes," he said.

He pretended to fiddle with the window frame, looking through the glass into the black beyond. When he turned around again, the boy had gone.

FORTY-FOUR

Dryden wrote to Sarah when he got to Africa. On average he wrote every two weeks, and she replied to every letter. Her own life went on, and she tried to share it with him, to keep him a part of it by telling him little things, things that didn't really matter. Dryden wrote about little things too, but he never wrote about the school, only about his new experiences and how much he missed her. He wrote about the people at the bank and about Rhodesia and how it was changing and trying to stay the same. The exchange of letters went on for over six months, becoming almost routine. Then his letters stopped. She wrote two more letters, and a month had gone by when she decided to phone. He had never given her a number, but she got one from the bank's head office in London. A woman at the other end answered, and Sarah changed her mind. She put the phone down without saying anything because she didn't know what to say. She was sad, but she was also angry, angry that he had stopped writing, that he had cast her adrift again.

***

She heard the phone in her flat start to ring when she was at the front door. Her shopping bag split open as she struggled with the key in the lock. It did little for her mood. By the time she reached the phone it had rung seven times.

"Hello," she barked.

"Is that Sarah Crawford?" a man asked. He had a foreign accent.

"Yes."

"I'm sorry to phone out of the blue," the man said cautiously, hearing the irritation in her voice. "I'm a friend of Philip's, Philip Dryden."

Sarah said nothing. She just held the phone tighter.

"Hello?" the man said.

"Yes, I'm sorry; I haven't heard from him for quite a while," Sarah said.

There was silence at the other end, her turn to wonder whether the connection had been broken. She was about to say something else, to ask how Philip was, but the man spoke again before she could.

"I'm afraid to have to tell you that he's passed away," he said. "I'm sorry to break it to you over the phone like this."

She froze inside, but when she spoke she didn't really sound that shocked. Another part of her instantly took over the phone, the part that managed things and didn't need to care. "When did it happen?" she asked.

"About two weeks ago," the man said. He waited for her to react, to break down. When there was only silence he carried on. "I'd like to come and see you, if I may. I have some of his things, your letters to him and other items."

"Yes, of course," she said.

"I'm in the UK on holiday; I arrived this morning. I'm

staying in London, but I'd like to come down tomorrow if that's all right?"

"Yes, of course," she repeated mechanically.

She gave him her address and arranged a time. She only realised she hadn't asked his name after she'd put the phone down. It didn't seem to matter. He was coming anyway, a messenger from Africa to tell her how one of her dreams had died.

Sarah's other self kept busy for ten minutes, picking up the groceries and cleaning the mess a couple of broken eggs had made. It wasn't until all that was done and everything was tidied away that she sat down on the couch and wept.

The messenger's name was Anton Marais. He was actually South African, an Afrikaner, though he'd been living in Rhodesia since he was a boy, he told her. He was a big man, and he had big brown hands. He clasped them together, sitting on the edge of the chair, looking awkward and enormous in Sarah's small lounge. He belonged to Africa's big spaces, not to Worthing.

She poured him some tea, stirring in two sugars.

"How did you get to know Philip?" she asked.

He told her that they both worked at the same bank, that they had started at the same branch at about the same time.

"He really liked the bush. We went hunting together. He was a good shot, a natural, but he didn't like killing things," he said. He smiled properly for the first time, remembering the little duiker with half its head blown away and the Englishman's sorrow and remorse. He'd looked as though he was about to throw up.

Sarah smiled slightly too, thinking of Captain Quack.

"After the first time he just came to be in the bush, just to relax. He really liked the bush," Marais repeated. "He was a real rooinek but a very good man, very solid."

Sarah nodded, waiting. Marais stirred his tea. He put the teaspoon down in the saucer and his smile went away.

"He died in the bush; he was killed by a lioness near Vic Falls. It was a crazy thing to happen. People over here think it occurs all the time, that there are lions all over the place in Africa, but it hardly ever happens."

He waited for her to say something, to recoil in horror, to start weeping, but she just sat there staring at him.

"She had cubs: he must have walked straight into them down by the river. That's what we worked out from the spoor," he said.

"Was he on his own?" she asked.

Marais nodded. "Yes. He stayed in camp. The rest of us were out on the trail, two, three hours away on foot. He shouldn't have gone off like that, not without a rifle, not at all."

He told her it must have been very quick, that Philip wouldn't have suffered. He'd decided in advance that she didn't need the full story. She didn't need to know that Dryden had somehow managed to crawl half way back to camp leaving a dark trail in the red parched earth. He had crawled through the dry thorns, the dead haak-en-steek, with his guts hanging out. She didn't need to know about that or about the red ants in his eyes and the blowflies on his guts when they found him. It wouldn't help with anything, he thought. He wished he didn't have to know himself. He wished he could forget.

"Have you spoken to his parents?" Sarah asked.

"They were told some time back, soon after it happened. Someone from head office in London went to tell them," he said.

"I'm really grateful that you've taken the trouble to come and tell me," she said.

Marais smiled again briefly: "I didn't want to tell you over the phone but it had to come out that way; you didn't know me, of course. It was the least I could do, to come down and tell you what happened. I didn't know him long but he was a good friend, very solid."

He opened the canvas bag at his feet and took out a large brown envelope.

"It's just your letters and a couple of pictures he had," he said.

She took the envelope but she didn't open it. She knew she would start crying if she did. She just put it down beside her on the couch.

"Thank you very much," she said.

Marais stared at the envelope for a while and then he reached into his bag and took out something else. It was a roll of paper, held shut by an elastic band. He held it lightly in both hands, and he seemed embarrassed by it, undecided whether to hand it to her.

"I don't know what this is. It's a private thing. I didn't know whether to throw it away; I didn't know what it meant but I didn't think it should go to his parents. It must be from his teaching days, a joke maybe. It was among his things."

He abruptly held it out to her, like a baton, something to be rid of. He watched her face intently as she slipped off the elastic band and unrolled the paper. He was worried that he had been a fool not to tear it up; that his last act for a dead friend had been to betray something secret, a secret that should never have been, that needed to die with him. He was relieved when she smiled.

"It's Peter," she said.

Marais grinned when he saw the recognition in her face, when he saw the smile. It had been a joke after all, a source of joy and happiness, he thought.

"It's a boy Philip taught. He was very, very fond of him," Sarah explained.

"I thought it was something like that; I knew it must be a joke," Marais said happily.

"It must be one of Heathfield's drawings. Beautiful little Peter, young Dionysus, love and kisses," she said softly, reading the last words.

Marais sipped his tea, studying her face over the rim of the cup.

She let the paper roll back in on itself and put it down by the envelope.

"Thank you," she said.

Marais left soon afterwards. He gave her a big hug at the door and he wished her well.

***

The next day Sarah phoned Bruder. She told him what had happened to Philip. He had been shocked, of course, and although he said the predictable things, she could tell from his voice that the sadness was genuine. She said she wanted to come and take Peter Chapman out from school and tell him herself.

Bruder was cautious at first. He thought she was being overly dramatic. He thought that Chapman would be surprised, perhaps a little upset, but nothing more. He didn't say that to her, and he agreed in the end because he realised that it was something she needed to do, to put to rest.

"Can you please keep it to yourself until I've told him – just until Sunday," she said.

"Yes, I will," Bruder said.

When Sunday came, Sarah parked her MG in the same spot on Pond Road as she'd parked all those many months ago. It was colder than it had been then, but the seasons were changing again, spring giving way to summer. The morning sun shone on the shabby walls of St Mary's, and she remembered Philip's disparaging remarks about the old church, how much he'd always seemed to hate the view. She looked up at the school buildings and wondered which window had been his. She had never known that, never thought to ask.

There were other people waiting in parked cars, the parents of dayboys waiting for the service to end. A man sitting in a car on the other side of the street looked across at her and smiled. He tapped his watch and raised his eyes to the heavens. She smiled back then looked away.

Bruder had said the service normally ended at ten thirty but it was well after that already, almost a quarter to eleven. The parents were getting impatient. Several had climbed out of their cars to stand it silent protest. She debated whether to get out too, but in the end she just sat there staring into space, wondering whether she was doing the right thing; whether Peter needed to know; whether it would actually matter to him.

When the doors of the chapel finally opened, organ music wafted out. The masters came first, led by Bruder. A steady stream of boys followed, the oldest in front, spilling into the street, getting more boisterous as they descended in age and size. Sarah looked intently at their faces, looking for Peter, searching the scowls and the smiles. After a couple of minutes the stream of bodies thinned to a trickle and she knew she'd missed him. As she climbed out of the car she was startled to hear his voice behind her on the pavement.

"Hello, miss," he said.

He was just the same, just as beautiful, younger than she remembered.

"I was looking out for you. How did you get around there?" she asked.

"I waved," he said. "I thought you'd seen me."

Another boy was standing close behind him, much older, looking at her curiously, smiling slightly. The smile faded as their eyes met. She wondered who he was, why he was there at all. She decided to ignore him.

"It's really, really nice to see you again, Peter," she said and it was. It filled her with a sense of relief somehow, with happiness.

"It's great to see you, miss. Do you want me to change? Can I come like this?"

"That's fine, fine like that, but you can change if you like."

The older boy whispered in Chapman's ear and Sarah saw him slide his hand briefly into the boy's jacket pocket, putting something in or taking it out. Then he walked off towards the school entrance. Chapman didn't seem to take any notice.

"I'll stay like this if that's OK, miss," he said.

"That's fine – hop in," she said.

She climbed back in, wondering what had been whispered, what had been given or taken away.

The street was chaotic with cars trying to pull away and boys still crossing the road, running back and forth. She concentrated on her driving, remembering what a fool she'd made of herself with Philip. She wasn't sure of the way even now.

"Where are you taking me, miss?" Chapman asked.

She didn't know. She hadn't decided. *Where do you go to talk about death*, she thought.

"Wherever you want to go."

"What about the beach?"

"OK," she said, missing second, grating the gears. She grinned at him and pulled a face. Then they were free of Pond Road and the way was open and the school was behind them. She headed for the bridge over the river, passing the school playing fields on the right. Chapman seemed happy, relaxed, sitting back and enjoying the ride. She was glad she'd left the top down, even though it was still a bit cold.

"Can I take my tie off, miss?" he asked.

"Of course you can," she said.

He pulled it off and undid the top three buttons of his shirt. Then he held the tie up in his outstretched hand and let it stream behind, a thin snapping banner in the slipstream of the car.

"Don't let go," she said.

"I hate ties," he said. "When I finish school, I'm never going to wear one again."

"What are you going to do?"

"Surf," he said.

"Great," she said, and she meant it. She didn't mean it to be patronising or sarcastic. He was somehow meant to live a life like that.

"How is Mr Dryden, miss?" he asked.

"He went to Africa," she said.

Chapman pulled the tie in, bunched it up and stuffed it into his jacket pocket.

"I wish he'd stayed," he said. "The new bloke is a complete jerk."

"I wish he'd stayed, too," she said.

She glanced at him briefly, and he was smiling and looking at her.

"I told him he shouldn't go to Africa, miss. I said he should marry you," he said with a grin.

She was startled by his words and lost concentration, looking at him. She only saw the stop sign at the last moment and had to stand on the brakes. The tyres squealed in protest.

"Sorry miss, did I say something wrong?" he said.

"No, Peter, but Philip's dead; he was killed in Africa," she said. "That's what I came to tell you. I was going to tell you on the beach."

He carried on looking at her, his mouth slightly open. His bright eyes searched her face, lightly touching the raw edges of everything. Then he nodded slightly. He understood the reason for her coming to see him, taking him out of school. He had wondered about that but not known how to ask.

A car behind them hooted. She'd forgotten where she was for a moment, forgotten that life moved on. She had to concentrate on driving, and neither of them spoke again until they got to the sea. It didn't take long, just two or three minutes. Chapman got out of the car, leaving his jacket on the seat. He went down the steep shingle beach. He didn't wait for her. He picked up a stone and threw it, trying to clip the top of a wave before it broke. Sarah sat on a breakwater and watched, not following him down to the water's edge, wondering what he was thinking. She didn't pay any attention to the other people there, the couples with small kids. It was as though they didn't really exist.

Chapman tired of the game quite quickly and came to sit beside her. He sat very close, almost touching.

"Philip had a drawing of you," she said. "It must have been one of Heathfield's drawings."

He looked at her again and smiled. He didn't say anything for a while. The sound of the sea on the shingle beach suddenly seemed very loud to her, like countless voices all talking at once.

"Why do you think he liked me so much, miss?" he asked.

"Because you're a sweet boy; he really admired your spirit," she said. She didn't know what else to say.

"I thought he just fancied me at first, like the others," he said.

"Is that why you got into bed with him?" she asked. The

question was triggered by his nonchalance, his seeming self-assurance. She didn't mean to ask it. It was a demeaning and stupid thing to say. She wished she could have taken the words back the moment they were out of her mouth.

He didn't seem upset, though. He didn't get up or move away.

"Is that why you wanted to see me, miss?" he asked. "Do you want to know whether it was all true – about me and him and the photos and stuff?

"No, I'm sorry, Peter – I didn't mean it to sound like that – I know it wasn't true," she said. "He told me he loved you very much – that if he had a son, he'd want him to be just like you," she said.

Chapman picked up a stone at his feet, turning it over in his slim fingers before dropping it again.

"I don't think Mr Dryden really wanted to go to Africa. I don't think he knew what he really wanted at all, miss," he said softly.

"I don't think any of us ever really do," she said.

"I think he wanted to kiss me, but he never did."

Before she could react he startled her by taking her hand, holding it and trying to turn it over. She resisted instinctively for a moment, but then she let him, seeing his grin and realising it was part of a game. He peered into her palm, running the tip of his finger along the lines in the taut skin. It made her shiver and want to giggle.

"You'll get married next year and after that you'll have two children, a boy and a girl," he said with mock pomposity. "And you'll live until you're seventy-eight."

"Only seventy-eight?" she said, sounding disappointed.

"That's really old, miss," he said.

"And you can see all that in my sweaty palm?" she asked.

He let go of her hand and looked up into her face, still

smiling slightly, inches away. She saw him properly for the first time that day. He was astonishingly beautiful, as perfect as the sun. She felt his beauty filling her and draining her, ebbing and flowing like the pulse in her veins, like the wash of the sea. His eyes seemed to reflect all the beauty in the world, all the pain that made it and brought it into being. In that instant she imagined what Philip had seen, what had enchanted and consumed him so completely in the end.

"You'll never grow old, will you," she said. She wasn't sure what she meant, whether she was talking to the boy or a being shining through him, not sure whether they were one and the same.

Chapman looked away, down towards the sea. Then he stood up.

"Never," he said. "Can we get something to eat please, miss? I'm starving."

STEALING TH

SAMANTH.

Chapter One

A sound that could only be described as a loud *raspberry* ripped through the drawing room. Rosamunde winced and covered her eyes briefly with a hand. Well, she could describe the sound in worst ways, but she was a lady and she certainly did not talk about bodily noises in such a way. Aunt Petunia leapt from the chair, her cheeks pink, and picked up the offending windbag.

"George Hampton, are you behind this?" she demanded.

George, Rosamunde's nine-year-old cousin, fought to keep a straight face. His cheeks bulged until he crumpled into laughter, clasping his stomach.

His sister raced over, snatched the windbag from Aunt Petunia, and tossed it to George. "That was the best yet, George!"

Aunt Petunia reached for the back of George's jacket, but he dodged his aunt's grasp and darted out of the drawing room, followed by his sister and the two other younger cousins. Aunt Petunia sank onto her chair but not before checking there was nothing else that would make such a rude noise.

Rosamunde's mother patted the back of Aunt Petunia's hand. "They are in high spirits today."

As were they always. Rosamunde adored her younger cousins and could not even blame them for their behavior. She had been similar when she had visited her father's house as a child. The grand rooms of Westham House always provided such a wonderful playground for children. Even now, she rather fancied sneaking off into the library and hiding on the upper

1

balcony or tiptoeing through the servant's hallway and hoping not to get caught. Anything other than sit around and listen to her four aunts and her mother talk of Rosamunde's future marriage prospects.

Goodness, she had married once already. Was that not enough?

"What about Sir Bellmont?" her mother suggested.

"Ohh." Aunt Janey nodded. "He's eligible."

"Not rich enough," said another aunt.

Rosamunde wrinkled her nose. His wealth wasn't a problem. Sir Bellmont was almost as old as her late husband. If she married him, she'd likely be a widow for a second time and what sort of a reputation would she have then?

She pursed her lips. People would call her *The Black Widow*. Or *The Wicked Widow*.

No, *The Killer Wife*.

She smiled to herself. Actually, that would not be so bad. It might even be exciting. Not that she had any desire to bury another husband, but it would be rather exciting to be known as something more than Lady Rosamunde Stanley, heir to her father's fortune, widow to the Viscount Rothmere, and aunt to far too many naughty cousins.

She glanced at her hands. She shouldn't complain. There were many in much worst circumstances to her. Her arranged marriage had been acceptable, if incredibly dull. The Viscount always treated her respectfully, though she supposed visiting a mere two times a year left him with little chance to treat her any other way. His passing had been no shock. Only a year into their marriage, his health began to fail, and she gave up hope of conceiving any children from it. It was a miracle he lasted five years.

Her cousins darted back into the room, followed by her young sister Ellie. George dashed past the delicate table next to Rosamunde and it wobbled precariously. She snatched the cup of tea from it before it could topple with a crash and watched George dart between the thick, damask curtains while the rest of the younger cousins followed.

Aunts, uncles, sisters, and older cousins exclaimed their dismay as the children barged around everyone, racing about the room as though it were a horse track rather than the elegant drawing room of a most expensive London house. Several dogs in the room began barking.

Rosamunde closed her eyes briefly. These gatherings at Westham happened at least every Saturday. It was rare the house was ever occupied by just her parents and her sister. And as much as she adored her family, sometimes she suspected it would be nice to have a little peace.

Or would it?

No. Maybe something, well, different. Something other than tea with her aunts and discussions of her future. Something more than watching her cousins knock over the Wedgewood vase every time they visited. Something different to eating shortbread and sipping tea.

She glanced to the open doorway and silently waited. One day, it would happen, she was certain. That something different and exciting would occur. A pirate would charge through the door, thrust his finger at her, and say, *yes, this is it. Yer coming on an adventure with me, lassie.*

She scowled. No, that wasn't right. Pirates said *me heartie*. She had been thinking of the braw Scotsman who would demand she come to his castle in the Highlands immediately and help him see off a siege of thousands of Englishmen.

Today, though, she rather fancied an adventure on the high seas. She could swab decks as well as the next man, she reckoned, and she was an excellent swimmer, not to mention she could handle a sword. Her pirate would be handsome, of course, with a full set of white teeth and smelling like fresh sea air and soap. His eyes would be blue like the tropical seas she had heard tale of and his hair a sort of sandy color, bleached by the sun. Not to mention, he would be terribly strong and able to sweep her up in his arms or hold her fast to the deck when a storm hit.

Rosamunde sighed when the doorway remained empty and no handsome man with strong arms and sun-kissed hair stepped through.

"Rosamunde, are you daydreaming again?" her mother asked, leaning over from the sofa.

"No."

"You were."

"I was merely thinking, Mama."

Her mother tutted. "Daydreaming. You really should cease that. It is unbecoming of a lady, especially in good company."

Rosamunde did not mention that her family were well used to her flights of fancy and were far too preoccupied with discussing her future to care whether she was paying attention or not.

"You are far too like Uncle Albert," muttered Aunt Janey. "We are lucky she's pretty or else she would still be a spinster with her nose always stuck in a book or her head in the clouds."

Rosamunde resisted rolling her eyes. Her aunts were not bad people but none of them were any good at holding their tongues. It was rather a family trait unfortunately. If one of them thought it, they usually said it aloud. Even she did it at times.

"Has anyone heard from Uncle Albert?" asked her mother.

Aunt Janey shook her head. "No, but you know what he is like. He is probably hiking up Scarfell or has made friends with some reclusive lord."

Rosamunde scowled. "No one has seen him this week?"

Mama shrugged. "Albert often vanishes for a period of time, you know that."

"Yes, but it has been three months." Rosamunde pushed her glasses up her nose. "That is a long absence, even for him."

Aunt Petunia waved a hand. "He has always been his own man."

And Rosamunde envied that. Of all her family members, Uncle Albert was the one she most understood. He didn't always attend the weekly gatherings and more often than not, would be gallivanting about the country or frequenting his gentlemen's club then bringing back tales of fistfights and daring wagers. She suspected he was the only one who understood her too. He had that same desire to see more, do more. He loved to travel around the country and always brought her back a little something.

Last time it had been a sharp-shaped rock from Cumbria that he claimed was some ancient tool used by humans thousands of years ago. She had heard of such discoveries but could not figure out if hers was the genuine thing. But it didn't matter. She treasured her collection of worldly belongings, regardless. After all, it was the story behind them that created the value rather than the objects themselves.

"Do you think we should hire someone to find him?" Rosamunde suggested. "It has been quite a while since we saw him last."

Her mother shook her head. "He will return soon enough, with lots of grand tales no doubt."

"But he could be hurt," Rosamunde protested. "Or in some sort of trouble. What if someone has—I don't know—kidnapped him?"

Mama laughed. "Why on Earth would someone want to kidnap Uncle Albert?" She tapped Rosamunde's knee. "Rosie, you really must cease with your imaginings. We shall never find you another husband if you continue to behave like a child."

Rosamunde blew out a breath, not least because she loathed being called Rosie. It reminded her of being a child and getting told she could not do the things boys could do.

Oh no, Rosie, little girls do not go swimming in the lake.

No, Rosie, young ladies cannot learn to fence.

Absolutely not, Rosie, women your age should not smoke or drink liquor.

Pfft. She didn't see why. She could fence with the best of them, having learned by copying her Uncle Frederick when he practiced. She could smoke too but actually it was not very pleasant and she had spent much of the night coughing after trying a cigar. She was a strong swimmer and she did not wrinkle her nose when she drank liquor like many young ladies. She could do all those things, and she did so with relish.

At least she would, if her family would let her.

But, no, it looked as though she would be sitting here for the rest of her days whilst married to another old man.

She eyed the open doorway hopefully. If there was ever a time for Laird Macfarlane to come and rescue her, it was now. She would even accept Mr. Hunter, the intriguing archaeologist who just desperately needed her help in Egypt to decipher the hieroglyphs of a long lost, cursed tomb.

Her younger cousins hastened out of the room in a long line, breaking her reverie. She sighed. No laird or adventurer was coming, which meant she would have to figure out a way of having an adventure herself. The trouble was, she hardly knew where to start. None of her friends had the same desires and most were married or having children. If only Uncle Albert were here. He could surely give some fine advice.

"Oh, Rosamunde," said Aunt Petunia, "will you come with me to Lady Lockwood's tomorrow? I was meant to go with Mabel but as you know, she is too busy with wedding preparations and everyone wants to visit with her now that she is engaged."

Well, it was not an adventure, but she always liked visiting Lady Lockwood. The rather forthright woman had a lovely old house in the country and several dogs. Rosamunde somewhat envied her isolated state.

There were no aunts nagging Lady Lockwood about remarrying or cousins racing around the hallway. It was just her and her dogs, and a house that surely housed several ghosts and secret corridors. Sometimes when Rosamunde visited, she pressed her fingers to the walls in the hopes of finding secret doorways, but she had yet to find any.

"I'd be happy to accompany you, Aunt."

No great adventure would be occurring tomorrow but at least she would get to travel a little and escape the discussion of her next marriage.

"I hear Lord Woolhurst will be visiting," her mother said in an urgent whisper. "You should catch his eye. He would make you a fine husband."

Rosamunde suppressed a groan.

Chapter Two

Marcus Russell adjusted the scarf across his nose and clasped the pistol tight. His hand remained steady, his breaths slow and calm. He clasped the reins of his horse and peered down the lane.

"Any time soon," he murmured to the horse.

So long as there were no animals this time, the kidnapping should go smoothly.

So long as there were no damn cats. That last ugly, horrible thing had clawed the inside of the carriage and left little pulls in the fabric. He was hardly carriage-proud—the vehicle was used to carry women to and from their hideout and it showed plenty of wear and tear, but he didn't need anymore blasted animals clawing up the inside of it.

He snorted to himself. Miss Beaumont had been the first and only woman to bring a cat, and he doubted any other woman would think to bring their ugly pet with them on a 'kidnapping'.

Of course, she wasn't Miss Beaumont anymore and Russell found it rather amusing to see Nash head-over-boots in love with the interesting woman, even if she did have the most hideous cat in the world.

The rattle of carriage wheels on the dry road made his heart give a little jump. He took a breath and glanced down the road. A closed carriage, shining glossy black under the summer sun with gold trim. Most certainly his prey.

"Come on, Junior," he urged the horse forward into the middle of the road. "Time for action."

Holding the pistol straight out, he kept his stance firm. Junior had enacted plenty of these kidnappings before and remained perfectly still. The carriage drew to a halt and the driver scrambled to climb from the seat, but Russell focused his weapon upon him.

"Stay where you are or I shall shoot," he ordered firmly.

The driver nodded, his hands trembling around his loose grip on the reins. Russell moved around the carriage and glanced through the window to find two women clutched together. He eyed the younger one. Dark-haired and attractive, just as Guy had described.

Very attractive. Russell clenched his jaw. Miss Heston looked a little older than the one and twenty-year-old he had expected but Guy had certainly downplayed her looks. She peered at him with wide eyes then murmured something to her older companion.

Before he pulled open the door, the woman shoved it and pushed her head out, meeting his gaze head on. Without the hazy glass between them, he had a full view of generous lips, a slightly stubborn chin, and wire-framed spectacles that emphasized a warm, nutty gaze. However, there was nothing warm about the way she looked at him.

He let a brow rise. The woman was an excellent actress.

"Come with me." He kept his voice low, just in case her companion did not know of their arrangement.

"Like hell!"

He blinked at the blasphemy. As far as he knew, the woman they were kidnapping was gently bred and trying to escape the persistent overtures of a gentleman. Still, perhaps she was trying to play the role of helpless victim for her companion's benefit.

Very well. She wasn't the only one who could act. He had not read every one of Shakespeare's plays for no reason. "Come with me or I shall shoot," he warned her, keeping his tones low and aggressive.

Miss Heston scanned the length of him and lifted her chin. "If it is money you want, I am quite wealthy." She put her hand to a broach at the neckline of her crimson gown.

Russell's gaze tracked the movement, unintentionally. He only realized her cleavage had caught his attention when she began to undo the gold and ruby broach. He swiftly looked away and blinked, feeling as though the image of soft skin, dark shadows, and generous curves might well be burned into his mind. Every time he blinked from now on, he suspected he would see the image there again.

Fool. He'd seen many a cleavage in his lifetime. A little glimpse of what appeared to be a most excellent cleavage wouldn't be the undoing of him. If he could survive on the streets and forge a life for himself from nothing, he could most certainly rid himself of the image of the faintest glimpse of not even a third of a breast.

Or two.

Damn it. He blinked a few more times then scowled when she handed over the broach.

"Here, this is worth far more than you could get for me from ransom."

He ignored it, letting his frown deepen. Why the devil was she dragging this out? Much longer and the driver might get the courage to fight him or someone would happen along and Russell could end up getting shot.

"If that isn't enough..." She hitched up her skirt, revealing pale stocking that encased a shapely leg.

Well, the cleavage image no longer bothered him so that was something. He swallowed hard and frowned as she revealed the lacy edge of her stocking and the garter holding them up. Her hand moved slowly to the band, and she tugged out a bank note.

Why the hell did this woman keep banknotes in her stockings?

She reached for the note then curled her fingers around something else—a jeweled handle.

A bloody penknife.

She grabbed it swiftly and thrust it outward. Russell dodged back, the blade skimming past his stomach and catching briefly on the fabric.

"Bloody hell, woman." He grabbed her wrist. This play-acting was becoming far too dangerous. This needed to end now.

She squealed and the blade dropped from her grip. He used the hold on her wrist to pull her toward him then latched an arm about her waist. The woman inside the carriage screamed and grabbed for Miss Heston's skirts but Russell tore his captive away easily and hauled her over the saddle, her legs kicking against frothy skirts and petticoats, her fists bashing against his thigh. He glanced down at the woman sprawled across his lap and shook his head.

No cats this time. Instead he had a she-beast who seemed likely to shred *him* to ribbons with her claws.

THE GROUND RUSHED past her so fast, Rosamunde grew dizzy. The man's thighs pressed hard into her stomach and she imagined if she were not being jostled about so aggressively, she might find the desire to vomit.

If only she could. Maybe then her kidnapper would fling her away in disgust.

He moved fast and she could scarcely breathe, let alone fight her way from the saddle. Even if she did, she would likely end up trampled. Far better to live and fight another day. If only she had not dropped her knife. She could have hurt the blaggard and bought them enough time to run away.

Or not. The man was an excellent horseman and would likely have caught up with them. Curses, she should have tried to fit a bigger knife in her garter.

He slowed the pace, and she gulped down breaths. "Put me down," she managed to gasp.

The world tilted and for a moment, she thought he might have changed his mind, but she found herself flung into the interior of a dark, creaky carriage, her bottom landing hard on the floor.

The door slammed shut, and he thrust a finger at her. "Stay," he ordered, his words slightly muffled by the glass.

She frowned. *Stay.* What sort of a kidnapper was he that he expected her to simply stay? She eased herself up from the floor with a hand to the velvet seats and wrinkled her nose. The interior smelled of perfume. Just how many women had this man kidnapped?

Rosamunde pressed a hand to her bruised ribs and winced. The brute likely did it all the time. She recognized fine clothing and fabric when she saw it. No doubt all his poor victims funded quite the luxurious lifestyle.

She watched her kidnapper through the window, keeping an eye on the pistol in his hand. He could have shot her earlier, but she took a gamble on his greed. Would he shoot her now, though? Oddly, the man had strangely soft blue eyes—not the eyes of a cold murderer, but if she knew anything from the many, many books she had read, one should never judge a man by appearance and especially not by a pair of intriguing eyes. He might well shoot her if she tried to escape too soon.

He hitched up the horse next to another. She had to admit, when she heard of highwaymen, this was not what she pictured. Of course all of them were dark and charming with rakish smiles and a flattering tongue. She couldn't see if he had a rakish smile underneath the scarf, but she had seen no hint of amusement or flirtation around his eyes.

Nor had she imagined a kidnapper might have a carriage. She twisted around. Set out with cushions and a blanket, nonetheless. Maybe he wouldn't shoot her.

The carriage jolted forward, and she fell back onto the seat. She pushed herself up and readjusted her glasses. This was all her fault. She should not have been dreaming of adventure. Perhaps God was playing a perverse trick on her and giving her what she had been craving.

"Not this sort of adventure," she muttered to the ceiling of the vehicle.

Admittedly, she had thought of being taken away by many a man but certainly not involuntarily.

Drawing in a breath, Rosamunde eyed the passing scenery. They moved swiftly, aided by the dry roads. If it was autumn or winter, he would have a much harder time moving so swiftly. It seemed as though everything was in his favor.

Except, she would not go easily. No doubt he was used to women who would swoon at the mere sight of a gun. Well, she knew how to shoot thanks to Uncle Albert giving her secret lessons and she had never swooned in her life. Maybe this was not God playing a trick on her but giving her a chance to prove herself. She would get out of this situation alive and without this wretch of a man getting any coin from her family.

She shoved open the door and watched the ground pass by in a blur. It would hurt, there was no doubt about that. Her main problem would be jumping far enough so that she did not get run over by the carriage wheel. Her useless gown would not help matters much.

Rosamunde eased off her slippers and flung them aside. As tempted as she was to fling them out of the carriage so she could find them later should she need to walk far, it might draw his attention so she would have to walk barefoot. Then she bunched up her skirts as best as she could, holding them in one arm while she gripped the edge of the door with the other.

The grassy verge whipped by. If she could just land carefully enough, she could miss the hard road and be somewhat cushioned by the grass. She had heard that one should relax when one fell to prevent breaking bones, but she was not certain she had it in her. Every muscle felt tight already. The sound of the wheels rattling and the creaking of the vehicle competed with the heavy thud of her heart in her ears.

"Well, I have to try."

It was jump or put her fate in her kidnapper's hands and he was no beautiful pirate or braw Scotsman. Just a regular criminal with hauntingly blue eyes.

She uttered up the briefest prayer, clutched her skirts tightly, and jumped.

Chapter Three

"Damn it."

Russell glanced over his shoulder and hauled the carriage to a halt. He thought he'd been imagining it when he heard the thud and the carriage door slamming hard against the side of the vehicle. Nothing about capturing Miss Heston felt normal and he was simply on edge.

But no.

The bloody woman had fallen from the carriage.

Or most likely jumped.

He leapt down from the driver's seat and sprinted back down the road. He cursed under his breath—repeatedly. What the bloody hell was wrong with her? First, all the play-acting, then nearly cutting him. Guy, the leader of their kidnap club, never told him he was kidnapping a madwoman.

He cursed some more when he spied her crumpled form on the side of the road. Great. Now he had an injured madwoman to deal with.

Or worse.

He kneeled next to the spread of petticoats and crumpled fabric and touched the curve of her neck. A pulse beat strongly.

Not dead. One thing to be grateful for, he supposed.

Her hat was long gone, a splash of straw tucked in a tree some distance away. Well, he had no plans to retrieve that. The woman deserved to lose it as far as he was concerned. Behind her glasses, her eyes remained closed, dark lashes splayed against pale skin and the occasional freckle dashed across her nose.

He leaned in. If this was a trick, she was damned good at pretending. He ran his gaze down her, noting the rise and fall of her breasts and the gentle curl of her fingers. He'd met many a women who enjoyed playing pretend in his lifetime. Mostly, they were trying to get into his pocketbook. But why this one wished to make this kidnapping far too real, he could not fathom. Anyone would think she didn't want to be kidnapped.

At least it didn't look like anything was broken. All limbs were at the right angles and when he pushed a hand under the mesh of dark hair, his fingers came away clean. She'd likely received a good knock to the head but nothing a little rest would not cure.

Or she'd awaken even more crazed.

When this was over, he was demanding danger pay, for certain. Facing down armed drivers and hired brutes was far less dangerous than this woman.

Sighing, Russell eased an arm under her shoulders and legs. He braced himself for some tirade from the madwoman or perhaps another knife, stashed away in her bodice, only to be revealed as she came alive and slashed at him, but she remained limp.

He stashed her in the carriage, laying her out on the seat. He paused a moment.

God damn, bloody hell, hellfire and brimstone. Who cared if she was pretty? He'd kidnapped pretty women before. Beautiful ones, even. All that mattered was he got her to Nash and then he could wipe his hands of the crazed creature.

Stomping back to the front of the carriage, he climbed up to the driver's seat and urged the two horses on. He kept the pace slower, not daring to jostle her any farther. A traveler's inn was only a mile or so up the road, so he'd stop there until she woke up. With any luck, she'd be suffering a mild headache and nothing more and then they could be on their way.

And he'd be rid of her.

Once he arrived at the inn, he drove through the gates into the carriage entrance and eased open the door. Miss Heston remained knocked senseless, a curled-up bundle of silk and lace. He scooped her up once more and stared down the stable hand who gawped at him. Moving swiftly, he barged through the doorway and stopped in the taproom. "A room. With haste. My, uh, wife is injured."

Wide-eyed, the chap behind the bar nodded and handed over a key. "Y-you'll have to sign in."

"Later." The innkeeper didn't argue with him or try to stop him as Russell navigated the stairs to the room and fought to get the door open through the masses of fabric that curled around his arms and tickled his nose. "You could have worn a simpler dress," he muttered. What sort of a woman wore silk and petticoats and fine broaches to a kidnapping?

Oh, yes, a mad one, remember?

He laid her on the bed and spread out her skirts. He paused. Her breaths were steady, and she showed no signs of being in pain. But he should probably check properly for injuries.

That meant touching her, though.

He smirked at himself. He'd touched plenty of women. Hell, he was hardly a rake like Nash had been before settling down, but he was no trembling virgin either. Running his hands over a little silk to ascertain she was well hardly counted as being sordid.

He glanced down at his hand. "You can stop that," he ordered the limb when he saw the slight quiver.

Not a virgin, but still trembling, apparently. What a fool.

Shaking his head, he started at the top of her, running his hands down each arm, feeling for breaks or swelling.

Damn it, he should have started from the bottom. Then he wouldn't be trying to steal a look down the inviting shadows. Madwoman or not, he should certainly not be using this opportunity to lust over her.

No, not lust. He didn't do lust. He occasionally had brief relationships with women to satisfy his basic needs, but he would never go so far as to say he lusted over a woman. He appreciated them—occasionally—and that was that. Entanglements were most certainly not for him.

He forced his gaze onto the expensive fabric of her gown while he felt down her ribs, following the curve of a shapely waist, down to hips that sat perfectly in his hands.

Not. Bloody. Lust.

It had been a while, that was all.

When he got down to her legs, his difficulty was no longer looking down, but up. He'd seen that flash of thigh above her garter and spotted the shapely length of her legs when she'd waved that knife at him and even then, he'd been intrigued. Now she was all spread out for the taking, and trying to keep his gaze from darting up to the darkness between her thighs made his chest tight.

He curled a hand around an ankle. No breaks here. He moved his hand up to her calf. Nor there. She stirred and released a slight moan when he moved his hand up.

Good Lord. She almost sounded as though she enjoyed his touch.

He snatched his hand back swiftly. If she was waking, she could tell him if she hurt anywhere. He was no gently bred man but even he had little desire to touch a woman without her permission.

Nor did he want to touch her with it, he reminded himself.

The Kidnap Club made a rule. They did not touch the women they took.

Well, Nash touched the last one and had ended up married to her.

Russell sure as hell wasn't going to let that happen. He did not do marriage. He certainly did not do love.

And he was not, under any circumstances, going to lust over this woman.

ROSEMUNDE SMILED. IT had been a while since she'd dreamed of a new hero. This one had dark, tousled hair—a little long perhaps but she rather liked it that length—and piercing blue eyes. Her imagination was really quite spectacular, even if she did say so herself. Who would have thought she could make up a little scar on the forehead of her hero and another pale line just by his ear? Or the stubble sprouting on his chin. In fact, this had to be about the most accurate daydream she had enjoyed for a long time.

She stretched and winced. Goodness, her head hurt. What on Earth—

Oh.

The carriage.

The fall from the carriage.

The rush of ground and a hard *thwack* then darkness.

Oh.

Her kidnapper! She blinked a few times and fixed her gaze upon the man.

The man who currently straddled her.

Good God, he had kidnapped her to ravish her!

"Let me go," she demanded breathlessly. His weight practically crushed her, pinning her down to the bed of some unknown place. "Let. Me. Go," she insisted, wriggling against him.

"Keep still, damn it, you hit your head."

She opened her mouth then shut it. Why should he care if she hit her head if he had simply taken her to ravish her?

Rosamunde pushed against a firm chest. "You may take my body, but you will never possess my soul."

"What?"

When he failed to budge, she tried to swipe at him, her nails extended, but he grabbed her hand and pinned it onto the bed by her head. She tried with the other hand, but he did the same, keeping her pinned and vulnerable against the mattress.

Her heart pounded hard, her breaths coming fast. It didn't matter if he was handsome, didn't matter if his brute strength made something deep inside her twinge. This was not a fantasy, she reminded herself. He would not be gentle with her or make love to her then declare he must have her help him on his quest to find a lost treasure in South America.

Here was a criminal. A blackguard. The scourge of society. And it did not matter if he smelled like soap and a little ginger, nor should she let it confuse her that his generous lips appeared rather kissable or that she was extremely aware of his muscles straining the seams of his jacket.

"Leave me be," she uttered, wriggling her hips while trying to free her legs from the confines of her skirts. If she could just lift a knee, she could connect with his ballocks and he'd go down, surely? She'd heard men found it quite excruciating to be struck there and had imagined using such a method when she had to go and rescue her pirate or help the archaeologist escape the band of ruffians who wished to steal the antiquities.

"Will you keep still?" He grunted. "You hit your head, woman. You need to stay still."

"So you can take advantage of me? I think not."

"I have no desire to take advantage of you," he muttered but a flash of something in his gaze made her heart jolt.

"You're lying. I can tell. I know when people are lying."

"I am not damn well lying," he said through a clenched jaw. "Now keep still."

"No. Never. I shall never be still. I shall fight and fight until my last breath." She twisted and thrashed until she could scarcely breathe against his weight and the tightness of her stays. She paused and gulped down a breath. "You haven't won. I merely need to rest."

What a silly thing to admit to her kidnapper.

"Yes, you bloody well do." He kept his hands pinned around her wrists, his weight atop her, but he eased his grip slightly.

She swallowed when she met his gaze. His eyes darkened and the air around her felt thick, as though the room had suddenly filled with water and she could not breathe nor move. In her fantasies, her heroes tended to have rather vague features. There was nothing vague about this man. His face was an arrangement of hard angles—his eyebrows fierce slashes upon a furrowed brow. The only softness that existed were those lips. Lips that she could not stop herself from looking at.

When she met his gaze again, she saw he was doing the same. His gaze darted down to her mouth then back up.

God Lord, surely she wasn't going to let her kidnapper kiss her?

He lowered marginally so that she felt the warmth of his breath. She frowned. It smelled like mint. What sort a kidnapper chewed mint leaves before ravishing his captive?

She lifted her chin. They were mere inches apart. If she closed her eyes, he might do it.

No. No, no, no. This was no fantasy. This was dangerous and real.

She wrenched her hands suddenly from his grip and shoved him back. Grappling with her skirts, she tried to squeeze out from underneath him, but he pinned her again, this time forcing his hand up her skirts. She scrunched her eyes shut. "You'll never possess my soul," she murmured.

"What is it?" he said. "Another knife? Another bloody weapon concealed in your garter?"

She opened her eyes and scowled. He fumbled around her garters, half buried in her skirts.

"There's no more knives," she admitted.

He shoved down her dress and blew out a ragged breath. "Good. I didn't sign up to this to be stabbed, Miss Heston, no matter how much you enjoy this play-acting."

Rosamunde pushed up onto her elbows. "Miss Heston."

"Keep still," he ordered. "You really should not be moving in your condition."

"But I'm not Miss Heston." She shook her head and winced when a dull pain thudded through her head. "Do you not see?"

He eased back from her, moved off the bed, and folded his arms. "See what?"

"You have kidnapped the wrong woman!"

Chapter Four

"If this is part of your game..."

"What sort of a game would I be playing?" She shoved her skirts down and sat upright then adjusted her spectacles. "What sort of game did *you* think we were playing? Because I must tell you, sir, I did not find it amusing."

Russell scraped a hand over his face. The wrong woman. He had the wrong damned woman. Unless, she really was insane, and she thought it would be funny to trick him. He eyed the rosy-cheeked woman and curled a hand as he briefly recalled the feel of soft thigh on his fingertips.

Slightly older than he had expected her to be. *Check.*

Fought him like a damned wolf. *Check.*

Flung herself out of a carriage with little regard for her own life. *Check.*

Oh, yes, don't forget she had nearly stabbed him.

Which meant, the little hellcat had every intention of hurting him and it hadn't been part of her act.

He narrowed his gaze at her. "Who exactly are you?"

She drew up her chin. "Lady Rosamunde Stanley, Dowager Viscountess Rothmere."

Bloody hell. Bugger it all. Damn him to hell. "Fu—" He caught himself. "Fudge," he muttered.

"I think the first word was more correct." She clambered up from the bed and straightened the bodice of her gown.

Now that she stood upright, he had a better view of her figure. When she wasn't flinging knives at him or throwing herself

26

to the ground, she carried herself like a viscountess—her shoulders proud, her generous breasts thrust outward. He couldn't resist skimming his gaze down her person and noting the curve of her waist and hips. Though the petticoats disguised her legs and rear, he had a good idea of what laid underneath them now.

A far too clear and accurate idea.

He'd had his damned hands thrust up the skirts of the wrong woman. He'd been laid on top of her, his body lined up just so with hers. He'd been able to feel everything.

Russell drew in a heated breath between his teeth. He was like a camel. He could go without female company for months, even years. There had certainly been a lack of decent female company when he'd been fighting in France and he'd survived. So why the hell did he feel as though he were a man in the middle of a desert, and she was the only oasis?

"Who precisely are you? And what did you want with my cousin?"

"Cousin?"

"Miss Heston. She's my cousin."

He cursed. Fully this time. Then he grimaced. "Forgive me, my lady."

She tilted her head. "Considering you are a kidnapper, I should rather think you do not care much for my forgiveness." She took a few steps forward and peered up at him.

He met her gaze, maintaining a cool expression, despite feeling as though she had lit a fire at the bottom of his feet. This was one giant mess and even his quick mind could not chase a way to fix this.

"Why are you not threatening me? Or tying me down or something?"

He sighed. "Because I did not intend your cousin harm nor do I intend the same for you."

"Then...I may go?"

"I suppose."

What else was he going to do? Keep her locked here and force her to keep his movements a secret? Somehow persuade her that he had good intentions toward her cousin and actually, he had intended to help her?

He knew how he looked. Too tall, too rough. No amount of rich clothing could hide the fact he'd once been a gritty soldier and an orphan on the streets. Rough living had left its mark on his face, his accent, and his manners.

The Dowager Viscountess inched closer. She eyed him closely as though studying a painting and trying to see the individual brushstrokes. Well, there was no work of art here. Just a man making coin by helping women escape whatever fate befell them. Unfortunately for him, he had royally effed this up, and his role in The Kidnap Club would likely come to an end. After all, he couldn't pretend to be a kidnapper now someone had seen him.

"You're not a very good kidnapper, are you? Kidnapping the wrong person."

"Well, you weren't meant to be in that carriage. I can't be held responsible for her change of plans."

"That's true, actually. I took my cousin's place." She wrinkled her nose. "Why exactly were you intending to kidnap Mabel?"

He looked into her dark eyes. When she wasn't fighting him, he saw intelligence behind that gaze. She might be rich and probably entitled, but she was no fool. He could try to make up some story, but he couldn't fathom anything that might satisfy her.

"Because she wanted to be kidnapped."

Her lashes wavered a few times. "She wanted to be kidnapped?"

"Yes."

"But...why?"

"You would have to ask her that, but I believe it was something to do with a proposal."

She put a hand to her mouth. "Dear Lord, Mabel thought she was going to be forced to marry Mr. Dixon." She shook her head. "But Mr. Gosford proposed just yesterday, and she has been in love with him forever."

"That would have been useful to know," he muttered.

Lady Rothmere put hands to her hips. "So, forgive me if I seem confused but my head still hurts...my cousin *wanted* you to kidnap her, so she did not have to marry Mr. Dixon?"

"Indeed."

"But why would you do such a thing? And why all this trouble?"

He lifted a shoulder. "I'm paid to do it. Nothing more."

ROSEMUNDE DIDN'T BUY it. Maybe it was the romantic in her and she was being a fool but there was more to this story than a man simply paid to hide a woman away. Even her mind could not make such a thing up.

And she needed to know more.

She craned her neck to study the man. Admittedly, she had never been able to conjure such a man in her imagination, but he would certainly make a good pirate. He had a sort of hardened look behind his shockingly blue eyes and his disheveled hair combined with the long length of him added an air of mystery. Though she'd felt the strength behind his body, he was more long than broad, filling out his tailored clothes perfectly.

And he had a story.

She needed to hear it, so, so badly.

Her head throbbed a little and concern flickered behind his gaze when she put a hand to the back of her head. Sure enough, a sizeable egg was forming. She plucked out the pins from her disheveled mass of hair and finally tugged out the jeweled comb then flung them onto the table nearby.

"Where are we anyway?"

He took a moment to answer while she shook out her hair. He jolted as though he had been lost in thought. "An inn. I thought it prudent to ensure you were rested before we continued onward."

She moved over to the window that looked out onto a road. Would her aunt be looking for her? Worried out of her mind? Rosamunde needed to bring this adventure to a conclusion and ensure her family knew she was safe. But first she had to know more.

She twisted to face him. "When you say you are paid to kidnap people, at their behest, what exactly do you mean?"

He shoved his hands into his trouser pockets and glanced briefly at the wooden floor. "I am not certain I can tell you, my lady. Suffice to say, I had little desire to kidnap an unwilling woman today."

Now he had her really intrigued. Why the secrecy if her cousin wanted to be kidnapped?

"Mr., um, what did you say your name was?"

"I did not."

She lifted a brow.

"Russell. Marcus Russell."

"Mr. Russell, may I assume that you might wish to keep this incident quiet? That kidnapping young ladies is not something you wish to be known for?"

"You might assume that, yes."

"In which case, I want to know it all." She seated herself on the bed, laced her fingers in her lap, and leaned forward. "Every last detail."

He scowled.

"I do so love a story," she said.

She swore she heard him groan. Or maybe he uttered another *F* word under his breath. It was hard to tell.

"If you tell me, I shall keep this incident entirely quiet. I shall tell them I fought you off and you ran away, and I never saw a thing."

"You really think they would believe you fought me off?"

"Well, they would hardly think I simply sweet-talked you into letting me go. Also, I might well have another knife hidden in my garter."

"You most certainly do not," he growled.

Oh yes. He had done a thorough exploration of her person. Her cheeks heated when she considered just how far up her skirts his hands had gone.

"Why did you keep a penknife there anyway?"

"For precisely what happened today. Who knows when one might need to defend oneself?"

A dark brow lifted. "Have you had many occasions in which you have had to use it?"

"Actually, this was the first time." She waved a hand. "But it does not matter. I'm more interested in why you, Mr. Russell, play at kidnapping."

"Russell," he corrected. "No one calls me mister."

"In which case—and most especially because you kidnapped me today—I think you can call me Rosamunde. But, please, cease trying to be elusive."

"Trying? I am fairly certain I *am* elusive."

"Oh yes, you certainly have the air of it."

He blew out a breath. "You are not easily dissuaded, are you, my lady?"

"Rosamunde," she corrected. "And no."

"Very well." He shoved fingers through his hair, which explained why it was so disheveled. She'd wager that was quite a habit of his. "I am part of a group of men who assist women in escaping."

"Escaping?"

"Marriage, delicate situations...anything in which it is imperative they disappear, be it for a while or forever."

"Goodness."

It was a strange sort of a service, but she could imagine there was quite a need for it. She had been lucky never to have been trapped in some terrible situation, but she was not ignorant to the plight of many women of the gentry in difficult situations.

"So you kidnap these women? But why? Why not simply aid them in their escape? Sneak them out."

His lips quirked upward. "One would think that might be easier, yes. However, we found there was a need to keep the women innocent in their actions. That way, should they be discovered or need to return home, they were faultless."

"No doubt people would assume they were ruined too," she mused. "I imagine that might scare away a suitor or two."

"No doubt."

Interesting. She had always thought of Mabel as a little whimsical, but this was rather ingenious. She could have returned home, having been kidnapped and potentially ruined and waited for her true love to propose rather than be pressed into an engagement with a man she did not like. She almost wished such a service had been known to her when she married five years ago. Although her marriage had been entirely acceptable, if a little dull, a kidnapping would have been far more exciting.

"Let me ensure I fully understand. There is a group of you who do this?"

"Yes."

"And you are paid for this service?"

"Yes."

"Well, then, Russell, I should very much like to hire you."

Chapter Five

No. No, no, no, no. There was no chance he was kidnapping this woman. She had trouble written all over her. Even if she had not pulled a knife on him and flung herself from a moving carriage, he'd still see that in her. He wasn't fooled by the sweet pout of her mouth or the innocent freckles scattered across her nose.

"I'm not helping you escape your husband," he said.

"Oh, I'm still a widow."

He shouldn't feel relieved at that. In fact, it should aggravate him more. It meant he had not been thinking of a married woman's breasts or wondering how her soft thighs would feel against his lips.

"Well, I'm not helping you escape whatever it is you wish to escape."

No matter how much he really, really wanted to help.

For all the wrong reasons.

Russell didn't do relationships. Hell, he barely did friendships. Guy and Nash—the other members of The Kidnap Club—were about his only friends and he liked it that way. Even then, he hardly shared much with them. It wasn't in his nature and never would be. Nor did they expect anything more from him.

But, somehow, he knew this woman could take everything from a man. He wasn't fooled by the neat little glasses perched on her nose or the freckles dancing just underneath the wire frames. She had the looks, figure, and boldness to wrap herself around a man and suck him dry.

Not for him.

No, thank you.

Definitely not.

"I do not need to escape, actually."

"You're asking the wrong man."

She rose from the bed, cocked her head, and peered up at him. "You seem like exactly the right man."

How wrong she was. How wrong he was. For her, that was.

He was tempted. And Russell didn't do temptation. He'd learned the hard way that giving in to your heart's desires left a man open and vulnerable. Fine, so perhaps it was not his heart talking so much at present but there was a whole lot of desire wrapped up in this situation.

"I can pay you," she pressed.

"I don't need your money."

True, but he could not deny the word money always caught his attention. When one has been an orphan on the street, starving with an aching belly, it was hard to not let his ears perk up at the mention of coin. Even as he had accrued more money—more than he would ever need at this point—he constantly found himself lured in by the idea of more. That way there was no risk that he would ever, ever go hungry again.

"You do not even know what I want to hire you for."

"It doesn't matter." He raised a hand and ticked off a finger. "Firstly, I do not work alone and therefore cannot make decisions like this on my own."

She made a little scoffing noise. "You cow to other men? I doubt that."

She wasn't entirely wrong. While he would certainly not make decisions that might affect Guy or Nash alone, he could not claim that he hung on their every word either. Guy and Nash had been friends since college and were raised in the same social set. It wasn't hard for Russell to feel like an outsider, so he kept his independence from them and avoided sharing too much of his life with either of them.

"Secondly, we offer a very specific service." He ticked off another finger. "We're not just hired brutes."

Rosamunde reached out and folded down his fingers. He drew his hand back sharply. It was insanity that the mere touch of her hand—that was still gloved, no less—should make him feel anything, but it did. For Christ's sake, he'd just plunged his hands up her skirts. A touch of gloves was nothing.

"I do not need the assistance of hired brutes, or in fact, the rest of your club. I want you."

I want you.

He groaned inwardly. Perhaps he had been wrong about her. Maybe the glasses and freckles were a true reflection of her, and she had no idea what she did to a man.

I want you.

Somehow, he knew, even after he'd returned her home and assured himself, he would never set eyes on Lady Rosamunde Stanley again, that those words would haunt him at night.

It was no good. He needed out of this situation. And fast.

"Lady Rothmere."

"Rosamunde."

He sighed. "Rosamunde, I can only apologize for the misunderstanding today, but I cannot offer you help. All I can do is return you safely home to your family."

"But really you owe me."

He arched a brow. "I thought you could pay."

"I can. Most generously. And I still will." Her lips curved. "But you scared me today, Russell. I thought I was going to be kidnapped and...and ravished!"

He shoved a hand through his hair. He'd been right. The glasses and freckles were false. Underneath them, was a bright and manipulative mind.

"I should think," she continued, "that you might feel a little honor bound to offer me assistance."

"Well, there you are wrong. I'm a kidnapper. I have no honor."

"You kidnap women to help them. That sounds honorable to me."

"No," he said again.

He helped for the money. Plain and simple. When the Earl of Henleigh had approached him, he'd been looking for something new, some more interesting way to earn, so he'd leapt at the chance. Investing in stocks and businesses and speculations had grown dull, and frankly too easy. It always seemed ridiculous to him how easy it was to make money when one had vast sums of it. How was the average man meant to pull himself up out of the dirt when the richest ones were hoarding it all? He'd been one of the few lucky ones.

"I'm very rich. An heiress, actually," she persisted. "My family is wealthy, and my husband left me with a sizeable income."

"Lucky you."

"My point is, I cannot only pay you generously but I can ensure this kidnapping is never talked of again and you suffer no...unwanted consequences from this misunderstanding."

He stared down at her and made a sound in the back of his throat. "Are you threatening me?"

IT SEEMED RIDICULOUS threatening this coarse man who towered over her. Insane to even say such a thing when he had her alone and technically kidnapped. But she could not stop herself. Here was her chance. He could help her track down Uncle Albert and, well, she might even enjoy a little adventure doing it.

The fact was, no one thought anything of Uncle Albert's disappearance. Even today, Aunt Petunia dismissed Rosamunde's fears for him, waving her worries away as though they were one of her usual flights of fancy. Yes, she was prone to being far too imaginative, but he had been gone too long, and it would at least be prudent to try to track him down.

She swallowed and met his gaze. "Yes, I suppose I am."

She forced herself to remain still, even while a little tremble threatened to shoot from head to toe. She could not say if it was because she had never threatened a man before, or because he towered over her and she was mightily aware they were in a room alone, or maybe because she kept recalling how firm his body had been atop hers.

Perhaps a combination of them all.

He blew out a breath and shook his head. "I can't help you."

"You do not even know what I want to hire you for!"

"It does not matter. I can't help you."

"Even if I threaten to expose you?"

He eyed her. "I don't think you would."

Rosamunde lifted her shoulders. "You do not know me."

He pressed his lips together. "I know you. I know plenty of women like you. You are rich, spoiled, have led an easy life. You think you can get whatever you wish. Well, Lady Rothmere, you cannot have me."

But she wanted him.

Oh. Goodness. Not in that manner, she reminded herself. She hardly knew the man and was not the sort to take lovers. Her one and only experience of men had been with her late-husband and it had certainly not lived up to any fantasy. She didn't think any man could if she was honest.

So she had remained relatively innocent for a once-married woman. It felt a little silly sometimes. Almost childish to be a grown woman of twenty-five with such little experience but even if a man flirted with her, she hardly knew how to respond. One of the unfortunate side effects of being married at eighteen meant she had minimal experience with the opposite sex.

She did understand a few things about this man, though. He was not like any of the *ton*. And that intrigued her to no end.

"Mr. Russell, please hear me out." She lifted a hand before he could reply. "You are a kidnapper by trade. Or whatever you wish to call it. And I have someone who I believe may have been kidnapped. I should very much like to pay for your expertise."

"I'm not interested."

"My Uncle Albert," she continued, ignoring him, "has been missing for several months. Usually, he returns home by now, but I fear something has happened to him. Could it not be that he has been taken by someone?"

"Your uncle vanishes a lot?"

"He does, unfortunately." She wrinkled her nose. "He is a little...eccentric."

"So you wish me to chase down a man you think is kidnapped but often goes missing so is, in actual fact, probably not kidnapped at all?"

She knew it sounded paranoid, but he didn't have to be so rude about it. Folding her arms across her chest, she tried not to pout. "I know my uncle and I know he would not be gone this long without at least a letter."

"As I said, I cannot help. I don't know what sort of flights of fancy—"

"This is no flight of fancy." She unfolded her arms and jabbed a finger at his chest. "But you, sir, owe me. You kidnapped me, scared me half to death, injured me—"

"You injured yourself..."

"Made me lose my knife. Not to mention terrified my poor aunt." She jabbed again. "You. Owe. Me."

He rubbed the spot on his chest she'd prodded. "Lady Rothmere..."

"Rosamunde."

"Rosamunde, your uncle is a grown man and I am certain—"

"No. *I* am certain you are going to help me. I am not a fool, no matter what anyone thinks. You are not wrong that I am rich and have probably been spoiled. My life has been relatively sheltered. But I also know this—deep in my gut—my uncle needs help, and you are going to help me."

He eyed her for several moments while her heart pounded in her ears. He had to help her, he just had to.

"If you do not help me, I shall try to track him down myself," she added for good measure, though why she thought he might care for her welfare, she did not know.

Perhaps it was because underneath his rough manner she had seen a glimpse of an honorable man. Despite his protests, he had some honor. No man would risk his life to help women simply for money, surely?

His shoulders dropped a little. He pushed both hands through his hair and eyed her as though she were causing him great pain. "Fine," he finally said.

"Fine?"

"Fine, I shall help you. No doubt he is holed up somewhere in a club or something similar and your mind shall be put at ease within days."

Rosamunde couldn't resist the smile that burst across her lips. She flung her arms around his neck. "Oh, thank you, thank you, thank you!"

Russell pried her hands away from his neck and set her firmly back from him.

She bunched her hands at her side, her cheeks warm. She would have to behave much more professionally now she had hired him. This was important and it could be dangerous. Certainly not the time to hug her hired kidnapper.

"So where do we start?"

"First, I return you home. You can tell me all about your uncle on the way back. Then, I shall make some enquiries."

"And then?"

"Then I shall find you."

"Discreetly?"

His brow furrowed. "I take it your family does not have the same concerns about your uncle."

She shook her head.

He sighed heavily. "I will find you. Discreetly." His lip curled slightly. "Believe it or not, Lady Rothmere, I am excellent at discreet."

Chapter Six

"How the devil did you kidnap the wrong woman?"

Russell removed his hat, shoved a hand through his hair, and set it on the table in the busy inn. He peered around the empty inn before sitting opposite Guy. He leaned back in the chair and shrugged. "She matched the description. Not to mention she was riding in the correct carriage."

Guy shook his head. "Damn it, Russell, at this rate we'll have to quit the club."

Nash strode over to the table, three ales in hand, and dumped them onto the table. "He can hardly be blamed for the woman changing her mind."

Russell didn't need Nash to defend him, but he appreciated it nonetheless. "Look," he said to Guy, "I'm not happy about it either."

Especially considering he was now obliged to help a woman with pretty freckles and soft skin.

"But Lady Rothmere isn't going to say anything," he continued. "She understands the need for our service to remain secret and she would hardly reveal her cousin's intentions."

Guy blew out a breath and reached for the ale. "All this could have been avoided if Miss Heston's message had reached me in time."

"I didn't much enjoy kidnapping the wrong woman, to be certain."

"Are you certain about that?" Nash flashed a grin. "Lady Rothmere is a pretty thing if I recall rightly."

"You shouldn't even be thinking about who is pretty," Russell snapped. "Your wife is the only pretty thing you should be looking at."

"Grace would think it entirely logical that I should notice if someone is symmetrically proportionate and appealing," Nash said smugly.

Russell groaned. "You are sounding more and more like her every day."

"I know. I rather like it." He lifted his ale and took a drink.

Russell eyed Nash. The rakish lord had a way with women and his manner hadn't changed but their last kidnapee, Grace, had been a steadying influence on him. He'd never seen Nash so...fulfilled, he supposed. In some ways, he envied Nash that sense of peace, but it wasn't for him. He kept moving. Always. It was the only way he knew how to be. The idea of being steady made his feet twitch even just sitting here.

As for Guy, the man hadn't changed, even after their last adventure looking after Grace. The dark, brooding earl remained deadly serious about everything. Hell, he made Russell look practically chirpy. He understood the need for it at times. The earl was in sole charge of their operation and dedicated himself to helping women in need after aiding a cousin escape a vicious marriage. But, damn, the man could cease glowering for at least one moment.

"Well, I didn't enjoy it," Russell said.

Didn't enjoy the feel of her thighs. No, sir. Certainly not how her body was beneath him. Didn't like looking at her freckles and certainly didn't admire her gumption. Not one jot. Not at all. Most certainly not.

It was all quite inconvenient really.

"We're lucky she was able to return home and cover for you," Guy said. "If she had revealed you..."

"I know." Russell clasped the cool ale close. "I'd be out."

"We'd all be out," Guy corrected. "I don't blame you, Russell, but it would be too dangerous to continue."

"Oh so he messes up and he's fine to stay but I mess up and I almost get kicked out?" Nash leaned back in his chair and laced his fingers behind his head.

"You did not mess up, Nash. You bedded the woman we were meant to be helping," Russell pointed out.

"Yes, but can you blame me? Besides, I tried my best to resist her, but she can be damned persuasive."

Russell rolled his eyes. He did know that Nash had tried his hardest to resist her, but he'd seen early on that the man was falling for Grace. It had amused him at the time.

Now he was feeling even more sympathetic. He knew all too well how one could be living life normally only for it to be blown apart by a woman.

He lifted his drink and drained it, closing his eyes briefly while he let the warmth of alcohol simmer through him. No, his life wasn't blown apart. Nor would he let it be. He'd make a few inquiries, discover where Lady Rothmere's uncle was, and be on his way and forget he ever met her. He certainly would not do a Nash and wind up bedding her or worse...marrying her.

Not that he anticipated a lady of gentle breeding would want him. Beneath his fine clothes, he was nothing more than a bastard orphan who had become good at mimicking everything nobility did. Simply because he walked and talked a little like them did not mean he deserved a woman like her.

Nor did he want to. He'd learned a few things in life.

First, eat whenever there is food.

Second, never fall asleep on the streets.

Third, do not form attachments.

Fourth, do not form damn attachments.

Make that the fifth and sixth point too.

Make it the one vow that he would have tattooed onto his skin alongside the other ugly etchings from his boyhood. Engrave it on his headstone perhaps. No damn attachments.

They made a man vulnerable and weak, something he didn't wish to be ever again.

"So, what's next, Guy?" Nash asked, removing his hands from behind his head and leaning forward. "Grace is itching to help."

Guy shook his head. "Nothing. You go back to your wife and rebuilding your country pile and Russell does...whatever Russell does."

Nash leaned in, "Yes, what is it you do, Russell? I don't even know where you live."

"And that's the way it will stay," Russell said.

"Some friend you are," Nash muttered. "Won't even invite a chap over for a drink."

"Who says you're my friend?" Russell said with a slight grin.

"Ouch, you do wound me so." He pressed a hand to his chest.

Russell pushed his chair back and rose from the table. "Gentlemen, I have business to see to. Let me know if you need my aid. You know where to find me," he told Guy.

"What business?" Nash asked but Russell ignored him.

The less they knew about him, the better. The less anyone knew about him, the better. Including Lady Rothmere.

ROSAMUNDE DROPPED THE penknife with a clatter, wincing when it landed on the porcelain bowl. Her cousin Mabel barreled into her bedroom, her pink cheeks almost matching the bright hue of her gown. Rosamunde glanced at the bowl. At least it hadn't cracked on impact. She retrieved the knife and tucked it into her hand.

"What were you doing?" her cousin asked, peering at her hand.

"Oh, um just..." Pretending to fight off an attacker? No, that sounded ridiculous, even to her. "You know...reading letters." She gestured vaguely about the room, knowing there were no letters to be seen.

Mabel lifted the tiny dog she held in one arm onto the bed. Rosamunde didn't bother to say anything as the dog rolled about on the plush blanket. Much of her family owned dogs and it was not uncommon for visitors to bring theirs and let them roam around. There was scarcely a day when she did not find dog hairs upon her person. She loved them but sometimes she wouldn't mind just having one dog at a time.

"I wanted to make sure you were well," Mabel said, hastening toward her and lashing her arms about Rosamunde's waist.

Rosamunde peered down at her petite cousin and received a face full of feathers. She eased her cousin back before the feathers ended up thrust up her nose. "I am well," she assured her.

Mabel flung herself down on the bed and the dog climbed onto her lap, putting its paws up on her shoulder to lick her face. "I am so, so sorry," she said between licks. "If I had realized Mama was going to ask you to accompany her, I would have said something. Apparently, my letter to the men involved in this did not get there in time." She eased the dog away and frowned. "I paid the messenger generously too."

"You do not need to apologize. I am quite well."

More than well. She was...excited. It had been a week since she had been 'kidnapped', and she had yet to hear from Mr. Russell. However, it did not stop her anticipating him. She wondered if he was lurking somewhere, watching her perhaps, waiting to get in contact at the right moment. She kept trying to ensure she was alone but that was hard with her family.

She couldn't wait to see him again.

For her uncle, of course. No other reason. She knew virtually nothing of Mr. Russell and there was no sense in letting her imagination carry her away. Even if she did sometimes wonder what would have happened if she'd let him continue searching her person for the knife. Or if she had fought back and flipped him over and kissed him hard...

"You must have been terrified," Mabel cried. "I was nervous enough when I considered doing it and I knew what was happening." She sighed. "If only we did not look so alike."

"We do not look that much alike. It's only our dark hair."

"I suppose to a man we must do, though." Mabel leaned forward. "Was it very scary? Mama said you threatened him with a knife."

"It was sort of scary, but I didn't have much time to think about it."

Mabel grinned. "You are so brave, Rosie. I wish I could be the same. Of course, everyone thinks you fought him off and now they are determined you marry before you become too independent."

Rosamunde rolled her eyes. "Why they should see me fighting off a kidnapper as a bad thing, I do not know."

"Oh you know this family. They aren't happy unless there's a wedding happening." Mabel tilted her head. "Besides, do you not want to marry again? You've been widowed for over a year now and I know you found marriage to George terribly dull." She clapped her hands together. "What if you married one of Hugh's friends? Then we could spend even more time together."

Rosamunde closed her eyes briefly. She adored Mabel but there was a limit to the amount of time she wished to spend with her. Or with Hugh's friends. He was a lovely man but rather too sweet for her and she didn't expect his friends to be much different. She preferred men with a little roughness about them. Men who would argue with her and challenge her.

Men like Mr. Russell.

No, do not go down that path, Rosamunde.

"Well, we have your wedding to look forward to." She sank down onto the bed next to her cousin and the Pomeranian slunk over to Rosamunde's lap and nudged her hand with its wet nose. She gave in and rubbed the dog's head. "I am sorry that you thought you had to enlist the services of these men, though. You know you could have come to me."

"I know." Mabel glanced at her hands in her lap. "I was scared I was going to have to marry Mr. Dixon and it seemed as though Hugh would never propose. Then I heard rumors of these men from Lady Ellis and it just seemed the perfect answer. I could escape for a while and give Hugh time to miss me and then he would certainly propose by the time I returned."

Rosamunde winced. It wasn't the best reason to risk ruin and put her family in such distress but as much as she adored Mabel, her cousin did not always think things through thoroughly. If anyone had a reason to marry, it was Mabel. She almost needed someone to look after her.

Which was one of many reasons she did not wish to marry again. She could look after herself, thank you very much, and did not need a husband to do it for her.

All she needed now was to get much, much better at knife fighting.

Chapter Seven

Russell eyed her from afar, feeling oddly like an intruder. Which was ridiculous. Lady Rothmere perched on a bench overlooking the Serpentine River. Hardly some secretive spot. The paths flowed with people and carriages while children played on the grass, enjoying the warm summer weather. Yet he had this inkling Rosamunde wasn't watching the children or the various park goers.

She tilted her head to the sun and though he couldn't see her expression, he knew what she'd do. She'd have her eyes closed.

He knew this because this wasn't the first time he'd seen her in the park. Nor the second. For three days now, he'd come here after discovering she enjoyed visiting the park unaccompanied. Three days and he'd yet to approach her.

What went on behind those closed eyes, he did not know. Nor did he wish to know.

Nope. No. Definitely not. The less he knew about Lady Rosamunde Stanley, the better. He'd already done a little digging into her. She came from a large, wealthy family with a history of old money and plenty of clever marriages. Her father was the Marquess of Hopsbridge and she had several titled uncles by way of marriages. She would inherit a sizeable sum upon his death and the family had singlehandedly sucked up much of the wealth in the country.

The last thing he wanted to do was be involved with people like that. Those who took and took and took, leaving people like him to have to scrabble around for the scraps.

He clasped his hands behind his back and rocked onto his heels. Not that he had mere scraps these days. Even his wealth could compete with several members of the gentry, but he hadn't been simply born or married into it. He'd worked for every coin. He'd wheedled and plotted and rubbed his fingers raw. He'd lifted and hauled and slogged until every part of his body hurt. Thankfully, he didn't need to do much of that anymore, but he'd never be complacent. It only took one mistake for a man to lose it all and he could never let that happen.

He'd never let himself be poor again.

His gut itched. It had been doing that ever since kidnapping Rosamunde. He trusted his gut. It had been what helped him survive the cruel streets of London as a child. It had helped him escape the slums.

That one mistake could well be Lady Rothmere, it told him.

So today he'd finally march over to her and tell her in no uncertain terms that he would not help her. She would have to seek out her uncle on her own. After all, a man was entitled to his privacy. Simply because he'd been unable to find any trace of the man didn't mean much. Admittedly, Russell had a knack of finding people, and he'd been surprised none of his connections across the country knew anything of his whereabouts, but it still didn't mean anything.

He drew up his shoulders and marched over to the bench. No more waiting. He'd just tell her, *Sorry, Lady Rothmere, but I cannot help you. I'm a busy man and I'm certain your uncle shall turn up soon.*

He paused behind the bench and eyed her uptilted features, just visible above the brim of her hat. Her dark lashes fanned across pale cheeks, but he couldn't see the freckles thanks to the sun glinting off her glasses.

Fool.

Why did he even care to see them again? If anyone was to ask him what his favorite feature of a woman was, he might say her breasts or her waist. If he was feeling gentlemanly, he'd perhaps say her mouth or her eyes. Never before had he been interested in freckles.

Shaking his head at himself, he cleared his throat.

"Oh." Rosamunde jolted, straightened, and twisted on the bench to look at him. "*Oh.*"

"Lady Rothmere." He dipped his head briefly.

"I was beginning to think I would never hear from you." She rose from the bench and came to his side. "I've been waiting for news."

"Don't tell me you have been waiting here for me?"

Her cheeks reddened. "Well, you said that you would find me and I had little idea how or when, and I decided that you would want to meet with me on my own, in a busy place, so it seemed sensible to come to the park and ensure you could make contact."

"Sensible?" he repeated. As far as he could tell, there was not much sense in her plan at all.

"It is better to be seen here, surely? Where no one shall question why we might be together."

He scowled. "I am no titled gentleman, but I doubt anyone shall accuse me of trying to scandalize you, my lady. After all, no one knows who I am."

"No, that's not what I meant at all." She smiled up at him. "It's just that, if anything has happened to my uncle, we must be secretive, surely? I would not wish to give away the fact that I am hunting him to anyone nefarious." She whispered the last part, leaning in as though they were two spies discussing wartime secrets.

Russell straightened. At least she wasn't ashamed to be seen with him, a man of low birth and with no reputation—rake, gentleman, or otherwise.

"Well, the thing is, Lady Rothmere—"

"You really must call me Rosamunde," she insisted.

"Rosamunde," he corrected himself. "The thing is—"

"I really am so grateful you are going to help. You must tell me what you have discovered." She stilled and her brow creased. "Oh dear, you look as though you are going to tell me terrible news. Is it awful? Should I be sitting? Oh, poor Uncle Albert. He really was the best of men." She put a hand to her mouth and her eyes grew damp. "I do not know what I shall do without him."

He blew out a heavy breath. He couldn't fathom such an attachment to a mere uncle but then he'd never had an uncle to attach himself to. However, he still didn't want Rosamunde crying.

Damn it. All he had to say was a quick *sorry, I cannot help you*. How hard could that be?

A tear trickled down the side of her face.

God bloody damn it.

"I just wanted to tell you that I would help you," he said in a rush.

Inwardly, he groaned. What a fool he was.

ROSAMUNDE ALREADY KNEW Russell was not the sort of man who would appreciate a woman flinging her arms around his neck or beaming beatifically at him, so she forced herself to keep her expression neutral. After all, if she didn't prove herself to be entirely comfortable with what she imagined Russell's rather secretive world was, he would never let her help.

She'd been sitting on this bench for days, watching everyone stroll by, waiting for a signal from him that they could start their investigation. When he hadn't made contact yesterday, she started to give up hope. But now he was finally here, and they could begin searching for Uncle Albert.

"Thank you so much," she murmured. "I just knew you would be the answer to my troubles."

He gave her a sort of pained look, which she didn't quite understand.

"So, where do we start?"

"We?" he echoed. "No—"

"Oh." Rosamunde snatched his arm and hauled him behind a tree, pressing herself flat against the bark.

"What the—"

She grabbed his arm tighter and gave another tug, forcing him close to her. He stumbled a little, pressed his hand to the tree trunk, and peered down at her.

Swallowing, Rosamunde craned her neck to look up at him. A mere couple of inches separated them. She'd brought him in too close, but they had no choice. If she had not, they would have been spotted.

He peered down at her, a line of confusion creasing between his brows. She opened her mouth to explain but words vanished. She could not deny that a few of these days spent whiling away the hours on the bench had been occupied by her recalling when he'd pinned her to the bed. What would have happened if she'd reacted differently? If she had perhaps leaned up and brushed her lips across his mouth? If she had seduced her way out?

She sighed. But that had not happened, and she would do well to keep her thoughts where they belonged—on finding her uncle. Everyone always told her she let her imagination get away from her and she could not do that with Russell. It would be too dangerous.

Dangerous. The word repeated through her mind, bouncing around until it lodged there.

Lord, everything about Russell screamed danger. From the little scars to the stubble on his chin to the mussed hair that was so at odds with his refined clothing. Not to mention his strong, lean body. Oh yes, and she could not forget the darkness of his eyes that contrasted so captivatingly with the bright blue. His pupils were wide now, his expression unreadable.

The way he looked at her made her chest tight and her skin prickle beneath her gloves. She absolutely should most certainly not like the way he made her feel. Certainly shouldn't be excited by the danger. She knew how easily she could get swept away in her imaginings and now was not the time for this. She had to prove that she was right about her uncle, that he had not simply vanished off on an adventure, and it would not do to convince herself that Russell was like the pirate or the archaeologist and simply could not live or breathe without her.

She inhaled slowly. His gaze snapped from hers and jerked back.

"Why are we hiding?" he demanded.

"My Aunt Effie," she explained a little breathlessly. "I could not let her see me."

A dark brow rose. "You are a widow, are you not? And you already said no one would question why we are here together."

"Oh, it's not that." Rosamunde wrinkled her nose. "My family does not agree with me that Uncle Albert could be in danger. They think it, well, a flight of my imagination."

"I see."

"But it is not," she added quickly. "I always hear from him on his adventures. He never fails to write to me. Never," she said firmly.

"Indeed."

"You think it is my imagination too." She looked down to her feet.

"I tried to find some trace of him and failed." He tapped a finger to her chin, forcing her to look up at his unreadable expression. "It could be nothing but there should be some trace of the man."

"So you believe me?"

He whipped off his hat, thrust a hand through his hair, and nodded. "I believe you."

"And you *are* going to help me?"

"I said I would; did I not?"

"You did." She couldn't help but beam at him.

Russell's scowl deepened. She just knew he was the sort of man who wouldn't appreciate a woman grinning at him. She straightened and tugged her bodice back into place. Now was not the time for childish excitement or silly smiles. She needed to be sensible, focused. With any luck, there was a simple explanation for his disappearance, and they would track him down and she could be assured he was safe.

And Russell could go back to kidnapping women and doing whatever else the mysterious man did.

"So," she clapped her hands together, "what do we do first?"

"We talk to your family. Then *I* follow up any leads."

"No."

"No?"

"My family thinks I am a fool and I insist on helping."

He pinched the bridge of his nose. "Your family is the sensible place to start and I do not need your help, my lady. You hired me to help find your uncle and I'm quite capable of doing that myself."

"Yet, you found no leads in the time we've been apart."

"I made a few, quick enquiries. That is all."

"But I know my uncle better than anyone. My expertise will be invaluable."

He eyed her for a few moments then his shoulders dropped. "Fine. You can help. But you do as I say. No getting into trouble."

She widened her eyes. "Do you think there'll be trouble?"

"Of course not. But I still don't want you in any."

"I can look after myself."

"Rosamunde," he pressed through a tight jaw.

"I shall keep out of trouble."

"And we do need to speak with your family."

She grimaced. He likely wasn't wrong. As much as she had tried speaking with them about Uncle Albert, they had given her little information, and no one could pinpoint when they had last seen him. Perhaps if Russell came in in all his imposing presence, they would give him some actual information.

"Very well. But be warned. They like dogs."

Chapter Eight

They like dogs. She hadn't been exaggerating. As soon as he pulled the bell on the door to the generous London townhouse, a cacophony of barking and yapping started up. The door opened and a young woman who he almost mistook for Rosamunde dashed past him. It was only when he glanced back did he realize a dog had darted out ahead of her. She scooped up the small pile of ginger fur and made an apologetic face.

"Forgive Mr. Pompadour. He gets excited when visitors are here." She glanced him over, narrowing her gaze in on his face, and gasped. "You must be the investigator Rosie spoke of."

Investigator? Well, that was one way of describing him. "That's me." He didn't offer his name. He avoided giving it considering his role in The Kidnap Club. Far better for him to skirt around the edges of society than be identified accidentally by someone.

"You must come in!" the young woman declared and grabbed his arm, hauling him in past the butler.

Russell scarcely had time to remove his hat and gloves and fling them at the butler before being dragged into a large drawing room. The barking continued and several dogs wound themselves around his legs whilst a large black and white dog propped his paws on his chest. He blinked at the dog and gave it a little pat. "Um, good boy."

"Down, Rusty," a woman commanded.

He peered around the dog to see Rosamunde trying to herd all the dogs back toward their various owners.

Various owners who were all staring at him, cups paused halfway to mouths or biscuits clasped in their frozen hands. He scanned the room that housed several sofas and chairs—none of them matching—and grimaced inwardly. There had to be at least a dozen women in here but no men. In another room somewhere, he heard the giggle of children. Exactly how many family members did Rosamunde have?

He dipped his head. "Forgive my intrusion."

Rosamunde met his gaze and he concluded he must have looked panicked indeed. "Maybe I should speak with Mr. Russell—"

"Oh you must sit, Mr. Russell." The young woman scooted over and patted the seat beside her.

Well, so much for his anonymity. Considering how against him meeting her family Rosamunde had been, she had given up on the idea of this being secretive fairly quickly. He supposed there would be no more hiding behind trees after this.

Shame, really.

No. No, it wasn't. It was for the best. The last thing he needed was to be pressed up against her yet again, looking down and trying to count those freckles or glancing at her lips and wondering how they would taste.

He did not do relationships or entanglements. How many times did he need to remind himself of that?

He especially did not do entanglements with wealthy women from huge families who owned far too many dogs.

Hesitating, he glanced around the room. The offered seat was now occupied with another ball of fur, this one white and slightly curly. A single chair remained empty, so he sank onto that one. A loud sound that could only be described as an excretion of gas from a person ripped through the room. He jumped up and a young boy dashed in.

"Oh that was the best." The boy lifted the cushion seat and drew out a wind bag and waved it in front of Russell. "You must be heavy, sir, because it never makes that loud a noise with my aunts."

"George!" Rosamunde scolded. "Aunt, tell him he should not do that to guests."

"Oh it is only a joke. I'm sure Mr. Russell played many a trick when he was younger," one of the older ladies said with a wave of a hand.

Actually, he didn't. He had no time for jokes or playing when he was a child. He'd spent most of his childhood wondering where his next meal would come from then when he was older, where his next coin could be earned.

Rosamunde's cheeks reddened and she gestured for him to sit again. "It should be safe now."

He eased himself gingerly down, relieved when no more bodily sounds burst from the chair. Rosamunde took the seat up next to the young woman who looked similar to her.

He glanced around, finding all eyes upon him. This had been a mistake. A big, huge mistake. He couldn't recall the last time he had been in a room with this many people, especially ladies of the wealthier variety. His idea of socializing was meeting with the other members of The Kidnap Club for an ale. Hell, he'd even avoided the wedding breakfast for Nash and Grace, keeping himself quietly at the back of the church then slipping out once their vows were complete.

"Rosie says you are looking into Uncle Albert's whereabouts?" the young woman with...Mr. Pompadour?...asked.

"I am."

"There's no need," said the lady to his right. "He's perfectly safe. He does so love to vanish off at a moment's notice. He's always been that way."

Another woman nodded. "Indeed. This is quite normal behavior."

"Lady Rothmere does not think so," he interjected.

"Rosie doesn't think anything is normal," the older woman in the chair next to Rosamunde said.

"Mama," Rosamunde hissed.

"Well, it's true," her mother said. "I do not think Rosie has ever had a normal thought." Her eyes widened—eyes that were similar to Rosamunde's, if a little faded with age. "That is, not that she is addled or anything, Mr. Russell." Her mother reached over and patted Rosamunde's hand. "She has quite the vivid imagination and I have had many a man tell me they do so enjoy a woman with imagination."

Russell stiffened. There was no chance Rosamunde's mother realized quite what she was saying but his own imagination could not help but dart to the bedroom, where even he who avoided the opposite sex these days could not help but think of how an active imagination could certainly be to a man's benefit.

"Mama," Rosamunde said through gritted teeth.

"Anyway, Mr. Russell, enough about this Albert business." Rosamunde's mother leaned forward. "Tell us of you. Where do your family hail from? What does your father do? Do you own property?"

EACH TIME HER mother spoke she could swear a little bit of her died inside. Soon she would be a husk of a woman with no soul left. Just a dried up, wrinkled case of skin, barely held together by bones.

It didn't help that Russell had this constant uncomfortable expression. Nor did it help that her cousin had concealed a wind bag under his chair. If only she had realized.

This had been one huge mistake. She could have questioned her family on her own. She *should* have. Instead, her mother was eyeing him up as a potential suitor. If she was honest, she almost didn't blame her mother. Russell might look a little rough in places, but his clothing screamed wealth and he was mightily handsome. He'd even shaved today.

Not that she should be noticing such things.

She glanced at the parlor room door. If only she had put her foot down and said in no uncertain terms that they were not meeting with her family. She supposed she had thought Russell might be better at getting useful information from them. Whenever she conversed with her aunts, it inevitably turned to talk of marriages or if she was eating enough or whether she had stayed in the sun too long and goodness, why did such a pretty girl have to have freckles?

No one could deny Russell had a certain imposing sort of presence. Surrounded by her aunts and cousins in varying feminine shades and the muted pastel tones of the parlor, he was like a tall oak tree surrounded by spring flowers, casting his shadow and drawing the attention of each and every one of them. Even Mabel seemed a little breathless and Rosamunde didn't think anyone could tear her attention away from her beloved fiancé.

"I have no family," Russell replied curtly.

Oh. A pang of sympathy struck her. As much as her family drove her to the edge of madness, she could not imagine life without them.

"I'm sorry," she murmured.

He shrugged and swung a quick glance her way. "It doesn't matter."

Her mother straightened a little. "So it is just you? No...wife or children?"

Good Lord. Rosamunde resisted the desire to drop her head into her hands. "Mama," she said, clenching her teeth.

"Just me," he replied.

"Interesting." Her mother pressed fingers to her lips. "Would you like a cup of tea, Mr. Russell? Or some cake? We have plenty."

He shook his head. "No, thank you, my lady. I really must ask you—"

Aunt Effie interjected then another of her aunts and even Cousin Emily began asking him questions. He evaded all of them, revealing little about himself. She did not blame him for avoiding the questions, but she had to admit, it left her a little curious.

How long had he been without family? Had he ever been married? He was surely old enough to have once had a wife. She didn't know precisely how old he was, but she had concluded he was edging toward his thirtieth year. Maybe he had some tragic story where his family were lost in a shipwreck and now he couldn't even look at the sea that he had once loved.

No. Preposterous. There were plenty of people with no family and no tragic tale.

Nevertheless, she could not deny her curiosity had been piqued.

"This is terrible," she murmured to Mabel.

"They like him," she said. "That's no bad thing."

Rosamunde shook her head. "I do not need them to like him. I need them to answer his questions."

And he tried his best. For every question he avoided, he asked one, but no one could say when they had last seen Albert or even heard from him. It seemed likely that she had been the one to last speak with him and that was three months ago.

"He is quite handsome, in a sort of rugged way," Mabel observed. "I can see why you like him."

"Like him?" Rosamunde said, keeping her voice low. "I don't like him. That is, I don't *not* like him, but he is not here to be liked. He is helping me investigate."

"Do you really think your Uncle Albert is in trouble?"

"I do."

"Well, I think if anyone could find him it would be Mr. Russell. He has a determined look about him."

Rosamunde couldn't resist glancing at his firm jaw and strong shoulders. Determined was one way to put it. She kept finding her mind drifting to words like *attractive, powerful, intriguing*. Maybe even *dashing*. She doubted Russell would appreciate being called dashing but she could see him performing heroic deeds with ease, racing to save his love or drawing his sword to fight off a horde of enemies.

He managed to remain a good hour before making his excuses to leave. All the dogs began barking and jumping from seats and climbing up his legs when he rose. Rosamunde fought her way through to see him to the door and followed him out onto the pavement.

"I am sorry you did not get more information." She twined her hands in front of her. "And for my family. They can be a little intimidating."

A slight smile curved his lips. "I have faced worse."

"I should like to hear that story sometime."

He eyed her for a moment then seemed to snap to attention. "They are not for a lady's ears," he said tersely, the smile vanishing.

"I am hardly—"

"It was not a complete waste of time anyway. One of your aunt's made mention of The Alfred Club."

"Oh yes, it's a writer's club. Gentlemen only. Though Uncle Albert always said there was more drinking and cards than actual conversation."

"I think it would be worth visiting there and speaking with some of his acquaintances. Perhaps he confided in one of them about wherever he was going."

She nodded. "That sounds an excellent idea. When shall we go? Tonight?"

"I shall go tomorrow. Alone. In case you have forgotten, Rosamunde, you are most certainly not a gentleman."

She opened her mouth then closed it.

"I'll let you know what I find out."

"But I could—"

"I'll be in touch."

He turned away and headed off down the road, his long limbs carrying him away from her so quickly that even when she called after him, she doubted it reached his ears.

"Oh pooh," she muttered to herself.

A gentlemen's club. How interesting it would be. If only she could think of a way of getting in. Maybe she could find a rear entrance or climb in through a window. But then how would she actually get any information from anyone? She pressed a finger to her lips. There had to be some way she could be involved. There was no chance she was letting Russell do all the investigating alone.

Chapter Nine

"You'll have to pull tighter."

Mabel stepped back from Rosamunde and eyed her critically. "I can pull as much as I like but there's no disguising your, um, assets."

Rosamunde blew out a breath and eyed herself in the long mirror. White fabric crushed her breasts tight, but they still curved outward. "I'll never pass for a man now."

"I'll try again," offered Mabel.

Rosamunde nodded and prepared herself. Mabel pulled hard on the ends of the fabric and Rosamunde winced as it pinched into her skin. "I never thought I'd curse having curves," she muttered.

"Are you certain you should be doing this? Do you not have to be a member of the club to get in?"

"Male family members are allowed to visit. I'll just use Uncle Albert's name."

Mabel peered up at her. "I'm really not certain you are at all masculine enough. Not even with my brother's clothes."

"Just keep pulling."

"If your mother finds out I have been involved in this..."

"No one will know," Rosamunde assured her cousin. "I shall sneak out the servant's entrance whilst the staff are eating their dinner."

"You could just let Mr. Russell do his job?" Mabel suggested softly.

"And let him have all the fun? Not likely."

"I do not see what is fun about crushing one's breasts and sneaking into a stuffy old gentlemen's club," Mabel muttered.

"I have to do this, Mabel. I have to find Uncle Albert."

"I thought the point in hiring someone to help was so you did not have to."

"I hired Mr. Russell for his expertise. Plus, you cannot deny having a man's assistance does open some doors."

"It opens the doors to gentlemen's clubs, which is precisely why I do not see why we are doing this!"

"Tighter," Rosamunde urged.

"You never did say where you found Mr. Russell. He is frightfully handsome. No wonder your mother was enamored with him."

Rosamunde grimaced. She should have kept him far away from her batty family. It seemed Mama had decided Mr. Russell had enough wealth and good looks for him to be good enough for her daughter and now her mother would not cease speaking about him. Or maybe her mother had simply got tired of Rosamunde paying no attention to men and figured this was as good a shot as any to have her daughter remarried. Either way, her mother was wrong. Russell might be wealthy as near as she could tell but he hardly seemed the marrying sort.

"Mr. Russell was meant to be your kidnapper."

Mabel sucked in a breath. "Oh goodness." She tucked in the ends of the fabric and stepped back to admire her work. "That's better, I think."

"I can scarcely breathe so it had better be."

"I'm not sure how I would have felt about being kidnapped by Mr. Russell."

Rosamunde frowned. "You knew it was coming. Why would you have felt anything?"

"Well, he does have that sort of dark, dangerous air about him, does he not? I think it could have been quite intimidating."

"It was, I suppose." And a little exciting, and invigorating.

"I still paid them, of course, with a long note of apology, but I do feel utterly terrible about the change of plans."

"I imagine there are plenty of other women for them to kidnap."

"I wonder how on Earth a man gets involved in such a thing." Mabel offered Rosamunde a shirt and helped her slip her arms into it.

Rosamunde fought with the buttons, releasing a frustrated sound. "I do not know how men do these all the time. They're backwards!"

"They do not," Mabel reminded her. "They have valets."

"I doubt Russell has one. He strikes me as the independent sort."

And now she was picturing him dressing, drawing on his shirt over strong arms and a taut chest. If she wasn't already struggling to breathe, she had made it worse.

Mabel aided Rosamunde with the buttons and cravat then the rest of her clothes. Rosamunde twisted her hair into a tight knot and shoved a simple comb into it then added the hat.

"What if you need to remove your hat?"

Rosamunde grimaced at her reflection. "If only I had time to buy a wig." She eyed herself and drew up her chin. She did look masculine, if a little young. In the lamplight of the club, surely she could pass for a man?

"Perhaps you should leave this to Mr. Russell."

"Never."

"There's nothing wrong with letting a man help, you know," Mabel said as she handed Rosamunde gloves.

"I don't need help."

"So why did you hire Mr. Russell?"

Rosamunde blew out a breath. Mabel would never understand. She adored men and adored relying on them. When Rosamunde considered having men in her life, they were rather like her Uncle Albert. Not old and a little portly, of course, but they respected her and her opinion. They certainly didn't marry her then spend as little time as possible with her. They considered her an equal and wanted her help.

No, they *needed* her help.

Russell didn't know it yet, but he would need hers too, she was certain of it. And whilst she would bow to his experience and the doors he could open by way of his sex, she had little intention of letting him have all the fun.

RUSSELL GRIMACED. THE woman had to be mad. It was the only explanation.

Dressed in men's clothing, she paced the entranceway of the club. He shook his head. How she hadn't been removed already, he did not know, but there wasn't a chance she passed for a man. Or even a boy, for that matter. Her curves were disguised well enough but there was no mistaking that pretty face, even behind heavier glasses than she usually wore.

He strode over to her and took her arm. She released a decidedly feminine squeak.

"What are you doing here?" he murmured.

Her eyes widened when she realized it was him. She glanced him up and down. "You look very fine."

It was hardly the response he expected, and he never usually considered how he looked in evening wear or if it even appealed to women. He wore fine clothes because there had once been a time when he'd had none. Hell, he'd scarcely had shoes that fit let alone top-quality fabrics. Wearing these clothes had nothing to do with impressing anyone.

But some strange piece of him liked that she thought he looked good.

He shook his head to himself. "Let us get out of here before someone realizes who you are, and you are utterly scandalized."

"No one has noticed me yet." She resisted the pull on her arm toward the door.

"Trust me, someone will notice you soon enough. You make a terrible man."

"But—"

"I've made enquiries already. There's no need for you to be here."

"But—"

"Come." He pulled on her arm again and she sighed, allowing him to lead her out onto the darkened streets.

He released her arm and she huffed and straightened her waistcoat. He frowned at her chest.

"I had my cousin bind my chest," she explained.

His gaze shot up. Bugger. He'd been caught. "I wasn't even thinking..."

She tugged her jacket tighter about herself. "How did you get in anyway? You are not a member, surely?"

He gave a wry grin. "You don't think I'm clever enough?"

She frowned. "No. I do not have you pegged as the sort to enjoy other men's company."

He fought for a reply. She wasn't wrong there.

A carriage pulled up outside the club door and two gentlemen exited the vehicle before it moved on. The men nodded in greeting and one gave Rosamunde a confused look.

He took Rosamunde's arm again and drew her into the shadows of the building. "What were you thinking?" he demanded. "You can't pass for a man."

"I thought I looked quite good." She lifted her chin.

"You are far too pretty."

"Oh."

"Not to mention, there are no disguising some things."

"Some things?"

"Your, uh..." He made a curving motion with his hands. "Your jacket is too short to conceal, um..."

"Oh!" She clapped hands to her face. "I only really looked at myself from the front." She frowned. "Curses. Why did Mabel not say anything?"

"Even if she had, would you have listened?"

She gave a begrudging smile. "I suppose not."

Russell guided her deeper into the shadows when a man stepped down the steps from the building, whistling. Tucked against the side of the building, he could make out her expression but little else. "You should return home quickly, before anyone spots you. Did you take a carriage?"

She shook her head. "I walked."

"Walked? Christ, woman, you are even madder than I thought."

She folded her arms. "I'm not mad. My house isn't far from here and I would have thought one of the benefits of being a man is everyone leaves you alone."

"Even men are set on by footpads."

"I would wager you have never been."

"I had my share of encounters when I was younger."

"But not now you are older."

He shrugged. "I suppose not." He gestured to her. "But even if someone thought you to be a man, you make a very different sort of man to me."

Very different. She was still wide-eyed and youthful. Her lips were still too curved, her nose too petite. Her jawline too smooth. And, of course, he couldn't forget that arse. All women should wear trousers, he concluded. It was far more enticing than any dress, seeing the fabric cling to her rear. He drew in a breath and forced his attention to her face. He sighed. "I'll walk you home."

"There really is no need."

"There really is."

"I suppose you can tell me what you discovered."

"Not much I'm afraid."

He offered an arm and she nearly took it, but they must have both recalled she was meant to be a man and created some distance between each other. They walked along the streets at a leisurely pace. The roads were still relatively busy, with carriages rolling past every few minutes. Fewer people were walking, however, than one would normally see in the day, for which he was grateful. Less chance of anyone recognizing Rosamunde.

"I spoke with several of your uncle's acquaintances, but none could tell me much, only that they had not seen him in a while."

"Maybe he went and got into some kind of trouble." She bit down on her lip. "I do hope he is well."

"I'll find him," he assured her.

"*We'll* find him," she corrected.

Before he could argue, she gasped and snatched his arm. He scarcely had a moment to figure out what was happening when she pressed him up against the wall. She flung off her hat, pulled out a comb that clattered to the ground, and slung her arms around his neck.

"What the—"

She pressed her lips to his. Hard.

His mind raced to catch up with what had occurred. But all it could latch onto was the fact she had her mouth pressed to his. And that she tasted sweet. And that all he needed to do was skim his hands down and he could take two handfuls of that arse that had him so preoccupied.

So, he did what any red-blooded man would do and glided his hands down, taking her rear in his palms and squeezing her flesh. She moaned against his mouth and he used the opportunity to take a deeper taste of the sweetness.

Dear God, did she taste sweet. And so warm.

She moved against him, pressing her strangely firm chest to his. He kept her gripped tight and her fingers twined into the hair under his hat. She moaned again when he drew back and nibbled briefly on her bottom lip before taking her in a deep kiss once more. She angled her head so that the kiss moved deeper, and he met her sounds with a groan.

He ached fiercely. More fiercely than ever before, he could swear. He used his grip on her rear to move her closer, so close that their hips collided. He supposed he should be grateful she didn't have the added barrier of skirts. He rubbed against her and moved his lips from her mouth to her neck, taking little bites along her flesh and feeling her shudder.

She tapped his shoulder and drew in a long, shaky breath. "I think they are gone now."

He lifted his head and glanced around the street. A young couple strolled along the opposite side of the road, doing their best to ignore them. "Who?"

"A friend," she said. "I feared they might recognize me."

He eased his hands away from her, feeling as though she'd just thrown a bucket of ice-cold water over him. She'd been trying to hide. *That* was why she had kissed him.

"So you thought that was the best way to hide?"

"Well, no one wants to look at a couple kissing, do they?"

"Right. Of course."

"I think it worked." She grinned at him. "I had to think quickly there."

He straightened his jacket and retrieved her hat and hair comb for her, giving him a moment to draw in a long, cool breath of night air. He adjusted his breeches before he turned back to her but there was little he could do about it, especially considering she had felt every inch of him pressing against her only moments ago.

He handed her the hat and comb. "Let's get you home before you feel the need to do anymore kissing."

She blinked at him, her brow furrowing briefly. "Of course," she said brightly. "Shall we investigate my uncle's house tomorrow?"

"We?"

"You did not think I was letting you go on your own, did you?"

Of course he didn't. But he had rather hoped. That way, he could get a grip on himself and not think about how damned good her body had felt against his, and certainly not wonder if he would get another chance to kiss her again.

Chapter Ten

Rosamunde hauled the large bag over her shoulder. Russell eyed the cumbersome thing with a scowl. "You can leave that in the carriage."

She pressed the ugly thing to her side. "Goodness, no. We might need it."

Why they should need a bag that looked like it had been made of a faded rug that had been trampled on by many, many muddy boots, he did not know, but he wasn't going to argue. Not today. In fact, if he could avoid all conversation with her, it might be better. Hell, if he could manage not to look at her, that would be perfect too. Then he might have a chance of feeling absolutely nothing with regards to her.

How nice that would be. To go back to moving through life with zero feelings toward a woman.

Well, not just any woman. A crazed, freckled, curvaceous, beautiful woman who kept prodding at some soft spot he didn't know he possessed and made him want to do things he'd never been interested in before.

Like...converse, for God's sake.

He shuddered as they made their way around the side of her Uncle's townhouse. The few lovers he'd been with previously had known little about him and he learned zilch about them. That was the way he liked it.

Christ. He shook his head. She wasn't his lover. Wasn't ever going to be either. Entanglements were not for him. He did not desire one and he knew full well he'd be awful at one, especially with someone like Rosamunde who deserved a hell of a lot better.

"He certainly has not been home in a while," Rosamunde murmured, looking back at Russell. She kicked a large dandelion. "Look, he would never let his garden get like this."

"He has a gardener to attend to it, surely?"

She shook her head and went onto tiptoes to peer through the slightly cloudy-looking window at the side of the house. "He only keeps a butler and a cook. Uncle Albert always said there was nothing like dirt under one's fingers to make one feel human."

He was inclined to disagree. He'd spent far too many a day filthy, sitting on the streets. Whilst his busy schedule and inability to remain in one place for long meant he was often unshaved and his hair tended to grow a little long, he was always, always clean. He hated going without a wash.

"The butler and the cook, where are they?"

"They're at my Aunt Petunia's. They split their time with the households when Uncle Albert isn't here. Which is often."

"We should probably speak with them if this leads nowhere."

She nodded. "I had thought of that, but Aunt Petunia is my biggest skeptic."

"Skeptic?"

"She thinks I should have remarried as soon as I was out of mourning and that I am too busy dreaming of something different and am entirely impractical." She wrinkled her nose. "Aunt Petunia never did like me much."

"Well, I can go alone," he offered. This Aunt Petunia could not accuse him of being impractical, that was for certain. He didn't think anyone had ever accused him of being anything but a realist and if anything he was often accused of being far too cynical.

"I would not wish to inflict Aunt Petunia on you."

"If it saves you from having to face her, I don't mind." He shrugged. "I've faced far worse than a sour-faced aunt in my lifetime."

"That is very gallant of you." She gave a light laugh. "And Aunt Petunia is exceedingly sour-faced and known to scare many a man."

He hadn't been trying to be gallant. Mostly, it would be good if he could keep Rosamunde away for a little while, give him some breathing space. Even now, as they skulked around the outside of the house to the rear door, she felt too close. He smelled her vanilla fragrance and his gaze kept straying to her rear as he recalled how soft and delicious she had felt.

He closed his eyes briefly, took a breath, and forced his attention on the door. A simple, boring, dull door. Black with a gold knocker. Nothing exciting here. A few scratches as though a cat or dog had been trying to get in. Dull indeed. Nothing that could make him think of Rosamunde.

And her rear.

Curses, he was doing it again.

He tried the doorknob. "Locked. Do you have a key?"

"One moment." She opened the bag and delved deep, her whole arm vanishing into the unsightly fabric. He saw her hand move around inside and something jangled until she produced a small, jagged metal thing. "Here it is."

He peered at it. "A lockpick?"

She nodded and motioned for him to move aside. "I've been looking forward to using this."

He blinked as she kneeled and pushed the pick into the lock. Her lips pursed in concentration as she moved it swiftly in an up and down motion.

"Rosamunde, perhaps I should—"

The door clicked and swung open. "Ah ha." She rose, a wide grin on her face, and shoved the pick back into the bag.

He shook his head and followed her in. "When the devil did you learn to lockpick?"

"Oh goodness, a while ago now. It seemed a handy sort of skill, but this is the first chance I've had to use it."

He shook his head again and followed her into the drawing room. The house certainly looked as though it had been occupied by an eccentric old bachelor. A brandy glass sat empty by a worn armchair, a brown stain in the bottom of the glass indicating it had been a while since it had held any liquor. Most of the furnishings were unmatched and tired. He swept his finger through the fine film of dust on the nearest bookcase.

"It's certainly been a while since he had been home."

Rosamunde nodded. "Everything looks normal. No signs of a fight."

Russell picked up an empty wine bottle, discarded in front of a row of books. "French," he murmured. "Hard to come by this stuff after the war."

"Yes, it's his favorite."

"I tried it in France. Didn't do much for me but you could get a pretty penny for it if you found some."

"You fought?"

He nodded.

"Will you tell me about it?"

He stiffened and peered closer at the titles on the bookshelf, too aware of her gaze upon him.

OH DEAR. PERHAPS she shouldn't have asked. She had a few male cousins and an uncle who had fought and told tales of the grim nature of battle. Maybe Russell went through some traumatic ordeal.

"Forgive me for intruding."

He shook his head. "It doesn't matter. War is war. Violent, messy, and confusing."

She nodded. "I can imagine."

"I hope you never have to," he said, his mouth pulled into a grim line.

"Why did you leave the army?"

Russell fixed her with a look. She understood it easily enough. It was one she saw often when she asked too many questions. *Be quiet, Rosie. Cease your queries, Rosie. That's quite enough of that, Rosie.* Why her noisy family ever expected her to behave any differently, she did not know. After all, they were hardly the timid sort.

"Perhaps I should see if he has packed some clothes. Then we shall know if he went voluntarily."

His lips quirked. "Most people do not really get kidnapped you know, Rosamunde."

"If it can happen to me, it can happen to anyone," she replied with a grin before leading the way upstairs.

The winding stairs creaked underfoot, and the second floor sloped slightly, making one want to hug the wall. She moved past the guest bedrooms to the master one and twisted the doorknob then pushed.

It refused to move. She frowned. "Must be locked."

Russell stepped in front of her and tried the door himself. "No lock, though, and if there's a bolt on the inside, he'd have been forced to leave by the window or something."

Though her uncle prided himself on being the adventurous sort, she could not imagine him climbing from the window. He suffered aches in his joints these days and had grown a little portly with age. "I do not believe he would do such a thing."

He gave the door handle an experimental wiggle then pressed the door with a shoulder. "It's stuck fast. I can get in, but I might break the door."

She debated it for a brief moment. Would Uncle Albert mind coming home to a broken door? "Do it." If anyone would understand, it would be him, especially if he really was in trouble as she feared.

Hand to the doorknob, Russell backed up a little then shoved hard with his shoulder. The door splintered, a sharp crack ricocheting through the silent house. He put a finger to the broken door frame and a bit of metal hanging from it. "A bolt."

Maybe Uncle Albert really had left through the window. She inched open the door and narrowed her gaze into the gloomy room. The curtains were drawn, and the window remained shut.

"Uncle Albert?" she called softly into the darkness, even though she saw no sign of human occupation.

She stepped forward. At least she would have done. Russell thrust an arm out, latching it around her waist. "Wait!"

He hauled her back and she was faintly aware of a metal clanking sound as her hands landed on his chest. His heart beat hard against her palm and she peered up at him, eyes wide. "What..." she managed to mutter on a breath.

He held her for a moment, completely wrapped in his arms. One latched around her waist, the other banded about her shoulders. Even if she wanted to put some distance between them, she could not. Rosamunde let her gaze linger briefly on his stubbled chin whilst drawing in the scent of soap and a little woodsmoke. She realized now she knew so little about this man. She could talk of the scars on his face or how his body felt against hers. She could now even say how he tasted.

How he kissed.

And good Lord, the man could kiss.

But she could say little else of him. She did not know where he resided, if he did anything other than kidnapping women for a living or if he had any friends. All she could say of him was that his body felt utterly perfect against hers and that she had not been able to cease thinking of their kiss.

Who could blame her, really? It was the sort of kiss that one imagined since girlhood. The sort of kiss that made her tremble with the mere thought of it. The sort one told all of one's friends about and they all gasped and sighed.

Of course, she hadn't told anyone of it. They would imagine she was having an affair and if she let herself, she might imagine it too, and that would be foolish indeed. She doubted a man like Russell spent much time dwelling on kisses and how they made his toes curl. Goodness, she doubted his toes had ever curled from a kiss, not even hers.

She had tried to be light about it after she threw herself at him and that was how she needed to remain. They kissed because she needed to hide, nothing more.

He peered down at her, his eyes unreadable. She glanced at his mouth and recalled how warm it had been against hers. He smirked slightly, as though she were amusing him, then eased his grip. Were it not for the wall behind her, she might have fallen over entirely. She pressed both hands to the fabric wall covering and tried her best to surreptitiously suck in a deep breath. She glanced up at Russell through her lashes and felt her insides twist.

"Must you look at me that way?" she snapped.

He frowned. "What way?"

"I'm not certain. It is a puzzling way and it makes me feel, well, puzzled."

His lips tilted. "I shall try my best, my lady."

She glowered at him. "Don't mock me."

"Never," he vowed, his eyes growing dark once more.

"You are doing it again."

He straightened slightly and gestured into the darkened bedroom. "You nearly lost a foot."

She looked to where he pointed and gasped. A rusty metal trap sat in front of the door, its jagged teeth pulled tightly together. "Goodness." She had almost forgotten he must have grabbed her for a reason and hadn't simply been overcome with the need to kiss her again.

If only he *had* kissed her.

She shook her head and peered through the doorway to the bedroom, careful to keep her person on the other side. "Uncle Albert had no enemies, but he did like to think of himself as rather intriguing." She gestured to the trap. "This doesn't surprise me especially but maybe there is some clue as to why he might leave it set up."

He put an arm in front of her before she could step over the threshold. "Let me take a look," he ordered. "Wouldn't do for you to lose a foot, especially not after I managed to return you unharmed from a damned kidnapping."

Chapter Eleven

"Only *just* unharmed," Rosamunde pointed out before Russell could step into the room.

He glanced at the animal trap. One second more of inaction and he'd have been holding her down while someone sawed off her mangled leg. His gut roiled. Foolish. Stupid. He should have been paying better attention and thinking less about kissing her or dragging her down onto the bed and burying himself in the scent and feel of her.

Of course, she was referring to the fact she'd hit her head when jumping from the carriage.

He twisted to view her. "Why did you jump from the carriage? You could have been killed."

She lifted her chin. "Better than being taken alive by a kidnapper."

"Was it really?"

"I had little idea you were not really a kidnapper, did I?"

"Were you not scared?"

"Naturally. But I was less scared of jumping than being taken captive by you." Her eyes crinkled at the corners. "You can be quite intimidating, Russell. Especially when masked."

He gave a begrudging smile. The woman was mad, there was no escaping it. She'd knocked herself senseless leaping from a moving vehicle and still couldn't bring herself to regret it. He'd never met a woman like her.

"You know, you never did seem that contrite."

He blinked. "For what?"

"For kidnapping me, of course."

He scowled and thought back. He remembered touching her. A lot. Recalled the feel of her body beneath his, the softness of her thighs. The determination in her gaze, the courage in her struggles. He couldn't, however, recall giving her anything other than a brisk apology.

"I guess I am deeply, deeply sorry then."

She shook her head with a grin. "You were not made for groveling, Russell."

"I've never groveled a moment in my life."

"I do not doubt that."

"Still, I suppose you helping me is almost apology enough."

"You are paying me," he reminded her.

"That must mean you still owe me, then."

He groaned inwardly. Russell didn't want to owe the woman a thing. He'd never had a debt in his life and the last thing he needed was a reason to remain wrapped up in Rosamunde's odd life. He'd already experienced too much of it for his liking. If he wasn't careful, he'd begin to like it and then where would that leave him? Hankering for something that would never be? He shook his head to himself. The sooner he found the uncle, the better. Then he could go back to his nomadic, kidnapping ways.

He stepped cautiously into the room and peered around. A faint cloud of dust danced in the slit of light sneaking through the curtains. He glanced up, half expecting some medieval torture instrument to swing down from the ceiling or for flaming arrows to shoot from the sides of the room, but no other traps revealed themselves when he stepped farther in. He gestured for Rosamunde to follow him.

"Just be careful," he urged.

She nudged the trap aside with a foot. "Uncle Albert has many prized possessions, but I cannot fathom what needed protecting in his bedroom."

Russell pressed the door shut and fingered the broken door bolt. "It doesn't even look like this was affixed properly. It might have slipped in accidentally."

"I do not think the trap was accidentally left there, though."

"No," he agreed.

She moved about the room, running a finger around the edge of a painting, skimming the mantelpiece with a hand, eyeing the corner of each room.

"What are you looking for?" he asked.

"At the viscount's house, he had several hidden doors."

"I doubt a house of this size has one, surely?"

She shrugged. "Some smaller houses had priest holes." He tensed at the sound of a click. She gave a smug smile and eased open a panel in the wall, barely big enough for a boy to fit in. "See?" Her head vanished into the hole. "I cannot believe my uncle never showed me this." Her voice echoed. "It's a little dark."

He shoved open the curtains. "Better?"

"Better." She withdrew her head. "I can fit in. Just give me a little lift."

"You don't need to go in."

"Well, you can hardly fit in, can you?" She gestured with a thumb toward the hole. "And I thought I saw something."

He blew out a breath. "Fine."

She pressed her head back through the small opening and Russell took hold of her legs, her rear nestled on his shoulder while he maneuvered her in. He fixed his gaze upon the poorly painted scenery to the right of him, scowling at the ugly green splotches that were meant to look like trees, while he did his best to ignore the feel of her arse so damned close to his face. She made little sounds of effort as she wriggled her way in, and he closed his eyes.

Bad idea.

He snapped his eyes open. Behind his closed lids, it was too easy to imagine those sounds were meant for him. Too easy to picture hauling her over his shoulder, laying her on the bed and lifting those skirts so he could see that arse in its full glory. He'd taste her too. Spread her wide and...

"Oh."

Her legs flew from his grasp suddenly and she toppled into the hole. He shoved his head into the gap to find her sprawled at the bottom of a hole several feet deep. She twisted and managed to rise to standing.

"Are you well?"

She nodded and pressed her glasses up her nose. "Just a little mussed."

"Mussed," he repeated, absently. He rather liked mussed. It made his fingers itch to muss her farther. He shook himself. "What's in there?"

She bent and picked up a stash of letters. "Just these and a few bottles and trinkets." She picked up a bottle. "More French wine."

"Take the papers. We'll look at them properly shortly."

She folded them and stuffed them into her bodice then held up her hands for him to grab. He eyed where the papers had vanished and swallowed.

"What?"

"You couldn't have found a better home for them?"

"Well, there is always my garter..."

He resisted the desire to bury his head in his hands. What was he going to do with her? "Is there still a knife there?"

"A new one, yes." Her gaze narrowed in on him. "You made me lose my last one."

With a sigh, he grabbed her arms and hauled her halfway out of the hole. Once she was almost free, he grabbed her waist and set her on her feet.

"What am I going to do with you?" he asked.

"I COULD THINK of a few things."

Oh no. She hadn't meant to say that aloud. Maybe he had not heard her.

No. From the arched eyebrow, he certainly had. He removed his hands from her waist as though he had been handling fire.

Which was not far from true. Every part of her felt scalding hot, as though he'd been dangling her over flames. She blew a strand of hair from her face and gulped down a giant breath then held it for a few moments.

She had lied too. She couldn't think of a *few* things. Oh no, she could think of lots of things. Maybe hundreds if she had the time to dwell on it. He could kiss her, for one. Touch her again, for two. Carry her over to the bed, for three. Maybe remove his jacket and shirt, for four.

Well, this wasn't helping with the heat rushing through her veins. She released the breath and straightened her bodice. "That is, um—"

"What did you find?" he asked abruptly.

"Oh yes." She tugged the papers from her bodice and unfolded them. "Looks like letters. We should read them for clues."

"You can read them." He glanced behind her. "Anything else?"

She shook her head. "Nothing that looked important. Some wine, a wooden box, and old jewelry. It probably belonged to my grandmother, but it didn't look as though it was of value."

"Hardly worth setting a trap for then..." Russell mused.

"Maybe there is something in these that can tell us why he might set the trap."

He straightened his jacket sleeves. "Read them and we can meet tomorrow."

"There's still a whole afternoon left for investigating."

His lips moved into that odd, elusive smile she was beginning to recognize. It did not crop up often, but it was almost as mysterious as that look in his eyes. "I have other things to do, Rosamunde, but I am certain you are capable of reading a few old letters on your own."

"What other things?"

His lips tilted farther. "Am I to divulge my every move to you?"

"Well, I am paying you."

"So I suppose you own me now, then?"

What a thought. She would not mind that at all. She would command him to do a great many things.

No. She gave herself a mental shake. She'd heard of women doing such things, paying young, handsome men to be their lovers, just like courtesans. She had little desire to do that. If Russell ever...made love to her, she would never wish him to do so because she had paid for him.

Not that he would do such a thing and to think so was folly. Yet again, she had let her imagination run away with her. The job was keeping him here, nothing more.

"I did not mean that," she murmured.

"I should hope not." His gaze grew dark, his posture almost menacing. "No one will ever own me. Not again."

"Again?" She blinked at him. "You mean when you were a soldier?"

"Something like that."

Rosamunde opened her mouth to ask more but the menacing posture had not faded so she closed it. Whatever was in this elusive man's past would stay there it seemed but, sweet Mary, did he pique her curiosity. What stories he would have to tell. No doubt they were a hundred times more exciting than her Uncle Albert's tales.

"Where shall we meet?" she managed to ask, instead of the hundreds of other inappropriate questions burning through her mind.

"Somewhere quiet."

"So not at my house then?" she said with a smile.

"No." His posture relaxed, and his lips twitched marginally.

She allowed herself a breath. "Perhaps Harris's subscription library in Piccadilly? It shall be nice and quiet there. I always thought it would be a good place for a..." She clamped her mouth shut.

"For a what?"

"Rendezvous," she said softly and braced herself, waiting for his admonition.

"Rendezvous," he repeated. "Do you have a frequent need for secretive meetings?"

Now she did not know how to respond. Was he suggesting she took lovers? Or something else. "I have never used it for meetings," she said hastily. "That is, I do not really meet with people." She blew her hair from her face. "Well, of course, I meet people. But not in a secretive manner, of course. Especially not men." She clamped her mouth shut.

Lord, now she had made this ten times worse. Perhaps she ought to go thrust her foot in that animal trap and end it all. A good amputation would certainly put a stop to this conversation. It should not even matter if she had taken lovers. She was a widow. So long as she was discrete, it would not matter. She doubted Russell cared either way.

She lifted her chin. "I could if I wanted to, though."

His gaze held hers for so long that she grew breathless. A clock ticked somewhere in another room and birds chirped outside.

"I have no doubt you could," he said finally. "No doubt at all."

"Good."

"Good."

She pressed her lips together. "So..."

"Tomorrow then."

"Oh yes. Tomorrow. At the library. Shall we say noon?"

He nodded. "Noon it is."

"Perfect."

"Excellent."

He gestured to the door. "After you then."

"Right. Yes." She moved swiftly through the house, almost tumbling down the stairs and spilling out into the fresh air. She drew in several breaths and willed away the heat in her cheeks. This man had such an ability to make her feel unsteady, as though she was standing in a rowboat, waiting to topple into the Serpentine. And the most foolish thing was, if it were not for her ridiculous inability to hold her tongue, she might well like it.

Chapter Twelve

He needed to end this as soon as possible. Which meant finding Albert as soon as possible too.

Russell clasped his hands behind his back and strolled past the bookshelves, eyeing the gold letters upon red, green, and blue spines. The scent of parchment and a little dust swirled in the air. He paused to peer at a title and withdrew it, gingerly opening the stiff leather and running a finger along the title on the inner page. Interesting. He'd have to see if he could find a copy of his own.

He snapped it shut when the door to the library squeaked open, feeling guilty for even picking up a book. He blew out a breath. Not that he needed to. He could read perfectly as an adult. Hell, he read faster than most men he knew and with greater understanding of the text but it didn't stop that gnawing ache in his stomach that reminded him a man like him should never have been able to read, let alone enjoy books. It was only through pure determination as a boy that he'd taught himself.

That, and a few carefully curated books that ended up in his possession by way of what one might consider illegal means.

Very well, he'd stolen them. But he sure as hell didn't regret it. As far as he was concerned, education should be for anyone, regardless of wealth.

Rosamunde gave him a little wave and hastened over, a far too pleasing smile upon her face.

Oh yes, he needed this over.

Most especially when her smile made his insides do odd things. Who'd have thought a man like him could get excited over a mere smile?

"I was not sure you would be here yet. I thought I might have to grant you access." She undid the bow on her hat, and he found himself distracted with the quick movement of her fingers and then the glossy dark curls under the dull lamplight.

"I know some people."

She peered at him and set her hat on the nearest table. "People?"

He shrugged. "People know me, I suppose. Or at least of me. Makes it easy to get into places."

She shook her head and grinned. "For a man who behaves so mysteriously, that seems surprising."

"Mysteriously?"

"You know, this whole rather brooding, tight-lipped thing."

"I hardly brood."

"You do a little. Not to mention you give away as few details as possible about yourself, and you are rather, well, sneaky, I suppose."

He arched a brow. "I hadn't expected a whole dissemination of my character today." He gestured around. "I rather thought you wanted to discuss our plan."

"Believe me, Russell, I do not have your character marked yet, so it would be impossible for me to disseminate."

He could not help move a little closer. Only because the lamplight was so low, of course. Not because he wanted to look more closely into her eyes or remind himself of those freckles that hopped across her nose. "Why should you wish to?"

That smile danced on her lips. "Oh, you must know I love a story by now. And you, Mr. Russell, most certainly have one."

"Not an interesting one."

"I doubt that."

He shook his head, allowing himself the smallest of smiles. There was no escaping it—the woman was mad. No other woman had ever been interested in his history. They certainly did not want to hear about his life on the streets or the army. None even got as far as figuring out he was likely richer than half the people they knew. Which was perfect. He liked it that way. If they didn't know him, they wouldn't get attached, and neither would he.

"Shall we make a start?" He drew out a chair for her.

"Absolutely." Rosamunde sat, laid out the letters, and patted the chair beside her. "Will you sit? It is hard enough craning my neck up to look at you normally, let alone from a seated position."

He jerked into action and lowered himself onto the chair next to her, grimacing when his leg brushed hers through her skirts. A bolt of heat flashed through him. It was pure insanity. A mere brush of a leg and he felt like a young man catching his first glimpse of a woman's thigh.

He drew in a deep breath through his nostrils and regretted it instantly. The scent of orange blossom lingered on her, combined with the clean fragrance of soap. She must have bathed this morning and—

Damn it, now he was picturing her in the bath, all soapy and wet with her dark hair trailing down her damp skin. He gritted his teeth and focused on the shiny surface of the mahogany table. He was not some whelp at the mercy of his newfound libido, nor was he some wet-behind-the-ears man, in desperate need of the feel of a woman. He was Marcus Russell—orphan turned soldier turned entrepreneur, and he controlled every aspect of his life, including his desires.

"So, a few of these letters were a little, um, saucy." Rosamunde's cheeks colored in the dull light.

She tapped a finger at a line in the top letter and the words *breast, taste,* and *lick* caught his attention.

He groaned.

"WHAT IS WRONG?" Rosamunde peered sideways at Russell. He seemed a little pained, his brow furrowed.

"Nothing." He gave a tight smile. "Just hoping this gives us a lead."

"Well, I think it does. These letters are from a lover of my uncle's. He never mentioned her to me, which is curious."

Russell eyed her. "Your uncle is in the habit of telling you the sordid details of his love affairs?"

She tugged off her spectacles, rubbed them on her sleeve, then put them back on. "Well, honestly, I did not know he really had any love affairs, but he never usually kept anything from me." He gave her a skeptical look. "I am a widow, Russell. A grown woman. I am quite aware of how love affairs work and am hardly in need of protection from such knowledge."

"Don't remind me," he murmured.

"Pardon?"

He jabbed at the date at the top of one of the letters. "These are from fifteen years ago."

"Yes, but my uncle kept them hidden. I have to wonder why."

"The lady was married perhaps."

"She fails to mention a husband."

"It's hardly romantic to write to one's love of one's husband, is it?" he pointed out.

"True." She pressed a finger to her lips. "Do you think a jealous husband has had a hand in his disappearance? Lord, what if he is harmed or has been challenged to a duel? He's a good shot but his eyesight is not much better than mine!"

"Let's not run away with ourselves. This could be nothing. If you didn't find any newer letters, then surely the affair is not ongoing."

"There were only these. They span a year." She spread out the letters.

"It would still be worth looking into. Did you find out who the lady is?"

"Yes and no. Her name is Mary but there is no last name. However, her address is scrawled on the outside of most of these letters." She flipped one over to show him.

"That's on the west side of London."

"So not far from here."

"Of course, there is nothing to say she still lives there." He pulled a letter close and scanned it. "It seems a, uh, passionate affair."

Rosamunde nodded. It felt a little odd thinking of Uncle Albert being embroiled in such a match, but he had been a handsome man once upon a time and he was full of personality.

It made sense that this woman would be so enamored with him. It also made her a little envious.

"What's the matter?" Russell asked, his gaze narrowing in on her and making her feel a little breathless.

"It's nothing."

"Rosamunde..." he pressed.

Well, he was insisting so she supposed she might as well say it. "I was wondering what it must be like to have a passionate love affair."

"Ah." He scanned her face. "I take it your marriage was not one of those."

"It was...fine." She lifted her shoulders. "More than most women could expect from an older husband I believe. He was pleasant enough, but we didn't spend much time together and I think I bored him."

"More likely he didn't have the energy for you."

She pursed her lips. "You think?"

"I'd be hard-pressed to neglect a beautiful bride like you unless there was good reason. And you are hardly the sedentary type."

"I suppose not."

She shouldn't but she could not help but latch onto his words. He thought her beautiful. And she liked that. Far too much. She had been called pretty or handsome before but usually by family members and that didn't really mean much. After all, they were biased. But coming from Russell, she could not help but believe it. He had no reason to say such a thing and hardly seemed the sort to hand out compliments willy-nilly.

"I pity your husband in a way."

She wrinkled her nose. "You do?"

"Stuck with a beautiful woman but not knowing what to do with her."

"Well, I'm sure he knew..." Her cheeks warmed. She was no prude, but she certainly did not expect to be discussing her late-husband's prowess or potential lack of in the bedroom department.

"I'm sorry you were neglected, though. That should never have happened." His eyes took on that dark, unfathomable look as though she were looking into a deep well of darkness and unable to see the bottom no matter how far she leaned over.

If she wasn't careful, she was going to lean too far and fall in. Her heart pounded fiercely at the unspoken words that seemed to linger in the air.

I wouldn't neglect you.

He'd be an excellent lover. Even with her lack of experience, she felt that certainty throbbing through her body. He moved with such confidence, spoke as though he had never once had to worry whether he was wrong or not. Not to mention, he had kissed her with such skill that if she closed her eyes, she could recall it and find herself all hot and bothered and ready to sneak off to her bedroom again.

"Russell..." she managed to mumble, not even sure why she needed to say his name.

He jerked back a little. "We should visit here then." He jabbed the address. "But we also need a list of where else your uncle likes to visit, in case we come up emptyhanded."

There it was. She'd leaned too far and tumbled down the hole, landing at the bottom with a cold, wet splash. Simply because she was imagining kisses, and there being more behind his complimentary words, did not mean any of it existed. When would she learn? Real life was nothing like her imaginings.

And Marcus Russell did not want her. Not now and probably not ever.

Chapter Thirteen

Russell handed Rosamunde down from the hack and paid the driver. He was rather relieved she hadn't had access to the family coach today as he'd feel a damned fraud riding along in the luxurious vehicle. Not to mention, meeting away from her home meant he could avoid her family and their inquisitive nature. Why they should even be interested in him, he had no idea.

He also had little idea if that was the way families always were. He'd ask Guy or Nash but neither of them had much contact with their families either. Nash more so of late but his relationship with his father was still in its tentative stages.

If they didn't press him for information, he'd probably find their boisterous, noisy manners amusing.

Perhaps.

The truth was, he didn't know how to feel about them. Or if he even wanted to feel anything. It certainly would not help this whole desiring Rosamunde a great deal thing. After yesterday at the library and learning of her neglectful husband, he'd been unable to cease thinking of her.

He smirked to himself. Well, that was not that uncommon at present, but the ruminating was worse now. Now, he couldn't stop thinking about what a damned waste her marriage had been. Couldn't cease picturing her, all alone, untouched. He gritted his teeth. She was no virgin but by the sounds of it was close enough. It was enough to drive a man to the edge of madness.

She put a hand to her hat and peered up at the tall, cream townhouse. He glanced up too. Though not in the fashionable part of London, Grovesnor Street was still respectful enough with clean pavements and access to a small green over the road.

"I hope she still lives here."

He did too. And that she could lead him to her Uncle Albert, and he could return to doing what he did best—kidnapping women and making money—and *not* being far too wrapped up in some knife-wielding, freckled woman's life.

He also hoped she didn't live here, fool that he was.

Russell pulled the bell and stepped back, motioning for Rosamunde to move in front of him while the ring of the bell echoed throughout the house. "You look less threatening than I do."

"I would not say you look threatening," she murmured. "More...intimidating."

"And that's better?"

"Maybe."

The door eased open slowly and a man with bushy white brows, a thick white beard, and a few strands of hair clinging to his head appeared in the gap. He narrowed tired eyes at them while remaining stooped low.

"Certainly not Mary," he muttered under his breath.

"Yes?" he barked, the volume of his voice making Rosamunde jump.

"Forgive the disturbance but does, um, Mary live here?" Rosamunde asked.

The man frowned. "Wary? Why do I have to be wary?" he bellowed.

"Mary." Rosamunde raised her voice. "I'm looking for Mary."

The door inched farther open and an attractive woman with a sizeable bosom and faded pale hair smiled at them. "I'm Mary. Can I help?"

"Oh wonderful." Rosamunde's eyes lit up. "We are looking for Sir Albert Wood. We thought you might know him."

"Sir Albert Wood?" she repeated softly, glancing at the old man.

"Yes." Rosamunde laced her hands together. "He's my uncle," she explained.

"Perhaps we had better take a little walk." Mary tapped the old man's arm. "Go inside, I'm going to just talk to this lady."

"A baby? Who's having a baby?" the man asked.

Mary smiled softly and shook her head. "You need to stop losing your hearing tube. Especially when you do it on purpose."

"I do not do it on purpose," he muttered, "but I would lose it less if you would cease your rabbiting."

Mary folded her arms. "Oh, so you heard that perfectly."

"Yes, I'd like some lemon curd." He shuffled around and winked at Rosamunde before retreating into the house.

"Forgive him," Mary said. "He likes to play games with me. It keeps him amused."

Rosamunde winced. "We didn't realize you were married."

Mary laughed. "Oh, that's my father. He came to live with me after my mother passed. He's good company most of the time." She snatched a shawl from behind the door, looped it over her shoulders, and shut the door behind her." She glanced Rosamunde over. "So you are Albert's niece?"

Rosamunde nodded.

"I can see the family resemblance." Mary looked to Russell. "And is this your husband?"

"No," Russell replied swiftly.

Her brows lifted. "If I were you, I would change that," she said to Russell. "You won't get a prettier girl and if she's anything like Albert, well...let's just say you won't ever be bored."

Good God were all the women associated with Rosamunde's family so bold? He glanced at his feet and avoided her inquisitive gaze.

"Come," Mary ordered. "I have little desire to talk about my lover here. Knowing Father, he's found his hearing tube and is holding it up against the door."

They obediently followed Mary over to the small green. Despite the fine weather, few people occupied it, most likely preferring to head to Hyde Park where they could be seen.

"So you are my uncle's lover?" Rosamunde asked.

Mary peered at Rosamunde. "You are quite young. I am not certain you should be hearing this."

Rosamunde lifted her chin. "I'm a widow."

Mary made a noise. "Married women rarely know anything about what it is like to have an affair. God knows, their husbands are useless. That is why I never married." She sighed. "Though I might have married your uncle had he asked."

"When did you last see him?" Rosamunde pressed.

"Oh goodness." She furrowed her brows. "It must have been a good fifteen years ago or so."

"Oh."

"Why? What has happened?" Mary asked. "Is he in trouble? And, I must ask, however did you find me?" She looked to Russell. "Are you some sort of investigator? You have the clever look of one."

ROSAMUND COULD NOT help but smile as Russell eyed Mary. The man didn't know how to take her compliment at all.

"Uh..."

"Mr. Russell is helping me find Uncle Albert," Rosamunde said. "He has been missing for some months now."

Mary wrinkled her nose. "He did have a tendency to vanish for a while."

Rosamunde nodded. "But never for this long, and he always wrote to me. I haven't had a single letter this time."

"Which niece are you?" Mary paused to peer at her.

"Lady Rosamunde Stanley."

"Rosamunde," she repeated. "Oh yes, the little girl with the big imagination. I recall him doting upon you." Mary sighed. "Albert was quite the man." A soft smile lingered on her lips. "He knew how to make a woman feel, well, divine."

Rosamunde eyed the attractive older woman and tried to picture her uncle as some suave rake-type character and failed. Uncle Albert was not without his charm and his big personality drew people to him, but he had a large nose, a rounded belly, and a sore knee.

"So you haven't seen him recently?" Russell pressed.

She shook her head. "I wish I could say I had but, alas, neither of us were the marrying sort and our courtship ended when my mother died, and Father moved in. There isn't a day that goes by when I do not think of him." Mary wrung her hands together. "I do hope he is well."

"So do I," Rosamunde agreed.

"However did you find me anyway? We kept our *tête-à-tête* extremely quiet."

"He kept letters from you," Rosamunde explained.

"Goodness." Mary cinched the shawl closer around her neck and smiled. "I forgot about those. How wonderful he still has them. I might not have his letters anymore, but I cannot deny, he is still close to my heart."

Rosamunde smiled back. "You must have meant a lot to him. He kept them with other prized possessions."

"That is nice to know." Mary sighed. "I wish I could be of more help but, unfortunately, I have not seen him since our last time together."

Rosamunde blew out a breath. She felt certain Mary would know something of her uncle. It seemed their one lead on his whereabouts had come to nothing and she could find no reason Mary would lie to them. She certainly did not seem the dishonest sort and as much as Rosamunde had a habit of seeing things that were not there, she could usually make out a liar.

"Will you let us know if you hear from him?" Russell asked.

Mary nodded. "Is the family still at Westham House?"

"Yes. You can write to me there."

They stopped near the entrance gate to the green and Russell rubbed a hand along his jaw. "Can you think of anywhere he might be?"

"He went to so many places." Mary shrugged. "Though he did like to frequent the Queen's Head whilst visiting with me.

They had some rather pleasant ales apparently, despite its location. I would hardly think he is there, though."

Nor did Rosamunde. Uncle Albert rather considered himself a connoisseur of alcohol but was not the sort of man to get into some drunken stupor and disappear for months on end in a pub of all places.

"I know the place," Russell said.

"I think we should at least see if he has been there recently," Rosamunde declared.

Russell stiffened. "We can talk about that in a moment."

"I should be returning to my father." Mary twisted on her heel and paused. "Do let me know once you find him. And maybe suggest he tries to find me again." She gave a coy smile.

"I will, thank you." Rosamunde watched the woman hasten back toward the house and shook her head. "I never thought of Uncle Albert as some sort of passionate lover."

"We all have hidden depths."

She eyed Russell and rubbed the end of her nose. "I'm not certain any of mine are hidden. I was never very good at being secretive and alluring."

He lifted a shoulder. "I wouldn't expect a woman like you to have a knife in her garter." He leaned in. "Some might even find that fact alluring too."

Her cheeks warmed as she recalled his hands splayed on her thighs, searching for the knife.

"I prefer my women unarmed, though," he added swiftly.

The heat swiftly doused. Of course he did. No one was interested in a woman with a mind full of adventure. She often suspected it was because men feared they could not live up to her expectations. They were not wrong, if she was honest. Russell, however...

Well, he certainly lived up to some of them. Mysterious, handsome, rather reckless...

She shook her head. "Shall we go to the inn?"

"*I* will go to the inn."

"Where is it?"

"Not far from the docks."

"We could even walk from here."

He shook his head. "I'll see you home and then make inquiries."

"But that makes no sense," she protested. "We could walk there in half an hour."

"Rosamunde, the docks are no place for a lady, and I doubt this establishment is either if it is based there."

"I want to come."

"Have you ever even set foot on the docks?"

She lifted her chin. "Once."

"And a tavern?"

"I've been to plenty of traveler's inns."

"These sorts of places are vastly different from the posh traveler's inns you likely frequent."

She waved a hand. "I do not see how. They serve food and ale. How different can they be?"

He fixed her with a look. "Vastly different, as I just said."

"If you do not take me, I shall go on my own."

"You are not going, Rosamunde, and that's final."

Chapter Fourteen

She was going. Why Russell ever thought he could persuade Rosamunde to return home, he did not know. Had he learned nothing about the stubbornness of this woman yet?

He briefly debated flinging her over his shoulder and stuffing her in a hack, but he doubted Rosamunde would remain in it. The damned woman would likely fling herself from it again and he couldn't have her injured because of him once more.

"Let's get this over with," he muttered.

It seemed unlikely Albert would be holed up in some inn for months on end, but it was worth seeing if anyone had seen him. If they could only figure out his last movements in London, it would make it a darn sight easier to find the man.

He shook his head. Why did Albert frequent such a rough area? Fine ale be damned, as soon as Russell could get out from the slums, he did, and he only set foot there if absolutely necessary.

He led the way down the busy streets, passing through the market. Rosamunde scurried to keep up and he offered out a hand. Mostly because he didn't want to lose her in the crowds. Not because he enjoyed holding her hand or anything foolish like that. The stalls were crowded with sellers shouting their wares, making it impossible to communicate with Rosamunde until he ducked into one of the alleyways. He released her hand, flexing his fingers.

No chance he missed her fingers entwined with his. Not at all.

"Not everyone has long legs and can walk as fast as you," she said breathlessly, keeping pace with him.

"We need to keep moving. If you look at all lost, you'll draw attention."

"*You* certainly do not look lost."

"I'm not."

"How do you know this area of London so well anyway?"

He stilled briefly, glancing around at the filthy alleyway. Dirty rags of clothing hung from windows and the wail of several likely starving children echoed about the soot-blackened walls. "I've spent a lot of time here."

"But why?"

He continued on, ignoring her question, and she scampered behind him.

"Is it to do with kidnapping?"

"No."

"You work somewhere nearby perhaps?"

"No."

"Ah, you volunteer at the workhouse and do not want me knowing you are soft and kind!"

"Certainly not."

"I still think you are secretly soft and kind," she muttered.

"I am damn well not."

"Very well, then you must own some institution here or perhaps a ship." She peered up at him. "I think you must have cocoa plantations somewhere or trade in coffee."

He had many different ventures to his name, so she was not entirely wrong. However, he did as little owning of things as possible. *Things* meant planting down roots and making attachments. Life was far too fragile for that.

"Rosamunde," he said in a warning tone.

"I could see you as a sea captain actually."

"Rosamunde..."

"No, perhaps not. I think it more likely you work with orphaned children. You bring them gifts and sweetmeats but do not want anyone knowing, lest they think you have a heart."

"Damnit, Rosamunde. I grew up here. In these dirty alleyways. And believe me, I have no heart. I think I lost it here, in these very streets."

She stilled, forcing him to come to a stop.

He ground his teeth together. "Can we keep moving?"

"You cannot tell me such a thing and expect me not to wish to know more."

"Rosamunde, for once in your life, can you not be curious?"

She shook her head vigorously. "I'm not sure I'm capable of that."

Despite himself, his lips tilted a little. He shouldn't like her curiosity. It was the exact opposite of what he needed from her. Could she not be one of these meek, mild women who were too scared to ask questions and let him get on with this job?

"Fine. You have three questions. That's it."

"Three questions?"

He held up three fingers. "One, two, three. And once you have asked those, you may never ask me a personal question ever again."

She pressed a finger to her lips. "I do not see what is so harmful about personal questions. No one ever died from talking about themselves."

"I'm certain there were a few prisoners in the tower who would have fared better by keeping their mouths shut."

She waved a hand. "Those are exceptional circumstances and I'm certainly not keeping you prisoner."

Wasn't she? He could not help but feel the moment he'd grabbed her from the carriage, she'd caught him, and wrapped him up in her world where he most definitely did not belong. He was incapable of refusing her. He swore it was worse than torture in the Tower of London.

"Three. Take it or leave it."

"Fine. I'll take it."

They continued along the alleyway until they came out onto the road that led toward the docks. A little mist seeped in off the water, swirling about their ankles, contrasting strangely with the warm day.

"Well?" he asked when she remained quiet.

"I'm thinking," she said. "If I only have three, I must use them sensibly."

He rolled his eyes. He shouldn't have even offered three. No one wanted to hear the grim story of his life anyway and he did not much enjoy speaking of it. Guy Huntingdon, the Earl of Henleigh, knew a little of it, only because they'd met through a shared business interest and before offering him the job with The Kidnap Club, he'd asked of his past. Even Nash had no idea of his roots.

"What age were you orphaned?"

"Five."

"Blast, that was a waste of a question." She glanced up at him. "Can you not tell me more?"

"That's question number two. And no, I cannot."

"That was not a question and you know it. I still have another two."

He looped an arm around her waist and drew her into him. "They will have to wait." He nodded toward a building ahead where several men lounged in the streets outside, clearly deep into their cups. "We're here."

ROSAMUNDE EYED THE building. The once-white walls were grimy, marked with soot and dirt from the road. The front door had a boot print on it. She frowned. Why someone had put their foot so high up she could not fathom. There was no doubting this was unlike the clean traveler's inns in which she sometimes stayed. Most of the time, if they went to the country, they found someone obliging who would put them up for a few days in one of the many elegant country homes.

The tavern looked rather like one of those ones she pictured by the coast, on some rugged cliff top with the wind howling, rather than tucked in between warehouses and tumbling down buildings. She anticipated someone bursting through the door at any moment, a pistol brandished or maybe some customs men barreling through the entrance and arresting smugglers.

No one left or entered and a man who lounged against the building let out a huge belch.

She looked to Russell who eyed her reaction. He expected her to be frightened. He expected her to be the privileged lady and balk at entering.

How little he knew her. She couldn't wait to step through into this other world. It might only be in a different part of London and not an hour from her family home, but it was the unknown—and nothing excited her more.

Lifting her chin, she pushed open the door and stepped in, her eyes taking a moment to adjust to the dull light. The grimy windows let in little of the daylight that seeped through the gaps in between the taller buildings that crowded around it. Her shoes stuck to the floor as she walked in and several heads whipped around at the sound of the door shutting. She inhaled deeply and drew up her shoulders. No, she did not belong here, but she'd be damned if she'd let anyone scare her away.

Not only because she wanted this but because she could not let Russell think she had a distaste for his past.

He remained close, a hand to the small of her back. The touch was intimate, but she liked it. That large hand, pressing lightly against her, removed any worries she might have for her safety.

Not that she intended to have any. Here was one small chance to prove to herself that she did not just dream of exciting situations, but she could actually follow through.

She kept her chin raised and headed toward the bar of the taproom, the hairs on the back of her neck pricking at the feel of all the eyes on her. Even Russell, in his fine clothes, did not look like he belonged here, however, she doubted anyone would question his presence. Despite the fine fabrics and well-cut clothing, he never failed to have an air of intimidation.

She supposed that was because of his past. Gosh, how fascinating the man was. How had he gained wealth? Was it simply because of the kidnapping? Was it something else? How had he been orphaned? What happened next? Of course, she only had two questions now so she would have to think them through exceedingly carefully.

A short man with a thick head of faded red hair and a matching moustache stood behind the bar, cleaning a tankard with such dedication she imagined he would wear through the metal before long. He didn't look at them until he rubbed it several times, lifted it to the dim lamplight, and rubbed it again then set it on a shelf behind him.

"What can I do you for?"

"Two ales," Russell replied before Rosamunde could say anything.

She shut her mouth. She supposed it would be best if they purchased a drink, then the innkeeper might be more obliging. He poured the drinks and shoved them over then Russell pushed some coins across the bar. The exchange happened so swiftly she hardly had time to breathe let alone catch up with Russell as he made his way to a table in the corner by the empty fireplace.

He put the drink on the table then drew out a chair, cocking his head toward it. "Sit."

"But—"

"Just sit. We'll ask our questions soon enough."

She glanced around and frowned. Why they could not ask now, she could not fathom but Russell knew this inn better than her, so she sank reluctantly onto the chair.

He followed suit and grabbed the ale, taking a lengthy gulp then swiping the foam from his upper lip.

Rosamunde peered at the froth on top of the drink. She enjoyed a nice glass of wine or sherry, but she'd never partaken in ale. It looked rather refreshing on such a warm day, so she pulled the tankard toward her.

"You do not have to drink it."

"I want to." She lifted it and took a long sip. The bitter tang danced on her tongue and she gulped it down. A warm sensation soon reached her fingertips.

Russell watched her, a brow raised.

"It's quite nice actually."

His lips tilted. "You have a little..." He leaned forward and swiped what had to have been froth from her lip then licked it from his thumb.

Eyes wide, she watched the movement, frozen. It wasn't anymore scandalous than them already having kissed yet she could not help think on how his thumb had touched her mouth. And how his tongue had then touched his thumb. It was as close to kissing as one could get without actually participating in the act.

He cleared his throat, glanced around, and took another drink.

"Why are we not asking about Albert?" she whispered.

"Because the innkeeper does not trust us. He'll tell us nothing."

"How can you tell?"

He shrugged. "I just know."

"So if we have a drink, he'll trust us."

"If we spend enough, he will."

"Could we not just, you know, bribe him?" she murmured.

Russell shook his head. "I know men like him. He makes fine ale and takes pride in it. He won't take coin for information on his patrons."

"I see." She looked to the innkeeper who had returned to polishing tankards. How he knew all that, she couldn't fathom, but she trusted Russell to be right. He had so much more experience of life and people than she did. "So it looks as though we are drinking ale for the rest of the afternoon." She lifted her drink. "Cheers."

Chapter Fifteen

Halfway down her third pint, Russell put a hand to Rosamunde's arm. "When I said we needed to earn the innkeeper's trust, I did not mean you had to drain every barrel in this place."

"Nonsense! Besides, you have drunk as much as I have."

"I drink ale on regular occasions. You do not."

"I drink wine! Even whiskey sometimes." Her voice grew louder, and he motioned for her to hush. Although the patrons had returned to their drinks and card games, he didn't want to draw unnecessary attention, given that both of them had already drawn plenty as it was.

Not that he blamed anyone for watching Rosamunde. In the dark, dank corner of the inn, she offered up a spark of beauty in her green gown and shimmering fabrics. His presence put an end to any attention, but he had no doubt if he was not here, she would be fighting off admirers.

And now the bloody woman was sozzled. When he put an ale in front of her, he certainly never expected her to drain it more swiftly than some men he knew then demand another as though she were a Viking at a feast. He shook his head. Would she never cease to surprise him?

"I suggest you drink it a little more slowly," he murmured.

"It's quite delicious though and thoroughly refreshing." She looked to the innkeeper and lifted the tankard. "This is quite refreshing, sir," she bellowed at him.

The man shook his head, a slight smile on his lips. Perhaps her enthusiasm was working. With any luck, by the time they left, they'd be able to wheedle some information from him.

"You know I have thought of my second question." She leaned forward, jabbing a finger at the table. "How did you get involved with the kidnapping?"

Well, it was an easy enough question. At least it was not about his past. "I met a friend through one of my business ventures..."

She lifted a finger. "So you have friends? Interesting. But I think, in fairness, you should elaborate on this business venture. It is hardly fair to answer my question vaguely."

He sighed. "Very well. This friend invested in a speculation at the same time I did."

"Invested. So you *do* have money."

Quite a lot but he was not going to admit that.

"Continue," she ordered, gesturing with her hand.

"He needed someone with few connections and lack of fear." Russell gestured to himself. "He had me marked out as that sort of man and he was not wrong."

"You do look fearless," she agreed.

"His cousin needed help escaping a violent marriage, but it is not easy for a woman of stature to escape such things. So he arranged to have her kidnapped. That was where I came in."

"So you spirited her away and prevented her husband from tracking her down."

"Yes, she ended up in Ireland I believe." He paused. "That was your third question."

She shook her head, sending curls bouncing around her face. "No, that was a statement not a question." She leaned back and sipped her ale. "Then you found that other women needed such a service."

He nodded.

"It seems a great shame that such a thing is needed but I can understand why, and I must say, I think you are a fine man for doing such a thing. Even if you do sometimes kidnap the wrong woman." She grinned.

"I'm not a fine man. It pays handsomely." He shifted forward. "And I would rather you did not mention the kidnap thing." He looked around. "Someone might get the wrong idea."

"Oh goodness." She sucked in a breath. "Someone might try to rescue me from you." Rosamunde laughed. "Though I do not think anyone would be brave enough to go up against you. You are very strong. I know, because I remember you pinning me down. I could tell you were strong then and I felt your muscles."

Russell had little vanity and being strong merely meant it was easier to survive in life. That didn't mean, however, that he did not like she had noticed. He closed his eyes briefly and regretted it when images of her wriggling beneath him flared through his mind.

It didn't matter what she thought of him. He didn't care. Not one jot. He just had to remember that.

"I think you've had enough ale." He tried to reach for the drink, but she moved it away from him.

"Let me just finish this."

"No more after that." He nodded toward the innkeeper. "I think we can ask our questions soon enough."

"Oh good. I so hope he has information on Uncle Albert."

"Why is it you are so worried about him, but your family is not?"

She pouted. "I already told you they think I'm silly and over imaginative."

"But why do you care so much? He's a grown man and, by the sounds of it, experienced in the world. Surely he can look after himself?"

She sighed and traced a scratch on the table with a finger. "Have you ever felt alone?" She grimaced. "Of course you have."

Russell didn't reply. He'd been alone for as long as he could remember. It had been easier that way, though. He didn't have anyone else to worry about. Sometimes, he was even grateful for it. If he'd had a sibling to look after, life on the streets would have been even harder.

"Uncle Albert understands me. He *sees* me."

Russell frowned.

"He sees who I want to be, not just a young, noble woman who is destined to marry and embroider and play the piano. Through him, I can live." Her eyes glistened slightly. "Truly live."

"I see."

"You likely do not. You have always done whatever you want."

"There are few choices given to an orphan on the streets of London."

She paused. "No, I suppose there aren't." Her mouth curved. "We are alike then. You understand what it is like to have little choice in your future."

"We are not alike," he said, more to himself than her.

Rosamunde sighed and patted his hand. "We are, Russell. We really are."

"YOU KNOW, I'M not certain why we have to drink wine at dinner." Rosamunde swayed a little as they headed toward her family home. "I think we should drink ale instead."

Looping an arm around her waist, Russell pulled her tight into his side before she could get in the way of an elderly couple ambling along the pavement. "I think you should avoid any drink for a while."

"It's a shame they hadn't seen my uncle in a while." She gave a dramatic sigh. "Everyone thinks I'm being silly. Even you, I'd wager. Everyone always says what an active imagination I have."

"I do not think you are silly."

"Is it my fault that life is so terribly dull? I do not think it is." She hiccupped. "Everyone expects women to stay at home and take tea and run the household and look pretty and stay quiet."

His lips quirked. "I do not think you possess the ability to remain quiet."

"Well, precisely." She leaned more heavily into him. "I was never meant for this dull life, I'm sure. I was meant to sail on the high seas. Or explore uncharted territory."

She glanced up at him, enjoying being in his hold far too much. The world swayed a little. Perhaps she should not have partaken in that third ale, but it really had been most refreshing, and she had felt so daring, gulping down such a masculine drink.

"I think you'd miss your family too much," he said.

She shook her head from side to side in exaggerated movements. "They are so noisy and always just...*there*. Do you know what I mean?" She grimaced. "Oh I suppose you do not." Pausing, she tugged away from his side and turned to face him, clasping her hands in front of her and dropping her gaze. "Sorry."

"You have nothing to be sorry about. It is hardly your fault you have family and I do not."

"But you must think me selfish."

"Not one jot."

She cocked her head. It was hard to fathom what it must have been like to grow up on one's own with no one to rely on. She had to admit, she did appreciate their support even if they drove her mad at times.

"Do you not wish you had family? Even a quiet one without hundreds of dogs?"

He shrugged. "Why would I? I am beholden to no one. I like it that way."

She closed the gap between them, stumbling slightly and placing her hands upon his chest to steady herself. He peered down at her, his brow slightly furrowed. Their kiss flashed through her mind and it took all her willpower not to rise up on her toes and press her lips to his.

"You must find such an existence lonely, surely? After all, no man is an island."

"John Donne's Devotions," he murmured.

"I didn't even know that was from that sermon. You are curiously well read."

"For a penniless orphan you mean," he said dryly.

She scowled. "Certainly not. I always had you marked as a clever man."

"Even when I mistakenly kidnapped you?"

"Well, I shall admit that was not your cleverest moment."

He nodded toward her house. "Come, we are not far, and I suspect you shall want your bed soon."

"Not at all. I feel quite awake." A yawn overtook her, and she tried to mask it behind a hand.

Russell chuckled. "You should most certainly sleep, or you'll awaken with a sore head."

"It is not like I drank *that* much."

"You certainly drank enough." He pulled her into him again and led her to the front door.

When he unhooked his arm from around her, she could not hold back a disappointed sigh. They might have made no progress on finding Uncle Albert, but she had rather enjoyed today. The ale had been delicious, and she had enjoyed being somewhere different. More to the point, she learned a lot about Russell, and she had enjoyed that more than anything.

He leaned past her and twisted the doorknob, gesturing for her to go inside. "Go get some rest."

"What shall we do next?"

"We still have other locations to explore. Let's concentrate on those."

"You are not tired of my presence yet then." She beamed at him.

"I am exceedingly tired of your presence," he said, his lips pressed together.

She narrowed her gaze at him, seeing the tiniest spark of something in his gaze. She gasped. "Goodness, you are teasing me. I had no idea you were capable of such a thing."

"I'm capable of many things, Rosamunde."

The air in her lungs froze. Had he meant for his words to have another meaning? The glint in his eyes vanished and she saw his jaw flex. She parted her lips and leaned in. It was no good, she had to try again, had to see if a second kiss would be as wonderful as the first.

"Rosie!"

Russell jerked back and Rosamunde whirled to find her mother in the doorway. She glanced between the two of them then smiled broadly.

"And Mr. Russell. How lovely to see you again."

He ducked his head. "And you, Lady Hopsbridge."

"Good afternoon, Mother," Rosamunde said formally. She might be a widow and entirely capable of making her own decisions, but she rather felt like a child at the moment who had been caught stealing slices of cake from the kitchen.

Her mother gave her a bemused look. "Good afternoon, Rosie." She turned her attention to Russell. "Mr. Russell, I am glad to see you actually. I was hoping you might join us for a dinner party tomorrow night. Just a small gathering."

"*Not* a small gathering," Rosamunde muttered. It was likely to be much of the family and Russell would probably loathe it. She twisted to view him. "I'm certain Mr. Russell—"

"Mr. Russell can speak for himself, I am sure," her mother said.

Rosamunde held her breath while waiting for his response. He'd say no. There was no chance he wanted to spend extra time with any of them, even her.

He looked toward Rosamunde, not taking his gaze off her when he responded, "I'd be delighted, my lady."

Chapter Sixteen

Russell eyed the shiny door knocker, just able to make out his reflection in the brass. He grimaced to himself. What was he doing here? Why had he even said yes to dinner?

Hell, why had they even invited him?

Perhaps he was there for their amusement. Maybe Rosamunde had even told them about his background. *Let's all get our entertainment from the orphan who likely has no idea how to behave at a dinner party.*

Well, he did not do dinner parties, but he knew how to pretend with the best of them. It was how he'd survived this long.

He blew out a breath and tried to ignore the thud of his heart beating in his ears. He'd faced the enemy in battle, slept on the streets, and kidnapped countless women—willing women, naturally. So why the hell did a mere dinner terrify him so?

Likely because he wasn't pretending when it came to Rosamunde.

He shook away the thought as the door opened and a butler gestured him inside. He handed over his hat and gloves and glanced around, hating that he immediately sought out Rosamunde. His heart gave a little skip as soon as he spotted her. He almost suspected he'd said her name aloud because her attention immediately shot to him. Her lips curved, her eyes warmed, and he swore there was no feeling on Earth like having Lady Rosamunde Stanley's full attention. It should be damn well bottled and sold for hundreds of pounds.

She hastened over, her dark blue silk skirts moving elegantly with her body, clinging to her curves. He forced himself to unclench his jaw and keep his expression neutral.

And *not* damn well leer over her.

"You came!"

He inclined his head.

"I shall admit, I thought you might not. I know Mama bullied you into this."

"No one can bully me into doing anything I do not wish to do."

"So you are telling me that the elusive Marcus Russell really wants to come to a dinner party with my far-too-noisy and inquisitive family?"

"Yes," he replied stiffly.

"For a man who prides himself on mystery, you are a terrible liar."

He wasn't actually. At least, not usually. Apparently being around Rosamunde made him incapable of being anything but truthful.

She glanced him up and down. "You look very handsome."

"For a man raised in the gutters you mean."

Her brows knitted. "That's not what I meant at all."

Russell drew in a breath through his nostrils and released it. Of course she hadn't. Rosamunde certainly did not lie or flatter. He doubted she was even capable of it. She and her family seemed to simply open their mouths and say whatever they wished. It should annoy him.

After all, it was the privilege of wealth and status to say whatever one wished and get away with it, but he could not help admire it. He'd never met people like them and while he wasn't sure he could say he wanted to repeat tonight, he was curious to watch her family in action.

"You look beautiful," he murmured.

Too beautiful. If he was going to have one regret tonight, it would be seeing Rosamunde in her evening gown with jewels glittering around her neck. Now, he'd be stuck with the image of her in all that silk and wondering what it would feel like against her body. Would he feel the heat of her skin through it? He dropped his gaze down.

"What is it?" she asked.

He let his lips curve. "I was wondering how you would manage to fit a knife under that gown."

"I have a special one for evenings." She grinned.

He couldn't tell if she was jesting or not, but he didn't manage to prevent his responding smile. The woman was mad.

And he couldn't help like her for it.

"Ah, Mr. Russell." A woman looped her arm through his and dragged him away from Rosamunde before either of them could say anything. He glanced at the petite, older lady and tried to recall her name. Aunt Elsie perhaps? Maybe it was Aunt Petunia? He furrowed his brow. Usually, he was excellent with names and faces but Rosamunde's vast family made it difficult to keep track.

"You must come and meet Uncle Billy and Aunt Clementine. And Lady Grandmother is here. She is so keen to see you."

"I cannot fathom why," he muttered.

"Oh you are funny, Mr. Russell," the aunt said, thrusting him toward a group of people that included a refined older woman he had never met. She eyed him coolly, her chin lifted as though she were looking down upon him despite the fact he had a good couple of feet on her.

"So you are Mr. Russell then?" she said. "I have heard a great deal of you."

"This is Lady Newhurst," the aunt said. "And Sir William Grant and Mrs. Latham." The aunt gestured to Russell. "And this is Mr. Russell. He is the one we told you about."

Russell dipped his head. What the devil had they been saying about him? More to the point, why the hell was he here, and why did this family have any interest in him at all? He'd never met people like them, especially in the upper echelons of society. As far as he was concerned, they tended to keep their ranks close and avoided inviting anyone in, wealthy or not. And none of them could have any idea how wealthy he was.

"I hear you have been assisting with looking for Albert," Lady Newhurst said, lifting a pair of spectacles to her face to peer up at him then dropping her hand by her side.

"I have."

"And have you had any progress?"

"Not yet."

She pursed her lips. "How exactly does one become an investigator of sorts?"

"I am not an investigator by trade," he admitted, maintaining eye contact with her.

"Indeed."

"Indeed?"

"I know of you, Mr. Russell. I have done my research."

He stiffened slightly.

"You have several business dealings with good friends of mine. It seems they believe you to be quite the businessman." She lifted her chin. "My granddaughter is an heiress. She gained a significant amount of wealth when her husband died and will gain more once her father does. She is quite the interesting prospect, do you not think?"

"I imagine there are many who would feel that way."

"But you do not?" A thin white brow arched.

"Come now, Hettie," said Sir William, "leave the poor man be."

"Oh that poor man does not mind a few questions, do you?" Lady Newhurst asked.

"I do not." Especially not when she was questioning his motivations. Was he ruthless in business? Yes. Had he amassed coin by being an unfeeling bastard? Most likely. But he sure as hell would not hurt Rosamunde for all the wealth in the world.

Christ. Was that true? He grimaced. It had to be. He couldn't fathom doing anything other than protect her. After all, why else was he here but to spare her feelings?

"Lady Rothmere is an interesting prospect, my lady," he said. "Not for her wealth but for her heart. She is a determined and clever woman, and I would pity any man who tried to take advantage of her. Most likely they'd end up with a knife to their throat."

Lady Newhurst narrowed her gaze at him for several moments. Finally, a smile broke across her face. "I see what my granddaughter sees in you, Mr. Russell. You are quite different to the usual men who are interested in her hand." A sparkle lit in her eyes. "And I can see that you do not like the thought of there being other suitors, so I suppose the only thing I must say to you is, what will you do about that?"

"LET YOUR LADY Grandmother speak with him," Rosamunde's mother said. "She can do no harm."

From the way Russell's face had paled, Rosamunde could not help but think otherwise. She shook her head and forced her attention back to Mabel and her aunt and uncle. Russell was a grown man with much more experience of the world than her. He could manage the matriarch of the family, surely?

"He is quite handsome," said Mabel. "Especially in his evening wear."

Rosamunde nodded vaguely. Quite handsome was an understatement.

Of course, she had already seen him in his evening wear. She'd also kissed him in his evening wear. Seeing him dressed so brought back memories of that darkened street and his lips upon hers, his body pressed up against her breasts. Merely seeing him in a well-tied cravat and smart evening jacket made her limbs feel like liquid.

"What could Grandmama be saying to him?" she murmured to Mabel.

"No doubt she is ensuring you are protected from him."

"I do not see why anyone thinks I need protecting from him. After all, we are not courting."

"But you could be." Mabel grinned.

"Honestly, I thought everyone wanted me to marry a duke. You were saying that only a few weeks ago, Mama, were you not? That I need a man of high rank."

Her mother lifted a shoulder. "Mr. Russell is handsome, and I hear tell that he is quite wealthy."

"But he's no duke," Rosamunde protested.

Why she felt the need to say that, she did not know. Perhaps because if her family liked him, it would make it all the harder to cease letting her imagination run away with her. Like right now, he would turn to her, and look at her as though she were the most beautiful woman in the world. Then he would stride over, and take her hand, and declare his unending love and ask her to join him in rescuing some poor defenseless princess who must escape her brute of a husband, and then they would don masks and hold up a carriage—

"Rosamunde, I hear tell that he is exceedingly wealthy," Mabel said, leaning in.

Rosamunde snapped her head around and peered at Mabel as she nonchalantly took a sip of champagne. "Where have you even heard such things?"

"Lady Grandmama knows everything, and we have been talking of Mr. Russell and how much time you are spending with him."

"We are investigating Uncle Albert's disappearance," she reminded Mabel.

"But he would be quite capable of investigating himself, surely? And what sort of a man wants a woman's opinion all the time?"

"I think he rather values my opinion, actually."

"All I am saying is there is a reason he has not sent you home and kept you out of the way." She gestured wildly, sending a little champagne spilling over the edge of her glass and forcing Rosamunde to take a step back lest it spill onto her gown.

"He has not sent me home because I would not let him."

Mabel looked to Russell then back again. "You think a man like that could not force you to remain away?"

Rosamunde released a breath. He had been surprisingly co-operative with letting her assist him. At least after their initial few investigations. Now, he seemed to accept that she would be accompanying him everywhere.

But that meant nothing. None of this did. Not even their kiss. It had been one of pretense, used to hide. Russell did not want her, and he did not want to be part of this family. Who would? They were noisy and inquisitive and pure madness half the time. Even she needed to escape them on occasion. A man like Russell would never willingly join such a family.

She frowned as her grandmother's expression softened. Was he really exceedingly rich? After their conversation yesterday, she concluded he had done well for himself, which was interesting but not surprising. He was a determined sort of man and though he did not reveal it often, she had come to the conclusion he was exceptionally clever. When she thought he wasn't looking, he had picked up several books in the library to borrow and none of the titles were simple reads.

Russell glanced her way and her heart juddered to a halt. He offered a slight smile and she stepped forward to join him, but Aunt Petunia took his arm and dragged him off to speak to another set of cousins. Her grandmother gave her a knowing look and motioned for her to join her. Reluctantly, Rosamunde traipsed over.

"Yes, Grandmama?"

"Quite an interesting fellow, that Mr. Russell. He must think highly of you to follow on this fool's errand of finding Albert."

"Uncle Albert is missing, Grandmama."

She waved a hand. "Albert is off doing his usual adventuring but if this keeps you happy, I see no harm in it."

"I am not doing this for entertainment, Grandmama."

"He seems to have a good heart," she commented, looking Russell's way.

Rosamunde nodded. "I think he does, even if it is a little buried."

"You seek to dig it out?"

"Oh no." She shook her head vigorously. "Mr. Russell is merely working for me. I know he has no interest in—"

"Nonsense." Her grandmother lifted her spectacles to her face and squinted up at Rosamunde. "He has interest, as do you."

"But, Grandmama, why are you even encouraging such a thing? I thought Mama wanted me to marry—"

"A titled fellow, yes." Her grandmother shook her head. "As if we need more connections in this family. But, my dear, I am not entirely without ambition for you."

Rosamunde frowned. "Grandmama?"

"I did a little investigating into Mr. Russell. His name had me curious, I will admit."

"His name?"

She nodded. "I knew a Marcus in my youth. Frightful cad of a man. The Earl of Henleigh at the time."

"I do not see—"

"He bedded a young maid—the sister of my lady's maid, and unfortunately got her in the family way."

"How terrible."

"Her name was Russell."

Rosamunde froze. "Russell..." she whispered. "And the father of the child was...Marcus?"

"Indeed."

"So you are saying that Mr. Russell is the natural son of the late Earl of Henleigh?" Rosamunde put a hand to her mouth. "Dear Lord."

"The maid was let go from her position of course but she married quickly to some other chap."

"But Russell said he was an orphan."

"Oh, he is." Her grandmother leaned in. "My maid lost track of her sister after they moved to London. We were in Hampshire at the time, you see. But years later, she discovered her sister had died of consumption shortly after the child was born and the husband vanished."

"And the child...?"

"No one knew what happened to him."

"The Earl of Henleigh, does he know he has a half-brother?"

"They have business dealings together." Her grandmother lifted both palms. "I have to conclude he does."

"Goodness." She looked to her grandmother. "You are more of an investigator than I am."

Her grandmother grinned. "I simply have nearly eighty years of knowledge to draw upon, Rosie. That is all."

She looked back to Russell. "Do you think he knows?"

"I would not know. But if anyone should ask, it should be you."

Chapter Seventeen

Ducking under the rafters of the tavern, Russell could not help but recall the last time he'd been in a place like this. Rosamunde had drawn all the attention from the patrons and then drunk far too many beers.

He had to admit, she did make a rather charming drunk, though.

He made his way to the table where Nash and Guy were seated.

"What's the smile for?" Nash asked, peering up at him.

Russell clenched his jaw. "What smile?" He lowered himself into the wooden chair and drew the small glass of amber liquid close. He'd drunk rather too much champagne last night and the stronger liquor was a welcome change. He was decidedly not the sort of man who enjoyed champagne.

The dinner had been *interesting* though. He couldn't decide if he had actually enjoyed himself, but Rosamunde's family were a large, interesting lot, with less airs and graces than he might have expected. In fact, after the initial interrogation from the grandmother, he'd been welcomed like one of the family. It had felt almost...nice.

He shook his head to himself and took a sip of the whiskey. Nice or not, he would be wise to avoid being with them again. Once he found her Uncle Albert, he'd never see any of them again anyway.

"He's doing it again," Nash said.

"I'm doing nothing," he snapped.

"You did look as though you were smiling," said Guy.

Russell narrowed his gaze at Guy. "Whose side are you on anyway?"

Guy lifted both palms. "No one's."

"It's Lady Rothmere that's making him smile." Nash grinned.

"I'm not damn well smiling," he said through gritted teeth. "Christ, I'm regretting coming here now."

"What a short memory you have," Nash said. "I recall you finding it rather amusing that I was falling for Grace."

Russell nearly choked on his sip of whiskey. Good Lord, he wasn't falling for Rosamunde. Hell, he'd only known her for a few weeks. Besides which, she'd never have him. Even if her family were pleasant to him, they were likely pleasant to everyone. It might explain why they were so goddamn huge. They sucked in family members like a hole in a ship taking on water. That did not change that he was an orphan with no lineage and even less experience of being part of a family.

"This is a job, that is all," he muttered.

"An attractive job." Nash's smile grew smug. "Lady Rothmere is handsome indeed."

Russell gave Nash a cold stare. "If I cared for handsome, I'd have gone after Grace."

"If you'd have touched her, I'd have damn well chopped off your hands."

Russell let out a laugh. "Never took you for the possessive type, Nash."

Nash shook his head. "Enough about Grace. Let's talk of Lady Rothmere."

"Or we could talk business," Guy suggested.

Russell turned his attention to the earl. He could always be relied on to be the serious member of the group, making Russell seem practically cheerful at times. "Happily."

"First, I'm away to the country this afternoon." He jabbed a finger at the table. "Estate business," he explained. "Secondly, I have heard murmurs that our services might be requested next month. Will this Lady Rothmere business get in the way of that?"

Russell shook his head. "I intend to have found her uncle by then."

"Only you could wind up getting another job by kidnapping the wrong woman." Nash leaned in. "Is she paying you well?" A brow arched. "Or perhaps she is paying you in other methods..."

Russell slammed a hand on the table. "Damn it, Nash, she's a lady."

"Well, you're not a gentleman." Nash shrugged. "And ladies have needs."

"What would Grace say if she heard you talking like this?" Russell said.

"She would say that Russell here deserves a fine woman and she would congratulate me on asking many questions and quiz me on the answers for her notebook."

Russell scowled. "Grace writes about me?"

Nash lifted his shoulders. "She writes about everyone. You know what she is like."

Russell blew out a breath. Nash's wife had a tendency to always be writing in a notebook—an odd quirk to his mind—but it seemed to keep her happy. He wasn't sure he liked that he might be written about, however.

"Anyway," Guy continued, "so long as you are done, we should have another job. I have yet to speak with the woman involved but she has been asking about us, and it looks like a case with which we would want to be involved."

Russell nodded. "Fine with me."

"I'm in," Nash said. "And I know I can speak for Grace when I say she'd be happy to assist."

"Good." Guy rose from the table and lifted two fingers to the barkeep. "Two more if you will." He retrieved his hat and jacket from the nearby coat stand. "I'm on a tight schedule but I'll make contact upon my return to discuss this next job further." He paused. "Oh and if you hear from a Miss Haversham, do not respond."

"A Miss Haversham?" Russell eyed Guy. The man avoided women at all costs so it would not be a mistress he was avoiding or a love interest.

"She is a reporter and a damned nosey one at that," Guy explained. "I have heard she is investigating the disappearance of several society ladies and is asking around about them. I do not see why she would come upon you two, but we can take no risks."

"I doubt she would come to me," said Russell.

"You don't think she would reveal us?" asked Nash. "I have little desire to put Grace in any danger."

Guy shook his head. "She has nothing. She's just an over-ambitious little fool." He put in his hat and paused again. "Curses, that reminds me. I spoke to several acquaintances of mine—after all, I've known Lady Rothmere's family for some time—and the word is Albert Wood might have been in Bath recently. You would do well to search there."

Russell accepted the second drink from the barmaid and lifted it in salute. "With any luck, I'll have found Albert within the week, and we can get back to normal."

"I'll see you soon, gentlemen."

Russell watched Guy leave then took a sip of his drink. He met Nash's amused gaze. "What is it?"

"I pity you."

"What?"

Nash's lips curved. "You think you can go back to normal after Lady Rothmere."

Russell rolled his eyes and drained his drink. He did think that, and he would. Rosamunde would have no lasting effect on him, of that he was certain. None at all.

"DO YOU THINK he knows?" Mabel put a little tea on a teaspoon and offered it out to Mr. Pompadour, who lapped at the liquid.

Rosamunde shook her head. "How can he? Russell talked of being an orphan. Surely he would have said if he was the natural son of an earl?" She reached for a biscuit and stuck her tongue out at the dog as he eyed every movement of the shortbread. "Mr. Pompadour is going to get fat," she said when Mabel offered him a nibble of her biscuit instead.

"Never. He has excellent breeding. He simply isn't capable of getting fat." Mabel drew the dog close and kissed his nose. "Are you, Pompie? You are simply too handsome for your own good. Besides, mumsie will still love you, even if you do get a little chubby."

"It would be hard to tell under all the fur, but he is looking a little rounder."

Mabel put her hands over his ears. "Do not say that! He is a sensitive soul."

Rosamunde finished the biscuit and retrieved a napkin to wipe her fingers on and dab her mouth. She set it back down on the delicate walnut coffee table. She came here to confide in her cousin, not to discuss Mr. Pompadour's greedy inclinations. She still had no idea what to do about this new information. Should she tell Russell? Keep it from him? After all, it was really none of her business.

"Have you spoken to him since the dinner?" Mabel asked.

"He bid me goodnight briefly but that is it. I received a letter this morning saying he had news and we are to meet in the park later today."

"I wonder what the news could be..."

"Hopefully it is about Uncle Albert."

Mabel wrinkled her nose. "Uncle Albert might well be in the Outer Hebrides and what are you going to do? Chase him all the way there?"

"If I get information that he is in the Outer Hebrides and is safe, I will not need to."

"So you could ask Mr. Russell about this earl business today," Mabel mused. "I saw there was breeding there, you know." She pressed a finger to her lips. "He has an air about him."

Rosamunde did not think that was anything to do with being the illegitimate son of an earl and more to do with his experiences in life.

"I feel as though I am lying to him if I keep it from him." Rosamunde sighed. "But how do we even know it is true? All we have is Grandmama's assumption that he is the son because of his name."

"Grandmama is never wrong."

"True."

"*And* when it comes to her granddaughter she is infinitely protective. Surely she has dug up more information on Mr. Russell to confirm it?"

"She didn't say." Rosamunde made a face. "And I did not think to ask more. I was so surprised by the revelation."

"You are certain he does not know?"

Rosamunde shrugged. "He could know and be ashamed perhaps? Or simply keeping it quiet because that is the sort of man he is? He rarely speaks of himself."

Mabel sighed and tilted her head. "He is so mysterious. If it were not for my lovely Henry, I would be quite enamored with him."

A slight prick of jealousy jabbed at her heart. Rosamunde straightened and shook the sensation away. She had no claim over the man and she very much doubted he wanted anyone to claim him, not even pretty Mabel.

"I am not enamored with him."

"I did not say you were," protested Mabel. "But it cannot be a hardship to spend time with him, Rosie."

"It is not terrible, no," she admitted. "But it will be all the more difficult now I know this." She paused and eyed the grandfather clock in the corner of the drawing room. "I will be meeting him in an hour. I need to decide what to do."

"You have a knack for investigation. Perhaps you should investigate this. Ask him some questions, ascertain what he knows and maybe how he would react if he found out."

Rosamunde shoved her glasses up her nose. If he did not know, she could not see him reacting well. He seemed to almost take pride in his lack of attachment to anyone. She had a suspicion that being an orphan was as much a part of his identity as her being over-imaginative.

"I already tried to get an audience with the Earl of Henleigh, but he is in the country." She pursed her lips. "I cannot think of anyone else I can speak to whilst being discrete. After all, it is hardly something many people would know of and I would so hate to cause any rumors or problems."

"Then you must keep this to yourself," Mabel said firmly. "At least until you can either get him to admit he knows or speak with the earl."

Rosamunde blew out a breath. She did not much like the thought of keeping anything from Russell. Being dishonest always made her uncomfortable anyway but lying to Russell would be a hundred times worse, especially about something as important as family. But what other choice did she have? She could not reveal such a thing and risk scandal without at least confirming the truth behind it. Not to mention, she had little idea if the earl even wanted such a thing revealed.

"What a rotten situation," she muttered more to herself than anything.

"Well, at least no one would ever be able to protest the two of you courting," Mabel said, her smile wide. "He is wealthy *and* has noble blood in him."

Rosamunde looked to the ceiling. "We are not going to court," she replied firmly.

"We shall see," Mabel said. "Shall we not, Mr. Pompadour?" She pressed several kisses to the dog's head. "We shall see."

Chapter Eighteen

Something was wrong.

No. Not wrong.

Different.

Rosamunde kept twitching in her seat. Or fiddling with the buttons on her gloves. Or toying with the latch on the carriage window.

Russell didn't usually mind different. In fact, he usually did well with it. He stayed in different places all the time, ate different meals. Hell, spending time with Rosamunde was about the most time he'd spent with anyone with the exception of The Kidnap Club.

He was comfortable with different. Different meant no chance of attachment.

At least until now.

"Is something the matter?"

Her head whipped around. "No. Of course not. Why would you ask?"

He fixed her with a look. "That is the sixth time you have redone that button." He nodded to her glove.

She dropped her hand from the glove and offered a swift smile. It didn't reach her eyes and that was different too. Rosamunde's smile always reached her eyes, and Russell had to prevent himself from curling a fist when he considered the fact that someone might have done something to upset her and stop those little crinkles around her eyes.

"Nothing is wrong," she said tightly.

Nothing. Christ. Something really had to be wrong. His gut bunched at the words. He might not do entanglements with women but even he knew *nothing* was dangerous. Even worse than her being different.

"Rosamunde..."

"I am perfectly fine, Russell. I promise." Her smile broadened slightly but he still didn't see any eye crinkles.

She turned her attention to the passing scenery. As soon as he'd contacted her with the information that her uncle might be in Bath, she'd demanded they depart. They would stay in the family townhouse, she had announced, though Russell rather hoped he'd be able to escape to a nearby inn. The last thing he needed was to be staying with her family. It wouldn't do to get comfortable with them.

With any luck, they'd find her Uncle Albert holed up in Bath somewhere and he'd never see Rosamunde or her family again. He most certainly did not want to find himself almost enjoying hers or their company.

Because, oddly, he had almost enjoyed his dinner with her strange, noisy family.

They were all mad, of course. Just like Rosamunde. They spoke when they wished to, talked over each other, laughed readily, and could be counted on to have some of the oddest ideas. Like the uncle who was convinced the world was to end in the year two thousand and twelve or the aunt who insisted on reading everyone's fortune from their palm and could only tell them all that they were to meet a tall, dark stranger.

In his case, he probably was the tall, dark stranger and if he let himself, he almost didn't feel like a stranger. It made no sense really. Why should they welcome him, someone of no lineage and no obvious connections?

He shook his head and eyed the back of Rosamunde's hat. There was no sense in dwelling on her family. Especially when he had a woman who had spoken the dreaded *nothing* aloud in his presence.

"Is it your uncle?" he ventured.

She twisted around. "Pardon?"

"Your uncle? Is that what is wrong? You are worried for him?"

"Oh. Yes. That's it. I'm terribly concerned for Uncle Albert."

"We'll find him."

"Yes, I've no doubt we will."

So if she thought that, what the devil was wrong? He blew out a lengthy breath. He never regretted not taking the time to understand women. Until now. He didn't like the slightly concerned creases on her brow or the way her lips kept pinching. Not one jot. And he wished to hell he could figure out how to fix it.

She opened her mouth, then closed it.

"Rosamunde?"

Rosamunde tilted her head slightly and peered at him. "When you say you are an orphan, did you mean you have no one at all? Not even any siblings?"

Goddamn it. He thought she'd forgotten the whole sorry story. "Rosamunde," he warned.

"I have at least one more question," she protested. "Consider that my final one if you must." She sighed. "I do not see what the problem is with talking of our pasts between friends."

"You hardly speak of your husband," he reminded her.

"Well, there is nothing to say! He was acceptable, he did not treat me poorly—"

"He neglected you and your needs. I'd say that was poor treatment. Hell, if I was your husband, I would—" He stilled. "Anyway, I am not the only one who does not speak of the past."

"Because my past means nothing."

There it was again. The dreaded nothing. "That simply is not true, Rosamunde. It shapes us into who we are now. I have no doubt your miserable marriage shaped you."

"It wasn't miserable," she protested. "Just a little dull. And if you think the past is so important, why will you not speak of yours?"

Blast, she had him there. "There's nothing to speak of."

"Nothing," she repeated. "How can that possibly be true?"

Nothing. He was really beginning to loathe that word. "Why should anyone want to hear the sorry story of an orphan?"

An eyebrow arched, telling him that she really did want to hear the story.

"I was an orphan, grew up on the streets, worked hard to get out of poverty, and now I am the man you see before you. The end."

"The end?" She pressed a palm to her face. "Russell, you skipped, oh, at least twenty years there."

"Is this what the problem is? That you do not know my story?"

"Yes. No. Well, in a way."

He tightened his jaw. So, he could fix the nothing if he just told her it all. Spilled his guts to her. And, God, was he tempted, but that part of his life was behind him. He barely gave it a moment's thought unless he had to. He'd rather not think about his aching belly, or the fights on the streets to survive, or even his time as a soldier. Why she should even want to hear such awful stories, he could not fathom.

As much as he wanted to see her smiling properly again, he couldn't do it.

"Rosamunde," he started, "I—" The carriage came to a sudden halt, cutting him off. "What the—" He looked out the window and cursed under his breath.

"What is it?"

"Highwaymen," he muttered.

"HIGHWAYMEN?" ROSEMUNDE ECHOED.

Russell's mouth set into a grim line. "Yes."

She peered out of the window to spy two men on foot, one with a pistol pointed at the driver. She couldn't make out the words being flung back and forth between the driver and the men through the closed window, but it did not sound like a pleasant exchange.

She narrowed her gaze at Russell. "This is not to do with you, is it?"

"Why the devil would I have something to do with this?" He bent over to look under the carriage seat. "No gun?" he said, rising. "Doesn't your family learn?"

"We hardly expected yet another kidnapping attempt!" She gripped her skirts and began to lift them. "You are certain these are not part of your kidnapping club?"

"The Kidnap Club," he corrected. "That's what we call ourselves."

"Well?" she demanded.

"This is nothing to do with me." He tossed off his hat and pushed a hand through his hair. "I should have brought my pistol," he muttered.

Hoisting her skirts to her thighs, she slipped the pretty, jeweled penknife from her garter. "Will this help?"

He shook his head and shoved down her skirts with one hand. "Likely not but it's better than nothing."

Rosamunde's heart picked up speed when the men walked over to the carriage.

"Just do as they say," Russell said through gritted teeth. "Do not give them a reason to harm you."

"Are we not going to fight back?"

"*You* are going to do nothing," he ordered.

The carriage door swung open and Rosamunde found herself staring at the end of a pistol. She swallowed hard. It had been instinctual to fight Russell off when he'd grabbed her but this time, she remained frozen, her limbs unmoving. Why would they not work? Why could she not spring into action? Had Russell's presence turned her into some helpless female?

"Good afternoon, ladies and gentlemen." The man with the pistol peered into the carriage. "Well, lady and gentleman," he corrected. "All your finest goods, please. Jewelry, coin, and the like." He gave a gap-toothed grin.

Rosamunde touched the ruby necklace she wore. It had been her great-grandmother's and she wasn't certain she wished to part with it.

"Now!" the man snapped whilst his companion lingered back, a wary eye on the driver.

"Rosie," Russell urged. "Give the man what he wants." He flicked a glance at the knife concealed in her hand. "Give him everything, yes?"

"I do like a man who can take orders," the highwayman quipped.

She nodded slowly and gave a shaky smile. He had something planned, she just was not certain what. "Yes. Of course. Everything." She opened her palm on the penknife, revealing the jewels. The man's eyes lit upon it, his grin widening.

"That will make a good start."

As he went to grab it, she flicked it open and thrust it forward. The knife rammed into his outstretched palm and he released a howl of pain and snatched his hand back, ripping the handle of the knife from her grip.

Russell rose and flung himself from the carriage, landing on top of the man. The pistol flew from the outlaw's hand and skittered across the dry road. Rosamunde rose from the chair and thrust her head out of the carriage. She eyed the brawl occurring on the ground. The second man had joined in, thrusting a fist into Russell's side in an attempt to get him off his friend. What should she do? The driver clambered down but Mr. Wimpole was old, and she did not think he could do much in the tussle that was currently occurring.

"Stay there, Mr. Wimpole," she ordered, jumping from the carriage. She dashed over to the gun, but the second man snatched her ankle, flinging her hard against the floor.

"*Oof.*" Her chin met ground, sending sparks behind her eyes. She rolled over and pressed her stinging palms together whilst trying to focus through the slight haze. Where had that pistol gone now?

But she didn't need it. Like a beast rising from the mist, Russell stood, shoving off the second man and throwing a punch. It connected with his jaw and he staggered back, landing on his rear. A swift kick to the first man had him flopping around like a fish. The other outlaw rose once more but Russell turned, meeting his face with another punch that knocked him to the ground, prone and senseless.

Rosamunde gaped. She'd known Russell was strong and capable, but she had never seen anything like this.

"Let's go before anyone else gets here," he ordered the driver, giving the first man one last kick then turning to Rosamunde.

He offered her a hand and she slipped her fingers into his, feeling the rough warmth seep through her gloves. Before she could take a step, he swept her up into his arms and carried her into the carriage.

"They might have friends," she heard him say to the driver. "Move fast."

Her skirts awry, her glasses halfway down her nose, and her white gloves filthy, she gaped at Russell as he climbed in and slammed the door shut. The carriage moved off swiftly, leaving behind the injured men.

"Rosie, are you well?"

She blinked at him a few times and he shifted closer to her on the seat. A finger under her chin, he lifted her face to peer into her eyes. Was she well? What a question. She had never seen anything so...so exciting!

"Rosie?" He swept a thumb across her chin. "Can you hear me? Are you harmed?"

She blinked a few more times.

"Rosamunde!" he barked.

"Oh. Yes. I am fine. I think."

"Good." He tilted his head and eyed her chin. "You have a little cut." Russell untied his cravat and dabbed her chin a few times, revealing a tiny red stain. "Nothing serious though."

She eyed the bloodied fabric. "I have a perfectly good handkerchief, somewhere."

His lip tilted. "Well, I'm not about to search your person for it."

"No, of course not." She remained frozen, captured by the one little finger he kept under her chin. His gaze searched hers.

"You seem a little dazed."

"Well, one might be after being held up by highwaymen." She released a long breath. "Not to mention stabbing a man."

His lips curved. "You did well."

Not as well as he did. Gosh, she wished she could fight like that. Had he learned that in the war? Or on the streets of London perhaps? Her worry about trying to find out if he knew about his brother had vanished and all she could think of was how ridiculously handsome and wonderful he seemed right now with his hair tussled, his cravat gone, and his fists dirty.

There was something very, very wrong with her, but she suspected she had never been so attracted to a man in all her life.

"You did well," he repeated then dropped a swift kiss to her lips.

She gasped at the contact, but it was gone in mere seconds and she did not seem to have the energy to draw him back into her and demand he make it a proper kiss.

"You'll have to get a new knife, though."

"My knife...?" He glanced toward her bunched skirts and she shoved them down hastily. "Oh, my knife. Well, I think I want a bigger one for next time."

He chuckled and shook his head. "There better not be a next time."

He meant the highwaymen, she knew that much, but she could not help feeling he also meant the kiss. Even with how brief it had been, she wished he'd do it again. And again. And again. She sighed and unbuttoned her messy gloves to peel them off and inspect her sore palms. Trust her to turn a meeting with highwaymen into some romantic story that would never exist.

Chapter Nineteen

The flashing of lights behind his eyes roused Russell. He groaned inwardly and put a hand to his neck as he straightened and peered outside. Squinting at the lit lamps that moved past, he concluded they'd reached Bath. When he spied the Pump Room, he knew they had. He tilted his head this way and that to ease the ache from sleeping awkwardly in the carriage and glanced down at Rosamunde.

He shook his head to himself. Her glasses dangled from a gloved finger and her head lolled against his shoulder. The dark confines of the carriage and dull lamplight meant he couldn't make out her freckles but, as always, they taunted him with their presence, especially while she remained asleep. He wanted to flick a finger over her nose then kiss each freckle now that her glasses were gone.

He plucked her spectacles from her fingers and folded them carefully then tucked them into his waistcoat pocket. Any other woman would be fretting about travelling two days on the road to Bath after such an incident but not Rosamunde.

No, the bloody woman could only talk about where she might find a bigger knife or if she needed to practice her archery. There was no denying she was utterly mad.

And he damn well liked it.

He eyed the buildings as they passed, great stone monoliths that all looked the same. He'd been to Bath several times for work but never for pleasure.

Not that this was for pleasure, he reminded himself. There was no pleasure to be had here, none at all. Aiding Rosamunde was work. After all, he was being paid handsomely to find her uncle.

The carriage came to a halt outside of a tall townhouse on one of the finest streets. A small front garden, blooming with flowers, was fenced off from the stone pavement, but no lights shone behind any of the windows. He scowled. With the size of Rosamunde's family, they'd expected at least a couple of her family members would be here.

She stirred, blinked a few times, and rubbed her eyes. "Oh." She straightened and leaned over to look by their feet. "My glasses."

He tugged them out of his pocket, unfolded the arms, and set them upon her nose.

She eyed him sleepily, a little crease between her brows. "Oh."

He cursed silently. He could have handed them to her. That would have been the easiest thing to do, surely? But no. Of course he could not resist a chance to touch her, even if it was a mere skim of hair.

Just like he had not been able to resist a quick kiss to her lips after their encounter with the highwaymen. It had been a minor miracle he hadn't bundled her to him and kissed every inch of her, including the thighs where that stupid knife had been pressed. He'd received several hits to his ribs, and they ached even now but he had barely felt the blows at the time. His only concern had been Rosamunde and her safety.

"We're here," she murmured, leaning around him to look at the house. She scowled. "Where is everyone?"

"Perhaps they're asleep."

"What time is it?"

He plucked out his pocket watch and turned it toward the light of the streetlamp. "Twenty past eight."

She shook her head. "They wouldn't be asleep so early. Besides, the servants would still be awake."

The driver opened the door and Russell climbed out then offered a hand to Rosamunde. "I'll take a look around," he said. "Don't unload the luggage," he told Mr. Wimpole. "Not yet at least."

"Need me to come with you?" Mr. Wimpole suggested.

"You do not think it is dangerous, do you?" Rosamunde's eyes widened. "Could this be to do with Uncle Albert going missing?"

"I couldn't say." He gestured to Mr. Wimpole. "Stay here with Lady Rothmere." He opened his palm. "You have a key?"

She nodded and fished in her reticule for it. "I wish I still had my knife."

Russell shook his head with a sigh and headed toward the house, careful to keep to the shadows. He turned the key in the lock slowly then inched open the door, braced for an attacker. The house sounded empty and as he moved through each room, he realized there was no nefarious plot but simply that none of her family were in Bath and thus there were no servants needed. Sheets still covered the furnishings and shutters remained closed. He made sure to check each room before heading back outside.

"It simply seems as if no one is home."

"Oh dear." Rosamunde chewed on her bottom lip. "Mama had been certain at least Uncle Barnaby would be here."

"We could stay at one of the inns," Russell suggested. "I was intending to find a room at the Crown and Rose. It's a decent establishment."

She wrinkled her nose. "It seems silly when we have a perfectly good house." She glanced up at the building. "No, we'll stay here," she said firmly.

"I can't play no lady's maid," muttered Mr. Wimpole as he unloaded the luggage. "And I can't cook."

"I should have brought Mrs. Lambert with me but she's been unwell, and I thought Uncle Barnaby would have his staff with him."

"I don't think you should stay here alone." Russell followed her into the empty drawing room, watching as she lit a lamp and threw open the shutters. "It could be dangerous if it is known it is just you."

"I have Mr. Wimpole."

He glanced back to see the driver slowly unloading the luggage. "Mr. Wimpole can barely climb down from the carriage let alone protect you."

"I am quite capable of looking after myself." She pottered around and lit a few candles, warming the cool, blue toned room.

"Even without servants?"

"Especially without servants," she declared. "One should be prepared for any circumstance and should be able to rely on just one's self."

He could not help but let his lips curve. Of course she thought she could look after herself. God, if there was ever a demonstration of how different their worlds were, this was it. She probably couldn't even unbutton her dress while he had survived alone since the age of five.

Russell released a breath. "I'll stay here with you."

She grinned and he could not help but wonder if he had fallen into some sort of trap.

WELL, SHE HAD not planned things this way, but she would not complain about how they worked out. It made far more sense for Russell to stay with her. Not to mention, the idea of staying alone in the vast house did not much appeal, no matter what she said about looking after herself.

It wasn't a lie. She really could, she was certain of it. She'd cultivated many skills should the need ever arise.

Once Mr. Wimpole had brought in their luggage, he tugged out a handkerchief and wiped his brow. "All set, my lady, but I daren't unpack for you. I've little idea how to, uh, handle a lady's garments. Should have brought your lady's maid with you," he muttered.

"Thank you, Mr. Wimpole."

"I'll set up the horses in the stables and turn in shortly."

"Do you not wish to eat before turning in?"

He shook his head vigorously, his eyes wide. "I cannot cook, and I certainly would not have you or Mr. Russell waiting on me, my lady." He shook his head again. "Perish the thought."

She suspected it was less to do with propriety and more to do with him doubting either of their cooking skills. "But—"

"I'll get a pie just down the road." He thrust a thumb. "I have a hankering for some meat and potato pie."

"If you are certain."

"Oh yes, my lady. Most certain." Mr. Wimpole hastened out of the house and shut the door behind him.

She stared at the door for a moment. "It seems Mr. Wimpole does not trust us to feed him," she said to Russell as he came back downstairs, having deposited the bags in the bedrooms.

He lifted a brow. "Should he trust us?"

"I can cook."

His brow lifted higher.

"I can," she protested. "I have practiced many times."

"I doubt there'll be much to eat here but I can put together a few things."

"You can cook too?"

"Do you doubt me?"

After what she had seen yesterday with the highwaymen she did not think she could ever doubt him. If Russell could cook as well as he could brawl, they would have no problems. "Not at all."

"Let's see what we have." He patted his stomach. "I'm famished. Or...we could always find rooms at an inn."

"No, we should stay here. Maybe if Uncle Albert is in town, he will come here."

He shrugged. "Lead the way to the kitchen."

They traipsed downstairs and Russell lit a few candles and the large lamp on the table in the center of the room. She peered into the cold storage and grimaced. "Not much, though it looks as though there's some dried meat, and a few vegetables." She drew out a limp-looking carrot.

"Plenty of honey and jam." He lifted a few jars from one of the cupboards.

"We could make a cake."

"A cake?" he repeated.

"Well, we have plenty of flour. That will do for dessert and we can even make some dumplings if there's any butter."

"There is." He came from behind her and pointed out the butter jar. "And we can make a stew of sorts."

She twisted and smiled. "See? We can have quite the acceptable meal."

He peered at her for a few moments and she realized how close they were. One mere step back and she would be in his arms. That was, if he put his arms around her. Which he would not. Most likely, she would bump into him and he would think she was merely being clumsy instead of romantic.

He cleared his throat and stepped back. "We had better get started."

Well, he could not make it anymore obvious. He did not want anything romantic from her, and she would do well to remember that.

"Yes. Of course." She turned away from him so he could not see her warm cheeks then gathered up all the ingredients.

Russell set to work on the vegetable stew whilst she put together the ingredients for a jam sponge. By the time she had the cake in the oven, the stew was well under way. She inhaled deeply. "That smells divine."

"Being in the army taught me a thing or two about cooking with few ingredients."

"I can imagine."

"The cake smells excellent too." His stomach grumbled. "Really excellent."

She leaned back against the table. "When I was young, I would sneak into the kitchens and force the kitchen maids into letting me help. I was determined I would know how to feed myself should I ever need to."

He smiled softly. "Why did you think you would need to?"

"Well, I always intended to escape."

"Escape?"

"I love my family dearly but growing up with them was...intense. I always wanted to run away, even if it was simply to some remote Scottish island and fend for myself." She lifted a shoulder. "I knew I would need to be able to cook for myself."

"I think you would miss your family."

"I probably would, but that does not mean I would not mind the occasional break from them. You've met them, after all. I would wager you were grateful you only had to spend a mere evening with them."

"They were interesting."

She fixed him with a look. "Interesting or simply awful?"

"No, I mean interesting. I've never seen a family like it. Or any family, really, but I know not all families are filled with that much love. Your aunts and uncles and cousins, they all actually want to spend time with each other. It's quite remarkable."

"I suppose it is." She shook her head to herself. She'd never thought of them as remarkable. Mostly they were just too noisy and always prying into her affairs. But seeing them through Russell's eyes, it did make her appreciate them all the more. At least she always had someone she could turn to. Which reminded her...she really needed to find out what he knew of his lineage.

"Russell—"

He turned away and stirred the pot. "Looks like the stew is ready. The bowls are over there." He nodded toward the dresser.

Rosamunde opened her mouth then closed it. It seemed their conversation was at an end. What a pity, especially when she was on the verge of finding out more about him.

And, boy, did she want to know more.

Still, they had time. If Uncle Albert was not here, they would have to do some searching, and she almost hoped he would not be easy to find, just so she could spend more time with Russell.

"Sorry, Uncle Albert," she muttered under her breath.

"Pardon?"

"I was just saying it smells delicious," she said with a smile as she handed him a bowl.

Their fingers brushed and a rush of sensation ran up her arm. She exhaled slowly. Keeping her head about this man was going to be more difficult than ever but she could not bring herself to wish it to end.

Chapter Twenty

"So I thought that we could—"

Russell whirled around at the sound of Rosamunde's voice. Her eyes widened and her lips parted. He muttered a quick curse, tightening the towel around his hips. Her gaze raked over him.

"I, um..." Her cheeks grew rosy, but she didn't move.

"Rosamunde," he said, the word a growl of warning. She needed to leave. Now. Before he made them both extremely uncomfortable.

Because, hell, she was too pretty this morning. The morning rays slipping in through the gap in the curtains warmed her skin and she wore a slightly crinkled gown of rich purple. The high bodice emphasized her curves.

Hell, who was he kidding? It wasn't just how she looked this morning that he found so appealing. Last night, the whole cooking debacle, sharing stew and cake with her...it had tweaked something inside him. Maybe even softened him. She was still as beautiful and as tempting as ever but he felt weaker, like she'd punched a hole in his bruised ribs and was working her way inside.

"I did not realize you were hurt," she whispered, her gaze lingered on the bruises on his torso.

He shrugged and swept a hand through his damp hair. "It's not painful," he lied.

His ribs throbbed and had kept him awake but it was nothing compared to the agonizing ache of need she caused inside him.

She unfroze and closed the distance between them. He gritted his teeth, wishing like hell he could bark at her, tell her to scram, but somehow, the woman held a power over him that he couldn't deny. He even let her put her finger to his ribs to inspect the bruises.

He sucked in a breath through his teeth.

"Forgive me, does that hurt?" Her gaze met his, wide and wary, but too beautiful.

Yes, it hurt. All over. Wanting her hurt him in so many ways. Physically and mentally too. He couldn't want her, shouldn't want her. He had nothing to offer. She didn't need his money and if he was honest, she barely needed his help. The bruises weren't just outside but inside too. He had no idea how to be a person to rely on and even less idea how to give someone like Rosamunde everything she needed. She came from this loud, boisterous, loving family, and he simply couldn't match that.

"It's fine," he said tightly.

She gave him a little prod in the side, and he gave a little groan. "Your ribs could be broken," she gasped.

"They're not broken."

"Let me just check."

He tried to twist away to grab his shirt and put an end to this, but she moved around him, blocking his path.

"I just want to check the other side," she said, matter-of-factly.

Damn it. He closed his eyes briefly and offered himself up to her. The sooner he let her check him, the sooner this could be over. Russell had learned quickly there was no arguing with Rosamunde.

She ran her fingers over his ribs.

He tensed his abdomen and forced himself to focus on a spot of wallpaper where birds flittered about the branch of a tree.

"Does that hurt here?" she asked.

"No," he lied.

Just being near her killed him. Cooking with her, living as though they were practically married, was draining him of every barrier he'd ever put in place. Rosamunde kept smashing through somehow, impressing him then enchanting him.

"Rosamunde, I am fine, I promise."

"I wish you had said something. You should have rested." She glanced up at him. "Perhaps you should take today to rest. I can quite easily—"

"I don't need rest."

He needed to be busy. Needed to put an end to their time together as swiftly as possible. Much longer with her and he had no idea what sort of a man he would turn into. She already tested his usually excellent self-control and he found himself wanting—no, craving—things he'd never wanted before. More dinners with her. More carriage rides together. The scent of her on his clothes, the feel of her beneath his fingertips.

If he wasn't careful, he would no longer be satisfied with the life of a wandering bachelor, and he could not afford to imagine there might be anything else for him. Their circumstances were too different, and nothing could convince him otherwise.

"You have a tattoo." She followed the faded pattern with a fingertip, her eyes wide.

"A misspent youth."

"You have so many scars," she murmured. Her finger traced down his side.

"The war," he muttered, flinching at her touch.

"I have a similar one."

He lifted a brow. "I doubt you were sliced by the end of a bayonet."

"Well, no but it was a sword."

He shook his head, unable to keep the smile from curving his lips. "Of course it was."

"I challenged Cousin Joseph to a fight when I was twelve."

"And he won?"

"Hardly." She wrinkled her nose. "He mocked me, saying I couldn't fight dirty, so I punched him. As he fell over, his blade caught my side." She motioned to her ribs. "I doubt it was nearly as deep as yours, however." She sighed. "I was never allowed near the armory again."

"Good."

She pressed a finger near his clavicle. "I have one here too."

"Let me guess, you challenged someone to a duel."

Rosamunde shook her head with a smile. "Nothing exciting. I fell from a tree and skewered myself on a branch."

"Skewered? Good Lord, woman."

She laughed and loosened her fichu to tug down the neck of her dress. "See, it goes from front to back?"

He touched the puckered scar then turned her around to see the other side of it. "Christ, I bet that hurt."

She nodded. "Much more than the sword, especially when they had to pull it out."

"You're lucky you didn't die of infection."

"I am lucky it did not hit anything important. And that my mother ever let me out of the house again."

He eyed her. "How is it a young, well-brought up lady found herself climbing trees and challenging cousins to sword fights?"

"It was more exciting than embroidery or piano, I suppose." She sighed. "I always did want more."

She moved marginally and he realized his fingers lingered on her skin. He snapped his hand away swiftly. But not quickly enough.

MORE. SHE'D ALWAYS wanted more. Now, she wanted more, well, Russell. Wanted his fingers on her more, wanted him to look at her like that more. His gaze dropped to her shoulder then back to her lips then scanned her gaze. Her chest tightened and the room filled with this odd sort of thickness. Her skin tingled where he had touched it.

Her gaze fell to his chest, to the scars littering his tight abdomen. A tiny trail of hair led down into his pantaloons. Her fingers twitched with the need to trace it. Only moments ago, she'd been touching his body, feeling his warm flesh. She needed to touch him more. Slowly, she reached out, landing on a tiny white scar not far from his hip. He drew in a breath between his teeth and she saw his muscles flex.

"How did you get this one?" she asked softly.

"Knife fight."

"And this?" She moved to a tiny round one, covering his heart.

"When I was a boy. I don't remember how."

She flattened her palm over it. How awful it must have been to be a child on the streets, struggling to survive alone. His heart beat fiercely against her palm. She longed to take the pain away from him, the pain that lingered in his gaze. The pain of the scars and the experiences.

Russell put his hand over hers then tugged her fingers away. "Rosamunde," he said.

A warning.

Well, she never listened to warnings before and she was not going to listen now. She tugged her fingers from his and splayed both hands over his chest. "Yes, Russell?" she murmured, lifting her chin.

His gaze dropped again, and his lips parted. She wasn't wrong, he wanted to kiss her. And she could not think of anything she wished for more.

He lowered his head then paused, his gaze searching hers. Perhaps he expected her to retreat but she'd never been capable of surrendering and she would not start now. Kissing Russell was an adventure she craved almost more than anything, regardless of their suitability for one another, irrespective of whether he would want her again.

His breath smelled minty and was warm upon her lips. She lifted her chin higher.

He closed the gap in a rush, the sudden heat of his mouth making her cry out. His hands curved around her waist as if to hold her in place and prevent her escaping.

As if she would ever wish to. His mouth slanted across hers and she moved her hands upward to grip onto his shoulders. He urged open her lips with his and swept his tongue into her mouth. Her legs trembled at the contact, her insides knotted. He held her firm and strong and as carried away as she was by his kiss, he kept her rooted. She tangled her tongue with his, over and over, losing herself to the sensations.

His hand skimmed up and squeezed her breast through her bodice. She moaned against his mouth and moved into the touch, receiving it gratefully. He moved his fingers up then pressed them down, underneath her stays. She gasped when his fingers met her hard nipple.

"Hell's teeth," he muttered, drawing back and flicking her nipple with his fingers. He ducked his head and covered her breast with his mouth.

"Oh."

Her eyes widened at the heat and dampness. The sight of his dark hair against her skin made her body pulse. She splayed her hands over the taut muscles of his back and offered herself to him. He eased her other breast out and lavished attention there too, murmuring sweet words against her skin, sweet words she would never have expected to hear from such a stoic man. Talk of her beauty, how delicious she tasted, how much he craved her.

He moved away from her breasts and down, dropping to his knees. She watched, wide-eyed, as he lifted her skirts and she heard him suck in a breath once she was revealed to him. She glanced in the mirror and a flood of dampness settled between her legs at the sight in front of her. Her breasts were revealed, rosy and wet from his kisses. Her skirts were hitched high. She couldn't see Russell in the reflection, but his fingers were curled into the fabric of her gown. She had never seen anything so...so erotic.

He lifted her skirts higher and moved between her legs. She felt the heat of his breath upon her tender flesh. Digging her fingers into his shoulders, she held her breath and waited for that first touch. His tongue swept over her flesh in one swift movement and she cried out.

"Oh my." She gripped onto him tighter.

Russell made a rumbling sound of appreciation, sending tiny tremors through her. He urged a leg up and over his shoulder then licked again. She tilted her head back and clung onto him for dear life while he licked and tasted and nibbled, running his tongue in circles around that sweet, sweet spot until she feared she would collapse. His hands curved over her bare rear, keeping her firmly against his mouth until the pleasure crescendoed and burst over her.

Gulping down breaths, she closed her eyes and waited for the pleasure to dissipate while he licked gently, coaxing every ounce of it from her. Gradually, it faded, leaving her feeling as though she could sleep for a week. He eased away, dropping his grip from her rear then lowering her skirts and finally standing. He swiped a hand over his mouth.

"No one..." She sucked in a breath. "No one has ever done that to me before."

His gaze took on that strange intensity that she never quite understood. He twisted away and splashed his face with water. "Gentlemen probably don't do that to their wives," he muttered.

As he turned, his mouth stretched into a grim line. Rosamunde swiftly tugged up her bodice, feeling suddenly exposed.

"I'm not a gentleman, if you recall," he reminded her.

"I do not...that is—"

"I'll be ready in a moment. Then we can get on with our search."

She tried to swallow the knot in her throat. She was no fool. She read what he was trying to tell her. He regretted making love to her with his mouth. It was a warning, a reminder not to get too close to him, not to let her imagination run away with her. Russell did not want her, and that wouldn't change.

Chapter Twenty-One

"Rosie!"

Russell paused in the hallway of the townhouse and peered down at the petite dark-haired woman.

She giggled. "Oh, you are definitely not Rosie, Mr. Russell." Mabel peered around him. "Where is she?"

"I'm not certain, Miss Heston," he muttered to her cousin.

Truth be told, he had done his best to avoid her this morning. They had not broken their fast together and he had dressed with haste, intending to search Bath without her. They had already decided Rosamunde would call upon friends and acquaintances to see if anyone had heard from or seen Albert and he would search the gentlemen's clubs and any less savory areas.

So there really was no need for them to even see each other. He released a breath through his nostrils. Especially when he had seen far, far too much of her yesterday.

She stepped around him, coming to the bottom of the stairs. "Rosie," she called up the stairs. "Mabel is here." She twisted. "Whatever have you done to my cousin?"

"Nothing," he snapped quickly. "That is, your cousin is perfectly well."

Confusion flitted briefly across her face then she smiled swiftly. "I only meant she is not normally late to rise."

He cursed inwardly. Neither of them had been late to rise. He half-wished he had been. Then perhaps he wouldn't have ended up with his face under her skirts and his tongue buried in...

"She'll be down in a moment." He snatched his hat from the hat stand in the hallway. "Now, if you'll—"

Mabel stepped in front of him, hands to her hips. "Wait!" Her gaze narrowed. "Are you two alone here?"

He lifted a shoulder.

"Goodness me." She ran her gaze up and down him. "You seem a good, dependable sort of a man, and my family likes you." Her pursed lips broke into a smile. "Well, I like you too."

"Good, now if you'll—"

"But," she lifted a finger, "I feel I must warn you, Mr. Russell, I do not wish to see any unsavory behavior toward my cousin."

"Unsavory?" he repeated.

Like kissing her and touching her and tasting every inch of her? Unsavory like that? Because it was far too late to take back his behavior now, even if he wanted to. Which he did. Absolutely.

Didn't he?

Christ, he couldn't help thinking he'd take that moment to the grave with him, even if it was a huge mistake. What if he'd given her the wrong impression? He was a damned cad, touching her like that. Once more, he had proved to them both he was nothing more than a kid from the gutters in fine clothing. There was no disguising who he was at the heart of it all.

"Rosamunde is a handsome woman. Not to mention clever and humorous," Mabel said. "Many a man would be quite content to be in your shoes."

"Believe me, I—"

She stepped closer, lifting her chin to view him. "I need to know what your intentions are toward my cousin."

He stared down at the little woman and groaned inwardly. What was it with this family and their utter pig-headedness? He could move her aside with a mere flick of a finger, yet she was trying to intimidate him?

"I have no intentions."

"No intentions?"

"None."

She shook her head. "Well, that isn't possible. I have seen the way you look at her."

"It is entirely possible, I assure you."

"No."

"Yes."

"Miss Heston, I am merely the hired help. I know full well there is no future for Rosamunde and me."

"Ah."

He didn't want to ask. He *shouldn't* ask. "Ah?"

"You think you are not good enough for her."

"I did not—"

She shrugged. "You are probably right. There are few men good enough for her. But I think she likes you."

"No." He couldn't let himself believe it. Even if she did like him just a jot, it was no good. The divide between them was enough to prevent anything happening between them but add in his inability to form relationships, and it was a disaster waiting to happen. He wasn't willing to put Rosamunde through such a thing.

"She had a rather miserable marriage, you know."

He nodded. "I know."

"I always hoped she would find someone more exciting, someone who would treat her like the wonderful person she is." Mabel pursed her lips. "It could be you."

"No."

"Yes."

"Rosamunde is titled. Your family is wealthy," he pointed out.

"You are wealthy." She nodded toward his waistcoat. "No one wears such buttons unless they have a large amount of excess wealth."

"I could be in debt."

"A man like you? No, certainly not." She looked up at him. "You are a very in-control sort of a man. I know because my father is similar. I doubt you have ever had a debt to your name."

Good Lord, who was this woman? He had certainly underestimated Rosamunde's cousin. Apparently quite a shrewd character hid behind the easy laughs and charming smile.

She waved a hand. "Anyway, it comes down to this." She pointed at him. "Rosamunde deserves all happiness."

"I agree."

"Good, so you will agree with me that you will not ever, ever hurt her."

He blinked. "Are you...threatening me, Miss Heston?"

She released a laugh. "Oh, I suppose I am."

He inhaled slowly. "Well, I can assure you that I shall never hurt Rosamunde."

Her shoulders relaxed. "Oh good." She tapped his arm. "Because I do like you, Mr. Russell, I really do. But you must understand, Rosie is almost like a sister to me and she deserves the world."

"I agree."

"Excellent." She beamed at him. "I'm so glad we had this little talk."

"If you'll excuse me, Miss Heston." He put on his hat, dipped his head to her, then left swiftly before she could issue anymore threats.

Which were entirely unnecessary. He wouldn't hurt Rosemond, because he would never put himself in the spot of being able to do so. All he had to do was ensure he never touched her again. Easy enough, surely?

THE SLAM OF the front door echoed through the house. Rosamunde scurried downstairs and paused on the bottom step, breathless. "Mabel, what are you doing here?" She eyed the closed door. "Did Russell leave?"

Mabel nodded. "Quite abruptly too. Whatever did you do to the man?"

"What did I do? I haven't seen him since..." Heat rushed into her cheeks and she paused. "What are you doing here?" she repeated.

"Mama heard you were coming to Bath and decided we should join you. She wants to take a look at fabrics for the wedding whilst we are here, but I think there's quite enough of a selection in London." She wrinkled her nose. "I hope Mama does not choose something too old-fashioned."

Rosamunde glanced between her cousin and the closed door. She was not even certain what she would have said to Russell had she caught up with him. He'd been avoiding her since their, um, meeting this morning but she had at least hoped to discuss their plans for the day.

And perhaps had a chance to gauge how he was after their...time together.

He likely feared she would turn into some lovesick debutante who had never felt the touch of a man before.

Well, she supposed that was not a wholly inaccurate description. She was no debutante, nor was she lovesick, but no man had ever touched her there before with his *tongue,* for goodness sakes. Even now, the warm flow of pleasure rung inside her, simmering through her insides and making her face warm.

"Rosamunde?"

She snapped her attention to Mabel. "Yes?"

"I was asking if you two are alone here."

"Well..."

"Goodness, I cannot wait until I am married. Being engaged has certainly afforded me a little more freedom but once I am married..." She grinned. "I shall be able to go anywhere and do anything."

"I'm not certain Hugh will wish to let you out of his sight."

Mabel squeezed her hands together. "Well, that is true. He is quite devoted to me and hardly wanted me to come to Bath for a few days, but I said you needed me, and you know he thinks highly of you."

"I'm perfectly well."

"Rosie, you are *alone* with Mr. Russell. I think even your mother will be a little scandalized by it."

"I hardly expected to be alone and you know Mrs. Lambert is unwell at present. It did not seem fair to bring her when I expected some of the family to be here."

Mabel wrinkled her nose. "I did think Uncle Barnaby mentioned coming to Bath. It is getting far too hot in London now. I wonder where they are?"

Rosamunde shrugged. "They might be with friends. I have yet to find out. We only arrived yesterday."

"Well, I am here now so I can ensure nothing untoward happens." Mabel reached for Rosamunde's arm and tugged her toward her. "That is, unless you wish me not to be here." A smile curved her lips.

"Why on Earth should I want that?" Rosamunde managed to force herself to say, the words a little tight in her throat.

"Because Mr. Russell is handsome, and he cares for you."

Rosamunde shook her head from side to side. "He is here for the money."

"He is here for you," her cousin insisted.

Lord, how her breath caught when she heard such words. But she could not let herself believe it was true.

Because it was not.

For once in her life, she would not let herself be guilty for following the wild trail of her imagination. Not when it could really, really hurt.

"With any luck, we shall find Uncle Albert in Bath and then I shall likely never see Russell again."

"How sad that will be." Mabel tugged Rosamunde into her side. "But I do not think that likely. The man cannot take his eyes off you."

"I do not see how that can be true. He's not even here!"

"I saw him at the dinner party. Plus he gets this odd look when he speaks of you. His eyes go all dark and mysterious."

"He *is* dark and mysterious." Rosamunde sighed. "And believe me, he likes it that way."

Twisting around to face her, Mabel withdrew her arm from hers and clasped Rosamunde's upper arms. "Mr. Russell is many things, but he is also utterly enraptured with you."

"No."

"He is," she insisted.

"I cannot let myself believe that, Mabel."

Mabel gave a soft smile. "Why?"

"Because..." She released a breath. "Because I might like it too much."

"How can it be a bad thing to believe a man adores you?"

"You do not know him, Mabel. He is a man used to being alone. He does not want a lover in his life let alone someone like me, someone who cannot help but spend most of her waking hours dreaming." She bit down on her bottom lip. "What if I dream that he is in love with me and wants more?"

"What if he does want more?"

She fixed her cousin with a look. "Now you are starting to sound like me."

"I always knew I would marry a sweet man and settle down and have babies, but you were always destined for something else, I just knew it. Even after your marriage to the viscount, I was simply waiting to see what was next. Perhaps some exotic prince from a faraway land would take you away..."

"Mabel," she warned.

"But now I see it is a roguish kidnapper who looks at you as though you are some rare treasure."

"Mabel—"

"And he's not wrong. No one is like you, Rosie, and he would be a fool to let you go."

"That's just not true."

"It is. It's why your mother embraced him so fully. Even she saw how excited you were by life again when you started working with him."

"My mother told you that?"

"I overheard her talking to Aunt Janey when she expressed a little surprise about her encouragement."

"Goodness."

Mabel squeezed her arm. "I never took you to be scared, Rosie."

"I'm not," she protested.

"Then you should let yourself go down this path. See where the adventure leads."

"I never quite pictured this sort of adventure," Rosamunde admitted.

"You've never put your heart at risk before. It is the scariest of adventures."

"My heart?"

Mabel nodded sagely. "You are falling for him."

"Oh Lord." Rosamunde pressed a palm to her forehead. Could that even be true?

"Anyway, what are your plans for today? Let us get some fresh air and sun and we can figure out how we will persuade the elusive Mr. Russell to never let you go again."

"I really do not think—"

"We could have a double wedding after all," her cousin exclaimed.

Rosamunde closed her eyes briefly. This was not going to help her keep her feet on the ground at all.

"We are calling on our friends to see if anyone has seen Uncle Albert," Rosamunde said.

"Excellent. Perhaps seeing all the dry old husbands out there will remind you how wonderful Mr. Russell is."

Rosamunde shook her head. She didn't need reminding.

Chapter Twenty-Two

Either Rosamunde didn't hear him enter the kitchen or she was ignoring him. Russell stilled on the last step. She kept her back turned away while she chopped the fresh vegetables, the rhythmic sound of the knife striking wood nearly hiding another noise.

Nearly but not quite.

Rosamunde was crying.

He drew in a careful breath and eyed her shoulders. Yes, definitely crying. Her body moved in odd little jerks, as though she were trying to keep sobs at bay. She sniffed and swiped her face with the back of a hand.

Damn it. What the devil had made her cry? Or who? If he found out, he'd beat the cad to a pulp.

He moved off the final step and her head lifted but she didn't turn. "Russell?"

"It's me."

He slowly closed the gap between them, feeling as though he was approaching a frightened pup who might skitter at any time. He'd never seen Rosamunde cry. He'd never wanted to see her cry. Hell, she was about the most positive person he'd met in his life. It was hard to imagine what might have caused such upset and he couldn't say he was good at helping crying women—Lord knew plenty of their kidnapped women cried for various reasons and he left the comforting up to Nash and Grace. But he had to try for Rosamunde.

"Did you..." She took a long breath in. "Did you find out anything?"

"No."

"Oh." A little sob escaped her.

"Rosie," he said, putting a hand to her shoulder. She didn't turn. "Rosie, what's the matter?"

"Nothing." She sniffled. "Nothing at all. I am just being silly."

"I don't care if it is silly. I don't wish to see you cry."

She dropped the knife onto the table and waved a hand, keeping her head lowered. "Then perhaps you should wait upstairs. I'll bring dinner up."

"I don't think so." He took her shoulders in his hands and twisted her around. Using a finger on her chin, he lifted her face. His heart gave a painful pang at the sight of puffy eyes and tear tracks on her face. She'd been crying for some time. "Rosie," he said softly, "what's the matter?"

Her watery gaze met his and she bit down on her bottom lip. He kept a hold of her arms in case she tried to turn away from him. Whatever was the matter, he had no intention of letting her suffer on her own.

Finally, she drew in a long breath. "I'm just...tired."

"Tired?"

"Of not finding out anything. Of not knowing where Uncle Albert is." She dropped her head to his chest. "Oh, Russell, what if he is harmed? Or dead? I do not think I can bear this not knowing."

He looped his arms around her, drawing her fully into his embrace and cradling her against his body. "We will find him," he vowed. "I promise."

"I cannot believe we have found nothing yet. That no one seems to know anything." Her voice cracked. "And that I am the only one who seems to care."

"You are not the only one who cares." He eased her back slightly and cupped her face to look into her eyes. "I care. And we will find him." He offered a slight smile. "I do not offer promises lightly, you should know that by now, but we will find him."

"But what if we don't?" Her chin quivered.

God, all he wanted to do was to make this better. To find her Uncle Albert and ensure she never cried ever again. If he had to tear apart the whole of England to find the man, he would. Anything for her.

"We will," he assured her, easing off her glasses, setting them aside, and swiping a thumb across a damp cheek. "Rosie, we will."

She drew in a long breath and scanned his gaze. He continued smoothing his thumb across her face, swiping away tears and catching new ones. He had to fix this. In any way he could. He dropped his gaze to her lips and the air in his lungs grew thick, his skin heated. Then he lowered his head.

Her lips rose to meet his and he had the permission he needed. Their lips met in a fierce and sudden clash, the heat inside him reaching boiling point. She gasped and he groaned at the contact. He pressed the kiss deep instantly, giving her no chance to retreat. Not that she seemed to want to. Her fingers looped around his neck, drawing him as close as humanly possible.

"Oh, Russell," she moaned against his mouth.

"Christ," he muttered, using both hands to angle her chin so he could kiss her again and again, over and over. Her tongue tangled with his and he explored every inch of her lips, her mouth. He hurt. So badly. His heart thrust against his chest in an agonizing ache and his body pulsed fiercely, painfully.

Moving his lips to the corner of her mouth then down, he felt her quiver. He kissed along the soft skin of her cheek and down to the crook of her neck. She moaned as he nipped lightly, curling her hands around his arms and digging her fingers into his flesh to draw him closer. Russell drew back only briefly to search her gaze, to ensure she was as lost to this as he was.

"Russell," she begged.

He had no doubt now. He grabbed her waist forcefully and drew her flat against him, then pressed her up against the table as he took her mouth again, her lips hot against his. In one swift motion, he lifted her onto the table, and she coiled her legs around his hips, urging him closer. With a groan, he rocked his aching cock against her while he kissed her deeply, feeling as though he would never get enough of her. He'd never taste enough, never feel enough.

He had to have more.

"GODS'S TEETH," RUSSELL uttered as he drew back, both hands clasping her face. "What are you doing to me?"

"About the same as you are doing to me, I suspect," she replied breathlessly.

Rosamunde's body throbbed all over from her swollen lips, to the little pulses where he'd nipped her skin, to the ache between her thighs. She could scarcely draw breaths let alone conjure up a comprehension of what was happening. One minute she'd been worrying about Uncle Albert and the next Russell was kissing her like a crazed man.

She tightened her grip on his arms and urged him closer once more. Locking her ankles around his waist, she angled herself to feel the hard heat of him bearing down upon her. A growl rose in his throat and he rocked against her, sending sensations pulsing through her.

"Ohhhh."

"You're so beautiful," he said. "These freckles drive me to the edge of insanity." He kissed her nose then her cheek and her lips, delving deep once more.

Freckles? What was he on about? How could freckles drive a man crazy? But she couldn't even find it in her to ask. He rocked into her and she closed her eyes, giving herself up to the blissful sensations. Not one of her wild imaginings had led her here, to being taken in his muscular arms on a kitchen table of all places. To listening to his growled compliments. To being kissed like she'd never been kissed in her whole life.

"Your body, Rosie...It's all I've been able to think about. And your mouth. And kissing you."

For a quiet man, he certainly had a lot to say. And while she could not deny such compliments warmed her inside and out, she didn't need them right now. All she wanted was him. She opened her eyes and wound her hands up to his shoulders.

"Less talk, more action."

His eyes twinkled with amusement. "Anything you say."

Of course, Russell was a man of action so she should not have expected anything less than perfection from him. He bundled her close so she could feel every inch of his hard body against hers. Her nipples pressed agonizingly against her stays, chafing on the fabric. Dampness gathered between her thighs. His arousal rubbed between her legs, jutting up against the thick fabric of her skirts.

He muttered a low curse and shoved her skirts up, his hands curving up her thighs and coming to cup her bare rear. The new angle had her eyes practically rolling back in her head. Hardly any layers separated them now and she felt the shape of him against her, desperate for release.

She needed to feel it. Fully, completely.

Rosamunde reached down between them and fumbled with the buttons and layers. He hissed when her fingers connected with hot, solid flesh. He tilted his head back briefly and sucked in a breath through his teeth then his gaze met hers.

"Rosie..." he warned.

She usually hated that name but not on his lips. Not when he was looking at her with that dark expression she had seen so many times. Now she understood what he'd been thinking. He'd been imagining them flesh to flesh, picturing them together, visualizing touching her. She hadn't been the only one with fanciful thoughts.

"Take me," she urged. "Make me yours."

"Make you mine," he repeated. "God, I want nothing more."

His lips met hers, his tongue clashing with hers over and over. His fingers dug into her rear and kept her just *there*, just at the point of torturous pleasure. His cock met her flesh and she released a whimper. How much longer was he going to make her wait?

"I should make you ready."

She shook her head. Ready? She didn't think she could be anymore ready.

"It's been a while for you."

She shook her head again. "Now," was all she could manage to vocalize.

Russell shifted slightly, kissing the crook of her neck, and she gasped at the feel of his solid arousal pressing against her. Gripping him tight, she urged him forward. He gave one hard thrust and she stiffened, the sudden hardness filling her so deeply that she could scarcely breathe. He froze too, his breaths hot and heavy in her ears. His arms were tense under her grip and the veins in his forearms pulsed.

Then he moved. A slight shift back and forth and she sucked in a breath. He retreated again and slammed back into her. The table rocked underneath her, thudding against the tile floors in rhythm with his pounding. All she could do was hold on and let him take her, let him unleash himself upon her body.

She threw her head back, her eyes scrunched tightly closed while the pleasure built with each hard, primal thrust. This was no sweet touch of pleasure. This was a hot, searing touch that had her barely able to tell where he ended, and she began. She couldn't escape and certainly did not even want to. No imaginary world could draw her away from what he was doing to her body.

He grunted and thrust hard, over and over. She opened her eyes and met his gaze. Sweat sheened on his forehead and his brows were furrowed. He leaned forward and kissed her fiercely, moving hard inside her. There was no escaping the pleasure, no running from the steely thrust of his cock.

She moved her hands down his arms and dug her fingers in while the sensations surged, building to a pinpoint that sapped her breath and stole her thoughts. His gaze never left hers as the crescendo hit. Rosamunde opened her mouth, releasing a silent cry and stiffening while the pleasure rolled over her.

Finally, it passed, leaving a warm, buzzing sensation behind. She dropped her head forward and he gave a few hard thrusts then drew out.

He groaned and she lifted her head to watch his climax. He closed his eyes shut and threw his head back, the tension in his body palpable. His eyes opened as he spilled onto her bare thigh and, slowly, the tension eased from his body. A half-smile flittered over his lips while she rubbed her hands soothingly up and down his arms.

"You're a madwoman," he muttered. "Letting me take you here, on a damned kitchen table."

"I did not exactly plan it."

"Neither did I."

"I do not regret it, though."

His smile broadened. "Neither do I." He leaned in and gave her a sweet kiss. "Neither do I."

Chapter Twenty-Three

Rosamunde hefted her bag onto the dining table and fished a hand around inside it. Peering at her with a raised brow, Russell tried to keep the bemused smile from his face. He also had to force himself to keep his hands at his sides and not heft her onto the table and make love to her again.

He clenched his jaw. Easier said than done. Anyone would have thought he'd be satiated after a night with Rosamunde but apparently not. The damned woman had made him obsessed.

"Whatever are you looking for?" he asked.

She pulled out a scroll of paper and chucked it onto the table, ignoring him. A spare pair of spectacles followed, then several handkerchiefs, the lockpick, and several pocketbooks. He eyed the titles. "Why do you have a book about poisons?"

"They're useful reading," she muttered, peering into the bag. "And I cannot find my rope anywhere."

"Rope?" He folded his arms, leaned back against the table, and shook his head. "Why the devil do you need rope?"

"I don't. Yet."

"Rosie, I have little intention of tying anyone up." He came to her side and took the compass she clasped from her hand then set it on the table. "We'll find him," he vowed.

She blew out a breath. "I'm not even certain where to start now. We shall have to scour the whole country."

"You still have your list of his favorite places to go?"

She nodded.

"Well, we shall start on that now."

"He could be in Scotland for all we know!"

"Then we'll go to Scotland."

Her lips tilted. "We will?"

"We'll go wherever we have to until we find Albert," he vowed.

"And you do not mind coming with me?" she asked hesitantly. "I know you did not expect to be helping me this long."

He smirked. "I do not mind one jot." He dropped a gentle kiss to her lips, holding back deliberately. His self-control was but a thin wire threatening to snap.

She relaxed into him. "Thank you," she murmured and kissed him again.

Russell could have sworn he heard it snap. His self-control vanished in an instant. The moment her lips connected with his, the spark lit, and he pushed a hand around the nape of her neck and looped an arm about her, hauling her into him. She gasped, allowing him to push the kiss deep.

"Oh," she moaned, clawing his arms.

He moved his mouth down her neck, leaving a trail of little bites. Rosamunde shivered and inclined her head back, giving him better access.

"Coo-ee!"

Russell tore away, letting his hands drop. He turned as Mabel entered the room. Her gaze swung between them, a slight smile upon her lips while Rosamunde readjusted her gown beside him.

"Did I interrupt something?"

"Not..." The words failed in his throat. He coughed. "Not at all."

Mabel swept into the room, her dog under one arm, pulled out a chair, and sank onto it. "I only wanted to speak with my cousin." She gave a dramatic sigh and set the fluffy dog on the table. He sniffed his way along the shiny surface, stopping by a discarded wine bottle and giving it a lick.

Rosamunde snatched the empty bottle and put it back on the drink's cabinet. Russell cursed under his breath. If it wasn't enough that Mabel had caught them decidedly flustered, she had also seen the wine they had finished together after hours of lovemaking. All they needed now was to have left one of Rosamunde's stockings slung somewhere and she would have a clear picture of how they had occupied themselves last night.

"Mama is talking of having yellow in the wedding," Mabel wailed. "Yellow!" She looked to Rosamunde. "She knows yellow is not my color at all."

"Perhaps I should..." Russell inched toward the door.

"Oh, Mr. Russell, how I wish my Hugh was like you. You would never let your bride have a color she detests, would you?"

He had met Hugh briefly at the dinner party and he seemed a patient and doting sort—perfect for Mabel in his opinion. He shrugged and shared a look with Rosamunde. "I do not know much about weddings, I'm afraid."

"I'm certain your mother will come around," Rosamunde assured her.

Mabel released another dramatic sigh.

"Perhaps I should...go and make some tea?" Russell suggested. Anything other than stay here and try to advise Mabel on wedding colors. He was most certainly out of his depth.

"An excellent idea," Rosamunde said.

"I would rather have something stronger." Mabel dropped her head to the table.

Hesitating, Russell retrieved the nearly empty bottle of wine and poured a small glass, sliding it across the table.

Mabel lifted her head and smiled. "Thank you." She sipped it and released a long breath. "That's better." The dog tippy-tapped across the table and lapped at the glass. "Even Mr. Pompadour is finding this stressful." She took the dog's face in her hands and pressed a kiss to his snout. "Are you not, Pompy-wompy? You need a nice lap of wine, do you not?" She leaned to peer around Russell. "Is there anymore?"

He lifted the empty bottle. "I'm afraid not."

"Oh yes, that's Uncle Albert's favorite. It's so hard to buy." Mabel set the dog on the floor. "What a shame as it is so delicious. No wonder he goes to such lengths to get it."

"The wine." Rosamunde gasped. "Of course!"

Russell frowned. "The wine?"

"Uncle Albert covets fine alcohol, and this is his favorite French wine. It's hard to come by since the war."

Mabel nodded. "Aunt Janey was complaining only a few weeks ago that he spends time with unsavory sorts all for some silly wine."

"That's it," Rosamunde declared. "I know where he must be."

"You do?" Russell asked.

"The Isle of Wight." She pressed a hand to her forehead. "I should have realized." She pressed her palms to the table and eyed her cousin. "When Aunt Janey was complaining, was it because Uncle Albert was going there?"

Mabel lifted a shoulder. "I was not really paying attention, but I believe so." Her mouth formed an 'o' shape. "So that's where he is!"

Rosamunde twisted to face Russell. "We need to go to the Isle of Wight," she announced. "He must be there, I'm certain of it."

ONCE RUSSELL LEFT to fetch Mr. Wimpole from his lodgings, Rosamunde sank onto the dining chair next to Mabel. "Why did you not say anything?" she asked her cousin.

"About the wine?"

"Well, yes."

"If I am honest, my mind was a little preoccupied with Hugh and his lack of a proposal. Not to mention my kidnapping!"

Rosamunde put a hand over Mabel's. "I know, forgive me. I cannot believe I did not think of it either. I saw some of the wine at his house and it never occurred to me how much he covets it."

"Just think, if you had figured it out then, you would have had no time with Mr. Russell, and how awful that would have been."

"Mabel..."

"You were kissing, were you not?" Her lips curved.

Rosamunde hesitated. There was no sense in lying to Mabel. She would see through her in a heartbeat. But it was hard to admit anything had happened between them, even to herself. It was so new and fresh and wonderful but there had been no time to discuss it or even fathom what it all was. All she knew, was that she craved Russell almost more than her next breath.

"We were kissing," she finally admitted.

"Oh, how wonderful." She clapped her hands together. "I knew he was desperate for you."

"I would not say desperate." Or perhaps she would. He had seemed mightily desperate for her when he'd lifted her up onto the table in the kitchen. And when he had taken her to bed, actually. It had been quite something to feel the desperation in his touch and taste it on his lips. Even with her vivid imagination, she had never been able to picture such moments.

"Gosh, you are quite smitten with him."

Rosamunde looked at her cousin and allowed herself a small smile. "I suppose."

"We really could have a double wedding then." She scooped up Mr. Pompadour. "Do you hear that, Pompy? A double wedding! What a wonderful day it will be, and you will look so handsome walking down the aisle."

Rosamunde lifted a hand. "We really have not discussed the future, Mabel, and I'm not even certain Russell is the marrying type." She pressed her lips together. "In fact, I would say he is most decidedly not."

"Oh pfft. Men change. Look at Hugh. I thought he would never propose but lo and behold, he did!"

"Hugh was always going to propose. The poor man was just terrified you would say no."

"Well, that just goes to show...men have no idea what they are doing."

Rosamunde scowled. "I'm not certain that's at all comforting."

"What I mean to say is, they think one thing but in reality, it's something else."

She let her frown deepen. "Mabel..."

"Mr. Russell thinks he is an independent, mysterious bachelor sort, but he is not." She grinned. "At least not when it comes to you."

"I'm not certain..."

"Well, I am." Her cousin gave her a little nudge. "He will want to marry you, I am certain."

"Enough talking of me, what about this yellow business?"

"Oh, I hardly care now." She waved a hand. "What does a little yellow matter when your favorite cousin is utterly in love?"

"I did not say I was in love."

"You must be. Your cheeks are all flushed and your eyes sparkle. What else could it be other than love?"

Likely satisfaction but Rosamunde certainly was not going to tell her cousin that. "Please do not get carried away," she warned Mabel.

Mabel made a motion of sewing her mouth shut. "I shall not say a word, I promise, but you must, must write to me if anything happens in the Isle of Wight. Especially as I am going to be stuck here looking at ancient patterns with Mama when I would far rather be shopping in London."

"I am certain your mother will not choose anything awful," Rosamunde assured her.

"I wish I could tell her of you and Russell. Then we could plan a much bigger wedding!"

"Mabel," Rosamunde said tightly.

"I know, I know, I will not say a word." She pressed a kiss to the top of her dog's head. "Mr. Pompadour and I shall remain deathly silent until you are engaged."

"I really do not think that will happen. Besides, who says I even wish to marry again?"

"Why would you not? Imagine spending every waking hour with Mr. Russell." Mabel's smile grew mischievous. "Not to mention every sleeping hour too."

"Mabel!"

"What? I am going to be married soon. I will have to come to you for some advice anyway. Goodness knows, Mother said just to lie back and think of England and that sounds horribly dull."

"That does," Rosamunde agreed.

"I would wager Mr. Russell would not wish you doing such a thing either."

Rosamunde shook her head and pinched the bridge of her nose. She was beginning to wish she hadn't admitted a thing to her cousin.

"Your mother shall be pleased, you know."

"Do not—"

"Say anything." Mabel lifted a hand. "I know. I'm simply saying, your mother saw the attraction between you two. Now she has decided that he is a fine man, it's simply perfect."

"I'm not certain—"

"Your father won't say no either. How can he? He might be the *natural* son of an earl, but Mr. Russell still has noble blood in him."

"I have what?"

Rosamunde whipped her head around to find Russell standing in the doorway, his expression thunderous.

"Oops," said Mabel.

Chapter Twenty-Four

"That can't be true." Russell looked between the two women and shook his head. "Where did you hear such a thing?"

"Oh everyone knows," Mabel said. "Well, at least all of our family does. Grandmama knew your father."

"Mabel," Rosamunde hissed.

He swept a hand through his hair, recalling the dinner party with Rosamunde's family and her grandmother's keen interest in him. No bloody wonder. She'd been trying to see if her assumption was correct. Which it was not. How could it be? Guy would have said something.

"It's not true," he insisted.

Rosamunde glanced at her cousin then rose and took Russell's arm, leading him into the drawing room and closing the door behind her. She nibbled on her bottom lip and eyed him.

"It's not true," he repeated.

"It might be."

He narrowed his gaze at her. "How long have you known about this?"

"Since the dinner party," she admitted softly. She stepped closer but he backed away, pausing by the window to peer out. "I tried to find out for certain if it was true. That was why I didn't say anything. I did not wish to cause you any distress."

He whirled on her. "It certainly explains all the damned questions."

"Do you not think I want to know of you anyway, Russell? But I needed to see if you knew." She glanced down at the floor. "There did not seem a good way of broaching the subject."

He moved closer. "Perhaps you could have said before we..." He blew out a breath.

Her eyes widened, her cheeks going hot. "I hardly planned that now, did I?"

"How can I know that? It certainly explains your family's interest in me. Did they have me lined up as your next husband perhaps? I might be the bastard son of an earl, but I'd imagine that's good enough for some people."

She opened her mouth then closed it.

"I imagine it was quite amusing to you all. Laughing at the orphan with little idea of his heritage."

He drew in a long breath, but it was no good. Every inch of him felt hot, dangerous. Just when he thought he might even quite like her family, they'd been amused at his expense, gossiping of his past behind his back. He'd been nothing more than a free bit of entertainment for the rich family.

"My family only found out when I did."

"You think that makes it better?"

"Russell..." She tried to reach out to him, but he ducked her touch. "I knew it would be a shock, which is why I said nothing. I wished to confirm it first."

"Do you not think it might have been better if *I* had been able to confirm it?"

"Maybe, but it's a bit late for that now, is it not?"

"Yes, just a bit," he spat out.

He looked out onto the streets, watching a few pedestrians pass by. How he envied them, continuing on their life as normal. For a brief, blissful moment this morning, he'd thought something had changed. That he and Rosamunde, they could...Well, it didn't matter now. If she could hide such a thing from him, what else was she hiding? Was the uncle missing even real? Goddamn, how could he even be sure this was not some flight of fancy of hers?

"Are you certain you heard correctly?" he asked, motioning with his hand.

She nodded and laced her fingers together in front of her. "You are named for your father, and your mother was a maid in his household. My grandmother knew her sister and the tale of your birth."

"It cannot be true," he muttered.

"I think you should be open to the possibility that it is." She smiled slightly. "Just think, you have a family."

"I don't want a family." He raised his voice. "I don't need a damn family."

"I know this is shocking, Russell, but can you not see this might be a good thing? Surely having these connections is no bad thing?"

"I've done quite well without connections, Rosamunde." He curled his lip. "I survived on my own for long enough. No, in fact, I thrived. I certainly don't need 'connections' now."

"That's not what I meant."

"I know well enough what you meant."

She put a hand to his arm, and he left it there only because he didn't have the energy to fight her off right now. If Guy knew of this, it meant he'd known when he'd approached him to join The Kidnap Club. It meant the work had been some sort of act of charity, most likely.

Well, he didn't need damned charity. He'd done fine on his own.

"If it is true, then you have a brother," she said quietly. "You have a history. Surely that pleases you?"

"What would please me was if people were not discussing my supposed past behind my back." He met her gaze. "It would please me if you were not lying to me, not laughing behind my back."

She frowned. "Come now, do you really think that little of me? You think that I am a gossip, that I enjoy such secrets?"

He searched her pained gaze. He hadn't. At least until now. But maybe he was wrong.

He lifted a shoulder. "Perhaps you are more like your family than you realize."

She took a few steps back. "My family has their flaws, but they are good and kind people. They would never wish hurt upon another and they greeted you with open arms."

"They greeted me because I'm the natural son of an earl."

"If you really believe that then you are more jaded than I realized."

He smirked. "Darling, if you haven't realized that already, then you are more foolish than you look."

ROSAMUNDE SUCKED IN a sharp breath. He did not mean it, she reminded herself. He was lashing out because the bloody silly man could not cope with the idea that he might not be alone in the world. None of his hurtful words were meant.

That did not mean it didn't hurt, though.

"Russell..." She tried to reach for him, but he dodged her touch again. She fisted her hands at her sides. "No one was laughing at you, no one had any designs on you."

Which was sort of true. Her family had seemed to take a liking to him for her. And, well, she had taken a liking to him for herself now. But that had little to do with his heritage.

He folded his arms and eyed her.

"Goodness, my mother was hoping I'd marry a duke not long ago!"

Russell gave a dry laugh. "Of course she was." He shook his head. "I forget how the rich work sometimes. I imagine they thought you were really scraping the barrel with me."

"No one thought anything!" She curled her fists tighter and concentrated on drawing in breaths and not giving into the heat that flowed through her. "They were merely being nice."

He cocked his head. "Is it nice to talk of someone's past behind one's back?"

"It is not like we were all gossiping about you."

"I struggle to believe that. Your family is quite skilled in that area."

"My family talks a lot, I will give you that, but they are certainly not malicious." She took a step forward. "Russell, please, I know you are hurt but—"

"I am not hurt," he snapped. "To be hurt, one has to care. I do not care if your family gets enjoyment from the lowborn situations of others. I do not care what they think of me." He folded his arms. "Hell, I do not even care what you think of me, Rosie. Because it doesn't matter so long as you pay me."

"Well, I had thought it might matter a little."

"I'm hired help, nothing more." He lifted his shoulders. "And for all I know, you hired me as some form of entertainment. Well, I hope you got your money's worth, my lady."

She let her brows furrow. "Entertainment? Russell, I—"

"For all I know, this uncle doesn't even exist. I know you find life dull so why not create some mystery?"

"Well, that's quite rude."

"Need I remind you I grew up on the streets. I'm not a gentleman." He moved closer, unfolded his arms, towering over her. He dropped his voice. "Why not fuck the bastard son of an earl?"

Rosamunde staggered back a few steps, the coarse word ringing in her ears. Heat flowed into her cheeks and she felt as though she had been struck. Her heart throbbed painfully against her chest while she peered up at him, not quite able to believe he had uttered such words. What they had done had been more than a f...Well, it was more than that. It had been special. Goodness, she had even thought that maybe...

"You clearly do not know me at all," she said, her voice tight.

"I know you are a bored little miss with little to do but make up stories about missing uncles merely to gain some excitement in life."

"How...how dare you!" Tears burned in her eyes, blurring her vision, and she swiped them away angrily. Out of everyone, Russell had been the one person to believe her. Had been the one person not to think her foolish.

"I dare, my lady, with ease." His lips curled. "I should never have indulged your fantasies."

"You said you believed me."

"Because you were paying me, or have you forgotten that part?"

"Uncle Albert is missing," she insisted. "You even said yourself you thought something was amiss or else you would never have accepted the job."

"Or perhaps I said that so I could get paid."

"No." She shook her head vigorously. "You would not have taken it. Besides, everyone says you are wealthy. You don't even need the money."

His expression darkened. "So not only was I the bastard son of an earl, but I was wealthy too. No wonder your family took a liking to me."

"We did not even know that at first!" she protested. "And I can think of a few more suitors they would rather court me over you."

His lips twisted into a bitter line. "Yes, I don't suppose I would ever be good enough for you."

"I thought you might be," she whispered.

He stilled, his jaw working. For a moment, she thought it might be over, that he would take her into his arms and apologize for his hurtful words and accept hers for not speaking up sooner. For a moment, that possibility existed, and she held her breath. The moment fled. He turned away, allowing her a brief glance into a cold expression.

"I think it is high time we put an end to this farce. I have other business so see to."

"But what about the Isle of Wight?"

He paused by the door. "Go home, Rosie. You don't belong on some foolish adventure. Go home where you belong."

"I still need to pay you," she said hastily, searching her mind for reasons to prevent him from going.

"Consider last night payment."

She took a few steps back until the backs of her knees met a chair. He glanced briefly at her, his gaze meeting hers, and for a short second, she could have sworn she saw regret. But he left anyway. Left her with a searing pain in her chest. Left her with words that singed her to her soul.

Sinking on the chair, she buried her face in her hands. Tears wouldn't come and she almost wished they would because surely that would be better? Surely it would help to get the pain out? How could he say such things? Infer that she was some sort of...sort of whore! How dare he.

She lifted her head as the door creaked open, the hope in her chest quickly disappearing when Mabel slipped into the room.

"Has he gone?" Rosamunde asked, her voice tight.

Mabel nodded. "He seemed angry."

"He was."

Mabel sank onto the chair next to her. "What shall you do now?"

She straightened her shoulders. Damn him. If he wanted to be an ass about all of this, then let him be. It didn't mean Uncle Albert had to suffer. She'd wanted to find him, and she could do that without Russell's help. "I'm going to the Isle of Wight," she said firmly, "and I'm going to find Uncle Albert."

Chapter Twenty-Five

He wished it hadn't taken him so long to track Guy down. The days of travelling to Suffolk estate then back to London had given Russell too much time to ruminate. Especially on how he'd dealt with Rosamunde. He fisted his hands and pushed past a group of people meandering along the pavement by Regent's Park.

He couldn't forget the hurt on her face.

He couldn't forget that she'd still tried to appeal to his better nature.

As if he had a better nature. Their argument had only served to highlight their differences—to highlight how little he belonged in her world. No matter how much money or fine clothes he accrued—and even if he had the blood of an earl running through his veins—he couldn't remove the touch of filth from his past. He'd been born in the gutters and the stench still clung to him. After speaking so crudely to Rosamunde, that much was extremely apparent.

He stopped outside Guy's London house and peered up at the building that spanned much of the street. Calling it a townhouse seemed ridiculous when the building would sit quite easily on a generous estate in the middle of the countryside and still dominate the landscape. He'd known where Guy spent time in London ever since they'd met but he never visited thanks to trying to keep their association with The Kidnap Club secret. Now he could not help but wonder if it was because Guy had been trying to keep *him* a secret.

A butler answered the door, took his name, and vanished, leaving him in the middle of a lavish hallway, scattered with paintings and looked over by a giant chandelier.

He allowed himself a small smile. If his father had claimed him, he might have something close to this for himself. In truth, he could probably afford a nice home anyway but the thought of coming home to the same house all the time...well, until recently the thought had made his gut clench.

Until Rosamunde, that was. Until that damned night in the kitchen.

Tapping a foot, he folded his arms. He should never have given in to his needs. It had clouded everything, it had twisted him up inside so that he hardly knew who he was anymore. Bastard? Lover? Orphan? Who the hell knew?

Guy stepped into the hallway, his brows raised. "I didn't really expect it to be you." He gestured for Russell to follow him.

"You know many men called Marcus Russell?" he asked dryly as he followed him into a wood-paneled study.

Letters were scattered across a large mahogany desk and books lined shelves behind it. Guy's fingers were ink-stained, and his cravat was askew. Whatever business Guy had been attending to, it was stressful.

Whatever business his *brother* was attending to, he corrected himself.

"I thought you understood that you should never be seen here," Guy said, pouring a dram of brandy and handing it to Russell. Russell ignored the drink and remained standing while

Guy perched on the edge of his desk. He eyed Russell. "It must be something grave indeed."

He ground his teeth together. He'd pictured this meeting over and over. Imagined demanding an explanation. Even visualized slamming Guy against a wall and telling him their association was over, that he did not appreciate being lied to.

But all the fight had gone out of him. It might well have deserted him the moment he spoke to Rosamunde in such a way. He blew out a breath. "Tell me truthfully, did you know?"

Guy's brow furrowed. "Know?"

"Damn it, Guy."

Guy gave a slight smile and pushed away from the desk. "Did I know we are brothers?"

"Half-brothers," Russell corrected.

"I knew."

Russell pressed a hot breath out between his teeth. "Why did you not say something?" He rubbed a hand over his face. "Did you track me down deliberately? Hell, have you been pulling strings all this time?"

"Pulling strings?"

"Ensuring my business dealings went well," he muttered. "I never needed charity, you know."

"I know that, Russ. I know you probably have more spare wealth than me and Nash combined."

"Hardly."

Guy lifted his hands. "I had nothing to do with any of that."

Russell released a breath. The thought that maybe everything he'd achieved had been nothing to do with his smarts or ambition had been etching a hole inside of him ever since he'd found out about Guy.

"I did know, though, before I invited you to join The Kidnap Club."

"So that was charity?"

Guy shook his head. "I realized you were clever. Exceedingly clever. Plus you had the background that I needed. Someone willing to get dirty and who could hold his own."

"It is true then," Russell murmured, more to himself than anything.

"You are my brother," Guy confirmed. "I realized it as soon as we met. You have our father's eyes." He nodded toward a portrait of a man who looked like an older version of Guy. "Plus you carried his name. It was no stretch of the imagination to think my father might have sired you—he was not exactly faithful to my mother."

Russell took a step forward and eyed the painting. Though Russell didn't see much of himself in there, they had the same piercing blue eyes that so many women commented on. He moved back, his chest tight.

"I did a little research and found out about your mother. It looks as though my father had a brief moment of conscience before his death and tried to track you down, but you were lost to us then."

"I wasn't lost."

Guy shrugged. "By the time I got to know you, I knew you'd not take this news well. I'm sorry that I kept it from you, but you might understand why."

"Rosamunde knew," he said. "She and her family. They figured it out."

"I'm sorry for that too. You should have heard it from me." Guy stepped forward and put a hand to his shoulder. "I won't give you anything you do not wish for, but I would like to claim you as a brother."

Russell clenched his jaw. He'd been so set on remaining how he was—an orphan with no family, a self-made man. He hardly knew how to be a brother, let alone the son of an earl. But everything had been changing recently.

Thanks to Rosamunde.

"I—"

The door opened and the butler thrust out a platter with a card on it. "Forgive me, my lord, but there is a loud young woman here demanding to speak with you."

Guy took the card but barely had time to glance at it before Rosamunde's cousin barged into the study. She gasped when her gaze met Russell's. "Oh goodness. I came here looking for Lord Henleigh to see if he could find you but here you are." She paused and drew in a long breath. "I have been looking all over Bath then London for you."

Russell's gut twisted. "What is it, Mabel?"

"It's Rosie. She's gone to the Isle of Wight alone. I thought she might be fine—you know how tough she is—but she promised to send me word as soon as she arrived, and I have heard nothing. I'm worried she has become tangled up in whatever has happened to Uncle Albert."

Damn it. Of course she'd go off on her own. He should have anticipated it. No one could match Rosamunde's determination.

He looked to Guy. "We'll have to finish this conversation later. I'm going to the Isle of Wight."

Guy lifted a brow, his gaze lighting with amusement. "Naturally."

Chapter Twenty-Six

Russell froze when he saw her, his heart following suit.

Her eyes widened when she spotted him at the top of the stairs. Rosamunde stilled in the inn doorway. "Russell!"

He closed the distance in three quick strides. "I'm sorry," he managed to murmur before curving a hand around her neck and pressing his lips to hers.

He hadn't planned it this way. Lord knew, nothing ever worked out as planned when it came to Rosamunde. For the first time in his life, he didn't care. His plans could go to hell so long as he had Rosamunde.

She gasped and flung her arms around him, returning his kiss with the same hunger he felt. They'd been apart for mere days, but it felt like an eternity. Too long without touching, too long without seeing her. He backed her up into the room and kicked the door shut.

"I'm sorry," he repeated between kisses.

She tugged at his cravat.

"I was a fool."

"Yes," she murmured, drawing the cravat from his collar and flinging it aside.

"I thought I might have lost you."

"No." She worked loose his waistcoat buttons while he fought to find the ribbon at the back of her gown and untie it. He peppered kisses down her face, her neck, her décolletage, then started work on the tiny buttons at the front of her dress.

"God, I missed you." He claimed her mouth again, her lips hot against his. She moaned and wound herself closer, pressing her breasts against his chest. He groaned in response.

"I missed you too."

He tore off his jacket and she shoved his waistcoat from him then started unbuttoning his shirt. The tiny buttons on her gown did not seem to want to cooperate and he broke the kiss briefly so he could concentrate on removing the bloody thing from her. She kissed his neck, trailing little bites down his skin that made him shudder.

"You are not making this any easier," he murmured.

"Good. You do not deserve easier."

"I know." He shoved her dress down her arms to her hips. "I said terrible things."

"You did." She wriggled the gown from her hips, leaving her clad in her stays and petticoat. He issued a harsh breath at the sight of her breasts straining at the corset, her curves highlighted by the gentle boning.

Grasping her waist in both hands, he drew her into him, taking her mouth again. She surrendered instantly, giving him everything he craved and more.

"I don't even deserve your forgiveness," he said against her mouth while he worked at the lacing of her stays.

She shoved his shirt from his shoulders and spread her palms across his chest. He hissed at the feel of her warm fingers and closed his eyes briefly. To think he'd nearly lost this, lost her. He had to be the biggest damned fool in the world. He opened his eyes when she pressed a hot, open-mouthed kiss to his chest.

Briefly, he held her there, his hand cupping the back of her head, allowing himself a brief moment of relishing her being so close.

Rosamunde looked up at him, her hands dropping to his trousers. "Probably not," she agreed.

"I will do whatever it takes." He kissed her lips. "Whatever you want of me. I don't care. I'm yours."

She stepped back and pushed her petticoat down, then slipped off her shoes and peeled down her stockings. The corset went next and he feared something must have happened to him on the journey here. Because surely he had died and gone to heaven.

The early morning light slipped over her skin, highlighting the generous curve of her breasts, the slight softness of her belly, the length of her thighs, and the shadows between them. Her dark hair was awry, spilling over one shoulder and her glasses slipped down her nose.

"And I'm yours," she finally said.

"Christ."

In what had to be the fastest undressing in the history of mankind, he undressed, then scooped her up. She latched her legs around his hips while he gripped her rear. Her body was hot against his. Hot and damned perfect. His arms shook, not from exertion, but from sheer disbelief that he had this amazing, beautiful, utterly mad woman in his arms.

And she wanted him. After all he had done, she wanted him. He'd never met a woman so loving and loyal. For all the awful things in the world he'd experienced, she was the cure. She was the heaven to his own personal hell.

He never wanted to lose her again.

Carrying her over to the bed, he laid her down on the deep red blanket, her milky skin a stark pale contrast against it. He scarcely had time to admire her before she wrapped her arms around him and drew him down to her.

Their kisses grew frantic and he could hardly fathom how he'd survived a day without her, let alone several. When this was over, he never wanted to be apart from her. It would be amusing if the thought of losing her again didn't make his heart pound painfully. He, the lone orphan, now had a brother and a woman he loved.

Because there was no denying it. She'd chiseled through his every barrier and was deep in his hard heart.

He slipped a hand between them and found her wet and ready. She released a small cry when he touched her, moving his fingers over the core of her.

"Do not make me wait," she urged.

"Tell me again."

"What?" she asked, kissing his jawline.

"Tell me you're mine."

"I'm yours." She kissed his chin. "I'm yours," she repeated, pressing her lips to his.

He pulled off her glasses and tossed them onto the table at the bedside then positioned himself between her legs. He kept his weight braced on his palms and met her gaze.

"I'm yours," she repeated, her gaze never wavering. "I'm yours."

He pushed inside her with a groan.

"I'm yours." Her voice grew in pitch. "Oh God, I'm yours."

ROSAMUNDE SUSPECTED SHE'D been his long ago. Maybe even when he'd first kidnapped her.

He shifted inside her, stealing her breath. She clung on, moving with the waves, unable to do anything but meet his intense gaze and thank the Lord he was here.

After days of waiting for the winds to die down so she could catch the ferry to the island, she had never anticipated seeing Russell again but the sight of him in the hallway, his expression contrite, had undone any anger she'd held. He'd been hurt and had lashed out like an injured animal. She'd known that at the time but seeing this strong, tall man so vulnerable had made it impossible not to forgive him.

She gripped his arms and he surged forward. The tendons in his neck stood out in stark contrast to the planes of his shoulders. She gasped and took everything he could give her, over and over.

The bed rattled beneath them while the sweet, steely heat of him pressed inside her. He never looked away, his gaze locked on hers. He'd ceased apologizing now, but she saw everything she needed in his eyes. Gone was the doubt. This was nothing to do with her imagination. He needed her as much as she needed him.

As much as she loved him too.

She slipped her hands down his spine, curling one hand around his taut rear, the other splayed over this back. His muscles flexed with tension and he groaned her name, burying his head into her neck. He nipped and nibbled, sending shivers through her.

Meanwhile, pleasure built with each delicious push of his body. She arched her back, moving into the sensations. He pushed back up onto his arms and rocked forward, hard. Then again and again, thrusting into her with such force, she scarcely knew how to hold onto her sanity.

"You're mine," he said, his voice hoarse. "And I'm yours."

"Yes," she moaned. "Oh yes."

"Mine, mine, mine," he said each time he pressed into her.

"Yes!"

The pleasure peaked swiftly, quicker than she'd anticipated, crashing around her like the ocean waves. It thundered through her and she gripped Russell's body tight, clinging on for dear life while it ebbed up and down her body until it seeped away, and she was left satiated and limp.

Russell bundled her to him and stilled, his body frozen in pleasure. With a deep groan, he released into her, moving gently inside her until his muscles relaxed. He dropped a gentle kiss to her lips and Rosamunde smoothed her palms up and down his damp skin.

"I am so sorry."

She smiled. "For that? There is definitely nothing for which to apologize there."

He hesitated. "I meant for leaving you. And for my words. But I shouldn't have..." He indicated between them.

"Oh."

"Unless..." He blew out a breath.

"You don't need to apologize. I wanted that."

His lips tilted, the slightest hint of a smile upon them. She pressed her fingers to his mouth and traced the curve. "You should smile more often."

"Don't get used to it." He eased out of her and rolled onto his back, drawing her with him so that she was cradled in one arm.

She lifted up to view him, tracing a finger across his chest and the puckered scar that sat over his heart. "You're still smiling," she teased.

"Fine. Maybe get used to it. Occasionally."

"You are quite handsome when you smile."

He lifted a brow. "Are you saying there are times when I'm not handsome?"

"Goodness, I did not mark you as a man of vanity. Perhaps I have you all wrong."

He shook his head and rubbed her shoulder. "You seem to understand me better than anyone. Somehow, you knew precisely why I was such an ass when you told me of my father."

"You think you are all mysterious, but I do not believe you are as elusive as you'd like to think."

He eyed her, that smile still hovering on his lips. "You would be the only one to think that."

"I'm the only one to know you," she declared.

"That might very well be true."

She dropped her head to the crook of his shoulder and took a moment to absorb the feeling of being so safe in his arms. "Did you speak with the Earl of Henleigh?"

"I did."

She lifted up again to look at him. "And?"

"It's true."

"I see."

"I didn't get much chance to hash it out with him because I thought someone was in trouble."

"Me?"

He nodded. "Mabel said she hadn't heard from you and was worried." He blew out a breath. "I thought I might have lost you."

"Gosh. I did send a letter. Perhaps it is simply delayed, but I am not sad it brought you back to me."

"Neither am I, but it doesn't make me any less of an ass for leaving you in the first place."

"Perhaps not but I can think of a few ways you can make it up to me." She kissed the very corner of his mouth, where his lips were curved upward.

"Oh?"

"Or maybe *many* ways." She kissed his chin, the side of his face, even the tip of his nose.

"Many ways," he echoed. "I think I can do that."

Suddenly, he shifted, rolling her onto her back and covering her body with his. "Many, many ways actually. After all, I do have a lot of apologizing to do."

Chapter Twenty-Seven

"Take off your coat."

Rosamunde's eyebrow arched as Russell entered their room at the inn.

Russell chuckled. "Not like that. I just mean we aren't going anywhere today." He pulled off his jacket and slung it over the back of the wooden chair.

Tucked into one end of the building, the room in which they were staying was split into two, with a dressing room just past the fireplace. He'd thanked God Rosamunde had booked herself into a relatively respectable establishment but many of the hotels on the coast served sailors and other coarse types, so he didn't regret rushing to her side.

He didn't regret a damned thing. Not even spilling inside her many a time last night. After this was all over, he was going to ask for her hand in marriage.

He allowed himself a smile.

"What is it?"

"Nothing." If he was going to do it, he'd do it properly. Approach her father and buy a house somewhere. He might be no gentleman, but he'd treat her like the lady she was.

"I take it it's too windy again."

He nodded and set his hat on the hat stand. "No ferries today."

She blew a strand of hair out of her face. "Why is it England can never make up its mind when it comes to the weather? We've had such warm, sunny days recently."

He peered out of the window that overlooked the docks. "It's still sunny, just damned windy. The waves are too big for such a small boat."

"I missed the one pleasant day because of you." She slunk over toward him, looping her arms around his waist. "I was about to catch the ferry when you arrived."

"I know you're keen to find your Uncle Albert and we will, I promise. Chances are he's staying on the island and could not get a message to you with the seas being the way they are."

"I'm beginning to conclude you are right." She nibbled on her bottom lip. "And at least you made it worthwhile."

"Minx."

She pressed herself up against him and kissed him lightly, leaving him wanting more. He inhaled slowly and fought to slip back into his usual mode—the all business Russell that was not entirely infatuated with this crazy, wonderful woman. It was a fight, but he needed to keep his head level while he was protecting her. As much as he was certain Albert wasn't actually in trouble anymore and this was all just a lack of communication, he couldn't afford to lower his defenses.

God knew, he'd done enough of that yesterday.

"Rosie," he warned when she slipped her hands between them.

"You know I used to hate people calling me that, but it feels nice to hear you say it."

"I could always call you Lady Rothmere," he offered.

She wrinkled her nose. "I'd rather not think about my late-husband when I am with you, thank you very much."

"I'd certainly rather you not think of him either." A knock at the door snared his attention and he strode over, letting in the maid.

"Food?" Rosamunde asked.

He nodded. "As we're not going anywhere, I thought it best we have a decent meal." He pressed a hand to his stomach. "Some of us haven't eaten since yesterday lunchtime."

And some of them had used up a ridiculous amount of stamina making love to the most beautiful woman in the world. He didn't say it aloud, but her eyes crinkled at the corners and he knew she was thinking the same.

The maid set out the food and left them to it. He motioned for Rosamunde to sit then dropped onto the chair opposite her. A slightly overcooked pie nearly spilled over the edge of the plate, its crust thick and flaky. They'd also been provided with a jug of ale and two cups.

"Remember the last time we shared an ale?" She gestured to the jug.

"*An* ale? If I recall correctly, you had several and were quite merry afterward."

"You know, I never did get around to asking you that last question," she mused.

He paused, his knife halfway through the pie. "You had better make it a good one."

"I think I should be allowed many more questions after last night."

"Was it not enough to satisfy you, my lady?"

"I was certainly satisfied." A lovely blush creeped into her cheeks. "But only in one way. My curiosity will never be satisfied I suspect."

"You always do seem to enjoy getting into trouble."

"I do not intend to!" she protested. "But I cannot help myself. I have always wanted adventure, and no one seems to understand that."

"I can, in a way."

"But you've had a lifetime of adventure. Surely you do not want more?"

"Not more adventure, no, but I always wanted more. Ever since I was a boy, all I could think of was having everything I never had."

"And now you have it."

He nodded. "I do, and more than I could have imagined, but it never seemed enough. At least not until—"

"Until?"

No, he couldn't say it. Not yet. If he was to do this, he'd do it properly.

"That was a question," he pointed out.

"No!" She shook her head vigorously. "That scarcely counts as a question."

He smirked. "Fine. Ask away. After my behavior, I cannot deny you anything."

"Any question?" She pressed a finger to her lips. "Goodness, I must have millions."

"Go on then, but I'm going to eat while you think." He took a bite of pie and despite the slightly burnt crust, it melted in his mouth. He ate swiftly and she watched him for a few moments, her eyes wide.

"I never noticed how rapidly you eat."

He shrugged. "I cannot help myself. I guess it comes from the days when I didn't know when my next meal would be."

"I would have to agree." She cocked her head and eyed him. "What will you do, now that you know you have a family?"

"I haven't thought about it much, but I cannot see that things need change. I don't need charity."

"But will you try to have a relationship with your brother?"

He stilled. He had lost any anger toward Guy now, but it was hard to consider having a real brother. Having said that, Guy was about the closest thing to a friend he had, and he did not much want to lose that, despite himself.

"I suppose I will."

Her lips curved. "You are softer than you realize, Marcus Russell."

He was. Softer than she realized too because he knew now, he'd do anything for her. He'd settle down and play the son of an earl and see his brother for dinner parties in the country and take walks in the park and attend charity balls or whatever the hell gentlemen did. He'd do it all. But only for her.

ROSEMUNDE COULD NOT quite fathom why he kept getting that odd little smile on his face, but she rather liked it.

"I think I should get to ask you questions too."

She furrowed her brows. "Me? But you know everything."

He leaned in, his smile growing wicked. "I know many, many things about you but I want to know more."

She glanced at the made bed.

He chuckled. "I appreciate your belief in my stamina, Rosie, but even I need sustenance and rest occasionally."

Her cheeks warmed. "Forgive me. It has been a long time since...well...and it was never like that."

"Good." He took a long gulp of ale. "It might make me a barbarian, but I'll be damned if I like the thought of you being with another man."

"It definitely makes you a barbarian, but I quite like it," she admitted.

"Good to know. I'm not a gentleman," he reminded her.

"I am aware of that," she said primly. "But I am barely a lady."

He shook his head. "You are most definitely a lady," he said. "An unusual one but still a lady."

"I do not feel much like a lady after, well..." She gestured to the bed.

"Why did you marry?" he asked abruptly.

Rosamunde blinked a few times. "It was what I was meant to do."

"I don't think I could ever persuade you to do anything against your will."

"I was young. Only eighteen. I hardly knew any different."

"And yet you wanted more?"

"I did." She pushed the remainder of her meal around the plate with a fork. "But I did not know how to get it." She released a long breath. "I did not enjoy being married much but I do not regret that I have freedoms now that most women do not. Besides, it could have been much worse. You must know that with what you do for women."

His mouth stretched into a thin line. "That I do." He met her gaze, seeming to search for something. "Your family talked of your remarrying."

"Apparently one marriage isn't enough for them. They mean well, though, they only want to ensure I'm looked after."

"Despite the fact that if there is one woman who does not need looking after it is you."

She rubbed the end of her nose. "It's hard to imagine being married again."

"Ah."

"Ah?"

He shook his head. "Nothing."

"How is it you ended up questioning me? You offered me full access, if you recall?"

Russell opened his arms wide. "I'm at your disposal."

Goodness the thoughts that rushed through her mind at his words. At her disposal. To think she had spent all night with this man in her bed and she would likely get more. They had not spoken of the future, but he wanted her as his. She was hesitant to let herself think of anything more. They would be lovers, maybe for the rest of their days, was her conclusion. How could she let herself think of anything more when she knew how averse to the idea of family he was?

"How did you gain your wealth?"

"Lots of business deals and investments."

"Yes, but how did it begin?"

He hesitated. "Pickpocketing to start with." He watched her reaction, so she concentrated on keeping it neutral. "Then I managed to get a job at the docks. I saw the goods coming in and made note of those products that were most in demand. It was easy to figure out what the next big thing would be. So once I had enough saved, I invested."

"That's mightily clever of you."

He shrugged. "I've always been one to observe. It came naturally to me."

"Why do you still live modestly?"

He motioned to his clothing. "None of this is modest."

"You have never spoken of a house or arrived in a carriage, and I am certain my family would know if you had some great country pile somewhere. I have to assume either you do not wish to show them to me, or you have neither."

"I don't do possessions particularly, no," he agreed.

Another reason why she should not picture a specific future for them.

"Do you wish to?" she could not help herself asking.

His eyes took on that odd intense look, the one that said he was keeping his feelings to himself. Perhaps she had asked too much. He'd already surprised her with his candor.

"You do not have to answer that." She offered a quick smile. "You have already answered more than I anticipated."

He shrugged. "I can deny you nothing, Rosie. You should know that by now." He finished his ale. "And there is certainly one thing of which I wish to take possession."

His eyes darkened and her breathing quickened in response. Her body was already attuned to him, still warm and flushed from his touches and kisses last night. She moistened her lips with a quick dart of her tongue and fought for a response through her desire-muddled brain. How she could feel such a way after a night of lovemaking, she could not fathom, but she had a suspicion this would never abate. They would always be able to light the fire with the tiniest spark.

Russell saved her a response, standing up so quickly that his chair fell to the floor with a thud. He scooped her up in one swift movement and carried her over to the bed then laid her down. He moved over her, his gaze hunting hers. "You said you were mine, do you remember?"

"I remember."

"Good."

"You thought I had forgotten?"

"Perhaps."

She shook her head. How a man like Russell could seem so vulnerable at times, she did not know. Creases were etched between his brows and she smoothed them out with a finger. "I'm yours, Russell. To do with as you wish."

"As am I," he muttered, coming down for a kiss. "As am I."

Chapter Twenty-Eight

The white cliffs of the island gleamed under the morning sun. Wind threatened to tear the hat from Russell's head, so he kept one hand on that and another around Rosamunde's waist. Despite the clear day, the seas were still unpleasant, and he regretted he'd ignored his gut and allowed the ferryman to take them out. Still, they were nearly to the shore and in one piece. He jumped out when they reached the beach and aided the old man in dragging the boat up onto the shore then aided Rosamunde onto the soft, damp sand.

A hand to her bonnet, she peered up at the cliffs. "There's nothing here."

The ferryman shrugged. "The tides have taken us about a mile from Fishbourne. It's not too far a walk." He gestured toward the small cluster of buildings that could just be seen farther along the island.

Russell peered at the town. "It won't take us long," he assured her.

She gave a tight smile and took his offered hand so he could aid her across the sand toward a narrow path that cut through the slope of the grass. Unease ate into his gut, but he couldn't tell if it was because something was amiss or that this would soon be over.

Not over, though, he told himself. She'd talked of being uncertain about marriage, but she still wanted to be his. That had to mean something surely? He blew out a breath. These were uncharted waters for him, and he could scarcely recall the last time he'd been doubtful of his next move.

"I hope he's there," Rosamunde said once they were away from the unsheltered coastland, nodding in the direction of the town.

"The island's small. We'll find him," he assured her.

"I have little idea what to do if he's not here."

He squeezed her hand and pulled her into him. "We'll figure that out together."

Her expression softened a little and she nodded. "Yes, we will."

Just as he hoped they'd figure out their future together. He just had to consider how to broach the subject. But first, they had to find her Uncle Albert.

Once they reached Fishbourne, they headed toward the dock where the majority of the inns were clustered. The scent of fish lingered in the air and the main street was cluttered with market stalls and carts filled with produce. Most of the buildings were painted white with blackened window frames and wooden beams.

Keeping hold of her hand, Russell carved a path through the crowded, narrow roads until they emerged out near the sea once more. Several masted ships were docked and wooden crates and barrels cluttered the main road. He gestured to the first inn.

"Let's try here. The ferryman said this was the finest inn on the island."

She nodded. "I hope he's here," she murmured as he led her into the tall white building.

He approached the main desk and rang the bell. The low murmur of conversation could be heard from the room next door, which he assumed was the dining room. His stomach grumbled and Rosamunde chuckled.

"Hungry again?"

He gave her a look. "Someone made me miss the morning meal."

"If you had arisen earlier, we would not have missed it."

He leaned on the desk and gave the bell another ring. "If someone had not kept me up late, I would have been able to rise earlier."

She folded her arms. "Are you complaining?"

"God, no." He shook his head with a grin. "Never." He scowled and peered around. "Where the devil is everyone?"

"Likely still serving the morning meal." She peered through the glass window of the door to the dining room. "Let us go see."

She nudged open the door and he followed her into a narrow dining room that occupied much of the front of the building, making the most of the morning sunlight. He shut the door behind him and nearly crashed into Rosamunde when she froze.

"Rosie?"

"Uncle Albert..."

"What?"

"Uncle Albert," she repeated, loudly enough for a gentleman to lift his head from eating his meal.

"Little Rosie!" The man waved his hand vigorously.

Rosamunde marched over to the older gentleman. Russell had seen paintings of him at Albert's house, but the man was a little more ruddy-faced than the pictures and his faded red hair sat at all sorts of strange angles.

He showed no signs of some awful ordeal, though. His clothes were clean and neat, and he caught the glimmer of a pocket watch chain hanging from his waistcoat, so he had not been robbed it seemed. He followed Rosamunde over, keeping back slightly.

"What are you doing here?" he asked, gesturing for them to join him. He glanced up at Russell. "And who is this chap?"

She opened her mouth then shut it, peering at the large meal before him and what looked to be a nearly empty bottle of wine. "This is the man I hired to help me find you." She exhaled. "Uncle Albert, I thought you were in trouble."

A white eyebrow lifted. "Trouble? Goodness, no. Well, sort of, but that's all over now." He motioned to the chairs. "Sit, sit. You look a little tired."

"That's because I have been searching for you." She dragged out the chair, sitting with a huff, and Russell sat next to her. "I received no word from you, Uncle. I would normally have received at least two letters from you by now."

He grimaced and waved a hand. "I know, I just didn't get the time." He leaned in. "I went to France," he confided.

"And there is no post there?" she demanded.

"Not where I was." He cracked a wide grin. "I came here to retrieve some wine but the chaps who bring it in got in a little pickle, hiding from some customs men. The next thing I know, they're taking off and I'm still on their ship. Ended up in France, can you believe it?"

She shook her head slowly. "You were on a ship with smugglers?"

Uncle Albert nodded vigorously. "Quite the adventure, do you not think?" He patted her hand. "I'll tell you all about it when I come home."

"I was worried for you," she said. "I thought you were dead!"

"Me? Dead?" He poured another glass of wine, filling it halfway then peering into the end of the empty bottle. "It takes a bit more than a quick trip across the channel to kill me off."

She narrowed her gaze at him. "How long have you been here? On the island?"

He pressed a finger to his lips. "Oh, about two weeks."

Her cheeks grew rosy and Russell recognized the tension in her body. Rosamunde was not happy at all and he did not much envy Albert being on the wrong side of her.

"So enough time to write me a letter," she declared.

Uncle Albert waved the empty bottle at a nearby barmaid. "Well, the seas were a little choppy so I wasn't certain I could get one to you, and, if I'm honest, I got a little tangled up in a new business venture." His smile broadened. "I've commissioned a ship."

"A ship?" she repeated.

"There's a high demand for French wine and no one can meet it considering the restrictions still in place on the country." He looked to Russell. "You look like a gentleman of the world. Fancy an excellent investment?"

"Uncle, you're considering..." She glanced around. "Smuggling?" she murmured.

He shrugged. "Well, we are no longer at war with France so it's hardly the terrible crime it was before."

She stared at him for a few moments then rose suddenly from the table. "Russell, I think I wish to leave."

ROSAMUNDE DIDN'T WAIT to see if Russell had followed her out of the inn.

She strode a few paces from the building and paused by a galley ship that towered over her to take a breath. She felt a fool.

And she felt a fool in front of Russell. Of course her uncle was fine. Of course her family had been right. Trust her to take her imaginings too far and think he was in trouble when he was merely sitting in a hotel dining room, drinking wine and apparently entirely unbothered by her concern.

Russell put a hand to her shoulder. "Rosie?"

She twisted. "You must think me foolish."

"Never."

"I cannot believe he is here. Just...just eating and drinking without a care in the world."

"I know."

"He could have at least sent a letter."

"He could have."

She glanced around. "I should have listened to my family. Now I have dragged you all the way here and for what? To watch my uncle drink a whole bottle of wine?"

He grasped her shoulders, forcing her to look at him. "You did the right thing. You followed your instinct."

"My instincts were wrong!"

He shook his head. "They were not wrong, Rosie. He was involved with smugglers. That sounds dangerous even to me."

She shoved her glasses up her nose. "Everyone always talks of Uncle Albert vanishing and getting up to adventures and I always wanted to be a part of that. It sounded so exciting, you know?"

"I know."

"But I'm aggravated by how careless he's been. How he did not consider how I might feel not hearing from him." She paused and drew in a long breath. "And I'm annoyed at myself for wanting similar."

"You're not wrong to dream, Rosie," Russell insisted. "There's never anything wrong with that."

"I am certain you have never had a flight of fancy in your life."

"I've had many—mostly about warm beds and large meals."

"But not about silly things like...like taking off with an archaeologist or being taken by a pirate."

His lips tilted. "You were kidnapped by me, does that count?"

She could not help but smile. "Almost." She shoved a strand of hair from her face. "I am sorry to have wasted your time."

A dark brow lifted. "Do you consider it a waste of time?"

She eyed him, seeing the hesitancy in his gaze, and shook her head. "No. Not at all."

"Good." He gave her a firm kiss. "What do you wish to do now?"

She let her shoulders drop. "I think I want to go home. I have little intention of staying around and watching my uncle drink the island dry."

"You should probably at least let him know you are leaving."

"I suppose."

"Rosie, if there's anything I know about you, it's that you love your family, no matter what. Don't let this misunderstanding get in the way of your relationship with your uncle." He chuckled and shook his head.

"What is it?"

"An orphan giving advice on family...It's a little ironic."

"You're not wrong though." She sighed. "I'll let him know we are leaving."

"I had better find out when the next ferry is. Shall I meet you back here?"

"Yes." She twisted then paused, turning back and looping her arms around his neck then giving him a long kiss.

"What was that for?"

"For being a wonderful man." She grinned. "Who would have thought this is where we'd end up when you kidnapped me?"

"I think I was simply lucky to get away with my life," he said dryly. "You and that knife are quite a vicious combination."

"I have another," she told him.

He rolled his eyes. "Of course you do. Are you ever weaponless?"

"Never."

He pressed his lips to her forehead. "Meet me here. Don't go wandering. There could be rough sorts in this area."

"I won't."

She watched him head back in the direction of the beach then drew up her shoulders. He wasn't wrong. Uncle Albert needed to know she was departing, and she could not leave things like this.

As frustrated as she was, she should have expected as much. She envied her uncle's life so much sometimes but the irresponsibility of it...she had never seen it highlighted so strongly before. It made her all the more grateful for the stability of her huge, boisterous family.

It made her grateful for Russell. And made her wish for other things from him.

A hand clapped over her mouth and another around her waist as she twisted to head back to the inn, hauling her to a halt. She released a scream, but it was muffled by the strong palm, pinching at her face.

The scent of sea salt mingled with the stench of stale sweat. She screamed and writhed against the vicious hold that crushed against her ribs. Her glasses slipped from her nose and she heard a crunch as they hit the ground.

"Take her to the ship," someone said, his voice low and gruff.

Rosamunde kicked out, meeting shin and hearing a satisfying grunt.

"She bloody hurt me," her kidnapper said.

Another man moved into her line of sight and snatched her skirts, grabbing one leg then the other. She tried to kick out of his bruising grip but to no avail. They carried her toward a ship and up a gangplank and dropped her feet onto the deck. She stilled for a moment, casting her gaze about.

The man behind her kept her held firm whilst the other eyed her and curled a rope around his fists. Her pulse pounded in her ears, her breaths came fast. As tempted as she was to lash out, she needed to try to remain calm and assess the situation.

There were only two men—both fairly strong, wearing ragged clothes. The man in front of her had sunbeaten skin and a large floppy hat that must do a terrible job at protecting him from the sun.

"We'll tie her up," he said, "then send word to her uncle."

Uncle? What on Earth was going on?

Chapter Twenty-Nine

"Tie up her wrists," said the man holding her.

Rosamunde concentrated on breathing, drawing each steady breath in and out through the gap between the man's hands. His sweaty fingers pinched her face and almost blocked her nostrils, leaving her lightheaded. There were still only two men on the ship as far as she could tell, and they were most certainly stronger than her but if she could just get to her knife...

She tried to evade the man with the rope, but he grabbed one wrist and bound it tightly. She cried out against the hand across her mouth when the coarse rope chafed her skin.

Then he snatched the other and bound her hands together in front of her. Wriggling against the hold the burly man had on her, she bit down on his fingers and he released her with a yelp.

"She bit me!"

Spinning on her heel, she raced toward the gangplank. She came mere inches from escape when an arm banded around her waist, winding her. She gasped in a breath and screamed as loud as she could. The back of a hand connected with her face, the sting burning through her cheek and disorientating her.

"She's Wood's niece to be sure," the man holding her muttered. "She's as much a pain in the arse as he is."

"What do you want with me?" she gasped.

He dropped her onto the deck, and she landed heavily on her rear, unable to brace herself with her bound hands. Her cheek throbbed and she tasted the bitter tang of blood. Both men towered over her, their shapes silhouetted against the sun.

Perhaps if she could understand what they wanted, she could negotiate her way out. Clearly, making a run for it wasn't going to work and she needed to gather her senses. She tried to swallow the knot gathered in her throat and forced herself to talk calmly.

"Whatever it is you want, I can help. I have money if that's—"

The smaller man chuckled. "We have money. And we'll have more if your uncle keeps his nose out of our business." He folded his arms. "As yet, he has been unpersuaded but now we have you, I think he'll be willing to leave the island rather swiftly."

"I do not understand."

The man crouched to eye her. "All you need to do is behave and we'll release you."

She glanced from man to man. "I can speak with my uncle if you wish. I'm sure I can persuade him to leave."

He shook his head. "The man is oblivious. No manner of threats work on him. But I reckon he'd do anything to save a pretty woman like you." He stroked a finger across her cheek.

She shrank away from his touch. "What are you going to do with me?"

"Nothing, if you behave, as I said." He straightened. "We're not in the habit of hurting women, not if we can help it. Draws too much attention to our...business, you see."

"You're smugglers."

He smirked and nudged the second man. "She's a clever one."

The other man nodded. "I'll hurt her if you need me to, boss."

Her chest tightened. The man who had snatched her had a ruthless air about him and she had no reason to believe otherwise. She needed to get off this ship, and fast.

"We're not drawing attention to ourselves, Bowcher, like I just said," the man said through gritted teeth. "I swear your mother must have dropped you on your head when you were a babe."

"Please release me," she begged. "I would not wish you to get into trouble."

"We won't," the boss said. "Islands like this one rather like our types. We bring in plenty of money and look after our own. It's only the damned customs men that have a problem with us."

"But you just said—"

"Look," he thrust a finger at her, "I don't want to go killing some posh lady type but there's nothing to say we can't get away with hurting you a little, so I suggest you behave, unless you want another slap?" He rose a threatening hand.

She twisted away from the threat of his hand and shook her head.

"Excellent." He grinned, revealing gappy teeth. "All you need to do is behave, then we'll send word to your uncle and you can go free, got it?"

She nodded vigorously.

He jerked his head toward Bowcher. "Tie her up properly over there. Don't want her making another run for it." He rubbed a hand over her face. "At least she was easier to grab than her uncle. That damned man is never alone." He chuckled. "I'm afraid you were rather in the wrong place at the wrong time," he told her. "We'd been hoping to snatch your uncle and ensure he...listened to us, but we couldn't pass up an opportunity to grab his niece."

Bowcher snatched her arms, his fingers digging into her upper arm. Her heart pounded hard, nausea rolling up in the back of her throat. She couldn't let them tie her up. She just couldn't.

WHEN RUSSELL ARRIVED back at the inn, he saw no sign of Rosamunde. He scowled to himself, scanning the docks. Perhaps she had decided to make up with her uncle. He ducked into the building and found Albert at the same table, polishing off another glass of wine. He peered up at Russell as his shadow crossed the table.

"Join me for a drink? I should like very much to know how you met my niece."

"Is she here?"

"Here? No, dear chap. Rosie has such a strong head, it would take more than a few minutes to get her to forgive me."

Russell blew out a breath. Rosamunde had her moments, but he didn't think she would have wandered off after promising to stay where she was.

"She'll come around," her uncle said. "I find it best to give her a little time," he confided.

Russell shook his head. "She's hardly the sort to run off sulking, sir."

He lifted a shoulder. "I suppose you're right." He finished off the last sip of wine, dabbed his mouth with a handkerchief, then rose from the table.

Russell tightened his jaw, a knot building in his chest. He didn't like it. Rosamunde was alone on an island known for housing smugglers and blackguards. And his palms itched. Something wasn't right.

He strode out of the building, ignoring Albert's protests about his pace, and scanned the docks again. No pretty woman in a blue gown stood out amongst those working.

"Where the bloody hell is she?"

"Perhaps she decided to take a wander along the docks and look at the ships?" Albert suggested, panting. "She does rather like ships."

"Perhaps." He paced down past one ship, his heart beginning to beat harder. Why the devil would she walk off? He didn't like this one jot.

Albert scurried to keep up while Russell moved past a few small fishing boats, toward a tall ship.

"Rosie always did get herself into trouble," murmured Albert. "She's probably exploring somewhere she shouldn't."

"I'm well aware of her inclinations but she's no fool," he snapped back.

"Oh no, Rosie, is the cleverest of us all. But you know what women are like. It's why I could never bring her along with me. Couldn't have her getting into trouble. Her mother would never forgive me for one."

Russell froze. His heart kicked into overdrive, ricocheting against his chest. "Did you hear that?"

Albert blinked. "Hear what?"

"A scream."

He didn't wait for her uncle to respond again. He knew what he'd heard, and he would recognize her scream anywhere.

Lord knew, he'd heard it loudly enough when he'd kidnapped her.

"Goddamn it," he muttered, picking up his pace and moving in the direction of the sound. He stopped by the gangplank of the ship. "Where are you, Rosie?" he muttered to himself.

Movement snared his attention. He glanced up at the deck to see a flash of blue. He raced up the gangplank to find Rosamunde near the aft side by the water, confronted by a man. Another lay prone on the ground, grasping his hand. Rosamunde held her penknife between bound hands.

"I'll stab you too," she threatened the man as he inched toward her.

Russell closed the distance. Her gaze flittered to him and a relieved smile broke across her face. "Russell!"

The man used her distraction to smack the knife from her fingers, sending it skittering across the deck. Russell rushed forward, his fist ready, but the blow made her lose her balance. She knocked into the side rail of the ship and her eyes widened. For a moment, time slowed. Her tangled skirts caught around her legs and she spilled over the railing. He grabbed for her, the fabric of her gown catching between his fingers then tearing out from them. He heard a splash.

"I never meant to do that," her captor said, leaning over the edge of the ship.

"Bloody bastard," he said, shoving the man back and punching him in the jaw so hard his knuckles made an awful crunching sound.

Russell kicked off his boots and hauled off his jacket, all the while watching the spot where she'd gone under, willing her to come back up. Her hands were bound, and she wore a God-awful amount of clothing.

"Come on, Rosie," he urged, as he flung his jacket aside.

His chest constricted. She likely couldn't get to the surface. Climbing up onto the side of the ship, he dove in.

The cold pricked his skin, making the air in his lungs shrink. He dove deeper, feeling around in the murky water for her. He wouldn't lose her. Not now. Not when he hadn't told her everything. Hell, he hadn't even told her he loved her yet.

The salt water stung his eyes, it filled his mouth. Movement from boats kept the silt constantly stirred up so he could see little. He fumbled around blindly, aware of each second ticking by. She wouldn't be able to hold her breath much longer.

He kicked deeper, his fingers connecting with the wood of the hull, and pushed farther from it. Goddamn it. This could not be how it ended.

His lungs screamed, his eyes burned. He didn't dare rise to the surface, not until he found her. He spun around and stilled. Blue. It had to be her. He kicked forward, stretching an arm out and his fingers grazed fabric. He snatched it. He wouldn't miss her this time.

Fisting the fabric, he hauled her into him. Thank God. An arm latched around her waist, he hauled her to the surface. He broke through, dragged in a lungful of air, and brought her to the surface. When he scanned around to get his bearings, he spied Albert waving at him from the dock. Russell swam swiftly to the nearest steps, his breaths coming hard, too aware Rosamunde remained limp in his arms.

Albert clambered down the steps and helped him haul her onto them. Russell shoved her hair from her face and pressed fingers to her neck. His hands shook when he took in her closed eyes. He could scarcely tell if she had a pulse with his numb, trembling fingers.

"Rosie," he urged. "Don't die on me. I love you."

He moved his hands down her bodice and tugged at her garments, tearing her gown asunder. Then he grappled with her stays, ripping them as loose as he could.

"Russell."

His gaze shot up. Rosamunde smiled weakly at him. He dropped his head to her chest and released a long breath. "Thank the Lord."

She wrapped her hands around his head. "I can't believe it," she said weakly.

He lifted his head. "Can't believe what?"

"I lost another knife!"

Chapter Thirty

Rosamunde tugged the blanket around her shoulders and tightened her jaw.

Another shudder wracked her, and she had to fight from preventing her teeth chattering. Russell handed her a small glass of something amber and motioned for her to drink it.

"It will warm you up."

She gulped back the liquid and gasped, feeling it burn the back of her throat then sliding down into her limbs. She passed the glass back to Russell and he took a seat next to her by the fireplace of the inn.

Despite it not being that cold, he had demanded a fire be lit and the tendrils of warmth were slowly seeping through her soggy, ripped garments. If only they had not left their luggage back in Portsmouth. She certainly had not anticipated needing a change of clothes after a dip in the sea.

She narrowed her gaze at him. "How come you aren't cold?"

He shrugged. "I'm used to the cold."

She cinched the blanket tighter with one hand and he took her other in between his two large palms. She sighed at the feel of his warm skin. Despite everything, she could not help but appreciate the sight of Russell wet, his shirt molding to his body, his hair damp and curling. If she were in a slightly better state, she might be unable to resist begging him to get a room for them but every part of her was exhausted and she suspected she would only pass out between the sheets from fatigue.

She tensed to fight off another shiver, this time caused not by the cold but by how close she had been to drowning. As soon as she had plunged into the cold sea, her clothes had dragged her down. Everything tightened around her, and her lungs seemed to shrink. No matter how much she clawed and kicked, she couldn't make it to the surface. That was one adventure she could have quite happily done without.

Uncle Albert approached the table, his expression sheepish. He pulled out a chair and sat. "The men are in the local jail." He grimaced. "Seems they were rather unhappy about my upcoming plans to get involved in trade with France. Feared my legitimacy would rather, um, spoil their own trade."

"They said as much," Rosamunde said. Russell's jaw tightened and she squeezed his hand. As frustrated as she still was with her uncle, he could not have predicted some local smugglers would kidnap her in an attempt to persuade her uncle to cease his business activities.

"Anyway, I think perhaps I might turn my attention elsewhere. I have the ship commissioned and I'm working on getting the crew together, but I was rather thinking some warmer climes might be more appealing."

She peered at her uncle. "You are planning to go too?"

"Why, of course? No sense in sitting around here." He pressed a finger to his lips. "I was thinking the Caribbean. I've never been there and there's some healthy profit to be made in sugarcane."

"Uncle Albert, that journey will take months."

"Indeed." He grinned. "It should be quite interesting to see if I can make it as a sailor."

She shook her head with a small smile. "So long as you write to me."

"I can do better than that, dear girl." Uncle Albert's grin widened.

"Whatever do you mean?"

He leaned in. "I saw you brandish that knife. Got that blaggard good in his hand, did you not?"

"Well, I—"

"You've proved to me you are more than capable of holding your own, and, well, you're a grown woman now. Who cares what the rest of the family says? Besides, it seems I have some making up to do."

"Uncle?"

"Come with me, Rosie. Come have an adventure. I know you've been hankering for one."

Rosamunde opened her mouth. She eyed her uncle for several moments. This was it. What she had been waiting for. She could travel the world, visit an exotic country, meet different people, and do things she could never do in England. She looked to Russell.

He avoided her gaze, his posture stiff. She saw his throat work.

"Uncle, I—"

"You should go," Russell said quickly, his gaze meeting hers.

"But—" Her heart gave a painful thud.

A crease formed between Russell's brows. His gaze darkened. There was no chance he really wanted her to go, of that she was certain. And unless she had been entirely addled, she could have sworn he told her he loved her at the docks.

He gave a tight smile. "Your uncle is right. All you've wanted is adventure. Now you can have it."

"We'll have so much fun, Rosie," Uncle Albert said. "We can drink rum on the beach and try one of those...what are they called? Coconuts!"

She swung her gaze between the two men. Her heart ached. But not for the reasons she thought it might. Russell wasn't wrong. Here was everything of which she had dreamed.

Drawing in a breath, she took her uncle's hand and gave it a squeeze. "Uncle Albert, I appreciate the offer, I really do. I think we would have a wonderful time together. But—"

She heard Russell inhale.

"But I think I should like a different sort of adventure now."

Her uncle frowned. "What could be more adventurous than the Caribbean?"

She turned to face Russell. A hesitant smile tugged at the corner of her lips.

"I want an adventure here. In England. With you," she said softly.

"Are you certain?" Russell asked.

"I've never been more certain of anything in my life."

"I cannot offer you more knife fights."

She shook her head and laughed. "I'm quite over knife fights I think."

"You always wanted adventure. I would not wish you to stay here just because of me."

"You know full well you cannot persuade me otherwise. I wish to stay."

He leaned forward, taking her hands in his. "I love you."

She pressed her forehead against his, closing her eyes briefly to take in the words fully. When she opened them, his gaze was warm on hers. "I love you too. So, so much." She turned to her uncle. "Sorry, Uncle Albert, but Russell is all the adventure I need."

Epilogue

He let his lips curve and Russell shook his head to himself as he rode to catch up with Rosamunde. She was already a good way ahead of him on the country lane. He came alongside her. "There's no rush."

She twisted to eye him. "We cannot miss the carriage!"

He gripped the reins in one hand and pulled out his pocket watch. "We will be perfectly on time, I promise."

"I hope so. This is my first time. It cannot go wrong," she said, emphasizing each word.

He gave his wife a look. "Have you forgotten I've done this a few times now?"

"Yes, and the last time, it went grossly wrong."

He chuckled. "I wouldn't say that."

Her posture eased a little. "Forgive me. I'm just nervous."

"I know."

"I'm glad Guy let me accompany you."

He nodded. Guy had been hesitant about getting Rosamunde involved but he hadn't been able to refuse a request from his brother. He could not claim they were the most brotherly of brothers yet but both of them were adjusting to having family for the first time in a long time.

"We shall have to invite him over once the house is finished," she announced. "And Nash and Grace too, of course."

He grimaced. He rather liked that they owned a country house now, but he could hardly imagine taking tea with his brother in the parlor room or hosting a dinner party there.

"Do not make that face," she scolded. "It will be enjoyable, I promise, and I will make it worth your while."

Russell shook his head with a smile. Married life had been an oddly easy adjustment. Mostly because being with Rosamunde meant there was never a dull day and if he ever felt like withdrawing, she understood. And now he was part of a family. It was never something he'd anticipated enjoying but her family had enveloped him into theirs. He still had little idea how to handle their noise and excitement, but it always amused him to stand by and watch the patent love they had for one another.

"Are you sure you would not wish to trade it all in for the Caribbean?"

"And miss out on this?" She gestured to her masculine clothing. "Never."

He ran his gaze down her form, appreciating the way the breeches hugged her curves. Her outfit reminded him of their first kiss. Once this was over, he was going to take her home and—

"Russell, concentrate."

"I have no idea what you mean."

"I saw where your mind was going." A tiny smile played on her lips.

"That's impossible."

"It's entirely probable, especially when I have been holding back similar thoughts."

"Minx," he muttered. She was not making this easy on him, and she wasn't wrong, he really did need to concentrate.

He nodded toward the crossroads, where a group of black-berry bushes would provide good cover. "Here will be good." They moved their horses into the sideroad.

"Goodness, I'm nervous." She tugged her hat off her head, swept a few strands of hair back, then put it back on.

"You will do wonderfully, I'm certain." He glanced down at her. "Where's your knife?"

She flashed a grin. "In my pocket." She patted her jacket. "I do so envy men with all their pockets. Much easier than stashing it in my garter."

"Do not stab anyone this time, though."

"Need I remind you that the man I stabbed had taken me captive."

A shudder ran down his spine. "You do not, and if I'd had it my way, he would not have lived."

"They shall rot nicely in jail I'm sure. Your connection to the earl made sure of that."

"I nearly lost you," he said through clenched teeth. "They deserve to rot in hell."

She waved a hand. "I knew you'd rescue me."

He peered at her for a few moments. No wonder he loved her more than anything. Somehow, she always remained positive no matter what life threw at them. Even when they had been forced to postpone their wedding due to a fire at the church or when it had turned out there was a leak in the roof of their new house and several of the upper rooms had to be completely re-done. She didn't care. She simply ploughed on, completely un-scarred by life. He might not quite understand that ability, but he admired it, and, he had to admit, it had begun rubbing off on him.

"What?" she asked.

He'd been staring at her. He blinked. "Am I not allowed to look at my wife?"

"You may, but you're doing that dark, mysterious look. Is something the matter?"

"Not one jot. I was simply thinking how much I love you. Have I ever told you that?"

"Oh." She pressed her lips together. "No, I don't think so. I might need to hear it again."

"I love you, you bloody madwoman."

She rolled her eyes. "If I'm mad then what does that make you?"

"Utterly insane." He pressed fingers to his lips. "That sounds like the carriage." He leaned over and pressed a brief kiss to her lips. "You ready?"

"Absolutely." She tugged the scarf over her mouth, following his suit. "Let the kidnapping begin!"

THE END

About the Author

USA TODAY Bestselling Author Samantha Holt lives in the middle of England with her twin girls and a Dachshund called Duke plus too many cats. She's known for steamy historical romance featuring unique heroines and roguish heroes.

www.samanthaholtromance.com

Read on for a sample of Married to the Earl

Chapter One

"Bloody hell," Joanna groaned.

"Joanna!" Her mother sucked in a sharp breath and scurried around to Joanna's bedside as though she might somehow be able to push the curse back into Joanna's mouth.

Joanna squinted into the sunlight that poured through the open curtain and threw an arm over her eyes, sinking back into the much welcome darkness there. "If ever there was a time to curse, Mama, it is now," she grumbled.

"There is never a suitable time to curse." Her mother's voice was full of irritation—the sort that would send her on an hour long lecture on refined language, so Joanna removed her arm and eased herself up the bed.

She grimaced while her mother fussed with the pillow behind her head. Every inch of her ached, her mouth was dry, her eyes felt as though they were filled with dust. She put a hand to her hair and shuddered. Knotty and matted. *Just wonderful.*

This illness had taken her swiftly, making her delirious. She did not remember much apart from feeling overwhelmingly hot and dreaming of odd things—odd people too. People she hardly knew.

She frowned to herself. Or more to the point, men. Or one man. She couldn't fathom why. The Earl of Newhaven had been in her general social circle for many years, but they rarely spent time together. As far as she was concerned, he was an arrogant, rakish sort of man, and while she had time for many an interesting person, he was obviously one of those men who lived off their good fortune and handsome looks without there being anything particularly interesting underneath the façade.

"You can stop fussing, Mama." Joanna batted her hands away from behind her. "I can manage now."

"You cannot blame me."

Joanna eyed the darkened rings around her mother's eyes. The creases in her face seemed more pronounced too. She sighed. "I know, but I am well now. You do not need to worry, I promise."

Her mother bit down on her lip. "We thought we had lost you, Joanna. How could we have coped? First Noah—"

Her eyes widened and her mother clamped her mouth shut and moved over to the dresser to fold some cloths that had been discarded there. Joanna tried to push away the pang that struck her at the mention of her late-husband's name. None of them ever talked about him—and for that she was grateful.

Well, she thought she was grateful. It was a strange thing to lose the man she had pictured spending the rest of her days with so suddenly. All that one had hoped for had gone—swept away by a silly riding accident.

It was easier not to speak of him really. It was simply too exhausting to linger on what could have been had he lived.

She forced herself to sit further up in bed, closing her eyes briefly as her head swam. Opening them and peering around her childhood bedroom, her gaze landed on the dolls that were propped up on the dresser. Why she had ever liked those ugly things, she did not know. Now, they peered hard at her through their lifeless eyes with their ugly dresses that were poorly patched by her own hand as a child, making her skin crawl. If she stayed here much longer, she really ought to at least put them out of sight.

She really ought not to be here at all. She was far too old to be sleeping next to dolls. After Noah's death, her mother had swept her up and dragged her back home, leaving the house she and her husband had lived in empty. She'd been too grief-stricken to protest but she regretted letting her over-protective mother coddle her. The house had been willed to her as part of her dowry, but she had yet to return.

In truth, she had been considering going back to the house lately. Her two closest friends had married, and it left her with rather more time on her hands. There was no reason to put it off any longer.

Except she was not sure how to tell her mother that. She had been close to death these past few days and knowing her mother, she had fretted non-stop. Not that she was not grateful for her mother's care. If there was a mother more involved in her children's lives, Joanna had yet to meet her, but it was too much sometimes. Here she was, a grown woman, a widow, with a house of her own, and yet she was still being cosseted like a child.

"Well, I shall leave you to rest a little longer," her mother announced. "Mrs. Giles shall bring you some supper shortly. Maybe some hot broth and bread shall do it."

Joanna pressed a hand to her grumbling stomach. "That would be wonderful."

Mama tilted her head. "I am so glad you are well, Joanna." She leaned in and gave her a soft kiss on the cheek. "I shall check back on you later and I'll send your father up when he's home."

"Yes, Mama," Joanna said meekly, rubbing the spot where her mother had kissed her. Wonderful. Now she felt simply awful about wondering if she could flee as soon as she was well.

She stilled, frowning and twisted her arm into the light, her gaze coming upon red marks that lined her wrists. She sucked in a sharp breath. They'd bled her. Touching her wrist, she ran a finger across the wounds. No wonder her mother had been so scared. She must have been closer to death than she realized.

"Well, that is not very attractive," she grumbled, letting her fingers linger on the marks.

"You never look anything other than beautiful."

Joanna snapped her attention upward and grinned at the sight of Chloe entering the bedroom followed swiftly by Augusta. Both women beamed down at her.

Joanna reached a hand out to Augusta. "I must look a sight, but I am so glad you are here."

Augusta sank onto the chair next to Joanna's bedside and squeezed her hand tightly. "You had us worried," she admitted. "But you look so well already."

"Indeed," Chloe agreed, "it shall not be long before you are out of this bed and back to normal, I'd wager."

Normal. Joanna grimaced. She had become friends with Chloe and Augusta because they were the only unmarried women in their social circle and had become far too close to being wallflowers for Joanna's liking.

Joanna didn't have much say in being one, but she'd recognized Augusta and Chloe had other options—mostly in the form of some handsome, rather adoring men. She, however, was still in her mourning period and therefore could do little at balls and parties apart from sit and watch. She was not so certain she wished to go back to normal.

"Why that face?" Chloe asked, pushing a curl of red hair from her forehead.

She paused for a moment, glancing between her two young friends. There was no denying the loving glow in their cheeks. She could not begrudge them their happiness with their new husbands—they were wonderful women who deserved every drop of joy. Not to mention she may have had a tiny hand in ensuring they had time with their beaus. However, it meant she had lost what had become somewhat of a matchmaking hobby for her *and* she was the only unmarried one now.

The last thing she wanted to do was say something that would upset them when they were at their happiest, though.

"Joanna?" Augusta pressed.

Joanna released a sigh. "You know how tired I am of being a widow." She held up a hand. "I am not saying I am desperate for another husband," she added swiftly. "But the pity, and the sitting around as though all one is allowed to do is mourn."

Augusta nodded. "I understand the sitting around part at least."

"You know what I am saying then." Poor Augusta had been forced to wait around whilst her fiancé gallivanted off around the world for years. "I am not used to doing nothing at the best for times. I just cannot help..." She swallowed the knot in her throat. "I just cannot help feel Noah would not like to see me like this. This..." She waved a hand down herself, "is not the woman he fell in love with."

Augusta lifted a dark brow. "I highly doubt that, and you can forgive yourself for taking bedrest after such an illness. Goodness, Joanna, you nearly died."

"I did," she agreed. "And it made me realize I cannot simply sit around and be the grieving widow." She glanced toward the window, picturing the spring weather, the flowers blooming, the clear blue sky, a sprinkle of fresh air touching her skin. "I miss him every day but to continue to be so confined by the role of widow..."

Chloe nodded. "Well, what can we do to help?"

Joanna lifted both shoulders. "I am at a loss."

"It sounds to me like you need something with which to keep you busy. Some sort of project or hobby perhaps," Augusta suggested. "What about learning a new instrument?"

A little shudder tracked up her spine. "I am far too old for that."

"You are only two years older than us!" Chloe said.

"Besides, instruments come too easily to me. How will that keep me occupied?"

Chloe rolled her eyes. "I forgot you are ridiculously accomplished. If only you could pass some of that onto me."

"Chloe," scolded Augusta. "You are accomplished."

"Not in the traditional sense."

"Brook loves you as you are," Joanna pointed out.

"Oh I know." She waved a hand. "But it would not hurt to be able to play the piano or paint beautifully. At the very least, it would shock my family," she said with a wicked grin.

"I think you shocked them enough with your choice of husband," Augusta pointed out.

Chloe smiled. "I suppose I did."

"Can we return to the subject at hand?" Joanna asked with a teasing smile. "I do believe we were discussing me."

Chloe rolled her eyes again while Augusta gave a bashful smile. Augusta's naturally meek temperament meant Joanna occasionally shocked her, but she was pleased to see her recent marriage to Miles was making her a little more outspoken. Chloe, on the other hand, was inclined to be more argumentative and stubborn.

Augusta pursed her lips. "You have such a way with people. Why do you not use those skills in some way?"

Chloe pressed a finger to her mouth. "It is true. You could convince anyone of anything, of that I am certain."

"Whilst I do not mind this flattery, I am not sure what it is you want me to do." Joanna smothered a yawn and tugged the blankets up around her shoulders as a sudden chill swept through her. She was not as recovered as she had hoped, it seemed.

Augusta rose from the chair and aided Joanna with the blankets, tucking her in until she was rolled up like a big ball of hay. "You would make an excellent nurse," Joanna commented.

"That's it!" Augusta snapped her fingers.

"I am not becoming a nurse." Joanna shook her head vigorously. "I do not have the stomach for it."

"No, but you could help sick people."

Joanna glanced at Chloe who merely shrugged.

Augusta sat down again. "Charity work," she said simply.

"Charity work?" Joanna echoed.

"Oh, yes," Chloe said, nodding eagerly. "It would be perfect."

"You are a natural organizer and you are excellent at charming anyone," Augusta pointed out.

"It is not like I go out of my way to charm people...it just happens."

"Precisely." Augusta's grin widened. "You would be perfect at it."

Joanna wrinkled her nose. "At what exactly?"

"Find a worthy charity—one for sick people perhaps—and help raise funds for it."

Joanna nibbled on the end of a finger. She had never really been involved with charity with the exception of giving alms at Christmas. Would she even know what to do? She could not deny the thought did appeal, however. She would get to spend time with people, organize charity events, and most importantly be entirely occupied with something worthwhile instead of sitting around and mulling over a lost life.

"I think you have struck on the perfect plan, Augusta." Joanna grinned. "I hope everyone in Hampshire is ready to hand over all their funds to me because I shall be the best charity advocate England ever saw."

Chapter Two

Ambrose winced when the butler set the tray down on the coffee table. The ache thudding in his temples heightened and he pressed fingers to either side of his head.

This is what he got for indulging in too much whiskey, he supposed.

He groped for the cup of tea the butler had just poured and drained the delicate cup in mere seconds before placing it back upon the tray.

"Another, my lord?" Bram asked.

He nodded vaguely and rested his head upon his knuckles, his elbow propped upon the arm of the chair. His mouth was hideously dry. When was it he ceased being able to drink until the morning and still get up for a ride? Being thirty was not nearly as interesting as it was meant to be, especially when one could no longer tolerate alcohol.

He peered around the parlor room and glowered at the midday sunlight as it dripped in through the windows, highlighting the golden frames around paintings and making the glassware on the console table glisten.

Ambrose resisted the need to groan. He should have stayed in bed but his need for sustenance had defeated him and he hauled himself downstairs in the hopes that the physical activity might remove the cobwebs from his brain.

The pot of tea clattered against the tray. Ambrose narrowed his gaze at the spry elderly man who swiftly moved out of the path of his glare and busied himself with the empty bottles discarded on top of the drinks cabinet.

Glass clinked. He winced. "Must you be so loud, Bram?"

"Forgive me, my lord."

The man did not sound contrite one jot and if his disapproving look this morning was anything to go by, the noise was deliberate. Ambrose couldn't fathom why. It was hardly the first time he'd enjoyed many, many drinks with friends, and he doubted it would be the last.

Or perhaps it would. He grimaced and threw back a second cup of tea. His stomach rolled in protest and released a slight grumble. He was thirsty and he could swear famished too, but his stomach was telling him otherwise. This was the most beastly of hangovers.

"Any chance of some food, Bram?"

The butler came to stand in front of him, a brow raised.

"What is it?" Ambrose snapped.

"Are you certain his lordship can manage some sustenance?"

His gut rolled again but he would be damned if he was going to sit here and suffer an empty stomach. He'd choke down some food and drag his behind from this chair even if it killed him. Hell, he was thirty—not ancient. The last thing he wanted to do was act like some feeble old man.

"I think I know if I can eat or not," he grumbled.

"Very well, my lord. Do you wish to eat in here?"

Ambrose drifted his gaze once more around the generously appointed room. Tall windows looked out onto the London streets, framed by thick green velvet curtains. It would be less bright in the dining room, but he was not certain he could bring himself to move yet.

"It's a beautiful morning. I think I shall stay here."

"Indeed." The butler's expression hardly changed but that slight quirk of disapproval was upon his lips again as he moved past him and out of the room.

Once Bram was gone, Ambrose let his head loll back. He closed his eyes and swiftly realized his mistake when his head began to spin, so he snapped them open. Memories of the previous night were hazy. It had been fun, had it not? He and several excellent friends had gathered together for drinks and games. It must have been fun.

Except, he could not recall much and now it left him with that strange itching feeling. It was a sensation that had been taking over him for some time now. A sort of tickling in his feet that made him want to leap up and do something different. But what the devil could an earl in London do that was different? He was hardly a coward and had pursued some interesting hobbies in the past. Heck, he'd even climbed Ben Nevis in his early years at Cambridge.

If he could get rid of this damned headache, he could go riding down on the row. Or he could gallop out to the surrounding countryside. If he was feeling particularly foolish, he could walk through some of the dangerous parts of London and see if he survived.

He was not, however, *that* foolish, no matter how much whiskey still lingered in his body.

There was always Mrs. Calvert. Or even Lady Anne. They would welcome a visit from him. What better way to recover from a night's drinking than in the arms of an experienced widow?

He curled a lip. "There really must be something wrong with me," he muttered. The idea didn't raise the slightest flutter of interest. He glanced down at his breeches and grimaced. Not even where it was supremely easy to raise a man's interest.

Damn it, if he was honest with himself, the party last night had left him with that same empty feeling. Was this just what being thirty was about? Or was it something else? He had everything a man could want. Wealth, friends, good looks...a winning personality, if he did say so himself. He wasn't exactly stupid either. So why oh why could he not be content?

Bram pushed open the door and let it thud on its hinges.

"Bram," Ambrose hissed, pinching the bridge of his nose.

"Food will be served shortly, my lord." The butler paused, withdrew a penknife from his pocket and scooped something up from one of the sofas with the tip of it.

Ambrose frowned at the slip of fabric.

"Should I see this returned to one of your lady friends, my lord?"

He peered at it and recognized it as a stocking. He vaguely recalled some game of stripping one's clothes off occurring and could only assume it had come from that. He waved a hand. "I could not be certain which lady friend it was from."

"Then I shall...dispose of it, my lord." Bram tightened his lips and carried it at arm's length out of the room.

He watched the butler leave, his long legs making quick work of the strides to the door. Bram moved with a litheness that Ambrose envied right now. He snorted to himself. It was ridiculous to be envious of a man who was likely thirty years his senior.

He frowned. At least, he suspected Bram was around sixty years of age. The butler was notoriously tight-lipped about everything. The long, slender man revealed little about his life and the few snippets Ambrose had garnered had been from other servants. Even Ambrose's mother knew little of him, but then she had spent many a year at the estate in the country, away from her estranged husband so it could be said she had spent little time with the man.

Regardless, he couldn't fathom being so closed about everything. His life was out there for all to see and had been for many years, even before he took on the title of earl. If he had any secrets, it was news to him.

Bram returned to the drawing room for the third time, this time with a platter of food. Ambrose pressed a hand to his stomach at the sight of freshly cooked sausages, bacon, and large hunks of bread slathered with butter. He usually had a hearty appetite in the morning but today...He groaned and waved the food away.

Bram tutted and moved the tray to the console table.

Ambrose rolled his eyes to himself. Bram had been with the family for years and had served the previous earl. He was somewhat like an old piece of furniture that one kept thinking one should give away but couldn't bring oneself to.

Ambrose could not fathom what he would do without him but, at the same time, he did not much appreciate all the judgmental looks. It was hardly like he behaved any differently to his father or many men before him. His father had been known to have many a mistress and enjoy a good drink, after all.

"You really should eat, my lord," Bram muttered.

Ambrose released a long breath. Now he recalled why he kept the man on. Despite his tight-lipped, disapproving attitude, there was no one he could rely on more than Bram and deep, *deep* down, he could swear the butler actually cared for him.

"I will try once my stomach has settled," he promised.

Bram continued to move around the room at a speed far too quick for Ambrose's liking. The butler tweaked curtains, pushed chairs back into place, and maneuvered ornaments until they were just so. Ambrose shook his head at the butler's efficiency, now more than envious at his ability to actually move from a chair. His head still pounded, that dryness in his mouth had yet to dissipate, and his damn heart felt as though it was going to explode through his chest.

"You can leave that to one of the maids, you know."

Bram's lips tightened while he adjusted a painting that had somehow been knocked askew during the previous night's frivolities. "I should rather those young ladies not have to witness the aftermath of...such evenings."

"I am not certain why they would be scandalized by a crooked painting or vase."

"They may be scandalized by what they find, and I would not wish such a thing on those young women." Bram lifted the edge of a curtain and indicated to what appeared to be another stocking with a raised brow. Whichever lady had removed them was apparently missing both this morning.

Ambrose made a dismissive noise. "'Tis only a stocking."

"Those girls are hard-working and respectful. I should rather it stay that way."

"If you fear they will gossip, you need not worry, Bram." Ambrose waved a hand. "There is enough gossip about me that a pair of stockings would read most tiresomely."

The butler kicked aside the stocking in question with a pinched expression. "As you say, my lord."

Watching the man for a few moments more as he finished tidying the room, Ambrose pressed a finger to his lip. "Do you enjoy your job, Bram?"

"Enjoy, my lord?"

"Is it satisfying?"

He stilled. "It is."

"Hmmm."

"My lord?"

"Is there anything else you find satisfying?"

Bram straightened and creases appeared on a surprisingly line free face for his age. "I am not certain what you mean, my lord."

"If you were looking for something interesting to do, what would it be?"

The lines deepened. "I should think his lordship knows enough about 'interesting' things in life."

"I am hardly asking if you have a lady lover, Bram." Ambrose held back a chuckle when the butler's skin paled a little. "I just meant, is there anything else in your life aside from...butlering? Anything that you find brings you a sense of...I don't know...fulfillment."

"I enjoy a good game of solitaire, my lord."

He groaned inwardly. He should have known Bram would not be able to offer much advice. The man was as plain as a man could get in his tastes—preferring water to ale, and bread to cake. And this was not much helping his conundrum. He could feel it, twisting deep in his gut. These parties and his life in general...well, they simply didn't bring him the enjoyment they used to. He needed to find something to stop that ache, to appease this need to do something new or useful.

"Do you do anything else, Bram?" Ambrose demanded.

"I enjoy the occasional stroll in the park. When it is not too busy, of course."

"Of course," Ambrose intoned.

"My life is lived in service to you, my lord."

"Well, now you have me feeling guilty indeed."

Bram's shoulders stiffened. "That was not my intention, my lord. You know I live to serve."

"I should think it is about time you found something else with which to occupy your time. Why do you not take the rest of the day off?"

The butler's eyes widened, and his posture grew so stiff that Ambrose feared he'd given the man a heart attack and he was going to keel over. "There are things to be done...," he spluttered.

"I am hardly in a state to demand much today and Mrs. Locke can take care of anything else I need." Ambrose shooed the butler with a waving motion. "If I cannot at least do something interesting, then you should."

"But, my lord..."

"Bram," he insisted.

His shoulders slumped. "Very well, my lord," he muttered.

"Where shall you go?"

He pursed his lips. "I suppose I shall visit my niece. She has been sick of late and needs tending to."

"Sick? Niece? Damn it, Bram, why did you not say something?"

He lifted a shoulder. "There was little to be said, my lord."

"Does she need anything? Is there anything I can do?"

Bram shook his head vigorously. "Nothing at all, my lord. In fact, your family charity has already offered aid."

"Charity?"

"The Creasey Children's Charity?"

"Oh yes, that thing." Ambrose frowned. "You know you need not rely on charity, you can come directly to me for assistance."

"You are busy, my lord..."

Too busy to help an employee out when their family member was ill apparently. Bitterness rose in his throat. Lord, what sort of man was he?

"The charity...what exactly are they doing at present?" Ambrose asked. He was aware of it and how his family had established it some forty years ago, but he had little knowledge of what they did or even how much of his money went toward it.

"I believe they are trying to establish a hospital at present near your estate in Hampshire."

"Interesting..."

"Interesting, my lord?"

Ambrose waved the butler away. "Go and see your niece, Bram. I think we should make a trip to the Hampshire estate this week so it will be your last chance to see her for a while."

Printed in Great Britain
by Amazon

61013128R00170